THE
FEDERAL RESERVE
SYSTEM

THE
FEDERAL RESERVE
SYSTEM

AN ENCYCLOPEDIA

R. W. Hafer

Greenwood Press
Westport, Connecticut • London

Library of Congress Cataloging-in-Publication Data

Hafer, R. W. (Rik W.)
   The Federal Reserve System : an encyclopedia / R. W. Hafer.
       p.   cm.
   Includes bibliographical references and index.
   ISBN 0-313-32839-0 (alk. paper)
   1. Board of Governors of the Federal Reserve System (U.S.)—Encyclopedias.   2. Banks
and banking, Central—United States—Encyclopedias.   3. Banks and banking—United States—
Encyclopedias.   4. Federal Reserve banks—Encyclopedias.   I. Title.
   HG2563.H235 2005
   332.1'1'097303—dc22   2005006189

British Library Cataloguing in Publication Data is available.

Library of Congress Catalog Card Number: 2005006189
ISBN: 0-313-32839-0

First published in 2005

Greenwood Press, 88 Post Road West, Westport, CT 06881
An imprint of Greenwood Publishing Group, Inc.
www.greenwood.com

Printed in the United States of America

The paper used in this book complies with the
Permanent Paper Standard issued by the National
Information Standards Organization (Z39.48-1984).

10   9   8   7   6   5   4   3   2   1

*To my parents
and
to Gail and Cait*

CONTENTS

PREFACE AND ACKNOWLEDGMENTS

The entries in this encyclopedia deal with the Federal Reserve System, the central bank of the United States. This book does not, however, deal solely with how the Federal Reserve operates or its current institutional structure. Even though focusing on these issues could fill a book, such an approach misses the rich history and development of the Federal Reserve, the dramatic changes that have occurred in the banking industry and the evolution of monetary policy over the past century. The entries that comprise this book, therefore, represent an attempt to cover a broader spectrum than merely what the Federal Reserve is and how it developed.

With this in mind, the entries chosen range across Federal Reserve operations and how monetary policy functions in the United States. The entries also cover points that may at first seem unrelated to the Federal Reserve. For example, how could a discussion of something as arcane as "real business cycle theory" fit in a book about the Federal Reserve? The answer is because this theory has important implications for how monetary policy is conducted. In this discussion, and in others like it, what might seem as unrelated issues are tied to monetary policy, to the Federal Reserve's regulatory oversight duties, or how the System operates. In each and every case there is an explicit connection between the entry and the Federal Reserve.

Some of the entries deal with complex issues or concepts. At times, economic jargon will creep into the discussion. On both points, every effort has been made to present the material in a fashion that makes it accessible to the general reader. The purpose of the book is to provide an introduction to the Federal Reserve and related topics, not to frighten you away from the subject matter. If successful, this will be the first, not the last, book that you'll read on the subject of the Federal Reserve.

A number of people provided suggestions and comments at various stages of this project. I would like to thank Stu Allen, Jerry Dwyer, David Hallidy, Joe Haslag, Scott Hein, Bob Hetzel, Mack Ott, Anna Schwartz, and Dave Wheelock for helping me decide which entries to include. I also would like to thank the numerous economists whose work I relied upon for most of the entries.

This book wouldn't have been completed without the help of my wife, Gail Heyne Hafer. Her editorial comments and insights as an economist greatly improved my earlier attempts. To her I owe my greatest debt of gratitude.

INTRODUCTION

The purpose of this introduction is to put the Federal Reserve and monetary policy in an historical perspective. Most countries around the world have a central bank. Some central banks developed over time from private commercial banks that served their governments. In addition, some are quite old. The Bank of England, for example, fits both descriptions: it started as a private bank operating in the time Sir Isaac Newton, who was a member of the Bank's board of governors. Other central banks, like the Federal Reserve, are comparatively new, having been in existence for less than a century. How is it that it was not until the twentieth century that the United States created its central bank? How has the Federal Reserve developed, both institutionally and in terms of policy actions since its inception? These two questions form a common thread to this introduction.

Because this introduction briefly covers a wide swath of history, it is necessary to compartmentalize it. I have chosen the following scheme. In the first section I examine the rise of central banking in the United States beginning in the late 1700s through the signing of the Federal Reserve Act in 1913. The next section examines the events impacting the development of the Federal Reserve through the Great Depression. The Great Depression (1929–1933) was a watershed event in the history of the Federal Reserve. To understand some of the problems that the Federal Reserve and policy makers faced in the 1960s and 1970s, it is instructive to recognize that many of the policies originated as reaction to the events of the Great Depression.

The third section skips ahead to look at changes in the Federal Reserve and monetary policy beginning in 1951, the date of the famous Treasury-Federal Reserve Accord. The accord is a natural point to begin, because it gave the Federal Reserve policy freedom from the U.S. Treasury. This section covers a long period of Federal Reserve policy. This discussion highlights the major debates and important economic events that challenged monetary policy. The fourth section explores the period since 1980 with a focus on the Federal Reserve's reaction to a number of financial and economic crises. Beginning in the early 1980s, major banks failed, a major financial crisis involving the default of numerous countries occurred, the savings and loan industry in the United States collapsed and the stock market experienced two "crashes," just to mention a few. The Federal Reserve and its approach to regulating the financial system were intimately affected by each of these events. The final section closes the chapter with some final comments and observations. By the time you get to this final section it is my intention that you will have gained an appreciation for the complexity of monetary policy and the diverse roles played by the

Federal Reserve. I hope you agree with me that the dynamic (and sometimes un-predictable) nature of setting monetary policy makes it a fascinating subject.

THE DEVELOPMENT OF CENTRAL BANKING IN THE UNITED STATES

The history of central banking in the United States began in the late 1700s. Alexander Hamilton, the secretary of the U.S. Treasury, was an early proponent of creating a central bank. Hamilton argued that a central or national bank would provide a standard currency that would promote trade between states. Such a currency also would lessen dependence upon foreign trade as a means to regulate the money stock: Since money consisted mainly of gold and silver, increasing these precious metals relied on increasing exports to other countries that would, in turn, pay for the goods with gold. Hamilton's idea of a national paper currency would eliminate that need and promote commerce. The bank also would serve as the government's "bank," housing government deposits of tax revenues and making sure that funds were transferred between the states.

Congress passed and President Washington signed the legislation granting the charter for the First Bank of the United States in 1791. The charter was for 20 years, at which time it could be renewed. The debate over the bank was heated and acrimonious. A key element in the debate, one that would resurface over and over in the development of banking in the United States, is the idea that creating a central bank would grant the federal government monopoly control over the nation's supply of money. This may seem bizarre today since we have long lived with the fact that only the federal government has the ability to print money. But it has not always been that way. Many believed that money—currency—should be competitively provided, determined by the changing supply of gold and not left to the whims of government officials. Under a monetary system based on some commodity, such as gold, it is much harder for individuals to manipulate the money supply for political gain.

The First Bank of the United States seemed to fulfill the role of a central bank. It acted as the government's fiscal agent, as it was supposed to, and it served as lender of last resort. This latter activity is often viewed as *the* reason for having a central bank. Having a lender of last resort—a banker's bank, as it were—means that when banks experience problems, such as deposit outflows that are greater than deposit inflows, the central bank's job is to step in and provide funds. The idea that a central bank behaves as an emergency lender remains one of the more persistently debated aspects of central banking.

During the early 1800s, not only did the debate over government monopolization of the money supply dog the bank, but it also came to light that a large portion of the bank's outstanding stock was owned by foreign investors. Even though the bank's charter made it clear that only U.S. residents could hold positions of control within the bank, some argued that the bank was being used for the benefit of foreign owners over the U.S. public. Even though there is little foundation for this, the political fallout severely damaged the bank's reputation. With mounting pressure to reconsider the usefulness of the bank, Congress in 1811 voted 65 to 64 to postpone rechartering the bank. The Senate vote was deadlocked: 17 to 17. The tie-breaking vote was caste by Vice-President George Clinton who voted against renewing the charter more for political than economic reasons. America's first experiment with central banking was over.

The decision not to renew the bank's charter was not productive. Without a central bank the United States government found it difficult to finance the War of 1812. Following the war there occurred a period of inflation that some felt would not have occurred if a central bank could coordinate monetary policy. Support for another bank arose and, after more debate, a charter for the Second Bank of the United States was passed in 1816. The second bank, like its predecessor, was set up to operate as the government's fiscal agent and to provide a uniform currency. And like its predecessor, the second bank almost immediately was embroiled in controversy.

In 1819 there occurred a financial panic that some attributed to the Bank. For example, the bank often took in the notes (currency) of state banks in exchange for its own. Because the state bank notes were backed by gold and silver (specie), the bank would redeem its holdings of state bank notes in exchange for specie as a way to check any overissuance of state notes. Some argued that this policy led state banks to issue too few notes, thus exacerbating the panic of 1819.

After weathering that storm, the second bank entered a period of near-constant turmoil when Nicholas Biddle was appointed its president in 1823. Biddle was an aggressive manager of the bank and, by extension, the nation's banking system. Even though some of Biddle's actions had positive economic outcomes, they put him squarely in the sights of the bank's long-time opponent: Andrew Jackson. Jackson, hero of the War of 1812 and presidential candidate who represented Western (at the time Tennessee *was* the West) and agrarian interests, opposed any action that would centralize power in the East. Consequently he openly opposed the second bank, which was located in Philadelphia. During the campaign of 1828, Jackson publicly decried the dangers of the second bank and of banks in general. After defeating Henry Clay for the Presidency, Jackson stepped up his campaign against the bank. This began the so-called Bank War, with Jackson discrediting the bank and Biddle, suggesting that the bank was being run by Easterners who cared not for the needs of ordinary citizens.

The bank became a centerpiece of the 1832 presidential campaign, which again pitted Clay against Jackson. Clay was able to bring renewal of the bank's charter into the political debate by introducing a bill to renew the charter four years early. Even though Congress passed the bill, Jackson vetoed it and Congress could not override his obstruction. With his victory in 1832, Jackson began to gut the bank of any influence, notably by directing the federal government to withdraw its deposits from the bank. By 1836 there was not enough political support to support renewal of the bank's charter.

The demise of the Second Bank of the United States launched an era in which no central bank existed until the creation of the Federal Reserve in 1913. With no federal oversight of banking, states quickly established the legal framework in which banks could operate. In 1837, Michigan passed laws that allowed individuals to open banks without the need of a bank charter. To operate a bank, owners needed only to meet certain minimum capital requirements established by the state bank regulators. To issue currency, banks acquired state bonds as collateral for their note issue. The passage of the Michigan law began the period in United States known as the "free banking" era.

Free banking laws popped up in a number of states. Eighteen different states passed free banking laws by 1860. There were varying levels of participation, however, usually mimicking the political climate regarding banks in general. In Illinois, for example, over 100 free banks were operating by the beginning of the Civil War. Iowa, in contrast, had few. Once free banks opened, they competed for business. Notes from individual banks carried the name of the bank and, if the bank was noted for trustworthiness and good management, its notes would trade for a premium relative to others. For example, a dollar bill issued by the First Bank of Geneva may trade for a dollar's worth of goods in the local store, but a dollar from the Bank of Wahoo may not. To be successful, it was important for banks to maintain reputations as well-managed businesses.

Although free banking was a viable bank system on many fronts, stories spread about nefarious bank practices. In fact, until fairly recently stories about "wildcat" banks and bankers disappearing with depositors' money predominated discussions of the era. Recent investigations into such stories, however, reveal that free banks were, much as their modern counterparts, operated by owners and managers seeking to maximize profits, stay in business and provide a service to the local community. If this is so, what ended the free banking era in the United States?

The free banking system was devastated by the onset of the Civil War and the banking legislation that followed. Free banks around the country held state bonds as backing for their note issue. If the value of the state bonds dropped in market value, the bank would either increase the amount of bonds deposited with the state, or reduce the amount of notes in circulation. Although their values had begun to deteriorate with the nomination of Lincoln, in April 1861 when Fort Sumter was fired upon, the value of the Southern bonds plummeted. The decline in these states' bond prices meant that many free banks were required to increase bond deposits with their state regulators. This became an economic impossibility as was the recall of notes outstanding. Instead, many free banks closed their doors. By 1862 the free banking era in the United States was, for all intents, over. Within the next few years nearly every free bank had closed.

Although the collapse of Southern bond prices decimated the free banking movement, the National Banking Act, passed during the Civil War, was the final blow. The act was the latest attempt to nationalize the banking system and centralize its regulation in the federal government. One part of the act imposed a tax on free bank notes. This tax made issuance of notes by banks unprofitable and doomed their existence. Into the void the government allowed only national banks to issue U.S. currency, effectively restoring the government's monopoly power over currency. This act thus instituted a uniform currency for the entire country.

The National Banking Act also began some aspects of modern banking. It precluded banks from branching, a constraint that was revived during the Great Depression and only recently removed. National banks were required to hold reserves against their customers' deposits at specified reserve city banks located in New York, Chicago, and St. Louis. Because the act also specified the nature of what would constitute reserves, the national banking system created by the act was flawed in one important way: the act specified that reserves would consist of gold and gold certificates, greenbacks and U.S. Treasury currency. Missing from this list is national bank notes. In times of financial crisis, commercial banks did not have access to their reserves to meet unexpected deposit demands. Held in reserve city banks, the funds were not readily available to meet customers' demands. When customers were not able to access their funds quickly, fear of bank failure spread quickly and bank runs occurred. The reserve system established in the national banking era is accused of creating just such an effect, one that the Federal Reserve Act sought to correct. Put differently, the Federal Reserve Act sought to create an elastic currency, one that would change (increase and decrease) to meet the needs of the economy.

The late 1890s sometimes is referred to as the Golden Age in U.S. history. It also was a time of economic turmoil. Commitment to the Gold Standard following the Civil War meant that prices, especially agricultural prices, fell steadily from 1879 through the mid-1890s. Even though there were major advances in industry and transportation, some sectors of the economy were not advancing at all. This uneven progress led to much political fighting, not only between Republicans and Democrats, but also between regions of the nation.

In 1896 there occurred a steep decline in economic activity. Politicians and economists argued the merits of the gold standard over a free coinage of money by allowing silver to be used. Some blamed the gold standard for the recession, arguing that if the government could use silver for coinage it could expand the money supply and avert the economic downturn. In one of the more interesting presidential elections, William Jennings Bryan, the Democratic candidate, campaigned on a platform that called for dual coinage, using both silver and gold. His opponent and eventual winner of the election, William McKinley, staunchly backed the gold standard. McKinley's victory in 1896 established the gold standard as the monetary standard for the next 40 years. That overarching monetary rule, in conjunction with the national banking system established after the Civil War, led to a continuation of financial strains.

The Panic of 1907 is sometimes viewed as the economic event that brought about the creation of the Federal Reserve. Even though the economy was expanding before 1907 and there appeared to be no major problems prior to the downturn, events unfolded in late 1906 through 1907 that hastened the decline. In spring 1907 there were a series of stock price declines related to questionable practices by some of the country's major companies. During the first half of the year there also occurred a reduction in gold inflows which caused the money stock to decline. By fall of 1907 the economy was in a full-fledged panic. Bank depositors tried to withdraw funds in an attempt to increase liquidity. A key reason for this was the increased uncertainty about the stock market. The effect was a run on banks. The regulations of the era simply could not prevent the same type of bank panics that prevailed in earlier times. The money stock declined and with it went economic activity.

Although dramatic, the panic actually was short-lived. A consortium of financial institutions, led by financier J. P. Morgan, provided a pool of funds to troubled banks and trust companies. During the fall his consortium distributed funds that helped shore up public confidence: depositors returned to banks. By February 1908 the panic had subsided and the economy once again began to expand.

The Panic of 1907 left a permanent mark on the financial and economic landscape of the United States. To many it clarified the need for changes in bank regulation, especially breaking the link between banks and the stock market. (This tie would not be severed until the 1930s.) It also demonstrated anew the need for a central bank. The first push of this reformation movement took shape in the Aldrich-Vreeland Act of 1908.

The act focused on two areas. One was how to deal with the inelastic currency issue. In times of panic, banks faced deposit outflows that could not be countered by any emergency issuance of currency. The act sought to remedy this. The other major accomplishment of the act was to create the National Monetary Commission. The charge of the commission was to study and analyze the banking systems of the United States and other countries to see if a "best practices" model could be developed. Out of this analysis and many volumes of published work, the commission provided three key recommendations: first, formation of a central bank that would create and hold reserves; second, creation of a coordinated system of check clearing and collection; and third, establishing a fiscal agent that could satisfy the needs of the federal government. While some of these are obvious replications of earlier attempts at central banking in the United States, they seemed to take on a new life following the Panic of 1907.

Out of the debate surrounding the work of the National Monetary Commission the legislation that created the Federal Reserve Act grew. Between 1908 and 1913 the discussion focused on how to create a central bank that would meet the economic needs of the country and satisfy parochial political desires. Many in the expanding West and South—reminiscent of the Jacksonian days—feared the concentration of financial power in the East. Amidst this debate, the election of 1912 put the Democratic candidate Woodrow Wilson in the White House and gave the Democrats controlling majorities in both the Senate and the House. This victory changed the political dynamic of the central bank movement. Representative Carter Glass (D, VA) and Senator Robert Owen (R, OK) sponsored legislation for bank reform and a central bank. After extensive political debate and compromise, the Federal Reserve Act was ready for President Wilson's signature in December 1913.

The Federal Reserve Act is a political document based on economic considerations. By that I mean that while the act sought to remedy the problems besetting the economy and the banking system, the final document reflects political compromise. For example, to gain the support of representatives of the Western and Southern areas of the country, the System is geographically dispersed. The Board of Governors did not exist in its current form: the policymaking power of the System was in the hands of the numerous Reserve banks (eventually 12) that were to be spread around the country. The dispersion of the Reserve banks meant that the long-standing fear of concentrated power in the East was compromised. The Reserve banks exercised this power through use of the discounting mechanism: To get a loan from the Federal Reserve, a local bank could bring in, say, $100 of U.S. securities for which a loan of $95 would be made. This was one way in which, acting as the lender of last resort, the Federal Reserve System could address the problems of an inelastic currency.

The act also delineated the role of the new central bank. From rediscounting paper brought in by member banks and thus serving as lender of last resort to buying and selling government securities in the open market, the Federal Reserve was seen as the solution to financial panics and economic downturns. Although this hubris was misplaced, the new system was a large step in the nation's economic and financial development. Although there was much to learn, and significant policy mistakes would be made, the United States now had its central bank.

THE GREAT DEPRESSION AND REFORM OF THE FEDERAL RESERVE

Between the signing of the Federal Reserve Act and the late 1920s, Federal Reserve officials were engaged in some on-the-job training about being central bankers. There were many issues that they dealt with; the Federal Reserve's role in financing World War I; how to deal with the inflationary aftermath of the war and the effects of returning to prewar parity in a gold standard world; and how to use the power of open market operations (the buying and selling of government securities). This list is an oversimplification of the learning curve that Federal Reserve officials faced. In some ways the policies established in the period, such relying on the real-bills doctrine to guide policy, would later become the foundation for disastrous policy decisions made during the Great Depression.

The Great Depression and the sweeping changes that it created stand out as a turning point in the development of the Federal Reserve and monetary policy. Even though the stock market crash in October 1929 is often considered as the start of the depression, economic growth actually had already slowed several months earlier. In fact, today we date the beginning of the economic downturn as August 1929. The Federal Reserve, trying to fight the speculative excesses in the stock market that characterize the late-1920s moved to raise interest rates in summer 1929. Although it is debatable whether the Federal Reserve's actions were the only reason that the speculative activity slowed, it along with a mounting concern that the market had become grossly over valued caused stock prices to fall: between August and October stock prices fell about 25 percent. In addition, the growth of the economy continued to decline. If Federal Reserve officials were pleased by the slowing in stock price increases, they did not anticipate the plunge that occurred on October 29, 1929—Black Tuesday. Newspaper headlines noted that the stampede to unload stocks was widespread. Since much of the earlier speculation was fueled by borrowed funds, the drop in stock prices meant that financial institutions were calling for additional funds from investors to meet their margin requirements. These calls were not met, pushing stock prices even lower. As in earlier financial panics, individuals sought refuge in liquidity by draining deposits from banks.

Based on its policy of determining monetary ease or tightness by watching market interest rates, the Federal Reserve did not act quickly to avert economic disaster. In October 1930 there was a wave of bank failures in the South and the West. On December 11, the Bank of the United States, one of the largest New York City banks, failed. In light of this, the Federal Reserve still did not infuse sufficient funds into the banking system. The official policy of the time was that troubled banks were mismanaged and should fail. When it became apparent that the Federal Reserve would not step in, a broad-based bank run occurred. Even though bank failures increased at alarming rates—5,000 banks failed between 1930 and 1932—the Federal Reserve did much too little to avert the consequence.

The failure of banks and the Federal Reserve's policy led to a sharp reduction in the supply of money, about 25 percent between 1929 and 1932. The decline in the stock of money, on top of the financial calamity that existed, simply exacerbated the economic downturn. While the Federal Reserve's policies are not the sole reason for the Depression, many economists believe that their restrictive actions and failure to act as lender of last resort turned a relatively normal economic downturn into the nation's worst economic catastrophe, before or since.

In the wake of the Great Depression a number of institutional and policy reforms were made. In 1932 Congress passed the Glass-Steagall Act, which expanded the ability of Federal Reserve policy to be more flexible in times of crisis. For instance, the act allowed the Federal Reserve to lend funds to banks based on their use of commercial paper as collateral: prior to the act this was not permitted. In 1933 President Roosevelt also signed into law the Banking Act that aimed at stabilizing the banking system. The act created the Federal Deposit Insurance Corporation (FDIC) to provide deposit insurance as a means to ward off future bank failures that arose from bank runs by depositors. The act also established Regulation Q which, enforced by the Federal Reserve, removed the explicit payment of interest on checking accounts. An important institutional change was creation of the Federal

Open Market Committee (FOMC), the policymaking arm of the Federal Reserve. The act formally established the Committee, its composition and that it would meet regularly in Washington, D.C.

Two years later, the Banking Act of 1935 was passed. Unlike the 1933 version, the 1935 act significantly overhauled the Federal Reserve System into what we recognize today. The act centralized policy decision-making authority in the newly named Board of Governors of the Federal Reserve System in Washington, D.C.; it strengthened the Federal Reserve's independence from the government, removing the Secretary of the Treasury and the Comptroller of the Currency as members of the Board of Governors; it established terms for the Chairman of the Board (4 years) and proscribed the number of governors (7) and their terms (14 years); and it codified the voting pattern on the FOMC: seven governors plus 5 of the 12 District Bank presidents (the New York Bank president was given a permanent vote). Having the FOMC make policy decisions gave the majority position to the Board of Governors while giving the process some degree of openness by allowing the District Bank presidents some say in the matter.

The Banking Act of 1935 completed the Roosevelt Administration's reform of commercial banking and the Federal Reserve System. It resuscitated the banking system and established the Federal Reserve as the authority in the oversight of the banking industry and as the source of monetary policy. Perhaps just as importantly, it centralized the power of the Federal Reserve System in Washington, D.C.

MONETARY POLICY COMES OF AGE: POLICY INDEPENDENCE, INFLATION AND MACROECONOMIC SHOCKS

If the period from 1913 through the end of the Great Depression and World War II can be characterized as one in which the Federal Reserve was evolving institutionally, the period since 1951 is one in which the Federal Reserve changed more on the policymaking side as it faced many economic events that tested its decisions. To recognize this, in this section I will examine the development of monetary policy. In the next section I turn to the impact that various crises in financial markets and a series of banking failures had on Federal Reserve regulatory policies.

During the 1940s the main objective of monetary policy was to peg the interest rates on U.S. government securities. The Federal Reserve kept rates low to lower the cost of financing the war effort. Following the war, this policy was maintained for fear that unemployment would increase sharply as the war-induced production of goods subsided with the cessation of hostilities. A policy of pegging interest rates at artificially low levels meant that during the late 1940s the Federal Reserve was expanding the money supply at rates that put upward pressure on prices in the economy. As the rate of inflation began to rise—due in part to the removal of war-time price controls—Federal Reserve officials argued that pegging interest rates precluded them from following policies to fight inflation. Although in 1949 and 1950 inflation subsided and the controversy seemed to cool, the outbreak of hostilities in Korea led to another round of surging prices and calls by Federal Reserve officials for a policy change.

In early 1951 the controversy came to a showdown between the Truman administration and the Federal Reserve. In January 1951 the Treasury Secretary announced that government securities would be issued with interest rates no higher than 2.5 percent. The implication was that the Federal Reserve would follow policies necessary to keep rates at this level. The Federal Reserve had not, in fact, agreed to such a policy and made this point publicly. After a series of internal meetings and some public finger-pointing, the Treasury and the Federal Reserve came to an agreement about the conduct of monetary policy. On March 4, 1951, the Treasury and the Federal Reserve issued a joint statement—the so-called Accord—that forever changed how the Federal Reserve conducts monetary policy.

The accord gave the Federal Reserve autonomy and flexibility. Now it could follow policies it deemed necessary to achieve its dual policy objectives of sustained economic growth (and low unemployment) and low inflation. During the period following the accord, the Federal Reserve tried to achieve these goals by manipulating short-term interest rates. During the 1950s and most of the 1960s, the Federal Reserve paid little attention to movements in the money supply when setting policy. This focus on interest rates as the key tool of policy was flawed, as it had been during the Great Depression. This time, however, as the 1950s turned into the 1960s such policies gave rise to an upward drift in the rate of inflation. This steady increase in inflation is so pronounced that the period 1960–1980 sometimes is referred to as the "Great Inflation" in the United States.

The rate of inflation varied in the 1950s between 2 and 4 percent. Beginning in the 1960s, however, the rate crept upward. By the end of the decade the rate of inflation stood at nearly 6 percent; by the end of the 1970s the rate of inflation was in double digits. The underlying cause of the increase in the rate of inflation was the increase in the average rate of growth of the money supply. With monetary policy trying to reign in rising interest rates, the Federal Reserve's attempt to keep rates low forced it to pursue a policy that continuously raised the growth rate of the money supply. As mentioned earlier, Federal Reserve officials put little consideration into the behavior of the money supply at the time. In fact, the prevalent view was that inflation was caused by firms passing on rising costs of production. This view, along with the popular notion that there was an exploitable tradeoff between the rate of inflation and the unemployment rate (the Phillips curve) set into motion a monetary policy that paid more attention to the level of the unemployment rate and interest rates than inflation and the money supply growth rate.

Not all economists believed that the Federal Reserve's policy approach was appropriate. During the late 1960s Federal Reserve policy was challenged by a group of economists that focused on the behavior of the money supply as an explanation for economic fluctuations and inflation. As the rate of inflation rose, the credibility of the so-called Monetarists increased in a widening circle of economists and policymakers. Nobel Prize economist Milton Friedman, one of the Monetarist's leading spokesmen, argued that relying on the Phillips curve tradeoff would lead to disastrous policy choices *if* a shock occurred that negatively impacted inflation and unemployment. In the 1970s, just such a shock occurred. In the mid-1970s the Organization of Petroleum Exporting Countries, better known by its acronym OPEC, tripled the price of crude oil. This shock brought about a simultaneous increase in inflation and an increase in the unemployment rate. Within its existing policy framework, the Federal Reserve was perplexed: if it tried to counter the rising unemployment rate with an expansionary policy, it would worsen the inflation problem. If it tried to counter the rising rate of inflation with a contractionary policy, this would push the unemployment rate higher. In reality, the Federal Reserve tried both approaches. The aftermath of this episode, as well as a similar oil price hike that began in 1979, was a higher underlying rate of monetary growth and a higher average rate of inflation.

The high average rate of inflation in the late 1970s increased pressure, both domestically and from abroad, on the Federal Reserve to alter its policies. Some changes were being made: passage of the Federal Reserve Reform Act in 1977 and the Humphrey-Hawkins Act in 1978 required the Federal Reserve to preannounce in testimony delivered by the Chairman of the Board of Governors its intended targets for the monetary aggregates and its policy objectives for the coming year. Although such testimony increased policy transparency, it is widely believed that policymakers paid little attention to the targets: movements in short-term rates, primarily the federal funds rate, still dominated policy discussions.

The pressure to alter its approach mounted. In response the Federal Reserve announced on October 6, 1979 that it would henceforth follow policies aimed at achieving "better control over the expansion of money and bank credit, [that would] help curb speculative excesses in financial, foreign exchange, and commodity markets, and thereby serve to dampen inflationary forces." With this statement, the Federal Reserve said it would henceforth try to achieve this goal by placing more emphasis on the behavior of bank reserves—and hence the money supply—than on movements in short-term interest rates. Thus began the "Monetarist experiment" in monetary policy.

This announcement initially was viewed as a major change in the direction of monetary policy. Many believed that monetary policy would now take a longer view, less concerned with the short-term wiggles of the economy and more with the inflationary effects of their actions. As the experiment ensued, actual policy did not follow the path that many had hoped for: the volatility of money growth and of interest rates were higher now than when policy tried to keep the federal funds rate in a relatively narrow band. Monetarists quickly reacted, arguing that Federal Reserve officials never really intended on a policy change, but used the experiment only as camouflage to increase interest rates. Those more sympathetic to the Federal Reserve pointed to swings in the public's holding of money as preventing the Federal Reserve from successfully targeting on the growth of the monetary aggregates in a manner consistent with overall policy objectives. Regardless of who was correct—and the debate continues to this day—the change in policy was associated with the steepest decline in economic activity in the postwar period. The Federal Reserve's policies had succeeded in wringing inflation out of the economy, but the price was a heavy one. By October 1982, monetary policy abandoned the use of monetary targets and switched back to a focus on the behavior of interest rates.

Monetary policy in the era following the Monetarist experiment resembles the earlier time when movements in the federal funds rate predominated policy discussion. Even though the Federal Reserve returned to manipulating interest rates, some significant changes were made. One was the increased openness of policy discussions. Today the FOMC, the policymaking arm of the Federal Reserve, announces its policy intentions immediately after each of its meetings (it meets eight times a year). In earlier times, such information was not made public for months, thus leaving the public to guess about the direction of policy. Increased transparency has reduced the amount of guessing that takes place and, arguably, means that policy changes create less uncertainty in financial markets.

The other major change is the use of a policy rule. Before the 1979 policy experiment, changes in the federal funds rate were made on the basis of what the policymakers felt were appropriate. Their decisions were founded in forecasts provided by mathematical models of the economy, but there often was no firm indication of which way, or by how much, rates should go to achieve those goals. By the 1990s, it became apparent that the Federal Reserve was employing a policy rule to guide its deliberations. This rule, called the Taylor Rule after its creator, John Taylor, established parameters for how much policymakers would need to change the federal funds rate given changes in real output growth and inflation. The announcement that the Taylor Rule was part of the policy analysis added even more transparency to policy deliberations. Those changes have led some to argue that even though the Federal Reserve returned to the use of interest rates as their main policy tool, some of the earlier criticisms of policy have been adopted. In this sense, policy has evolved since the accord in ways that reflect changes in our understanding of how policy affects the economy, and what its limitations really are.

FINANCIAL CRISES

The previous section gave an overview of how monetary policy developed over the past 50 years. During this time there were a number of financial crises that tested the Federal Reserve's stance on bank regulation and how it reacts to financial emergencies. In this section I take a brief look at these events and how they shaped changes in regulation and the Federal Reserve's role as lender of last resort.

About the time when policymakers abandoned the Monetarist experiment and returned to targeting the federal funds rate, there were several developments, none good, in banking. Prior to 1980, banks were unable to pay explicit interest on checking deposits. Because of high inflation during the 1970s, many nonbank financial firms began to compete with commercial banks for deposits. Credit unions, for example, offered interest-bearing checkable deposits. Money market mutual funds did likewise. Even though deposits were not covered by FDIC protection, individuals were willing to gamble on the loss of deposits for the chance to earn interest income.

Banks argued for an overhaul of those regulations, many in place since the Great Depression, which put them at a competitive disadvantage. A major shift in bank regulation and Federal Reserve oversight took place in the form of the Depository Institutions Deregulation and Monetary Control Act (DIDMCA) of 1980. This act was a major step in dismantling many of the regulations that negatively affected banks. Altering the regulatory landscape in which banks operated led to widespread restructuring in the form of consolidation and bank closures.

Although a number of banks closed their doors, none were more famous than the collapse of Penn Square Bank in 1982 and Continental Illinois in 1984. Penn Square is the poster child for the banking excesses of the late 1970s and early 1980s. Located in a strip mall in Oklahoma City, Penn Square grew rapidly as it aggressively loaned to regional oil and gas speculators. With the price of oil and gas at high levels, the successes in the oil fields of Texas, Oklahoma and Louisiana pushed the value of Penn Square's loan portfolio higher and higher. Between 1977 and 1982, the value of Penn Square's loans increased from about $30 million to over $430 million. Although some questioned their lending decisions, bank regulators allowed Penn Square to continue its aggressive practices. That is, until oil prices fell sharply in 1982. The fall in oil prices brought bankruptcy to many oil and gas producers, exactly the ones that had outstanding loans with Penn Square. Unable to meet loan payments, these firms defaulted on their outstanding loans. With asset values falling below liabilities, Penn Square was left insolvent and closed for business on July 5, 1982.

How does this bank's failure fit in with a story of the Federal Reserve? Part of the answer is because the Federal Reserve did not step in to curtail Penn Square's activities. This regulatory forbearance showed up soon after Penn Square failed but in a slightly different form. Perhaps the most celebrated bank failure of the time was that of Continental Illinois.

Continental Illinois, home office in Chicago, also followed an aggressive lending strategy. By 1981 Continental became the nation's largest commercial lender by taking a below-market strategy to encourage borrowing from them. By late 1981 and 1982, however, events outside the control of Continental's management took their toll on this strategy. Like Penn Square, Continental's loan portfolio was weighted heavily to the oil and gas sector of the economy. Continental even participated in some of Penn Square's lending activity. When oil and gas prices fell, Penn Square tumbled and Continental went soon after. Not only did Continental have much of its outstanding loans tied up in the oil and gas business, but it had made substantial loans to less developed countries, especially in Latin America. Problems in the oil industry coupled with the default of several Latin American countries (the so-called LDC debt crisis) pushed Continental Illinois into bankruptcy.

Unlike Penn Square, however, the Federal Reserve rushed in to prop up Continental. This policy, known as the too-big-to-fail policy, was followed because Federal Reserve officials and other governmental regulators felt that if a bank the size of Continental failed it would set off a chain reaction of bank closures reminiscent of the Great Depression. Even with assistance from the Federal Reserve and the FDIC, Continental could not be saved. Surprising to some, the collapse of Continental did not create a shock wave of defaults. While the infusion of funds from the Federal Reserve no doubt helped curtail this possibility, it is not clear that the Federal Reserve's actions accomplished that much. In fact, some argue that such actions merely gave rise to future problems as other bankers now believed that they too would be bailed out in times of distress.

The change in bank regulations also precipitated problems in the savings and loan industry. Although outside the regulatory purview of the Federal Reserve, the systemwide failure of the S&L industry during the 1980s had a large ripple effect on other financial institutions and financial markets in general. The collapse of the S&L industry, tied directly to changes in bank regulations stemming from the DIDMCA, put further pressure on the Federal Reserve in terms of maintaining stability in the banking industry.

These financial crises pushed to the fore the role of the Federal Reserve as lender of last resort. Although widely agreed that the Federal Reserve should step forward in times of financial distress to provide liquidity to the market, its actions in the case of Continental Illinois fueled a debate over when such a role should be taken. That is, if a poorly managed bank goes bankrupt, should the Federal Reserve bail it out or simply let the private market deal with it? Even as this debate ensued another financial shock hit the Federal Reserve: the stock market crash of 1987.

When stock prices fell on Monday, October 19, 1987, some wondered whether this signaled the beginning of another Great Depression. With a 23 percent decline in the Dow Jones Industrial Average in one day, the Federal Reserve publicly announced that it was stepping in to meet the needs of the financial market. Through a series of announcements Federal Reserve officials made it clear that it was not going to stand by as it had during the 1929 crash. This time the Federal Reserve would "meet promptly any unusual liquidity requirements of the economic and financial system" in the days following the crash. The fact that the Federal Reserve moved aggressively in its role of lender of last resort calmed the markets. In fact, by the end of 1987, the stock market averages actually had returned to their precrash levels and economic growth did not suffer any significant decline.

Testing the Federal Reserve's mettle was repeated in the late 1990s. In 1998 the hedge-fund company Long Term Capital Management "bet" that the spread between long-term government bonds and corporate bonds was unusual and would soon return to some normal level. They bet wrong and, facing huge losses, could have been forced to sell its portfolio of securities worth an estimated $80 billion and $1 trillion in derivative securities. Fearing that such a fire sale would disrupt financial markets, the Federal Reserve again moved aggressively. This time it acted to lower the federal funds rate by 75 basis points. This action was taken to signal markets that the Federal Reserve recognized the seriousness of the situation and was moving to calm the markets by injecting funds into the system. These actions, along with a Federal Reserve Bank of New York engineered bailout plan, prevented Long Term's failure and reassured jittery financial markets that the Federal Reserve could be counted on to maintain stability in financial markets.

As if these problems were not enough, during the next couple of years financial markets were rocked with the collapse of stock prices beginning in late 1999 and the terrorist attacks in September 2001. In each case the Federal Reserve moved to provide liquidity to the market in an attempt to stave off any further deterioration. Regarding the stock market decline, there remains a question concerning the Federal Reserve's failure to forestall the surge in stock prices during the late 1990s. Although Federal Reserve Chairman Alan Greenspan had warned of "irrational exuberance" as stock prices climbed, he also led the Federal Reserve at a time when their expansionary policies may have fueled the rally that ended with a massive loss of wealth.

As a final note, it is important to recognize that actions taken by the Federal Reserve in one area often impact another. That is, facing the massive loss of wealth associated with the stock market crash the Federal Reserve soon undertook an very expansionary policy in late 2000. This direction of policy was enhanced following the terrorist attacks of 9/11 as Federal Reserve policy pushed the federal funds rate down from 6 percent to 1 percent, a level not seen since the 1950s. Of course, the logical question to ask is whether this policy would ignite inflationary pressures in the economy? At the time of this writing (summer 2004) the Federal Reserve has begun to reverse this policy, increasing the federal funds rate in small steps.

CONCLUDING REMARKS

I hope that you have a better appreciation for the complexity of monetary policy and the dynamic environment in which the Federal Reserve System operates. The remainder of this book provides a wide-ranging collection of items associated with the Federal Reserve and monetary policy. I do not, however, think that you should consider this your final source. To that end, below is a list of books dealing with the Federal Reserve, its history and how it makes monetary policy. While I am sure that others would add some books or remove some in my list, those listed will get you started on your study of what I believe to be one of the more fascinating topics in economics.

FURTHER READING

Anderson, Clay. *A Half Century of Federal Reserve Policymaking*. Philadelphia: Federal Reserve Bank of Philadelphia, 1965.

Beckhart, Benjamin H. *Federal Reserve System*. New York: American Institute of Banking, 1972.

Board of Governors. *The Federal Reserve System: Its Purpose and Functions*. 8th edition. Washington, D.C.: Board of Governors of the Federal Reserve System, 1994.

Broaddus, Alfred. *A Primer on the Fed*. Richmond: Federal Reserve Bank of Richmond, 1988.

Burgess, W. Randolph. *The Reserve Banks and the Money Market*. 2nd edition. New York: Harper, 1936.

Dunne, Gerald T. *A Christmas Present for the President: A Short History of the Creation of the Federal Reserve System*. St. Louis: Federal Reserve Bank of St. Louis, 1985.

Friedman, Milton, and Anna J. Schwartz. *A Monetary History of the United States: 1867–1960*. Princeton: Princeton University Press, 1963.

Garcia, Gillian, and Elizabeth Plautz. *The Federal Reserve: Lender of Last Resort*. Cambridge: Ballinger, 1988.

Goodhart, Charles. *The Evolution of Central Banks*. Cambridge: MIT Press, 1988.

Grieder, William. *Secrets of the Temple: How the Federal Reserve Runs the Country*. New York: Simon and Schuster, 1987.

Hammond, Bray. *Banks and Politics in America from the Revolution to the Civil War*. Princeton: Princeton University Press, 1957.

Hadjimichalakis, Michael G. *The Federal Reserve, Money, and Interest Rates: The Volcker Years and Beyond*. New York: Praeger, 1984.

Harris, Seymour E. *Twenty Years of Federal Reserve Policy*. 2 volumes. Cambridge: Harvard University Press, 1933.

Johnson, Roger T. *Historical Beginnings...The Federal Reserve System*. Boston: Federal Reserve Bank of Boston, 1989.

Kettl, Donald F. *Leadership at the Fed*. New Haven: Yale University Press, 1986.

Maisel, J. Sherman. *Managing the Dollar*. New York: W.W. Norton, 1973.

Melton, C. *Inside the Fed: Making Monetary Policy*. Homewood, IL: Dow-Jones Irwin, 1985.

Meltzer, Allan H. *A History of the Federal Reserve: Volume I: 1913-1951*. Chicago: University of Chicago Press, 2003.

Meulendyke, Anne-Marie. *U.S. Monetary Policy and Financial Markets*. New York: Federal Reserve Bank of New York, 1998.

Newton, Maxwell. *The Fed: Inside the Federal Reserve, the Secret Power Center that Controls the American Economy*. New York: Times Books, 1983.

Patrick, Sue. *Reform of the Federal Reserve System in the Early 1930s*. New York: Garland, 1993.

Strong, Benjamin. *Interpretations of Federal Reserve Policy in the Speeches and Writings of Benjamin Strong*. Edited by W.R. Burgess. New York: Harper, 1930.

Timberlake, Richard H., Jr. *The Origins of Central Banking in the United States*. Cambridge: Harvard University Press, 1978.

Warburg, Paul M. *The Federal Reserve System, Its Origins and Growth*. 2 volumes. New York: Macmillan, 1930.

Wicker, Elmus R. *Federal Reserve Monetary Policy, 1917-1933*. New York: Random House, 1966.

Wooley, John T. *Monetary Politics: The Federal Reserve and the Politics of Monetary Policy*. Cambridge: Cambridge University Press, 1984.

LIST OF ENTRIES

LIST OF ENTRIES

TOPICAL LIST OF ENTRIES

Fed Watcher
Financial Intermediaries
Liquidity
Money Market
Primary Dealer
Secondary Markets
Mark-to-Market
Random Walk

FINANCIAL MARKET INSTRUMENTS
Bond Rating
Bonds
Commercial Paper
Eurodollars

FINANCIAL MARKET PANICS
Asian Crisis
Black Monday of 1929
Black Monday of 1987
Crash of 1987
Credit Crunch
Financial Bubble
Great Crash
LDC Debt Crisis
Long-Term Capital Management
Morgan, J. P.

**FOREIGN EXCHANGE SYSTEM
AND MARKETS**
Bretton Woods System
Exchange Rate
Gold Standard
Gold Window
International Banking Facilities
Special Drawing Rights
Sterilized and Unsterilized Intervention

FRACTIONAL RESERVE BANKING
Excess Reserves
Free Reserves
Reserve Accounting
Reserve Requirement
Reserves
Vault Cash

GOALS OF MONETARY POLICY
Countercyclical Policy
Full Employment Act of 1946
Full Employment and Balance
 Growth (Humphrey-Hawkins) Act of
 1978
Price Stability
Stabilization Policy

INFLATION
Deflation
Disinflation
Great Inflation
Phillips Curve
Price Index
Purchasing Power of Money
Seigniorage
Wage and Price Controls

INTEREST RATES
Basis Point
Ex Ante and *Ex Post* Real Rate of Interest
Expected Return
Fisher Effect
Interest Rate Spread
Nominal Interest Rate
Real Rate of Interest
Term Structure of Interest Rates

INTERNATIONAL AGENCIES
Group of 5, Group of 7, Group of 8, and
 Group of 10
International Monetary Fund

INTERNATIONAL AGREEMENTS
Basel Accord
Louvre Accord
Plaza Agreement
Smithsonian Agreement of 1971

MACROECONOMICS
Equation of Exchange
Monetarism/Monetarist
Monetary Versus Fiscal Policy Debate
New Classical Economics
New Keynesian Economics
Quantity Theory
Rational Expectations

MEASURING ECONOMIC ACTIVITY
Business Cycle
Economic Growth
Econometric Model
Gross Domestic Product (GDP)

MEMBERS OF CONGRESS
Aldrich, Nelson Wilmarth
Glass, Carter
Patman, John William Wright
Vreeland, Edward

MONETARY MEASURES
Commodity Money
Currency

ADVERSE SELECTION. Suppose two individuals apply for a **loan** from a bank to buy a car. One of them intends to make payments on time, but the other does not. Before the bank makes the loans, it must determine if either of the two borrowers is likely not to repay the loan. As is clear, while the two individuals know with certainty how each will behave after receiving the loan, the bank does not. Not knowing with certainty borrowers' willingness to pay off the loan *before* making the loan illustrates the problem of **asymmetric information** between borrowers and lenders.

Adverse selection is a condition that occurs when there is asymmetric information. Adverse selection occurs when a lender cannot distinguish between a high-risk borrower and a low-risk borrower. When both types of borrowers actively seek a loan, a lending institution will try to determine which is the riskier borrower. If the bank can determine the borrowers' risk level, it charges each borrower an interest rate commensurate with their risk: the higher the risk, the higher the interest rate. If a bank is unable to determine the riskiness of the two borrowers, it simply charges an interest rate on *both* loans that reflects this fact: because the bank may be lending money to a high-risk individual, it will assume that both are high-risk loans and the interest rate charged will be higher than if it could differentiate between the borrowers. These higher interest rates may discourage low-risk borrowers from applying for loans. This is bad for banks, because riskier borrowers are more likely to agree to the higher rate: they have no intention of paying off the loan anyway. As a result, the bank's loan portfolio contains a higher than desired share of high-risk loans. Even though banks may be charging high interest rates on loans, their profitability could suffer if the high-risk borrowers start to default on the loans.

The existence of adverse selection explains the growth in information gathering activities by banks and other lending institutions. If banks are unsure about the risk of lending to an individual, they may not make the loan. What if this company or individual would have paid off the loan? Due to adverse selection, the company that would have expanded its business and hired more workers with the loan now will not do so. Adverse selection has clear negative implications for overall economic activity: Lessening the existence of adverse selection through increased information gathering means that banks will make loans more efficiently. That is, low-risk borrowers will pay lower interest rates compared with high-risk borrowers. This leads to a more efficient allocation of funds.

Banks and other lending companies adopt a variety of strategies to reduce the problem of adverse selection. First, most lenders require credit checks on potential borrowers. Using companies that specialize in checking your credit history (Have you paid off previous loans on time, defaulted on credit card balances, etc.?), banks assemble information that allows them to assess the possibility that a borrower will not repay a loan. The higher the risk of default (i.e., the greater the likelihood that a borrower will not repay the loan), the higher the interest rate the lender will charge. This helps explain why customers get different rates on the same types of loans. Another method that lenders use to deal with adverse selection is to require collateral on loans. For example, when someone takes out a car loan or a home mortgage, the car or the house is the collateral for the loan. If the borrower fails to repay the loan, the bank takes ownership (repossesses) the car or house and sells it to recoup the funds loaned. By requiring collateral, the bank shifts some of the risk of default back to the borrower and reduces the problem of adverse selection. Additionally, banks may try to reduce the cost of adverse selection by charging up-front fees for loans, charging fees for processing the loan, or requiring that borrowers establish deposit accounts with the bank with some minimum balance.

FURTHER READING

Clement, Douglas. "Beyond Supply and Demand." Federal Reserve Bank of Minneapolis *fedgazette* (May 2002); Wheelock, David C., and Subal C. Kumbhaker. "Which Banks Chose Deposit Insurance? Evidence on Adverse Selection and Moral Hazard in Voluntary Insurance Systems." *Journal of Money, Credit and Banking* (February 1995): 186–201.

AGGREGATE SUPPLY SHOCK. When someone uses the term "supply shock," the term generally refers to a situation in which some event has caused the cost of producing a specific good to rise. For example, if pumpkin seed prices increase in the spring, then the cost to a farmer of producing pumpkins increases, which is likely to result in an increase in pumpkin prices in the fall. The shock here is an increase in pumpkin seed prices. The term *aggregate supply shock* applies when some event causes the cost of producing a wide variety of goods to change. A negative shock usually is associated with an increase in the general level of prices, whereas a positive shock has just the opposite effect. For example, a "negative" aggregate supply shock occurred in the mid-1970s when the Organization of Petroleum Exporting Countries (OPEC) agreed to limit production of crude oil and thereby raise its price.

This "oil price shock" reverberated throughout the world. The increase in the price of crude oil generated an increase in the price of refined oil products, such as gasoline and diesel. These price increases raised the cost of producing a vast number of goods because oil and gas are important components in almost any production process—from plastics to fertilizer to home heating; the majority of production process depends on oil and gas in some way. This supply shock caused the general level of prices, measured by the Consumer Price Index (CPI), to increase rapidly: In the mid-1970s, the rate of **inflation**—the percentage change in the CPI—increased at a rate greater than 15 percent. To make matters worse, such a negative aggregate supply shock often leads to a reduction in the pace of business activity, measured by the rate of change in real **gross domestic product (GDP)**. In the mid-1970s, for example, with general prices rising due to the increase in oil prices, incomes were unable to keep pace and there occurred a reduction in business activity—the growth rate of real GDP turned negative—and an increase in the **unemployment rate**. Economists refer to this combination of rising rates of inflation and rising rates of unemployment as **stagflation**.

A "positive" aggregate supply shock, on the other hand, generally has just the opposite effects on the economy. The positive shock reduces costs of production of a broad range of goods and enables higher levels of economic activity without increases in the rate of inflation. Many economists believe that the growing use of computer technologies during the 1990s is an example of a positive supply shock. The increased use of computers helped lower the cost of production in most sectors of the economy. The outcome of this positive aggregate supply shock was a reduction in inflation rates, falling from double digits in the early 1980s to around 2 percent in the late 1990s. Additionally, real output rose throughout the 1990s and the unemployment rate fell to levels not seen since the 1960s.

FURTHER READING

Abel, Andrew B., and Ben S. Bernanke. *Macroeconomics*. 5th edition. Boston: Pearson Addison Wesley, 2005; Meyer, Laurence H. "The New Economy Meets Supply and Demand." Remarks before the Boston Economics Club, Boston, MA, June 6, 2000. Website: www.federalreserve.gov.

ALDRICH, NELSON WILMARTH (1841–1915). Nelson W. Aldrich was born in Foster, Rhode Island, on November 6, 1841. After attending school in Connecticut and Rhode Island, Aldrich entered the wholesale grocery business in Providence, and served with the First Regiment of the Rhode Island National Guard during the Civil War. Aldrich began his political career as a member of the Providence city council and soon entered state politics, serving as a state assemblyman in 1875–1876. From 1879–1881, Aldrich was a U.S. Representative. Aldrich resigned his position as U.S. Representative on October 4, 1981, when he became Senator, a position he held from 1881 through 1911.

Aldrich dominated Republican politics at the state level and was a national figure in Republican politics, especially on issues that affected big business. During the late 1800s, Aldrich promoted protective tariffs to stem the import of foreign goods into the United States. During his time in the Senate, Aldrich actively campaigned against the progressive policies of Theodore Roosevelt and his administration. This helped solidify Aldrich's position as a promoter of big business, because much of Roosevelt's progressive policy platform was aimed at controlling the activities of big business.

In addition to his support of business, Aldrich focused a great deal of his attention on monetary matters. In 1897 he took the helm and guided Republican administrative legislation. From this position he was able to force the "Silver Republicans" out of the party. The Silver Republicans favored the addition of silver to back the money supply of the United States. Supporters of a bimetallic system in which both silver and gold would be used to back the money supply argued that it would help ensure the stability of the dollar's value. Although popular with a wide variety of groups, the push for silver pitted the **gold standard** interests, generally viewed as East Coast establishment bankers, against the agrarian West. Silver supporters knew that by allowing silver to back the money supply, prices would rise at a faster rate. Because prices for commodities, especially agricultural goods, suffered declines throughout the late 1880s, this was seen as a panacea for the woes of the agrarian sector of the economy. The "eastern establishment," of which Aldrich was considered a member, viewed this as a break from the gold standard and argued against the change. In the end, the power of the gold interests prevailed and the silver movement died.

With the passage of the Gold Standard Act of 1900, the silver movement was effectively quashed. This act defined the dollar only in terms of gold and required the Secretary of the Treasury to maintain a gold reserve of $150 million. In essence, this act committed the United States to the gold standard. [For an interesting treatment of this episode, see Rockoff (1990), who suggests that L. Frank Baum's book *The Wonderful Wizard of Oz* is a metaphor for the debate over the usefulness of gold and silver.]

In a history of the Federal Reserve, Aldrich is best remembered for his work during the early 1900s. He, along with U.S. Representative **Edward Vreeland**, shaped the **Aldrich-Vreeland Act of 1908**. The act was passed in the aftermath of the **Panic of 1907**, a downturn that exposed many problems in the U.S. banking and monetary system, a key one being the so-called inelastic supply of money. This means that increases and decreases in the money supply were determined solely by changes in the gold stock. That and the prevailing view of the time that the money supply would be self-regulating as business demands dictate meant that during emergencies, like the Panic of 1907, the money supply could not adjust to offset an economic downturn. The Aldrich-Vreeland Act sought to remedy this problem by allowing for the emergency issuance of currency in times of distress. In that sense, the act was viewed as providing a mechanism by which the supply of currency could be changed to meet the needs of the economy.

This act also created the **National Monetary Commission**. The commission's charge was to study the banking practices of the United States and other countries, and to examine the structure and activities of foreign central banks to see what best practices from these others' could be adapted to the U.S. monetary system. Aldrich headed the National Monetary Commission from 1908 through 1912. The commission produced the "Aldrich Plan" in 1911, a plan that called for many changes in the U.S. banking system and for the creation of a central bank. Although the Aldrich Plan was not made into law, it did, in many ways, form the foundation upon which the **Federal Reserve Act of 1913**, was based.

Following his service on the commission, Aldrich retired to Providence, Rhode Island. Nelson W. Aldrich died in New York City on April 16, 1915.

FURTHER READING

"Biographical Directory of the United States Congress." Website: http://bioguide.congress; Rockoff, Hugh. "The Wizard of Oz as a Monetary Allegory." *Journal of Political Economy* (August 1990): 739–60; Stephenson, Nathaniel W. *Nelson W. Aldrich: A Leader in American Politics.* Port Washington, NY: Kennikat Press, 1971; Aldrich's papers are housed at Rockefeller University. Website: www.rockefeller.edu/archive.

ALDRICH-VREELAND BILL, OR ACT, OF 1908. The Aldrich-Vreeland Bill, which was passed by Congress on May 30, 1908, was named after its two sponsors: Senator **Nelson W. Aldrich** and Representative **Edward B. Vreeland**. The act followed closely on the heels of the **Panic of 1907**, an economic downturn and banking panic that illustrated problems in the banking and monetary system of the United States.

The Panic of 1907 demonstrated the difficulties that a banking system faces when there is an "inelastic," or nonresponsive, stock of money. At the time, the main cause for changes in the money supply was changes in the stock of gold, since the United States operated on the **gold standard**. This meant that increases and decreases in the amount of money in the economy came about primarily through increases and decreases in the flow of gold into and out of the United States. When individuals chose to convert deposits at banks into gold coin, this had a detrimental effect: converting deposits to coin caused drains on bank deposits, which generated a contraction in the money supply. The end result was often a slowing in economic activity, sometimes even a severe **recession** like that which culminated in the Panic of 1907.

A popular economic theory at the time was the so-called **real bills doctrine**. This notion held that the pace of economic activity and business trade determines the changes in the supply of money. As business activity picks up, the money supply simply expands to meet business needs. Another aspect of this view, one that was totally discounted in later years, was that banks would make only self-liquidating or short-term loans. In short, supporters of the real-bills doctrine believed that the central bank should control credit flows in the economy and should not be concerned about the behavior of the self-regulating money supply. (The events of the **Great Depression** would prove this view to be dramatically incorrect.)

The act contained two key provisions. Each provision aimed at the problems inherent in controlling the stock of money in the economy. One was to increase the responsiveness of the money supply to changing demands. The other was to create the **National Monetary Commission**.

The main thrust of the Aldrich-Vreeland Act in the area of monetary reform was to allow for emergency issuance of **currency**. The idea was that in times of increased demand for money, unless there was a method by which banks could meet these demands, **bank runs** would occur and economic activity would suffer. Thus the act sought to provide for a more elastic supply of currency and, therefore, money.

The remedy was to allow banks to form "associations" that had the power to issue currency in emergency situations. An association was described as any 10 national banks with a total equity fund equal to or in excess of $15 million. The association had the ability, with oversight by the U.S. Treasury, to issue emergency currency. To obtain currency from an association, banks could use as collateral a variety of government **bonds**, such as U.S., state or local, corporate bonds and **commercial paper**. In this manner, the act eased an earlier restriction that collateral for issuing currency could only be U.S. government bonds. This aspect of the act provided the banking system with much more flexibility to respond to emergency needs. At the same time, the act included a provision that its sponsors believed would prevent overissuance of currency. For example, the privilege of issuing currency was limited to those banks with outstanding notes already secured by government bonds. The act also limited the amount of currency issued by any one association to be a specified fraction of their capital. The idea was that while provision of currency in times of an emergency was good, allowing banks to flood the economy with money would have longer-term detrimental effects and should be avoided.

The number of bank associations grew slowly after the act passed. The first association was the National Currency Association of Washington, which formed in 1908. It was not until 1910 that other associations began to form. In that year, 13 associations were formed, with six more in 1911, one in 1912 and three in 1913. By the end of 1913 there were a total of 21 national currency associations that included about 350 banks. Although the total number of banks in the associations amounted to less than 5 percent of the banks operating in the United States at the time, the total capital comprised by these banks was about one-third of the total for the whole banking industry.

The emergency currency provision in the act was used on only one occasion, that being the outbreak of World War I. On July 31, 1914, due to uncertainties circulating in the financial markets, trading on the New York Stock Exchange was halted. The reason for the trading halt was the large-scale selling of securities by Europeans, which, it was believed, would lead to widespread uncertainty and panic selling by domestic stockholders. As a response to this action, country banks began withdrawing currency from New York City banks. Such currency drains, if left unchecked, would lead to problems often associated with the bank runs that occurred during the Panic of 1907. On August 3, 1914, in response to this event, the New York Clearing House issued loan certificates—currency substitutes—a response that was soon followed by other clearing houses and associations. By November 1914, about $400 million of emergency currency had been issued. Unlike the events that unfolded in 1908, the ability of the clearing houses and associations to provide currency to meet the demands of anxious bank customers prevented any widespread bank run. Indeed, **Milton Friedman** and **Anna Jacobson Schwartz** (1963, p. 172) argue that "the availability of the emergency currency issue probably prevented a monetary panic and the restriction of payments by the banking system."

The other major component of the act and the one that has left the longest shadow over U.S. monetary policy was the creation of the National Monetary Commission. Chaired by Senator Nelson W. Aldrich, with Representative Edward B. Vreeland as vice-chair, the commission was made up of nine senators and nine representatives. The broad charge of the commission was to investigate and report on the development of banking systems both in the United States and in other countries, to examine U.S. financial laws, to study banking practices, and to investigate the origins of the national banking system. Based on this wide-ranging investigation, the final report filled a total of 47 volumes. In 1912 the commission recommended many changes in the banking and monetary system to improve its efficiency and reduce the likelihood of further bank panics and economic recessions. These suggested reforms to the banking and monetary system became known as the Aldrich Plan, after the chairman of the commission. In many ways, the Aldrich Plan became the template for the **Federal Reserve Act of 1913**.

FURTHER READING

Friedman, Milton, and Anna J. Schwartz. *A Monetary History of the United States, 1867–1960*. Princeton: Princeton University Press, 1963; Groseclose, Elgin. *Fifty Years of Managed Money*. London: McMillan Press, 1966; Warburg, Paul. *The Federal Reserve System, Its Origins and Growth*. New York: Arno Press, 1930.

ANDERSEN, LEONALL (1924–1985). Leonall Andersen was an economist in the research department of the Federal Reserve Bank of St. Louis. While this alone would not qualify him for inclusion in this volume, his research published while employed there does. Andersen and **Jerry Jordan** co-authored one of the most important economic studies of the 1960s. Their article, "Monetary and Fiscal Actions: A Test of Their Relative Importance in Economic Stabilization," which appeared in the Federal Reserve Bank of St. Louis's *Review* in November 1968, set off a maelstrom of debate over the comparative usefulness of fiscal policy—changes in government taxation and spending—and monetary policy. At the time, the conventional wisdom among most economists and policymakers was that fiscal policy was the government's main tool to stabilize economic activity.

Because it was widely believed at the time that the government could "fine tune" the economy—keeping it neither too much above nor too much below full employment—the very fact that Andersen and Jordan's study suggested otherwise was grounds for argument.

Essentially, the Andersen-Jordan model posited that movements in nominal income, (measured by **gross domestic product**, or **GDP**) were better explained by previous changes in the stock of money than by changes in government spending or taxation. Even though the study indicated that fiscal policy had some short-term influence on nominal economic activity, Andersen and Jordan found that these affects disappeared after less than a year. That is, an increase in government spending might increase nominal GDP over the course of a few months, but its effects then dissipated so that in the long run, the net effect was zero. Monetary policy actions, on the other hand, were shown to have long-lasting effects. For example, an increase in the stock of money was shown to increase nominal GDP by a proportional amount, an effect that took about a year to be fully reflected in GDP, but one that was permanent.

This was an important finding for the so-called **Monetarist** movement. This group of economists believed that changes in the supply of money were critical in explaining economic activity. It had been demonstrated previously by a number of economists, including **Milton Friedman**, **Anna Jacobson Schwartz**, **Karl Brunner** (who coined the term Monetarism), and **Allan Meltzer**, to name a few, that changes in economic activity and inflation were related directly to movements in the money supply over time. What Andersen and Jordan did was to show that in the short run, movements in the money supply also contributed to observed changes in nominal income. Given these two results, it was easy to demonstrate that short-term fluctuations in the money supply were directly related to short-term fluctuations in real economic activity, measured by nominal GDP adjusted for price level changes. If this were true, then monetary policy, not fiscal, should be the dominant policy tool used to achieve full employment.

As the debate over Andersen-Jordan continued, Andersen extended this work by producing an economic model that was considered a prototype Monetarist model. This work, co-authored with Keith Carlson and published in 1970 under the title "A Monetarist Model for Economic Stabilization," also appeared in the Federal Reserve Bank of St. Louis's *Review*. This article demonstrated that the Monetarist idea of money's importance could be translated into a model of the economy; one that proved to be much more compact than the other economic models being built and discussed at the time. Indeed, the Andersen-Carlson model consisted of fewer than a dozen equations, much smaller than the conventional models that sometimes exceeded several hundred equations. This model demonstrated the Monetarist idea that movements in the money supply dominated all other policy variables in explaining movements in the rate of inflation and real GDP.

Although the Andersen-Jordan and Andersen-Carlson studies became some of the most cited works in economics, their message—that changing the money supply could be used to fine-tune economic activity—fell into disrepute in the early 1980s. Unforeseen changes in the technology of transacting, changes in the nature of why people hold cash and checking balances, and changes in the relation between movements in the supply of money and the economy all helped to weaken the message that Andersen and his colleagues had promoted. While it still remains an economic fact that money and inflation are related in the long run and that money and real output are not, there is little support for the idea that changing the growth rate of the supply of money has predictable short-run effects on the real economy.

Nevertheless, the contributions of Leonall Andersen remain important steps in the development of our understanding about how monetary policy affects the economy.

After retiring from the Federal Reserve Bank of St. Louis in 1978, Andersen accepted a position as professor of banking in the College of Business Administration at the University of Florida, a position he held until 1981. At that time he accepted the position of professor of economics at Gustavus Adolphus College in Minnesota, his undergraduate alma mater. He held that position until his death on October 27, 1985.

FURTHER READING

Hafer, R. W., and David Wheelock. "The Rise and Fall of a Policy Rule: Monetarism at the St. Louis Fed, 1968–86." Federal Reserve Bank of St. Louis *Review* (January/February 2001): 1–24; Federal Reserve Bank of St. Louis *Review* (October 1986) commemorative issue.

ANNOUNCEMENT EFFECT. Prior to 1994, the decisions made by the **Federal Open Market Committee (FOMC)** regarding its objectives for the **federal funds rate** were not made public. (*See* **Asymmetric Policy Directive**.) To interpret Federal Reserve policy, analysts watched movements of interest rates, especially the federal funds rate, to get an idea where policy was headed. After 1994, the Federal Reserve began announcing its target level for the federal funds rate immediately following each meeting. The **announcement effect** measures the market response that results from the Federal Reserve's announcement of a new target for the federal funds rate. Prior to 1994, unanticipated changes in policy, changes that so-called **Fed Watchers** did not expect beforehand, had large impacts on the behavior of various interest rates. With the increased openness of Federal Reserve policy since 1994, dramatic shifts in policy—unexpected changes in the economy—occur less often, thus producing less policy-induced volatility in interest rates. The fact that such announcements today have smaller effects on interest rates suggests that the more open reporting by the Federal Reserve enables the public to better understand and predict changes in the direction of monetary policy.

FURTHER READING

Demirlap, Selva, and Oscar Jorda. "The Announcement Effect: Evidence from Open Market Desk Data." Federal Reserve Bank of New York *Economic Policy Review* (May 2002): 29–48.

ASIAN CRISIS. During the 1990s, many of the East Asian economies experienced rapid **economic growth**. These economies also enjoyed relatively low rates of **inflation** and high savings and investment rates. As this combination of positive economic factors continued, there also were sharp increases in the value of stock and land prices. Although many of the Asian economies were expanding at rapid rates, certain events external to their economies led to a sudden decline in the foreign exchange value of their **currencies**. For example, both the Chinese yuan and the Japanese yen were devalued sharply; that is, their value in exchange with other currencies fell. In addition, changes in the global market place had direct, adverse effects on these economies. Perhaps the most important external shock was the reduction in the price of computer semiconductors, a key export product of several Asian countries.

This confluence of economic factors and continued pressures in the foreign exchange markets first led to a collapse in the foreign exchange value of the Thai baht in July 1997.

The collapse of the baht set into motion a series of currency reevaluations throughout Asia. Along with the currency devaluations came reassessments of the Asian financial systems that had supported and encouraged the rapid economic growth and, in hindsight, unbridled financial speculation. By the summer of 1998, stock indexes in many of the affected countries had fallen to less than half their values before the crisis began. In general, the value of East Asian currencies fell 30 to 80 percent against the U.S. dollar. Similar to the **financial panics and crises** that occurred in other countries and the United States, these events ultimately resulted in widespread bankruptcies and contractions in economic activity across many Asian economies.

Many researchers have analyzed the causes of and effects from the Asian crisis. Besides an interest in the crisis as another event study in the long history of financial panics, the lessons learned from the crisis can aid central bankers and policymakers to select policy actions that can prevent similar crises from occurring in the first place and to determine what actions to take in the future if and when such a crisis occurs. One interesting aspect of the Asian crisis was the speed at which the difficulties in one economy spread to other countries, much like the problems that affected banks in the United States during the **Great Depression**. What started out as a problem in one area of the country quickly spread throughout the economy. Aside from the lessons to be learned, the Asian crisis thus is important in a discussion of central banking.

One lesson learned from the crisis, and one that specifically lends itself to a discussion of the Federal Reserve, is how bank regulations, or the lack thereof, may have contributed to the events of 1997. Some economists have noted that many of the financial institutions in the East Asian countries were holding a significant amount of liabilities due to foreigners. That is, they had incurred liabilities—financial promises owed to others—and had not backed them with significant amounts of liquid assets, items easily converted into cash. This is a recipe for financial panic: Once the owners of those liabilities decide to convert their liabilities into liquid assets, such as currency, the financial institutions simply cannot meet all of their demands at once. A comparable event occurs when depositors at a bank all decide simultaneously to convert their deposits into cash. With limited reserves on hand, a bank simply cannot meet everyone's request and must deny funds to some depositors. Once word of the bank's inability—or unwillingness—to convert deposits to cash reaches the general public, it is possible that a **bank run** begins. If a run occurs, depositors attempt to withdraw their funds not only from the troubled bank but from others as well. Because depositors cannot tell if their bank does or does not have adequate funds to meet depositors' demands, and because no one wants to risk their savings, everyone tries to get their money out, causing a financial panic. If allowed to spread, as in the Great Depression, the banking system effectively collapses.

The evidence indicates that not all countries in East Asia were affected equally by the crisis. For example, Indonesia, South Korea, and Thailand, three countries with the most troubled financial sectors, experienced the most severe effects of the crisis. Other countries with financial institutions that implemented better protection against such runs, Singapore, for example, suffered less, while they still experienced some of the negative consequences of the crisis.

Moreno (1998) notes that there are two characteristics common among the East Asian economies that experienced the most severe financial crisis in the late 1990s. First, the decision on how credit is allocated was not always based on standard business practices. In other words, credit often was allocated not based on potential loss or gain by the lender but on the informal connections of borrowers. This meant that even firms that had demonstrated poor management and posed significant risk of collapse often received **loans** or credit simply based on who the management knew or based on some government-imposed quota determining which firms/industries would get credit. Second, many financial intermediaries were protected against loss from bad loans. In other words, some of the governments in the East Asian countries simply guaranteed the loans of firms so that financial institutions cared little about potential losses or risk of the borrower. Because financial institutions did not bear the cost of failure, the incentive to effectively manage the riskiness of the loans being made disappeared. Bad loans were made with little regard to the affect of their default. This, Moreno writes, "was confirmed by events in 1997, when the government encouraged banks to extend emergency loans to some troubled conglomerates which were having difficulties servicing their debts and supplied special loans to weak banks. These responses further weakened the financial position of lenders and contributed to the uncertainty that triggered the financial crisis towards the end of 1997."

The events that transpired during the late 1990s in East Asia provide several lessons for policymakers. First, increased integration of banking and financial activities across international borders increases the possibility that changes in market perceptions may affect financial institutions around the globe. In an economy that permits a relatively free flow of capital and depends somewhat on international trade, increasing available funds to the banking system to prop up troubled banks, may have adverse long-term effects. With the inflow of **liquidity**—the central banks acting as **lender of last resort**—the exchange rate may become destabilized. This in turn could lead foreign holders of the domestic currency to try to reduce their holdings by demanding other, more stable currencies. If the government cannot meet these currency demands, then there could be severe impacts. Indeed, during the Asian crisis, those countries that were able to satisfy currency demands—those countries with relatively large foreign exchange reserves, such as the Philippines, Malaysia, and Taiwan—suffered less during the crisis than those countries without sufficient foreign currency reserves, such as South Korea, Indonesia, and Thailand.

The upshot is that the Asian crisis illustrates the need for soundness in the financial sector. Although the crisis had the classic conditions of a panic, the differential effects across countries illustrate the role of bank regulation in mitigating some of those effects. In those countries where sound lending practices were used, the crisis had a much smaller effect than in those countries where "cronyism" and government guarantees against loan default ruled.

FURTHER READING

Moreno, Ramon. "What Caused East Asia's Financial Crisis?" Federal Reserve Bank of San Francisco *Economic Letter* (August 7, 1998); Moreno, Ramon, Gloria Pasadilla, and Eli Remolona. "Asia's Financial Crisis: Lessons and Policy Responses." In *Asia: Responding to Crisis*. Tokyo, Asian Development Bank Institute; Radelet, Steven, and Jeffrey Sachs, "The Onset of the East Asian Financial Crisis." Harvard Institute for International Development (March 1998).

ASYMMETRIC INFORMATION. The notion of asymmetric information is fairly straightforward: individuals have different amounts of information upon which to base decisions. For example, when two parties enter into a contract without knowing for sure the other's intention, this is an example of asymmetric information. An example of this problem occurs in banking when a firm applies for a **loan** from a bank. (*See* **Adverse Selection**.) In this case the firm may have better information than the bank does about the riskiness of its business and the likely return related to the investment project for which it wishes to borrow funds. Also, the firm knows whether it intends to repay the loan. To address this problem of unequal information, banks use the services of certain firms, such as credit report agencies, that specialize in collecting background information about borrowers' and supplying this to lenders (for a fee) before loans are made.

George Akerlof, a professor of economics at the University of California-Berkeley, is generally credited with recognizing the importance of asymmetric information in economics. In fact, his initial discussion of asymmetric information and how it pertains to market transactions form the basis for awarding him the Nobel Price in economics in 2001. To see just how valuable was Akerlof's discovery, consider his assessment (Akerlof, 2001) of the problems associated with asymmetric information:

> I first came upon the problems resulting from asymmetric information in an early investigation of a leading cause for fluctuations in output and employment—large variations in the sales of new cars. . . . I discovered that the informational problems that exist in the used car market were potentially present to some degree in all markets. In some markets, asymmetric information is fairly easily soluble by repeat sale and by reputation. In other markets, such as insurance markets, credit markets, and the market for labor, asymmetric information between buyers and sellers is not easily solvable and results in serious market breakdowns. For example, the elderly have a hard time getting health insurance; small businesses are likely to be credit-rationed; and minorities are likely to experience statistical discrimination in the labor market because people are lumped together into categories of those with similar observable traits. The failure of credit markets is one of the major reasons for under-development.

FURTHER READING

Akerlof, George A. "Behavioral Macroeconomics and Macroeconomic Behavior." Nobel Prize Lecture (December 8, 2001). Accessed at Nobel Prize Website: www.nobel.se/economics/laureates/2001

ASYMMETRIC POLICY DIRECTIVE. In January 2000, the **Federal Open Market Committee (FOMC)** made an announcement that helped to increase the **transparency** of monetary policy. Beginning with that meeting, the FOMC announced that it would, at the conclusion of future meetings, make known any change in the stance of policy. In addition, the FOMC would make public any change in their assessment of the risk of **inflation** or weak **economic growth** over the immediate future. These two actions reflected quite a change from past FOMC behavior. What this change accomplished was to provide **Fed Watchers** an official, immediate statement of FOMC policy interpretations. And while the new information does not indicate the likely direction or timing of future policy actions, it does give the public a better understanding of the basis upon which future policy actions will be based.

Why was this change so important? Historically the FOMC made decisions about the growth of the money supply or changes in interest rates in a highly secretive manner. For instance, the **blue book** and the **green book**, documents that provide the Board staff with estimates and forecasts of the economy and financial markets, are not made public until some years after the meetings have taken place. These aspects of setting policy meant that many resources were expended trying to determine what the Federal Reserve was going to do. Once the FOMC had met, Fed Watchers tried to decipher any change in the direction or emphasis of policy through observed changes in market interest rates, especially the **federal funds rate**, or by changes in bank **reserves**. Both measures reflect Federal Reserve policy, because they are related to **open market operations**, the main tool by which the Federal Reserve brings about its desired policies.

Although still secretive—cameras and reporters are not allowed in the meetings, for instance—the recent change is another step by the FOMC toward greater transparency. As documented by Wheelock and Thornton (2000), this recent move is one in a series of actions taken to increase awareness and immediacy of Federal Reserve decisions. For example, following each meeting the FOMC issues its **directive** to the open market **trading desk** of the New York Federal Reserve. The directive is the document that guides individuals at the trading desk (the "desk") in New York, indicating whether to undertake trading actions consistent with an expansionary or contractionary policy. For example, the directive may call for the desk to take actions that would increase the federal funds rate in an attempt to slow economic activity, something that may be desired if inflation is perceived as a greater risk than slow economic growth. Between 1983 and 1999, the directive included language that revealed the FOMC's expectations for possible changes in the stance of policy. Wheelock and Thornton (2000, p. 1) note that "the statement pertaining to possible future policy was known as the 'symmetry,' 'tilt,' or 'bias,' of the directive. The directive was said to be symmetric if it indicated that a tightening or easing of policy were likely in the future. Otherwise, the directive was said to be *asymmetric* toward either tightening or easing"(emphasis added).

Beginning in 1999, the postmeeting announcement by the FOMC did not indicate whether an asymmetric directive had or had not been issued to the market trading desk at the New York Federal Reserve. Beginning with the May 1999 meeting, however, the FOMC began to announce what it thought was a likely direction of policy actions *in the future*. Even though the FOMC did not announce what actions had been decided upon at the meeting, it now provided a glimpse into what may occur down the road. This change ended with the January 2000 announcement.

How should one interpret the January 2000 announcement? Why did the FOMC do away with the asymmetric directive? First, the January 2000 announcement ends a long history of the FOMC not providing much information about what its actual policy or what it might be in the future. Issuing an asymmetric directive provided the FOMC with enough flexibility that intermeeting changes in policy, sometimes large deviations from the last directive, could be undertaken in necessary. Wheelock and Thornton (2000, p. 1) suggest that "an asymmetric directive ... granted the chairman authority to make larger intermeeting policy changes in the direction specified by the asymmetric language than he otherwise was permitted to make." In other words, the asymmetric directive gave policymakers more leeway to engage in policy changes if they believed that conditions warranted it. Wheelock and Thornton (2000) also note that an asymmetric directive was often used to build a consensus within the FOMC, especially if there was dissention over the future direction of policy. For example, an asymmetric directive allowed those FOMC members who dissented from the majority view to still vote along with the majority, knowing that the possibility of a policy change could still take place in the future.

While these possible interpretations are not necessarily exclusive, they do suggest reasons why the asymmetric directive lasted for so many years. In the end, the 2000 change signifies a move toward more openness in the setting of monetary policy.

FURTHER READING

Thornton, Daniel L., and David C. Wheelock. "A History of the Asymmetric Policy Directive." Federal Reserve Bank of St. Louis *Review* (September/October 2000): 1–16.

AUTOMATED TELLER MACHINE (ATM). Increased efficiency in providing banking services to the public came with the revolution in telecommunications. One example is the automated teller machine, or ATM for short. An ATM allows bank customers to deposit money into accounts, move funds between accounts, and make cash withdrawals electronically. Because ATMs make use of modern telecommunications systems, customers can engage in these activities at locations far from their bank, even overseas. While ATMs increase convenience for customers, ATMs also allow banks to avoid certain banking regulations. For instance, ATMs allow a bank to offer its services in many places—even fast-food restaurants—without the need to build a new branch office.

How does an ATM work? An ATM is just a data terminal that links the customer with his or her bank. For example, suppose someone wants $80. When the ATM card is inserted into the machine and the PIN number is entered, the host computer then sends a message to that individual's bank and funds are transferred electronically from the bank to the host computer's account (assuming the bank does not own the host computer). Once this step is completed, the host computer sends a message to the ATM to authorize the dispensing of cash. The $80 in bills is dispensed and the individual's bank account is reduced electronically by $80.

Although ATMs seem to be everywhere, this was not always the case. The American Bankers Association provides many useful statistics about the rapid rise of ATMs. For example, when and where was the first ATM transaction? The answer is 1971 at the Citizens & Southern National Bank in Atlanta, Georgia. How many ATM machines are there? The American Bankers Association reports that in 1990, there were about 80,000 ATM machines in operation in the United States. By the end of the 1990s, that number stood at almost 190,000, an increase of nearly 140 percent. Along with the increased number of machines came an increase in volume: in 1990, there were an estimated 5.8 billion transactions. By 1998, that number had grown to over 11 billion. In other words, the number of ATM transactions increased from 184 transactions *per second* in 1990 to 355 transactions *per second* by 1998. Who owns the most ATMs? Bank of America. What is the average size of the withdrawal? $80.

There has been some debate over issues regarding the accessibility of ATM services. That is, some argue that anyone should be able to access cash from any ATM without having to pay a service fee from the bank that owns the machine. One reason why banks charge fees to customers of other banks is because ATM machines are not costless to operate, and the availability of ATMs change the cash reserves that a bank must hold, especially in tourist areas. Based on information from the American Bankers Association, the cost of an ATM machine ranges from $15,000 to $50,000, depending on the functions required by the machine. More important, the annual maintenance cost of an ATM ranges from $20,000 to $30,000. This maintenance cost includes service fees, cash replenishment, telephone line costs, repair, rent, etc.

FURTHER READING

American Bankers Association. Website: www.aba.com ATM Connection. Website: www. atmd.com

BALANCE SHEET. A balance sheet is a financial statement that lists the assets and liabilities of an individual or a firm at a specific point in time. For example, stocks, a car, and a collection of stamps are assets to those who own them. Assets have some market value and may generate an income to their owners. At the same time, if someone is paying off a home mortgage or credit cards, those payments represent liabilities. A liability is something that is owed to another. The dollar difference between the two—assets minus liabilities—is referred to as net worth. For instance, if assets add up to $1,000 and liabilities add up to $500, then net worth is $500.

For a **commercial bank**, it is a little different. Its balance sheet still lists assets and liabilities, but they may have a different meaning. For a bank, its liabilities are its source of loanable funds. That is, the funds that customers have in a checking account at the bank, while an asset to the customer, are a liability to the bank: it owes the money to the customer, because the bank is liable for the money should the customer ever request it. Even so, such deposits are an important source of funds that the bank can use to make loans. On the other side of the balance sheet, the bank's assets are how it uses customers' deposits. For example, a bank uses deposits to make **loans** and buy government securities. Assets generate income for the bank. If the total value of the bank's assets exceeds the total value of its liabilities, the bank has a positive net worth.

Below is the aggregate balance sheet for all commercial banks in the United States as of April 2003. The entries in the balance sheet are reported in billions and given in parentheses as a percent of the total. This is a very streamlined version of the banking systems' balance sheet. For example, the "Loans and leases" category includes commercial and industrial loans, real estate loans, and consumer loans, among other items. Similarly, "Deposits" includes transaction deposits—checking accounts—and nontransaction accounts, such as savings and other time accounts.

This level of simplification is useful to illustrate a balance sheet, especially as it relates to the banking system. On the asset side, the banks' loans and leases represent the largest source of income for the average bank. In 2003, this component amounted to almost 60 percent of the banks' assets, with securities a distant second at 25 percent. Banks generate revenue from loans and leases by making loans at interest rates greater than that paid to acquire funds.

Although smaller than loans, the securities component of the bank's balance sheet also is an important source of revenue. Securities held by commercial banks are limited to

Balance Sheet of All Commercial Banks in the United States

Assets (Uses of Funds)		Liabilities (Sources of Funds)	
Cash items	$ 317.6 (4%)	Deposits	$4,613.4 (64%)
Securities	1,765.6 (25%)	Borrowings	1,406.5 (20%)
Loans and leases	4,206.5 (59%)	Other	591.5 (8%)
Other	843.3 (12%)	Capital	575.7 (8%)
Total	$7,187.1	Total	$7,187.1

Source: Federal Reserve Statistical Release H.8, June 6, 2003.

debt instruments (**bonds**) because banks are prohibited from owning stock in companies. The securities held by banks are comprised largely of U.S. government securities and state and local government securities. Of these, U.S. government securities are the most easily converted to cash in times of need, and thus are sometimes referred to as secondary reserves. The final component of assets, although not necessarily in size, is the cash assets held by banks. This entry reflects banks' **reserves** deposited at the Federal Reserve and **vault cash**, cash held in the bank's vault. It also includes something called "cash items in the process of collection." When a check written upon a bank is deposited into an account at another bank, an account called "cash items in the process of collection" is credited until those balances have been collected by the receiving bank. The receiving bank views this amount as an asset, because it represents funds owed to it from the other bank that will be collected in a short time.

The liability side of the balance sheet reflects the sources of loanable funds for a bank. As you can see in the table, the largest single component (64 percent) is deposits. Deposits, including checking accounts, such as NOW accounts or simple checking accounts, savings accounts, and time deposits, are owed to depositors. In that sense they are a liability to the bank but an asset to you. Of the two primary types of deposits, nontransaction accounts (e.g., savings) are the primary source of funds that banks use to make loans and purchase securities. The other major component on the liability side is borrowing. Banks often borrow funds from other banks, for example, through the federal funds market, or from the Federal Reserve. (The latter are referred to as discount loans.) Banks also may borrow funds from corporations through **repurchase agreements** or, if they are part of a bank holding company, through the parent corporation. Borrowing has become an increasingly important source of funds for banks. While borrowing today accounts for about 20 percent of banks' total liabilities, 40 years ago it was less than 5 percent of the total.

The last entry on the liability side of the balance sheet is something called capital. Bank capital is simply the difference between assets and liabilities. It is the bank's "wealth" position. When bank capital is positive, as it is in the above balance sheet, this means that the total value of a bank's assets exceeds the value of its liabilities. This is good: bank capital is a cushion of funds that banks use in case the value of their assets falls. When bank capital is negative, the bank technically is insolvent or bankrupt. As shown in the balance sheet above, the level of bank capital for the aggregate banking system in April 2003 was about 8 percent, although the actual value varies across individual banks. Banks determine the amount of capital they hold partly on the basis of capital requirement that are determined by the Federal Reserve. (*See* **Capital Requirements**.)

FURTHER READING

"Balance Sheet." Website: www.BusinessTown.com/accounting/basic-sheets.asp; Mishkin, Frederic S. *The Economics of Money, Banking, and Financial Markets.* 7th edition. Boston: Pearson Addison Wesley, 2004.

BANKERS ACCEPTANCES. A bankers acceptance is perhaps best explained by example. Suppose that a U.S. importing firm would like financing from its bank and it cannot obtain financing from the exporting firm located in another country. The importer may ask for acceptance financing from its bank. The acceptance agreement drawn up between the importer and its bank essentially is a contract by which the bank agrees to accept drafts (like a promise to pay) from the importer and that the importer agrees to repay drafts that the bank accepts. In this case, the importer receives a draft from the exporter; the bank accepts the draft and pays the importer some percentage of the face value. In other words, the bank "discounts" the draft, giving the importer some but not all of the draft. The importer then uses this money to pay the exporter for the goods.

An acceptance of this type is quite common in international trade where firms do not have close working relationships. Banks step in and effectively guarantee payment to one of the firms with the other agreeing to terms of the acceptance. Once an acceptance is created, the bank may hold it or sell it in a secondary market (re-discounting). As LaRouche (1993, p. 76) describes it, "In the former case, the bank is making a loan to the importer; in the latter case, it is in effect substituting its credit for that of the importer, enabling the importer to borrow in the money market. On or before the maturity date, the importer pays the bank the face value of the acceptance. If the bank rediscounted the acceptance in the market, the bank pays the holder of the acceptance the face value on the maturity date."

Another type of acceptance financing involves a letter of credit being extended to the importer. Essentially the bank agrees to extend a line of credit on behalf of the importer to the exporter. The bank accepts the exporter's draft and the bank is presented with the title to the goods shipped. The goods shipped thus become the collateral for the "loan," which is the acceptance. After the goods are shipped, the bank, assuming all documentation is in order, accepts the draft and discounts it for the exporter. The exporter has been paid and now the transaction turns to the relationship between the bank and the importer. The acceptance, which the bank may hold or sell in the open market at a discount, is a liability for the importer. Whether the bank holds it or sells it off to another party, it is the importer's responsibility to pay off the debt on or before its maturity date.

This type of transaction may seem familiar. Indeed, it is very similar to that carried out when someone uses a credit card. Suppose you buy a pair of shoes at a store in the mall and use a major credit card to make the purchase. The credit card company pays the shoestore some percentage of the final sales price—a discount for the credit card service—and extends to you a loan for the money to buy the shoes. At this point the shoestore is done with the transaction: it was paid by the credit card company. Now it is up to you to pay off the debt, either in total or over time. The only real difference between an acceptance and your credit card purchase is that the credit card company does not sell off your liability to some third party.

FURTHER READING

LaRouche, Robert K. "Bankers Acceptances." Federal Reserve Bank of Richmond *Economic Quarterly* (Winter 1993): 75–85.

BANK FAILURE. A bank is like any other firm: if it is poorly managed, or if it experiences extreme distress, it will go out of business. When a bank fails, it is unable to meet its obligations to depositors. That is, it is unable to pay back to its customers the full amount of their deposits. Because much of the cost of bank failure falls on depositors, the banking industry is one of the most heavily regulated in this country.

Number of Commercial Banks in the United States, 1930–1933

	National Banks	State Banks			Total Banks
		Federal Reserve Member Banks	Nonmember Banks	Total State Banks	
1930	7,247	1,068	15,364	16,432	23,697
1931	6,800	982	13,872	14,854	21,654
1932	6,145	835	11,754	12,589	18,734
1933	4,897	709	8,601	9,310	14,207

Source: Federal Reserve Bank of Boston.

During the **Great Depression**, bank failures were common. The table above illustrates the massive number of bank failures that occurred during the years of 1930–1933. During this four-year period, at least 2,350 institutions, or about one-third of all national banks in the United States, closed their doors. Although the absolute number is smaller, 359, or 34 percent, of Federal Reserve member banks ceased operations between 1930 and 1933. In contrast to these numbers, state banks experienced the largest number of failures. These banks, which were not members of the Federal Reserve System, suffered a failure rate of 44 percent during the Great Depression. With over 15,000 banks in 1930, their numbers declined sharply to almost half that number in a few short years. Indeed, of the almost 9,500 banks that failed, nonmember state banks account for over 70 percent of the total.

Following a comprehensive change in bank regulation in the 1930s (*see* **Banking Act of 1933**), the number of bank failures decreased substantially. Between 1960 and 1980, bank failures averaged fewer than 10 per year. During the 1980s, there again occurred a wave of bank failures, increasing to over 200 by the late 1980s. This more recent period of increased failures is explained by changes in the regulatory environment in which banks operated (*see* **Depository Institutions Deregulation and Monetary Control Act [DIDMCA] of 1980**) and banks' attempts to increase profitability through riskier lending activities. Beginning in the early 1990s, the annual number of bank failures once again returned to single digits. (*See also* **Bank Panic of 1907, Financial Crises or Panics.**)

FURTHER READING

Eisenbeis, Robert A., and Larry D. Wall. "Reforming Deposit Insurance and FDICIA." Federal Reserve Bank of Atlanta *Economic Review* (First Quarter, 2002): 1–16; Federal Reserve Bank of Boston. *Closed for the Holiday: The Bank Holiday of 1933.* Website: www.bos.frb.org; Kaufman, George G. "Bank Failures, Systemic Risk, and Bank Regulation." *Cato Journal* 16 (1996).

BANK HOLDING COMPANY. Corporations that own several different companies often are referred to as a holding company. During the early 1950s, in part due to government regulations that prohibited banks from opening branch offices in other states, banks avoided regulatory restrictions by forming bank holding companies. Because each individual bank was not considered a branch of the holding company, the holding company enjoyed the benefits of **branching**—operating banks in different states—without violating the existing regulations. Because of their unique position in the banking market, bank holding companies also were able to offer more services than a traditional bank. As specified under the Federal Reserve's Regulation Y, these activities include providing investment advice, leasing and credit card services, and data processing and transmitting services. Today, bank holding companies, like Citicorp and BankAmerica, own and operate some of the largest banks in the country.

FURTHER READING

See Further Reading for **Bank Holding Company Act of 1956.**

BANK HOLDING COMPANY ACT OF 1956. The Bank Holding Company Act, passed by Congress in 1956, directed the Federal Reserve to regulate the behavior of multibank holding companies. The act was one of a number of measures used by Congress to regulate the activities of so-called group banks. Numerous hurdles faced previous legislation, not the least of which was deciding whether bank holding companies and their activities actually needed further regulation over and above the rules that existed already. In some sense, therefore, the act was passed as a precautionary measure to preclude abuses and to provide some delineation of the holding companies' markets and operations.

The act had three major purposes. The first was to establish a legal definition of a **bank holding company**. The act defined a bank holding company as a company that owns, controls, or is able to vote 25 percent or more of the shares of each of two or more banks or of a company that becomes a bank holding company. In other words, the act attempted to define ownership of an affiliate bank based on control of its stock and to establish how many banks a company may own before it is officially defined as a bank holding company. Fischer (1961) notes that this definition, although stricter than previous attempts, failed to cover the majority of bank holding companies. Still, it helped limit expansion of bank holding companies, which was one reason for the act.

The second major provision of the act was the requirement that bank holding companies divest themselves of ownership or voting control of stock in any business engaged in nonbanking business activities. A predicament created by this aspect of the act was that while it required two-bank holding companies to divest nonbanking companies, it did not make this a requirement for one-bank holding companies. One reason for this differential treatment is that there were many more one-bank holding companies and requiring them to divest their nonbank activities would have made passing the legislation impossible.

Finally, on the regulatory side, the act also brought holding companies under the purview of the Federal Reserve. Bank holding companies now were required to register with the **Board of Governors**. The board was charged with the supervision and examination of bank holding companies, activities that already had been assigned to it in a limited manner under the **Banking Act of 1933**. In addition, the board was given the authority to grant or deny applications for holding company expansion. The board, with secondary opinions required from the **Comptroller of the Currency** or state banking officials as dictated by the request, would make its decision to accept or reject the application.

This provision in the act raised an important issue that the board would confront following its passage. In Section 3(c) of the act, the board was required to consider "the convenience, needs and welfare of the communities and the area concerned; and whether or not the effect of such acquisition or merger or consolidation would be to expand the size or extent of the bank holding company involved beyond limits consistent with adequate and sound banking." Stated briefly, this portion of the act required the board to determine the sometimes conflicting impacts of allowing for expansion of a bank holding company. On one hand, the expansion might expand available services and increase competition. On the other, the increased competition might threaten the stability of existing banks in the market.

In addition to defining a bank holding company, the act also defined a bank as a financial institution that made commercial loans and accepted deposits. Defining a bank in this manner created an unforeseen loophole: If a financial institution engaged in making loans but did not take deposits, then technically it was not a bank. Similarly, an institution that accepted deposits but made no loans was not, by law, a bank. And if not a bank, then by law these limited service or **nonbank banks** as they would be called were not subject to the **branching** restrictions facing other, traditional full-service commercial banks. This loophole created a way by which some banks could effectively branch across state lines without violating any existing regulation. A series of amendments and new laws since 1970 closed this loophole.

FURTHER READING

Fischer, Gerald C. *Bank Holding Companies*. New York: Columbia University Press, 1961.

BANK HOLIDAY OF 1933. When **Franklin Roosevelt** was elected to the presidency in November 1932, the U.S. economy had already suffered through several years of severe economic hardship. By the end of 1932 the **unemployment rate** stood at almost 25 percent, much of the industrial sector was operating well below its capacity (steel was operating at only 12 percent of its capacity), and there was **deflation**, a condition in which the general level of prices are falling. This latter condition hit the agricultural side of the economy especially hard. With prices falling, farmers were unable to generate enough revenue to pay their mortgages, forcing banks to foreclose. It also meant that banks were often unable to recoup their **loans**, putting pressure on their profits.

Although the outgoing Hoover Administration had encouraged the Federal Reserve to do something to stem the plight of the banking community, **bank failures** continued apace with no end in sight. Depositors withdrew whatever funds were left in banks, or simply bypassed the banking system altogether. As discussed elsewhere, some attempts were made to resuscitate the banking system. The **Glass-Steagall Act of 1932**, for example, allowed the government to provide credit to banks that faced closure. But other proposed rescue attempts either did not materialize or were defeated. Overall the mood was that the economy, and the banking system, would continue to spiral downward.

During the period between the election in November 1932 and inauguration day, March 4, 1933, there were some startling developments in the banking system. Because the federal authorities seemed frozen into inaction, state banking authorities moved to quell the tide of bank failures. In November 1932, the governor of Nevada declared a statewide bank holiday, a time when all banks would close their doors and no depositors would be allowed to withdraw funds. In January 1933, Huey Long, the governor of Louisiana, also closed the banks in his state. Other states followed suit: By the end of February 1933, governors in the states of Indiana, Maryland, Arkansas, and Ohio had all declared bank holidays.

The beginning of March 1933 brought the banking system's problems to a head. The nationwide outflow of deposits from banks and the consequent increase in the demand for gold—something that individuals felt was a safe haven in these troubled times—severely strained the ability of New York banks to remain solvent. Because New York banks often held deposits for smaller banks in other areas of the country, deposit withdrawals in other parts of the country meant that there were increased withdrawals from New York banks as well. The problem in New York was magnified because they effectively faced the combined problems from the other banks throughout the country. This increased demand for gold caused the New York Federal Reserve Bank's gold reserves to fall below its legal limit. Because the gold reserves were used to back the paper **currency** of the United States, once gold reserves fell below the legal limit, the New York Federal Reserve Bank would be hard-pressed to redeem paper currency for gold. George L. Harrison, the head of the Federal Reserve Bank of New York, called for a national bank holiday to stem the outflow of gold.

The increasing number of bank closures and failures forced a decision. On March 4, 1933—inauguration day—every one of the 12 Federal Reserve Banks chose not to open, and banks in 37 states were closed for business or operating with limited withdrawals. In his inaugural address, Roosevelt declared his "firm belief that the only thing we have to fear is fear itself—nameless, unreasoning, unjustified terror which paralyzes needed efforts to convert retreat into advance." On March 5, the new president called on Federal Reserve officials, Cabinet members, and Treasury officials to meet and establish the ground rules for a nationwide bank holiday. On March 6, 1933, President Roosevelt issued a proclamation declaring that all bank transactions would be suspended effective immediately. The Bank Holiday was a reality.

As noted by the Federal Reserve Bank of Boston in *Closed for the Holiday: The Bank Holiday of 1933*, the official declaration of a bank holiday "specified that no such banking institution or branch shall pay out, export, earmark, or permit the withdrawal or transfer in any manner or by any device whatsoever of any gold or silver coin or bullion or currency or take any other action which might facilitate the hoarding thereof; nor shall any such banking institution or branch pay out deposits, make loans or discounts, deal in foreign exchange, transfer credits from the United States to any place abroad, or transact any other banking business whatsoever" (p. 16). The holiday was scheduled to run for four days until March 9, when Congress was scheduled to consider legislation to restore order and confidence in the banking system. During the holiday, officials from the Federal Reserve and Treasury worked on the emergency legislation.

On March 9, 1933, the Emergency Banking Act was sent to Congress. Not meant to extensively reform the banking system, the Emergency Banking Act was really meant to restore public confidence in the banking system and to establish an orderly procedure by which closed banks could reopen. This latter aspect was perhaps the most important. As noted in the

Boston study, "Federal authorities divided banks into three categories. Class A banks were solvent institutions in little or no danger of failing. They would be the first allowed to reopen. Class B banks were endangered, weakened, or insolvent institutions that were thought to be capable of reopening after an indefinite period of reorganization. Class C banks were insolvent institutions that would not be allowed to reopen" (p. 20).

Four days after the Emergency Banking Act was passed, banks began to reopen. The first to open were member banks in cities with Federal Reserve Banks. Two days later, on March 15, even more banks were permitted to open. With this additional surge of reopenings, the banking system was almost fully in operation. The Bank Holiday and the Emergency Banking Act had accomplished their goals: when banks resumed operations the amount of deposits exceeded the withdrawals. Confidence had been restored in the banking system. With confidence restored, Congress and other public officials turned their attention to massive reforms of the banking and financial system. Within months of the bank holiday, major pieces of legislation were passed that represented comprehensive reforms to banking. Not only did the bank holiday mark a key turning point in Great Depression, it also marked a major turning point in the regulation of the U.S. banking system. Indeed, legislation passed on the heels of the bank holiday would affect banking practices in the United States for the next 50 years.

FURTHER READING

Burns, Helen M. *The American Banking Community and the New Deal Banking Reform, 1933–1935*. Westport, CT: Greenwood, 1974; Eccles, George S. *The Politics of Banking*. Salt Lake City: University of Utah Press, 1982; Federal Reserve Bank of Boston. *Closed for the Holiday: The Bank Holiday of 1933*. Website: www.bos.frb.org; Friedman, Milton, and Anna J. Schwartz. A *Monetary History of* the *United States, 1867–1960*. Princeton: Princeton University Press, 1963; Meltzer, Allan H. *A History of the Federal Reserve, Vol. 1: 1913–1951*. Chicago: University of Chicago Press, 2003.

BANKING ACT OF 1933. President **Franklin Roosevelt** signed into law the Banking Act of 1933 only three months after Congress passed the Emergency Banking Act of 1933. The Emergency Banking Act was essentially a stopgap measure to help restore public confidence in the banking system. (*See* **Bank Holiday of 1933.**) The Act of 1933, in contrast, attempted to overhaul the banking and financial system, which many believed was to blame for the severity of the **Great Depression**.

One aspect of the banking system that Congress attacked in the act was the excessive stock speculation that contributed to the stock market crash in 1929. The 1933 act separated commercial and investment banking. Senator **Carter Glass** led the effort on this portion of the act, because he was convinced that the difficulties faced by the banking system in the previous few years were due in large part to commercial banks financing investment bank activities in the volatile and unpredictable stock market in the 1920s. Following passage of the act, commercial banks had to divest themselves of any securities affiliates and could not underwrite securities. Congress believed that the separation would protect depositors from the speculative nature of the stock market by insulating commercial banking from the potential effects that in 1929 ran from stock market declines to the banking system in general. The separation of activities forbade **investment banks**, which deal in securities, from accepting deposits and commercial banks from dealing in securities.

There were several other aspects of the 1933 act that were aimed at increasing stability in the banking system. One is the creation of the **Federal Deposit Insurance Corporation (FDIC)**. The act required Federal Reserve Banks to provide capital for the newly created FDIC. Although there had been state and private insurance funds to cover losses of bank deposits, the massive collapse of the banking system in the early 1930s led many to argue that only a nationwide, federally controlled insurance program would be sufficient to protect depositors' holdings. The 1933 act created this safety net for depositors, with the federal government insuring bank deposits up to $2,500. This insurance coverage, which began on January 1, 1934, had a dramatic affect: **Bank runs** almost ceased to occur, and the number of bank failures declined dramatically, from more than 4,000 in 1933 to only 62 in 1934.

Following passage of the act, commercial banks were no longer allowed to pay interest on checking account balances. (*See* **Regulation Q**.) Some argued that this activity led to increased competition among banks and that this is in part to blame for the number of bank failures during the previous few years. The argument was that banks, paying higher and higher interest on deposits simply to attract them from other banks, would put themselves into a vulnerable condition if there was a unforeseen increase in deposit withdrawals. Strongly influenced by the events of the recent past, anything that reduced potential destabilizing competition for banks was viewed as positive. Even though this argument suggested that bank managers would engage in activities that they could see were potentially harmful, it carried the day. And it was supported by the banking community because it made checking account deposits almost costless to banks. Other than the cost of maintaining the accounts and any expenses derived from attracting accounts to a bank, checking account deposits were low-cost funds that banks would use to make loans at a higher level of profitability.

Another key provision of the 1933 act was that it created the **Federal Open Market Committee (FOMC)**. This part of the act made official that the Federal Reserve could determine monetary policy through the purchase and sale of U.S. Treasury securities. This aspect of the act formally established the Committee and its composition. The FOMC was given the authority to meet regularly in Washington, D.C., even though they were not yet given the authority to implement their policy decisions until passage of the **Banking Act of 1935**.

While these are the major components of the 1933 act, there were other changes brought about by its passage. For example, the act weakened the constraints on banks for establishing branches. Some argued, correctly, that by allowing more **branching**, banks could diversify unforeseen negative shocks in one area across several banks. The act also gave the board the authority to regulate interest rates paid on time and savings deposits at its member banks. Finally, the act also attempted to control the spread of **bank holding company** activities by extending the spirit of legislation designed to avoid interlocking directorships by requiring board approval.

The Banking Act of 1933 ushered into existence a number of regulations that altered commercial banking in the United States for many years. To a large extent, most of its provisions were designed to limit competition among banks and to restrict their activities in financial markets. The act, in other words, attempted to force commercial bankers to focus on commercial banking. These provisions, it was thought, would forestall a repeat of the disaster that befell banks in the early 1930s.

FURTHER READING

Eccles, George S. *The Politics of Banking*. Salt Lake City: University of Utah Press, 1982; Friedman, Milton, and Anna J. Schwartz. *A Monetary History of* the *United States, 1867–1960*. Princeton: Princeton University Press, 1963; Meltzer, Allan H. *A History of the Federal Reserve, Vol. 1: 1913–1951*. Chicago: University of Chicago Press, 2003; Moore, Carl H. *The Federal Reserve System: A History of the First 75 Years*. Jefferson, NC: McFarland and Company, 1990.

BANKING ACT OF 1935. The Banking Act of 1935 overhauled the Federal Reserve System. Passed on August 20, 1935, the Act of 1935 moved the effective power center of the Federal Reserve from New York to Washington, D.C. During the period since its establishment in 1913, the 12 District Bank presidents (then called governors), especially the president of the New York Federal Reserve, overshadowed the Federal Reserve Board in Washington, D.C. The Act of 1935 changed that and produced the system that exists today. In addition to relocating the power of the Federal Reserve—in effect centralizing its activities in much the same way that the Roosevelt administration federalized other heretofore dispersed government activities—the act renamed the Reserve Board to the **Board of Governors** of the Federal Reserve System.

The act strengthened the Federal Reserve's regulatory oversight powers and helped established it as an independent central bank. This latter aspect was accomplished by giving the Federal Reserve increased independence from the White House, Congress, and the banking community. For example, the act removed the Secretary of the Treasury and the **Comptroller of the Currency**, who had previously served as *ex officio* members, from the Board of Governors. By amending Section 10 of the Federal Reserve Act, the 1935 legislation also produced changes that, although seemingly innocuous, cemented the hierarchy within the Federal Reserve. For example, the act changed the title of governor to chairman and set the term for the chairman at four years, subject to renewal. The title of vice governor also was changed to vice chairman. The act also proscribed changes in how many governors there would be (seven) and how long the governors would serve (14 years without reappointment after a full term was served). How governors were selected also was established: nomination by the president with confirmation by the U.S. Senate.

Amending Section 4 of the Federal Reserve Act, the title of governor, once held by individuals running the district banks, was changed to president. The president and the first vice president of each district bank would be appointed by the bank's board of directors with final approval by the Board of Governors. The presidents would serve five-year terms subject to renewal. This change in the operating aspects of the Federal Reserve System focused the power of the Federal Reserve in Washington, D.C. Because the final decision on who would be district bank presidents ultimately resided with the board in Washington, it could work to pack the banks with individuals agreeable to their points of view. Although this view does have some merit, the observed independence of district bank presidents over time suggests that there is little support to the notion that the board has or could dominate policy views throughout the System. The very fact that several district banks—St. Louis in particular—have long held positions quite contrary to the official board view is one indication of independence within the System.

While the act centralized power in the District of Columbia, it also kept much of the Federal Reserve's independent character intact. That is, while power flowed to Washington, the decision process was counterbalanced by how the voting membership of the **Federal Open Market Committee (FOMC)** was established. The act required that the FOMC be composed of the seven governors plus the president of the New York Federal Reserve plus four of the remaining the District Bank presidents, the latter serving on a rotating basis. (The New York Federal Reserve Bank president was given a permanent voting position on the FOMC because that bank oversees operations of the open market **trading desk**.) Having the FOMC make open market decisions would give a majority position to the board but also kept the decision process decentralized because bank presidents could sway the discussion and eventual vote on policy actions. The act also gave the FOMC greater latitude to alter the level of bank reserves through its open market operations, the buying and selling of government securities in the financial market.

The 1935 act thus completed the Roosevelt administration's reform of the banking industry. With a more independent Federal Reserve, the administration thought that the problems that had characterized the banking industry and monetary policy during the 1929–1933 period could be alleviated. Although some components of the 1933 and 1935 Banking Acts would later be overturned, the changes that established the Federal Reserve as the central authority in its oversight of the banking industry and as a policymaker largely independent of the federal government and the political process survive relatively intact to this day. Perhaps more important, these acts resuscitated a banking and financial system that had nearly stopped functioning.

FURTHER READING

Federal Reserve Bank of Boston. *Closed for the Holiday: The Bank Holiday of 1933*. Website: www.bos.frb.org; Meltzer, Allan H. *A History of the Federal Reserve, Vol. 1: 1913–1951*. Chicago: University of Chicago Press, 2003; Moore, Carl H. *The Federal Reserve System: A History of the First 75 Years*. Jefferson, NC: McFarland and Company, 1990.

BANK PANIC OF 1907 (*See* **Panic of 1907**)

BANK RUN. A bank run occurs when depositors, fearing that their bank will not be able to settle up on their deposit accounts, attempt to withdraw their funds. U.S. banks operate in a fractional reserve system; that is, they have on reserve only a small fraction of each dollar on deposit. If all depositors attempted to withdraw their money, banks would not be able to meet everyone's demands. During a bank run, banks are forced to pay on a first-come basis, so not all depositors get reimbursed before the bank exhausts its reserves and closes. This is referred to as a suspension of payments. Although often thought to be an event associated only with the **Great Depression**, bank runs were not uncommon before the 1930s and even have occurred in modern times.

What causes a bank run? One view is that bank runs are caused predominantly by a decline in "economic fundamentals." In other words, bank runs are thought to occur when the economy experiences a **recession** or a downturn in the economic activity. To see if this view is supported by the facts, Gorton (1988) compared the timing of **business cycle** dates, as determined by the National Bureau of Economic Research (NBER), and periods in which bank runs were common. Focusing on the pre–Federal Reserve period, Gorton found some but not complete support for the notion that economic downturns are associated with increases in bank runs (panics). Of the 11 business cycles studied, bank runs occurred in seven of them. Because such **financial panics** do not occur with every recession and because the number of bank runs varies across recessions, some argue that this view is not a general explanation of bank runs.

It also has been suggested that bank runs are more likely to occur at certain times of the year, when the **liquidity** needs of depositors stress banks' ability to meet their needs. For example, demands for liquidity by depositors may rise during the fall, a time usually associated with agricultural harvests. Miron (1986) examined this notion and found that financial panics and the associated bank runs in the United States tended to occur most often during the spring (March–May) and fall (September–November) months—periods associated with planting and harvests—and least often during the summer (June–August).

Finally, it also has been suggested that bank runs occur because depositors, regardless of the current economic conditions, experience an increase in uncertainty. The idea is that even if an event does not affect the economic fundamentals that affect the profitability of a bank, such as a poor harvest that reduces the return on farm loans, depositors may believe that it does. If depositors act on this belief, based in fact or not, they will attempt to convert their deposits into currency: a flight to liquidity. The underlying notion of this "expectations" view is that *if* depositors believe that their bank is suffering and may fail, then they will opt to withdraw their deposits and hold currency until the uncertainty is resolved. What makes this explanation more interesting from the others is that it does not exclude external effects, such as a deteriorating economy, from impacting depositors' decisions. At the same time, negative external effects are not necessary for a bank run to occur. In this case, the expectations view is more general.

Why is there this research into the possible causes of bank runs? The occurrence of bank runs is economically costly. When a bank run occurs, customers attempt to convert their deposits into currency. This has the effect of lessening banks' ability to make loans, leading to a potential slowing in the pace of business activity and, if prolonged, a recession. Because banks act as **financial intermediaries**, a bank run also reduces their ability to efficiently facilitate the needs of borrowers and savers. Severance of this tie also has adverse economic consequences. Indeed, the severity of the Great Depression is linked in no small measure to the widespread bank failures that resulted from bank runs. The extent of the problem was so serious that President Roosevelt declared the **Bank Holiday of 1933**—a nationwide closing of all banks—in March. This action, many believe, broke the fear-based runs on banks, restored confidence in the banking industry, and helped the economic recovery process.

FURTHER READING

Ennis, Huberto M. "Economic Fundamentals and Bank Runs." Federal Reserve Bank of Richmond *Economic Quarterly* (Spring 2003): 55–71; Gorton, Gary. "Banking Panics and Business Cycles." *Oxford Economic Papers* (December 1988): 751–81; Miron, Jeffrey. "Financial Panics, the Seasonality of the Nominal Interest Rate, and the Founding of the Fed," *American Economic Review* (March 1986): 125–40.

BARTER. Barter is the simplest form of trade. When barter takes place, both parties agree to trade one good for some other good. For example, a hog farmer and a cabinet maker might agree to trade hogs for cabinets and cabinets for hogs. Or, a dentist trades a free checkup for some trim work by a housepainter. In both cases, the trade does not involve any money. And in both cases what each person trades is what the other party wants: a condition referred to as a double coincidence of wants. If the condition of double coincidence of wants is not met, trading will not take place.

This aspect of barter makes it very costly. Why? Because now anyone wishing to trade must find someone else who has what they want and is willing to trade. For example, what if the hog farmer wants dental work but the dentist does not want hogs? Then no trading takes place. The only way for trade to occur is when the two parties can agree on what good trades for what good. Of course, someone might act as a broker. That is, they know that the hog farmer wants dental work and that the dentist wants cabinets and that the cabinet maker wants hogs. Using this information, a broker could arrange for the trades to occur. But how would this type of trading occur? The broker must be compensated for this activity and what is the payment? Cabinets? Hogs? As you can see, barter is a very costly form of trading once the number of traders extends beyond just a few.

Barter also imposes another significant cost on trading. Suppose that there are two goods in an economy: coffee mugs and music CDs. What is their exchange value? That is, what is the "price" of each good in a barter economy? The answer depends on how badly someone wants mugs or CDs, and therefore how many of each they are willing to part with. If through negotiation it turns out that it takes three mugs for the owner of CDs to part with just one of them, then the "mug price" of a CD is three. Conversely, the "CD price" of a mug must be 1/3. So, with two goods, there really is only one price pair.

Now suppose that there are five items in the simple economy. In addition to coffee mugs and CDs, there are laptop computers, pencils, and automobiles. How many price pairs are there in a barter economy with five goods? Because each price pair in a barter economy is a relative price—the price of each good relative to each of the other goods—the answer turns out to be 10 prices. In other words, there are 10 pairings of the goods (CDs and laptops, CDs and pencils, laptops and automobiles, etc.) and therefore 10 prices. As this example shows, barter increases the cost of buying and selling. Put another way, barter increases the cost of transacting.

To further illustrate the cost of barter, how many price pairs would be necessary in a barter economy if you bought 20 items at the grocery store and were trying to check out through the fast lane? With 20 goods in the basket, the number of price pairs is 190. An even more dramatic illustration can be made by using a grocery store to represent the economy. Suppose there are 5,000 different items in our representative grocery store. With 5,000 items, there would be a whopping 12,497,500 price pairs! Because this number of goods is about average for a large grocery store, the example still does not come close to capturing the transaction cost of a barter system of exchange. The high cost of barter exchange once you move beyond a simple economy explains why it has given way to monetary exchange. In an economy where money exchanges for goods and goods for money, the number of prices is reduced dramatically. In our example above, a 5,000-item store in a monetary economy would have only 5,000 prices (stated for example in dollars) compared with the almost 12.5 million required under barter.

FURTHER READING

Jevons, Stanley. *Money and the Mechanism of Exchange*. New York: Appleton, 1896.

BASEL ACCORD. The Basel Accord represents a major attempt by domestic regulatory agencies to coordinate relations across national borders. In 1988, in the town of Basel, Switzerland, representatives from countries comprising the **Group of 10**—the major industrial countries of the world—adopted the Basel Capital Accord. The Accord, developed by the Basel Committee on Banking Supervision, represented an important development in the growing international banking industry.

What the Accord did was to create **capital requirements** that were based in part on the credit risk of internationally active commercial banks. By linking capital requirements (the amount of funds that a bank would be required to hold as a reserve against unforeseen losses) to credit risk (the possibility of losses due to borrower default on outstanding loans), the Accord was able to create a more uniform and comparable capital standard across countries. With this set of capital standards, investors, regulators, and depositors could compare the relative riskiness of commercial banks regardless of the country in which they reside.

Specifically the Accord created four risk weights, or "buckets." The first bucket comprised claims against governments that are members of the Organization of Economic Cooperation and Development (OECD), such as claims against the U.S. government in the form of government securities. This bucket received a zero weight because such claims are generally considered to be risk free. The second bucket included claims on banks incorporated in OECD countries. The third was made up of claims against residential mortgages. Finally, the fourth included claims against consumers and corporations. Following passage of the Basel Accord, the amount of capital held by banks generally increased.

Over time there have been numerous amendments to the original Accord. Given the dynamic nature of financial markets and the constant development of new financial instruments and trading technologies, such evolution is expected. In April 2003, in fact, the Basel Committee on Banking Supervision released for comment a new Basel Capital Accord to replace the original 1988 version. The new Accord, commonly known as Basel II, focuses on making bank capital requirements even more risk sensitive than the original version, refines existing bank supervisory processes that are specifically aimed at capital adequacy issues, and increases public disclosure requirements that focus on capital adequacy. In large part, these changes, especially those regarding the disclosure requirements, are aimed at increasing the transparency of bank operations. Lopez (2003) comments that, "In order for market discipline of banking institutions to be effective, banks must be sufficiently transparent; that is banks must provide a sufficient amount of accurate and timely information regarding their conditions and operations to the public."

Attempting to ensure the viability of banking systems within the major industrial and financial countries was the original intent of the Basel Accord. Over time, the Basel Accord served to, even though crudely, set minimum capital requirements that reflected the inherent riskiness of a bank's activities. In an attempt to further reduce the **moral hazard** problem in banking, a new set of standards have been developed that tie capital requirements to a bank's risk management. These standards, if fully implemented, will help regulators and markets to discipline those institutions that are not meeting capital adequacy requirements and, therefore, are raising the probability of failure and potential loss to owners and to depositors, not to mention government insurance agencies, like the **Federal Deposit Insurance Corporation (FDIC)**.

FURTHER READING

Lopez, Jose A. "The Basel Proposal for a New Capital Adequacy Framework." Federal Reserve Bank of San Francisco *Economic Letter* (July 30, 1999); Lopez, Jose A. "Disclosure as a Supervisory Tool: Pillar 3 of Basel II." Federal Reserve Bank of San Francisco *Economic Letter* (August 1, 2003).

BASIS POINT. A basis point is 1/100th of a percentage point. The term is used primarily when discussing **interest rates**. For example, an interest rate of 7.53 percent can be stated as 753 basis points. The term basis point also is used to describe changes in interest rates. If an interest rate increases, say, from 5.50 percent to 5.73 percent, then the interest rate increased 23 basis points.

BEIGE BOOK. The "beige book" is a publication of the **Board of Governors** of the Federal Reserve System. It really is not a book but a summary of economic activity across the 12 Federal Reserve districts. Its name is derived from the fact that the covers of the release are beige. It is one of three documents generated for the purpose of discussing monetary policy (the other two are the **green book** and the **blue book**) by the **Federal Open Market Committee (FOMC)**, the policymaking arm of the Federal Reserve. The beige book is released to the public eight times a year (this coincides with the number of meetings of the FOMC) and contains anecdotal evidence compiled by each of the Federal Reserve System's districts. This evidence is based on conversations with individuals in various areas of business, including manufacturing and finance. This publication often is used to gauge the state of economic activity in each district and, taken as a whole, in the nation.

To provide a feel for its content, below is an excerpt from the April 23, 2003 Beige Book. We reprint here part of the summary prepared at the Federal Reserve Bank of Cleveland, which is based on information collected from the other District Banks before April 15, 2003.

> Reports from the 12 Federal Reserve Districts suggested that the pace of economic activity continued to be lackluster during March and the first two weeks of April. Although Richmond observed continued modest growth, reports from Boston, Cleveland, Atlanta, St. Louis, Dallas, and San Francisco characterized economic conditions as still mixed or soft. Since the last Beige Book, New York, Philadelphia, Chicago, Minneapolis, and Kansas City noted that the recent pace of economic activity had been slower than reported earlier. The onset of the war with Iraq appeared to have some effect on sales and spending, although it is too early to ascertain the full effect of the war on both consumer and business confidence.
>
> Reports on consumer spending were generally weak in March, but respondents attributed part of the weakness to poor weather and the onset of war. Contacts also cautioned that year-over-year comparisons of sales for March were difficult because Easter fell in late March last year but falls in the third week of April this year. Optimism remained that the retail environment would improve within the next six months.
>
> Most Districts continued to report weakness in manufacturing, although some pockets of growth were noted in most of the reports. Businesses continued to report a cautious attitude toward spending, and commercial real estate was reported to still be in a slump. In contrast, homebuilding activity remained strong across all Districts. Mortgage lending, buoyed by refinancing activity, remained strong, and a few Districts noted some improvement in commercial

loan demand. Agriculture conditions generally improved as rain and snow eased drought conditions in several Districts. Labor markets remained soft, but some Districts noted moderating layoffs or improvements in demand for temporary labor.

FURTHER READING

Fettig, David, and Arthur J. Rolnick. "The Federal Reserve's Beige Book: A Better Mirror than a Crystal Ball." Federal Reserve Bank of Minneapolis *The Region* (March 1999). Available online at: www.minneapolisfed.org; Ginther, Donna K., and Madeline Zavodny. "The Beige Book: Timely Information on the Regional Economy." Federal Reserve Bank of Atlanta *Economic Review* (Third Quarter, 2001): 19–29.

BILLS ONLY. The Federal Reserve attained policy freedom with the **Treasury-Federal Reserve Accord of 1951**. Prior to the Accord, monetary policy actions tried to peg interest rates on Treasury obligations at low levels. This allowed the U.S. government to fund its activities at a relatively low interest cost. This made some sense during World War II, but soon after the war this policy was recognized as inflationary. Even so, it was not until the Accord (1951) that the rate-pegging constraint was lifted. Only two years after gaining freedom from this policy constraint, the Federal Reserve announced that it would follow procedures that focused their purchase and sale of securities on short-term Treasury securities—**open market operations**—those with maturities of less than one year. This approach was dubbed the "bills-only doctrine," because Treasury securities with less than one year to maturity are referred to as Treasury bills.

The bills-only approach to conducting policy was made public in a speech in 1953 delivered by **William McChesney Martin, Jr.**, the chairman of the Federal Reserve at the time. In his speech, titled "The Transition to Free Markets," Martin laid out the rationale for the change in policy. Basically, once the constraint of having to peg government interest rates was lifted, the Federal Reserve sought to maintain order in the financial markets. Because the Federal Reserve was no longer pegging rates, it makes sense that there would be some time of adjustment as investors other than the Federal Reserve began to determine market prices for government securities. This weaning process stopped with Martin's speech.

Why would policymakers abandon the longer end of the Treasury securities market and focus on short-term securities to carry out policy? There are several possible answers. One is that by buying and selling long-term securities, the Federal Reserve would expose government securities dealers to greater potential losses that stemmed solely from changes in policy. A second reason is that continued dealing in longer-term securities would not be far removed from their previous policy of pegging rates, something that Federal Reserve officials attempted to distance themselves from as much as possible. Finally, as suggested by the title of Martin's speech, Federal Reserve officials often stated that they wanted interest rates to be set in open, orderly markets for longer-term securities. Even though changes at the shorter end of the maturity spectrum was thought to influence longer-term rates, it was not the same as having the Federal Reserve actively involved in establishing long-term interest rates. Officials hoped that this would be done by market participants reacting to economic factors.

Although the full extent of the debate is too vast for this entry, the announcement and enactment of a "bills-only" type of policy was not without detractors. Many argued that a bills-only policy restricted monetary policy makers from realizing their ability to achieve policy objectives, such as sustained economic growth and low rates of inflation. The argument against bills only was that it hampered policymakers from following whatever policy was needed, and if that meant influencing long-term government interest rates, then that was the policy to follow. A bills-only approach prevented this from occurring. On the other hand, some economists believed that the restriction was good: If the Federal Reserve did not try to operate in all sectors of the Treasury securities market, their powers would be constrained and the possibility for policy mistakes would be, if not minimized, reduced.

To a large extent, the Federal Reserve successfully followed their bills-only policy. Although it deviated from it in 1955 and in 1958, each time purchasing newly issued government securities when it appeared that the issues would be undersold, it has maintained this rule ever since. Although the controversy is now dated, it remains an interesting episode in the development of monetary policy in the United States.

FURTHER READING

Ahearn, Daniel S. *Federal Reserve Policy Reappraised, 1951–1959.* New York: Columbia University Press, 1963; Friedman, Milton, and Anna J. Schwartz. *A Monetary History of the United States, 1867–1960.* Princeton: Princeton University Press, 1963 (especially Chapter 11); Goldfeld, Stephen M., and Lester V. Chandler. *The Economics of Money and Banking.* 8th edition. New York: Harper and Row, 1981; Mayer, Thomas. *Monetary Policy in the United States.* New York: Random House, 1968.

BLACK MONDAY OF 1929. Stock prices of U.S. firms increased dramatically during the late 1920s. In 1929 alone, one measure of stock prices, the *New York Times* index of 25 industrial firms, increased by almost 350 points, rising from 110 in January to 452 by September. Worried about excessive speculation in the stock market, the Federal Reserve took actions to increase the cost of borrowing by raising the **discount rate** in August 1929. Part of this worry stemmed from the practice of purchasing stocks on margin; that is, purchasing stocks using borrowed funds. The Federal Reserve's action slowed stock purchases slightly and prices fell modestly in September. Some financial market experts warned that stock prices had risen too far too fast. On October 23 and 24, stock prices began to slide sharply. To avert panic in the market, a number of banks organized to buy shares. Even so, on October 28—Black Monday—stock prices plummeted. On this day and the next, the average stock lost about 25 percent of its value. By November stock prices had fallen to about 50 percent of their August level. For many, Black Monday marks the beginning of the **Great Depression** in the United States.

FURTHER READING

Chandler, Lester V. *America's Greatest Depression, 1929–1941.* New York: Harper and Row, 1970; Galbraith, John Kenneth. *The Great Crash: 1929.* 2nd edition. New York: Houghton Mifflin, 1961; Friedman, Milton, and Anna J. Schwartz. *The Great Contraction: 1929–1933.* Princeton: Princeton University Press, 1965; Sobel, Robert. *Panic on Wall Street: A History of America's Disasters.* New York: Macmillan, 1968.

BLACK MONDAY OF 1987. On Monday, October 19, 1987, the value of stocks traded on the New York Stock Exchange plummeted. The Dow Jones Industrial Average (DJIA), a widely used gauge of stock market performance, dropped 508 points or nearly 23 percent of the previous day's value. This plunge took place amid frenzied trading: the one-day trading volume was pushed to 604 million shares. For comparison, in September 1987 the average daily volume of trading was 177 million shares. This one-day decline in the DJIA was larger than that experienced on **Black Monday of 1929**. Although stock prices declined in almost every exchange around the world, the economic fallout associated with the stock market crash of October 1929 did not occur. In fact, stock prices in the United States rebounded after the 1987 decline and, by the end of 1987, had almost fully recovered to their precrash levels.

One reason why the 1987 stock market plunge did not have the same economic effects as the 1929 crash is because the Federal Reserve quickly and forcefully moved to stem further financial market effects. Prior to the 1987 crash, Federal Reserve policy was actively pushing interest rates higher in an effort to stem financial market activity. On the heels of the 1987 crash and unlike their behavior following the 1929 crash, Federal Reserve policy was reversed. Because of the drop in stock prices and the threat to other financial markets, the Federal Reserve's most immediate response in 1987 was to publicly guarantee liquidity to financial institutions and, by extension, to financial markets.

Following the crash, the **Federal Open Market Committee (FOMC)** conferred every day by conference call during the remainder of October. During these calls, the FOMC assessed the ongoing developments in financial markets and in the wider economy. Members of the Committee agreed "on the need to meet promptly any unusual liquidity requirements of the economic and financial system in this period." During this period, open market operations were directed to providing more reserves to the banking system as needed. By responding in this manner, the Federal Reserve fulfilled its role as **lender of last resort**.

At its November and December meetings in 1987, the FOMC undertook policies designed to forestall the potentially negative economic effects stemming from the stock market crash. Federal Reserve Board economists and private forecasters believed that one outcome of the crash would be a significant decline in economic growth caused by the widespread loss of wealth. The idea was that if the value of individual's assets (which included stocks) fell sharply, the individual would be inclined to reduce spending, thus reducing incomes in the economy. Federal Reserve policies aimed at reducing interest rates were one way to cushion the effects of the crash. At the November FOMC meeting, the paramount concern was to ensure the viability of the financial system and to offset the negative economic effects of the recent events. As the FOMC stated in its policy **directive**:

> In light of the uncertainties that continued to dominate financial markets and the risks that the recent developments could depress business activity ... policy implementation should remain especially alert to developments that might call for somewhat easier reserve conditions.

At the final meeting of 1987, incoming data suggested that the potential for recession stemming from the stock market crash was ebbing. Even so, the FOMC was alert to possible changes in the markets, as evidenced by the continued large daily fluctuations in stock prices. By December, the FOMC's discussion showed that it thought the main effects of the crash had been overcome by their early and swift response. The December directive stated that "the Committee [FOMC] recognizes that still sensitive conditions in financial markets and uncertainties in the economic outlook may continue to call for a special degree of flexibility in open market operations." Although this policy stance indicated that the

Federal Reserve was soon to return to its precrash policy, it also showed market participants that it was willing to respond quickly to new developments.

FURTHER READING

Meyer, Laurence H. *A Term at the Fed: An Insider's View*. New York: HarperBusiness, 2004; Shiller, Robert J. *Irrational Exuberance*. Princeton: Princeton University Press, 2000.

BLUE BOOK. The blue book is one of the three monetary policy documents provided to individuals attending the meetings of the **Federal Open Market Committee (FOMC)**. (The other two are the **beige book** and the **green book**.) The contents of the blue book—so named because its cover is blue—contains forecasts for the monetary side of the economy produced by the Monetary Affairs Division of the **Board of Governors**. Unlike the beige book, which is released to the public, the blue book is available only to the members of the FOMC and their staff. The blue book is made public only after several years have elapsed following the FOMC meeting for which it is prepared.

Prior to each meeting, economists in the Monetary Affairs Division put together projections of monetary aggregates and interest rates over horizons of a few months out to several years. These projections are normally grouped into three different scenarios for the direction of policy. For instance, a restrictive policy, one meant to slow the economy, a scenario of no change, and a scenario aimed at stimulating economic growth. (*See also* **Green Book** and **Beige Book**.)

FURTHER READING

Federal Reserve Bank of Richmond. "The Policymaking Process." Website: www.rich.frb.org/pubs/frtoday/process.html.

BOARD OF GOVERNORS. The Board of Governors of the Federal Reserve System as we know it today really came into being with passage of the **Banking Act of 1935**. With that act, Congress established the Board of Governors (hereafter, board) and the Federal Reserve System as a fairly independent central bank, at least much more independent from the federal government than central banks in other major economies. The 1935 act established that the board would be constituted of seven members who would be appointed by the president of the United States and confirmed by the U.S. Senate. The act also established that each governor could serve a full term of 14 years and that, after serving a full term, a board member may not be reappointed. If, however, someone resigns as a board member before his or her term expires, the person appointed and confirmed to serve the remainder of the term may later be reappointed to a full term. In addition, appointments to the board would be staggered so that one term expires on January 31 of each even-numbered year.

Why all of these complications? The main reason is that the above process and term limitations were created as an attempt to keep the board apolitical. By having terms last 14 years, almost all presidents would be required to work with board members appointed by previous administrations and no president would have the opportunity to appoint the entire board. Even though some recent presidents have been able to appoint the entire board, due primarily to governors who do not remain for their full 14-year terms, the board remains largely apolitical. The extended terms, the staggering of appointments, etc., are all designed to keep the board as independent from the political process as possible.

In addition to appointing the board members, the president appoints, subject to Senate confirmation, the chairman and the vice chairman of the board. Nominees to these positions are sitting members of the board or are simultaneously appointed to the board. The chairman and the vice chairman serve for renewable four-year terms. Because these individuals also are board members they still face the constraint of a 14-year term or some combination of filling out another's unexpired term plus the full 14 years. Indeed, there have been several chairmen who have served for extended terms. **William McChesney Martin** served from April 2, 1951, to January 31, 1970, and **Alan Greenspan** has served since August 11, 1987, to the time of this writing (2005). In sharp contrast to these lengthy stays, **G. William Miller** served as chairman only from March 8, 1978, to August 6, 1979, the shortest tenure for a chairman in the post–World War II era.

The Board of Governors has a staff of economists in Washington, D.C., that numbers about 1,700. These staff economists are responsible for the analysis of domestic and international financial and economic developments and reporting to the board. The board uses the staff to answer important policy questions that may impact the direction and the timing of policy actions. This activity is not done in a vacuum. Such analyses are carried out independently or in conjunction with economist located at the District Banks. The board also is responsible for the supervision and regulation of the **District Federal Reserve Banks** and their branches.

As described in the board's publication *The Federal Reserve System: Purposes and Functions*, the board is responsible, either completely or in concert with Bank presidents, for conducting monetary policy. The major tools used to accomplish this are as follows:

1. **Open market operations**—the buying and selling of U.S. government (mainly Treasury) securities in the open market to influence the level of reserves in the depository system
2. **Reserve requirements**—requirements regarding the amount of funds that commercial banks and other depository institutions must hold in reserve against deposits
3. The **discount rate**—the interest rate charged **commercial banks** and other depository institutions when they borrow reserves from a regional Federal Reserve Bank

Open market operations are conducted through the **trading desk** at the New York Federal Reserve Bank. The desk receives its instructions to buy and sell government securities from the **Federal Open Market Committee (FOMC)**, a 12-member committee on which the seven board members serve along with five Bank presidents. Although the board members represent a majority block on the FOMC, the Board of Governors has sole authority over changes in reserve requirements and discount rates. Changes in the discount rate occur only with approval by the board, even though any change in the discount rate usually is initiated by a Federal Reserve District Bank.

In addition to its roles in the setting of monetary policy, the board also is involved with the supervision and regulation of the nation's banking system. This role is shared with other federal regulatory agencies, most notably the Office of the **Comptroller of the Currency (OCC)**, which supervises national banks, and the **Federal Deposit Insurance Corporation (FDIC)**, which supervises state banks that are not members of the Federal Reserve System. As stated in *Purposes and Functions* (p. 5),

... the Board's supervisory responsibilities extend to the roughly 1,000 state banks that are members of the Federal Reserve System, all bank holding companies, the foreign activities of member banks, the U.S. activities of foreign banks, and Edge Act and agreement corporations (institutions that engage in a foreign banking business). Some regulations issued by the board apply to the entire banking industry, whereas others apply only to member banks. The board also issues regulations to carry out major federal laws governing consumer credit protection, such as Truth in Lending, Equal Credit Opportunity, and Home Mortgage Disclosure; many of these regulations apply to various lenders out-side the banking industry as well as to banks.

An important role filled by members of the Board of Governors is to publicize the board's decisions and policies. In this role, board members are constantly in touch with policymakers throughout the government. Many times each year board members testify before various House and Senate committees that oversee banking, financial markets, and related areas, such as consumer protection and fair housing.

Since the late 1970s, the board is represented by the chairman in what is referred to as the Humphrey-Hawkins testimony. Twice a year, in February and July, a report on the economy and the conduct of monetary policy is submitted to Congress by the Board of Governors. This report outlines the board's views on the state of the economy, its outlook for the economy, and its expected policy response. The testimony is given by the chairman of the Board of Governors before the Senate Committee on Banking, Housing, and Urban Affairs and the House Committee on Banking, Finance, and Urban Affairs. This testimony serves to increase the transparency of policy decisions by the board. Not only does it present the board's views on the economy, but it also allows the board to present its case for past and potential future policy decisions.

One of the areas in which the board helps establish policy is in the area of supervising financial institutions. In this vein, one member of the board is a member of the Federal Financial Institutions Examination Council (FFIEC). Comprising representatives from the Federal Deposit Insurance Corporation, the National Credit Union Administration, the Office of the Comptroller of the Currency, and the Office of Thrift Supervision, the FFIEC coordinates examinations of depository institutions and related policies.

The chairman of the board meets occasionally with the president of the United States and has regular meetings with the secretary of the Treasury. The chairman also is responsible for representing the United States in several international areas. Among others, the chairman is the alternate U.S. member of the Board of Governors of the **International Monetary Fund**, is a member of the board of the Bank for International Settlements (BIS), and is a member of the National Advisory Council on International Monetary and Financial Policies. When there are meetings of the finance ministers from the **Group of Seven** (G-7), the U.S. delegation oftentimes includes the chairman. The board also is represented by the chairman or another board member at meetings of the Organization for Economic Cooperation and Development (OECD) in France.

The board publishes a significant amount of material regarding monetary policy, economic activity, banking regulation and supervision, consumer protection, and other information about the System's activities and the economy. These publications cover the board's function, purpose and structure, and studies of monetary policy. A complete listing of available publications is provided at the board's website.

FURTHER READING

Federal Reserve Board of Governors. *The Federal Reserve System: Purposes and Functions.* 8th edition. Washington, D.C., 1994. (This publication is available on the Board of Governors' Website at www.federalreserve.gov.)

Bond Ratings by Moody's and Standard and Poor's (as of June 2003)

Rating		
Moody's	**Standard and Poor's**	**Description**
Aaa	AAA	Highest Quality
Aa	AA	High Quality
A	A	Upper Medium Grade
Baa	BBB	Medium Grade
Ba	BB	Lower Medium Grade
B	B	Speculative
Caa	CCC, CC	Poor
Ca	C	Highly Speculative
C	D	Lowest Grade

Source: Standard and Poor's.

BOND RATING. A bond rating is a summary measure of how likely it is that a firm or government (such as a local municipality) will not make total payment on its outstanding **bonds**. Two firms, Moody's Investor Service and the Standard and Poor's Corporation, provide this information to investors by rating the quality—in terms of likelihood of default or potential to not repay—of corporate and government bonds. Bond ratings are published and updated periodically. The table above lists the ratings and their description for each of the two bond rating agencies. Bonds with relatively low risk of default receive the highest ratings, denoted as Aaa by Moody's and AAA by Standard and Poor's. As the risk of default increases, the bond's rating goes farther into the alphabet. Bonds with a rating of at least Baa or BBB are referred to as investment grade bonds. Bond ratings below Ba or BBB have a much higher risk of default and are called junk bonds.

FURTHER READING

"Bond Rating." Website: http://invest-faq.com; Standard & Poor's. Website: www.standardand poors.com.

BONDS. A bond is a financial instrument that is traded among investors in financial markets. Firms that sell (issue) bonds to investors incur a debt. By selling a bond, a firm promises to make periodic payments to the investor over some prespecified period of time. Sometimes this payment is made only once. In other instances, the stream of payments from seller to buyer may last over many years. Bonds that make periodic payments over time are called coupon bonds. These bonds make fixed payments over time and, upon maturity, pay the face value of the bond. For instance, when XYZ Corporation issues a $1,000, 10-year bond with the promise to pay 10 percent interest (its coupon rate), the purchaser of the bond receives a payment of $100 (= $1,000 × 10 percent) per year and a final payment of $1,000 (the face value) at the end of 10 years. In this way, the size of the periodic payment determines the **interest rate** on the bond. Bonds are used by firms to raise funds to finance their activities, such as building a new factory, and by governments to fund projects, such as building roads or schools. The likelihood that the payments will be interrupted or stop—the bond's default risk—is reflected in the **bond rating**.

FURTHER READING

Mishkin, Frederic S. *The Economics of Money, Banking, and Financial Markets*. 7th edition. Boston: Pearson Addison Wesley, 2004.

BRANCHING. Branching refers to the act of banks operating in more than one location, not including **automated teller machine (ATMs)**. An argument in favor of branching is that a bank with many branches is better able to serve a wider market, both geographically and demographically, and thus enable it to cushion any ill effects of a specific problem. For example, suppose a bank headquartered in a major city like Chicago lends funds mostly to manufacturers and companies in that city. This is a limited market, both geographically and in terms of potential risk. If there is an economic downturn that happens to affect manufacturing more than other sectors of the economy, then this bank's loans are more likely to not be repaid than are the loans of a bank that is able to lend in a variety of areas outside of manufacturing alone. If it can open branches in the rural areas or in other parts of the country where the focus is on, say real estate lending, then the bank is able to diversity its loans across many different sectors of the economy and thus lessen the effects of the downturn in manufacturing.

Branching also is seen as a way to increase competition among banks. If a town has only one bank, that bank may operate in a manner that maximizes its profit at the expense of the customers. The appearance of another bank and the ensuing competition may force loan rates down and interest rates on deposits up. Even so, a number of government regulations historically were aimed at reducing this avenue of competition by limiting branching. For example, the **National Banking Act of 1863** allowed states to determine how much branching would be allowed. Some states required each bank to operate as a single entity (unit banking), some allowed banks to operate within a limited geographical area (limited branching), and others permitted banks to operate across the state (statewide branching). At the national level, the **McFadden Act of 1927** prohibited national banks from operating outside of their home state and required that they follow state branching regulations. Some have argued that this restricted branching contributed to the severity of the banking collapse in the United States during the Great Depression. Indeed, the Canadian banking system, which had nationwide branching, did not suffer the same catastrophic decline in the number of banks as occurred in the United States.

The thrust of these regulations has been dulled by numerous innovations in the financial market and recent changes in regulations. For example, **bank holding companies** allowed banks to branch without violating the letter of the law. With the spread of ATM machines, they also effectively act as branches, providing customers with more widespread locations at which to deposit and withdraw funds from their accounts. More recently, deregulation of the banking industry and a curtailment of the McFadden Act have enabled banks to branch across state lines. (*See* **Riegle-Neal Act of 1994.**)

FURTHER READING

Federal Deposit Insurance Corporation. "Bank Branching Trends and Prospects of Key Banking Sectors." Website: www.fdic.gov/bank/analytical/future/index.html.

BRETTON WOODS SYSTEM. The Bretton Woods System refers to a multilateral agreement that was initially proposed following World War II that would create a more stable international trade and payments system. It is named after the small resort town in New Hampshire where the delegates from 44 nations met to hammer out the agreement in July 1944. The underlying belief of most delegates was that the world's international monetary system would not return to the **gold standard** that prevailed for most of the century in one form or another. Although the gold standard system was outmoded and would likely cause economic harm for most countries, it was thought that there must be some system whereby governments rather than market forces could control foreign **exchange rates** in order to encourage international cooperation and trade. Indeed, the end of the gold standard era was one of sometimes wildly fluctuating exchange rates, devaluations that often ended in economic disaster, and the raising of trade barriers designed to thwart competition and the free flow of capital across national borders. All of these negative aspects of unbridled markets would, some believed, lead to economic fluctuations and, potentially, a return to the problems associated with the downturns of the 1930s.

At Bretton Woods, the signatory nations created an international monetary system, complete with its own "central bank" that would assist member nations. That organization—the **International Monetary Fund** (IMF)—would be the institution to administer the new monetary regime. In the Articles of Agreement of the International Monetary Fund, the delegates established a system of pegged though adjustable exchange rates. While this may seem contradictory, the idea was to get nations to maintain exchange rates within relatively narrow bands, bands that, according to the plan, would change infrequently. By establishing predictable exchange rates, exporters and importers could trade with some certainty regarding the relative prices of goods across borders. The IMF also was there to act as the international monetary system's banker. The IMF would provide a system of international credits that member countries could use to finance temporary balance of payments difficulties—trade deficits; it would maintain currency convertibility for current account transactions and it would prohibit discriminatory currency practices. Overall, the IMF was set up to act as watchdog for the international monetary system, much in the same way that the Federal Reserve was established to oversee the operations of the domestic banking system.

Although the Bretton Woods agreement was signed in 1944, the new regime did not become fully operational until 1958. The reason for the delay was the extended period of postwar reconstruction. Once the European countries had regained solid footing economically, the European currencies became fully convertible. During the 1960s, the strengthening of European currencies—the increase in their exchange values relative to the dollar—was accompanied by repeated challenges to the international monetary system. Even though the system called for governments to maintain certain exchange values for their currencies, more often domestic policies were at odds with the regime's requirements. This conflict between domestic economic objectives and the maintenance of exchange rates as outlined by the IMF led to a decline in the system's ability to guide the increasingly complex international monetary system.

The 1960s marked a period of dramatic challenges to the system. Although the gold standard had long disappeared as an effective control on the international monetary system, the U.S. dollar was still convertible to gold at a set price. During the 1960s, the dollar was overvalued relative to gold and other major currencies. Because Bretton Woods called on governments to maintain fixed exchange rates, large imbalances in trade deficits among countries arose.

Because the U.S. dollar was a linchpin in the system, the maintenance of the exchange rates required the United States to run balance of payment deficits in order to provide the funds needed by other countries. The end result was a continual outflow of U.S. gold reserves. As foreign countries began to hold more and more dollars, they in turn began to demand that the U.S. exchange these dollars for their equivalent in gold, then stated as $35 per ounce. Discussions by the **Federal Open Market Committee (FOMC)** during the early 1960s show that this imbalance was of great concern and frequently dwarfed domestic monetary policy issues.

To stem the erosion of confidence in the system, a number of remedies were proposed, but decisive action was not taken until March 1968. At that time the IMF created **special drawing rights** (SDRs), a new reserve asset to substitute for dollars. By this time, however, the strains on the system had almost reached the breaking point. The United States was running an overly expansive monetary policy, which meant that inflation rates in the United States were rising. Internationally, the rising rate of U.S. inflation meant that the dollars held by foreign governments were falling in purchasing power. This in turn prompted them to try to convert dollars to gold at even faster rates. By the end of the decade, the problems had grown so severe that there was some question about the convertibility of the dollar.

Reduced confidence in dollar convertibility combined with the increasingly difficult task of maintaining fixed exchange rates led to some startling changes. The first bombshell occurred in August 1971, when President Richard M. Nixon announced that the dollar would no longer be convertible to gold. In more euphemistic terms, Nixon closed the **gold window**.

Releasing the dollar from the constraint of gold convertibility truly meant that the international monetary system had become a pure fiduciary system. No longer was there some commodity, however remote, that established the trading value of national currencies. This initial break led to a series of attempted repairs. **The Smithsonian Agreement of 1971** called for devaluation of the dollar against gold, a multilateral realignment of exchange rates, and an increase in the width of the bands within which exchange rates could fluctuate. Under this agreement, currency movements in the European Economic Community countries were determined by the so-called Snake, a technical mechanism for aligning currency movements. Even with these changes, the system fell apart. By April 1973, the exchange rates of all major industrialized countries began to float against the dollar. The Bretton Woods System, established in 1944 to guide the international monetary system, ceased to exist.

The international monetary system has continued to evolve since the 1970s. Much of this change has occurred in order to keep up with economic, political, and technological changes. From a world once ruled by fixed exchange rates, now we live in a world of flexible exchange rates determined by market forces. While some have argued that a more laissez-faire system has not come without a cost—greater transactions costs as exchange rates are more unpredictable than before—there is no consensus on what would be a better model.

FURTHER READING

Cononi, Rachel E., and Rebecca Hellerstein. "50 Years after Bretton Woods: What Is the Future for the International Monetary System? An Overview." Federal Reserve Bank of Boston *New England Economic Review* (July/August 1994).

BRIMMER, ANDREW F. (1926–). Andrew Felton Brimmer is President of Brimmer & Company, Inc., an economic consulting firm located in Washington, D.C., and the Wilmer D. Narrent Professor of Economics at the University of Massachusetts–Amherst. Born on September 13, 1926, in Newellton, Louisiana, Brimmer moved to Bremerton, Washington, upon graduation from high school, where he worked in the naval shipyard. After being drafted into the Army in 1945 and serving until 1948, Brimmer entered the University of Washington, where he received his B.A. in economics in 1950. After a stint as a Fulbright Scholar to India, Brimmer entered the graduate program in economics at Harvard University, where he received his Ph.D. in 1957.

During the last few years of his time at Harvard, Brimmer worked for the Federal Reserve Bank of New York. During the Kennedy Administration, Brimmer served as the assistant secretary of economic affairs in the Department of Commerce, a post he held until 1966. It was in March 1966 that President Lyndon Johnson appointed Brimmer to the **Board of Governors** of the Federal Reserve System. This appointment marked a milestone: Brimmer became the first African-American to serve as Governor of the Federal Reserve System. Brimmer served as Governor until August 31, 1974, when he resigned to take a position at Harvard University. After two years in the academic world, Brimmer returned to Washington, D.C., to form his consulting company, Brimmer & Company, Inc.

In addition to his work at the board and his private consulting, Brimmer has held several positions of note. He was elected vice president of the American Economic Association in 1989 and president of the Eastern Economics Association in 1991–1992. He also has received numerous awards and recognition within the economics profession, including presenter of the Richard T. Ely Lecturer of the American Economics Association (AEA) in 1981, and the Distinguished Lecturer on Economics in Government of the AEA (joint with the Society of Government Economists) in 1988.

FURTHER READING

Biography. Website: http://www.cob.subr.edu/brimmer%20bio.htm.

BROKERED DEPOSITS. Federal deposit insurance currently has a deposit ceiling of $100,000; that is, deposits are insured only up to $100,000 per account. A **financial innovation** to get around that restriction is the brokered deposit. If someone has $1 million and purchases one **certificate of deposit** (CD) from the local bank, $900,000 (the amount in excess of the $100,000 deposit ceiling) could be lost if the bank went bankrupt and closed. To protect against such a loss, a broker can, for a fee, take the $1 million and purchase $100,000 worth of CDs from 10 different banks. Because each $100,000 CD is covered by deposit insurance, all of the $1 million is insured against possible loss due to **bank failure**. Although deposit insurance authorities attempted to prohibit brokered deposits in 1984, a federal court decision later overturned this ban.

FURTHER READING

Maloney, Dan. "Liquidity Risk: Banks Rely on Brokered Deposits, Jumbo CDs to Sustain Growth." Federal Reserve Bank of Cleveland *Fourth District Conditions*. Website: www.clevelandfed. org/bsr/conditions/v2n3/jumbo.htm; Office of the Comptroller of the Currency. "Joint Agency Advisory on Brokered and Rate-Sensitive Deposits." Website: www.ots.treas.gov.

BRUNNER, KARL (1916–1989). Karl Brunner left a lasting mark in economics, especially with his analysis of monetary theory and policy. After receiving his Ph.D. in 1945, Brunner held several positions, both in private firms and in academics. Granted a Rockefeller Fellowship Research Grant to study in the United States for the period 1949–1950, Brunner's research began to blossom. Brunner's research brought together the rigor of theory with the real-world concerns of applied empirical work. His time spent at the Cowles Commission and the University of Chicago introduced him to a number of stars in the economics profession. At the Cowles Commission he worked with **Irving Fisher** and Ragnar Frisch, both noted for their work in statistics and the nascent field of econometrics. At Chicago he was influenced by **Milton Friedman** and Frank Knight.

Brunner accepted a position as assistant professor at UCLA, where he rose to associate professor in 1953 and to professor in 1961. In 1966 he left UCLA to join the Economics Department at Ohio State University. While at Ohio State, Brunner was founding editor of the *Journal of Money, Credit and Banking*. This was an important accomplishment because there was no journal specifically devoted specifically to the analysis of monetary theory, monetary policy, and how these impact the economy and financial markets. Remaining as editor of the *JMCB* until 1974, Brunner put an indelible stamp on what was published in the field. Moving to the University of Rochester in the mid-1970s, Brunner founded the *Journal of Monetary Economics* in 1975, another academic journal devoted to the study of money and monetary policy. Through these journals, Brunner promoted the study of monetary economics and broadened the outlets through which such research could be published. Because many in the economics profession at the time believed in the Keynesian model and the notion that fiscal policy dominated monetary policy, Brunner's two journals helped change the nature of monetary research and the analysis of macroeconomics.

Aside from these important accomplishments, Brunner's research, often co-authored with **Allan H. Meltzer**, focused on the role of money and especially on the measurement of the stock of **money**. His work provided a theoretical framework in which the supply of money could be measured and understood under different institutional arrangements. Brunner generally is credited with creating the framework underlying the construction of the adjusted **monetary base**, today a product of the Federal Reserve Bank of St. Louis. This measure is often used to identify changes in Federal Reserve policy.

Brunner, along with Meltzer, did much to highlight the importance of money and its effect on economic activity and in financial markets. Unlike Milton Friedman, Brunner and Meltzer provided a theoretical framework in which monetary policy was transmitted through the economy. One of their early analyses questioned the approach to monetary policy used by the Federal Reserve. This study, "The Federal Reserve's Attachment to the Free Reserve Concept" (Washington: House Committee on Banking and Currency) was published in 1964. They also questioned the usefulness of the then-accepted Keynesian IS-LM model. Brunner and Meltzer generalized this model, allowing for asset substitution and explicitly considering the role of credit markets. Brunner was part of the so-called **Monetarist** movement and through his research contributed to the research showing the importance of money and the impact of monetary policy actions. Although his research took a different turn than other Monetarists, especially Friedman and his followers, they both had the same goal: understanding the role of money and monetary policy in modern economies.

Not only did Brunner's research, journals, and conferences attract and promote research in monetary economics, he also is credited with coining the term "Monetarism." In July 1968 Brunner published an article in the Federal Reserve Bank of St. Louis's *Review* titled "The Role of Money and Monetary Policy." In that paper, largely a critique of studies by economists who did not favor the use of monetary aggregates to guide monetary policy, Brunner lays out the conclusions of what he refers to as the "Monetarist critique." These are:

First, monetary impulses are a major factor accounting for variations in output, employment and prices. Second, movements in the money stock are the most reliable measure of the thrust of monetary impulses. Third, the behavior of the monetary authorities dominates movements in the money stock over business cycles.

While these views were not new or unique to Brunner, he crystallized the debate between the newly named Monetarists and those economists who disagreed with the preceding conclusions. For this and for his untiring devotion showed to pursuing economic understanding, Karl Brunner has left a deep mark in modern monetary theory and debate.

FURTHER READING

Brunner, Karl, and Allan H. Meltzer. *Money and the Economy: Issues in Monetary Analysis.* Cambridge, UK: Cambridge University Press, 1997. (See especially the biography written by Giovanna Nicodano.)

BRYAN, MALCOLM (1902–1967). Malcolm Bryan served as president of the Federal Reserve Bank of Atlanta from 1951 through 1965. Although being president of a District Bank may not warrant inclusion in an encyclopedia of the Federal Reserve, Bryan's contributions to the development of policy in the early 1960s set him apart from his peers. Bryan's pioneering development and use of monetary growth targets as a policy tool in the late 1950s and early 1960s was a unique contribution to the development of postwar U.S. monetary policy. The minutes of the **Federal Open Market Committee (FOMC)** meetings reveal that money market conditions were of uppermost concern for policymakers at the time. That is, policy analysis and decisions often were based on the "tone and feel" of financial markets. This approach, often associated with Federal Reserve Chairman **William McChesney Martin**, meant that "gut" reactions to market developments were used in place of statistical analysis and formal econometric forecasting.

Bryan's proposals to replace money market activity as the policy operating guide with policy rules based on the behavior of monetary aggregates faced a hostile reception in meetings of the FOMC, just as proposals to use monetary growth targets would a decade later. His campaign to change policy challenged not only the convention of maintaining orderly domestic financial markets but also the politically pressing need to deal with worsening conditions in the U.S. balance of payments.

Bryan's approach to conducting monetary policy was a dramatic departure for a member of the FOMC. He took new and controversial research results coming out of monetary economics and tried to implement them. Bryan's contributions, however, went beyond merely adopting others' ideas. Indeed, arguments for the use of monetary aggregates in the formulation of monetary policy were becoming a popular issue among a group of economists that would later gain the label "**Monetarists**." In his writings, it is clear that Bryan was influenced by the work of **Milton Friedman** and his students at the University of Chicago. There also was increased emphasis on the monetary aggregates coming out of the Federal Reserve Bank of St. Louis, a movement that was initiated by its director of research **Homer Jones**. But Bryan's contribution went beyond the call for watching the aggregates: Bryan introduced short-run aggregate growth targets—growth cones—to guide policy. This stands out as a significant and innovative development in monetary policy analysis. Even though his targets and procedures were not adopted by the FOMC at the time, his strategy for monetary policy would resurface when the high inflation rates produced by the policies against which Bryan fought reached unacceptable levels. Indeed, it is arguable that if the FOMC adopted Bryan's policy approach the so-called **Great Inflation** of the 1960s and 1970s would not have occurred.

What is Bryan's legacy? Bryan's singular contribution is the development and use of monetary aggregate growth targets. Discussions at the FOMC during the late 1990s and early 2000s indicate that some members, as in Bryan's time, remain concerned about the behavior of the money supply and its potential effects on economic activity and inflation. Still, the role of monetary aggregates in the formation of policy is as limited today as it was 40 years ago: Manipulating the market interest rates (by adjusting the **federal funds rate**) remains the primary instrument by which the Federal Reserve carries out policy.

Bryan's contribution also should be considered within a larger perspective. Bryan, along with a few other bank presidents, pursued a research agenda that resulted in policy prescriptions quite different from that of the board. His willingness to advocate a controversial view within the FOMC promoted an airing of diverse views and concerns over monetary policy. In his own way, Bryan helped to foster an environment in which alternative theories and approaches to economic analysis could be used for improving monetary policy.

FURTHER READING

Hafer, R. W. "Against the Tide: Malcolm Bryan and the Introduction of Monetary Aggregate Targets." Federal Reserve Bank of Atlanta *Economic Review* (First Quarter 1999): 20–37; Hetzel, Robert. "William McChesney Martin and Monetary Policy in the 1960s." Unpublished manuscript, Federal Reserve Bank of Richmond (April 1995); Meigs, James A. "Campaigning for Monetary Reform: The Federal Reserve Bank of St. Louis in 1959 and 1960." *Journal of Monetary Economics* 2 (November 1976): 439–53.

BUDGET DEFICITS (*See* Monetization)

BURNS, ARTHUR FRANK (1904–1987). Arthur Burns served as governor and chairman of the **Board of Governors** of the Federal Reserve from February 1970 to December 1977. Before his tenure at the Federal Reserve, he held other positions in the government, including chairman of the **Council of Economic Advisors** (1953–1956) under President Dwight D. Eisenhower. During his time as chairman of the Council, Burns established a relationship with then-Vice-President Richard M. Nixon, who, as president, appointed Burns to be the chairman of the Federal Reserve in 1970.

Burns is perhaps best known for two positions that he held in his professional career. Beginning in the 1940s, Burns served as director of research (1945–1953) and then as president (1957–1967) of the National Bureau of Economic Research (NBER). During his time as head of the NBER, Burns gained an international reputation for his path-breaking work on business cycles. His work with Wesley Clair Mitchell—the founder of the NBER—which was published in 1946 under the title *Measuring Business Cycles,* became a classic. From his analysis of business cycles, Burns reached the conclusion that recessions arise because of previous bouts of inflation. Hetzel (1998, p. 21) suggests that Burns "concluded that inflation itself sets in train forces that cause recession."

Burns's views on the causes of business cycles and inflation colored his approach to policy when he was chairman of the Board of Governors. For example, Burns believed that the economy is inherently unstable and subject to periodic collapses and booms. He looked at economic history and argued that unless the government took an active policy approach in correcting these built-in instabilities, the economy would experience problems such as the **Great Depression**. Instead of a rare occurrence, Burns's analysis suggested to him that events like the Great Depression were likely to recur without government intervention to correct the "imbalances" that naturally occur in the economy.

Even though Burns often gave the impression that he was a staunch inflation fighter, the record of his policy recommendations suggests otherwise. Burns, like many other economists of the time, believed in fine-tuning economic activity through demand management. That is, Burns believed that monetary policy should be used to achieve full employment goals, even if those policies produced higher rates of **inflation**. Because Burns believed that monetary policy had little to do with inflation, Burns favored incomes policies to help fight inflation while he was chairman of the FOMC. Such policies aimed at reducing the growth of nominal income and price level changes through direct government intervention most often were advocated by more liberal economists of the times who, like Burns, did not recognize the impact of money growth on the rate of inflation. So-called cost-push forces—increasing wages, for example—were considered to be the root cause of inflation. Eliminating or stemming these effects through price control programs was, therefore, viewed as the correct approach to controlling inflation. Indeed, it often is argued that Burns initiated the monetary policies of the 1970s that resulted in the upward climb of inflation rates that culminated in double-digit rates in 1979 and 1980.

Burns brought considerable attention to the Federal Reserve during his tenure as chairman of the Board of Governors. Unlike his predecessor, **William McChesney Martin**, Burns relied on scientific analysis to form policy decisions. Martin, whose background was mostly as a financial market participant, relied on the "tone and feel" of the market to determine the direction of policy. Burns, in contrast, increased the budget of the research staff of the board in order to develop and improve its econometric forecasting models, even though he had eschewed the use of formal models in his earlier days. Such models and the rigorous theoretical foundations upon which they are based provided Burns and policymakers with an approach to policy analysis that had not been used before.

Burns also developed a reputation for commanding respect for his positions and views. As quoted in Hetzel (1998), a magazine article of the time suggested that, "Where Arthur sits, there is the head of the table." When testifying before Congress, Burns often challenged the views of any questioning congressman or senator, especially when they disagreed with his own views. Burns believed in strong leadership and is quoted as saying, "What is the chairman supposed to be, a purely passive regulator, a policeman who keeps order, or a leader?" (quoted in Kliesen, 1996). Burns lived up to that example, even when it meant that the role of others in the decision process was reduced. For example, today the Federal Reserve makes available the **beige book** summary of the various District Banks' views on current economic conditions. This compilation of anecdotal information about district economic conditions was initiated under Burns's request. Although not made public and called the Red Book at the time because of its then red cover, the (apocryphal) story within the Federal Reserve System is that Burns started this collection of material to keep District Bank economists busy at something other than national monetary policy analysis. Burns's penchant for centering power within a small orbit also is suggested by the fact that during his time as chairman, the verbatim records of the FOMC meetings were discontinued.

In many ways, Arthur Burns was an enigmatic person. He was a believer in free markets who also advocated government intervention. He advocated the scientific pursuit of answers regarding economic policy but closely controlled the flow of information and input to the decision process. The complex nature of Burns's approach to economics and his role in the often turbulent economic environment of the 1960s and 1970s make him a fascinating character for study.

Burns received his Ph.D. from Columbia University in 1934. He taught economics at Rutgers University from 1927 until 1944, when he joined the faculty of Columbia University, where he became the John Bates Clark Professor of Economics in 1959. After his time as chairman of the Federal Reserve Board of Governors, Burns held several positions, most notably Ambassador to West Germany (1981–1985).

FURTHER READING

Hetzel, Robert. "Arthur Burns and Inflation," Federal Reserve Bank of Richmond *Economic Quarterly* (Winter 1998): 21–44; Kliesen, Kevin. "Book Review." Federal Reserve Bank of Minneapolis's *The Region* (September 1996); Wells, Wyatt C. *Economist in an Uncertain World: Arthur F. Burns and the Federal Reserve, 1970–1978.* New York: Columbia University Press, 1996.

BUSINESS CYCLE. Economic activity, measured as the growth of real **gross domestic product** (real GDP) or changes in the **unemployment rate**, changes in irregular patterns. That is, there are times when the economy is growing and other times when it is contracting or suffering negative economic growth. These ups and downs of economic activity are often referred to as business cycles. Although the notion of a "cycle" may conjure up the idea of a steady cycle—like the pattern on a heart monitor, or an oscilloscope—patterns of economic growth are anything but regular. For that reason, many economists prefer the phrase "economic fluctuations" to business cycles, although the latter term is the most commonly used phrase.

Business cycles are defined by the behavior of the economy relative to its potential level of performance. Potential real GDP is the level of output at which the economy is operating at full capacity. Potential real GDP often serves as the reference point for determining where in the business cycle the economy is. To see this, consider the hypothetical path of real GDP relative to its potential level in the figure below. What you can see is that there are times when the level of output is above potential, and there are times when it is below. This suggests the cyclical nature of economic activity. You also will note that there are specific points labeled on the path of actual output. When real GDP reaches its highest point, that is

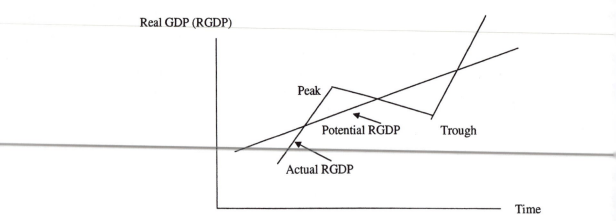

referred to as the *peak* of the business cycle. From that point, the level of economic activity falls until it reaches a low point, referred to as the *trough*. It is the trough of the business cycle, because from here the economy once again begins to grow. With the peak and the trough identified, a business cycle is thus defined as that period from peak-to-peak or from trough-to-trough—in other words, a complete cycle.

Of course, real GDP behaves much differently than this stylized version of the economy suggests. Still, the main points are the same: business cycle peaks occur after the economy has been expanding for a time, and business cycle troughs occur once the downturn in economic activity has ended. Economists call these periods economic expansions and recessions, respectively.

What does the behavior of real GDP actually look like? Below is shown the rate of growth (percentage change) of real GDP for the time since 1970.

As you can see, the pattern of real GDP growth is not very regular. Still, there is a noticeable pattern to its behavior over time. As a reference point, the figure also includes the recessions experienced by the U.S. economy. The shaded bars represent the time at which the economy enters a **recession** to the time when it reaches the bottom of the cycle and once again begins to expand. Note that in every instance, real GDP growth rates begin to decline before the onset of a recession and turn negative once the recession has begun. Indeed, the rule of thumb definition of a recession is two consecutive quarters (six months) of negative real GDP growth. Note also that the lowest (or most negative) growth rate for real GDP generally occurs at some point covered by one of the bars.

The unevenness of the recessions delineated in the figure below also points out the unevenness of the periods in which the economy is expanding. Compare the period before the early 1980s with the period since. Between 1960 and 1984, there were five recessions, the worst of which occurred in 1982–1984. Since then, a period of comparable length, there have been only two recessions, and by comparison, they have been relatively mild. The period since the 1980s has been characterized by **John Taylor**, a professor of economics at Stanford University, as the "Long Boom" in U.S. economic history. This is because the expansions of the 1980s and the 1990s are the second longest and longest periods of sustained economic growth in U.S. history.

Who decides the dates of the recessions? Putting an "official" date on business cycles is the job of the Business Cycle Dating Committee of the National Bureau of Economic

Quarterly Growth in Real GDP at Annual Rates, Percent

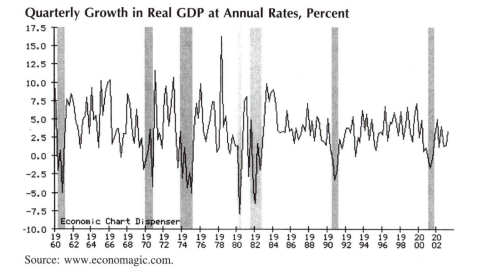

Source: www.economagic.com.

Research (NBER). This committee, composed of academic economists who specialize in business cycle analysis, determine the dates when a recession begins and ends. The NBER Committee defines a recession as "a recurring period of decline in total output, income, employment, and trade, usually lasting from six months to a year, and marked by widespread contractions in many sectors of the economy." The problem faced by the committee is that it is virtually impossible to know that a recession has begun at the time when it actually occurs. We can see the evidence only with a delay. Walsh (1999) notes that,

> First, recessions and expansions are, by definition, recurring periods of either decline or growth. One quarter of declining GDP would not necessarily indicate that the economy had entered a recession, just as one quarter of positive growth need not signal that a recession had ended. Second, the information that is needed to determine whether the economy has entered a recession or moved into an expansion phase is only available with a time lag. Delays in data collection and revisions in the preliminary estimates of economic activity mean the NBER must wait some time before a clear picture of the economy's behavior is available.

Even though there is a lag in the reporting of recessions, the NBER's dating is widely recognized as the official dates. In fact, even the U.S. government accepts these dates for its use in analyzing policy changes and effects. The NBER has dated business cycles extending as far back as the 1800s. Focusing on the period since World War II, the table below lists the NBER business cycle dates.

It is important to recognize that the occurrence of business cycles, their duration and severity, are sometimes linked to policy decisions made by the Federal Reserve and other government agencies. A long-standing debate has occurred over how much affect changes in monetary and fiscal policy actually have on the behavior of real GDP. Walsh (1999) suggests that

> ... understanding changes in the nature of the business cycle is important for policymakers. Most central banks view contributing to a stable economy as one of their responsibilities. Promoting stable growth has important benefits, and reducing the frequency or severity of recessions is desirable as part of a policy to ensure employment opportunities for all workers. Preventing expansions from generating inflation is also important since once inflation gets started, high unemployment is usually necessary to bring it back down.... Thus, one reason

Business Cycle Reference Dates		Duration in months	
Peak	Trough	Contraction	Expansion
November 1948	October 1949	11	
July 1953	May 1954	10	45
August 1957	April 1958	8	39
April 1960	February 1961	10	24
December 1969	November 1970	11	106
November 1973	March 1975	16	36
January 1980	July 1980	6	58
July 1981	November 1982	16	12
July 1990	March 1991	8	92
March 2001	November 2001	9	120

Source: NBER.

business cycles can change, even if the underlying economy or source of disturbances haven't, is because policymakers do a better (or worse) job of stabilizing the economy.

FURTHER READING

National Bureau of Economic Research. Website: www.NBER.org. Romer, Christina. "Remeasuring Business Cycles." *Journal of Economic History* 54 (September 1994): 574–609; Taylor, John B. "Monetary Policy and the Long Boom." Federal Reserve Bank of St. Louis *Review* (November/December 1998): 3–12; Walsh, Carl. "Changes in the Business Cycle." Federal Reserve Bank of San Francisco *Economic Letter* (May 14, 1999).

CAMELS. One role of the Federal Reserve is to supervise and regulate the nation's banking system. One aspect of this activity is to ensure that banks are operating in a safe and sound manner. This means that bank managers and owners are not exposing their bank to undue risk, whether it is risk from defaults on **loans** that they have made or risk related to how they manage their investment portfolio. To gauge the overall soundness of a bank's management, regulators use an evaluation system that is based on six measures. Although formally called the Uniform Financial Institutions Rating System (UFIRS), it is commonly known as the CAMELS rating. The term CAMELS is an acronym. That is, each letter stands for one component of the evaluation rubric. They are:

C   adequacy of *C*apital

A   quality of *A*ssets

M   capability of *M*anagement

E   quality and level of *E*arnings

L   adequacy of **Liquidity**

S   *S*ensitivity to market risk

The CAMELS system is used by Federal Reserve supervision personnel to rate each bank. After visiting and inspecting a bank's operations and its balance sheet, the institution receives a CAMELS rating between 1 and 5 for each area. A low rating indicates a "safe and sound" bank. The higher the rating, the more suspect is the management of the bank in terms of riskiness. A rating of 5 usually indicates that the bank is likely to fail. Banks receiving high CAMELS ratings are subject to increased scrutiny by regulators or even closure by authorities. The CAMELS ratings and a description of each are shown in the table below.

The CAMELS system originally did not include the last component, sensitivity to market risk. As described in the Federal Reserve Bank of Chicago's Fedwire (1997), "The sensitivity to market risk component (S) is designed to reflect the degree to which changes in interest rates, foreign exchange rates, commodity prices, or equity prices can adversely affect an institution's earnings or economic capital." How does the Federal Reserve go about making this determination? The Federal Reserve's supervision and regulation personnel consider several factors. One is the sensitivity of the institution's earnings to unexpected and harmful changes in interest rates, foreign exchange rates, commodity prices, or equity prices. Sometimes referred to as "market risk," banks must

CAMELS RATINGS

CAMELS Composite Rating	Description
Safe and Sound	
1	Financial institutions with a composite one rating are sound in every respect and generally have individual component ratings of one or two.
2	Financial institutions with a composite two rating are fundamentally sound. In general, a two-rated institution will have no individual component ratings weaker than three.
Unsatisfactory	
3	Financial institutions with a composite three rating exhibit some degree of supervisory concern in one or more of the component areas.
4	Financial institutions with a composite four rating generally exhibit unsafe and unsound practices or conditions. They have serious financial or managerial deficiencies that result in unsatisfactory performance.
5	Financial institutions with a composite five rating generally exhibit extremely unsafe and unsound practices or conditions. Institutions in this group pose a significant risk to the deposit insurance fund and their failure is highly probable.

Source: Gilbert, Meyer, and Vaughn (2002).

be prudent in managing their portfolio of loans and investments to avoid exposing the bank's earnings or its capital to possible loss from unforeseen changes. Because banks are by their very nature involved with balancing the risk between the returns on longer-term assets, such as loans, against the cost of shorter-term liabilities, such as checking accounts, they must be able to manage these two aspects of their portfolio in a way that does not expose their earnings to losses stemming from unexpected changes in market conditions. In order to manage their risk exposure, the CAMELS system means that managers of banks, regardless of the size of the bank, must identify, measure, monitor, and control exposure to market risk.

FURTHER READING

Gilbert, R. Alton, Andrew P. Meyer, and Mark D. Vaughn. "Could a CAMELS Downgrade Model Improve Off-Site Surveillance?" Federal Reserve Bank of St. Louis *Review* (January/February 2002): 47–64; Federal Reserve Bank of Chicago. *FEDWIRE* (February 1997).

CAPITAL MARKETS. This refers to the market for debt instruments, such as **bonds**, that have a time to maturity greater than one year. Also traded in the capital market are equity instruments—stocks—which have no fixed maturity. There is no separate, physical market for these instruments. Rather, the notion of a separate market for longer-term financial instruments is really for the purpose of distinguishing trading in these instruments from those with maturities of less than one year. Financial instruments traded in the capital market generally are thought to be riskier than those traded in the shorter-term market, commonly referred to as the **money market**. The financial instruments that make up the capital market consist of corporate stocks and bonds; federal, state, and local government bonds; residential mortgages; and various types of bank loans.

FURTHER READING

Mishkin, Frederic S. *The Economics of Money, Banking, and Financial Markets.* 7th edition. Boston: Pearson Addison Wesley, 2004.

CAPITAL REQUIREMENTS. A bank's capital is similar to the notion of an individual's net worth. Capital is the value of a bank's assets minus the value of its liabilities. Banks with greater amounts of capital are thought to be less likely to suffer bankruptcy and failure. This is because capital serves as a bank's cushion should it suffer losses on its assets (i.e., a number of loans are not repaid). If a bank has negative capital, then regulators may close it down, sell off the assets, and/or remove the management. In this case, investors may lose their money. Because of this, bank regulators set capital requirements to establish minimum requirements. (*See also* **Basel Accord**.) These requirements usually are measured as the ratio of capital to assets; the higher the ratio, the larger is the cushion. Forcing banks to keep minimum amounts of capital also prevents managers from using this money for overly risky investment activities.

An important aspect of setting capital requirements concerns the nature of how regulators measure the value of assets and liabilities. Consider a bank that makes a 10-year loan on a shopping center for $30 million. Three years into the loan, the shopping center falls on bad times. If the bank were to foreclose on the loan and sell the center, it would get only $20 million. Which is the correct value of the bank's assets to use when calculating its capital position: the $30 million for the original value of the loan—the value carried on the books— or the $20 million that the asset is really worth in the market today? Many economists support using the latter number (sometimes this is referred to as **"mark-to-market"**) because it provides a market-based measure of the asset's real value and therefore a truer picture of what the bank's assets are really worth.

Economists and some regulators have suggested that capital requirements vary across institutions based on the riskiness of their activities. Such risk-based capital requirements recognize that banks engaging in riskier activities—making loans to start-up tech firms in the late 1990s, for example—should hold more capital compared with banks making loans in low-risk, stable markets.

FURTHER READING

Bris, Arturo, and Salvatore Cantale. "Bank Capital Requirements and Managerial Self-Interest." Yale School of Management IFC Working Paper (September 1998); Federal Deposit Insurance Corporation. "Risk-Based Capital Requirements for Commercial Lending: The Impact of Basel II." April 21, 2003. Website: www.fdic.gov/bank/analytical/fyi/2003/042103fyi.html.

CENTRAL BANK INDEPENDENCE. Economists often discuss the relative independence of a central bank and how it may or may not affect both its policymaking decisions and the outcomes of policy actions. But we must be clear on what is meant by the term "independence." MacLaury (1976) states that

> independence does not mean decisions and actions made without accountability. By law and by established procedures, the [Federal Reserve] System is clearly accountable to congress—not only for its monetary policy actions, but also for its regulatory responsibilities and for services to banks and to the public. Nor does independence mean that monetary policy actions should be free from public discussion and criticism—by members of congress, by professional economists in and out of government, by financial, business, and community leaders, and by informed citizens. Nor does it mean that the Federal Reserve is independent of the government. Although closely interfaced with commercial banking, the Federal Reserve is clearly a public institution, functioning within a discipline of responsibility to the 'public-interest.' It has a degree of independence within the government which is quite different from being independent of government.

This description of independence is unique to the Federal Reserve. Other central banks, such as the Bank of England or the Bank of Japan, often have much closer ties to their governments in terms of accountability and the composition of the decision-making bodies. Unlike the Federal Reserve, others are not so well insulated from the political process.

In recent years the degree of central bank independence has become a topic of much debate. The Reserve Bank of New Zealand, for example, moved to a much more independent role in the past few years. The establishment of central banks for the newly emerging nations of eastern Europe offer a new landscape upon which to build the type of central bank one wishes to have making policy. And the development of the central bank overseeing the monetary policy decisions of the European system offers another situation where this discussion has raised important questions about the degree of independence a central bank should enjoy.

Although this may suggest that central bank independence is a new topic, it hardly is. Writing in the early 1800s, the British economist David Ricardo suggested that the government not be granted the power to issue paper money. Such power, he argued, would mean that the control over the monetary policy discussion would be conducted among politicians seeking to enhance their own reelections and not with a longer-term goal in mind. Even though Ricardo recognized the need for some accountability, the actions of the monetary policymakers should be outside the political arena.

In discussing this topic, it is useful to first compare the arguments for and against central bank independence. The argument for independence generally rests on the issue already mentioned: independence from the political process. Why is this important? It is commonly agreed that price stability or a low-inflationary environment is a key goal of monetary policy. Indeed, some argue that it is the only goal that, in the long run, the Federal Reserve or any other central bank can actually achieve. If this is true, then monetary policymakers must take a long-term outlook to setting policy.

To achieve a goal of low **inflation**, for example, this may mean going through a period of slow economic growth or even **recession**. As one example, this is exactly what transpired during the early 1980s. Led by Federal Reserve Chairman **Paul Volcker**, the Federal Reserve geared policy to rid the U.S. economy of high inflation by pushing interest rates up and slowing the rate of growth of the money supply. These actions brought about the worst recession of the postwar period, lasting from 1982 through 1984. But this action also reduced inflation from approximately 15 percent to single digits. Since then, the Federal Reserve has aggressively acted to keep inflation low and, during the early 2000s, the rate of inflation was around 2 to 3 percent.

Could the Federal Reserve achieve low inflation even if it was not independent? The argument is that if driven by political pressures, then the Federal Reserve's policies would become much more shortsighted. This is because most politicians can only achieve their goals if they are reelected to office. For Congress this means a window of only two years; for presidential aspirants, four years; for senators, six. The goal of getting reelected may refocus policy actions away from solutions that take many years to accomplish. Trying to achieve short-run policy objectives like lowering **unemployment rates** before an election can have disastrous long-term consequences. There is some evidence to suggest that during the 1960s and 1970s, there existed a so-called **political business cycle** in which expansionary economic policies were pursued prior to an election with contractionary policies following the election. If the Federal Reserve was under the direct control of Congress or the president, it could be used to further these short-term political goals over the prospects of longer-term damage. As B. W. Fraser (2004, p. 2), governor of the Reserve Bank of Australia put it, the two main threats that relate to the issue of central bank independence are "the tendency for policy makers and politicians to push the economy to run faster and further than its capacity limits allow, and the temptation that governments have to incur budget deficits and fund these by borrowings from the central bank."

Another aspect in this debate is that putting monetary policy in the hands of nonexperts could have negative effects. Members of the **Federal Open Market Committee (FOMC)**, the Federal Reserve's policymaking body, generally are either economists or individuals from the banking and financial sectors of the economy. While being an economist with a Ph.D. does not provide one with foolproof insights, such individuals are highly trained in understanding the links between economic activity, **financial markets**, and monetary policy. The need for such expertise and the constant pull of political pressures favor an independent monetary policymaking body.

Even with these warnings, an independent central bank is not without its problems. The most important issue of having an independent central bank is accountability. While you know who is the president and probably know who represents you in Congress or the Senate, it is unlikely that you know the members of the FOMC, except perhaps the Chairman of the Federal Reserve. Although politicians face accountability for their actions (votes on certain legislation, ability or lack thereof to bring projects to the local district, etc.) at the ballot box, members of the FOMC—the body that determines monetary policy—remains largely unknown. This means that when bad decisions are made, the public has no recourse to remove those policymakers. During the 1970s, for example, the economy experienced high rates of inflation, due in part to oil price increases engineered by the Organization of Petroleum Exporting Countries (OPEC) oil cartel but also due in large part to expansionary monetary policies. Even though the FOMC at the time saw inflation rates rising, they did not take actions that would curtail those increases. In their collective view, the cost of reducing inflation, in terms of reduced economic growth and higher unemployment rates, was not a worthwhile tradeoff. As mentioned above, it was not until the early 1980s when inflation rose to almost 15 percent that the Federal Reserve, under Paul Volcker, took actions to reduce inflation.

The **Great Depression** is another episode in the Federal Reserve's history that warns against unchecked independence. At that time, the Federal Reserve's independence meant that it could pursue policies that helped exacerbate the economic calamity that befell the U.S. and other economies. This is not to imply that the Federal Reserve's policymakers acted maliciously in their decisions. In fact, they generally applied the economic theories of the time. But a less independent Federal Reserve may have been forced to move to an expansionary policy stance more quickly than it actually did, perhaps reducing the severity of the downturn.

While there is no consensus over the issue of central bank independence, there is some evidence that suggests that independence is related to overall economic performance, especially inflation. One of the earliest tests of this relationship was made by Alberto Alesina and Lawrence H. Summers (1993). Alesina and Summers developed a measure of central bank independence. The more the central bank was independent of the government, the higher was its "independence" rating. This rating was then compared with several measures of economic activity. One was the average rate of inflation over the period 1973–1988. A reason for using this extended time horizon is that the two economists did not want the inflation numbers to be unduly affected by some short-term event, such as a bad harvest or an external shock, that may have caused inflation to be higher than average in some years.

The figure below shows the relationship between Alesina and Summer's measure of central bank independence and average inflation for a sample of 17 counties. Each dot represents a country's average level of inflation and its level of central bank independence. What the figure indicates is that, at least over this timespan, there was an obvious, negative relationship between a country's average rate of inflation experience and the level of independence of its central bank. For instance, Spain was gauged to be the least independent central bank and had one of the highest average rates of inflation. Other countries with similar levels of bank independence include Australia and Italy. At the other end of the spectrum, Germany with the most independent central bank and had one of the lowest average rates of inflation. As shown, the United States falls toward the higher end if the independence rankings (relatively more independent) and was one of the lower inflation countries. Along with the United States and Germany, Japan and Switzerland experienced low average rates of inflation and had relatively more independent central banks.

Does this evidence conclusively mean that increased independence leads to better economic performance? Although the relationship between inflation and central bank

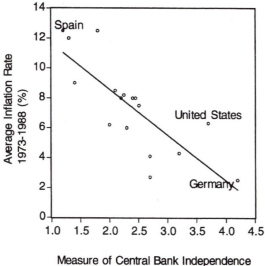

Measure of Central Bank Independence
(Least Independent to Most Independent)

Source: Alesina and Summers (1993).

independence is suggestive, other studies have found that the link may not be as strong as indicated in the above figure. Moreover, in the Alesina and Summers study, no relationship was found between the degree of central bank independence and the average rate of growth of the economy. In other words, over time, a central bank, independent or not, probably has very little control over the average rate of real economic growth in an economy.

Finally, central bank independence is not achieved without cost. If central banks are to be independent from their governments, there must be some measure of accountability. This logically leads one to the issue of policy **transparency**, that is, the notion that policy decisions are made with greater openness so that decision makers in the economy understand the direction of monetary policy and reasons for any change. With that information, individuals can alter plans so as not to be unduly affected by a change in policy. Such transparency reduces the costs of unexpected policy changes and increases the likelihood that there will be less interference with monetary policy decisions. Indeed, in recent years the Federal Reserve has made significant moves in the direction of increased disclosure of policy actions, including the immediate dissemination of policy decisions following its FOMC meetings.

FURTHER READING

Alesina, Alberto. "Macroeconomics and Politics," in NBER *Macroeconomics Annual*, Stanley Fisher, ed. Cambridge, MA: MIT Press, 1988, 13–52; Alesina, Alberto, and Lawrence H. Summers. "Central Bank Independence and Macroeconomic Performance: Some Comparative Evidence." *Journal of Money, Credit, and Banking* (May 1993): 151–62; Fraser, B. W. "Central Bank Independence: What Does It Mean?" Reserve Bank of Australia *Bulletin* (December 1994): 1–8; Friedman, Milton. "Should There Be an Independent Monetary Authority?" in *The Federal Reserve System After Fifty Years*, Hearings Before the Subcommittee on Domestic Finance of the House Committee on Banking and Currency. Washington, D.C.: Government Printing Office, 1964; MacLaury, Bruce K. "Perspectives on Federal Reserve Independence—A Changing Structure for Changing Times." Federal Reserve Bank of Minneapolis *Annual Report* (1976); Weintraub, Robert E. "Congressional Supervision of Monetary Policy." *Journal of Monetary Economics* (April 1978): 341–62.

CERTIFICATE OF DEPOSIT. Commonly referred to as CDs, certificates of deposit are financial instruments sold by banks. When you buy a CD, the bank agrees to pay you a fixed interest rate and you agree to leave your money with them for a specified period of time. For example, a bank may advertise that it is paying 5 percent for five-year CDs with a minimum deposit of $5,000. Rates on CDs are reported in the financial pages of most newspapers, including rates on CDs ranging in maturity from one month to several years. Beginning in the 1960s, banks started offering large CDs ($100,000 or more) that could be sold in the secondary market. In other words, if you purchased the CD, you could sell it to a friend and they could redeem it at maturity or even sell it to someone else. In general, these CDs (called *negotiable CDs*) have become important sources of funds for banks.

CHAIRMAN OF THE BOARD OF GOVERNORS. The chairman of the Board of Governors of the Federal Reserve System is appointed by the president and confirmed by the Senate. The chairman is one of the governors of the board. The term of the chairman is four years and is renewable, up to the maximum the individual may serve in their capacity as governor. Even though the chairman has, on paper, no more power than any of the other governors, this is misleading. Most chairmen have influenced policy in very direct and meaningful ways. For instance, the chairman directs the allocation of research resources among the other governors, assigns the governors to special task forces, and in general oversees the operations of the **Board of Governors**.

This power comes partly from the fact that the chairman directs the discussion at the **Federal Open Market Committee (FOMC)** meetings, of which he also is chair. As chair of the FOMC, the chairman influences the discussion and direction of monetary policy. In a long-time tradition, the chairman usually initiates the discussion at FOMC meetings, often leading off with presentations by board staff economists on various aspects of economic and financial events that have occurred since the last meeting. Of course, the tone of these discussions also is affected by the chair since he or she has the ability to direct the staff research agenda. With those presentations over, the FOMC engages in what is call the "go around." At that time, governors and presidents of the banks have time to offer their views on the current state of the economy and the direction of monetary policy. Once this general discussion is completed, the meeting often closes with the chairman providing his or her opinions and observations of the issues. This allows the chairman to frame the policy discussion and make clear his or her position before any votes on policy are cast.

Aside from the operational power that the chairman wields within the System, the chairman also is widely considered to be one of the most influential people in the world, sometimes even put right up there alongside the president of the United States. How does an appointed official achieve such a position? Because the Federal Reserve oversees the regulation of the U.S. banking system and directs monetary policy for the United States, it has dramatic affects on the U.S. and other nation's economies. In an understatement of vast proportions, the board's Website describes the chairman's position thus: "As the individual who presides over the organization deciding monetary policy in the world's largest economy, the Chairman has a great deal of stature in economic, financial and political affairs, both domestically and abroad." This stature also derives from the fact that the chairman serves as the U.S. representative on a number of international organizations. For instance, the chairman serves as the alternate U.S. member of the Board of Governors of the **International Monetary Fund** (IMF). The chairman also sits as a board member of the Bank for International Settlements (BIS) and is a member of the National Advisory Council on International Monetary and Fiscal Policies.

The chairman is not only the most visible spokesman for U.S. monetary policy abroad but also actively represents the Federal Reserve Board and the System before domestic government bodies. The chairman often testifies before congressional committees and in hearings on topics as diverse as banking regulation, fair lending, recent events in financial markets, and, of course, monetary policy. As proscribed by the **Humphrey-Hawkins Act of 1978**, the chairman testifies in January and July before the Senate Committee on Banking, Housing, and Urban Affairs and the House Committee on Banking, Finance and Urban Affairs. In these appearances, the chairman provides legislators with an overview of the Federal Reserve's views on the economy, the conduct of monetary policy, and the direction of policy in the near future.

Although the foregoing provides an overview of the chairman's role in the Federal Reserve, it does not do justice to the individuals and their unique characters and problems faced. Those discussions are left for the biographical entries. Past chairmen and their terms in office are listed in Appendix B.

FURTHER READING

Blinder, Alan. *Central Banking in Theory and Practice*. Cambridge, MA: MIT Press, 1999; Grieder, William. *Secrets of the Temple*. New York: Simon and Schuster, 1987; Jones, David M. *Fed Watching and Interest Rate Projections: A Practical Guide*. New York: New York Institute of Finance, 1986 (Chapter 1); Mayer, Martin. *The Fed: The Inside Story of How the World's Most Powerful Financial Institution Drives the Markets*. New York: Free Press, 2001.

CHARTERING. Chartering is the process used by banking authorities to regulate the number of banks. When an individual or group of individuals wishes to open a bank, they must file an application with the Office of the **Comptroller of the Currency** for a federal charter. It may also be necessary to file an application with state banking authorities for a state charter. Essentially, this application procedure allows the bank regulators to determine if the owners have sufficient capital to back the bank and to gauge the qualifications of the proposed managers. Chartered banks are required to file quarterly reports to the appropriate authorities. In these reports, the bank reports its earnings, assets, and liabilities. Chartered banks may be subject to periodic examinations by the **Federal Deposit Insurance Corporation (FDIC)**, the Federal Reserve, the Comptroller of the Currency, or state banking regulators.

FURTHER READING

Bodenhorn, Howard. "Bank Chartering and Political Corruption in Antebellum New York: Free Banking as Reform." NBER Working Paper No. 10479 (May 2004); Fenimore, Chet A. "Organizing Your Bank." (1999) Website: www.denovobanks.com/chartering.

CHECKABLE DEPOSITS. This is the phrase used to describe several types of bank deposits, including checking accounts, negotiable order of withdrawal (**NOW**) **accounts**, super-NOW accounts, and share drafts at credit unions. Although each of these deposits have slightly different characteristics—some pay rates of interest and others do not, some have limitations on the number of checks you can write per month—the common aspect is that they are *payable on demand*. That is, if the account includes adequate funds, the bank where you hold such an account must pay account holders cash immediately (*on demand*) when they write a check on the account or present the bank with a check for funds. Use of checkable deposits is a common method to buy goods and services or to pay bills.

Checkable deposits account for about one-quarter of banks' liabilities, a source of funds. The distribution of checkable deposits between non–interest-bearing checking accounts and those checkable deposits on which some interest is paid has changed over time. Prior to the passage of the **Depository Institutions Deregulation and Monetary Control Act (DIDMCA) of 1980**, the majority of banks had been prohibited from paying interest on checking accounts since the 1930s. After passage of DIDMCA, however, all banks could pay interest on checkable deposits and many developed new deposits that had characteristics of both checking accounts and savings accounts: you could write a check against the account for your groceries and get paid interest on the balance.

To see how this change in the regulations affected the distribution between these two types of deposits, consider the fact that in 1975, non-interest-bearing checking accounts amounted to $211 billion, whereas there were only about $1 billion of the other checkable deposits. Together checkable deposits totaled about $212 billion. By 1985, five years after the regulatory change, non–interest-bearing checking accounts have grown to only $267 billion, but other checkable deposits had jumped dramatically to $180 billion. By 1985, total checkable deposits were $446 billion, over a 200 percent increase. This surge reflects the fact that once banks could pay interest, depositors shifted funds between these checkable deposits and from other types of deposits. At the end of 2002, checkable deposits stood at $576 billion, of which $278 was accounted for by interest-bearing checking accounts and $298 by non–interest-bearing accounts. Clearly, the growth over the past 20 years in this component of the money stock occurred primarily in the interest-bearing component. This shifting of funds from savings-type accounts to checkable deposits just makes economic sense: individuals sought more liquidity and a positive return, two aspects that could be achieved with interest-bearing checkable deposits. And, unlike money market mutual funds, accounts at banks are protected by FDIC insurance.

FURTHER READING

Carraro, Kenneth C., and Daniel L. Thornton. "The Cost of Checkable Deposits in the United States." Federal Reserve Bank of St. Louis *Review* (April 1998): 19–27; Stavins, Joanna. "Checking Accounts: What Do Banks Offer and What Do Customers Value?" Federal Reserve Bank of Boston *New England Economic Review* (1999): 3–14.

CHIPS. CHIPS is an acronym for *C*entral *H*ouse for *I*nterbank *P*ayments and *S*ettlements. CHIPS is based in New York and works to clear transactions that have been carried out instead of writing a check. CHIPS electronically transfers (wires) funds, typically for amounts in excess of $1 million, between banks, both domestic and foreign, to settle accounts upon which checks have been drawn. So, when one corporation buys something from another, it does not exchange a check as an individual might for groceries. Rather, CHIPS wires funds between the banks of two firms. This lowers the cost of transactions because it occurs much faster than it would take to write a check and clear it through the various bank accounts.

FURTHER READING

Federal Reserve Bank of New York. "CHIPS." *Fedpoint* (April 2002).

COMMERCIAL BANKS. Commercial banks are financial institutions that bring together, "intermediate," that is, borrowers and savers. While this role is shared with other financial institutions, commercial banks historically were special in that only they could offer demand deposits (checking accounts) to customers. Demand deposits are an important component of the **money** supply and, therefore, banks play a key role in determining the size and growth of the money supply. Until the 1980s, however, banks were not allowed to pay interest on these accounts. In the 1970s, other financial institutions began to offer customers accounts that had characteristics almost identical to checking accounts and paid market rates of interest. This led to funds flowing out of banks and into other institutions. (*See* **Disintermediation**.) Passage of the **Depository Institutions Deregulation and Monetary Control Act (DIDMCA) of 1980** and the **Garn-St. Germain Act** in 1982 helped restore banks' ability to attract funds by lifting regulations that prevented them from paying interest on **checkable deposits**.

Commercial banks provide needed financial services to many sectors of the economy. For those borrowers unable to raise funds in other sectors of the financial market, banks are often the sole source of funds. This is because banks reduce the information costs of raising funds faced by potential borrowers. Banks specialize in gathering information about borrowers, determining the potential for loan default, and monitoring borrowers' activities to ensure repayment of loans. This role is especially important for small firms and households, segments of the economy that rely on banks as their primary source of financing.

At the end of 2001, there were over 8,000 banks in the United States. This number is down considerably from the 12,000 banks that existed in 1990. This decline reflects the consolidation that has occurred during the past decade and the fact that banks today often rely more on branches: the number of branches was over 66,000 in 2001, up from about 50,000 in 1990.

FURTHER READING

Mishkin, Frederic S., and Stanley Eakins. *Financial Markets and Institutions*. 4th edition. Boston: Addison Wesley, 2003.

COMMERCIAL PAPER. Commercial paper is the term used to refer to "unsecured promissory notes" that are issued by corporations, and typically mature in 270 days (nine months) or less. What is an unsecured promissory note? Suppose a corporation needs to borrow money in order to finance its operation. To do this, it sells a financial asset (a note) to an investor. That note is a "promissory" note because the corporation promises to pay the investor some amount at the time when the note matures, say in six months. Finally, the note is "unsecured," because the investor has no claims on the corporation should the corporation default on paying the investor. Even so, most corporations issuing commercial paper back these notes with a line of credit. In other words, should the corporation not meet its obligations, the bank with which the line of credit is established will loan the funds needed to meet the investor's demands. Commercial paper is usually issued in large denominations, such as $100,000, although face amounts in multiples of $1 million are not uncommon.

Commercial paper usually is issued as a discount security. When someone buys a $100,000 commercial paper note, they may pay only $90,000. When the note matures, the corporation then reimburses the investor the full face value, or $100,000. The difference between face value ($100,000) and the purchase price ($90,000) is the discount. Because the investor receives $10,000 more at maturity than was paid at purchase, this is the interest received on the investment. In this example, the extra $10,000 at maturity translates into an 11 percent return on the investment (= $10,000/$90,000). In this sense, commercial paper is like a Treasury bill: both are sold at a discount from the face or maturity value, and their interest rates are quoted on a discount basis.

Because commercial paper is unsecured, it is usually issued only by large credit-worthy corporations. The interest rate paid by the corporation for the use of the investor's funds— the commercial paper rate—reflects both the relative demand and supply conditions in the market for credit and the riskiness of the corporation. A higher interest rate demanded by investors to purchase the corporation's paper, all other factors held constant, reflects the fact that investors consider there to be a greater risk that this firm will not reimburse investors or go bankrupt than some other firm.

Is there a reason why commercial paper matures in 270 days or less? The main reason is that by keeping the maturity to nine months or less, corporations skirt the requirement to register the security with the Securities and Exchange Commission. Hahn (1993, pp. 105–6) notes that "the Securities Act of 1933 requires that securities offered to the public be registered with the Securities and Exchange Commission. Registration requires extensive public disclosure, including issuing a prospectus on the offering, and is a time-consuming and expensive process. Most commercial paper is issued under Section 3(a)(3) of the 1933 Act which exempts from registration requirements short-term securities as long as they have certain characteristics. The exemption requirements have been a factor shaping the characteristics of the commercial paper market."

Even though the maturity of commercial paper is limited at 270 days, most commercial paper issued has a considerably shorter maturity horizon. Today, most commercial paper issued by corporations matures in less than two months' time. For this reason, commercial paper generally is used as a short-term finance tool, a way to acquire funds without committing to any long-term liability. For example, commercial paper often is used by nonbank corporations to finance loans. One such corporation is the General Motors Acceptance Corporation (GMAC), the financing arm of General Motors. When someone buys car from a GM dealer, it often is financed through GMAC. To lend customers that money, GMAC issues commercial paper to generate the funds loaned out. Using proceeds from commercial paper transactions in this manner does not violate any SEC rules over the issuance of notes. The SEC regulations require that proceeds from the issuance of commercial paper be used for "current transactions." While the funds acquired can be and are used for financing operating expenses, paying for inventories, etc., they may not be used for capital purchases, such as a piece of equipment or a factory.

The market for commercial paper has changed over the past few decades. Originally, commercial banks were the main issuers of commercial paper. With the advance of technology and the increased sophistication of financial markets, many corporations issue their paper directly to investors. This type of distribution of commercial paper, called *direct*

Commercial Paper of Nonfinancial Companies: Weekly Not Seasonally Adjusted

Source: www.economagic.com

placement, is more economical for the corporation because it lowers the transaction costs of issuing the notes. As shown in the figure above, the amount of commercial paper issued by nonfinancial corporations rose sharply during the past two decades. In part, this increase reflects the growing use by corporations of the commercial paper market to finance their business activities. As with many other aspects of the U.S. financial markets in the late 1990s, the sharp dropoff in commercial paper issuance following the stock market collapse in 2000 reflects the pullback in business activity, exacerbated by the events of September 11, 2001, and the recession of 2001.

Hahn (1998) provides a detailed discussion of the longer-term development of the commercial paper market in the United States. In summary, he notes that during the 1950s and 1960s, industrial firms began to shift from bank deposits to holding commercial paper. Why? The former "had regulated interest rates that at times were significantly below the market-determined rates on commercial paper"(p. 111). By holding commercial paper, whose rates could and did change with financial market forces, firms could actively manage their risk to interest rate changes. With interest rates during the 1970s becoming high and variable, due primarily to the high and variable inflation rates that characterize the period, firms shifted to holding their funds in short-term assets, such as commercial paper. "At the same time," Hahn notes, "many large businesses found that they could borrow in the commercial paper market at less expense than they could borrow from banks" (p. 111). For this reason, the commercial paper market expanded rapidly during the late 1970s up to the present (see figure).

The expansion of the commercial paper market over the past several decades came at the expense of commercial banks, which saw their traditional role of providing credit to business dwindle. Issuance of commercial paper often proved to be cheaper for large firms compared with borrowing funds from banks. In addition to the lower relative cost of using the commercial paper market as a source of funds, the increased use of securitization made commercial paper relatively more attractive than conventional bank loans. For example, asset-backed commercial paper freed the investor from wholly considering the riskiness of the investment by considering only the firm's operational or financial risk. Hahn (1998, p. 121) suggests that "with asset-backed paper, the paper's risk is instead tied directly to the creditworthiness of specific financial assets, usually some form of receivable. Asset-backed paper is one way smaller, riskier firms can access the commercial paper market. The advantages of asset-backed securities have led large, lower-risk commercial paper issuers to also participate in asset-backed commercial paper programs."

The growth in the commercial paper market has been rapid. Improvements in technology and information gathering have allowed investors to assess the riskiness of firms in ways that historically were accomplished by banks. Investors could lessen the **adverse selection** problem by acquiring more information, and this lessened the cost to firms of issuing commercial paper. In addition to this technological explanation for the growth of the commercial paper market, other innovations have increased its use among investors. The rise of **money market mutual funds** (MMMFs) also contributed to the increased use of the commercial paper market. Because MMMFs hold liquid, short-term assets, commercial paper is a natural component. Pension fund growth also has provided a ready outlet for commercial paper.

In summary, the commercial paper market is an important component of the financial market. As a source of short-term high-quality funds, investors and firms alike have turned to this market and away from the more traditional sources of funds, such as commercial bank loans. Statistics on commercial paper—interest rates, amount outstanding, etc.—can be found in the Federal Reserve Board of Governors' *Federal Reserve Bulletin* or at the Board's Website.

FURTHER READING

Hahn, Thomas K. "Commercial Paper." *Instruments of the Money Market.* Richmond: Federal Reserve Bank of Richmond, 1998; Mishkin, Frederic S., and Stanley Eakins. *Financial Markets and Institutions.* 4th edition. Boston: Addison Wesley, 2003.

COMMODITY MONEY. This term refers to those items used, generally in historical periods, to settle trades. Except for **barter**, trading occurs when one individual gives up some good or service in exchange for "**money.**" Commodity money, while used for trading, usually has some usefulness of its own. In the pre-Colonial times, shells of various kinds served as money. The shells met all the requirements of money. They were recognizable, portable, and durable. In addition, the shells were used in Native American ceremonies, which gave them value as a commodity. There have been many bizarre forms of commodity money. For example, on the island of Yap, giant stones serve as money. Although not portable, they are fixed and thus form a noninflationary base to the money supply. In the northwest United States, at one time it appears that the Karok Indians even used the scalps of woodpeckers as a form of money. Other, more recognizable forms of commodity money also have been used. For instance, gold, silver, and other precious metals served as commodity money and were used for jewelry. Other forms of commodity money include cattle (Africa and Greece), animal hides (China), and bales of cotton and tobacco (the U.S. colonies). Today, modern economies rely on paper forms of money. These pieces of paper, which have no intrinsic value—they are not good for anything else—are known as **fiat money.**

FURTHER READING

Angell, Norman. *The Story of Money.* New York: Frederick A. Stokes and Company, 1929.

COMMUNITY REINVESTMENT ACT. The Community Reinvestment Act, passed by Congress in 1977 and revised in 1995, is meant to encourage banks and other lending institutions to meet the needs of individuals in those areas that historically have been underserved. To a large extent, the act, known more commonly as CRA, was passed to prevent a practice known as "red lining." This practice occurred when a bank or other lending institution would draw a red line around those areas in which they would not lend. More often than not, those areas were low-income neighborhoods. While this action may have been based on the notion of the risk of making loans in the area was relatively greater, it also precluded individuals in the red-lined area from getting loans, regardless of their individual risk characteristics. In addition, the practice of red lining often took on more negative tones, sometimes being based as much on race as it was on economic characteristics.

What the CRA did was to allow regulators to examine each institution's record in helping meet the credit needs of its service community. CRA thus established periodic checks of the institution's books to determine if it was, within the limits of sound banking practices, doing what it could to provide credit to a wider set of borrowers. Regulatory agencies used this information to determine whether institutions would be granted applications for deposit facilities or be allowed to engage in merger and acquisitions activities. The list of federal agencies that conduct these CRA examinations include the **Board of Governors** of the Federal Reserve System, the **Federal Deposit Insurance Corporation (FDIC)**, the Office of the **Comptroller of the Currency**, and the Office of Thrift Supervision (OTS). In addition, the Consumer Compliance Task Force of the Federal Financial Institutions Examination Council (FFIEC) provides information to lending institutions regarding any changes in examination procedures and in data collection procedures. These publications are intended to promote the principles of the CRA and to provide data upon which the success of meeting CRA guidelines can be determined.

The CRA is not without its detractors. Some argue that CRA requires banks to make loans that are not in the bank's best interests. That is, under the CRA mandate—and the threat of increased regulatory supervision—banks may make loans that are of higher risk. If banks make loans that default—the borrower is unable or unwilling to make loan payments—this raises the possibility that the bank may face financial difficulty and/or reduce its profitability. If this occurs, banks may simply increase the rates it charges on loans to other, less-risky customers. Under the conditions of CRA, therefore, a bank must weigh its obligation to maintain viability and assurance to depositors that it will undertake sound banking practices together with its mandate that all customers, even those of questionable risk, be served.

FURTHER READING

Avery, Robert B., Raphael W. Bostic, Paul S. Calem, and Glenn B. Canner. "Trends in Home Purchase Lending: Consolidation and the Community Reinvestment Act." Federal Reserve *Bulletin* (February 1999): 84–95; Garwood, Griffith L., and Dolores S. Smith. "The Community Reinvestment Act: Evolution and Current Issues." Federal Reserve *Bulletin* (April 1993): 251–67.

COMPTROLLER OF THE CURRENCY. The Comptroller of the Currency heads the Office of the Comptroller of the Currency (OCC). Appointed by the president and subject to Senate confirmation, the comptroller serves for a five-year term. Similar to the appointment of a Federal Reserve governor, this five-year appointment helps insulate the comptroller from the political arena. In addition to heading the OCC, the comptroller serves as a director of the **Federal Deposit Insurance Corporation (FDIC)** and a director of the Neighborhood Reinvestment Corporation. Generally, when someone is discussing "the Comptroller," they really mean the OCC and not the individual in charge. In the discussion that follows, we shall follow that rule.

The OCC is one of the regulatory agencies of the federal government that oversees bank operations. The OCC has several roles in its official activities. In addition to granting charters and regulating and supervising all **national banks**, the OCC supervises the federal branches and agencies of foreign banks. The history of the OCC follows the trajectory of banking regulation in the United States. In 1861, the year the Civil War began, then Secretary of the Treasury Salmon P. Chase lobbied for a system of federally chartered national banks. One reason for this was to establish a uniform or standardized national currency. Issuance of national **bank notes**, based on U.S. bonds held by a national bank, was a direct response to the **free-banking** episode that had enjoyed some success in the United States up to this time. In 1863 Congress passed the National Currency Act of 1863, legislation that effectively gave the federal government monopoly control over the issuance of currency in the United States. As part of this legislation, the OCC was granted administrative oversight of the new national banking system. The **National Banking Act of 1864**, passed in 1865, enabled the comptroller to create a staff of bank examiners who would supervise and periodically visit national banks to determine their stability. The 1865 act further extended the comptroller's powers to regulate the lending and investment activities of national banks. This role continues today as the OCC oversees the activities of more than 2,200 national banks and 56 federal branches of foreign banks in the United States. These banks account for more than half of the total assets of all banks.

In carrying out its supervisory duties, OCC "examiners analyze a bank's loan and investment portfolios, funds management, capital, earnings, liquidity, sensitivity to market risk, and compliance with consumer banking laws, including the **Community Reinvestment Act**. They review the bank's internal controls, internal and external audit, and compliance with law. They also evaluate bank management's ability to identify and control risk" (OCC Website). Interestingly, the OCC's activities are funded not by Congress but by assessing the national banks for examinations and through investment income derived from their portfolio of Treasury securities.

The objective of OCC's examinations is to maintain a stable banking system. Through their decisions to approve or deny charters or allow banks to open new branches, the OCC also has a significant impact on the competitiveness of the banking industry. In sum, the OCC's ability to alter the management of banks who do not conform to federal regulations, or engage in unsound banking practices, makes them a powerful voice in maintaining and promoting stability in banking.

FURTHER READING

Further information about the history and operations of the OCC is available on their Website: www.occ.treas.gov.

CONTINENTAL ILLINOIS. Continental Illinois, more properly, Continental Illinois National Bank and Trust Company, stands out in the history of U.S. banking and in the Federal Reserve's approach to banking problems during the period since WWII. In the early 1980s, the banking system was beginning to show signs of problems. Although the brunt of the banking failures and bailouts would come later in the decade, the difficulties of Continental and **Penn Square** in 1982–1984 were omens of what was to come.

What happened, and how did the Federal Reserve respond? We have discussed Continental Illinois as part of the **too-big-to-fail doctrine**, so we will not repeat that discussion here. It still is instructive to see how Continental got into trouble and how the Federal Reserve responded.

Continental Illinois was noted for its aggressive management style during the late 1970s. The bank experienced rapid growth in the 1970s, especially in terms of commercial and industrial loans being made. In its publication "History of the Eighties—Lessons for the Future" (1998), the **Federal Deposit Insurance Corporation (FDIC)** reports that between 1976 and 1981, Continental Illinois's asset growth—income generating holdings—far outpaced that of other large banks in the United States, increasing from $21.4 billion in 1976 to $45.2 billion by 1981, an increase of 111 percent. As a result of this growth, Continental Illinois became one of the top 10 banks in the United States and the largest commercial lender. This growth was widely praised in the financial press. Investors also showed their favorable support by driving up the bank's stock price to over $40 by mid-1981.

Even though investors and market analysts glowed over the bank's success, some indicators suggested that the success had come with a cost: higher risk. One measure of this riskiness is the ratio of loans to assets. The idea is that as the ratio increases, an institution would not be able to cover losses stemming from a default of the loans with its existing assets. For Continental, this ratio increased sharply from the late 1970s into the early 1980s. By late 1981, Continental had the highest loan-to-asset ratio among the 10 largest banks in the United States. With an increase in this ratio, concerns began to surface that Continental faced greater default risk; if a proportion of those borrowers would fail to repay their loans, the losses would exceed the value of Continental's assets. Technically, it would be insolvent.

Another indicator of Continental's increased riskiness is the fact that the interest rates on loans being made in the early 1980s were lower than those on loans made in the late 1970s. This suggests that the bank had taken a below-market strategy to encourage even more borrowing. While Continental could boast of being the largest commercial lender in the United States, this goal was achieved by putting the bank at a higher risk of failure. Hindsight tells us that this is exactly the case.

By late 1981 and early 1982, events outside the control of Continental's management soon took its toll on their aggressive strategies. The bank's earnings dropped in 1981 due to losses incurred from oil- and gas-related loans. Oil prices in general were beginning to fall, and this was causing some problems with oil companies' incomes and their ability to repay their loans. For instance, one company, Nucorp Energy, an energy company in which Continental was heavily invested, lost $40 million. In another case, although not energy related, Continental made a bailout loan to International Harvester that turned out to be an ill-advised decision.

The big shock came in July 1982 when Penn Square Bank, N.A., an Oklahoma bank, failed. Penn Square had invested heavily (and it appears unwisely) in the oil and gas industry. It made millions of dollars of loans to oil and gas exploration companies at a time when oil and gas prices seemingly were headed nowhere but up. This is not what happened, however. Oil prices in the early 1980s began to fall. With the fall in oil prices, borrowers simply failed to repay their outstanding loans. The loans that Penn Square made to now-bankrupt oil and gas exploration firms were worthless. This affected Continental, because Continental had purchased $1 billion worth of participations in these ventures from Penn Square. When Penn Square's loans became worthless, so did the investment value of Continental's $1 billion. When other banks failed to help Penn Square out of this jam or give up their claims against the bank, Penn Square was closed down by the FDIC.

The failure of Penn Square set into motion a sequence of events that brought down Continental Illinois. Continental's stock price fell precipitously as investors viewed the bank's aggressive strategies in a new light. Investors now wondered whether previous strategies had placed the bank in jeopardy of bankruptcy. Bond rating agencies also took a renewed look at Continental's earnings and started downgrading its credit and debt ratings. On top of this, the debt crisis of summer 1982, highlighted by Mexico's default (*see* **LDC Debt Crisis**) exposed Continental's extended lending activities in Latin America.

Although Continental suffered substantial losses, it appeared to weather the storm—that is, until May 1984. On the rumor that the bank was going bankrupt, domestic and foreign depositors started shifting deposits out of Continental. Continental was unable to stem the tide of these deposit outflows and was forced to borrow $3.6 billion in emergency funds from the Federal Reserve's **discount window** to make up for the losses. The emergency funds were made available because the Federal Reserve and other regulators thought that the bank was simply too big to fail: that is, if it failed, it would set into motion a series of other bank failures, weakening the entire U.S. banking industry. Memories of the **bank runs** of the 1930s became fresh in the minds of Federal Reserve and other regulatory agencies.

Over the next few months, Continental received billions of dollars in government and private assistance in the hope that the bank could be saved from failure. The Federal Reserve announced that as **lender of last resort**, it would provide the bank with emergency funds through its discount window operations. While the regulators were announcing their willingness to support the bank, they also were searching for someone to buy out Continental. This search failed, and in July 1984 the bailout began in earnest: the FDIC announced that it would purchase over $4 billion in bad loans, and that it would purchase $1 billion in Continental preferred stock, although this action was blocked. Meanwhile the Federal Reserve kept supplying emergency funds through the discount window, loans that amounted to over $5 billion. During this time, there was a massive shake-up in Continental's management: the CEO of Continental and the board of directors were all removed from office and replaced with a new management team. In the end, however, the problems of Continental Illinois were simply too overwhelming. Not only did Continental Illinois cease to exist, but the policies to prop it up gave rise to a number of changes in how regulators deal with failing banks.

FURTHER READING

Federal Deposit Insurance Corporation. *History of the Eighties—Lessons for the Future* (Washington, D.C., 1998). This document is available online through the FDIC's Public Information Center: www.fdic.gov.

COOLIDGE, CALVIN (1872–1933). Calvin Coolidge was the 30th President of the United States (1923–1929). Born on July 4, 1872, in Plymouth, Vermont, Coolidge began his political career in Northampton, Massachusetts, after graduating from Amherst College. Coolidge's political career in Massachusetts began as a councilman in Northampton and continued all the way to the governor's mansion. Coolidge was made president of the United States when, on the morning of August 3, 1923, President Warren G. Harding died of a heart attack. Coolidge, on a trip to Vermont, was notified that he now was president.

As president, Coolidge was an economic conservative amidst the Roaring Twenties, a period of growing economic affluence and plenty for many, but not all, in the country. Unlike some of his predecessors, especially President Theodore Roosevelt, President Coolidge did not use the powers of his office to slow the growing boom. Rather, Coolidge called for tax cuts and for limiting government aid, even for areas such as agriculture, a sector of the economy that was experiencing economic hardship. In many ways, Coolidge earned his nickname of the "do-nothing" president. With the economy booming in many sectors, Coolidge more often was seen as the president who vetoed bills that would increase government activity in the economy than as the president who pushed for active government involvement.

During his time in office, Coolidge often sided with the banking establishment. For example, in his annual message to Congress in 1926, Coolidge urged the Senate and the House of Representatives to settle their debate and pass legislation that would "place the national banks upon a fair equality with their competitors, the state banks." The Eastern financial establishment generally favored increased power for the larger national banks, and this position drew the ire of the agrarian and Western banking interests. In some ways, Coolidge's position continued the discord between the East and the West that had been a hallmark of the U.S. political debate for many years.

Coolidge also viewed the Federal Reserve as a positive source of economic stability. Although he recognized that the Federal Reserve was not "a panacea for all economic or financial ills," he felt that the existence of the Federal Reserve System had likely stabilized the economy and that its policies followed during the 1920s were one reason for the prosperity of the country. Coolidge's belief in the ability of the business sector to operate and of the banking sector to run smoothly may have hampered his vision of the problems that many others saw arising in the economy as the 1920s progressed. Increased use of the stock market for questionable trading and the lack of a protective regulatory wall between commercial and investment banking were problems that increased in intensity as the decade rolled along. Coolidge's inaction, some suggest, may have contributed to the economic problems that befell the country soon after the Crash of 1929.

FURTHER READING

Fitzgerald, Carol B. ed. *Calvin Coolidge*. Darien, CT: Mecklu Publishing, 1988.

COUNCIL OF ECONOMIC ADVISERS. The Full Employment Act of 1946 created the Council of Economics Advisers. The act states that "the Council shall be composed of three members who shall be appointed by the President, by and with the advice and consent of the Senate, and each of whom shall be a person who, as a result of his training, experience, and attainments, is exceptionally qualified to analyze and interpret economic developments, to appraise programs and activities of the Government . . . and to formulate and recommend national economic policy to promote employment, production, and purchasing power under free competitive enterprise. The President shall designate one of the members of the Council as Chairman."

The council has not changed much in structure over the past half-century. What has changed is the influence that the council has on the debates over monetary and fiscal policy. The first CEA was appointed by a Democratic administration in a time when Keynesian economics took center stage. The CEA at the time was a source of economic policy advice on how to keep the economy—primarily through fiscal policy actions of raising and lower taxes, or increasing and decreasing government spending—running at full employment. Of course, time and many unsuccessful policies have tempered that objective since that time. Still, the CEA, especially through its chairman, acts not only as a policy advisor to the president and other officials of the federal government but also as a source for administration policy statements and positions. Unlike some government agencies, the CEA is viewed as part of the administration and, consequently, it generally makes policy pronouncements that help forward the administration's goals.

As stated on the CEA website, the duties and functions of the CEA include the following:

1. To gather timely and authoritative information concerning economic developments and economic trends, both current and prospective, to analyze and interpret such information for the purpose of determining whether such developments and trends are interfering, or are likely to interfere, with the achievement of such policy, and to compile and submit to the President studies relating to such developments and trends;
2. To appraise the various programs and activities of the Federal Government for the purpose of determining the extent to which such programs and activities are contributing, and the extent to which they are not contributing, to the achievement of such policy, and to make recommendations to the President with respect thereto;
3. To develop and recommend to the President national economic policies to foster and promote free competitive enterprise, to avoid economic fluctuations or to diminish the effects thereof, and to maintain employment, production, and purchasing power;
4. To make and furnish such studies, reports thereon, and recommendations with respect to matters of Federal economic policy and legislation as the President may request.

An important function of the CEA is preparation and publication of its *Economic Report*. This document, made available to the public following the president's State of the Union address each year, provides the CEA's overview of the economy for the past year and its outlook for the near future. In most cases, a chapter in the *Report* focuses on a topic that represents the administration's position. For example, in one *Report* it may be the role of international trade and why the establishment of trade zones, as in the case of the North American Free Trade Act (or NAFTA), is beneficial to the U.S. economy. In another *Report*, the focus may be on developments in the agricultural sector of the economy, and in still another it may be on changes in worker productivity. In any case, the focus deals with some topic that has implications for the economy and for policy debate.

The *Report* also makes available a large set of macroeconomic data. The tables that accompany the *Report* include data on real production in the United States, data on unemployment rates, prices and interest rates, among others. In that sense the *Report* is an excellent source of economic data, one that is used by many analysts.

The CEA is composed of three members, one of whom is nominated by the president to serve as the chairman of the CEA. The first chairman was Edwin G. Nourse, who served from

August 1946 until November 1949. Over the past 50 years, there have been a number of notable economists who served in the capacity as chairman: these include James Tobin (1961–1962) and Joseph Stiglitz (1995–1997), both of whom would later win the Nobel Prize in economics. CEA Chairmen **Arthur Burns** (1953–1956) and **Alan Greenspan** (1974–1977) each later became **Chairman of the Board of Governors**. In addition to the three members of the CEA, there is a staff of economists. The staff usually is composed of academic economists on leave from their universities, who serve as staff members for one or two years. The atmosphere is academic in nature, but also professional. As Martin Feldstein (1992), Chairman of the CEA under President Reagan notes, "the tradition of professionalist is so strong that even in a presidential election year the CEA chairman appoints members of the staff for the coming academic year with the clear understanding that they will continue to serve even if the party in power loses the presidential election ... the members of the CEA and their staff work full-time at their CEA responsibilities. Indeed, in December and January of each year, the pressure of working simultaneously on the Economic Report of the President, the budget, and the issues to be presented in the president's state of the union message seemed like much more than a full-time job."

Because the CEA acts as one of the economic policy arms of the administration, they often discuss policies made by the Federal Reserve. Indeed, there is a long history of debate, sometimes heated, between the CEA members and the Fedeal Reserve Board of Governors. This debate over policy often reveal different views on the role that monetary policy plays. For example, in the 1960s, the CEA, through its *Economic Report*, argued that the increasing rates of **inflation** did not stem from policy actions but from wage and price increases by unions and large firms. The notion that inflation was the product of "cost-push" phenomena—wage increases would cause firms to raise prices to maintain profits, which in turn caused unions to raise wage demands—was widely accepted in the Johnson administration. It also was accepted by many Federal Reserve governors, although the debate within the Federal Reserve System suggested a monetary explanation. (See Hafer and Wheelock [2001] for a discussion.)

Even though the CEA today is often considered to have a reduced role in the formulation of administration economic policies, its importance stems from its advisory role and as a source of administration views on economic issues. For more on the CEA, the offcial website of the council contains brief background information and links to other sources. For a personal reflection on the role of the Chairman, see Martin Feldstein (1992).

FURTHER READING

Feldstein, Martin. "The Council of Economic Advisers and Economic Advising in the United States,"*The Economic Journal* (September 1992): 1223–1234. (Reprinted at the Council of Economic Advisers Website: www.whitehouse.gov/cea.); Hafer, R. W., and David C. Wheelock. "The Rise and Fall of a Policy Rule: Monetarism at the St. Louis Fed, 1968–1986." Federal Reserve Bank of St. Louis *Review* (January/February 2001): 1–24; Hargrove, Erwin C., and Samuel Morley, eds. *The President and the Council of Economic Advisors: Interviews with CEA Chairmen.* Boulder, CO: Westview Press, 1984.

COUNTERCYCLICAL POLICY. Policy actions by the Federal Reserve often times are done to influence economic activity. Policymakers may alter policy to lower the rate of **inflation** or the **unemployment rate**. The notion of countercyclical policy is to undertake policy actions that offset the **business cycle**. Suppose the economy is in **recession**, a situation when the unemployment rate is high and the output of the economy is growing slowly or even falling. A countercyclical policy is one that attempts to reduce the unemployment rate by, say, lowering interest rates and increasing the growth rate of the money supply. In effect, this policy is geared to counteract the behavior of the economy. Similarly, if the economy is expanding too rapidly and inflation is a problem, then the proper countercyclical policy may be to raise interest rates and slow the growth of the money supply. It is argued that such policies are difficult to use, simply because it is hard for policymakers to know with certainty where in the business cycle the economy is operating. Policies aimed at spurring economic growth, pursued with the idea that the economy is growing to slowly, may require future policies that attempt to offset these actions. This on-again/off-again approach to policy has been criticized by some economists, most notably **Milton Friedman**. Friedman and others propose that policy actions be determined by a **policy rule** known to everyone. In his version, Friedman suggested that the Federal Reserve follow a policy that keeps the money supply increasing at some fixed rate of growth. The modern policy rule known as the **Taylor Rule** dictates that the Federal Reserve's actions are determined by what the inflation and unemployment rates are relative to policymakers' desired rates. When the actual and desired rates move apart—that is, when the inflation rate is higher than desired or the rate of **economic growth** is too slow—the Federal Reserve responds.

FURTHER READING

Chatrerjee, Satyajit. "Why Does Countercyclical Monetary Policy Matter?" Federal Reserve Bank of Philadelphia *Business Review* (Quarter 2, 2001): 7–14; Espinosa-Vega, Marco, and Jang-Ting Guo. "On Business Cycles and Countercyclical Policies." Federal Reserve Bank of Atlanta *Economic Review* (Fourth Quarter 2001).

CRASH OF 1987. The 508-point plunge of the Dow Jones Industrial Average on October 19, 1987, set into motion a number of events. First, it cast a pall over financial markets that had, up to that time, been enjoying a significant increase in stock prices. Because it occurred in October and followed such a significant run-up in stock prices, it was immediately likened to the stock market crash of 1929. As one story headline in the *New York Times* read on the following day, "Does 1987 Equal 1929?" Another suggested that "Frenzied Trading Raises Fears of Recession." Was the timing of the crash simply coincidence? Would 1987 turn into another 1929 with the calamitous aftermath of another Great Depression? Such questions quickly became the focus of discussions on news talk shows and in the financial press.

Of course, we now know that 1987 was not another 1929 and that the U.S. economy did not enter into another period of prolonged economic stagnation. In fact, by year's end, stock prices had recovered much of the territory lost in October. Why was the outcome of the two events so different? One explanation is that because of its earlier experience, the stock market had instituted a number of devices that would protect against the meltdown that occurred in 1929. Margin requirements were less liberal in 1987 than in 1929, although new, computer-based trading programs in 1987 could exacerbate the decline by spreading the effects from sector to sector.

For the purposes of this discussion, however, it also happens that the Federal Reserve behaved differently in 1987 than it did in 1929. In 1987 the Federal Reserve recognized that unless it acted quickly to offer emergency credit to financial institutions affected by the stock crash—in effect acting as lender of last resort—the one-day drop could expand and continue until the costs of intervening were much higher. Indeed, the Federal Reserve acted quickly to restore confidence in the financial system and to offset any effects that stemmed from the loss of wealth associated with the stock market crash.

At the time, many observers and economists warned that such a decline in the stock market would severely reduce individuals' wealth, defined as their assets less their liabilities. For instance, if an individual had a stock portfolio worth $1 million (their assets) and liabilities (what they owe to others, such as mortgages, credit card debt, etc.) equal to half that, their wealth position (assets minus liabilities) would be $500,000. That individual would determine spending decisions partly based on their wealth position. Once the stock market crashed, however, some originally wealthy people were no longer wealthy. If, for example, the crash lowered the value of the individual's assets to, say, $250,000, suddenly that person has a *negative* wealth position (assets < liabilities). A common belief was that such a negative wealth affect would cause households to dramatically cut back on their spending and cause the economy's growth to slow. Some predicted that the magnitude of the wealth effect could even lead to an economic recession.

Although this effect did not materialize—as mentioned, stock prices rebounded fairly quickly—the adverse threat to the economy and to financial institutions was a focus of Federal Reserve officials. On Tuesday, October 20, the Federal Reserve issued the following statement *before* the opening of the financial markets: "The Federal Reserve System, consistent with its responsibilities as the nation's central bank, affirmed today its readiness to serve as a source of liquidity to support the financial and economic system." The Federal Reserve announced that it recognized its role as lender of last resort and, unlike 1929, stood ready to perform its duties in this capacity. Parry (1997), then president of the Federal Reserve Bank of San Francisco, notes that the Federal Reserve took several important actions. In his words:

First, we added substantially to reserves through open market operations. The funds rate fell from 7½ percent just before the crash to 6½ percent in early November. This added liquidity helped prevent the crash from spreading to bond prices.

Second, we liberalized the rules governing the lending of securities from our own portfolio to make more collateral available.

Third, we used all of our contacts in the financial system to keep the lines of communication clear and open. In talking with banks, for example, we stressed the importance of ensuring adequate liquidity to their customers, especially securities dealers, and at the same time affirmed that they were responsible for making their own independent credit judgments. We also were in close touch with participants and regulators in the government securities market, officials at the various exchanges and their regulators, and our colleagues at central banks in other countries.

Finally, as a means of gathering real-time information, we placed examiners in major banking institutions to monitor developments—such as currency shipments—to identify the potential for bank runs.

To sum up, performing the lender-of-last-resort activity, and backing it up with close monitoring and close communication, did what it was supposed to do: it transferred the systemic risk from the market to the banks and ultimately to the Fed, which is the only financial institution with pockets deep enough to bear this risk. This allowed market intermediaries to perform their usual functions and helped keep the market open.

The crash of 1987 and the Federal Reserve's policy response helped clarify for many the role of the central bank in a financial crisis. More than offsetting any shock from the potential wealth effect, the fact that the Federal Reserve actively engaged in its role of **lender of last resort** helped calm volatile financial markets both here and abroad. As Parry (1997) sums it up, "The crash of 1987 and the Fed's swift and decisive response serves to reaffirm our understanding of what we need to do. While this should give confidence to the markets, I think it's worth repeating that it should be used sparingly. Such Fed actions must be limited to crises marked by systemic risk. Bailing out individual firms is *not* the job of the Fed, nor is it in the public interest since it would induce excessive risk-taking in the private sector."

FURTHER READING

Dwyer, Gerald P., and R. W. Hafer, eds. *The Stock Market: Bubbles, Volatility and Chaos*. Norwell, MA: Kluwer Academic Publishers, 1990; Parry, Robert T. "The October '87 Crash Ten Years Later." Federal Reserve Bank of San Francisco *Economic Letter* (October 31, 1997).

CREDIT CARDS. Credit cards are not cash, nor are they money. The name itself says what they are: credit. This means that when someone uses a card, the credit card company is making them a **loan** at a predetermined interest rate. When they pay off the balance on the account, funds are taken from bank deposits and transferred to the credit card company. In effect, a transfer is made from one checking account to another. Until that time, there exists an outstanding loan and the unpaid balance is being charged some rate of interest (the finance charge), a rate that usually is much higher than other short-term interest rates.

Although credit cards have been available from specific stores and oil companies since before World War II, their acceptance on a nationwide basis has come about only since the 1950s. The first such general use card was issued by the Diners Club. It was to be used in restaurants around the country. Soon to follow was the now familiar American Express card. The first bank credit card was made available by the Franklin National Bank in 1952. Because operating these programs was very costly, early credit cards were available only to a select clientele, individuals likely to make big purchases.

As computer and telecommunication technologies improved, the cost of operating credit card programs declined. Two bank credit cards appeared in the late 1960s: Visa, originally started by the Bank of America, and MasterCard (originally MasterCharge), offered through the Interbank Card Association. The overwhelming success of these credit cards lies in the fact that they make buying goods and services easier. On a visit to some far away city, a small store owner may not accept a check on your local bank but likely will take your Visa card. This is because the store owner is guaranteed payment (usually at a slight discount, around 2 to 5 percent) for the purchase by the card company. Once the transaction is electronically recorded at the store, the owner is paid whether you pay the balance on your credit card or not.

The success of credit cards and their profitability have led major card companies to make other services available to their card holders, including overdraft protection, insurance plans, and travel discounts.

FURTHER READING

Durkin, Thomas A. "Credit Cards: Use and Consumer Attitudes." Federal Reserve *Bulletin*. (September 2000): 623–34.

CREDIT CONTROLS. Credit controls are restrictions imposed by the government on the lending activities of banks. In effect, it is an attempt by authorities to make certain types of lending more expensive and, therefore, less desirable to certain borrowers. The best example is the attempt in 1980 by the Carter administration to reduce the amount of household and business borrowing. It was thought that this would slow economic expansion and lower the rate of **inflation**. In March, the Federal Reserve began its Special Credit Restraint Program, which, although voluntary, drastically reduced the amount of borrowing from the banking system. Major features of this program included increased costs for banks to borrow from the Federal Reserve (*see* **Discount Window**), imposition of **reserve requirements** on **money market mutual funds**, and raising reserve requirement on certain types of **certificates of deposit**. The overall effect of this program was to severely curtail borrowing by households and small businesses, which led to an overall downturn in economic activity. In fact, the economic impact was so severe that the controls were lifted in July 1980.

FURTHER READING

Hodgeman, Donald. "Credit Controls in Western Europe: An Evaluative Review." In Federal Reserve Bank of Boston *Credit Allocation Techniques and Monetary Policy*. (1973); Schreft, Stacey. "Credit Controls: 1980." Federal Reserve Bank of Richmond *Economic Review* (1981): 25–55.

CREDIT CRUNCH. A credit crunch occurs when banks become increasingly concerned about the risk of making additional loans. If this is widespread, banks reduce their lending, perhaps favoring more reliable although less profitable sources of revenue, such as government Treasury securities. The most recent credit crunch occurred in the 1990–1991 recession when bank loans to various sectors of the economy—most notably real estate development—dropped significantly. Because banks became increasingly concerned about the ability of borrowers to repay their loans, credit became harder to acquire, regardless of the borrower's credit history. Consequently, credit crunches help slow economic activity.

FURTHER READING

Wojnilower, Albert M. "The Central Role of Credit Crunches in Recent Financial History." *Brookings Papers on Economic Activity* 2 (1980): 277–326.

CREDIT UNIONS. Credit unions are financial intermediaries that usually are associated with one firm or industry, such as the credit union for Ford Motor Company employees or the credit union for employees of Union Pacific railroad. Credit unions are chartered by state or federal government agencies and generally take deposits from and provide loans. As a rule, the deposits of the employees—referred to as credit union shares—are invested in small loans or mortgages made to the members.

In the past, certain aspects of credit unions made them more attractive to depositors than banks. For instance, a credit union member writes "share drafts" (checks) against his or her account, which serves the same purpose as a check written by someone against his or her account at a commercial bank. Because a credit union share was not technically a **checkable deposit**, credit unions paid interest on these deposits while banks were unable to pay interest on checking accounts. With credit union deposits also federally insured, many individuals shifted their funds out of banks and into credit unions. This **disintermediation** stopped with the removal of **Regulation Q** in 1980, thus allowing banks to pay interest and checking accounts. (*See also* **Depository Institutions Deregulation and Monetary Control Act [DIDMCA] of 1980** and the **Garn-St. Germain Act**.) In addition, because members of credit unions often were dispersed across the country or even the world due to the location of their employer, credit unions were not subject to the branching restrictions faced by banks. These competitive advantages for credit unions have ceased with increasing deregulation of the banking industry. Still, credit unions continue to serve the financial needs of many depositors and borrowers.

FURTHER READING

Mishkin, Frederic S., and Stanley Eakins. *Financial Markets and Institutions*. 4th edition. Boston: Addison Wesley, 2003; National Credit Union Administration Website: www.ncua.gov.

CURRENCY. When someone uses the term currency, they usually mean cash and coin. In the United States, printing paper money—currency—is authorized by the federal government. This currency is considered **legal tender**; that is, it must be accepted for any payment of debt expressed in dollar amounts. If you look at a dollar bill, it even says so: "This note is legal tender for all debts public and private." The U.S. dollar has taken several shapes over time. When it was first adopted as our unit of money, back in 1785, the dollar was a coin, not paper. It was not for another 80 years that paper money was issued and authorized by the U.S. government. The basic version we have today came about in 1928.

Over the past 80 years, currency in the United States has changed in several ways. During this century, three types of currency have circulated. Up until 1934, when it was removed from circulation, gold certificates were issued. Silver certificates were issued until 1957. Since 1963, "Federal Reserve Notes" have been the currency in circulation. What makes them different? Gold and silver certificates were redeemable for their metal namesakes. Today these bills are mostly in the hands of collectors and are not convertible into gold or silver. Federal Reserve Notes, in contrast, never were: take one into a bank and ask to redeem it and what you'll get is coins or another bill. This reflects the fact that what "backs" our currency is only our belief in the reliability of the government, not any stockpile of gold or silver.

Other cosmetic changes have occurred recently. Beginning in 2000, the physical makeup and the design of the bills were altered to thwart counterfeiting. This took the form of changing the position of portrait, using new "microprinting" techniques, with so-called color shifting inks that alter appearance when bills are examined from different angles, and inserting security threads.

FURTHER READING

Angell, Norman. *The Story of Money*. New York: Frederick A. Stokes and Company, 1929; Federal Reserve Bank of Boston. *Currency Points: Understanding Our Money*. (1992).

CURRIE, LAUCHLIN (1902–1993). Born in the small fishing village of New Dublin, Nova Scotia, Lauchlin Currie rose to prominence during the 1930s, both as an academic economist and as an integral component of the reconstruction of the U.S. banking system during and after the Great Depression. After studying for two years at St. Francis Xavier's University in Nova Scotia, Currie traveled to London, where he studied at the London School of Economics. After receiving his degree in 1925, Currie entered the economics program at Harvard University, where he studied under the famous economists Allyn Young, Ralph Hawtrey, and Joseph H. Schumpeter.

After obtaining his Ph.D. in 1931, Currie remained at Harvard, where he constructed one of the first money supply series for the United States. Building on the work of **Irving Fisher**, Currie also created one of the first *income velocity* (GDP relative to the supply of money) series for the United States. Currie believed that the Federal Reserve's **real bills doctrine** was in large part responsible for the deeply contractionary monetary policy in 1929 that was not reversed quickly enough to prevent the **Great Depression**. Although not called this at the time, this approach to policy and the importance given the role of money was a foreshadowing of the **Monetarist** movement that arose after World War II. In fact, some modern economists claim that Currie's early work in the field of monetary economics was a forerunner to the monetary research often associated with the work of **Milton Friedman** and his associates.

Currie achieved some notoriety for his research and writing on the banking system. In 1934, he joined the U.S. Treasury and worked for Jacob Viner, the famous University of Chicago economist. While at the Treasury, Currie constructed a plan for banking system reform. One aspect of his plan was to give the Federal Reserve more control over movements in the nation's supply of money. Currie's plan was noticed by **Marriner Eccles**, who took Currie with him as his personal assistant when Eccles became governor of the Federal Reserve in November 1934. Although the draft proposals for what would become the **Banking Act of 1935** were circulated under the authorship of both Currie and Eccles, the brains behind them really were Currie's. In this piece of legislation, Currie was able to put some of his earlier academic ideas into reality. As discussed elsewhere, the 1935 act greatly altered the structure of the Federal Reserve and its role in the monetary system.

Currie's concerns were not focused solely on the monetary system, however. While at the Federal Reserve he constructed an economic series that demonstrated the effects of federal spending programs on the economy. Many economists and politicians at the time believed that the federal budget should be balanced at all times, but Currie demonstrated that large budget deficits—federal expenditures exceeding revenues—are desirable in times of economic hardship. Indeed, it is suggested that Currie was able to convince President Franklin Roosevelt of the need for federal budget deficits following the 1937 relapse into recession. By 1939, Currie had become Roosevelt's White House economist, advising the president on all economic policy matters.

During World War II, Currie served in several capacities. In 1941, he was sent to China as the administration's representative to the two main Chinese leaders, Generalissimo Chiang Kai-shek and Chou En-Lai, the latter the Communist representative. In 1943–1944, he oversaw the Foreign Economic Administration, and in 1945, he was appointed to represent the United States on a commission attempting to persuade the Swiss government to freeze Nazi bank accounts. During the period leading up to the **Bretton Woods System**, which created the **International Monetary Fund** and the World Bank, Currie also was involved with the preparation of the U.S. team.

Following the war, it was alleged that Currie engaged in espionage for the Soviet Union. With the takeover of China by the Communists and its leader Mao Tse-tung, Currie was among those blamed for "losing China." This period in U.S. history is replete with accusations and recriminations of sympathy toward the Communists, especially the Russians. Currie appeared before the House Committee on Un-American Activities in 1948 and was, on the basis of his testimony, able to refute the charges leveled against him. Still, although no charges were officially filed, the stain of this episode tarnished his record.

Currie was named in 1949 to head one of the World Bank's first country surveys to Colombia. Curried completed the study in 1950 and was asked by the Colombian government to return and oversee the implementation of the plan. During the early 1950s, Currie faced still more accusations as the hearings conducted by McCarthy began. When Currie attempted to renew his passport in 1954, he was denied on the grounds that he was living abroad, despite the fact that he became a naturalized U.S. citizen in 1934. Dogged by these unproved allegations, Currie chose to remain in Colombia to work for the government in an advisory role until 1953, when a military coup removed the government. In 1958, a civilian government returned to power in Colombia. This change in government brought about two events: one was that Currie was given Colombian citizenship. The other was that Currie was asked and agreed to once again act as an economic advisor, which he did until his death in 1993.

Currie's academic work on the money supply was published originally as *The Supply and Control of Money in the United States* (1934). There is a more recent (1968) reprint with a lengthy preface by **Karl Brunner** in which Currie's theory of the money supply is juxtaposed against modern views. Currie's views on how to fight the depression, along with a discussion of how this policy prescription foresees the later views, appeared in the *History of Political Economy* (summer 2002).

FURTHER READING

Currie, Lauchlin. *The Supply and Control of Money in the United States*. Cambridge, Mass: Harvard University Press (1934); Sandilands, Roger J. *The Life and Political Economy of Lauchlin Currie: New Dealer, Presidential Adviser, and Development Economist*. Durham, NC and London: Duke University Press (1990).

DEBIT CARD. Debit cards look just like a credit card, but they are not the same. When you use a credit card, the credit card company (e.g., Visa, MasterCard, etc.) is making you a loan. The credit card company pays the business where you just bought new shoes, and now you owe the credit card company the amount of purchase. When a debit card is used, however, you are immediately transferring funds from your bank account to the business. In this way debit cards are more like checks, except for the fact that no paper check is actually written. Instead, a debit card electronically transfers funds from one account to another. Often referred to as "point-of-sale" cards, the widespread use of debit cards reflects how the increased use of technology lessens the cost of transacting.

Debit cards have made the process of making monetary policy more difficult. Historical relationships between the growth rate of measures of the money supply like M1, which is composed primarily of currency and checking accounts, and measures of economic activity, such as **gross domestic product (GDP)**, changed with financial innovations such as the debit card. Above we mentioned that debit cards allow people to "economize" on their money holdings. Now one does not need to carry cash because debit cards allow one to withdraw funds from checking accounts immediately. This fact could alter the observed relationship between money and measures like GDP. This makes monetary policy more difficult, because it means that historical relationships are no longer a reliable guide to the future. (*See also* **Electronic Money.**)

FURTHER READING

Caskey, John P., and Gordon H. Sellon, Jr. "Is the Debit Card Revolution Finally Here?" Federal Reserve Bank of Kansas City *Economic Review* (Fourth Quarter 1994): 79–95.

DEFLATION. *De*flation is the opposite of *in*flation. Deflation is defined as a decline in the overall level of prices. Measuring the overall level of prices is difficult, which is why economists and others use price indexes, such as the Consumer Price Index (CPI). Price indexes, based on broad samples of available prices, attempt to gauge the general direction of prices in the economy. If the CPI were to fall in value over time, that would result in a negative percentage change in the price level—in other words, deflation. Sustained periods of deflation are rare in the United States. Bullard and Hokayem (2003) present evidence indicating that in the United States, most periods of deflation occurred prior to the founding of the Federal Reserve, except for the deflation that occurred during the Great Depression. For example, there were three periods of significant, sustained deflation in the United States: 1876–1879, when the CPI fell at an average rate of 3.82 percent; 1883–1885, when the CPI fell at an average rate of 2.34 percent; and 1930–1933, when the CPI fell at an average annual rate of 6.69 percent. Since the 1930s there has been no period in which the CPI has fallen for a sustained period of time. Other countries, however, have experienced short-term bouts of deflation. The most modern example is Japan, where prices fell during the 1990s. For example, between 1999 and 2001, the CPI inflation rate fell at an average rate of 0.71 percent.

What causes deflation? Most economists agree that *in*flation is a monetary phenomenon. That is, inflation cannot persist unless the central bank is actively expanding the amount of money in the economy. Historically, if money grows at a rate that is faster than the growth of real output in an economy, the rate of inflation tends to increase. The opposite also is true: When the supply of **money** shrinks, that is, when the growth rate of the money supply is negative, there tends to be downward pressure not only on economic activity but also on prices. Sustained negative money growth is often a key characteristic in economies that have experienced deflation. Indeed, in an examination of the Japanese monetary policies followed during the early part of this decade, Hetzel (2003) argues that the Bank of Japan's unwillingness to expand the money supply is a key factor in their deflationary problems.

FURTHER READING

Bullard, James B., and Charles M. Hoyakem. "Deflation, Corrosive and Otherwise." Federal Reserve Bank of St. Louis *National Economic Trends* (July 2003); Hetzel, Robert L. "Japanese Monetary Policy and Deflation." Federal Reserve Bank of Richmond *Economic Quarterly* (Summer 2003): 21–52.

DEPOSIT INSURANCE. Owners of cars and homes usually carry some form of insurance. In case of an accident or a fire, some proportion or all of the repair costs are paid for by the insurance company. Insurance thus allows an individual to lessen the risk of financial loss due to some unforeseen event. Deposit insurance works the same way for a depository institution, such as a bank. In the United States, depository institutions are members of some type of deposit insurance fund. For banks, it is the **Federal Deposit Insurance Corporation (FDIC)**. By paying an insurance premium into this fund, a bank insures its depositors against total loss of their funds if the bank were to close. Currently, the FDIC pays off depositors in full on the first $100,000 in their accounts. So, if someone has $250,000 in an account at the local bank when it fails, they are guaranteed to get back only $100,000 from the FDIC: the rest could be lost. Due to this limitation, **brokered deposits** have arisen. Brokered accounts split up deposits that are larger than the $100,000 maximum into multiple accounts that do not exceed the insurance limit at different banks.

Deposit insurance oftentimes is viewed as a safety net for depositors. Even so, deposit insurance may entice bank owners and managers to act in a more risky manner than they would if there was no deposit insurance. (This is referred to as **moral hazard**.) For example, if a bank fails and there is no deposit insurance, then the owners of the bank are liable for the deposits. That is, customers may seek legal remedies to regain their lost funds. In such a world, with the threat of personal loss affecting their behavior, bank owners may not take on projects that seem overly risky or projects that put the solvency of the bank at high risk. However, deposit insurance helps relieve that pressure. If bank owners are not liable for their customers' deposits, then bank owners may seek out projects that, if successful, are hugely profitable. If they fail, however, then the bank may be forced to close. With insurance, the loss to the owners is the loss of their capital invested in the bank.

This gambling aspect of bank behavior is thought to have helped inspire the bad loans made by banks during the 1980s. In the newly deregulated world of the 1980s, some banks saw their existence as hinging on increased profitability. One way to achieve that was to score big on loans, some made to questionable individuals and firms, both here and overseas. The consequence of this activity was, in some instances, increased bank failures and pressure on the deposit insurance fund. Indeed, this type of behavior was especially evident in the massive failure of savings and loans during the 1980s. If this problem arises, it forces the Federal Reserve and other bank regulatory agencies, such as the Comptroller, to take aggressive actions to ensure that banks are operating within the guidelines specified in the many regulations that govern their activity.

FURTHER READING

Calomaris, Charles W., and Eugene N. White. "The Origins of Federal Deposit Insurance." In *U.S. Bank Deregulation in Historical Perspective*. Cambridge, MA: Cambridge University Press, 2000; Vaughn, Mark D., and David C. Wheelock. "Deposit Insurance Reform: Is It Déjà Vu All Over Again?" Federal Reserve Bank of St. Louis *Review* (October 2002): 5–9.

DEPOSITORY INSTITUTIONS ACT OF 1982. This piece of legislation is more popularly known as the **Garn-St. Germain Act**, after the act's sponsors. By 1982, the phase-out of **Regulation Q** interest ceilings on **demand deposits** was in progress (*See* **Depository Institutions Deregulation and Monetary Control Act [DIDMCA] of 1980**.) Still, banks faced stiff competition for savers' deposits from **money market mutual funds**. These funds, which were not subject to Regulation Q ceilings, offered savers accounts that paid higher rates of interest and some limited check-writing ability. This act allowed banks to offer **money market deposit accounts**, which were similar in nature to accounts at money market mutual funds. Because these accounts fell under the umbrella protection of deposit insurance and faced no interest rate ceiling, banks vigorously offered these accounts to depositors. Depositors responded by plowing a significant amount of money into them ($400 billion by 1983).

Another component of the act allowed certain savings and loans to extend their lending activities into areas other than home mortgages. A consequence of this change was that savings and loans quickly entered into the more risky areas of lending, such as business real estate and commercial loans. Some argue that this change is partly responsible for the massive number of savings and loan failures in the late 1980s. (*See also* **Savings and Loan Crisis**.)

This piece of legislation, and the financial innovations that it helped spawn, created problems for monetary policy, especially in defining the money supply. Historically, economists and policymakers defined money along two main aspects: the use of money as a transactions medium and its use as a vehicle for savings. Once banks are able to pay interest on accounts that historically were thought to be used as a means to buy goods and services, then this delineation between transactions accounts and savings accounts becomes blurred and the appropriate measure becomes less certain. Indeed, it is partly this blurring of the distinction between transactions accounts and savings accounts that led the **Federal Open Market Committee (FOMC)** to abandon monetary targets as operating objectives during the 1980s.

FURTHER READING

Cooper, Kerry, and Donald Fraser. *Banking Deregulation and the New Competition in Financial Services*. Cambridge, MA: Ballinger Publishing Co., 1984; Garcia, Gillian G., et al. "The Garn-St. Germain Depository Institutions Act of 1982." Federal Reserve Bank of Chicago *Economic Perspectives* (March/April 1983).

DEPOSITORY INSTITUTIONS DEREGULATION AND MONETARY CONTROL ACT (DIDMCA) OF 1980. This legislation began the process of unwinding many banking regulations that by 1980 had put banks at a competitive disadvantage compared with other financial institutions. Passage of DIDMCA brought about several notable changes in banking. For one, the act phased out **Regulation Q**—which prohibited the paying of interest on checking accounts—between 1980 and 1986. A vestige of the **Great Depression**, this change also enhanced banks' competitiveness. In addition, DIDMCA raised to $100,000 from $40,000 the maximum deposit per account covered by **Federal Deposit Insurance Corporation (FDIC)** deposit insurance. The act also eliminated rate ceilings on mortgage **loans** and certain types of commercial loans. One of its most profound impacts came from the nationwide creation of interest-paying checking accounts—so-called **NOW accounts** and ATS accounts—at banks. This change made banks competitive with other depository institutions that were offering interest payments on checkable deposits. Removing this constraint on bank behavior brought about massive changes in how individuals held their deposits and helped stem the **disintermediation** that was occurring.

By allowing banks to offer NOW accounts, passage of the DIDMCA also created much uncertainty among Federal Reserve policymakers about the behavior of the **money supply**. In face of these changes, the Federal Reserve altered the definitions of the money supply, creating two versions of their narrow, or transactions-based, measure of money, called M1. The two versions, referred to as M1A and M1B, tried to sort out the accounts that the public were using for transactions purposes—the buying of goods and services—from those accounts thought to serve primarily as savings-oriented accounts. M1A was therefore defined as including currency and non–interest-bearing demand deposits. M1B, on the other hand, was defined as M1A plus NOW accounts plus ATS accounts plus checkable deposits held at thrift institutions (e.g., savings and loans, credit unions, etc.). These multiple definitions gave way within a few years to a more streamlined definition of money—simply M1—which was just like M1B. This meant that M1A disappeared from the Federal Reserve's list of money measures.

The process of redefining the monetary aggregates made setting policy actions more difficult. Historical relations between certain measures of money and the economy now were significantly altered. Policymakers relying on the old relations were getting mixed and sometimes incorrect signals from the monetary aggregates. As individuals shifted their funds out of non–interest-paying deposits into those that paid interest and allowed them to write checks against their deposits, there was a period when policymakers were unsure of which measure was giving the best indication of the direction of policy. Because of this, the FOMC switched its emphasis toward interest rates and away from monetary aggregates in determining the direction of policy.

DIDMCA affected all depository institutions by making certain rules and regulations more uniform. After 1980 all depository institutions—banks, savings and loans, credit unions, etc.—faced uniform **reserve requirements**. As a reward for going along with uniform reserve requirements, depository institutions gained access to services provided by the Federal Reserve, including **discount window** loans. The DIDMCA also had provisions aimed directly at activities on nonbank institutions. Following passage of the act, savings and loan associations and mutual savings banks were allowed to expand their lending activities beyond traditional areas. Thus, in addition to mortgage lending, savings and loans extended their activities into corporate bonds and consumer loans. Mutual savings banks also were allowed to enter the commercial loan market.

FURTHER READING

Cargill, Thomas F., and Gillian G. Garcia. *Financial Deregulation and Monetary Control*. Stanford, CA: Hoover Institution Press, 1982; Cooper, Kerry, and Donald Fraser. *Banking Deregulation and the New Competition in Financial Services*. Cambridge, MA: Ballinger Publishing Co., 1984.

DIRECTIVE. The "directive" is the formal statement of the **Federal Open Market Committee's (FOMC)** decision on the direction of monetary policy, voted upon at the end of their meeting, that is transmitted to the open market **trading desk** at the New York Federal Reserve Bank. In essence, it directs the activity of the trading desk in terms of increasing or decreasing the federal funds rate and, concurrently, changing the amount of reserves in the banking system. This streamlined description of the directive belies the nuances of the document and how the FOMC arrives at the language used in a directive and how it uses the directive to guide monetary policy.

The process by which the directive is determined is described in the discussion of the FOMC, found elsewhere in this volume. Briefly, when the FOMC meets, the discussion begins with the chairman calling for overview presentations by board staff economists. These presentations cover domestic financial market activity in the period since the last meeting, summaries of economic activity and price level developments, and reports on international economic issues, such as exchange rate changes or special events abroad. These reports may also deal with nonmonetary policy topics, such as recent changes in fiscal policies. These presentations provide the FOMC members with a common foundation of economic information. They also provide a glimpse into the issues and events that the chairman may believe are most important in guiding the discussion and eventual policy decisions at that time. Once these presentations have been completed and any questions have been addressed, FOMC members are permitted time to make statements reflecting their views and concerns about recent economic events and the affect of past policy actions. When this "go-around" is completed, the chairman summarizes the discussion—often shading the summary to reflect his or her own views and concerns—in preparation for determining the wording of the directive.

As Meulendyke (1998, p. 133), an economist who worked at the trading desk in New York for many years, observes, the decisions of the FOMC and the resulting directive are made in two key areas: "First, the FOMC has to decide whether to take some action to change the Federal funds rate at the meeting; if a change is selected, the Committee must then decide on the appropriate size of the move. Second, the FOMC chooses whether to express in the operating paragraph of the directive a predisposition to make a move between meetings." The latter of these decisions essentially asks whether an intermeeting change in policy is likely to occur, and in most instances it does not. The first decision, however, is more important. It essentially gives not only the direction of a possible change in the federal funds rate but also the magnitude of the desired change. In that regard, that decision forms the basis of the directive to the New York Federal Reserve's trading desk.

In general, once this decision is made, there begins a discussion amongst the members of the FOMC—the governors and the voting bank presidents—about their personal policy preferences. These preferences usually are framed by the alternatives laid out in the **blue book**, such as an increase or decrease in the federal funds rate by so many basis points, whether that change should be accompanied by a change in the discount rate, and how such a policy shift will be carried out. After everyone has had an opportunity to express their views on policy, there is a nonbinding ballot of the voting members. If the vote indicates a clear majority, the FOMC moves on to discussing the language of the directive. If the vote is not clear, then further discussion takes place. In the latter case, the chairman often guides the discussion, suggesting alternatives that may satisfy the alternative positions.

In the past, the directive provided much more detail concerning desired intermeeting ranges for the **federal funds rate**. For much of the 1960s, the directive provided narrow ranges for the federal funds rate. During the 1970s and 1980s, this changed. As summarized by Meulendyke (1998, pp. 136–137), "In the 1970s and early 1980s, it [the directive] listed conditions that could lead to an intermeeting change. It gave prominence to deviations in the behavior of the monetary aggregates. Later in the 1980s, as the demand for money became more variable, the Committee included a range of factors in addition to the monetary aggregates and periodically re-ranked the factors as its primary concerns shifted. In 1991, the Committee adopted a standard list, choosing to use the items presented to reinforce its longer term priorities."

The directive itself provides a general overview of the recent conditions in the economy and follows up on recent directives. In this sense, each directive, even when there are policy changes to be made, provides a measure of continuity from one meeting to the next. The directive provides guidance to the trading desk but also allows for some ambiguity. This is seen in the following directive, taken from the June 24–25, 2003, meeting of the FOMC:

> The Federal Open Market Committee seeks monetary and financial conditions that will foster price stability and promote sustainable growth in output. To further its long-run objectives, the Committee in the immediate future seeks conditions in reserve markets consistent with reducing the federal funds rate to an average of around 1 percent. The vote encompassed the following statement whose substance would be included in the press release to be made available shortly after the meeting:
>
> The risks to the Committee's outlook for sustainable economic growth over the next several quarters are balanced; the risks to its outlook for inflation over the next several quarters are weighted toward the downside; and, taken together, the balance of risks to its objectives is weighted toward the downside in the foreseeable future.
>
> *Votes for this action:* Messrs. Greenspan, Bernanke, Ms. Bies, Messrs. Broaddus, Ferguson, Gramlich, Guynn, Kohn, Moskow, Olson, and Stewart. (Mr. Stewart voted as an alternate member.)

Votes against this action: Mr. Parry.

Mr. Parry dissented because he preferred a 50 basis point reduction in the federal funds rate target as insurance against continued sluggishness in economic activity and further declines in inflation measures to undesirably low rates. While he believed that a significant increase in the pace of activity over the next several quarters was likely, he had not yet seen convincing evidence that this process was under way. Moreover, the current slack in labor and product markets was likely to persist for some time even with a significant pickup in real GDP growth, and this prospect threatened to reduce inflation further. Finally, recent declines in inflation expectations had raised the real federal funds rate. In order to offset that increase and provide additional stimulus, he saw a 50 basis point reduction in the rate as desirable.

As you can see from this example, the directive states the FOMC's objectives in terms of price stability and maintaining economic growth and then provides a short statement of how it expects to, over the near term, achieve those goals. At this meeting, it amounted to reducing the federal funds rate to 1 percent. The statement that follows, which is released to the press immediately following the meeting, provides the FOMC's assessment of the near-term risks faced by the economy. At the time of this meeting, the "downside risk" was determined by the FOMC to be more toward a sluggish economy than toward rising rates of inflation. Indeed, that explains the FOMC's actions: by lowering the federal funds rate, the FOMC was directing policy to be more expansionary and attempting to spur economic activity as the economy was still recovering from the 2001 recession. The directive also indicates that this policy action was taken with an eye toward changing it if conditions should warrant. Note that the directive deals with economic activity over the "next several quarters," indicating that policymakers' views may change as conditions warrant.

The directive from this meeting was selected also because it illustrates that not all directives are unanimously agreed upon. At this meeting, one member of the FOMC— President Parry of the San Francisco Federal Reserve Bank—dissented, that is, voted against the directive. In this instance, Mr. Parry did not vote for the directive because he believed that a further reduction in the federal funds rate to 1 percent was not sufficient. As this illustrates, dissents from the majority need not reflect disagreement on the direction of policy but may come from disagreements over the magnitude of changes.

FURTHER READING

Meulendyke, Ann-Marie. *U.S. Monetary Policy & Financial Markets.* New York: Federal Reserve Bank of New York, 1998, Chapter 5.

DISCOUNT RATE. The discount rate is the rate that **commercial banks** and other depository institutions are charged by the Federal Reserve to borrow funds from it. The discount rate is often considered to be one of the tools by which monetary policy changes can be achieved, even though today the role of the discount rate is very much diminished from earlier times. Still, by raising and lowering the discount rate, the Federal Reserve affects the quantity of loans made to banks and other depository institutions through the **discount window**. This affects bank **reserves** and, in turn, the supply of money and interest rates.

In the early years of the Federal Reserve, the discount rate was a key tool of monetary policy. Until the 1920s, the Federal Reserve conducted monetary policy primarily by *rediscounting* loans made by member banks. That is, banks would make loans to individuals or firms and use these loans to acquire funds from the Federal Reserve. The Federal Reserve would lend to the bank some amount less than the face value of the loan.

Discount Window Borrowing Rate (daily)

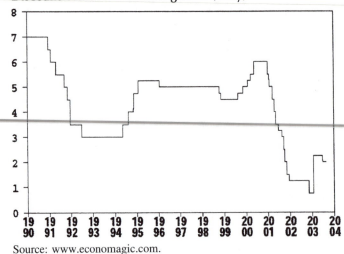

Source: www.economagic.com.

For example, if a bank brought to the Federal Reserve $100 of eligible loans, the Federal Reserve may lend the bank $95, thus discounting the loan. The size of the discount determined the *discount rate*. In this example, the discount rate was 5 percent.

A problem with this approach was that the Federal Reserve would lend funds to banks based on so-called productive loans. In essence, banks that brought loans used for the purpose of supporting the production of goods and services could get discount loans from the Federal Reserve. Known as the **real bills doctrine**, this approach was passive. As long as banks presented eligible paper to the Federal Reserve, discount loans were made. If business activity fell, so would discount lending, and the discount rate. The passive nature of the discount rate changed in the early 1920s when the Federal Reserve began to aggressively use the discount rate as a policy tool. In light of the inflation that soared following World War I, the Federal Reserve determined that its discount policy and the discount rate were not consistent with its long-term goal of price stability. In 1920 the Federal Reserve moved to raise the discount rate from 4.75 percent to 6 percent in an attempt to slow inflation. Although this move dramatically slowed money growth and led to a recession in 1920 and 1921, it has the desired affect of stopping the inflation.

The role of the discount rate today as a policy tool resides primarily in the fact that changes in the discount rate are often viewed as an indicator of a change in future monetary policy. Although the Federal Reserve emphasizes the federal funds rate as its main indicator of policy, changes in the discount rate also are used to emphasize policy actions. For example, an increase in the discount rate together with an increase in the federal funds rate may signal to the markets that the Federal Reserve is attempting to slow economic activity. Such a move may indicate that the Federal Reserve perceives the major threat to be increased inflationary pressures in the economy.

The frequency of discount rate changes varies. As shown in the chart above, the discount rate is changed infrequently in some time periods. This was the case during the period 1992–1993 and again during 1996–1999. For example, there was just one change in 1996 and none in 1997. However, from January to October 2001, when the Federal

Reserve was concerned about signs of weakness in the economy, it lowered the discount rate 10 times in a series of mostly downward steps, from 6.0 percent to the rate set in July 2003 of 2.0 percent. In other times, changes in monetary policy are not accompanied by changes in the discount rate. For example, the Federal Reserve left the discount rate unchanged when it lowered short-term rates in September 1998 and when it raised them in June 1999.

According to law, the directors of each **District Bank**, subject to the approval of the **Board of Governors**, set the discount rate. When a discount rate change is made, it must come from one of the District Banks: The Board of Governors, technically, does not set the rate. To see how the rate is determined, below is the official description of a request by the Federal Reserve Bank of San Francisco to lower the discount rate. In this instance, this request was denied. Although by law discount rate changes must be made by a bank, such changes often are initiated by the board or occur along with policy changes voted upon by the FOMC.

DISCOUNT RATES—Request by one Reserve Bank to lower the primary credit rate; requests by eleven Reserve Banks to maintain the existing rate. Existing rate maintained. July 21, 2003.

Subject to review and determination by the Board of Governors, the directors of the Federal Reserve Bank of San Francisco had voted on July 10, 2003, to establish a rate for discounts and advances under the primary credit program (primary credit rate) of 1-3/4 percent (a reduction from 2 percent). The directors of the Federal Reserve Banks of Boston, Cleveland, Richmond, Atlanta, Chicago, St. Louis, Kansas City, and Dallas had voted on July 10, and the directors of the Federal Reserve Banks of New York, Philadelphia, and Minneapolis had voted on July 17, to maintain the existing rate. At today's meeting, no sentiment was expressed in favor of a change in the primary credit rate, and the existing rate was maintained.

FURTHER READING

Friedman, Milton, and Anna Schwartz. *A Monetary History of the United States, 1867–1960.* Princeton: Princeton University Press, 1963; Meltzer, Allan H. *A History of the Federal Reserve, Vol. 1: 1913–1951.* Chicago: University of Chicago Press, 2003; Mishkin, Frederic S., and Stanley Eakins. *Financial Markets and Institutions.* 4th edition. Boston: Addison Wesley, 2003.

DISCOUNT WINDOW. The Federal Reserve Banks lend to **commercial banks** and depository institutions through the discount window. The rate at which these funds are borrowed is called the **discount rate**. Since its inception, discount window borrowing was considered to be a vital function of the Federal Reserve. Prior to the establishment of the Federal Reserve, there were large swings in interest rates, often the result of seasonal swings in credit demands. By allowing banks to borrow from the discount window, it was thought that the Federal Reserve could lessen the volatility of these demand changes and, therefore, reduce interest rate fluctuations. The fact that the Federal Reserve stood ready to make such **loans** and the fact that at times such loans were made to ensure the liquidity of the banking system (*see* **Lender of Last Resort**) made management of the discount window a key policy tool of the Federal Reserve.

As detailed in the Federal Reserve Bank of New York publication *Fedpoint* (2003), "discount window loans are secured by collateral that exceeds the amount of the loans. In 1999, the Federal Reserve expanded the range of acceptable collateral to include such items as investment-grade **certificates of deposit** and AAA-rated commercial mortgage-backed securities." Borrowing from the discount window generally fell under one of three categories. "Seasonal" credit is extended to depository institutions—mainly small and medium-sized banks—that demonstrate a recurring pattern of seasonal fluctuation in **liquidity** needs. As one might expect, such seasonality affects banks that do a large share of their business with agricultural or tourist-related businesses. The discount rate set on such seasonal borrowing is based on the current federal funds rate and the rate for 90-day certificates of deposit as determined in the secondary market.

The other two categories under which the Federal Reserve would lend were called "adjustment" and "extended" credit. Adjustment credit amounted to discount loans being made to banks that are deficient in liquidity. This type of lending usually amounts to overnight or weekend loans to banks that experience an unexpected shortfall in reserves. Such a shortfall generally is caused by unforeseen deposit outflows or insufficient reserves available in the federal funds market. Extended credit, on the other hand, represents loans made to institutions that are experiencing difficulties. Extended credit is usually made for periods longer than those under adjustment credit, and there are more requirements on banks if they are to get such loans. For example, a bank receiving extended credit from the discount window must provide the Federal Reserve Bank from which it is borrowing the funds with a business plan detailing how it will resolve the difficulties that gave rise to the loan request. In addition, even though the Federal Reserve Bank may charge the troubled institution the discount rate for the first 30 days, after which the discount rate is linked to market rates and must be higher than the official discount rate.

In January 2003 the Federal Reserve announced that it was replacing the adjustment and extended credit programs. In their place, the Federal Reserve announced that it would henceforth extend credit through its "primary" and "secondary" credit programs. The two programs instituted several changes. For example, the primary credit program allows depository institutions to use the funds for any purpose. In addition, the institutions are not required to try alternative sources of funding before making a discount window request. This represents a change from the historic belief that banks using the discount window may be unsound banks that could not acquire funds in the market for reserves. Even though the cost of acquiring primary credit is lessened from the past, this funding is available only to sound banks—that is, banks with **CAMELS** ratings of 3 or less. (These ratings indicate that the bank has met a set of regulatory guidelines regarding their capital adequacy and risk management: the smaller the number, the safer is the bank.) Secondary credit is available to banks that do not meet this criterion. A restriction on banks seeking secondary credit is that they do not use the funds to expand the bank's assets: make loans or purchase government securities.

The interest rate for primary credit is set above the target **federal funds rate**. (Gilbert [1979] discusses the benefits to banks when the discount rate is below market interest rates.) The secondary credit rate is set above the primary credit rate. Thus, the "discount rate" is viewed as a penalty rate to banks that borrow through the discount window. Wheelock (2003) notes that " ... the discount window should serve only as a backup source of funds for banks, as sound banks ordinarily will choose to obtain short-term funds less expensively from the federal funds market or other market sources." In the end, the discount window and the Federal Reserve's provision of credit through it remain a key source of liquidity to the financial system in times of crisis. As shown in the figure below, even though discount window borrowing has been relatively low in the past decade, there

Adjustment Plus Seasonal Borrowings

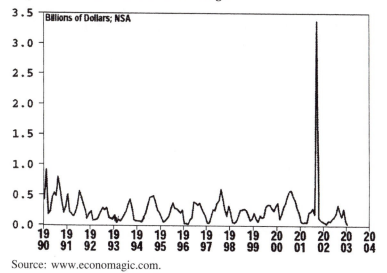

Source: www.economagic.com.

are times when it is a vital source of liquidity. *Fedpoint* (2003) notes that, "Following the attacks on the Pentagon and World Trade Center in September 2001, the Federal Reserve again encouraged depository institutions needing liquidity to borrow from the discount widow. Reserve Banks lent $45.5 billion to depository institutions on September 12, 2001, the record for a single day." By moving rapidly and expeditiously to provide needed credit, and reassuring the financial markets that it stood ready to provide such credit, the Federal Reserve fulfilled its role of lender of last resort.

FURTHER READING

Gilbert, R. Alton. "Benefits of Borrowing from the Federal Reserve when the Discount Rate Is Below Market Interest Rates." Federal Reserve Bank of St. Louis *Economic Review* (March 1979): 25–32; Federal Reserve Bank of New York. "The Discount Window." *Fedpoint* (February 2003). Available online at Website: www.newyorkfed.org; Wheelock, David C. "Replacement Windows: New Credit Programs at the Discount Window." Federal Reserve Bank of St. Louis *Monetary Trends* (May 2003).

DISINFLATION. *In*flation is defined as the persistent increase in the general level of prices. *Dis*inflation is when the rate of increase in the price level declines from, say, a rate of increase equal to 10 percent to a rate of increase equal to 5 percent. Disinflation is *not* a decline in the price level—that condition is defined as **deflation**—but a decline in the rate of increase in prices.

Is the notion of disinflation all that important in a book about the Federal Reserve? As noted elsewhere, one of the Federal Reserve's policy objectives is to keep inflation as low as it can without damaging **economic growth**. That means that when the rate of inflation is high, the Federal Reserve should take actions to bring it down. The question about how to achieve that goal is how disinflation fits in this volume.

In the early 1980s, following a decade of expansive monetary growth and two oil price shocks associated with policies of the Organization of Petroleum Exporting Countries (OPEC) countries, the Federal Reserve, under Chairman **Paul Volcker**, vowed to follow policies that would reduce inflation from its double-digit level. The difficult question facing policymakers was just how to bring about the desired pace of disinflation. Along with the desire to lower inflation was the knowledge that policies could cause a severe slowdown in the economy. Should monetary policy follow a "cold-turkey" kind of approach, one that would dramatically reduce the growth rate of the money supply, or should it follow a policy of gradualism, slowing the growth rate of the money supply in increments over time?

If the answer to this question seems like a no-brainer, it isn't. Even though the ultimate goal of the policies taken was to reduce inflation, policies that jammed on the monetary brakes would produce a severe slowdown in economic activity. With this possibility in mind, Volcker and the **Federal Open Market Committee (FOMC)** chose to quickly lower the rate of inflation, and bring about a dramatic disinflation. On the heels of the policy, the growth rate of real **gross domestic product (GDP)** plummeted and the **unemployment rate** jumped. In fact, the ensuing **recession** is the deepest in the postwar period. But the policy had the intended disinflationary effect: The rate of inflation fell sharply form its peak at nearly 15 percent in 1980 to about 3 percent within a few years.

FURTHER READING

Fellner, William, ed. *Essays in Contemporary Economic Problems: Disinflation.* Washington, D.C.: American Enterprise Institute, 1984; Meltzer, Allan H. "The Case for Gradualism in Policies to Reduce Inflation." In Federal Reserve Bank of St. Louis, S*tabilization Policies: Lessons from the '70s and Implications for the '80s* (available online at Website: www.stlouisfed.org); Meyer, Laurence H., and Robert H. Rasche, "Empirical Evidence on the Effects of Stabilization Policy." In Federal Reserve Bank of St. Louis. S*tabilization Policies: Lessons from the '70s and Implications for the '80s* (available online at Website: www.stlouisfed.org).

DISINTERMEDIATION. Disintermediation occurs when depositors withdraw their funds from banks and place them in other financial institutions. The effect is to reduce the amount of funds that banks have available for lending or for the purchase of securities. The end result can be a reduction in competition among financial institutions and a loss of profitability for banks. A notable period of disintermediation occurred during the 1960s. At that time, interest rates on deposits in banks and other depository institutions were subject to ceilings. (*See* **Regulation Q**.) These ceiling rates (sometimes equal to zero for checking accounts) were well below market interest rates available from other financial institutions, such as **money market mutual funds**. Seeking higher rates of interest on their funds, depositors shifted their savings out of banks and into other areas of the financial market. The effect of this disintermediation was to reduce funds available to banks for lending. When extensive, disintermediation can result in a **credit crunch** as borrowers, especially smaller firms, are unable to finance their activities. Such an outcome occurred during the mid-1960s and again in the early 1990s. In both instances, the result was a slowing in the growth of real GDP.

FURTHER READING

Gilbert, R. Alton, and Jean M. Lovati. "Disintermediation: An Old Disorder with a New Remedy." Federal Reserve Bank of St. Louis *Review* (January 1979): 10–15; Edwards, Franklin R., and Frederic S. Mishkin. "The Decline of Traditional Banking: Implications for Financial Stabilization and Regulatory Policy." Federal Reserve Bank of New York *Economic Policy Review* (July 1995).

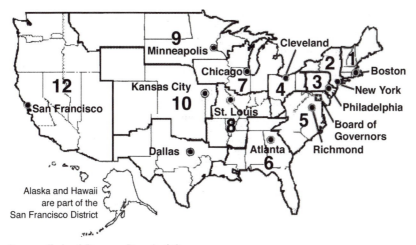

Source: Federal Reserve Board of Governors.

DISTRICT FEDERAL RESERVE BANKS. The Federal Reserve System is composed of 12 District Banks, each of which has several branches. As shown in the map above, the District Banks are located in major metropolitan areas. The size of the district covered by each bank varies greatly, from the second Federal Reserve District—essentially the state of New York—to the twelfth District, which includes all or portions of California, Oregon, Washington, Idaho, Nevada, New Mexico, Arizona, Utah, Hawaii, and Alaska. Why is there such disparity in the sizes of the districts? How were the cities chosen? To answer these questions, it is necessary to examine the history of the Federal Reserve System.

With the signing of the **Federal Reserve Act of 1913**, the blueprint for the nation's central bank had been drawn. Now the really hard work began as it was time to implement the various aspects of the legislation. The first question was how to lay out the system. The act provided some guidance. Section 2 of the act required the secretaries of treasury and agriculture and the **Comptroller of the Currency**—designated as the Organization Committee—to "as soon as practicable ... designate not less than eight nor more than twelve cities to be known as Federal Reserve cities. ..." In other words, this committee was given the charge to determine where the District Banks would be located and determine what the geographical makeup of the districts would be. The act provided little guidance. In deciding how to divide the nation into the Federal Reserve districts, the act suggested that the final choice be done "with due regard to the convenience and customary course of business and shall not necessarily be coterminous with any state or states."

The process by which the District Bank cities were selected and the Federal Reserve districts were laid out is an interesting study of how politics and self-interest often determine economic outcomes. The debate raged over both the number and the location. Some argued that more banks were preferable to fewer. Why? Because Western interests distrusted the Eastern banking establishment, centered primarily in New York City. If there were only a few banks, then the New York District Bank would dominate. After all, even then, New York City was the financial capital of the United States, and by this very fact, the District Bank located there would have the upper hand in Federal Reserve System activities.

Having determined the number of districts, how should one interpret the requirement that District Bank locations be determined with regard to the "due course of business"? At meetings held in January 1914 in New York City, leaders of the financial industry, including **J. P. Morgan**, made their pitch for a New York City bank. Locating a District Bank in the city was assured, but the amount of power given to it and the size of its district were not. Some argued that the New York Bank should be given a dominant position because it would be the bank dealing with foreign central banks. (Note: At this time, the **Board of Governors** in Washington, D.C., was not the center of power in the system that it is today.) The debate also raged on over how big the New York district should be. Some argued that it should include all of New England and states to the south of New York. It was even suggested that it should extend as far west as Ohio!

The New York City meetings were followed by similar visits to Boston and Washington, D.C., with representatives from other Eastern cities, such as Philadelphia, Richmond, and Baltimore. In each location, local interest groups made their case for a District Bank. In each meeting, the committee heard the same story: selection of (your city's name here) was paramount if the system was going to function properly and achieve the purpose of the act. After these meetings, the committee toured a number of cities away from the East Coast, including Cleveland, Cincinnati, Chicago, St. Louis, Kansas City, Denver, Portland, Seattle, San Francisco, Atlanta, New Orleans, Austin, and El Paso. Some cities were not visited—Dallas, Houston, Detroit, and Memphis—much to the dismay and consternation of their residents and business leaders. In each city, local dignitaries and leaders of business and finance all made their pitch for why their city deserved a District Bank. And, there often was an openly voiced concern that the power of the Federal Reserve be dispersed, that is, not concentrated in the Eastern states. As Moore (1990, pp. 14–15) quotes from a *New York Times* article of the day, "The hearings of the reserve bank organizers, generally speaking, have been more remarkable for the local jealousies they have disclosed than for the perception that there was anything of national significance in the new departure."

After further discussion and meetings in Washington, D.C., the committee released its decision on April 2, 1914. In that report the committee named the 12 cities that had been selected as Federal Reserve cities. Those cities are the 12 that today house the District Banks (see map). Once the district cities were named, the process then determined which cities would serve as branches of the 12 District Banks. In some cases, cities that had vied for but failed to get a District Bank got a branch. For example, New Orleans has a branch bank of the Atlanta District Bank and Memphis has a branch of the St. Louis District Bank. One of the more interesting outcomes of the process is that the state of Missouri garnered *two* District Banks: one in St. Louis and the other in Kansas City. Could it have anything to do with the fact that one of the Organization Committee members—David Houston, then the Secretary of Agriculture—was from Missouri?

In the end, the committee responded to critics by releasing the results of a poll they had conducted asking national banks which cities they preferred as reserve cities and a list of the criteria used in making their final selections. As detailed in Moore (1990), these criteria included

1. The ability of member banks within a district to provide the necessary capital.
2. The mercantile, industrial, and financial connections existing within each district.
3. The probable ability of the Federal Reserve Bank in each district to meet the legitimate business demands placed upon it.

4. The fair and equitable division of the available capital for the Federal Reserve banks among the cities.
5. Geographic factors, and the existing network of transportation and communication.
6. Population, area, and prevalent business activities of the districts.

The 12 banks and their districts remained essentially the same since the committee first designated them. Although there have been some minor changes over time—a county in some state here and there being moved from one district to another—the boundaries have remained intact for nearly a century.

The role of the District Banks has changed over the past century. Originally, the system was designed to diffuse power throughout the various banks, with no one bank dominating all actions or decisions. Even though the New York Bank was the preeminent bank, based simply on the fact that it was located in the country's financial center and that it was rapidly becoming an international money center, the other banks closely guarded their independence. As expressed in the process of selecting the districts, there was a definite feeling of distrust between banks located in the more agrarian West and South and the Eastern establishment banks.

In the early days, the District Banks conducted monetary policy on a much more localized basis than we experience today. Policy consisted primarily of rediscounting eligible paper from banks through the **discount window**. The District Banks provided funds to the banking and business communities through its lending practices, and by altering the local **discount rate**, the interest rate charged to banks that borrowed from the bank. As discussed elsewhere, this role diminished over time.

Monetary policy became centralized in the Board of Governors, and policy actions became dominated by the use of **open market operations**, the buying and selling of government securities by the Federal Reserve. Although the presidents of the District Banks still have a voice in the setting and conduct of policy—they serve as members of the Federal Reserve's policymaking body, the **Federal Open Market Committee (FOMC)**— the role of the District Banks today focuses on other functions of a central banking system.

Even though use of the discount rate and the discount window as a policy tool has declined over time, they still have some role. Changes in the discount rate are initiated by the boards of directors of the District Banks. A request for a change in the discount rate is initiated by a District Bank, but the change must be approved by the Board of Governors. So, even in this instance, the board has final say.

One of the more important roles played by the District Banks is in the supervisory area. This is a wide-ranging area of Federal Reserve Bank responsibility. For example, District Banks have regulatory authority over the activities of **bank holding companies** and state-chartered banks. The District Banks also oversee the field examinations of banks in their districts and the implementation of various bank regulations. Based on their examinations through the "sup and reg" departments, District Banks perform an important role in maintaining the stability and viability of the U.S. banking system. The banks also oversee changes in banking markets as they have the authority to approve or deny certain types of bank and bank holding company applications.

The District Banks also serve the banking community in other ways. For example, the banks serve as a centralized check-clearing system for commercial banks. Although this activity has declined over time—larger commercial banks with sophisticated computer systems now are able to furnish this service to smaller, correspondent banks—the system's

District Banks still processes a large volume of checks, about 18 billion a year. The banks sort the checks, route them to the banks upon which they are drawn, and transfer payments to those banks in which they are to be deposited. Through the banks' system of accounts, this process is done with great speed and efficiency, thus reducing **float** and increasing the efficiency of the financial payments system.

District Banks also offer other services to banks and other depository institutions located in their districts. District Banks offer wire transfer services by which depository institutions, electronically linked through the Federal Reserve Communications System, can transfer funds quickly and safely across the nation. The banks also operate clearinghouse systems through which participating institutions can electronically exchange payments. Examples of such clearinghouse activity include the U.S. Treasury Department's dispersal of social security payments and the widespread use of direct deposit of payrolls. Both of these services help the financial system work more efficiently.

Part of the reason for establishing the Federal Reserve System was to ensure an elastic **currency**: a supply of money that would respond to the needs of business. Although this aspect of the Federal Reserve's existence has changed dramatically over time, the banks still perform the function of distributing currency and coin to depository institutions within their districts. During periods of increased demand for currency, banks will request more paper money from their District Bank. It is the job of the District Bank to meet these demands. Because the District Banks are the source of currency, they also act as custodians of currency. Each District Bank has facilities to sort and count money, find counterfeit bills, and destroy unfit bills.

Finally, in addition to all of these roles that provide services to the banking industry, each District Bank has a research staff that analyzes economic data, gathers statistics pertaining to local and district business and financial activity, and provides advice to the president of the bank in advance of the FOMC meetings. The research departments, usually made up of professional economists and support staff, are an important source of analyses independent of the board staff's views usually presented at the opening of the FOMC's meetings. This again reflects one of the founding principles of the Federal Reserve System: a decentralization of ideas and viewpoints when making monetary policy. In addition to this internal advice and counsel, each District Bank publishes statistical releases, monthly and quarterly research reports conducted by the research staff, and current notifications of regulatory changes. (Visit any of the District Banks' web pages, and you will find a list of publications, most of which can be obtained free of charge.)

FURTHER READING

Groseclose, Elgin. *Fifty Years of Managed Money: The Story of the Federal Reserve, 1914–1963.* London: McMillan Press, 1965; Johnson, Roger. *Historical Beginnings—The Federal Reserve.* Boston: Federal Reserve Bank of Boston, 1977; Melzter, Allan H. *A History of the Federal Reserve: Volume I: 1913–1951.* Chicago: University of Chicago Press, 2003; Moore, Carl. *The Federal Reserve System: A History of the First 75 Years.* Jefferson, NC: McFarland & Company: 1990; Primm, James Neal. *A Foregone Conclusion: The Founding of the Federal Reserve Bank of St. Louis.* St. Louis: Federal Reserve Bank of St. Louis, 1989; Warburg, Paul. *The Federal Reserve System: Its Origin and Growth.* New York: Arno Press, 1930.

DUAL BANKING SYSTEM. The phrase *dual banking system* refers to the fact that banks in the United States are chartered at the state level or by the federal government.

One reason for the **National Banking Act of 1864** was to eliminate abuses by banks at the state level. A key component of the act was to prevent state-chartered banks, known as **state banks**, from issuing their own currency. To prevent this, the act imposed a severe tax on bank notes issued by state banks but not on bank notes issued by banks chartered by the federal government and supervised by the Office of the **Comptroller of the Currency**, known as national banks. This legislation was a direct attempt by the federal government to reduce competition between state and national banks. In response, state banks began to provide customers with a substitute for currency: the demand deposit or checking account. This financial innovation meant that state banks could accept deposits or checking accounts and remain in business, even though they were no longer issuing currency. The checking account became so popular that national banks adopted it.

FURTHER READING

Comptroller of the Currency. "National Banks and the Dual Banking System." (September 2003). Website: www.occ.treas.gov/ftp/release/2003–83a.pdf.

ECCLES, MARRINER (1890–1977). Marriner Eccles served as chairman of the Federal Reserve **Board of Governors** from November 15, 1934, to January 31, 1948. Eccles was replaced as chairman by **Thomas B. McCabe** in 1948 at the request of President **Harry S. Truman**. Although no longer chairman, Eccles remained on the Board of Governors until July 14, 1951.

Eccles rose to national attention during the **Great Depression**. Eccles, along with his brother George, controlled banks at numerous locations within Utah, Idaho, and Wyoming. In 1928, the Eccles brothers joined with E. G. Bennett of Idaho Falls to form the First Security Corporation, a holding company that managed the 17 banks. As president of the holding company, Marriner Eccles was one of the most prominent bankers in the Intermountain West (Arrington, 2004).

Eccles's ability to keep his banks open during the **bank runs** of the early 1930s pushed him into the national limelight. After serving briefly as a special assistant to Treasury Secretary Henry Morgenthau, Eccles was appointed to be head of the Federal Reserve System by President **Franklin Roosevelt** on November 10, 1934. Eccles's appointment was not without controversy, however. During his time at the Treasury, Eccles, along with **Lauchlin Currie,** drafted legislation that altered the structure of the Federal Reserve and the concentration of its power. This legislation flew in the face of the beliefs of one of the Senate's most powerful members, **Carter Glass**. Glass, the chairman of the Senate's Banking Committee, opposed the Currie-Eccles plan and opposed Eccles's nomination to head the Federal Reserve. Because Eccles's appointment was made during the congressional recess, he was not officially confirmed until April 1935. During the confirmation process, Eccles and Glass often sparred over the role and responsibility of the Federal Reserve System.

The opposition to Eccles centered around his desire to centralize monetary policy in Washington, D.C. Eccles supported a banking bill then circulating in the Senate and Congress, which would later become the **Banking Act of 1935**. Meltzer (2003, p. 470) notes that "Eccles wanted a central bank with authority concentrated in Washington, specifically in his hands." In addition to his preference for having power reside in Washington, Eccles wanted monetary policy to be determined by judgment, not rules. **Allan H. Meltzer** (2003, p. 470) argues that Eccles "preferred to rely on judgment and wanted a large measure of authority to do what he believed was in the public interest."

As governor of the Federal Reserve, Eccles was able to implement his own views on the appropriate course of policy. Many at the time argued that depressions were useful as a means to purge the economy of undesirable excesses. Eccles rejected that view. Instead, Eccles was an early advocate of government intervention and the use of unbalanced federal budgets to correct downswings in economic activity.

Eccles also believed that the Great Depression was as much a problem of uneven income distribution as any policy action. For example, Meltzer (2003, p. 465) notes that Eccles's "views help explain his decisions and his passivity as head of the Federal Reserve. Eccles did not blame the Federal Reserve for the depression or urge credit expansion. . . . Eccles opposed devaluation, silver purchases, or increases in money unless they increased consumers' purchasing power. He believed the money stock, though 22 percent below 1929, was adequate to support higher spending. . . . [He also favored] unification of the banking system under Federal Reserve supervision."

In many ways, Eccles approached the role of the Federal Reserve in much the same manner as the early Keynesian economists would: the central bank was really there to keep interest rates low and let fiscal policy actions guide the economy. Fiscal policy and altering income distributions through government intervention were the key to stabilizing economic activity. Eccles, testifying before the House Committee on Banking and Currency in 1935, stated, "One of the principle troubles or difficulties that brought about the depression was not the shortage in the supply of money altogether, but it was due in part to the inequitable distribution of income which contributed to the speculative situation in the security markets and to an expansion of productive capacity out of relationship to the ability of the people of the country to consume under the existing distribution of income" (quoted in Meltzer, 2003, p. 477).

In addition to his role in changing the power structure of the Federal Reserve System, Eccles is best known for his role in bringing about the Federal Reserve's independence from the Treasury in 1951. By this time Eccles was not the chairman of the board, but remained on as its vice chairman after President Truman did not renominate him for the chairman's position in 1948. Eccles's views on the role of monetary policy had changed somewhat by this time. Although he still favored fiscal policy as a means to redistribute income and maintain economic stability, he recognized the ability of monetary policy to check inflation. Following World War II, the Federal Reserve's policy responsibility was to peg interest rates on U.S. Treasury securities, a policy that kept financing costs of new government debt down so it could pursue expansionary fiscal policies. At the same time, it necessitated an expansion in the supply of money that pushed the rate of inflation higher than desired.

Eccles argued that the Federal Reserve should be given complete freedom to pursue policies that would keep inflation in check, policies that called for limiting the growth rate of the money supply. The problem is that such a policy would also likely push interest rates higher than the Treasury, or the Truman administration, desired. After a series of meetings in which the Truman administration and the Treasury pushed the Federal Reserve to maintain its policy of pegging rates, Eccles and others favoring Fed independence won the day. The so-called accord became fact on March 4, 1951. In the end, Eccles achieved the independence from the Treasury and the administration that he long believed should exist.

FURTHER READING

Arrington, Leonard J. "Marriner Stoddard Eccles." Utah History Encyclopedia, accessed at www.media.utah.edu (January 1, 2004); Hyman, Sydney. *Marriner S. Eccles: Private Entrepreneur and Public Servant.* Stanford, CA: Stanford University, 1976; Meltzer, Allan H. *A History of the Federal Reserve, Vol. 1: 1913–1951.* Chicago: University of Chicago Press, 2003.

ECONOMETRIC MODEL. To help explain the behavior of the economy and important economic variables, like **inflation**, unemployment, or economic growth, economists often use mathematics to capture or model the relationships between these measures. For example, economists believe that how much **money** you spend on clothes is partly related to your level of income, the alternatives available to you for using that money, and, of course, the price of the items. They also believe that producers of clothing take into account the price they can get for the item, the costs in producing them, the competition, etc., before actually going into production. Economists often express these relationships in terms of mathematical models, whose equations are estimated with statistical methods using observations on spending, production, prices, etc. The result is an econometric model, which borrows aspects from both economics ("econo-") and from statistical measurement ("-metrics").

Econometric models are used in the formation of monetary policy in numerous ways. They are used to provide forecasts of important variables, such as inflation, unemployment, and economic growth, and to conduct simulations of the effects of different policies on the economy. Econometric models are used to generate the policy alternatives discussed in the **blue book** and the **green book** during FOMC meetings. Econometric models also are used to provide businesses with forecasts of future economic trends. For example, companies like Ford Motor Company would like to know whether car sales will increase or decrease in the future before they decide on production levels. Based on statistical relations between variables, i.e., income, prices, interest rates, etc., economists can provide an educated guess that production managers then use to decide the number of automobiles to produce.

FURTHER READING

Carlson, Keith M., and Scott E. Hein. "Four Econometric Models and Monetary Policy: The Longer-Run View." Federal Reserve Bank of St. Louis *Review* (January 1982): 13–24.

ECONOMIC GROWTH. Economic growth generally is measured by the long-term trend in real **gross domestic product**, or real **GDP**. A thumbnail version of real GDP is that it measures the value of total output of all the goods, like cars and houses and textbooks, and services, such as haircuts and computer repair, produced in the economy and adjusted for price level changes. Economists concerned with economic growth want to know whether individuals in a country are better off, in a material sense, in one year compared with another. For example, are citizens in the United States better off today than, say, in 1920? One way to answer this question is to compare real GDP *per person* (real GDP divided by the number of people in the economy) now with that in 1920. A higher real GDP per person suggests that the average individual has access to more goods and services, prices being held constant.

Economic growth is determined by several factors, but perhaps the most important is productivity. Productivity measures how much output is produced in an economy per hour of work. Increasing productivity means that there are more goods being produced for the same amount of labor used. One way to increase productivity, therefore, is to supply more machinery to workers (increase the stock of capital) or to improve the existing stock of machines (increase technology). From manufacturing equipment to laptop computers, providing workers with more and better equipment raises productivity and, therefore, improves economic growth. Historically, increases in productivity usually are associated with improvements in technology and in education.

The onset of the industrial revolution in the late 1700s marked a major upswing in productivity growth. This surge in productivity arose with the introduction of new machines and production techniques. More recently, the increased productivity in the 1990s in the United States was accompanied by a marked increase in the growth of real GDP per person. In addition to producing goods more efficiently with new technologies, studies find that an increased level of educational attainment also is associated with increased economic growth. One reason is because higher levels of education are associated with greater advances in technology and its applications. Indeed, the evidence indicates that countries with higher educational attainment usually are also the countries with higher levels of real GDP per person.

FURTHER READING

DeLong, J. Bradford. "How Fast Is Modern Economic Growth?" Federal Reserve Bank of San Francisco *Weekly Letter* (October 6, 1998); Fischer, Stanley. "The Role of Macroeconomic Factors in Growth." *Journal of Monetary Economics* 32 (1993): 485–512; Kliesen, Kevin L., and Frank Schmidt. "Fear of Hell Might Fire Up Economy." Federal Reserve Bank of St. Louis *The Regional Economist* (July 2004).

ECONOMIC REPORT OF THE PRESIDENT. The *Economic Report of the President* is produced by the **Council of Economic Advisers** and is published annually. In addition to numerous tables of data on the economy, interest rates, prices, and measures of monetary and fiscal policy, the *Report* provides a guide to the administration's stance on major economic issues, such as welfare reform, agricultural programs, and international trade, to name just a few. The *Report* also provides economic forecasts that underlay the president's annual fiscal budget.

FURTHER READING

Copies of the *Report* can be obtained from the CEA's Website: www.WhiteHouse.gov.

EDGE ACT CORPORATION. Edge Act corporations are special subsidiaries of U.S. banks whose primary business is providing international banking services. Passage of the Edge Act in 1919 allowed banks to more effectively compete with foreign banks because it exempts these bank subsidiaries from some of the regulations that domestic banks faced. For example, during the time when interstate branching was not permitted, Edge Act corporations were allowed to have offices in different states. This exemption from interstate branching laws allowed these firms and their parent banks to facilitate the financing of international trade. For instance, with branches in New York, Seattle, and Miami, an Edge

Act corporation could finance trade with Europe, Asia, and Latin America, respectively. Edge Act corporations' activities are regulated by the Federal Reserve.

EFFICIENT MARKETS THEORY. A fundamental idea in economics is that individuals form their decisions by using all of what they believe to be relevant information that is available to them. That does not mean that everyone tries to collect every piece of information about all possible ice cream stores before selecting one from which to buy a cone on a hot summer day. Rather, it means that individuals will shop around until the benefits of looking some more are less than the costs of doing so. If it is a very hot day, prolonged search for the best ice cream store may be quickly outweighed by simply buying some refreshing ice cream from the nearest shop. Thus, if some individuals decide that search entails simply going to one shop only, then, by their estimation, that is sufficient.

In many ways, the same basic idea holds true in financial markets. Individuals make decisions about whether to buy this or that stock based on their expectations. It may have to do with expectations about the future earnings of the company or about the industry in which the company operates. Expectations about future **inflation** or whether the economy is entering a **recession** may affect not only stock-buying decisions but also the choice between stocks and other financial assets, such as **bonds**. In any event, prices for the different financial assets—stocks, bonds, etc.—are thought to reflect all publicly available information used by market participants in making their buy-and-sell decisions. Think of it: the stock of some corporation, such as Dell, is being bought and sold based on millions of buyers' and sellers' respective information sets and their interpretation of the information. For example, if I think Dell is not going to have a good year, I may wish to sell. Someone else has done more research into the matter (they have actually read experts' forecasts of Dell's profit outlook, for example) and believe that it is going to be a record-breaking year for computer sales and that Dell should prosper in such an environment. Unlike me, they decide to buy the stock. This buying and selling of financial assets based on differing information sets and differing expectations suggests that the observed market price—the one reported in the newspaper or on your computer screen—reflects how traders individually using publicly available information have come together to decide the price of Dell stock.

If financial market asset prices reflect publicly available information, why would prices ever change? Decisions to buy or sell a stock may be drastically affected by the arrival of some new information. For instance, what if Dell unexpectedly announces that they have discovered a new computer technology? This piece of new information is likely to drive up its stock price as buyers outnumber sellers. Once this announcement has been fully digested by the public, further price increases may not be as dramatic. For the future, further changes in Dell stock prices again are likely to reflect the arrival of new information: the new technology is yesterday's news. Or, as occurred during the first few years of the twenty-first century, announcements of management fraud and deceptive accounting practices caused investors to rethink the value of several large corporations, some of whose stock prices plummeted close to zero.

If changes in stock prices and other financial asset prices reflect the arrival of new information, then future *changes* in them are not very predictable. Otherwise, traders could predict future changes by simply looking at what happened in the past. In general, the evidence indicates that it is very difficult to accurately forecast future stock price and interest rate changes using past information alone. For example, the "best" forecast of tomorrow's close for the Dow Jones may simply be where it closed today. This reflects the notion that the change from day to day is close to random. Indeed, based on this observation, some have referred to observed movements in stock prices as a **random walk**. Here the analogy is that when following the footprints of a drunk on the beach, it is impossible to accurately predict, given the last impression, where the next footprint will fall. Hence, the best guess—which does not mean one that is accurate—is to extrapolate from where the last footprint was.

The idea that changes in market prices reflect new information suggests that individuals who acquire greater information or those who are more adept in analyzing an industry are likely to be better able to take advantage of profitable opportunities—new information events—as they arise. Because most of us have other things to do besides dig through company reports or watch the minute-by-minute activity of the stock market, some individuals become specialists in gathering this information, selling it to the rest of us. This is another example of specialization of labor within financial markets. Brokers, financial intermediaries who specialize in the collection of information, analyze and disseminate information pertaining to the movements in financial asset prices.

The notion that financial markets operate in this efficient manner also raises issues for monetary policy. If market participants watch every move made by the Federal Reserve (*see* **Fed Watcher**), then policy changes, when expected, actually may have little effect on interest rates or financial asset prices. In a sense, changes may already be "priced in" stocks or bonds. This has important implications for policymakers. The more transparent is policy—the more policymakers reveal their decisions and the logic behind them–market reaction will be less volatile when decisions are announced. On the other hand, if the Federal Reserve wants to change interest rates or asset prices, it may be necessary for them to act in an unexpected manner. This notion is especially true when it comes to policy actions that attempt to change real economic activity. Indeed, the **rational expectations** view of macroeconomics holds that the only way the Federal Reserve can raise or lower real economic activity is by increasing or decreasing, respectively, the growth rate of money in an unexpected manner. In other words, if the markets expect the rate of money growth to be 5 percent and the Federal Reserve wishes to stimulate the economy, then the Federal Reserve may increase the growth rate to 10 percent. Because the markets did not expect this higher growth rate, they may respond by increasing employment and production. Once they catch on, however, the economy returns to its normal rate of growth. As you can see, one view indicates that efficient markets and transparent policy go together to reduce fluctuations in the financial markets. The other suggests that to be effective, the Federal Reserve may actually want to surprise markets with their actions. (*See also* **Rational Expectations**.)

FURTHER READING

Fama, Eugene. "Efficient Markets: II, Fiftieth Anniversary Invited Paper." *Journal of Finance* 46 (December 1991): 1575–617; Malkiel, Burton. *A Random Walk Down Wall Street*. New York: Norton, 1990.

ELECTRONIC MONEY. This term is used to describe funds that are stored electronically. An example of electronic money is the **debit card**. As discussed elsewhere, debit cards allow individuals to purchase goods from stores simply by swiping their card at the register and entering a pin number. This activity electronically transfers funds from the buyer's bank account to the business's account. In this way, the debit card serves as a substitute for currency: hence the phrase "electronic money." There are other popular forms, such as *electronic cash*. Electronic cash, or e-cash, is used for Internet transactions. Backed by deposits in a bank, customers using e-cash simply transfer funds from their computer to the vendor's computer. Once the transaction is completed, the vendor can then have the funds transferred to the bank account from the buyer's bank account before shipping the items purchased. It is, in effect, similar to a debit card transaction except it is done over the Internet. *Stored-value cards* are another form of e-money. These cards usually are good for purchases up to some fixed amount. A $50 gift card to Wal-Mart, which entitles you to purchase up to $50 worth of merchandise, is an example of a stored-value card.

FURTHER READING

Dwyer, Gerald P., Jr. "Is There a Future for Electronic Cash in the United States?" *Journal of Banking and Commerce* (November 1998); Kelley, Edward C., Jr. "Developments in the Field of Electronic Money and Banking." Federal Reserve Bank of Minneapolis *fedgazette* (July 1996).

EQUATION OF EXCHANGE. The equation of exchange relates movements in **money**, output, and the price level. The equation most often is expressed as the relation

$$MV = PY.$$

In this equation, M is some measure of the money supply, P is the price level, Y is real output, and V is velocity. To use this equation, these terms need some counterpart in the real world, so M can be measured as the Federal Reserve's M2 definition of money; P could be some price index such as the Consumer Price Index or **gross domestic product (GDP)** deflator; and Y could be real GDP. That leaves the question of how to measure velocity. In the equation, the term PY actually measures nominal income, or nominal GDP. This is because, by definition, real GDP equals nominal GDP divided by the price level, or RGDP = NGDP/P. With a little algebra, it is easy to see that NGDP = P × RGDP. So, from the equation of exchange, velocity is just the ratio of nominal income (PY) to money (M). The concept of velocity is important. Velocity can be thought of as the number of times a dollar "turns over" during a given period of time to support a dollar of income. A larger value for velocity indicates that more income is being generated by each dollar in circulation. Each time someone purchases shoes, bananas, or haircuts, nominal income, often measured as nominal GDP, is affected. Used in this way, the faster the dollar turns over, that is, the greater is velocity, the more it supports the creation of income.

The concept of velocity is important in the equation of exchange. This can be seen by realizing that the equation of exchange is an identity: the quantity of money multiplied by the number of times it is spent is, by definition, equal to the amount spent on goods and services. The equation of exchange is used to investigate the relationship between changes in movements of the supply of money, the level of prices, and output. For example, the equation can be rearranged to be

$$P = V(M/Y).$$

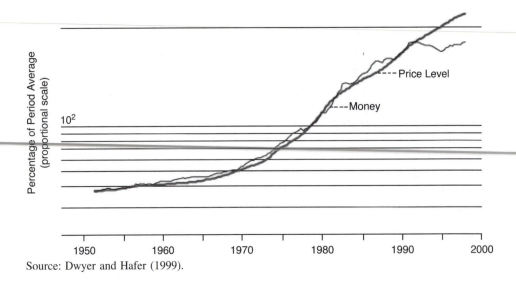

Source: Dwyer and Hafer (1999).

This version of the equation has an important policy interpretation. That is, if velocity is relatively stable over time—people maintain relatively constant patterns in how they buy goods—then the price level (P) is directly related to ratio of the money supply to output (M/Y). In other words, if the money supply (M) is increasing at a faster rate than real output (Y), *and* velocity (V) is relatively stable over time, the price level (P) will increase. This has a direct implication for monetary policy: policies that raise the growth rate of the money supply in excess of the growth rate of real output—velocity held constant—may lead to higher rates of inflation.

Is this conjecture true? The figure above shows the relationship between the ratio of money to real GDP and the price level in the United States between 1953 and 1997. Notice that, until the early 1990s, the relationship between the two lines was very close. In other words, when the money supply increased faster than the output of goods and services in the economy, the general level of prices also began to rise. What happened in 1990? There was a shift in velocity (V). This change meant that increases in the money supply relative to real GDP no longer had the same impact on prices as before. But this did not last long. As is evident in the chart, beginning in the mid-1990s, the two lines once again moved in parallel fashion, indicating that the relation had returned to normal.

Is this unique to the United States? On top of the next page is a chart for Japan, one that covers a longer time than the U.S. chart above. The Japan comparison is useful for several reasons. First, it again demonstrates that the money-output ratio and the price level still tend to track quite well over a longer period of time. Second, the relation is not terribly affected by events as dramatic as World War II: before and after the relation holds. Finally, Japan during the 1990s suffered an ongoing recession that often led to price deflation. One explanation for this low inflation environment is evident from the chart: growth in the money stock was low.

Another way to illustrate the relation is to compare average percentage changes in the money-output ratio with average percentage changes in the price level; that is, inflation. The chart on the bottom of the next page shows such a comparison using data from a large sample of countries for the five-year period of 1992–1997. The 45-degree line is

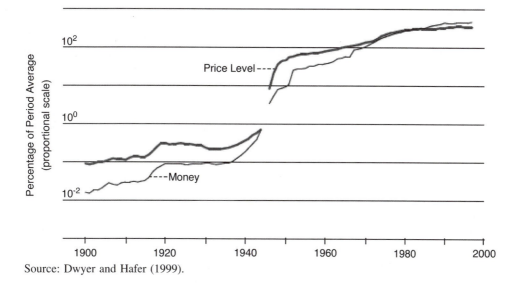

Source: Dwyer and Hafer (1999).

superimposed on the chart as a reference tool: points along this line indicate a one-to-one relation between money growth and inflation.

The chart below suggests that the equation of exchange holds. Since the majority of the points—each one represent a different country's experience—lie along the 45-degree line, then the average relation between money growth and inflation is upheld. Indeed, this comparison can be repeated for different time periods and the results are the same. Increases in money growth relative to output generally lead to increases in the general level of prices.

1992–97

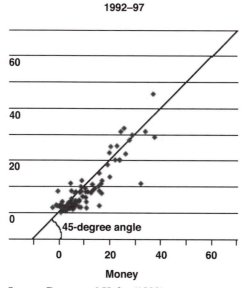

Source: Dwyer and Hafer (1999).

FURTHER READING

Friedman, Milton, and Anna Schwartz. *A Monetary History of the United States, 1867–1960*. Princeton: Princeton University Press, 1963; Dwyer, Gerald P., Jr., and R. W. Hafer. "Are Money Growth and Inflation Still Related?" Federal Reserve Bank of Atlanta *Economic Review* (Second Quarter 1999): 32–43.

EQUILIBRIUM. This term generally is used to describe a condition where the quantity supplied of some good is the same as the quantity demanded. The price at which this equality occurs is known as the equilibrium price. An example will help. As far as we know, there is only one Mona Lisa painting. It currently is displayed in the Louvre museum in Paris. Suppose the Louvre decides to sell it. With supply fixed (the single painting), its price will be determined by how much buyers are willing and able to spend for it. As art collectors compete with one another to buy the painting, which way does the price go? Of course, it goes higher and higher until only one buyer is left. The selling price—undoubtedly in the millions—represents the equilibrium price: the price at which the quantity supplied (here one) is equal to the quantity demanded (again one) at some price.

Why is that price an *equilibrium* price? The notion is that unless something changes, there is no reason for the price arrived at in the auction process to change. What if a week after the sale the curators discover another Mona Lisa in the basement of an Italian villa? What happens now to the price to acquire a Mona Lisa painting? Assuming the two Mona Lisa paintings are identical and experts cannot tell which came first, the supply of Mona Lisa paintings has doubled. In all likelihood the price that brings quantity supplied and demanded into equality in the next auction will be lower than when there was thought to be only one Mona Lisa. Once this new equilibrium price is established, it also will remain until some other outside force—changes in the number of buyers or their incomes, or the discovery of even more Mona Lisa paintings—causes it to change. In this way, equilibrium prices and quantities are stable unless affected by outside forces.

FURTHER READING

Taylor, John B. *Economics*. 4th edition. Boston: Houghton Mifflin Co., 2004.

EURODOLLARS. When someone deposits U.S. dollars in a foreign branch of a U.S. bank or in foreign banks outside the United States, those deposits are called Eurodollars. Eurodollar deposits are not converted into the **currency** of the foreign country, for example, Brazil, but remain denominated in dollars. This means that U.S. banks or their branches can borrow these funds from abroad when additional funding is needed. In recent years, Eurodollars have become an important source of funds for American banks. In 2004, for example, outstanding Eurodollars amounted to over $344 billion, compared with only $55 billion in 1980 and $92 billion in 1990.

An important aspect of activity in the Eurodollar market is that banks in this market compete for deposits with domestic banks. One reason is that the Eurodollar market is, compared with U.S. banking, relatively free of regulation. For this reason, the Eurodollar market has grown: participants use the market to avoid U.S. banking regulations. In this vein, **international banking facilities** (IBFs) and banks outside the United States are not required to hold reserves against their Eurodollar deposits. Because required reserves are a tax on bank deposits—that is, reserve requirements raise the cost to banks of offering deposits—Eurodollar deposits are more profitable relative to "standard" deposits.

Not only has interest in Eurodollars grown over time, but so has the geographical dispersion of the market. Initially, these deposits were held by European banks (hence the name). During the past few decades, however, Eurodollar deposits are held at U.S. IBFs and in the Bahamas, Bahrain, Canada, the Cayman Islands, Hong Kong, Japan, the Netherlands Antilles, Panama, and Singapore.

FURTHER READING

Goodfriend, Marvin. "Eurodollars." In *Instruments of the Money Market*. Richmond: Federal Reserve Bank of Richmond, 1998; Stigum, Marcia. *The Money Market: Myth, Reality, and Practice*. Homewood, IL: Dow Jones-Irwin, 1990.

EX ANTE AND *EX POST* **REAL RATE OF INTEREST.** The term *ex ante* is Latin for "before," and *ex post* means "after." These phrases are used in conjunction with the **real rate of interest** to specify how the real rate is measured. The *ex ante* real rate of interest is measured by subtracting the expected rate of inflation from a **nominal interest rate**. The *ex post* real rate of interest is measured by subtracting the actual rate of inflation from a nominal interest rate. Why the distinction? The *ex ante real rate of interest* adjusts the nominal rate for expected **inflation**, and it is this rate that is most important when one is making an economic decision, whether it is an individual who is deciding how much to save or a company deciding whether it should invest in a new factory. When making economic decisions, individuals and businesses try to weigh their best alternatives before selecting which action to take. Because the future is unknown, economic decisions must be based on expectations. In this case, the *ex ante* real rate of interest is most likely to be the interest rate that is used to make decisions. The problem is that it is very difficult for one person to measure another's expectation of future inflation. I can ask you today what you think inflation is going to be, say, next year, but that expectation could change very quickly if new information were made available to you tomorrow. In practice, therefore, many economists, policymakers, and financial market participants use the *ex post real rate of interest*, primarily because it is easier to calculate.

To measure the *ex post* real rate of interest, take the nominal rate of interest at some point in time and simply subtract the actual rate of inflation for the same period. For example, if the nominal interest rate on a three-month Treasury bill in January 2003 is 5 percent and the inflation rate for that month is 3 percent, then the *ex post real rate of interest* for a three-month Treasury bill for January 2003 is 2 percent (= 5 percent to 3 percent). Of course, one problem with this simple measure is that the interest rate actually is forward looking and the inflation rate is not. That is, the three-month Treasury bill rate in January is what market participants think the rate will be, given existing information, over the *next* three months. The inflation rate for January is just that: the percentage change in the price level, say the CPI, between January 2003 and December 2002. Thus, while the *ex post* real rate of interest is easier to calculate, it is obvious that it may not capture the exact characteristics of what one wants in an interest rate, especially the forward-looking aspect.

There have been several innovations in the market for U.S. Treasury securities that explicitly recognize the difference between nominal and real rates of interest. For example, in 1998 the Treasury began to offer savings bonds that promised to provide fixed

Inflation-Indexed Treasury Bonds
Percent, weekly data

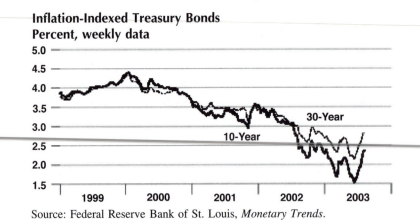

Source: Federal Reserve Bank of St. Louis, *Monetary Trends*.

real rates of interest to investors. As the Treasury stated in their press release, "The Series I Inflation-Indexed Savings Bonds (I-Bonds) offer Americans protection from inflation, insuring investors a real rate of return over and above inflation. The earnings rate an investor makes on inflation-protected bonds is the combination of two rates: (1) a fixed rate of return announced by the Treasury Department that remains the same for the life of the bond; and (2) a rate of inflation that is adjusted every six months by the Bureau of Labor Statistics to reflect changes in the Consumer Price Index for all Urban Consumers (CPI-U)." In this manner, the so-called I-Bonds served to protect investors from unforeseen future inflation.

The U.S. Treasury also issues an inflation indexed security call the Treasury Inflation Indexed Security, or TIIS. First issued January 1997, these securities—a type of financial innovation—are another example of how the Treasury attempts to protect investors from the affects of inflation. In effect, the TIIS adjusts the nominal rate of interest for changes in the inflation rate. In this case, the principal adjusts for inflation daily but is paid only at maturity. The recent behavior of the 10-year and 30-year TIIS securities is shown in the above chart.

FURTHER READING

Mishkin, Frederic S., and Stanley Eakins. *Financial Markets and Institutions*. 4th edition. Boston: Addison Wesley, 2003.

EXCESS DEMAND. Suppose that at a price of $35 a pair, consumers buy 100 pair of jeans each day, and the jean company produces 100 pair of jeans per day for sale. In that case, the quantity demanded by consumers (100) and the quantity supplied by the manufacturer (100) is the same. The $35 price at which the amount produced equals the amount purchased is called the **equilibrium** price. What happens if the price is *lowered*? What if tomorrow the price is set at $20? If income and preferences have not changed appreciably overnight, and the price of other competing goods, such as the price of khakis, has not changed, it is likely that people will respond to the lower price by trying to buy more. The manufacturer, however, produces fewer pairs of jeans because selling at this lower price is not as profitable as selling at the higher price. More people are willing to buy jeans at $20 than the manufacturer is willing to sell. At this lower price, then, the quantity demanded of jeans is greater than the quantity supplied. This condition defines excess demand. Excess demand is the same as a *shortage*. In this case, at $20 there is a shortage of jeans.

As with the notion of **excess supply**, the idea of excess demand is a useful concept in discussing monetary policy. For example, if the Federal Reserve undertakes a policy to decrease reserves in the banking system, during the initial stages of implementing this policy it may be true that there is an excess demand of reserves. If this is true, then the Federal Reserve may be attempting to raise interest rates. Why? Because when there is a shortage of something, in this case bank reserves, the "price"—in this case the federal funds rate—is pushed higher.

FURTHER READING

Taylor, John B. *Economics*. 4th edition. Boston: Houghton Mifflin, 2004.

EXCESS RESERVES. Banks are required by the Federal Reserve to hold **reserves** against their deposits. If a bank has $100 in checking deposits, the Federal Reserve may require the bank to hold $3 of it in reserve. Banks typically hold more than the required amount. If banks held $6 in reserves against $100 in deposits, the additional $3 is referred to as excess reserves. Reserves are deposited (electronically) with the Federal Reserve or are held as cash in the bank's vault. In either case, reserves earn no interest for the bank. Why then would banks hold more reserves than are required? The reason is that excess reserves are used by banks as an extra cushion against some unforeseen event when the bank may need that money. For example, if there is an unexpected withdrawal of deposits from a bank—everyone decides to convert their checking deposits to cash—the bank would use the excess reserves to satisfy this increased demand for **currency**. Indeed, in times of increased uncertainty, such as war or unsettled financial times, excess reserve holdings by banks increase. Even though banks are losing potential profits by not lending out this money or buying securities, the ability to meet unexpected demands by customers outweighs this cost.

FURTHER READING

Bindseil, Ulrich, Gonzalo Camba-Mendez, Astrid Hirsch, and Benedict Weller. "Excess Reserves and the Implementation of Monetary Policy in the ECB." European Central Bank Working Paper No. 361 (May 2004); Dow, J. P. "The Demand for Excess Reserves." *Southern Economic Journal* 67 (2001): 685–700.

EXCESS SUPPLY. This condition is exactly the opposite from **excess demand**, which is discussed earlier. So, let's use the same example as there. As in the example for excess demand, suppose that a pair of jeans sells for $35. At that price consumers are willing to purchase 100 pairs a day, and the company making jeans is willing to produce 100 pairs a day for sale. In that case, the quantity demanded by consumers and the quantity supplied by the manufacturer is the same. What happens if the price is *raised*? Suppose that tomorrow the price for a pair of jeans is set at $50, higher than the original **equilibrium** price. Because overnight incomes have not changed appreciably, nor has the price of competing goods, it is likely that people will respond to the higher price by buying fewer pairs. Seeing the potential for greater profits, however, the manufacturer produces more pairs of jeans and is willing to sell them at this higher price. But with fewer people buying jeans at $50 than the manufacturer is willing to sell, the quantity of jeans supplied is greater than the quantity demanded. This condition defines an excess supply. In everyday terms, an excess supply is the same as a *surplus*. In this case, at $50 there is a surplus of jeans.

As with the notion of excess demand, the idea of excess supply is a useful concept in discussing monetary policy. For example, if the Federal Reserve undertakes a policy to increase reserves in the banking system, during the initial stages of implementing this policy it may be true that there is an excess supply of reserves. If this is true, then the Federal Reserve may be attempting to reduce interest rates. Why? Because when there is a surplus of something, in this case bank reserves, the "price"—in this case the federal funds rate—is pushed lower.

FURTHER READING

Taylor, John B. *Economics*. 4th edition. Boston: Houghton Mifflin, 2004.

EXCHANGE RATE. The exchange rate is a price, just like the price of a movie ticket or a hamburger. The difference is that the price of a hamburger is the exchange rate of burgers for dollars. An exchange rate, on the other hand, is the price of one **currency** expressed in terms of another. If you pick up a copy of the magazine *The Economist* or the newspaper the *Wall Street Journal*, the exchange rate between the U.S. dollar and many other currencies is reported. Part of the table reported in the October 4, 2003, *Economist* is reproduced below. On the date that the table was selected, you can, for example, see that a Canadian dollar exchanged at a rate of $1.35 Canadian for each $1 U.S. In other words, it took 1.35 Canadian dollars to buy one U.S. dollar. Take the inverse of it and you get how much the Canadian dollar was worth in terms of U.S. dollars: $0.74, or 74 cents (= 1/1.35). That means that if you are planning a trip to Canada, at that exchange rate, when you exchanged U.S. dollars for Canadian dollars—Canadian shops do not accept U.S. dollars—you would have received one Canadian dollar for every 74 U.S. cents you had.

In a world that is becoming increasingly connected, foreign exchange rates are an important component to business. Foreign producers of goods we want, like Korean televisions,

Country	Currency Units (per $)*
Argentina	2.92
Australia	1.47
Canada	1.35
China	8.28
Japan	111
Sweden	7.72
Euro area	0.85
Russia	30.5
Turkey	1,390,000

*As of October 1, 2003.
Source: *The Economist* (October 4, 2003).

Japanese DVD players, or German cars, do not accept U.S. dollars for their goods. Rather, they wish to be paid in their own country's currency. In order to buy these goods, we must therefore exchange our dollars for their currency. This means that changes in the demand for goods across countries affects the demand for currencies and, as a result, exchange rates. If everybody suddenly wants Canadian timber, everyone will first try to acquire Canadian dollars to make the purchase. This increase in demand for Canadian dollars given the supply puts upward pressure on its exchange rate. If the Canadian government does not supply more Canadian dollars, the Canadian dollar's exchange rate rises relative to that of other currencies. Put differently, the Canadian dollar "appreciates" in value relative to other currencies. In our numerical example above, it now may take 80 or 90 U.S. cents to get one Canadian dollar. Of course, if no body wants Canadian goods, then the demand for the Canadian dollar sags and pushes its exchange rate downward, or a depreciation.

Movements in exchange rates also reflect the demand for things other than the timber or televisions a country might export. Individuals wanting to purchase foreign financial assets, such as bonds or stocks, also must first convert their currency into that of the country from which they plan to purchase the financial assets. As the financial assets of one country become relatively more attractive to investors, this also affects exchange rates. For instance, if foreign investors believe that potential returns from investing in U.S. government bonds is greater than the return from buying bonds in other countries, then foreign investors will demand more dollars in order to buy U.S. bonds. This drives up the exchange rate of the U.S. dollar.

These two examples illustrate the fact that movements in exchange rates often are explained by underlying factors, such as changes in the demand for goods or financial assets. It also should be noted that movements in exchange rates affect the competitiveness of one country's goods relative to another. For example, suppose everyone in the United States wants to wear shoes made in the Philippines. Due to demand shifts in the market for shoes, there is an increase in the demand for Philippine pesos by U.S. residents. This causes the exchange value of the peso to appreciate relative to the U.S. dollar. Can this affect financial markets? If investors' **expected returns** have not changed, Philippine financial assets are now at a competitive disadvantage to U.S. financial assets, because it now takes more dollars to get pesos in order to buy Philippine bonds. Investors must now get a higher return on a Philippine financial asset if they are going to continue investing in them. In this case, the increase in the exchange rate (an appreciation of the peso) makes Philippine financial assets less attractive to foreign investors, with all other factors being the same.

Exchange rates are affected by changes in the supply of national currencies, too. During times when the value of a currency is falling, as the dollar was in the early part of 2004, some central banks may attempt to "prop up" the dollar by purchasing dollars in the foreign exchange market. They do this by selling their own currency, or their holdings of other currencies. Why would they do this? Foreign central banks may wish to keep the value of the dollar high, because a falling value of the dollar translates into an appreciation of their own currencies and a change in the relative attractiveness of their goods compared with U.S. goods in the market. In its early years, the Federal Reserve actively intervened in the foreign exchange market to manipulate the foreign exchange value of the dollar. Beginning in the early 1980s, however, such activity was scaled back, allowing market forces to determine the market value of the dollar.

As this discussion suggests, it is important to understand what exchange rates are and how they impact purchasing and investing decisions.

FURTHER READING

Husted, Steven, and Michael Melvin. *International Economics*. New York: HarperCollins, 1995.

EXPECTATIONS. When students leave their homes in the morning for school, they make a choice of whether or not to take along an umbrella. Some look outside and see a bright sunny sky: they decide that an umbrella is unnecessary. Others, seeing the same clear blue sky may opt to carry along an umbrella. These are expectations based on observed factors and on information collected from different sources. Those taking umbrellas, for instance, may have listened to a weather report that called for afternoon thunderstorms. The others simply look outside and assumed that the weather later would be no different that it was in the morning.

Expectations impact almost all of our decisions when you think about it. From the mundane, like taking an umbrella, to more important ones, like which major to chose in college or which stock to buy, expectations influence our behavior in many ways. Expectations also affect the behavior of firms. If firms expect increased business activity, they may respond by building a new store or investing more in newer and bigger factories. Expectations also influence the level of interest rates in financial markets. This affect may come primarily from expectations of higher rates of **inflation**. If a bank makes a **loan** to be repaid in one year, it wants to get back its original loan amount (the principal) plus the cost of making the loan plus any loss in purchasing power. That is, the bank wants at a minimum to be repaid enough money to buy the same amount of goods and services it could have purchased at the time the loan was made. If banks expect inflation to increase in the future, then interest rates on loans are likely to rise to reflect these changing expectations.

Expectations also play a major role in monetary policy. At each meeting of the **Federal Open Market Committee (FOMC)**, for example, staff economists present detailed overviews of data relating to economic activity—growth of real GDP, **unemployment rates**, **inflation** rates, etc.—and developments in financial markets, both domestically and in other countries. Based on this information, forecasts of how the economy will likely respond to different policy actions are made and discussed. In this way, information about the past and forecasts of the future are used by the FOMC members to form individual expectations about which policy to take, or not to take. Of course, only when the future becomes known does the committee find out if their expectations were correct or not, just like the students who decided whether or not to take the umbrella.

For more on the role of expectations in financial markets, see **Efficient Markets Theory**.

FURTHER READING

Poole, William, Robert H. Rasche, and Daniel L. Thornton. "Market Anticipations of Monetary Policy Actions." Federal Reserve Bank of St. Louis *Review* (July/August 2002): 65–93; Poole, William, and Robert H. Rasche. "The Impact of Changes in FOMC Disclosure Practices on the Transparency of Monetary Policy: Are Markets and the FOMC Better 'Synched'?" Federal Reserve Bank of St. Louis *Review* (January/February 2003): 1–9.

EXPECTED RETURN. Suppose an investor faces two choices of what to do with some extra income: invest in the stock market or put the funds into a savings account at the local bank. How would you decide which to do? Is your decision going to be the same as mine? An important factor in this decision process is what each individual expects the return to be on the different financial assets. If the annual interest rate on the savings account is 10 percent, then $100 deposited today will be worth $110 in one year. If stock prices are expected to rise rapidly during the next year, then the expected return from this investment may be greater than 10 percent. That is, you might expect that investing $100 today will be worth $150 one year from now, or an expected return of 50 percent. Expected returns thus affect your decision about where, and whether, you invest or save.

Of course, in this example, the outcome is much less certain for investing in stocks than in the savings account. In such a case, investors factor in the risk of not obtaining some expected return. Changes in expected returns stem from a number of factors. Changes in tax rates on investments alter expected returns. So do movements in market rates of interest that reflect actual or anticipated changes in monetary policy. Regardless of the source, changes in expected returns have significant impacts on investment decisions.

FURTHER READING

Mishkin, Frederic S., and Stanley Eakins. *Financial Markets and Institutions*. 4th edition. Boston: Addison Wesley, 2003.

FEDERAL ADVISORY COUNCIL. The Federal Advisory Council is comprised of one representative from each of the 12 Reserve Banks. The directors of each reserve bank select a council representative. The council meets once every three months with the **Board of Governors**. As its name implies, the council serves in a purely advisory role. Other than providing an appraisal of local and regional business activity and serving as a sounding board for system proposals, the council today actually has very little impact on the making of monetary policy.

During the debate over the act, President **Woodrow Wilson** was staunchly opposed to creating a central bank that was under the control of bankers. Banking representatives, on the other hand, argued that only those with the training and expertise to understand and deal with banking and financial problems—that would be bankers—could guide the central bank. The Federal Advisory Council was thus established as a concession to banking interests when the **Federal Reserve Act of 1913** was being drawn up. The Federal Reserve Act gave the council the power "to confer directly with the Federal Reserve Board [and] to make recommendations in regard to the operations of the Board and Federal Reserve Banks." The Advisory Council, as documented in Meltzer (2003), often opposed board policy positions. Even so, there is little evidence that their opposition has caused the board to alter its course. Today the council is little more than an honorary appointment and plays virtually no role in the setting of monetary policy.

FURTHER READING

Federal Reserve Board of Governors Website: www.federalreserve.gov.

FEDERAL DEPOSIT INSURANCE CORPORATION (FDIC). During the period prior to the **Great Depression**, there were a number of approaches to insure customers' deposits held by banks. In some cases, such as during the **free banking** era (1837–1865), banks were required to deposit state or U.S. bonds with state banking authorities as a means to back their currency. Private insurance schemes also existed during the early part of the twentieth century. Like any other insurance plan, members paid a premium into the fund. In the event of a collapse or a **bank run**, the insurance fund would repay depositors of failed banks that were covered by the insurance fund. While these remedies had limited success, the onset of the Great Depression and the massive number of bank failures dwarfed the capacity of any private insurance fund to cover the losses of depositors around the country.

As a remedy to this situation, in 1933 Congress passed the **Banking Act of 1933**. This act led to sweeping changes in the banking system and its regulation. One aspect of the change was the creation of the Federal Deposit Insurance Corporation, or FDIC. The FDIC was created as the federal agency to provide nationwide insurance protection to depositors should their bank, assuming it was a member of FDIC, fail.

The FDIC's main function is to insure the bank deposits of individuals in all 50 states, the District of Columbia, the Virgin Islands, Guam, and Puerto Rico. That is, if your bank should close its doors and be unable to repay to you money deposited, your deposits would be covered by the FDIC. Today, deposits up to $100,000 held at member banks are insured by the FDIC. The catch is that your bank must be a member of the FDIC in order to have its deposits covered against loss. To be insured by the FDIC, a bank must pay a premium four times a year to the FDIC based on the amount of deposits it holds. The money collected by the FDIC is put into either the Bank Insurance Fund (BIF) or the Savings Association Insurance Fund (SAIF). As suggested by the names, today the FDIC insures savings and loan associations as well as banks. This is a change from earlier times when savings and loans were insured by the Federal Savings and Loan Insurance Corporation (FSLIC), which was separate from the FDIC.

After the near-collapse of the savings and loan industry during the 1980s, the FDIC assumed the duty of insuring savings and loans, in addition to banks. It is from the BIF or SAIF funds that the FDIC pays depositors to cover their losses. When a bank fails, FDIC staff arrive at the failed institution and use money from the BIF or SAIF to reimburse insured depositors. Once depositors have been repaid, the FDIC recovers a portion of these funds from selling the failed bank's loans and other assets, often times to banks in the same market.

The FDIC will insure a bank's deposits only if the bank can demonstrate that it is being run profitably and that the managers of the bank are not taking undue risks with the depositors' money. There have been many studies of the FDIC and the general nature of deposit insurance. One issue that arises in such a discussion is that insurance, whether it is for collision coverage on your car, accidental injury, or loss of deposit, creates something call **moral hazard**. The idea is that if an individual has collision insurance, then he may drive more recklessly than if any damage or injury claim would be borne solely by the individual. The same argument holds for deposit insurance.

To see this, consider the following scenario. Because a bank is not liable for your deposit money—the FDIC will cover any losses you incur if the bank closes—bank managers may be emboldened to make riskier but higher-return loans. By making riskier loans, the bank either enjoys greater profitability—the oil well hits a pocket of oil—or it loses everything, in which case the bank closes and the FDCI pays off the depositors. Because of moral hazard, some have called for the FDIC to alter the way in which insurance premiums are determined. Indeed, the **Federal Deposit Insurance Corporation Improvement Act of 1991** sought to do just that.

The FDIC, in its role as insurer of deposits, undertakes to make sure that banks are not only profitable but also being run within the regulations established by various regulatory bodies. To do this, the FDIC sends visitation teams to banks on a regular basis to determine if they are following the regulations. In addition to auditing the bank's books and examining its loan portfolio, the FDIC ensures that banks are meeting their social obligations by following the Equal Credit Opportunity Act. This act requires banks to treat individuals fairly, without regard to their race, gender, religion, or national origin. Lending decisions must be based on objective criteria, such as credit history and other economic factors, such as income and current debt outstanding, which help the bank determine whether the person will be able to repay the loan as specified in the loan contract.

In addition to overseeing banks, the FDIC is responsible for regulating certain savings banks and state-chartered banks that are not members of the Federal Reserve System. Overall, the FDIC attempts to prevent **bank failures** by closely monitoring bank performance and enforcing regulations intended to make sure that banks and other financial institutions operate in a "safe and sound" manner. Part of the FDIC's function also is to provide evaluations of economic conditions and how they might affect the banking industry. FDIC staff members are trained in economics, statistics, and finance, and they monitor many areas of the economy, from stock markets to home sales to barometers of business activity, in order to evaluate potential trends and their impact on the banking industry. For example, if it appears that a recession is imminent, the FDIC staff may use this information to predict the potential number of bank failures that may occur, an important piece of information for the organization whose job it is to help regulate bank activity and protect depositor's savings.

The FDIC's main office is in Washington, D.C., with eight major regional offices located in Atlanta, Georgia; Boston, Massachusetts; Chicago, Illinois; Dallas, Texas; Kansas City, Missouri; Memphis, Tennessee; New York, New York; and San Francisco, California. In addition to these offices, there are more than 80 small field offices located across the country and used by bank examiners when they are not conducting on-site bank examinations.

FURTHER READING

Federal Deposit Insurance Corporation Website: www.fdic.gov; Meltzer, Allan H. *A History of the Federal Reserve, Vol. 1: 1913–1951.* Chicago: University of Chicago Press, 2003.

FEDERAL DEPOSIT INSURANCE CORPORATION IMPROVEMENT ACT OF 1991. Commonly referred to as FDICIA, this legislation sought to strengthen the ability of the **Federal Deposit Insurance Corporation (FDIC)** to enforce sound banking. A number of reforms to FDIC policies were implemented or set into motion with the FDICIA. The major change instituted a switch to risk-based pricing of banks' insurance premiums. Historically, a bank paid a fee (an insurance premium) to the FDIC based only on the amount of its deposits. This approach meant that banks who were undertaking highly risky activities paid the same insurance as banks that took on very modest amounts of risk. This approach is comparable to charging smokers and non-smokers of the same weight the same premium for health insurance. (*See the discussion of* **Moral Hazard**.)

FDICIA established three different risk categories for banks, based on their capital. Banks that are "well capitalized" pay a lower premium than banks with "less than adequate" capital. In this way the FDIC shifted the burden of shouldering depositor loss to the banks. FDICIA also established a "prompt closure" rule that requires the FDIC to take quick corrective action when a bank's capital falls below required levels. This part of the act helped to reduce the **regulatory forbearance** that characterized earlier times, when examiners allowed insolvent banks to remain open, hoping that they could correct their problems and achieve capital adequacy. After the act, banks could be closed or put under the control of other individuals within 90 days.

The FDICIA also made other changes. FDICIA provided additional funding for the FDIC following the tremendous outflow of funds associated with the banking failures of the early 1980s. It limited **brokered deposits** so that individuals could not strain the insurance fund by creating multiple deposits of $100,000 in order to skirt the stipulation that FDIC insurance only covers deposits up to $100,000. The act increased the number of bank examinations and reporting requirements for member banks, and it strengthened the ability of the Federal Reserve to regulate the activity of foreign banks operating in the United States.

FURTHER READING

Eisenbeis, Robert, and Larry D. Wall. "Reforming Deposit Insurance and FDICIA." Federal Reserve Bank of Atlanta *Economic Review* (First Quarter 2002): 1–16; Mishkin, Frederic S., and Stanley Eakins. *Financial Markets and Institutions*. 4th edition. Boston: Addison Wesley, 2003.

FEDERAL FUNDS. Federal funds are funds made available over a very short time—usually overnight—between banks. For the most part, these funds are deposits at Federal Reserve Banks; that is, **reserves** of banks being held to meet their **reserve requirements**. Federal funds become available when a bank, upon closing its books for the day, finds that it is holding more reserves than required by law. Because reserves do not generate a bank any interest income, banks lend these excess funds out to other banks that are in the opposite position; that is, to banks that find themselves with fewer reserves than required. Even though trading in such funds began in the 1920s among a small group of New York City banks, it has grown to be the center of the market for short-term funds.

Federal funds can be distinguished from other short-term or money market instruments along two lines. First, as mentioned, they are funds that are immediately available, funds that can be transferred between depository institutions within a single day, usually overnight. Since passage of the **Depository Institutions Deregulation and Monetary Control Act (DIDMCA) of 1980**, or DIDMCA, the primary players in the federal funds market—both borrowers and lenders—are those depository institutions that are required by law to hold reserves with Federal Reserve Banks, including **commercial banks**, savings banks, credit unions, and savings and loan associations. Second, federal funds borrowed generally are exempt from both reserve requirements and interest rate ceilings, although this aspect of federal funds also closely matches the characteristics of **repurchase agreements**.

The existence of the federal funds market represents an efficient response by banks to variations in their assets and liabilities. For instance, an unexpected inflow of deposits into checking accounts may increase the reserves a bank is required to hold. Until it has altered its portfolio of deposits and loans to meet this change, it may use the federal funds market to meet the temporary imbalance. Not only are banks in need of funds able to acquire them in a very liquid market, termed a federal funds purchase, but they also are able to avoid borrowing funds from the Federal Reserve through the **discount window**. Similarly, banks can earn interest income by lending out their excess reserves, termed a federal funds sale.

How does a federal funds transaction take place? Suppose a bank finds itself without enough reserves to meet its required reserve position. In this case, the bank wishes to buy federal funds. It can accomplish this by locating a seller through an existing relationship, or it can work through a federal funds broker. Suppose that our bank has found a willing seller of funds. When the transaction is completed, if the banks are located in the same Federal Reserve District, the bank selling the funds authorizes the Federal Reserve to debit its reserve account for the amount of funds sold and to credit the reserve account for the bank purchasing the funds. In effect, the two banks are simply transferring—electronically—reserves being held by their District Bank. In this instance, the Federal Reserve's wire transfer system, known as **Fedwire**, is used to complete the transfer. If the two banks are not located in the same district, then the banks' transaction is carried out between the different District Banks. Although a bit more complicated, the end result is the same: The bank borrowing federal funds has its reserve account increased by the amount borrowed, and the bank selling funds has its reserve account decreased by the same amount.

Most of the large federal funds transactions, those amounting to trades of $25 million or more, are carried out through brokers. Federal funds brokers are intermediaries. They do not take positions themselves but simply facilitate the transfer of funds from one institution to another. In essence, their specialty is information: they bring together buyers and sellers. Maerowitz (1981, p. 3) describes federal funds brokers as those firms who "maintain frequent telephone contact with active buyers and sellers of federal funds. Brokers match federal funds purchase and sale orders in return for a commission on each completed transaction." Because of competition in the market, there generally is one interest rate throughout the market. Meulendyke (1998, p. 85) elaborates on the role of the brokers: "The brokers take bids and offers from banks by phone, charging each party to the trade a commission of 50 cents per $1 million. Generally either 1/16 or 1/8 percentage point separates the bid from the offer (with occasional spreads of 1/32). If the market is very one-sided or rates are changing rapidly, the spread may be much greater, as large as several percentage points."

Because federal funds transactions involve the trading of reserves, they are in effect unsecured **loans** between the two parties. That means that the trades are made without a formal, written contract. Sometimes, when the trade occurs between two known parties, an oral agreement or simply each bank's reputation is enough to satisfy any uncertainty about the party with whom the trade is taking place. When brokers are used, they provide information about the quality of a loan, another reason why brokers earn a commission for their services.

In addition to the market for overnight loans, there is a market for "term federal funds." In this case, the loan period is specified for a fixed term to maturity with a daily fixed interest rate agreed upon. Another type of federal funds loan is the "continuing contract." In this version the agreement is to make an overnight loan of funds on a continuing basis, automatically renewed, until terminated by the borrower or seller. This type of arrangement is used by banks that often purchase funds from correspondent banks. Until notified otherwise, the overnight loan takes place over and over. This is efficient for both parties: Neither needs to search for a trading partner and neither needs to engage a broker for each and every trade. In the case of continuing contract federal funds, the broker's fee is paid only at the time of initial purchase and ultimate sale.

The federal funds market plays a key role in the conduct of monetary policy. The trading of federal funds represents changes in the reserve position of the banking system. An increase in the demand for funds signals that banks are in need of reserves and may mean that business loan demand is on the rise. This increased demand for federal funds relative to their current supply affects the rate at which federal funds are traded. This rate, known as the **federal funds rate**, is a key barometer of money market pressures and is used by the Federal Reserve as a tool for monetary policy. For example, members of the trading desk at the New York Reserve Bank keep tabs on activity in the federal funds market by monitoring the information flows from financial market news services and by telephoning federal funds brokers routinely during the day to keep abreast of the rates and the volume of activity, which usually measures in the billions of dollars every day.

FURTHER READING

Goodfriend, Marvin, and William Whelpley. "Federal Funds." *Instruments of the Money Market.* Richmond: Federal Reserve Bank of Richmond, 1998; Maerowitz, Seth P. "The Market for Federal Funds." Federal Reserve Bank of Richmond *Economic Review* (July/August 1981): 3–7; Muelendyke, Ann-Marie. *U.S. Monetary Policy & Financial Markets.* New York: Federal Reserve Bank of New York, 1998; Willis, Parker B. *The Federal Funds Market: Its Origin and Development.* Boston: Federal Reserve Bank of Boston, 1970.

FEDERAL FUNDS FUTURES MARKET. Fed watchers and financial market participants constantly attempt to guess what the direction and level of future interest rate movements are going to be. Because the Federal Reserve relies on the **federal funds rate** as its primary policy instrument, this rate serves as the bellwether rate for anyone trying to predict the future course of interest rates and monetary policy. Prior to 1988, trying to predict future interest rates was difficult because observed changes in rates could and often did arise due to nonmonetary policy factors. Trying to predict what the monetary policymakers were doing often confused Federal Reserve policy actions with affects coming from changes in the economy, such as the onset of a recession or an increase in inflation rates.

In October 1988, this changed somewhat when the Chicago Board of Trade (CBOT) introduced trading in the Federal Funds Futures contract. Trading in this contract represents a market-based forecast by market participants of future interest rates on federal funds. Because of its narrowness, many consider the interest rate established in the futures market as an unbiased predictor of the expected federal funds rate. That is to say, because traders in this contract focus on the actions of the Federal Reserve, movements in the futures rate often reflect anticipated changes in monetary policy.

If someone wants to get a good forecast of what the market thinks the Federal Reserve's federal funds rate target is over the next several months, the Federal Funds Futures market is a good place to look. And it is freely available to anyone because the activity in the CBOT markets is reported in financial publications, such as the *Wall Street Journal*. To find the market's prediction of the federal funds rate, find the page reporting activity in futures markets, located in the "Money and Investing" section of the *Journal*. In the space labeled "Interest Rate Futures," there is reported information about 30-day federal funds. The information reported there is about trading in the Federal Funds Futures contract.

Several bits of information are provided: month of contract, the high and low prices, the volume of trading, etc. To find the market's forecast, look down the column labeled "settle." Because it is recorded as a price, subtract the listed price from 100 and that is the interest rate. For example, using the November 6, 2003, *Journal*, the settle price for the previous day's trading in the Federal Funds Futures contract for that December is listed as 98.99. Subtract 98.99 from 100 and the implied interest rate is 1.01. In other words, the market believed that the Federal Reserve would keep the federal funds rate at about 1 percent through the end of 2003. In fact, the federal funds rate held at 1 percent through the end of 2003.

What about farther into the future? The listing includes contracts that run as far as six or seven months in the future. In the November 6, 2003, *Journal,* for example, a contract for July 2004 is listed. Its settle price is 98.49, which yields an interest rate of 1.51. This means that, as of November 5, the futures market participants anticipated that the Federal Reserve would raise the federal funds rate from its current rate (1 percent) to about 1.5 percent. Such information can be used by individuals in a wide variety of situations, from businesses trying to plan future investment activities, to banks trying to determine what rates they may face in the future, both in terms of costs to acquire funds—deposit rates—or rates to charge on loans.

FURTHER READING

Chicago Board of Trade. *Insights into Pricing the CBOT Federal Funds Futures Contract.* 1997; Owens, Raymond E., and Roy H. Webb. "Using the Federal Funds Futures Market to Predict Monetary Policy Actions." Federal Reserve Bank of Richmond *Economic Quarterly* (Spring 2001): 69–77.

FEDERAL FUNDS RATE. The federal funds rate is the interest rate charged to borrow **federal funds**. Because federal funds are those **excess reserves** that banks lend each other in an overnight market, the federal funds rate is sensitive to **open market operations**, the buying and selling of government securities by the Federal Reserve that increases or decreases, respectively, the reserves of the banking system. This link to policy actions makes the federal funds rate one of the most closely watched interest rates in all financial markets. (A discussion of how the Federal Reserve goes about targeting the federal funds rate can be found in **Federal Funds Rate Targeting**.)

Historically the Federal Reserve limited borrowing from the **discount window**, so the federal funds market became banks' alternative source of funds to meet tempo-rary shortages. In the 1960s, banks were actively managing the liability side of their portfolios—the deposit side of their balance sheets—which led to banks more actively using the federal funds market. Prior to this time, the federal funds rate seldom rose above the **discount rate** (Maerowitz, 1981). This meant that the Federal Reserve was adminis-tering the discount window and the discount rate to act as a penalty to banks in need of temporary funds. But modern liability management techniques meant that banks were often using the federal funds market to meet reserve shortfalls. At this time they seemed willing to pay the higher rate for federal funds in order not to use the discount window.

Since that time, the Federal Reserve has actively used the federal funds rate as its principal operating target. By altering the available supply of reserves in the banking system through open market sales and purchases of government securities, the Federal Reserve tries to manipulate the federal funds rate to achieve its long-term goals of low inflation and stable economic growth. As noted in the Federal Reserve Bank of New York publication *Fednotes* (2002), "Movements in the federal funds rate have important implications for the loan and investment policies of all financial institutions, especially for commercial bank decisions concerning loans to businesses, individuals, and foreign institutions. Financial managers compare the federal funds rate with yields on other investments before choosing the financial assets in which they will invest or the term over which they will borrow." Moreover, the federal funds rate is often thought to establish the base borrowing rate upon which other rates depend. Movements in the federal funds rate are often paralleled by market interest rates on other short-term financial assets, such as **commercial paper** or short-term Treasury securities. Because changes in these rates affect a myriad of other rates, from bank loan rates to mortgage rates, movements in the federal funds rate are closely watched.

To see how the Federal Reserve has accomplished this, the next entry explains the process of targeting on the federal funds rate in more detail.

FURTHER READING

Maerowitz, Seth P. "The Market for Federal Funds." Federal Reserve Bank of Richmond *Economic Review* (July/August 1981): 3-7; Federal Reserve Bank of New York. "Federal Funds." *Fedpoint* (2002). Website: www.newyorkfed.org.

FEDERAL FUNDS RATE TARGETING. During the 1950s and 1960s, the Federal Reserve attempted to achieve its policy goals and objectives—promoting economic growth in a low-inflation environment—by focusing on activity in financial markets. That is, policymakers used an approach that has been dubbed "tone and feel" to describe how they would alter policy based on changes in financial markets, whether in terms of interest rate changes or in terms of changes to reserve holdings by banks. Easing and tightening conditions in the market often was gauged by changes in so-called free reserves in the banking system, equal to excess reserves minus discount window borrowings.

This approach to policy began to fail in the 1960s, especially in terms of meeting the objective of keeping inflation low. Although low by post-World War II standards, inflation began to creep upward in the 1960s. This led a number of economists, most notably the economists associated with the Monetarist school of thought, to argue for alternative policies. Led by Chairman of the Federal Reserve **Arthur Burns**, in 1970 it was announced that henceforth the Federal Reserve would focus its policy actions more on controlling the behavior of the monetary aggregates and less on free reserves. At the same time, policymakers were concerned about unwanted swings in interest rates. Policy during the 1970s was set by announcing relatively wide target growth rates for the monetary aggregates and fairly narrow ranges for the federal funds rate. Although monetary aggregate targets were announced, it became very clear that the policymakers gave movements in the federal funds rate top priority in setting and changing the direction of policy. Until 1979, the Federal Reserve was setting policy on the basis of a federal funds rate targeting scheme.

To see how such a policy operates, look at the diagram on top of the next page. In that diagram are shown the demand and supply curves for bank reserves. Because the federal funds rate represents the rate at which banks lend excess reserves on an overnight basis, this diagram depicts how changes in demand and supply determine the funds rate.

In the diagram on bottom of the next page, notice that the intersection of the demand for and supply of reserves is at the federal funds rate, for this example, 5 percent. Let's suppose that this is the rate that monetary policymakers are targeting. That is, any developments in

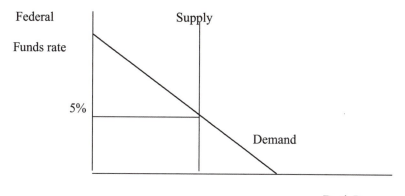

Bank Reserves

the market for bank reserves that push the federal funds rate away from 5 percent, up or down, will be offset. This is the sense in which the federal funds rate is being "targeted."

A major difficulty with this approach to monetary policy is that external factors often alter the conditions in the market requiring the Federal Reserve to intervene if the target rate is going to be maintained. For example, in the early 1970s the economy grew rapidly. Along with economic growth came higher rates of inflation. In terms of the diagram above, the effects of this economic boom was to increase the demand for bank reserves, as indicated by the higher demand curve, labeled D2 in the diagram below. If there was no change in the supply of reserves—something over which the Federal Reserve has direct control through its buying and selling of government securities to the banking system (*see* **Open Market Operations**)—the affect of this increase in demand for reserves is an increase in the federal funds rate. This is illustrated in the accompanying diagram as an increase in the federal funds rate from 5 percent to 10 percent.

The dilemma for the Federal Reserve is that to maintain the funds rate at the desired target level, the Federal Reserve was required to push more reserves into the banking system through its open market operations. This action had the effect of shifting the supply curve to the right, shown in the diagram as S2. Notice that while this action returns the funds rate back to the desired target level of 5 percent, it simultaneously increased the amount of

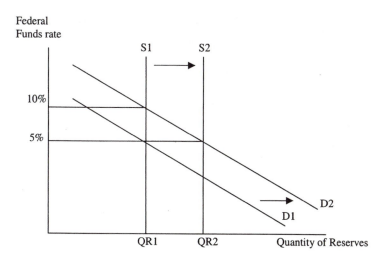

121

Fed Funds (effective)

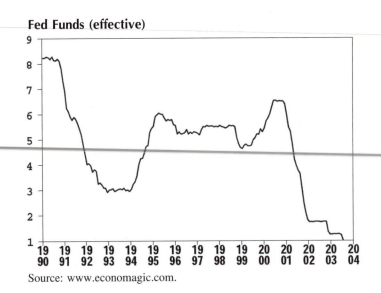

Source: www.economagic.com.

reserves in the banking system. As discussed elsewhere (*see* **Reserves**), because reserves do not generate income for banks, they attempt to reduce any excess holdings by making loans or buying securities. The effect, overall, is to provide further stimulus to the economy. This sets into motion a further increase in reserve demand, which precipitates another round of increased supply, and so on.

This episode illustrates the fact that a policy aimed at hitting a specific federal funds rate target requires that policy be procyclical. That is to say, when economic activity begins to put upward pressure on rates, the Federal Reserve must accommodate these demands by supplying more reserves. If it doesn't, rates rise and the targets are violated. (The same effects occur in reverse when there is a decline in economic activity which causes the demand for bank reserves to fall.)

Can targeting the federal funds rate work? After an ill-fated attempt during the period 1979–1982 to try to control monetary aggregates, the Federal Reserve returned to a funds rate targeting policy. What sets the most recent version of this policy approach apart from the earlier one is that the Federal Reserve has become much more proactive in changing the target rates. For instance, during the 1990s the Federal Reserve actively changed the funds rate target as dictated by economic events. During times when the Federal Reserve believed that inflation was a likely possibility, the funds rate was raised. As shown in the chart above, there were times when the Federal Reserve was able to maintain the funds rate at some desired level for relatively long periods. For example, between late 1992 and early 1994, the funds rate target did not change from 3 percent. More recently, however, the Federal Reserve actively reduced the funds rate from 6.5 percent to 1.0 percent between 2001 and mid-2003.

FURTHER READING

Federal Reserve Bank of New York. *Intermediate Targets and Indicators for Monetary Policy.* (1990); Gilbert, R. Alton. "A Case Study of Monetary Control: 1980–82." Federal Reserve Bank of St. Louis *Review* (September/October 1990): 35–58; Davidson, Lawrence, and R. W. Hafer. "Some

Evidence on Selecting an Intermediate Target of Monetary Policy." *Southern Economic Journal* (October 1983): 406–21.

FEDERAL OPEN MARKET COMMITTEE (FOMC). The Federal Open Market Committee, more commonly known as the FOMC, is the policymaking arm of the Federal Reserve System. The FOMC is comprised of the seven members of the **Board of Governors** and the 12 presidents of the **District Federal Reserve Banks**. Although each president is a sitting member of the FOMC, only five of the presidents vote on policy decisions at any one meeting. Thus, for each decision, the FOMC has a voting membership of 12: the seven governors and five of the 12 bank presidents. Of the bank presidents, the president of the Federal Reserve Bank of New York sits as a permanent voting member of the FOMC. The other presidents serve one-year terms as voting members in a rotation that is set by law. Nine of the Reserve Bank presidents vote one year out of every three, whereas the presidents of the Federal Reserve Banks of Chicago and Cleveland vote in alternate years.

Although in the past the FOMC met many times a year, sometimes even every couple of weeks, the FOMC is required by law to meet at least four times a year. Today the FOMC meets about every six weeks, or eight times a year. The scheduled meetings of the FOMC usually last one or two days and are held at the Board of Governors building in Washington, D.C. In addition to the Federal Reserve's Board of Governors (BOG) and the presidents of the 12 District Banks, the meetings are attended by some senior Federal Reserve staff members who make presentations about current economic and financial conditions. There are times, however, when the FOMC has an intrameeting discussion of policy. At some of these meetings, changes in monetary policy take place. More often than not, however, intrameeting changes in policy occur in response to some unforeseen event that may have direct consequences for the financial markets and the economy. For example, the September 17, 2001, meeting was convened in the wake of the September 11 terrorist attacks on the Pentagon and the World Trade Center.

Although the FOMC is the most powerful policymaking body within the Federal Reserve System, that was not always the case. In fact, the FOMC was not established until passage of the **Banking Act of 1935**. Creation of the FOMC is an interesting example of how the prevailing opinion at the time was split between a centralized bank and one that diffused power throughout the system. Under the original **Federal Reserve Act of 1913**, power was diffused throughout the 12 District Banks. This was probably due more to political motivation than to any underlying economic rationale. To a large extent, it reflected the framers' belief that many of the financial problems that had arisen in the past were due in large part to the concentration of financial power in the East, primarily in New York City.

The financial problems associated with the **Great Depression** changed some opinions. The collapse of the banking system and the failure of the Federal Reserve to engage in a sufficiently expansionary monetary policy to counteract the problems caused by the economic downturn led some to believe that a more centralized bank would be able to better coordinate policy and thus avert such events. This movement also was gaining momentum in other areas of government. The movement to centralize power at the federal level is exemplified by the number of national programs enacted to spur economic recovery that remained after the depression had ended.

The move to change the structure of the Federal Reserve System was spearheaded by **Marriner S. Eccles**, who became governor (prior to 1935, the chairman of the board was referred to as governor) of the Federal Reserve Board in 1934. As governor, Eccles pushed for major reforms to the system, not the least of which was a concentration of power in Washington, D.C., and not, as had evolved, in New York City. Although the political infighting is a fascinating story, covering it in detail here would detour us from our main purpose. (See Meltzer, 2003, for an excellent discussion of this episode.) Suffice it to say that the Banking Act of 1935, approved on August 23, led to several important changes in the makeup of the board. In the Federal Reserve Act, the Federal Reserve Board was to be composed of seven members—five were appointed; the secretary of the Treasury, who served as ex-officio chairman of the board; and the comptroller of the currency. The original term of office was 10 years, and the five original members appointed had terms of 2, 4, 6, 8, and 10 years, respectively.

Between 1913 and 1935, the board was altered twice. First, in 1922, the number of members appointed was changed from five to six. In 1933, the term of appointment was lengthened from 10 to 12 years. The Banking Act of 1935 produced the most dramatic change. It changed the name of the Federal Reserve Board to the Board of Governors of the Federal Reserve System. It also increased the number of appointed members from six to seven and further extended their terms to 14 years. Perhaps the biggest change, one that further increased the independence of the Federal Reserve from political persuasion, was removing the secretary of the Treasury and the comptroller of the currency as members of the board. Although the complete independence of the Federal Reserve from the Treasury would not occur until after the Korean War and the **Treasury-Federal Reserve Accord of 1951**, the Banking Act of 1935 to a large extent created the board as we know it today.

The act served to create a true central bank. Unlike many of its counterparts in the world, the Federal Reserve and the FOMC operate largely independent of the political process. The appointment process for both board members and the District Bank presidents is designed to minimize political influences on the FOMC, whether they emanate from Capitol Hill or the White House. For example, even though governors are appointed by the president of the United States with the approval of the U.S. Senate, they serve for 14-year terms, a period longer than any president can serve and longer than the term for any elected office holders. This and the fact that the 14-year terms are staggered—one expires on January 31 in every even-numbered year—in theory limits the ability of a president to name a majority of the board in a four-year presidential term. While this was the intent, today many governors do not serve their entire 14-year terms, thus leading to new appointments. Indeed, President Bill Clinton was able during his tenure to name all of the board members. In addition, the 12 Reserve Bank presidents are appointed by his or her bank's board of directors, with final approval by the Board of Governors. So, as you can see, there has been every attempt to erect a protective wall between the FOMC and the political process.

The typical FOMC meeting begins with a briefing of the committee by board staff economists. The contents of the briefing vary from meeting to meeting, but generally they cover domestic and international economic conditions, financial market developments since the last meeting, and perhaps some discussion of an event or events of current interest. One such topic in recent years was the September 11, 2001, attacks on the World Trade Center in New York City and the Pentagon in Washington, D.C. In addition to the material provided in the briefing, members of the FOMC also review the so-called **green book, blue book,** and **beige book**. These documents contain, respectively, the Federal Reserve Board staff forecasts of economic activity (output growth, unemployment, inflation, etc.) for the immediate future, forecasts and analysis of monetary policy alternatives, and economic conditions in each district. Of these, only the beige book is made available to the public, generally two weeks before each FOMC meeting.

In addition to being briefed by staff economists, the FOMC is apprised of developments in financial and foreign exchange markets by a senior official of the Federal Reserve Bank of New York. Because the New York Federal Reserve is the bank at which all **open market operations** are carried out, the trading activities conducted since the last meeting are discussed. These presentations are then followed by a go-around of opinions and outlooks of the governors and all of the District Bank presidents. This is a time when each member of the FOMC is free to express his or her opinion about the direction of policy and about the circumstances that they believe may warrant a change in policy. After the go-around, the board's director of monetary affairs presents the monetary policy options developed by the staff. Members of the committee then discuss their policy preferences, with the chairman usually waiting until the end to summarize the discussion. It is at this time that the chairman puts his emphasis on the discussion. With the discussion complete, the 12 voting members of the committee vote on the policy actions to be taken over the period until the next meeting.

Although the vote is often unanimous, there are times when someone dissents from the policy. Dissents occur when someone on the FOMC believes that policy should take a different course or be enacted at a different speed. For example, during 2001–2002, the Federal Reserve lowered the **federal funds target rate**, its primary policy tool, several times until it reached a low of 1 percent. During this period when policy was clearly attempting to offset the effects of the 2001 recession, some FOMC members voted against the persistent reduction in rates. Sometimes the dissent was based on the notion that the funds rate should not be pushed too low; at other times it was based on the belief that the FOMC was not pushing it lower fast enough.

The committee issues its policy directive after the vote is taken. The **directive** provides instruction to the open market **trading desk** at the New York Federal Reserve on the direction and thrust of policy. The desk uses the directive to determine open market operations. At the conclusion of its meeting, the FOMC makes public its monetary policy decision. At this time the FOMC states whether it believes that economic conditions pose a greater risk to higher inflation or to slower economic growth. This statement is considered by many to be the FOMC's statement on the direction of policy in the future and is, therefore, scrutinized by the financial community. Indeed, stock prices and interest rates often change dramatically if the statement issued by the FOMC does not match what was expected.

FURTHER READING

Meltzer, Allan H. *A History of the Federal Reserve, Vol. 1: 1913–1951*. Chicago: University of Chicago Press, 2003; Meyer, Laurence H. *A Term at the Fed: An Insider's View*. New York: Harper Collins Publishers, Inc., 2004; Muelendyke, Ann-Marie. *U.S. Monetary Policy & Financial Markets*. New York: Federal Reserve Bank of New York, 1998.

FEDERAL RESERVE ACT OF 1913. On the evening of December 23, 1913, President **Woodrow Wilson** signed into law the Federal Reserve Act. With his signature, the

Federal Reserve System was officially born and a new era of monetary policymaking in the United States was set into motion.

The act was in every way a compromise between competing views. The debate over the structure for the banking system and its regulation, and the oversight of the nation's monetary policy were hotly debated issues for more than a century. Two previous attempts at establishing a central bank—the **First** and **Second Banks of the United States**—had failed by 1836. Between 1836 and 1864, when the National Banking Act was passed, there was no national monetary policy as we know it today. During that time there were numerous experiments with banking that some argue gave rise to numerous **financial panics** and subsequent loss of confidence in banking.

Passage of the **National Banking Act of 1864** was seen by many as an attempt to federalize the nation's monetary system. For example, it taxed out of existence competing currencies that had arisen during the **free banking** era, 1837–1863. In that period banks could issue their own currency after meeting various state regulations and capital requirements. These currencies circulated alongside the national currency and thus competed with it. The National Banking Act, by placing a tax on each dollar issued by the banks, effectively monopolized currency production and circulation in the hands of the federal government. Even so, problems remained. Two key issues were the lack of a **"lender of last resort"** for banks if and when they encountered difficulties stemming from unexpected deposit withdrawals. The other was the "inelasticity" of the currency. This problem arose from the seasonal demands placed on banks, especially in rural areas where demands for credit and currency followed seasonal patterns tied to harvest and planting. Many argued that financial and banking panics—times when there were unexpected needs of currency to meet seasonal demands—often arose from the failure of the system to meet these needs. A centralized banking system, therefore, could supply currency elastically—that is, on demand—and thus thwart the cause of financial panics.

Although the late 1800s were turbulent in both financial and economic terms, it really was the Panic of 1907 that swung the balance in favor of a central bank. The **Panic of 1907** was the most severe of four banking panics that had occurred in the previous 34 years. On the heels of the panic, the **National Monetary Commission** was formed with passage of the **Aldrich-Vreeland Act of 1908**. The commission's charge was to study and analyze the U.S. banking system and the systems of other nations to arrive at some model that could be used for the United States. The National Monetary Commission's analysis indicated that a more substantial overhaul of the banking system was needed to fix the recurring problems of panics. To that end, the commission argued for establishment of a "rediscounting" process whereby banks in need of funds could borrow them—rediscount eligible paper—with the central bank. This would provide the flexibility in the money supply—the elasticity of the currency—that would meet the demands of the economy and avoid banking panics. Amongst other items, the commission also argued for changes in the regulation and supervision of banks.

It was out of the Panic of 1907 and the work of the National Banking Commission that the Federal Reserve Act grew. Although other attempts to reform banking were made between 1908 and 1913, they all failed for a variety of reasons, often political. For example, **Nelson W. Aldrich**, a Republican Senator from Rhode Island, proposed the National Reserve Association. This proposed reform failed as much for the fact that as part of the "Eastern establishment," the reform was rejected by Western and Southern politicians as they faced pressure from their banking constituents. This conflict between urban and rural interests would affect banking legislation and reform for years to come, and perhaps still does. Any plan that smacked of favoring the banks and financial interests of the East was doomed to failure among the agrarian interests in the West and South. Passing any legislation that would satisfy members of both political parties also found tough going because neither party controlled both the Senate and the House of Representatives prior to 1912. Ideas that actually had merit often were lost to the political fighting that took place. The election of 1912 put Woodrow Wilson, a Democrat, into the White House. The election also resulted in a Democratic majority in the Senate, thus providing the Democrats with a controlling majority in both houses. This political change set into motion the move for banking reform.

Carter Glass, the Democratic Representative from Virginia, was given the task of chairing the subcommittee of the House Banking and Currency Committee with instructions to devise a reserve banking system. Although Glass is sometimes called the "father" of the Federal Reserve System, and while he did have a prominent role in the development and eventual passage of the act, the act represents the debate and compromise of many individuals. Senator Robert Owen, a Republican from Oklahoma and chairman of the Senate Banking and Currency Committee, was the bill's sponsor in the Senate. Indeed, both men joined Wilson at his side as he signed the act into law.

The Minneapolis Federal Reserve (1988) observes that the Federal Reserve Act "was similar to the earlier plan launched by Senator Aldrich, except, of course, that private banks were not given as much control. Also, another primary difference in the Federal Reserve Act was the provision that all nationally chartered banks must be members of the Federal Reserve System. Many private banks, obviously, were opposed to certain provisions of the Federal Reserve Act because they reduced the banks' influence." Not only did the act cause some concern in the banking community over loss of power, but it also flamed the debate over the trustworthiness of bankers and the banking system. For example, an article in the *New York Times* suggested that the act "reflects the rooted dislike and distrust of banks and bankers that has been for many years a great moving force in the Democratic Party. . . . The measure goes to the very extreme in establishing absolute political control over the business of banking" (cited in Minneapolis Federal Reserve Bank *The Region* [1988])

Passage of the Federal Reserve Act created a central body—the Federal Reserve Board—and a system of geographically dispersed **District Federal Reserve Banks**. At the time, the board did not have the power that characterizes the Board of Governors today. The policymaking power of the system lied in the hands of the reserve banks. And the banks were given a direct role in solving the problems that had confronted the nation's banking system. As is stated in the preamble to the act: "To provide for the establishment of Federal reserve banks, to furnish an elastic currency, to afford means of rediscounting commercial paper, to establish a more effective supervision of banking in the United States, and for other purposes."

The act called for establishing a system of up to 12 Federal Reserve Banks that would coordinate policy with a seven-member Federal Reserve Board in Washington. As noted elsewhere (*see* **Board of Governors**; **Federal Open Market Committee [FOMC]**; and **District Federal Reserve Banks**), the system's makeup changed over the years, but the basic structure remained the same. The only major overhaul since the act was passed almost a century ago was the changes in the structure and power of the Board of Governors: In the mid-1930s, the board and the Federal Open Market Committee became the centralized decision-making bodies in the system. Much of the power that was once wielded by the District Banks now flows from Washington, D.C.

Aside from creating the structure of the Federal Reserve System, the act also delineated the role of the nation's central bank. As noted in the act, the District Banks now had the power to:

- Receive from any of its member banks, and from the United States, deposits of current funds in lawful money, national bank notes, Federal Reserve notes, or checks and drafts upon solvent member banks, payable upon presentation; or, solely for exchange purposes, may receive from other Federal reserve banks deposits in current funds in lawful money, national bank notes, or checks and drafts upon solvent member banks, payable upon presentation
- Discount notes, drafts, and bills of exchange arising out of actual commercial transactions
- Purchase and sell in the open market, at home or abroad, either to or from domestic or foreign banks, firms, corporations or individuals, cable transfers and banker's acceptances and bills of exchange
- Deal in gold coin and bullion
- Buy and sell United States government securities
- Establish from time to time, subject to review and determination of the Federal Reserve Board, rates of discount
- Establish accounts with other Federal Reserve Banks
- Issue Federal Reserve notes, obligations of the United States Government. (Moore, 1990)

This laundry list of activities spelled out the wide scope of the new Federal Reserve System. The District Banks could rediscount paper brought by banks—the **discount window** mechanism—and thus serve as a **lender of last resort**. That is, serve as the bankers' bank. This allowed the Federal Reserve to meet increased demands for currency as the need arose, thus enabling it to provide an elastic currency and offset the pressures that previously had given rise to banking panics. They also could buy and sell government securities—**open market operations**. Although this operation would eventually end up being a function of the trading desk at the New York Federal Reserve Bank, originally this function was shared by all reserve banks. And the banks could issue Federal Reserve notes, again allowing it to meet the demands of commerce. Although the notion that the Federal Reserve would stand ready to meet the currency demands of business would fall into disfavor over time—this approach created a procyclical policy, increasing funds when the economy is growing and reducing them when it is slowing—the very fact that the act made this a part of the change suggested that the new system was poised to meet difficulties in the banking system in a way that had not yet been attempted in United States.

The act represents a major milestone in U.S. economic history. Creation of the Federal Reserve was crucial to the economic growth of the United States. Although Carter Glass may have overstated the ability of the Federal Reserve—he opined that "it wrecked the old system of reserve deposits which was a breeder of panics" (cited in Moore, 1990, p. 8)—the system has evolved to meet new challenges. The evolution of the system was recognized by those who wrote the act. The last sentence of the act contains the caveat that the government has "the right to amend, alter, or repeal this Act is hereby expressly reserved." The Minneapolis Federal Reserve (1988) suggests that "the rules had to be developed as the game was learned—decisions were made as unprecedented situations arose . . . [while] Fed officials were seemingly unprepared to deal with [the Great Depression] and . . . was criticized as having failed in its mission. Nearly 60 years later, however, the Fed was largely credited with helping to stem the negative impacts of the October 1987 stock plunge.

The Federal Reserve Act is reprinted in its entirety in Appendix A.

FURTHER READING

Moore, Carl H. *The Federal Reserve System: A History of the First 75 Years.* Jefferson, NC: McFarland & Company, 1990; Federal Reserve Bank of Minneapolis. "Born of a Panic: Forming the Federal Reserve System." *The Region* (August 1988); Meltzer, Allan H. *A History of the Federal Reserve, Vol. 1: 1913–1951.* Chicago: University of Chicago Press, 2003; Laughlin, James Lawrence. *The Federal Reserve Act: Its Origin and Problems.* New York: Macmillan Publishing, 1933; Walton, Gary M., and Hugh Rockoff. *History of the American Economy.* 8th edition. Fort Worth, TX: Dryden Press, 1998.

FEDERAL RESERVE *BULLETIN*. The *Bulletin* is a monthly publication of the Federal Reserve **Board of Governors**. The first *Bulletin* was published in May 1915. In that inaugural issue, it stated that "The *Bulletin* is intended to afford a general statement concerning business conditions and events in the Federal Reserve System that will be of interest to all **member banks**." Each issue contains articles about monetary policy, regulatory issues, or international finance. In addition the *Bulletin* contains announcements of changes in banking regulations, reprints of speeches and congressional testimony given by the chairman and other governors, and recent data on various economic measures, such as interest rates, the money supply, output and unemployment. The *Bulletin* is available from the Board of Governors at the Federal Reserve Website: www.federalreserve.gov.

FEDERAL RESERVE NOTES. A Federal Reserve note is the official name for the paper money (**currency**) that we carry around in our pockets and purses. Look at any of the paper bills currently in circulation; the words "Federal Reserve Note" are printed along the top. Unlike previous forms of currency, such as "silver certificates" or "gold certificates"—the reference to a precious metal indicating that the piece of paper could be exchanged for that amount in silver or gold—today's Federal Reserve note is exchangeable only for another one or for coin. That is, go to a bank with a 10-dollar bill, ask to exchange it, and some combination of ones, fives, another 10, or a pocketfull of coins is what can be expected in return. (One can, however, go to a coin store and purchase gold coins with a sufficient number of bills, so in that sense it is exchangeable for a precious metal.) Even though the Federal Reserve note is not backed by gold or silver, businesses must accept it in transactions.

FED WATCHER. Put the term "Fed watcher" into your favorite search engine and you will find that the term is used by the Prudential Equity Group, Inc. as the title of their publication that discusses Federal Reserve policy and financial market activity. You also will find that it is used to describe a number of different individuals, an adjective that suggests that they spend a great deal of time trying to figure out what the Federal Reserve is up to. It is this latter usage that interests us here.

Why would anyone be employed to watch the Federal Reserve? Actually, "Fed watchers" are employed to watch for and interpret changes in the Federal Reserve's monetary policies. Their job is to interpret the potential effects of Federal Reserve policy actions on financial markets and the economy. In most instances, the term Fed Watcher refers to those individuals, mostly trained economists, employed at financial institutions whose responsibility it is to, as Meulendyke (1998, p. 204) suggests, "anticipate the effects of policy moves on interest rates and on the demand for credit because such information is important to the firms' trading and positioning strategies." This is not a simple task, nor unimportant. Because the Federal Reserve does not make all of its actions known to the public, a Fed Watcher must determine whether an unexpected purchase of government securities by the Federal Reserve represents a change in policy, an activity consistent with current policy, or simply a purchase to offset some technical change in financial markets.

Deciphering these actions and then trying to forecast their effect is necessary for financial firms to establish their trading positions. For example, if the firm's Fed Watcher, based on her reading of recent Federal Reserve actions, believes that interest rates will increase in the future, the firm may take a very different trading strategy than if it is expected that rates will fall. Obviously, an incorrect call by the Fed Watcher can be very costly, not only in terms of investment losses incurred by the firm and its clients but also in terms of the Fed watcher's employment status.

The role of the Fed Watcher has changed over time. During the 1960s and 1970s, Fed watchers tried to interpret the daily activity of the open market **trading desk** at the New York Federal Reserve Bank. Because all of the buying and selling of government securities takes place from "the desk," its daily activity was scrutinized to see if any change in policy could be gleaned from the data. This usually entailed watching movements in the **federal funds rate**, the interest rate that the Federal Reserve tries to target, and in **reserves** of the banking system. Because changes in reserves were used to move the funds rate, watching each provided information that a Fed Watcher could use to inform traders that the Federal Reserve was or was not changing the stance of policy (e.g., becoming more expansionary or more contractionary). Of course, oftentimes the signals from these two measures conflicted, thus giving Fed watchers little to go on when making a forecast.

As the conduct of monetary policy changed, so did the need for and the role of Fed watchers. Meulendyke (1998, p. 204) observes that "beginning in the late 1980s, as the **Federal Open Market Committee (FOMC)** gave increasing weight to the behavior of the federal funds rate in setting policy, reading the stance of policy became easier than it was over most of the preceding decade. Consequently, firms began to reduce the resources devoted to interpreting daily Trading Desk operations. In 1994, when the FOMC began to issue press releases announcing policy changes almost immediately after the decisions were made, Fed watchers no longer needed to provide analysis of daily Desk activity to interpret current FOMC policy."

Even though Fed watchers may not be predicting bank reserves with the same intensity as they once did, Fed watchers still play an important role for their firms. Today, most Fed watchers analyze economic events that may influence decisions made by the FOMC. For example, Fed watchers may study changes in economic activity, such as the growth rate of real **gross domestic product (GDP)** or in the **unemployment rate** or changes in the rate of **inflation**, and try to predict how the Federal Reserve will react. If there is an unexpected decrease in the unemployment rate, for example, how will the Federal Reserve respond? Will it attempt to raise interest rates or do nothing?

Fed watchers also keep track of public statements by Federal Reserve officials to see if there is any indication of a policy shift. During late 2003, for example, the public perception was that the economy was recovering from the 2001 recession but that there was not the same kind of job growth that had occurred with previous recoveries. The notion of a "jobless recovery" was widely discussed by the press and economic pundits. During all of this, many Federal Reserve officials were giving public speeches that indicated that they believed the recovery would continue along historical lines and that job growth would follow. If a Federal Reserve official had broken ranks from the "official" line, it would have been gobbled up by Fed watchers as a sign of disagreement among the policymakers. And that would have signaled possible internal dissention over the best course of policy. Determining how much weight should be put on such disagreement or differences of opinion is part of the Fed watcher's job.

FURTHER READING

Jones, David M. *Fed Watching and Interest Rate Projections: A Practical Guide.* New York: New York Institute of Finance, 1986; Meulendyke, Ann-Marie. *U. S. Monetary Policy & Financial Markets.* New York: Federal Reserve Bank of New York, 1998.

FEDWIRE. Fedwire is the name given to the system owned and provided by the Federal Reserve to facilitate the electronic transfer of funds between banks and other depository institutions. Technically, it is a "real-time gross settlement" (RTGS) system where users can make final payments. The use of Fedwire allows depository institutions to move balances from bank to bank or to send funds to other depository institutions on behalf of customers. This latter service could include transferring funds that are used for the purchase or sale of government securities or the transfer of deposits between banks. In addition to increasing the ability of depository institutions to move funds around the country with great speed, Fedwire is used by the U.S. Treasury and other federal agencies to disburse and collect funds. Fedwire, used in conjunction with the Clearing House Interbank Payment Systems (**CHIPS**), handles most large-dollar wire transfers. Because most CHIPS transfers stem from international transactions, CHIPS transfers can be settled on a net basis at the end of the day by using Fedwire funds transfers to and from a special settlement account on the books of the New York Federal Reserve Bank.

Fedwire is an extensive system. Fedwire is used by District Banks and their branches, the U.S. Treasury, and other government agencies. In addition, there are about 9,500 depository institutions that are able to initiate or receive funds over the Fedwire network. The system is available online to about 8,200 depository institutions with computers or terminals that communicate directly with the Fedwire network. In 2000, the Fedwire system processed almost 430,000 payments per day, with the median payment being $25,000. In 2000, about 10% of the Fedwire payments were for more than $1 million. In addition, only 120 of the Fedwire users accounted for 80 percent of all Fedwire transfers in 2000. These statistics suggest that the use of Fedwire is not uniform across all institutions but has several large institutional users who accounted for the bulk of Fedwire's use. This is evident by the fact that in 2000 nearly 40 million transfers, worth $209 trillion, occurred in the New York Bank's district alone.

Fedwire plays a significant role in the conduct of monetary policy. Because Fedwire transfers government securities electronically—no pieces of paper actually are exchanged—it increases the efficiency of **open market operations** by allowing the Federal Reserve and those institutions from which it buys or sells government securities to do so within a matter of minutes.

The use of Fedwire is an example of how technological improvements have affected the safety and efficiency of the financial payments system. (The following draws on "Federal Funds Transfer System" [2001].) Prior to an electronic means of transfer, settlement of interbank payments necessitated the physical delivery of the means of payment, for example, currency or gold. Obviously the transportation of these items was time consuming and entailed risks. As early as 1918, soon after the Federal Reserve System began operations, it developed a funds transfer network that connected the 12 District Banks, the Board of Governors, and the U.S. Treasury. This system relied on the Morse code communications system of electronic dots and dashes. Through this system, a precursor to the modern Fedwire system, Federal Reserve Bank balances could be transferred electronically.

The historical development of the Federal Reserve's transfer system mirrors the improvement in communications technology. Through the 1960s the system moved from leased-line public telegraph lines to telex to computer operations based on systems owned by the Federal Reserve. Until the 1980s, the system was decentralized, allowing each District Bank to operate separately from the others and to meet the localized needs of banks and other depository institutions in its district. As interstate banking grew in the 1980s, the need to create a more consistent provision of service became evident. Banks were stretching their services across district and state boundaries. To meet this need, the Fedwire operations became more standardized by the late 1980s and into the early 1990s. Standardized software was distributed across all District Banks, and most of the operations became centralized in the District Banks.

FURTHER READING

Federal Reserve Board of Governors. "Federal Funds Transfer System: Self-Assessment of Compliance with the Core Principles for Systemically Important Payment Systems." (2001). Accessed at Website: www.bog.gov under "Payments System."

FIAT MONEY. Historically, **money** has taken many forms. In the United States precious metals such as gold and silver, cattle, seashells, tobacco, and animal pelts have served as money. As economies developed and the need for more convenient and reliable forms of money became necessary, paper **currency**, often produced and circulated by governments, soon displaced these more cumbersome commodities. Initially, paper currency represented a claim on some amount of a precious metal, usually in the form of coin. For example, a 20-dollar "gold certificate" was convertible into $20 worth of gold. In most modern countries, however, this type of convertible commodity-backed paper currency has given way to fiat money.

Fiat money is distinguished from these other forms of money because it is not backed by any physical commodity and has no value in use. **Federal Reserve notes** are a form of fiat money, as is the Euro, the Canadian dollar, or the Japanese yen. If you ask a bank to redeem your piece of paper for something else, you will get another piece(s) of paper, or some coins. Why do we accept a piece of paper in exchange for goods or services provided? Fiat money is accepted in exchange for goods or for labor simply because everyone knows that when it is taken to the grocery store they also will accept it. Fiat money circulates and serves the purpose of a medium of exchange because the government declares that it is **legal tender** and must be accepted as payment for debts and everyone trusts the government to back the currency. This is why when governments collapse, so too does their currency.

FURTHER READING

Angell, Norman. *The Story of Money*. New York: Frederic A. Stokes Company, 1929; Dowd, Kevin. "The Emergence of Fiat Money: A Reconsideration." *Cato Journal* 20 (Winter 2001): 467–76.

FINANCIAL BUBBLE. This phrase describes a condition in financial markets when asset prices are far higher than can be explained based on "fundamental" factors. For example, in the now-infamous "tech bubble" of the late 1990s, many investors purchased stocks in firms that were entering the rapidly expanding field of computer technology without apparent concern for the firms' prospective revenues or earnings. The belief at the time was that shares of these firms could be bought and later resold for a substantial profit because their price was surely going to rise. Even though the price of many firms' stock was far greater than that predicted by the firms' profitability, investors eagerly purchased shares of such firms, thinking that someone else would buy them back in the future at a higher price. At some point, however, the ability to resell the stock at an even higher price began to slow. Whether investors realized that stock prices were far out of line with historical norms or it was some dramatic event—such as the corporate scandals of the late 1990s and early 2000s, or the onset of a **recession**—stock prices retreated in a dramatic fashion. For example, from its peak in the late 1990s, the tech-heavy NASDAQ stock index lost about 50 percent of its valuation. In other words, for those who had invested a dollar in the index in late 1999, by early 2003 it was worth about 50 cents.

Are financial bubbles the result of irrational behavior? In the 1990s, Federal Reserve Chairman **Alan Greenspan** coined the phrase "irrational exuberance" to capture the mood of the stock market during that time. The dramatic decline of stock prices in the early years of this decade would seem to bear this out. But were all stock purchases irrational? There is some evidence to suggest that investors were betting on the outcome of a new technological era. Consider how similar this episode is to historic periods that experienced similar advances in technology. In the early 1900s, there was a boom in the auto industry. Far more automobile companies were making cars than there are today. Was investing in those companies irrational? At the time, who knew if Hudson or Packard or Ford would survive the rigors of competition? Were investors in the now-defunct car companies of the past irrational in their decision or just unlucky?

History is strewn with the remains investment collapses. Some of the more notable are the "tulipmania" that occurred in Holland during the 1630s, the collapse of shares in the South Sea Company in Britain in 1720, the stock market crash of 1929 in the United States, the crash of Japanese stock prices that began in the late 1980s, and, as mentioned, the tumble of U.S. stock prices in the late 1990s. The events surrounding each of these episodes make for interesting reading, covering the political, cultural, and economic conditions that helped shape the outcomes.

FURTHER READING

Garber, Peter M. *Famous First Bubbles: The Fundamentals of Early Manias*. Cambridge, MA: MIT Press, 2000; Malkiel, Burton G. *A Random Walk Down Wall Street*. New York: W.W. Norton & Company, 1990; Shiller, Robert J. *Irrational Exuberance*. Princeton: Princeton University Press, 2000.

FINANCIAL CRISES OR PANICS. The term "panic" often is used to describe a period of extreme volatility in financial markets. These periods often have been associated with widespread bank failures and bankruptcies of firms. Historically, panics sometimes were ignited by the failure of a single firm. For example, the Panic of 1857 started when a large, Ohio-based insurance company announced that it was bankrupt. This surprise announcement led to a drain of money out of New York City banks as country banks across the nation drew down their reserves with New York banks in order to meet customers' unexpected deposit withdrawals. The fact that depositors in many areas sought to convert their depositors into currency—a flight to **liquidity**—widened the nature of the financial crisis. Another major panic occurred in 1893. At this time there was much agitation for the use of silver and gold as co-equal backing of the money supply. The election of Grover Cleveland in 1892, an avowed advocate of gold, sent financial markets tumbling. Stock prices declined throughout 1892 and into 1893. Individuals began hoarding gold and withdrew their deposits from banks, which led to bank runs.

Although the economy recovered and grew following the Panic of 1893, another panic occurred in 1907. One explanation for the start of the **Panic of 1907** was the collapse of New York's Knickerbocker Trust in October. Trying and failing to corner the market in the stock of United Copper—and to get in on the frenzied trading for copper, mining, and railroad stocks that was currently gripping Wall Street—Knickerbocker's stock prices fell sharply. The failure of the Knickerbocker Trust escalated concerns that other trusts, which also were engaged in questionable stock trading, would collapse. Based in fact or on whim, stock prices began a downward spiral as investors sought safer havens for their funds. In addition, once depositors feared that their bank would close its doors, **bank runs** started to occur.

Most panics historically gave rise to innovations in financial markets and banking. The Panic of 1907 precipitated the push for a central bank. The **Aldrich-Vreeland Act of 1908** paved the way for legislation that would establish the **Federal Reserve Act of 1913**, which was signed into law by President **Woodrow Wilson** in December 1913.

FURTHER READING

Schwartz, Anna J. "International Financial Crises: Myths and Realities." *Cato Journal* 17 (Winter 1998).

FINANCIAL INNOVATION. Innovation, whether it is in financial markets, automobile manufacturing, or computers, takes place because individuals seek profitable opportunities. Innovation allows them to make their product more desirable than their competitor's. In financial markets, innovation often comes in response to changes in the financial environment (for instance, following a panic) or in government regulations. For example, during the 1960s and 1970s, the rate of **inflation** began to rise. Because of the constraints of **Regulation Q**, which prohibited banks from paying interest on checking accounts, savers shifted funds out of bank deposits and into interest-bearing accounts at other financial institutions, such as credit unions. As inflation worsened, depositors began to search for alternative ways to hold money that paid interest high enough to offset the effects of inflation; that is, to avoid loss of purchasing power. One financial innovation that arose was the creation of **money market mutual funds** (MMMFs), which were offered by nonbank financial institutions. These mutual funds could pay market rates of interest on the checkable accounts because by law they were not banks and therefore not covered by Regulation Q. These mutual funds profited at the expense of banks as depositors shifted their deposits out of banks and into money market funds. (*See* **Disintermediation.**)

Banks countered this innovation with their own, partly to meet the competition of MMMFs and partly to circumvent Regulation Q constraints. Depository institutions in New England, for example, began to offer negotiable orders of withdrawal **(NOW) accounts**. NOW accounts paid interest and allowed depositors check-writing privileges. NOW accounts were legalized nationwide under the **Depository Institutions Deregulation and Monetary Control Act (DIDMCA) of 1980**. Banks also began to offer negotiable **certificates of deposit** (CDs) that paid market interest rates and allowed holders to sell them to a third party. This increased their attractiveness to investors and enabled banks to get around some of the existing interest rate regulations.

Financial innovations will continue to occur with changes in regulations and the desire of investors to reduce risk, increase **liquidity**, and seek the highest return for their investment. Other examples of financial innovations that have occurred in the recent past include adjustable rate mortgages, bank debit and credit cards, ATMs, securitization of home mortgages, and the increased use of derivative instruments now available in financial markets. In each case, the spur to innovate arose as a reaction to changes in the financial market and the desire to increase or maintain profitability.

FURTHER READING

Becsi, Zsolt, and Ping Wang. "Financial Development and Growth." Federal Reserve Bank of Atlanta *Economic Review* (Fourth Quarter 1997): 46–62; Furlong, Fred, and Simon Kwan. "Financial Modernization and Regulation." Federal Reserve Bank of San Francisco *Economic Letter* (December 31, 1999); Quinn, Stephen, and William Roberds. "Are On-line Currencies Virtual Banknotes?" Federal Reserve Bank of Atlanta *Economic Review* (Second Quarter 2003): 1–15.

FINANCIAL INSTITUTIONS REFORM, RECOVERY, AND ENFORCEMENT ACT OF 1989. This act, commonly referred to as FIRREA, was passed to reform the regulations governing the operation of savings and loans (S&L). It is arguably the most comprehensive overhaul of legislation for the savings and loan industry since the 1930s. The major objective of the act was to deal with the massive number of S&L failures that occurred during the late 1980s. (*See* **Savings and Loan Crisis.**) FIRREA accomplished this in several ways. First, the act abolished the Federal Savings and Loan Insurance Corporation (FSLIC), which had been the S&L industry's deposit insurer, much as the **Federal Deposit Insurance Corporation (FDIC)** insures deposits at commercial banks.

In its place, the act created the Resolution Trust Corporation (RTC). The job of the RTC was to deal with bankrupt thrifts and to sell off the real estate owned by the now-defunct S&Ls. It is estimated that the real estate sold following passage of this act amounted to over $300 billion.

A second change brought about by FIRREA was to create the Resolution Funding Corporation (RFC). This government entity was authorized to borrow funds through the sale of government debt to cover the cost of dealing with S&L insolvencies. By providing enormous funding to deal with the S&L crisis, FIRREA allowed regulators to close bankrupt institutions. FIRREA also replenished the reserves of the S&L insurance fund—the Savings Association Insurance Fund (SAIF)—by increasing insurance premiums paid by S&Ls against their deposits.

Finally, FIRREA also imposed new restrictions on the activities of thrifts. Passage of the act limited the activities of S&Ls in an effort to avoid a repeat of the problems of the 1980s. It also increased the powers of regulators to fire managers, issue cease-and-desist orders, and impose civil penalties.

FURTHER READING

Kane, Edward. *The S&L Insurance Mess: How Did It Happen?* Washington, D.C.: Urban Institute Press, 1989; Pilzer, Paul. *Other People's Money: The Inside Story of the S&L Mess.* New York: Simon and Schuster, 1989; Pizzo, Stephen, Mary Frickler, and Paul Muolo. *Inside Job: The Looting of America's Savings and Loans.* New York: McGraw-Hill, 1989; White, Lawrence J. *The S&L Debacle.* New York: Oxford University Press, 1991.

FINANCIAL INTERMEDIARIES. When you borrow money for a car **loan** or invest in the stock market, you seek out a bank or a stockbroker. Financial intermediaries specialize in bringing together individuals with money to lend or stock to sell and those who need to borrow or wish to purchase stock. Why do they exist? Think of how difficult it would be for you to get a loan if you had to canvass your friends, relatives, and neighbors until you could find someone or, more likely, a group of individuals willing to lend you the money for a car. Banks do this for you, first by collecting together funds—usually in the form of deposits—and lending these funds to borrowers. Financial intermediaries lower the cost of borrowing and saving. Because of this, individuals can spend more time building houses, teaching, or inventing the laptop computer. Financial intermediaries increase the efficiency of the economy and help promote **economic growth**.

The role of financial intermediaries can be seen in the figure below. When individuals do not attempt to borrow directly from others, they use financial intermediaries. For example, someone with funds that are not needed for current consumption—a saver—may deposit those funds in his or her local bank. The bank, in turn, is approached by a local business that wishes to expand its activity, open another store, or increase its inventory of goods. Banks serve as the "intermediary" linking savers and borrowers in the economy. Financial intermediaries also play an important role in providing funds to borrowers through financial markets. As shown in the figure below, banks and other intermediaries also may acquire funds, which are then used to purchase securities, such as stocks or bonds, of firms, governments at all levels, or foreign governments. Intermediaries thus play an important role in channeling funds from savers to borrowers. Specializing in this activity frees up resources that can be used in other areas of the economy. Instead of searching for the best

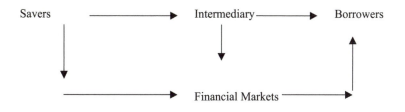

borrower, firms can use intermediaries to do this for them. This promotes economic growth and increases the liquidity of financial markets.

FURTHER READING

Wachtel, Paul. "How Much Do We Really Know about Growth and Finance?" Federal Reserve Bank of Atlanta *Economic Review* (First Quarter 2003): 33–47.

FINANCIAL MARKETS. Financial markets transfer funds from savers to borrowers. This is illustrated in the above figure. Financial markets allow savers—individuals who spend less than their income—to receive some positive return on their savings. Instead of putting their savings under the mattress, financial markets provide the opportunity to invest in the stock market, buy **bonds** from corporations, or deposit funds in banks. Financial markets channel these funds, directly and indirectly, to borrowers who need funds to buy houses, build new factories, or, in the case of governments, build roads and schools.

Financial markets also allow individuals to share the risk of an investment with other investors, increase the ease with which an investment can be converted into real goods (converting a share of Microsoft stock into groceries), and increase the gathering and communicating of information relevant for informed investment. This informational function sometimes is thought to be the most important aspect of what financial markets do. When borrowers and lenders possess unequal amounts of information—a condition known as **asymmetric information**—the return that an investor gets or that a bank receives after making a loan may be much different than they expected. Financial markets and **financial intermediaries** help reduce the problem of asymmetric information and thereby increase the efficiency of borrowing and lending.

FURTHER READING

Mishkin, Frederic S., and Stanley Eakins. *Financial Markets and Institutions*. 4th edition. Boston: Addison Wesley, 2003.

FIRST BANK OF THE UNITED STATES. The Federal Reserve was not the first central bank in the United States. There were previous attempts to create a central bank. Alexander Hamilton, the secretary of the Treasury, pushed for the establishment of a national bank. Hamilton argued that a national bank would provide a standard **currency** ("notes") and thus eliminate the need to increase exports in order to increase the size of the money stock. (**Money** was primarily gold and silver, and stocks of these could only be increased by exchanging goods for them.) Hamilton's idea was that by using paper currency issued by the central bank, commerce and trade would increase. Hamilton's central bank would lead to increased commerce and it would serve as the federal government's bank. That is, it would act as the government's fiscal agent, housing government deposits and transferring funds between regions of the country. (This role of the central bank is actually quite common, even today.)

Although there was much opposition to creating such a central bank—many believed that allowing the bank to issue currency would put too much economic power in the hands of the federal government—Congress passed the legislation that created the First Bank of the United States, signed by the president into law in 1791.

The bank was given a charter of 20 years. In the end, the charter was not renewed, for reasons that combine economics and political animus. On the economics side, many state banks started to use the bank's notes as reserves. Because the notes were valued in the market at face value—that is, a $1 bank note traded for goods just like $1 of gold and silver—using these as reserves allowed state banks to not use their holdings of gold and silver. In other words, the use of the paper currency was more convenient and pushed aside the use of gold and silver. This raised concerns by detractors about the bank creating a "money monopoly."

Opponents also resurrected arguments made during the debate over its initial charter. One argument was that the bank established virtual monopoly control over the money supply. At the time, many believed that responsible policy meant that changes in the money supply should be regulated by changes in the demand and supply of gold. Allowing a bank, whether a national bank or not, to issue currency would ultimately lead to an increase in the money supply that would ultimately ruin the economy through inflation. This argument was not new and would reappear in the development of the banking system during the 1800s.

As discussed elsewhere (*see* **Free Banking**), there was a strong tradition in the United States of trying to avoid a centralization of power, political or economic. The notion that the federal government controlled changes in the money supply—and hence the economy in many individuals' eyes—meant that personal and economic liberties were threatened. To many, the First Bank of the United States simply manifested that problem and should not be allowed to continue operation.

The vote to renew the bank's charter occurred in 1811. By this time, even though the evidence indicates that commerce did in fact improve during the bank's time, it became public knowledge that foreign ownership of the bank's outstanding stock stood at about 70 percent. Even though the bank's charter clearly forbade foreign individuals from serving as directors or voting on bank policy, raising this ownership issue was a red flag used by the bank's opponents. The very notion that foreigners owned a large block of the bank's stock was enough to push the vote against the bank. Another blow was dealt to supporters of rechartering the bank when past President Thomas Jefferson came out against renewing the charter of the bank.

In the end, the failure to recharter the bank was probably due more political animosities as it was clouded economic analysis. The vote in the House to recharter was postponed on a vote of 65 to 64. In the Senate, the vote on rechartering resulted in a tie: 17 to 17. The tie-breaking vote cast by Vice-President George Clinton, who voted against the bank largely because his earlier political enemies, James Madison and Albert Gallatin, Jefferson's secretary of Treasury, favored renewing it.

State banks quickly filled the gap left by the demise of the bank. Although there was no immediate effect from the failure to recharter the First Bank, the federal government faced difficulties in financing the War of 1812 that likely would have been more easily dealt with if the bank existed. That and the associated economic problems following the war (a significant bout of inflation) soon convinced many that a central bank was needed. In 1816, the Second Bank of the United States was chartered. (*See* **Second Bank of the United States**.) Like its predecessor, however, the Second Bank became the touchstone of economic and political debate.

FURTHER READING

Clarke, M. St. Clair, and D. A. Hall. *Legislative and Documentary History of the Bank of the United States.* Originally published in 1832; reprinted New York: Augustus M. Kelley, 1967; Timberlake, Richard H. *The Origins of Central Banking in the United States.* Cambridge, MA: Harvard University Press, 1978; Walton, Gary M., and Hugh Rockoff. *History of the American Economy.* 8th edition. Orlando: Dryden Press, 1998.

FISHER EFFECT. The Fisher effect, named after the noted U.S. economist **Irving Fisher**, relates the behavior of interest rates to expectations of future **inflation**. An example will help illustrate Fisher's insight. Suppose a bank lends a customer $100, with both parties agreeing that the **loan** is for one year. The bank therefore expects the loan to be repaid one year from now. If prices for everything go up (inflation), then the $100 the bank gets in a year actually has lost value. That is because inflation lowers the **purchasing power of money**. The bank wants to maintain purchasing power when it makes a loan. One way to try to prevent this loss in purchasing power is for the bank to ask for $100 plus interest to be repaid. Setting the interest rate—how much the bank charges for giving up use of the $100 now—depends on how high the bank's managers *think* the rate of inflation might be over the next year. If the bankers expect prices to increase 10 percent, then they will ask for $100 plus an interest charge of 10 percent to cover inflation, or $110 in a year. If they think prices are going to rise by 50 percent, then the bank will charge an interest rate of at least 50 percent and ask for $150 due in a year.

Fisher generalized this relationship between the **nominal interest rate** and the expected rate of inflation. More specifically, he suggested that when expected inflation increases, nominal interest rates also increase. Fisher argued that interest rates and expected inflation would move one-for-one; that is, if expected inflation rose by 10 percent, then so would interest rates. What actually appears to be the case is that interest rates and inflation are positively related but do not always move one-for-one. But as you can see in the figure on p. 140 which plots a measure of expected inflation along with the interest rate on three-month U.S. Treasury bills, they generally move together. Note how the general ups and downs in the inflation rate are mirrored in the nominal interest rate. This reflects Fisher's idea that movements in nominal interest rates are determined to a large extent by movements in inflation. This link between inflation and interest rates is one reason why many economists and policymakers favor anti-inflation policies as a means to keep interest rates low.

FURTHER READING

Fisher, Irving. *The Theory of Interest.* New York: Macmillan, 1930; Hafer, R. W., and Scott E. Hein. "Monetary Policy and Short-Term Interest Rates." Federal Reserve Bank of St. Louis *Review* (March 1982): 13–19; Keely, Michael C., and Michael M. Hutchinson. "Money and the Fisher Effect." Federal Reserve Bank of San Francisco *Weekly Letter* (August 7, 1987).

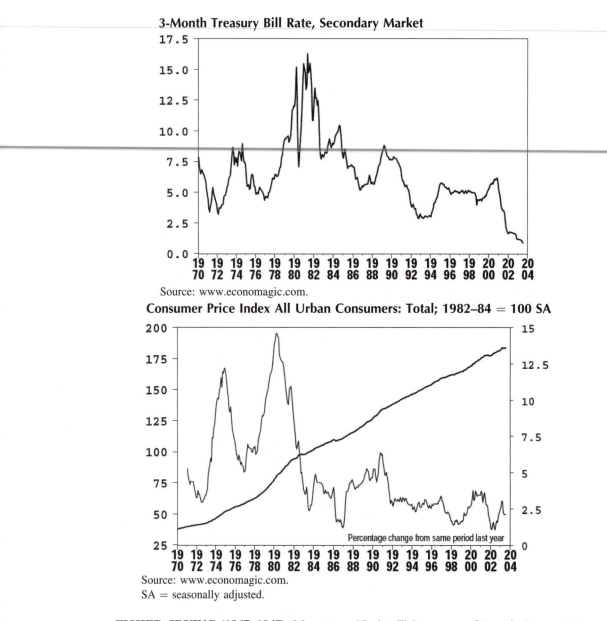

3-Month Treasury Bill Rate, Secondary Market

Source: www.economagic.com.

Consumer Price Index All Urban Consumers: Total; 1982–84 = 100 SA

Percentage change from same period last year

Source: www.economagic.com.
SA = seasonally adjusted.

FISHER, IRVING (1867–1947). Many regard Irving Fisher as one of America's greatest economists. Trained in mathematics, Fisher was one of the first American scholars to systematically use mathematical analysis and methods to develop and extend economic theories. He also stands out as an early pioneer in the use of statistical analysis to test alternative economic theories. Fisher joined with Ragnar Frisch and Charles Roos to found the Econometric Society in 1930.

Fisher's contributions to economics and monetary policy analysis are many. He was recognized as an expert on index numbers and the theory of their measurement (index numbers today are used in many areas, the most common in the measurement of price levels), was an early innovator in the use of statistical analysis, provided a foundation to modern treatments of investment and savings, provided the basic ideas that would later become the lifecycle saving theory, and more. For this entry, however, two of Fisher's many contributions will occupy us—his work on interest rate determination and his contribution to the modern quantity theory.

Fisher's work on interest rates stemmed from his earlier analysis of what economists call *intertemporal choices,* a fancy terminology for making choices over time. The idea is straightforward: Should I save my income today in order to spend it in the future, or should I spend it today? The decision you make depends on where you are in your lifecycle. In a relative sense, young people tend to spend and not save, middle-aged people tend to save more, and old people tend to spend and not save, each for obvious reasons. One of the key determinants in this decision process is the opportunity cost of choosing to spend or save. Fisher expounded upon the theory that the price that determined the tradeoff between current spending and future spending is the interest rate. The higher the interest rate, the greater is the opportunity cost of spending today and not saving for the future. Although this may seem trivial, the insights that Fisher provided in his work laid the foundation for much of modern capital and investment theories.

Fisher's ideas on interest rate determination were first provided in *The Rate of Interest* (1907), a book that was revised and republished in 1930 under the title *The Theory of Interest.* Fisher's theory of interest extended earlier work in capital theory by considering the importance of time in making the decision to save or spend. Earlier work, notably that of Leon Walras, had extended the discussion to a multicommodity structure but did not consider time. Fisher closed that loophole in the theory. Fisher's theory of individual saving remains a standard model today.

Not only did Fisher's work on interest rates provide a foundation for the modern lifecycle model of saving, but his work also provided a distinction between **nominal** and **real interest rates**, a distinction that remains known today as the Fisher equation. Fisher posited that nominal interest rates are directly linked to expectations about future inflation. That is, Fisher's equation indicates that nominal or observed interest rates can be thought of as the sum of the expected rate of inflation and the so-called real rate of interest. The real rate of interest is often thought of as the return to capital and is relatively stable over time. If so, then movements in nominal interest rates, such as the rates on Treasury securities, can be explained largely by changes in expected inflation. Fisher's insight into this relation provides one explanation for why nominal interest rates change so dramatically when there is an unexpected announcement about monetary policy. For example, an unexpected loosening of policy—one that may give rise to higher rates of inflation in the future—generally is associated with an increase in nominal interest rates.

Fisher's version of the quantity theory is expressed in his **equation of exchange**, or $MV = PT$. Even though Simon Newcomb, an American astronomer and economist, had written about the equation in the late 1800s, Fisher developed it and pushed its use to new levels. The equation is discussed at length elsewhere, so a brief entry is sufficient here. Essentially, the equation is a tautology: the money stock (M) times the number of times a dollar changes hands in a year (its income velocity, or V) must equal the dollar value of transactions (T) that occur in the economy, measured at current prices (P). This equation came to light in Fisher's *The Purchasing Power of Money* (1911). In many ways this book and its treatment of the relation between changes in the stock of money and the price level presage the post–World War II works of Monetarist economists, most notably **Milton Friedman** and **Karl Brunner**.

Fisher's equation of exchange allowed one to determine if changes in the supply of money affected its value in exchange for goods and services; that is, its purchasing power. To make this point, Fisher provided detailed discussion and analysis for his proposition that the velocity of money was relatively stable, in the sense that long-used, habitual methods of transacting and existing methods of payments meant that it would not vary much over time. With velocity relatively stable, changes in the stock of money must then be reflected in movements of the price level (P) or in the real volume of transactions (T). If the technology of transaction is exogenous (determined by forces not included in the model), then movements in the price level must be directly related to fluctuations in the stock of money. This is a very modern sounding relation, one that Monetarists touted during their heyday and one that forms the basis for the notion that monetary policy affects the price level in the long run. That is to say, Fisher recognized nearly a century ago that a sustained, expansionary monetary policy is more likely to push the rate of inflation higher than it is to lower the unemployment rate or sustain economic growth at a pace that exceeds its long-run potential.

Irving Fisher left a long and wide shadow on economics and the related fields of finance, statistics, and econometrics. Not only did his work impact modern economic theory, but it also affected the way we think about monetary policy.

FURTHER READING

Fisher, I. N. *My Father Irving Fisher*. New York: Comet Press, 1956; Tobin, James. "Irving Fisher." In *The New Palgrave: A Dictionary of Economics*, Vol. 2, John Eatwell, et al., eds. New York: Macmillan Press, 1987; *A Bibliography of the Writings of Irving Fisher*. Hartford, CT: Yale University Library, 1961.

FLOAT. When someone writes a check for groceries at the local store, the time it takes for the bank to decrease the checking account by that amount and the grocery store's bank to credit its account with the **money** is called float. Actually, the Federal Reserve describes float as "the difference between the total value of checks in the process of collection that have been credited to bank's reserve accounts and the value of those [checks] collected but not yet credited to banks' reserve accounts." Float is the amount of money that is in limbo between banks: An increase in float increases **reserves** in the banking system, a decrease in float reduces reserves in the system.

Why does float occur? Basically it represents banks operating efficiently. Consider the following. Every day millions of checks are written. In 2002, for example, over 16 billion checks (that's an average of about 66 million checks a day!) were collected and processed through the Federal Reserve System. When you deposit a check with your bank, it credits your account and expects to later collect from the bank upon which the check was written. Instead of dealing with each check, the bank may transfer its checks to the Federal Reserve for collection. That is, the Federal Reserve acts as the central processor for the checks in the banking system. The Federal Reserve pays the depositing bank for the total amount of the checks and collects the same amount from the banks upon which the checks are written. Until that process is completed, float exists.

Is float a problem? Historically, float was a major concern for Federal Reserve policymakers, especially over short intervals of time. Until there was an electronic means of transferring funds, the physical checks being cleared through the system were transported from banks to the Federal Reserve. Bad weather, often the cause of float problems, delayed the delivery of checks. Float would increase, and with it reserves in the banking system. If reserves increased unexpectedly, then there was downward pressure on the **federal funds rate** as the supply of reserves exceeded demand. When this occurred, the Federal Reserve, through the **trading desk** at the New York Federal Reserve, would undertake actions to offset this temporary aberration in reserves. Float is one of those "technical" problems that the Federal Reserve must deal with on a daily basis in order to maintain interest rates at their desired levels.

Because the transportation of checks is giving way to the use of electronic checks, the problems associated with float will to decrease in the future. In light of technological advances, Congress passed the Check Clearing for the 21st Century Act, which became effective on October 28, 2004. Check 21, as the Act is known, enables banks to handle more checks electronically, which lowers the time between using a check to buy goods and when the check is cleared through your bank account. This reduces float. For any float that remains, it likely will occur with enough weekly and seasonal patterns that the trading desk at the New York Federal Reserve can use these trends to forecast its level and smooth out any affects that it has on reserves in the banking system.

FURTHER READING

Federal Reserve Bank of New York. "Float." *Fedpoint* (October 2002); Federal Reserve Board of Governors. "Check Clearing for the 21st Century Act." Available at the Website: www. federalreserve.gov; Lacker, Jeffrey M. "The Check Float Puzzle: Check Collection in Banking." Federal Reserve Bank of Richmond *Economic Quarterly* (Summer 1997).

FOREIGN EXCHANGE MARKETS. The foreign exchange market is not located in any one city or at any one place. Unlike, say, the New York Stock Exchange, the foreign exchange market is a vast, worldwide network of traders engaged in the buying and selling of different countries' **currencies**. Such trading takes place largely anonymously as traders in London watch their computer screens for movements in the different foreign exchange rates, deciding whether to buy or sell. Today, even though there is no centralized trading location, the three main centers of trading are London, New York, and Tokyo. Singapore, Switzerland, Hong Kong, Germany, France, and Australia account for most of the remaining transactions in the market. Because of its worldwide nature, trading in foreign currency never stops. For example, the foreign exchange market opens in London as trades are ending in Singapore and Hong Kong. At 1 P.M. London time, the New York market is opening for business followed by trading on the West Coast of the United States in the afternoon. As the West-Coast market closes, a new day of trading is starting up in Singapore and Hong Kong. The very geographic size of the market suggests that it also is large in terms of the dollar volume. And it is: the foreign exchange market is the largest market in the world with well over a trillion dollars of currencies traded each day.

Why are foreign currencies traded? Individuals, firms, and governments all use foreign currencies for a variety of reasons. If you travel to another country, you must convert your dollars into the currency of the country you will be visiting. Travel to Mexico, and you'll need pesos. To Japan, and you'll need yen. And if you are going to Europe, you must exchange your dollars for Euros, the currency that now is accepted across Europe.

Although your exchange of, say, $1,000 for an equivalent amount of Mexican pesos does not affect the market, it still is part of it. And what the dollar–peso exchange rate is will determine how many pesos you get in return for your dollar.

Firms also are demanders of foreign exchange. If a business wishes to purchase a machine from a foreign producer, the payment usually is made in the foreign currency. For example, if the Coca-Cola Company buys a new bottling machine from Canada, it will pay for the machine with Canadian dollars. To do this, it must, just like you must when traveling abroad, convert U.S. dollars into Canadian dollars in order to make the payment. Domestic companies also may wish to acquire foreign currencies in order to make direct investments in another company. If the Coca-Cola Company wants to build a new plant in Canada, it may acquire Canadian dollars in order to pay for the new plant.

A major aspect of the daily trading that takes place in the foreign exchange market is done by traders who seek to profit from small movements in the exchange rates. Sometimes called speculators, oftentimes these traders buy and sell foreign currencies to try to lock in an exchange rate that is beneficial to their companies, or as part of a broader investment portfolio. Success in such trading requires that traders correctly predict movements in exchange rates. To do this, they must consider the underlying economic factors that movements in the exchange rates may reflect—for instance, one country's increasing inflation rates relative to others, thus putting downward pressure on its exchange rate—and how others in the market will react.

Even though individuals and firms may wish to purchase foreign currencies, trading in the foreign exchange market also is carried out by banks and other financial institutions, brokers, and central banks, like the Federal Reserve. About two thirds of all foreign exchange trades take place between banks. Sometimes banks trade directly with each other: one of their traders making a market with another by quoting a price at which he is willing to buy or sell the currency. Banks engaged in such trading are not always trading dollars for another currency. They may be trading British pounds for Japanese yen. Brokers are intermediaries between banks. As brokers, they specialize in information gathering. Brokers provide dealers and traders with prices and also provide some anonymity in the trading process. For this service, brokers earn a commission on the transaction. Central banks, such as the Federal Reserve or the Bank of England, also trade in foreign exchange markets. In these instances, the banks are acting on behalf of their governments. Historically, the Federal Reserve often traded in the foreign exchange market in order to affect the value of the dollar in the foreign exchange market.

How does trading in foreign currencies impact the domestic economy? Suppose that the Federal Reserve is selling some of its holdings of assets denominated in some foreign currency. To do this, it must first find a willing buyer. Assuming that a buyer is located, if the Federal Reserve sells $1 million in the foreign assets, it gets 1 million in U.S. dollars in return. This transaction is carried out through the foreign exchange trading desk at the Federal Reserve Bank of New York. The Federal Reserve's purchase of dollars lowers the amount of foreign denominated assets that it holds and, if purchased with currency, also decreases the money supply. (Recall that the money supply comprises currency in circulation and deposits held at banks. *See* **Money**.) If the buyer writes a check for the purchase of the assets, then the amount of deposits at banks is lowered, which also lowers the money supply. If the Federal Reserve is purchasing assets denominated in a foreign currency, then just the opposite affects occur. In either case, unless the Federal Reserve takes actions to offset its buying and selling of foreign denominated assets, it will impact the money supply of the United States.

In the modern world, most countries operate in what is known as a "managed float" system. In other words, with the demise of the **Bretton Woods System**—an international monetary system in which exchange rates were largely fixed—many governments attempt to buy and sell foreign exchange in order to manipulate the exchange value of their currencies. Although this was done in the United States in the past, today there is relatively little trading by the Federal Reserve with a goal of manipulating the exchange value of the dollar. Although there occasionally are times when the public pressures the Federal Reserve to raise or lower the exchange value of the dollar, the Federal Reserve's primary emphasis on achieving its long-term goals of low inflation and stable economic growth prevents it from allowing foreign exchange considerations to guide its actions.

FURTHER READING

Federal Reserve Bank of New York. "The Basics of Foreign Trade and Exchange." Available at the bank's Website: www.ny.frb.org/aboutthefed/.

FRACTIONAL RESERVE BANKING. This refers to the fact that U.S. banks hold a small fraction of deposits as **reserves** at the Federal Reserve and in the form of cash in their vaults. U.S. banks are required to hold these reserves as a cushion against unexpected withdrawals of deposits, or **bank runs**. In the event of a run, the Federal Reserve uses these reserves to rescue troubled banks and provide ready cash to meet the demands of depositors. Because banks hold a small fraction of deposits as reserves—less than 5 percent in many instances—the remaining deposits are used by the banks to make **loans** and to purchase government securities, both of which generate revenue for the bank.

Why is fractional reserve banking important to the conduct of monetary policy? When the **Federal Open Market Committee (FOMC)** votes to expand the money supply in an attempt to spur economic activity, it does so by buying government securities in the financial market. (*See* **Open Market Operations**.) The outcome of this action is to increase reserves in the banking system. Because banks hold only a fraction of their deposits on reserve, either electronically at their District Bank or in the form of **vault cash**, this infusion of reserves puts them in a disequilibrium position. That is, they have more reserves than they desire at the given level of market interest rates.

To rectify this condition, banks use the extra reserves to buy securities or, more important, make more loans. When a loan is made, often the bank creates a deposit upon which the borrower can draw funds. For example, a baker wishes to open a new outlet and borrows $100,000 to cover remodeling and equipment costs. Instead of giving the baker $100,000 in cash, the bank makes the loan and at the same time creates a checking account from which the baker can pay off carpenters, oven manufacturers, etc. In a fractional reserve banking system, what happens when this new $100,000 deposit is created? First, the bank holds some percentage of it on reserve. Currently the amount of reserves held against checkable deposits is 3 percent. (*See* **Reserve Requirement**.) So, in this case, the bank would increase its reserves as required by law by $3,000. That would leave $97,000 of the new deposit money for the bank to use.

Just like the initial increase in reserves generated by the Federal Reserve's actions, this initial increase in deposits sets into motion a sequence of increases in deposits and reserves.

But note that, unlike the initial increase, subsequent increases are progressively less and less. If the bank makes a $97,000 loan/deposit, reserves increase by 3 percent of this ($2,910) and the bank is left with $94,090 to lend again. In the next round, this loan creates $2,822.70 in required reserves and frees up $91,267.30 for the bank to lend out. The process continues until the bank has loaned out all of the funds. In the final analysis, the initial $100,000 increase in deposits will generate over $3 million in additional deposits. In the jargon of economics, this expansion of the money supply from an initial increase in reserves is referred to as the **money multiplier** process. Because deposits form part of the money supply, the Federal Reserve's actions have led to an increase in the money supply.

Fractional reserve banking is an important component to modern monetary policy. The Federal Reserve uses the existence of fractional reserve banking to affect changes in the money supply and, therefore, interest rates, prices, and economic output. It also can change the percentage that banks must hold against deposits. (*See* **Reserve Requirement**.) In the above example, raising the reserve percentage to 5 percent has the effect of reducing the ultimate effect on the expansion of deposits. If the reserve percentage is 5 percent, a $100,000 increase in deposits leads ultimately to only a $2 million change in deposits. Thus, small changes in the percentage of reserves held against deposits have dramatic affects on how the Federal Reserve brings about changes in the money supply and its conduct of policy.

FURTHER READING

Mishkin, Frederic S. *The Economics of Money, Banking, and Financial Markets*. 7th edition. Boston: Pearson Addison Wesley, 2004.

FRANCIS, DARRYL (1912–2002). Darryl Francis deserves special mention in this volume. Francis served as president of the Federal Reserve Bank of St. Louis from January 17, 1966, until his retirement on March 1, 1976. Like **Malcolm Bryan**, president of the Federal Reserve Bank of Atlanta (1951–1965), what separated Francis from his colleagues is the fact that he was an outspoken critic of the Federal Reserve's monetary policies. Francis, along with the St. Louis Federal Reserve Bank's Research Director **Homer Jones**, was instrumental in bringing together a research staff that promoted the ideas of the then-nascent view of **Monetarism**. The empirical analysis published by the St. Louis Bank and made publicly available through Francis's many speeches to various organizations promoted the idea that the Federal Reserve, through its insistence of focusing policy on the behavior of interest rates as a means to achieve low unemployment rates, was fostering inflation. Indeed, at the time when inflation had begun to increase in the mid-1960s, Francis strongly supported the goal of halting inflation and thought that the Federal Reserve's actions in late 1965 and early 1966 had been too timid. He attributed the increase in inflation which began at this time to the Federal Reserve's reluctance to allow interest rates to rise.

Francis's statements at meetings of the **Federal Open Market Committee (FOMC)** during his tenure always reflected his fundamental belief that the stance of monetary policy is measured appropriately by the growth rates of monetary aggregates, not the level of interest rates. It was his position that the Federal Reserve should keep the money stock growing at a steady pace, rather than allow it to fluctuate widely. Through the 1960s, Francis's support for targeting the growth of the money stock and for focusing monetary policy exclusively on containing inflation were gaining wider support in academic circles.

At the University of Chicago, such ideas were being studied by **Milton Friedman** and his students. Although the idea was gaining credibility, this viewpoint put Francis squarely at odds with most of his colleagues on the FOMC.

What is interesting about Francis's policy views is that they are not controversial today. The notion that monetary policy and not fiscal policy—government spending and taxation—is more effective now is widely regarded as true. During his time at the Federal Reserve, however, such ideas fell outside the mainstream. Indeed, the dominant view among policy makers at the time was that the government should respond to any shortfalls in employment or output growth by adjusting taxes and spending. Although reasonable stability of the price level was seen as desirable, many monetary policymakers in the Federal Reserve System, both governors and presidents, argued that modest inflation was an acceptable cost of achieving high employment. At the time, Milton Friedman's aphorism "inflation is always and everywhere a monetary phenomenon," today accepted by nearly all economists, was hotly debated.

Unlike his colleagues in and out of the Federal Reserve System, Francis agreed with the analysis that concluded that the Federal Reserve's persistent policy of trying to hold the unemployment rate below a level consistent with price stability increased the trend rate of inflation that began in the mid-1960s. Although economists today believe that the rate of unemployment associated with an economy operating at its potential was probably about 5 percent, many policymakers at the time thought that any unemployment rate above 4 percent engendered economic loss. Consequently, many argued for policies aimed at lowering the unemployment rate even though the consequence was rising rates of inflation. As early as 1970, Francis questioned whether following a policy to achieve a 4 percent rate of unemployment could be maintained without pushing the rate of inflation to unacceptable levels. As it turns out, Francis's view was correct: the period from 1965 through the end of the 1970s has become known as the **Great Inflation**.

Francis's views about monetary policy were based on a set of beliefs from which he did not waiver. There were four basic premises that guided his policy prescriptions. He enumerated these in a speech that was reprinted in the Federal Reserve Bank of St. Louis's *Review* in 1968. First, he advocated a "pre-dominantly market orientation." Francis believed that free markets were more efficient than government intervention to allocate incomes and goods and services. Francis also believed that "quantification is essential." Francis argued for quantifiable policy rules as the basis for sound monetary policy decision making. Today, the so-called **Taylor Rule** represents just such a quantifiable approach to making and assessing the success or failure of monetary policy. His third premise was that the "economic system is more stable than was believed a few years ago." Francis believed that the economy was inherently stable over time. That is, long-run real economic growth was determined by population growth, capital formation, and technology. Because monetary policy should, in his view, focus on the long-run impact it has on inflation, he believed that policy could not reliably improve on market outcomes over time. Although not the accepted wisdom in his time, today such a view is fundamental. Finally, Francis argued that "monetary management is more properly directed toward influencing changes in total spending." Although popular at the time, he did not believe that monetary policy could be used to affect specific markets or sectors of the economy: An efficient allocation of goods and services or resources should be achieved by market forces.

Francis had strong convictions about the efficacy of market forces and the limitations of government stabilization policies. Even though Francis believed that monetary policy could exert a powerful short-run impact on the growth of real **Gross Domestic Product (GDP)**, he was convinced that it could not be used to permanently steer the economy to any particular rate of growth. In the long run, he believed that monetary policy affected only the price level. Maintaining price stability, Francis believed, would help establish conditions that would foster maximum employment and economic growth. Although not widely shared among his contemporaries in the Federal Reserve, today such views are mainstream.

FURTHER READING

Hafer, R. W., and David C. Wheelock, "Darryl Francis and the Making of Monetary Policy, 1966–1975." Federal Reserve Bank of St. Louis *Review* (March/April 2003): 1–12; Jordan, Jerry. "Darryl Francis: Maverick in the Formulation of Monetary Policy." Federal Reserve Bank of St. Louis *Review* (July/August 2001): 17–22; Poole, William. "Eulogy for Darryl R. Francis, 1912–2002." Federal Reserve Bank of St. Louis *Review* (March/April 2002): 1–2.

FREE BANKING. When you use an **automated teller machine (ATM)**, what do you get? Have you ever looked at the cash it dispenses? If you do, you'll notice that printed along the front top of the bills is "**Federal Reserve Note**." This means that the bill is a product of the U.S. government. And the fact that it says on the bill that "this note is legal tender for all debts, public and private" means that it must be accepted as a means of payment, whether for a hotdog at the local deli or as payment for your federal taxes. While this is the accepted norm today, it wasn't always so.

During the 1800s, there was no central bank as we know the Federal Reserve today. The United States had tried to establish a central bank and failed in its two attempts. After the charter of the **Second Bank of the United States** expired in 1836, there was no federal oversight of the banking system. Into this void many states began to establish a legal framework for bank ingoperations. In 1837, Michigan passed the first set of laws that allowed private individuals to open banks, which, unlike today, had the ability to issue **currency**, or bank notes as the money is sometimes called. Many other states soon followed, with most state legislatures passing their versions of the Michigan law in the 1850s, as shown in the table below. The passage of the Michigan law thus began what is known as the free banking era in U.S. banking history. The free banking era ended officially in 1864, when the U.S. government passed the **National Banking Act of 1864**. This act ended free banking by imposing a tax on every bank note issued by a bank, effectively making it prohibitively expensive for banks to remain profitable while issuing notes.

One important characteristic of the free banking systems developed in the different states is that once the state's requirements for opening a bank were met—usually involving paying to the state banking regulator some minimum amount of funds—any group of individuals could open a bank. Unlike some state banking frameworks in which the legislature would "charter" banks, free banking took banking outside of the political process. Although opening a bank was by no means "free," it was much easier than gaining a charter to operate a bank. Once the bank's owners had paid a security deposit with the state banking authority, it could then issue currency, duly authorized by the state banking authority and bearing the name of the bank.

Free Banking by State and Year Passed

State	Year Law Passed
Michigan	1837
Georgia	1838
New York	1838
Alabama	1849
New Jersey	1850
Illinois	1851
Massachusetts	1851
Ohio	1851
Vermont	1851
Connecticut	1852
Indiana	1852
Tennessee	1852
Wisconsin	1852
Florida	1853
Louisiana	1853
Iowa	1858
Minnesota	1858
Pennsylvania	1860

Source: Dwyer (1996).

Free banks operated like any other bank. One difference was that they often competed for business. As individuals compared the trustworthiness of banks, the value of the different bank notes in circulation fluctuated. For example, a dollar bill from the Bank of St. Louis may buy you a dollar's worth of goods in the St. Louis area; if you try to use the bill in Chicago, it may be worth only $0.90. Because the value of currency changed over different geographical areas, newspapers that published the exchange values of the different bank notes, usually referred to as bank note monitors, became popular. Banks that were being poorly run would see the value of their bank notes fall in relation to those banks that had good reputations.

Free banks were subject to regulatory restrictions. For example, failure by a bank to convert its notes into gold or silver coin (specie) on demand could lead to closure of the bank by the state authority. Dwyer (1996) notes that "the requirement that banks convert notes into specie on demand created the possibility of a **bank run**." Banks could not convert all requests for gold or silver in exchange for its notes because, like banks today, they held only a fraction of deposits in reserve. This fact, Dwyer (1996) points out, means that "if note holders thought it likely that a bank would not be able to continue to convert its notes into specie at par, they had an incentive to exchange the bank's notes for specie. The note holders could then hold the specie or banknotes issued by another bank and wait to see whether the bank kept its notes convertible into specie." In this way, it was worthwhile for banks to maintain their reputations in order to forego the possible effects of a bank run.

In the past, some (e.g., Hammond, 1957) argued that free banking gave rise to unregulated gouging of customers. The notion of "wildcat" banking was popularized as the free banking era was characterized as one in which owners would take deposits from customers, give them their bank notes, and disappear with the assets, leaving the customers holding worthless pieces of paper. While such events no doubt occurred, more recent research suggests that, overall, most free banks were well managed and opened not with the intention of fraud but with the intention of profitable operation.

Bond Prices, December 3, 1858 to January 1, 1863

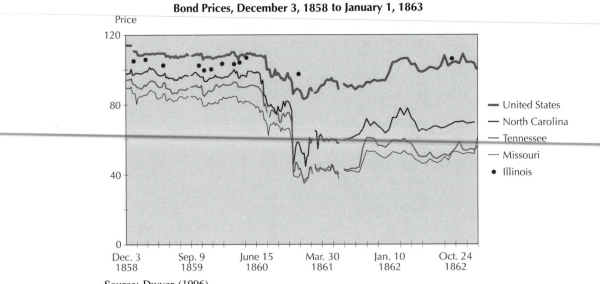

Source: Dwyer (1996).

Part of this "wildcat" notion of free banking stems from the fact that free banks largely disappeared with the onset of the Civil War. The reason for this collapse of free banking is largely due to the very framework in which the banks operated. To open a bank, owners were required to deposit assets with the state banking authority. Usually the acceptable assets included state or U.S. bonds, which at the time were referred to as stocks. Other assets accepted sometimes included real estate or corporate bonds, and gold. Because banks were allowed to issue notes up to some percentage of the market value of the assets deposited, any change in the value of those assets required banks to decrease the amount of outstanding (circulating) notes or to add to its security deposit by depositing more bonds with the banking authority. There were set rules about how banks had to respond to these changing conditions. For example, if the market value of the deposit with the banking authority fell below a specified value, banks had a limited time to correct the situation or the state regulators would close down the bank and sell the stocks on deposit to pay off the bank's depositors. (This is akin to the deposit insurance system used today. *See* **Federal Deposit Insurance Corporation [FDIC]**).

Given this framework, banks supplied regulators with **bonds** that were issued by any number of states, including those in the South and so-called border states like Missouri. With the election of Abraham Lincoln, financial markets anticipated conflict between the North and the South. The market value of southern bonds began to slide as investors worried about the riskiness of holding these assets. The culmination came in early April 1861 when southern troops fired on Fort Sumter, South Carolina. As shown in the figure above, the prices on state bonds fell sharply, with the descent of southern and border state bonds more pronounced than northern state bonds, or those of the U.S. government. As Dwyer and Hafer (2004) relate, the decline in state bond prices—and therefore the value of the deposits backing free banks' outstanding notes—was perhaps the most important contributor to the failure of free banks. For example, 44 percent of the free banks in Wisconsin and 87 percent in Illinois failed. Although differences in state laws and in how state regulators imposed the laws following the dramatic decline in bonds prices affected the magnitude of failure rates, the free banking system was for all practical purposes moribund by 1862. Passage of the National Banking Act in 1864, which created a federal monopoly over the issuance of currency and established the national banking system, simply finished the job.

FURTHER READING

Dwyer, Gerald P., Jr. "Wildcat Banking, Banking Panics, and Free Banking in the United States." Federal Reserve Bank of Atlanta *Economic Review* (December 1966): 1–20; Dwyer, Gerald P., Jr., and R. W. Hafer. "Bank Failures in Banking Panics: Risky Banks or Road Kill?" In I. Hasan and W. C. Hunter, eds., *Bank and Financial Market Efficiency: Global Perspectives.* Amsterdam: Elsevier, 2004; Hammond, Bray. *Banks and Politics in America from the Revolution to the Civil War.* Princeton: Princeton University Press, 1957; Rockoff, Hugh. *The Free Banking Era: A Reexamination.* New York: Arno Press, 1975; Rolnick, A. J., and W. E. Weber. "Banking Instability and Regulation in the U.S. Free Banking Era." Federal Reserve Bank of Minneapolis *Quarterly Review* 9 (Summer 1985): 9.

FREE RESERVES. Banks hold **reserves** against their deposits. These reserves are made up of required reserves held at the Federal Reserve (in the form of electronic entries) and **excess reserves**, so called because they are the amount of reserves held over and above required reserves. Banks can add to their reserves by borrowing funds from the Federal Reserve through the **discount window**. *Free reserves* are equal to these borrowed reserves minus excess reserves.

At one time, free reserves were thought to be a useful measure for determining monetary policy. Some Federal Reserve officials believed that if banks try to pay off their borrowed reserves before making **loans** or buying other securities, then free reserves may be a good indicator of whether banks are able to expand their assets. That is, if policymakers observed that free reserves in the banking system were increasing or decreasing, this was thought to indicate whether monetary policy was being "tight" or "easy," respectively.

In what is widely regarded as one of the definitive treatments of free reserves, Meigs (1962) describes the free reserve approach to policy as a direct descendant of the **Riefler-Burgess Doctrine**. The idea by the late 1950s was that if free reserves are high (low), then interest rates were expected to fall (rise) and the money supply to grow (decline). Even though official discussions of free reserves contained caveats suggesting that such interpretations may not hold at all times, the behavior of free reserves was an important policy variable often discussed in meetings of the **Federal Open Market Committee (FOMC)**—not because they thought it was a measure they could control, but as an indicator of policy tightness or ease.

What Meigs (1962) showed was that banks responded to movements is their free reserve positions and that these movements depended largely on market factors like changes in rates of interest. Meigs's analysis demonstrated that the level of free reserves is not a good policy indicator unless one knew what the banks' desired level of free reserves was. Simply observing changes in free reserves relative to some FOMC-chosen, desired level was not the basis of good monetary policy. Meigs's evidence showed free reserves to be an untrustworthy measure upon which to base policy decisions. In its place, he argued that a more reliable indicator of policy actions is total bank reserves adjusted for changes in reserve requirements (*See* **Monetary Base**.) Meigs argued that by using adjusted total bank reserves the Federal Reserve could exert relatively close control over the behavior of the money supply if it chose to do so.

FURTHER READING

Brunner, Karl, and Allan H. Meltzer. *The Federal Reserve's Attachment to the Free Reserve Concept.* Washington, D.C.: House Committee on Banking and Currency, 1964, reprinted in Brunner and Meltzer, eds., *Monetary Economics.* London: Blackwell, 1989; Meigs, A. James. *Free Reserves and the Money Supply.* Chicago: University of Chicago Press, 1962.

FRIEDMAN, MILTON (1912–). Milton Friedman, winner of the 1976 Nobel Prize in economics, stands out as one of the most influential economists of the twentieth century. In addition to his contributions in numerous fields of economics—from his work on the consumption function, statistics, scientific methodology, and economic theory—Friedman's contributions that are most important for this entry are those in the field of monetary economics and the analysis of monetary policy.

Economics after World War II is characterized by the popularity of **John Maynard Keynes**'s macroeconomic theory and the related policy analysis that had grown in popularity since the mid-1930s. In this view, money and monetary policy played a secondary role to fiscal policy. Monetary policy was viewed simply as a means to keep interest rates low in order to encourage investment spending. It was fiscal policy, according to the Keynesian model, that impacted economic activity. The Keynesian model assumed that inflation was caused by firms passing on to consumers increases in wages or other increases in production costs. The notion that inflation was a monetary phenomenon was dismissed.

Beginning in the 1950s there was a resurgence of interest in monetary economics. Much of the early work was based on refining the **quantity theory**, which established the relation between money growth and inflation in the long run. This approach, one examined by **Irving Fisher** and John Maynard Keynes earlier in the century, lacked statistical sophistication. In an academic world where mathematics was becoming an integral part of economic analysis and the subfield of econometrics was emerging, the quantity theory did not warrant much interest among many in the economics profession. Friedman changed that. What Friedman, his colleagues, and his students did was to refine the arguments inherent in the quantity theory, focusing on the stability of the public's demand for money. Indeed, the articles contained in *Studies in the Quantity Theory of Money* (1956), written by Friedman and his students at the University of Chicago, have a common thread: to demonstrate that the implications of the quantity theory—namely that changes in the stock of money have no long-run effect on economic activity but result in proportional price level changes—hold over time and across countries.

This work was important because it helped establish the role of money in explaining economic activity, especially the observed growth of nominal income. If changes in money growth were responsible for observed changes in inflation, were variations in the growth rate of money also related to observed fluctuations in an economy's real output? This question was analyzed by Friedman and his colleagues. For example, the study by Friedman and David Meisleman rejected the Keynesian model's underlying notion that the demand for money is inherently unstable. If the Keynesian hypothesis is true, changes in the growth rate of the money supply would have no predictable effect on income or prices. Refuting this notion allowed Friedman and others to argue that changes in the supply of money—and hence monetary policy actions—have important impacts on the economy. Friedman collaborated with **Anna J. Schwartz** to produce the monumental work *A Monetary History of the United States, 1867–1960,* published in 1963. This work, along with that of other monetary economists at the time (notably **Karl Brunner** and **Allan H. Meltzer**), addressed the question of whether **business cycles** in the economy were related to swings in the growth rate of the money supply. Were business cycles caused by monetary policy? With special emphasis on the **Great Depression**, Friedman and Schwartz's analysis could not reject the idea that monetary policy actions mattered and were the driving force behind observed changes in economic activity.

Friedman's assault on the Keynesian orthodoxy and the growing body of work indicating that monetary policy affected the economy led to significant changes in how economists thought about money. Empirical evidence on the importance of monetary policy actions in determining the path of the economy, in terms of showing both the effect of changes in the money supply and that changes in the money supply were largely due to actions taken by the Federal Reserve (here the work of Karl Brunner and Allan Meltzer stands out), began to undermine the Keynesian view and its policy prescriptions.

In the late 1960s, Friedman, along with independent work by Edmund Phelps, leveled another blow at the accepted wisdom. They showed that reliance on the tradeoff between inflation and unemployment—the so-called **Phillips curve** relation—was misplaced. Used as a foundation for much of the stabilization policies of the 1960s, the Phillips curve suggested that policies geared to lower inflation would push unemployment rates higher. The notion was that policymakers faced a "menu" of tradeoffs, meaning that a selected target rate of inflation would be associated with a certain unemployment rate. What Friedman (and Phelps) showed was that this tradeoff is not stable over time. That is, there is no unique relation between any rate of inflation and any unemployment rate. Friedman's argument, one that is now accepted as the conventional wisdom, is that in the long run, unemployment rates are determined by factors such as technology and growth of the labor force. Put another way, there was some long-run rate of unemployment around which the economy would fluctuate. Inflation, however, had no such natural rate to which it returned. Policies aimed at lowering the unemployment rate when it already was at this long-run level would only exacerbate inflation. Friedman's idea is supported by the data: Historical experience in the United States and other countries shows that a given rate of unemployment often was associated with a wide variety of inflation rates. The bottom line for policymakers was that they could do little to influence the unemployment rate—or potential output growth—in the long run. Rather, policy actions were more likely to impact the behavior of inflation over time. As in his earlier work, he again demonstrated the importance of considering the long-run consequences of policy actions.

Although much of Friedman's work criticized the Federal Reserve and other central banks for their policy choices, today many of them operate in a manner similar to that once advocated by Friedman. For example, most banks employ some type of policy rule instead of relying on the instincts of its policymakers to guide actions. Although the use of monetary aggregates has fallen into disrepute, largely an outcome of technological advances that rapidly changed the nature of what is considered to be money, Friedman's emphasis on the long-run effects of money growth today shapes policy analysis. Alan Walters (1987) sums up Friedman's activity in monetary economics this way: "By any standards—even those of [John Maynard] Keynes and the *General Theory*—Friedman's contribution to monetary analysis and policy must be ranked very high. Every economist, finance minister and banker felt his influence."

FURTHER READING

Friedman, Milton, ed. *Studies in the Quantity Theory of Money*. Chicago: University of Chicago Press, 1956; Friedman, Milton. *The Program for Monetary Stability*. New York: Fordham University Press, 1959; Friedman, Milton. *The Optimum Quantity of Money and Other Essay*. Chicago: University of Chicago Press, 1969; Friedman, Milton, and Anna J. Schwartz. *A Monetary History of the United States, 1867–1960*. Princeton: Princeton University Press, 1963; Friedman, Milton, and Anna J. Schwartz. *Monetary Statistics of the United States: Sources and Methods*. Chicago: Aldine Publishing, 1970; Friedman, Milton, and Anna J. Schwartz. *Monetary Trends in the United States and the United Kingdom: Their Relations to Income, Prices and Interest Rates, 1876–1975*. Chicago: University of Chicago Press, 1982; Friedman, Milton, and Rose Friedman. *Two Lucky People*. Chicago: University of Chicago Press, 1999; Walters, Alan. "Milton Friedman." in John Eatwell, et al. eds., *The New Palgrave: A Dictionary of Economics* (Vol. 2). New York: Macmillan Press, 1987.

FULL EMPLOYMENT ACT OF 1946. Following World War II, Congress passed legislation that required the federal government to follow policies that would ensure economic prosperity. With the successes of economic planning during the war and with the memory of the massive economic failure of the **Great Depression** still fresh in their memories, Congress passed and President **Harry Truman** signed into law the Full Employment Act of 1946.

The act represented a belief by its sponsors that the government not only had the duty to actively intervene to prevent economic downturns but had the means to do so. This latter belief was based on the then-new macroeconomic theories associated with the British economist, **John Maynard Keynes**. Keynes's theory of active government intervention was expounded in his most famous work, *The General Theory of Employment, Interest and Money*, which was published in 1935. Writing at the depths of the Great Depression, Keynes argued that the government, through programs of spending and reduced taxation, could influence the aggregate demand of an economy. That is, when the growth in the demand for goods and services in an economy was slowing, the government could step in and fill the void. By increasing government expenditures, incomes would rise, people would spend more and the downturn in economic activity would be avoided. More importantly, the government could thus avoid the dramatic increases in unemployment that characterized recessions and especially the Great Depression.

The act was one of hubris. Not only did the politicians and their economic advisors think that they could run the economy like one runs a machine—the term of the times was that they could "fine tune" economic policy to steer the economy away—but they also believed that they could foresee changes in economic conditions that would lead to needed changes in economic policy. The focus was on curtailing unemployment; hence the title of the act. (In fact, this focus would later lead to difficulties as policymakers, intent on keeping unemployment low, enacted a series of policies that led to increases in inflation. On this aspect, *see* **Great Inflation** and the **Phillips Curve**.) The initial version of the act, circulated under the title of the Full Employment Bill of 1945, suggested that unemployment could be attacked in two ways. First, the bill placed the responsibility of maintaining full employment on the federal government. Continuous full employment, especially in light of the Great Depression, could not be assumed in a system of pure private enterprise. This would be achieved by having the federal government provide "such volume of Federal investment and expenditure as may be needed . . . to assure continuing full employment."

The bill also provided a formula by which this goal could be realized. Essentially, the president would submit the federal budget to Congress and with it a forecast of the level of output required to keep unemployment at some desired low level. If output was projected to be below the necessary level, then the president was to recommend policy actions that would increase demand, stimulate production, and close the gap. This formula worked symmetrically: If the economy was projected to be growing too fast and unemployment would be pushed below its "full employment" level, the president would enact policies that would create a federal budget surplus.

Santoni (1986, p. 10) notes, "The sponsors [of the bill] believed that a continuous application [of such policies] was necessary because they interpreted [employment] data as indicating that high levels of unemployment were a natural consequence of free enterprise." Opponents, on the other hand, argued that basing future policy actions solely on the experience of the Great Depression was foolhardy. What if the Great Depression was not the "natural consequence" of a free enterprise system but an aberration? If economies naturally tended to full employment, then the intrusion of the government may upset these natural inclinations. And so the debate went.

Between the Bill of 1945 and the Act of 1946, there was much debate and many revisions. The final version enacted in 1946 eliminated the provisions that called for the government to ensure that anyone wanting to work would get a job. It also eliminated the requirement that the president submit a budget to Congress each year that outlined the response of the government to some projected shortfall in economic activity. In the end, the act was, as Santoni (1986, pp. 11–12) puts it, "a statement of intention rather than a requirement to act." Still, the Full Employment Act of 1946 set the tone for both fiscal and monetary policy discussions. This legislation and, perhaps more important, the economic theories upon which it was based established the role for monetary policy that would hold for the next three decades. With increases in unemployment generally at the top of the list of economic maladies to be feared, monetary policy during the period 1946–1980, and especially during 1960–1979, was inflationary. It was not until the early 1980s when inflation soared to a post–World War II high of nearly 15 percent did monetary policy shift gears and put greater importance on reducing inflation as its key policy objective. Indeed, since then, average rates of inflation have steadily declined, averaging less than 5 percent for most of the 1990s and thus far in the twenty-first century.

FURTHER READING

Assuring Full Employment in a Free Competitive Economy. Report from the Committee on Banking and Currency, 79 Cong., 1 Sess. (Government Printing Office, September 1945); *Full Employment Act of 1945.* Hearings Before a Subcommittee of the Committee on Banking and Currency, United States Senate, 79 Cong, 1 Sess. (Government Printing Office, September 1945); Keynes, John Maynard. *The General Theory of Employment, Interest and Money.* New York: Harcourt, Brace and Company, 1935; Santoni, G. J. "The Employment Act of 1946: Some History Notes." Federal Reserve Bank of St. Louis *Review* (November 1986): 5–16.

FULL EMPLOYMENT AND BALANCED GROWTH (HUMPHREY-HAWKINS) ACT OF 1978.

Referred to as the Humphrey-Hawkins Act in recognition of its sponsors, this legislation attempted to revitalize and expand the **Full Employment Act of 1946**.

Whereas the 1946 act set out the general policy guidelines of reducing unemployment, promoting **economic growth** and minimizing **inflation**, Humphrey-Hawkins was much more specific. In addition to these broad goals, it required the federal government to balance the federal budget and established set goals for the **unemployment rate** of not more than 4 percent and a target rate of inflation of not more than 3 percent. (See below for more specific details of the act.) In retrospect, none of these goals or the constraints on the federal government had a lasting effect on government actions. To a large extent, current policies are still directed by the broad notion of economic growth, low unemployment, and price stability.

One lasting aspect of the Humphrey-Hawkins Act affects the **transparency** of Federal Reserve policy deliberations. Historically, the Federal Reserve established monetary policy without providing any details on how decisions were reached or why different policy actions were taken. Minutes of the **Federal Open Market Committee (FOMC)** meetings were available only with an extended time lag, which made them useful only to historians. Humphrey-Hawkins increased the transparency of monetary policy—that is, the ability of the public to know and understand policy actions and decisions—by requiring the Federal Reserve Board to report to Congress twice a year on its monetary policies and the actions taken to achieve these goals. Today, the chairman of the Federal Reserve Board continues to testify before banking committees in the House and the Senate in February and in July. Although the chairman at one time was required under Humphrey-Hawkins to state the Federal Reserve's target growth ranges for its monetary aggregates, that requirement has been dropped as monetary policy deemphasized the growth of the monetary aggregates in favor of **federal funds rate targeting**. In testimony before Congress, the chairman of the **Board of Governors** usually takes this opportunity to provide the Federal Reserve's outlook on the economy and potential monetary policy actions in light of this forecast.

The following, taken from Santoni (1986, p. 14), summarizes the central provisions of the Humphrey-Hawkins Act:

Title I—National Goals and Priorities

1. Declares a national policy of promoting full employment, increased real income, balanced growth, a balanced federal budget, growth in productivity, an improved balance of trade, and price stability.
2. Declares a policy of primary reliance on the private sector for accomplishing the above economic goals.
3. Encourages the adoption of fiscal policy that would reduce federal spending as a percentage of GNP.
4. Requires the President to set budgetary goals so as to achieve an unemployment rate of not more than 3 percent among persons aged 20 and over, and 4 percent for persons aged 16 and over by 1983.
5. Requires the President to set a budgetary goal of reducing the rate of inflation to 3 percent by 1983. Furthermore, once the goal set in 4 above is achieved, the President is required to set a goal directed at reducing inflation to 0 percent by 1988.
6. Allows the President to modify the timetables for achieving goals set forth in 4 and 5 above.
7. Requires the Federal Reserve Board to report to the Congress twice a year on its monetary policies and their relationship to the goals of the act.

Title II—Structural Economic Policies

1. Permitted the President to establish "reservoirs of public employment," if he found that other policies were failing to achieve full employment goals.
2. Required that any reservoir jobs be useful and in the lower ranges of skill and pay, be targeted on individuals and areas with the worst unemployment problems and be set up so as not to draw workers from the private sector.

Title III—Congressional Review

1. Establishes procedures for Congressional review of Federal Reserve Board goals and policies.
2. Gives Congress the option of determining when the full employment goal could be reached should the President declare that the goal could not be met by 1983.

Title IV—General Provisions

1. Prohibits discrimination on account of sex, race, age, religion, or national origin in any program under the bill.
2. Provides that workers in reservoir jobs be given equal pay for equal work, but not less than the federal minimum wage.

FURTHER READING

Santoni, G. J. "The Employment Act of 1946: Some History Notes." Federal Reserve Bank of St. Louis *Economic Review* (November 1986): 5–16.

GARN-ST. GERMAIN ACT (*See* **Depository Institutions Act of 1982**)

GLASS, CARTER (1858–1946). Carter Glass was a newspaperman, a railroad man, a politician, and a pioneer in the formation of the Federal Reserve. After a successful career in the newspaper business, as both reporter and publisher, Glass entered politics in 1899 when he was elected to the Virginia Senate. During his time in the Virginia Senate (1899–1903), Glass was embroiled in several important political debates. One of these occurred when Glass was a delegate to the State Constitutional Convention in 1901. At the convention, Glass helped push through a proposal that would allow a new state constitution to be declared without submitting it to popular vote. This plan, which was defeated, would have effectively disenfranchised large segments of the population.

In 1902, Glass was elected as a Democrat to the U.S. House of Representatives to fill the vacancy caused by the death of Peter J. Otey. In 1904, Glass was appointed to the Committee on Banking and Currency, an appointment that would propel him into the forefront of the debate over resolving the nation's banking problems. The **Panic of 1907** brought with it increasing demands for a dramatic overhaul of the nation's banking system. The committee, with Glass as its chairman, began to consider the issues of most import; namely, that the banking system was prone to systemic failure and that the nation's **currency** was not responsive to changes in economic activity. (The work of the **National Monetary Commission**, discussed elsewhere in this volume, also was instrumental in this debate.)

Glass helped to draft the initial legislation that would create the central bank. Glass, who favored a decentralized system, used parts of failed legislation proposed by the previous Republican administration. As his proposals circulated, many suggested that Glass's ideas were retreads of the earlier Aldrich Plan, a charge that Glass denied. In the end, Glass was instrumental in ushering through the legislation that would become the **Federal Reserve Act of 1913**. The act reflected Glass's desire to decentralize the control over the banking system. At the same time, seeing the need for some overarching control, President **Woodrow Wilson** suggested a board of governors, members of which would be appointed by the president. Glass's promotion of the Federal Reserve Act and its eventual passage in 1913 earned him the title of "Father of the Federal Reserve."

Glass resigned from the U.S. House of Representatives in 1916 to become the secretary of the Treasury. Appointed by his long-time friend President Wilson, Glass served as secretary until 1920, when he resigned to accept the position of U.S. senator from Virginia, a position that he assumed on the death of Thomas Martin. He was subsequently reelected to the Senate in 1924, 1930, 1936, and 1942.

Glass was instrumental in other pieces of legislation that impacted the banking system. He cosponsored the **Glass-Steagall Act of 1932**, legislation that most notably separated commercial and investment banking activities. But Glass did not favor all of the banking-related legislation that stemmed from the **Great Depression**. For example, he opposed the development of the **Federal Deposit Insurance Corporation (FDIC)**, which was part of the Banking Act of 1933. Glass died in 1946 at the age of 88.

FURTHER READING

Friedman, Milton, and Anna J. Schwartz. *A Monetary History of the United States, 1867–1960.* Princeton: Princeton University Press, 1963; Meltzer, Allan H. *A History of the Federal Reserve, Vol. 1: 1913–1951.* Chicago: University of Chicago Press, 2003; Page, David. "Carter Glass." Federal Reserve Bank of Minneapolis *The Region* (December 1997).

GLASS-STEAGALL ACT OF 1932. The onset and duration of the **Great Depression** brought to light some problems with the limitations placed on the Federal Reserve in the **Federal Reserve Act of 1913**. For example, the act barred the Federal Reserve banks from using government securities as collateral for **currency**. The Glass-Steagall Act, passed on February 27, 1932, removed this ban. Originally, passage of Glass-Steagall was seen as a temporary move to enable the Federal Reserve to become more expansionary. Although the act was scheduled to expire in March 1933, it became permanent.

As discussed by Meltzer (2003), the Glass-Steagall Act had several effects on Federal Reserve activity. First, Federal Reserve District Banks were now able to use their holdings of government securities as collateral against Federal Reserve notes. Second, the act added Sections 10(a) and 10(b) to the Federal Reserve Act, which enabled Federal Reserve banks to lend through the **discount window** on **commercial paper** at a rate 1 percentage point above the **discount rate**. Previously such commercial paper was not eligible as backing for discount **loans**. This second aspect enabled Federal Reserve banks to lend to banks using a broader array of financial assets, thus giving the Federal Reserve banks more room to engage in expansionary policy actions. And third, the act allowed groups of five or more banks to borrow from the Federal Reserve based on the groups', not the individual bank's, credit. This portion of the act opened the window to existing clearinghouses and encouraged banks to form such clearinghouses.

FURTHER READING

Meltzer, Allan H. *A History of the Federal Reserve: Volume I: 1913–1951.* Chicago: University of Chicago Press, 2003; Moore, Carl H. *The Federal Reserve System: A History of the First 75 Years.* Jefferson, NC: McFarland, 1990.

GOALS OF MONETARY POLICY. The "official" goals of monetary policy are proscribed in two pieces of legislation: the **Full Employment Act of 1946** and the so-called **Humphrey-Hawkins Act of 1978**. In each of these, Congress established that the

Federal Reserve should follow policies aimed at maintaining steady **economic growth** (i.e., low **unemployment** rates) and stable prices (i.e., low **inflation**). In the Humphrey-Hawkins Act, Congress even went so far as to state specific numerical targets for the rate of economic growth and the rate of inflation.

Economists have come to realize that the Federal Reserve cannot follow policies that will, at all times, prevent economic downturns from occurring. Still, when such economic fluctuations occur, the Federal Reserve can follow policies that are aimed at stabilizing the economy. For example, if the economy experiences a slowdown in economic activity and an increase in the unemployment rate, the Federal Reserve can undertake policies that will help stimulate the economy and push it back to its full-employment level of output. Or, if the economy appears to be growing too fast, the Federal Reserve can pursue policies that help slow economic growth and once again return it to its full employment level. How successful the Federal Reserve is in achieving this goal is of course open to debate. Some economists argue that the Federal Reserve's actions to stimulate economic activity in order to offset a contraction often occur because the Federal Reserve had previously attempted to slow the economy. In other words, Federal Reserve policies are sometimes viewed as simply trying to correct previous mistakes. Still, in the short run, the Federal Reserve is concerned with trying to maintain the growth rate of output and levels of the unemployment rate that are associated with an economy growing at its long-term rate.

There is a great deal of evidence that monetary polices, while they may affect economic activity in the short run, have little impact on the economy over long periods of time. That is, if the Federal Reserve were to follow an expansionary policy even after the economy had achieved full employment, it is not able to make the economy grow any faster over time. In the long run, the growth of output and the level of employment are more likely to be explained by economic factors other than monetary policy. Such factors include the amount of investment in new plant and equipment, individual preferences for savings and work, and the growth or discovery of new technologies. A number of economic studies show that once these factors are accounted for, changes in monetary policy add no additional information to explain economic growth.

Studies show that monetary policies that persistently attempt to push the real economic activity beyond its long-run level lead to increased levels of inflation. This is why the objective of "price stability" or low rates of inflation is considered to be a key goal of monetary policy. **Milton Friedman**, the Nobel Prize laureate in economics, observed that "inflation is always and everywhere a monetary phenomenon."

Friedman's observation, based on a very large number of studies, means that sustained periods of inflation cannot exist unless excessive money growth occurs at the same time. By having monetary policymakers focus on the long-term effects of their actions, a goal of low inflation leads to some very beneficial results for the economy. First, in a low-inflation environment, prices act as a truer signal of demand and supply conditions in the market for goods and services. If inflation is low, individuals and firms do not have to spend valuable economic resources trying to predict what prices will be in the future. Indeed, in those instances when inflation gets completely out of control—episodes known as *hyperinflation*—the pricing mechanism of the market place simply breaks down. And in each case of hyperinflation, excessive money growth was the culprit. Second, when inflation is low and more predictable, there is less uncertainty in borrowing. Lenders's expectations of future inflation are embedded in interest rates on loans. When the rate of inflation is high, it frequently is also more variable and, therefore, more unpredictable. This means that there is more uncertainty about the level of interest rates in the future. In high-inflation countries, planning, contracting, and borrowing are all hindered, thus retarding economic development.

Because the various goals of monetary policy have different time horizons associated with them, they sometimes are in conflict with each other. For example, suppose economic growth is slowing sharply and the economy appears to be moving toward recession. According to the accepted wisdom, monetary policymakers should implement expansionary policies to ward off the downturn. But what if, at the same time, inflation also is increasing? This would call for a monetary policy that was more restrictive in order to fight inflation. The problem is that the goals are in direct conflict with each other. If the Federal Reserve were to fight the impending downturn, then it would likely increase the rate of inflation rate. If it fights the increase in inflation, then it could deepen the downturn and push unemployment rates even higher. Can such conflicting policy scenarios ever exist? Yes, with the best example being the economic events surrounding the recession that occurred in the mid-1970s. At that time, oil prices were being pushed up by the Organization of Petroleum Exporting Countries (OPEC), and the result was an increase in inflation rates and a slowing in economic activity.

What is the correct policy action? In the end, the answer depends on one's viewpoint. If one believes that the economy is self-stabilizing—it tends to self-correct when it is growing too slowly or too fast—then policymakers should focus on the long-term goal of price stability and low inflation. If, on the other hand, one believes that being in a recession is simply too costly in terms of lost output and the economic and social affects on people, then the policy for the Federal Reserve to follow may be one that focuses more on keeping the economy operating at full employment even if the cost is slightly higher rates of inflation. In the end, the Federal Reserve walks a thin line between trying to meet its competing goals.

FURTHER READING

Espinosa-Vega, Marco. "How Powerful is Monetary Policy in the Long Run?" Federal Reserve Bank of Atlanta *Economic Review* (Third Quarter 1998): 12–31; Dewald, William G. "Money Still Matters." Federal Reserve Bank of St. Louis *Economic Review* (November/December 1998): 13–24; Dwyer, Gerald P., Jr., and R. W. Hafer, "Are Money Growth and Inflation Still Related?" Federal Reserve Bank of Atlanta *Economic Review* (Second Quarter 1999): 32–43; Judd, John P., and Glenn D. Rudebusch. "The Goals of U.S. Monetary Policy." Federal Reserve Bank of San Francisco *Economic Letter* (January 29, 1999); Mayer, Thomas. *Monetary Policy and the Great Inflation in the United States: The Federal Reserve and the Failure of Macroeconomic Policy: 1965–1979*. Cheltenham, UK: Edward Elgar, 1999.

GOLD STANDARD. When people discuss the gold standard, they generally are referring to a period in time when a number of countries agreed to fix the "price" of their currencies to a specific amount of gold. In other words, the countries' central banks stood ready to buy and sell gold to anyone at the stated price. As an example, Great Britain fixed the price of gold at 3 pounds, 17 shillings, and 19.5 pence per ounce over the period 1821–1914. The United States fixed the price of gold at $20.67 per ounce from 1834 through 1933, excluding the so-called "Greenback era," which lasted from 1861 through 1878.

Gold emerged as an early form of commodity money because of several physical attributes. Among these attributes, gold is durable, storable, portable, divisible, recognizable, and easily formed into coin. This latter attribute makes it easy to standardize gold coins and maintain their exchange value. An important aspect that makes gold desirable as commodity money is that the stock of gold does not change very much over time. Because it is expensive to produce, it is difficult to increase the stock of gold in the short run. This makes it difficult for governments to actively manipulate the stock of gold, which gives rise to long-term price stability. Because gold exists both as a commodity—used in jewelry, dentistry, industry, etc.—and as a **money**, there are competitive pressures in the market that drive the price of gold—and the exchange value of a country's **currency**—up and down over time. Bordo (1981) notes that this property means that "the purchasing power of a unit of [gold] or what it will buy in terms of all other goods and services, will always tend toward equality with its long-run cost of production."

How does a gold standard work? Let's first suppose that our example economy does not trade with other countries and that only gold is used as money. In this country the government stands ready to buy and sell gold at some specified price. In this situation, prices in the economy will be determined by fluctuations in the supply of and demand for gold. In the long run, competitive pressures in the gold-producing industry will push the price of gold—and hence the average price of all goods and services—to equal the opportunity cost of producing one more unit of gold. Consider what happens when there is a discovery of gold such as occurred at Sutter's Mill in California in 1849. The discovery increases the stock of gold and therefore the money supply. Because the supply of gold coin is greater after the discovery, the prices of goods and services will tend to increase as well. This increase in the price level—and the simultaneous decrease in the purchasing power of gold coin—causes a shift from using gold as a commodity money to its other, nonmonetary uses. This shift in use and the reduced profitability of producing gold leads to a reduction in gold output over time. This eventual reduction in gold production serves to offset the initial effects of the gold discovery and reverse earlier price level increases. In this manner, changes in the production of gold, over time, leads to stability in the price level. To put it another way, under a gold standard it is common to see an average rate of inflation equal to zero over time.

If a gold standard has the properties of producing long-term price stability in a closed economy, what happens when we allow trade between countries to occur? In this case a gold standard system leads to a fixed **exchange rate** between currencies from different countries. For example, given the price of gold price as stated in British pounds and U.S. dollars, the pound/dollar exchange rate was determined to be $4.867 per pound. As long as the United States and Britain maintained their pound-gold and dollar-gold prices, then the dollar/pound exchange rate would remain fixed. Historically, because Britain and the United States were the dominant economies, their fixed exchange rate was referred to as the *par* exchange rate, or the exchange rate to which all others could be compared.

Fixing domestic prices of gold and therefore international exchange rates had the benefit of stabilizing prices across countries. This process, known as the *price-specie-flow* mechanism, worked in the following manner. Suppose there is an increase in the stock of gold in the United States. Initially, this will increase prices for goods in the United States as the stock of gold coin rises and its purchasing power declines. As the price of U.S. goods increase, this will result in a decrease in the demand for U.S. exports. Because prices in other countries have not changed, U.S. goods now are more expensive. This also means that there will be an increase in the demand for imports from abroad, because they are now relatively less expensive than before. These demand changes for imports to the United States and exports from the United States will induce gold to flow from the United States to other countries. This gold outflow from the United States helps to reduce the money stock here and cushion the effects of the gold discovery. Similarly, the inflow of gold into other countries has the effect of increasing their money stocks with the consequence of raising their prices. In the final analysis, this flow of gold from countries with increasing gold stocks (and price levels) to other countries not experiencing such a change serves to keep prices in line among countries that trade with each other. Thus, whether it is an economy closed to the rest of the world or one that freely trades with others, one aspect of the gold standard system is that it served to keep prices stable.

The gold standard existed in one form or another from 1821 through 1971. The period up to the establishment of the Federal Reserve, 1821–1914, often is referred to as the "Classical" period of the gold standard. The start date is associated with the end of the Napoleonic War, when Great Britain restored its pledge to convert gold to pounds at a predetermined rate. From this date through the 1800s, the number of countries operating under the gold standard expanded. By 1880 most countries in the world had ceased using silver coin and converted to the gold standard system. Bordo (1981, p. 7) describes the period from 1880 to 1914 as the "heyday of the gold standard ... a remarkable period in world economic history. It was characterized by rapid economic growth, the free flow of labor and capital across political borders, virtually free trade and, in general, world peace. These external conditions, coupled with the elaborate financial network centered in London and the role of the Bank of England as umpire to the system, are believed to by the *sine qua non* of the effective operation of the gold standard."

The role of the Bank of England—Britain's central bank—was critical for the success of the gold standard. During most of this period, the Bank of England acted to maintain the exchange value of the pound relative to an ounce of gold. When Britain experienced gold flows, the bank altered domestic interest rates to expedite the adjustment process. That is, it attempted to manipulate the domestic money supply and hence domestic economic activity in response to external gold flows. When gold reserves were declining, the bank raised interest rates to attract gold from abroad: Higher interest rates meant that British investments were more attractive to foreign investors and thus induced an inflow of gold. When there were inflows of gold, the bank would lower domestic interest rates, hoping to achieve exactly the opposite effect. In this manner, the Bank of England not only followed the rules of the game but also acted as the referee for the gold standard system (remember that the Federal Reserve did not exist at this time).

Even though the Bank of England played by the rules, Bordo (1981) suggests that most other countries on the gold standard did not. He notes that (p. 6) "there is evidence that interest rates were never allowed to rise enough to contract the domestic price level— that these countries did not follow the rules of the game. Also, many countries frequently followed policies of sterilizing gold flows—attempting to neutralize the effects of gold flows on the domestic money supply by open market purchases or sales of domestic securities."

The next significant period for the gold standard followed World War I. During the war, the gold standard did not function. Britain suspended payments for gold at the prewar ratio. Following the war, Britain attempted, unsuccessfully, to achieve prewar parities. In 1925, there began a period known as the gold exchange standard. Under this system, the United States and Britain held reserves only in gold. All other countries, in contrast, could hold reserves in the form of gold, dollars, or pounds. What this effectively did was to put the United States and Britain, the most influential and largest economies, squarely in the driver's seat when it came to international finance. This meant that the two countries were forced to act as the gold standard's "traffic cops." Even though they followed the rules of the game, most other countries continued to violate them by engaging in policies that protected their domestic money stocks from gold flows. This continued pressure on the system lasted until 1931 when, with the **Great Depression** well under way, Britain abandoned the gold standard.

From 1931 to the end of World War II, there was a managed fiduciary system. Following World War II, a new type of managed exchange system was attempted. Known as the **Bretton Woods System**, it was an attempt to restore to the world economy an exchange system patterned after the gold standard but this time with the U.S. dollar as the key currency. Except for those countries aligned with the British pound, all other counties settled their international balances in dollars. Because the United States fixed the price of gold at $35 per ounce and had vast gold reserves, the United States effectively became the modern-day version of the Bank of England in the 1800s. As did the Bank of England in the 1800s, the U.S. government agreed to settle external accounts in terms of gold.

The problem with this arrangement was that because the dollar became the de facto international currency, replacing gold, the use of dollars to settle international transactions meant that it put increased pressure on U.S. gold reserves. With the number of dollars in circulation increasing, there arose a concern that the United States would not be able to meet its obligations in terms of exchanging dollars for gold. Not only did the public's confidence in the ability of the United States to meet its obligations wane, but policy actions taken by the Federal Reserve during this time led to concern that the United States was exporting inflation. The United States was running a persistent balance-of-payments deficit—exports were less than imports—dollars were flowing abroad. Because the decade of the 1960s saw U.S. inflation rates rising, this meant that the growth rate of the money stock was increasing and the purchasing power of a dollar was falling.

After years of debate and argument, both domestically and with foreign governments, it was clear that the Bretton Woods System of managed exchange rates could not survive. The final blow to the gold standard system came in 1971, when President Richard M. Nixon announced that the United States would no longer peg the price of gold at $35 per ounce. This "closing of the **gold window**" marked the end of the gold standard system in any of its forms. Although there were several attempts to revive the exchange rate system that existed under Bretton Woods, in the end most countries chose to allow their currencies to float against the major countries.

FURTHER READING

Bordo, Michael D. "The Classical Gold Standard: Some Lessons for Today." Federal Reserve Bank of St. Louis *Review* (May 1981): 2–17; Cagan, Phillip. *Current Problems of Monetary Policy: Would the Gold Standard Help?* Washington, D.C.: The Free Enterprise Institute, 1982; Eichengreen, Barry. *The Gold Standard in Theory and in History*. London: Methun, 1985; U.S. Gold Commission. *Report to Congress of the Commission on the Role of Gold in the Domestic and International Monetary Systems*, 2 vols. Washington, D.C.: Government Printing Office, 1982.

GOLD WINDOW. This term is most often associated with the dramatic policy shift brought about by President Richard M. Nixon. On August 15, 1971, President Nixon announced the details of his New Economic Policy. In addition to several domestic policy changes—a phased-in wage and price control program, for example—Nixon's policy radically changed the way the United States and foreign nations met their trading obligations. In his address, Nixon announced that henceforth the United States would no longer agree to redeem dollars for a fixed amount of gold. This decision, which for all intents ended the **gold standard** system, closed the "gold window": that is, it ended the convertibility of dollars into gold.

Why is this action important in the discussion of the Federal Reserve? Prior to Nixon's announcement, U.S. dollars were convertible into gold at a fixed exchange rate. Foreign governments that ran trade surpluses with the United States could acquire gold for these balances. In the late 1960s, mounting U.S. trade deficits—the value of U.S. imports of goods and services exceeded exports to others—meant that U.S. gold reserves fell. This meant that dollar claims against the U.S. gold supply rose sharply, high enough in fact that potential dollar claims far exceeded the actual supply of gold. In some eyes, this condition helped foster a climate in which there was a loss of confidence in the U.S. government's ability to meet its obligations.

When Nixon closed the gold window and severed the convertibility of the dollar, he essentially left foreign governments holding about $70 billion in dollars. This meant that dollars, no longer convertible into gold, became worth whatever they could purchase. In effect, the closing of the gold window converted the monetary system into a true **fiat money** system, one in which the backing of the dollar was the pledge of the U.S. government to maintain the value of the dollar. In response to this change, foreign governments were left with little alternative but to hold U.S. dollars as reserves, thus raising the dollar to the status of an international medium of exchange. Gold became, at this time, separated from the Federal Reserve's decision process, a commodity whose value was determined solely in the market for metals, the same as silver, copper or tin.

FURTHER READING

Matusow, Allen J. *Nixon's Economy: Booms, Busts, Dollars, and Votes.* Lawrence, KS: University Press of Kansas, 1998; Yergin, Daniel, and Joseph Stanislaw. *The Commanding Heights.* New York: Simon & Schuster, 1997.

GRAMM-LEACH-BLILEY ACT. The Gramm-Leach-Bliley Act, also known as the Financial Modernization Act of 1999, was signed into law in November 1999. This act is significant for several reasons. First, the act impacts how financial institutions treat customers' financial information. Second, the act breaks down many of the barriers erected by the **Banking Act of 1933**, barriers that separated depository activities of banks from securities underwriting. The act thus affects the association between banks, securities firms, and insurance companies.

The act (hereafter referred to as GLB) authorizes eight federal agencies and states to administer the Financial Privacy Rule, a component of GLB. This rule applies not only to depository institutions, such as banks, but also securities firms and insurance companies. Who is covered by the Privacy Rule? The Federal Trade Commission (FTC) ruled that the Privacy Rule covers "any institution the business of which is engaging in financial

Banking Assets as Share of BHC Assets

Source: Furlong (2000).

activities as described in Section 4(k) of the **Bank Holding Company Act of 1956**." Which financial activities are covered? The FTC specifies these activities as including "lending money, investing for others, insuring against loss, providing financial advice or making a market in securities." The rule sets up a framework within which financial institutions can collect and disclose customers' personal financial information. The purpose of GLB was to restrain financial institutions from providing, unbeknownst to customers, personal financial information to third parties. In the event that a financial institution wishes to do so, it must request permission from the customer. In addition, GLB requires financial institutions to disclose to customers their privacy policies and practices.

While the privacy provisions of GLB are significant, perhaps more important is what GLB did to the landscape of the financial market. With the passage of GLB, the barriers that separated financial institutions were largely torn down. Breaking down the decades-old provisions of the Banking Act of 1933 that prohibited affiliations between banks, securities firms, and insurance companies, GLB significantly affects the provision of financial services. Still, it is well known that banks had successfully skirted the rules for some years. Furlong (2000) notes that "Section 20 [of the Banking Act of 1933] prohibited banks from affiliating with firms 'engaged principally' in underwriting and dealing in securities, like corporate bonds and equity. That phrase—'engaged principally'—left room for a bank holding company to form a subsidiary that conducted a large portion of permissible activities and a smaller portion of otherwise prohibited activities." This ability of banks to circumvent the 1933 law led to the formation of over 50 security subsidiaries by banking organizations in recent years. As shown in the figure above, banks successfully integrated to quite an extent prior to passage of GLB. This figure, reprinted from Furlong (2000), shows the banking assets as a share of **bank holding company** assets for some large financial organizations.

Another aspect of GLB is that it permits bank holding companies to become financial holding companies. To become a financial holding company, or FHC, the depository institution must show that it is well capitalized and well managed. This means that all

GLBA: Organizational Structure

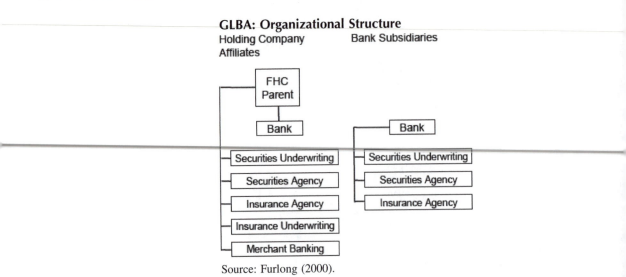

Source: Furlong (2000).

subsidiaries of the institutions must have a CRA (Community Reinvestment Act) rating of satisfactory or better. To become an FHC, the bank holding company must file for certification with the appropriate Federal Reserve Bank and the Federal Reserve Board declaring that its subsidiaries meet the same criteria of being well capitalized and well managed. Once the holding company achieves the designation of an FHC, it may engage in a variety of finance-related activities, including securities underwriting and dealing, insurance agency and underwriting, and merchant banking activities.

Another aspect of GLB is that it compromised on the structure of resultant FHCs and where various activities are housed. Furlong (2000) notes that, "While a number of activities, including underwriting municipal securities, can be done within the bank, most of the avenues for financial integration are pushed out to holding company affiliates or bank subsidiaries." As shown in the figure above from Furlong (2000), newly acquired financial activities could be conducted within the confines of the bank holding company or in a financial subsidiary of the bank.

Finally, regulatory supervision under GLB is placed under the umbrella of the Federal Reserve Board. The board serves as the supervisor of all bank holding companies and FHCs. Given this power, the board may require reports from and examine all bank holding companies, financial holding companies, and any subsidiary of the two. In fulfilling this role, the board relies on financial statements, reports submitted to regulatory agencies and examination reports provided by a subsidiary's functional regulator. There are limits to the board's influence. In general, the board is prohibited from imposing capital requirements on a regulated subsidiary if that subsidiary is already meeting federal and state requirements. In this sense, the primary regulators for banking activities are the Federal Reserve, the **Federal Deposit Insurance Corporation (FDIC)**, and the Office of the **Comptroller of the Currency** (OCC); for security activities, the principal regulators are the Securities Exchange Commission (SEC) and the Commodities Futures Trading Commission (CFTC); and for insurance activities, it generally is the various state insurance commissions.

Although the financial services industry has evolved dramatically over the past years, passage of the Gramm-Leach-Bliley Act of 1999 has helped clear the way for financial institutions to efficiently reorganize to provide a wider variety of financial services to customers. In addition, GLB has raised barriers to financial firms with regard to their use and reporting of personal financial information. Generally, the act recognizes that technological changes have made the laws passed in the 1930s operationally obsolete. It also deals with the ease with which new technologies can be used to gather customer information, even when its distribution is not granted. (A complete text of the act can be found at http://www.senate.gov/~banking/conf/.)

FURTHER READING

Federal Reserve Bank of San Francisco. "Overview of the Gramm-Leach-Bliley Act." Website: www.frbsf.org/publications/economics/letter/index.html; Federal Trade Commission. "Frequently Asked Questions About the Gramm-Leach-Bliley Financial Privacy Act." Website: www.ftc.gov; Furlong, Fred. "The Gramm-Leach-Bliley Act and Financial Integration." Federal Reserve Bank of San Francisco *Economic Letter* (March 31, 2000).

GREAT CRASH. The stock market crash of 1929—the Great Crash—remains as a vivid picture of financial chaos even today. One reason is because, aside from the stock market decline of 1987 and the more recent bursting of the stock bubble in 2000, the Great Crash stands out as a defining moment in U.S. economic history. Indeed, some have suggested that the crash brought on the **Great Depression**. While the stock market's role in precipitating the ensuing economic downturn remains a subject of academic study and debate, there is no question that the consequences of the stock crash were widespread. The crash helped define the policies implemented by the Federal Reserve, policies that may have exacerbated the decline in economic activity.

To put the 1929 crash in perspective, the chart below plots the daily closing value of the Dow Jones Industrial Average (DJIA) over the period 1920–1935. This chart is useful because it illustrates the tremendous run-up in stock prices during the "Roaring Twenties" and the equally dramatic decline in stock prices between 1929 and 1933. To put some numbers on the chart, the DJIA stood at about 65 on June 20, 1921. Although the rise is masked somewhat in the chart due to the scale, by June 20, 1925, the index had risen to 129, a 98 percent increase over the five years. Significant as this may seem, it palls in comparison to the steep climb that stock prices made in the next few years. By early September 1929, the DJIA surpassed 380, nearly a 200 percent increase since mid-decade. But that was the end of the ride. Over the next month the stock index would lose 14 percent of its value, dropping to about 330. By the end of 1929, the Dow would sink further, ending the year at 248. All told, from its peak value, the DJIA lost more than one third of its value in just three months. And, as the chart shows, even though there was an aborted recovery in stock prices in 1930, the DJIA continued to slide as the Depression worsened. By the middle of 1932, the index stood at less than 50, or only about 14 percent of its previous high value.

Those are the facts of the Great Crash, at least in terms of the stock market. And more detail can be found elsewhere about significant days that characterize the crash. What interests us here is to consider events leading up to the market crash, the Federal Reserve's role, and its response.

Dow Jones Industrial Average: Close

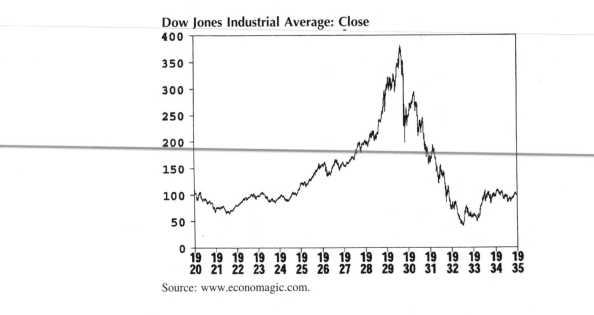

Source: www.economagic.com.

By the late 1920s, the Federal Reserve was concerned about the rapid run-up in stock prices. For the most part, statements by Federal Reserve officials indicated that they feared that prices were being driven by significant speculative behavior. While speculation is present in any asset market, in the late 1920s, as in the late 1990s, the fear was that speculation had become the dominant explanation for investors' stock purchases. In 1928 and 1929, the Federal Reserve attempted to temper this speculation by raising the **margin requirements** that investors faced. In effect, what the Federal Reserve did was to increase the cost to borrow money used to purchase stock. The Federal Reserve also raised interest rates in the hopes that these actions would redirect funds away from the stock market and into "productive" investments. For instance, it raised the **discount rate**—the rate that the Federal Reserve charges banks to borrow from it—from 3.5 percent to 5.0 percent during the first half of 1928. Because the price level was actually declining, the "real" discount rate actually was increasing to about 6 percent. (The real discount rate is calculated as the discount rate less expected inflation. A *negative* expected rate of inflation means that the real discount rate was increasing, even without Federal Reserve actions.) While it was raising the discount rate, the Federal Reserve also began to absorb reserves out of the banking system with an eye to slowing the growth rate of the money supply and, it was hoped, cooling off the economy and the stock market. As Hamilton (1987) reports, **open market operations** to drain bank reserves were accomplished by the Federal Reserve's sale of more than three quarters of its total stock of government securities. To put it mildly, monetary policy was very contractionary.

At this time, a number of countries had returned to the **gold standard**. One effect of this was that when the Federal Reserve followed a tight monetary policy, it impacted other countries' policy actions. Because the United States was the dominant economic power, when the Federal Reserve tightened, the rules of the gold standard necessitated that other countries follow suit. If they did not do so, they would face balance of payments deficits, which in turn gave them two options: devalue their currencies or abandon the gold standard altogether. Given these choices, most central banks chose to follow the Federal Reserve's lead and follow a contractionary monetary policy, even though, based purely on domestic policy needs, such an action was unwarranted. Many of the European countries, for example, were in the process of rebuilding from the ravages of World War I, and a tighter monetary policy was not their preferred course of action. As a consequence of the Federal Reserve's actions and the fetters of the gold standard, 1928 witnessed a global tightening in monetary policy. The consequence of this was that economic growth slowed in 1929 in the United States, reaching a **business cycle** peak in August and entering a recession in September. The crash of the stock market came a month later in October.

How did the Federal Reserve respond? Immediately following the crash, the Federal Reserve Bank of New York moved to ease conditions in credit markets because there was a squeeze in credit markets. This arose because the crash prompted calls from brokers and dealers to investors who had purchased stocks on margin to pay off their loans. Because a large amount of stock purchase was done on margin with a speculative intent, many investors simply did not have the funds available to meet margin calls. This led some lenders to call their loans to brokers. What the Federal Reserve did was to convince several large New York banks to take on the brokers' loans. It also allowed these banks to borrow freely at the **discount window**, much as the Federal Reserve did later in the 1987 crash. All of this was done to contain the liquidity crisis that emerged from the crash.

While this action is exactly what was called for if the Federal Reserve was to honor its role as **lender of last resort**, the problem was that the Federal Reserve did not maintain this policy very long. Soon after the crisis appeared to abate, the Federal Reserve returned to its contractionary stance, based on an argument by some within the Federal Reserve that not returning to its contractionary policy would simply reignite the speculative fever that had gripped the markets leading up to the crash. (Given the recession's start date, hindsight would show this policy to be inappropriate.) In 1930 the growth rate of the monetary aggregates turned negative and real interest rates increased. These policy actions on the heels of the crash no doubt deepened the recession that had begun in late 1929 and further contributed to the continued slide in the market. As Cogley (1999) has noted, "In retrospect, it seems that the lesson of the Great Crash is more about the difficulty of identifying speculative bubbles and the risks associated with aggressive actions conditioned on noisy observations. In the critical years 1928 to 1930, the Fed did not stand on the sidelines and allow asset prices to soar unabated. On the contrary. . . . The Fed succeeded in putting a halt to the rapid increase in share prices, but in doing so it may have contributed one of the main impulses for the Great Depression."

FURTHER READING

Cogley, Timothy. "Monetary Policy and the Great Crash of 1929: A Bursting Bubble or Collapsing Fundamentals?" Federal Reserve Bank of San Francisco *Economic Letter* (March 26, 1999); Friedman, Milton, and Anna J. Schwartz, *A Monetary History of the United States, 1867–1960*. Princeton: Princeton University Press, 1963; Galbraith, John Kenneth. *The Great Crash: 1929*. Boston: Houghton Mifflin, 1954; Hamilton, James D. "Monetary Factors in the Great Depression." *Journal of Monetary Economics* (1987): 145–69; Meltzer, Allan H. *A History of the Federal Reserve, Vol. 1: 1913–1951*. Chicago: University of Chicago Press, 2003.

GREAT DEPRESSION. The Great Depression was a defining moment in U.S. economic history. The depression, which generally is dated 1929–1933, created a more catastrophic decline in real economic output, increase in unemployment and decline in prices than any other economic downturn before or since. This discussion will attempt to provide a broad outline of the Great Depression, in terms of severity and possible explanations. Indeed, a complete discussion has filled books, several of which are referenced at the end of this entry.

The 1920s was a period of economic prosperity. The decade, known popularly as the Roaring Twenties, got this name for a variety of reasons. One is that the period following the end of World War I saw a significant increase in economic prosperity. For example, the percentage of homes using electricity for lighting increased from 35 percent in 1920 to almost 70 percent by 1930. More families owned automobiles: from 26 percent in 1920 to 60 percent in 1930. Radios went from being almost nonexistent in 1920 to 40 percent of households owning one by the end of the decade. (See Lebergott, 1962, for details.)

Along with the increase in standards of living, there was a dramatic change in how the economy operated. The use of credit was rapidly increasing as the mode by which consumers purchased an increasing array of goods from washing machines to cars. Employment was on the increase. Real earnings of workers increased for most of the decade, fueling the increased purchase of goods. By the end of the decade, the **unemployment rate** stood at a little over 3 percent. Although this is a rosy picture, not all sectors of the economy prospered. The agricultural sector, for example, faced hard times. Many farmers who incurred debt during the prosperous years before World War I now faced bankruptcy as land prices sagged. Prices for agricultural commodities also were falling as world markets faced surpluses.

Perhaps one of the most memorable aspects of the 1920s is the great run up in stock prices. Stock prices tripled between the early 1920s and 1929. But this is a bit misleading: Between 1922 and 1925, the Standard & Poor's Common Stock Index rose from 100 to 133, a 33 percent increase. From 1925 through 1929, however, the index increased from 133 to 309, a 132 percent increase in just 5 years. Why the take-off in stock prices? The rise cannot be explained by standard measures. During this period, stock prices increased at a much faster rate than can be explained by earnings increases, or even projected increases in earnings. Rather, it seemed as if stocks were being purchased not on the basis of an underlying valuation of the firms but on the pure speculation that stock prices would just continue to rise. Although some have argued that this buying of stocks was rational in the sense that many firms were producing new goods and investors hoped that they were buying into the newest Ford or RCA, it is hard to argue with the notion that many investors were buying stocks—and many on **loans** received from their banks—on the simple belief that stock prices would rise. This bull market and its abrupt end would not be repeated in U.S. economic history until the 1990s.

A common belief is that the Great Depression began with the stock market crash, which began in October 1929. While this is the first of several dramatic events associated with the depression, it does not mark the beginning of the economic downturn. As shown in the chart on top of the next page, industrial production of the economy began to slip several months earlier, peaking in August 1929. In fact, the National Bureau of Economic Research (NBER) designates August 1929 as the peak of the business cycle.

Why did the growth of economic output begin to slow in late summer 1929? Some argue that the slowing was due in part to actions taken by the Federal Reserve to stem the continued rise in the stock market. (See chart on bottom of next page.) Because a large part of stock purchases were being made with borrowed funds, in August the Federal Reserve

Industrial Production Index: Total index; 1997 = 100; Seasonally Adjusted

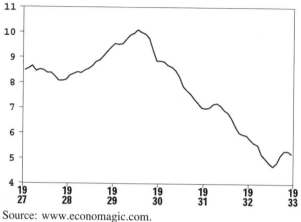

Source: www.economagic.com.

raised the **discount rate**—the rate at which banks borrow funds from the Federal Reserve. This increase, it was hoped, would curb speculation in the stock market and stem the flow of credit from banks to fund these purchases. Their efforts seemed in vain because stock prices continued to climb.

The Federal Reserve was not alone in its concern over the lofty stock prices. In September, a noted financial advisor, Roger Babson, predicted that the market was due for a correction. Whether Babson's predictions alone affected the psychology of investors or his comments together with Federal Reserve actions influenced investors' thinking is unknown. However, stocks did pull back slightly. By the end of August, the Dow Jones Industrial Average (DJIA) stood at 384, and one month later it dropped farther to 349. Sometimes referred to as the "Babson break," this decline was only a modest harbinger of what was to come.

Dow Jones Industrial Average: High

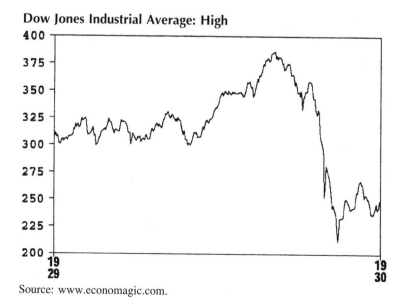

Source: www.economagic.com.

Dow Jones Industrial Average: High

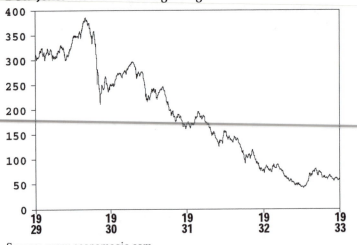

Source: www.economagic.com

By the end of October, stock prices had declined over 25 percent from their August levels. The biggest declines took place during the last weeks of October. (See chart above.) Stock prices dropped significantly, first on October 23 and 24 (Black Thursday) when trading was carried out at a significantly greater pace than ever before. On October 24, the number of shares traded exceeded 13 million, more than four times the average daily volume. Although a number of large banks organized the buying of stocks to prevent further declines, they could not stem the tide of selling: On October 28 and 29—Black Monday and Black Tuesday, respectively—stock prices continued their dramatic fall as investors dumped stocks. The *New York Times* headline for Tuesday, October 29, says it all: "Stock Prices Slump $14,000,000,000 in Nation-Wide Stampede to Unload; Bankers to Support Market Today." Even with this prediction of intervention, stock prices tumbled again on Tuesday. Although stock prices appeared to stabilize by the end of the year (see previous chart), further declines in stock prices would continue throughout the next several years (see chart above).

Although some consider the entire decade of the 1930s as the Great Depression, here the focus is on the period 1929–1933. How severe was the Depression? Let's consider several measures.

As shown in the above chart, stock prices declined in value for most of this period. From their peak value of 384 in August 1929, stock prices, measured as the DJIA, fell about 80 percent from their August 1929 level. The decline in stock values decimated individual wealth, which led to reduced spending and further downward pressure on the economy.

Other measures also show an economy in deep trouble. The chart on top of the next page shows the behavior of industrial production between 1929 and 1933. Following its peak in August 1929, industrial production declined steadily until late 1932 when it showed a slight rebound. At that time, industrial production was only about half of its 1929 level.

The decline in industrial production is mirrored in other measures of economic activity. Over the 1929–1933 period, gross national product (GNP) (today we use **gross domestic product [GDP]**), an overall measure of income generated in the economy, fell from $104 billion in 1929 to $56 billion in 1933, a decline of almost one half. Business

Industrial Production Index: Total index; 1997 = 100; SA

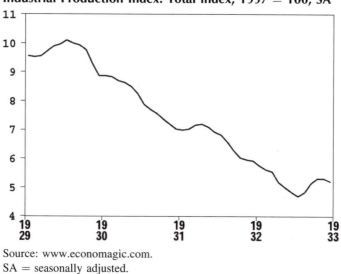

Source: www.economagic.com.
SA = seasonally adjusted.

investment in new factories and equipment also fell dramatically, dropping in real terms from about $35 billion in 1929 to slightly less than $5 billion by 1933.

These figures are startling. They indicate an economy that is collapsing. Two other statistics help drive this point home. One is the behavior of prices. As shown in the chart below, consumer prices, measured using the Consumer Price Index (CPI), fell throughout the 1929–1933 period. This decline in prices, technically referred to as **deflation**, meant that prices businesses received for their goods were declining. While this may sound like good news for consumers, it is not: declining prices mean that income derived from the sale of goods and services also is declining, as evidenced in the declining GNP numbers.

CPI: U.S. city average; All items - old base; 1967 = 100; NSA

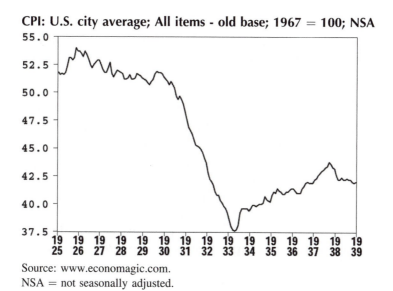

Source: www.economagic.com.
NSA = not seasonally adjusted.

The United States has not experienced another significant period of deflation since the period 1929–1933.

Finally, the unemployment rate during the Great Depression soared to heights that have not been revisited during any subsequent recession in the United States. At its peak, the number of unemployed stood at over 13 million people. By 1933, the official unemployment rate indicated that 25 percent of the labor force was unemployed. Keeping in mind that the gathering of official statistics on such measures was not as sophisticated as it is today, these numbers likely are not accurate: Unemployment during this time was probably higher than the "official" numbers indicate. To put these in perspective, during the recession year of 1982, the unemployment rate peaked at 9.5 percent, the worst in the post–World War II era.

Although many believe that the stock market crash of 1929 was *the* cause of the Great Depression, there are several other factors that help explain how a recession, albeit severe, turned into the calamity of the Great Depression. Even though the Roaring Twenties came to a sudden halt, could a reversal of the optimism that characterized the end of the decade explain, by itself, the next several years of economic decline?

Economists have long argued over the causes of the Great Depression. Several candidates have been offered in this discussion. One is passage of the Smoot-Hawley Act in 1930. Passed by Congress and signed by President **Herbert Hoover** in June 1930, the idea behind this act was to raise tariffs on imported goods, especially agricultural goods, thereby raising domestic agricultural prices and thus buoy the suffering agricultural sector of the economy. Although this bill was denounced by many policymakers and experts, it became law. Arguments against Smoot-Hawley focused on the detrimental effects that it would have on international trade. For example, by raising tariffs against foreign goods coming into the United States, residents here would be more likely to purchase goods produced domestically. While this would, the argument went, increase domestic purchases, it also would lessen incomes abroad. Because U.S. residents would reduce purchases of foreign goods, foreign incomes—and their ability to buy U.S. goods—would decline. This in turn meant that demand from abroad for U.S. goods would weaken, thus reducing incomes here. As you can see, the logic for the act was based on some spurious calculations. In reality, passage of Smoot-Hawley led to a round of retaliatory tariff increases by foreign countries with which the United States traded. As each country raised its tariffs on imported goods, international trade slowed. Indeed, some have argued that this upward spiral of tariffs partially explains the broad international impact of the Great Depression. (See Meltzer, 1976, for a discussion of this point.)

The failure of monetary policy to avert the severity of the Great Depression is another area of debate. Several possible areas of policy failures during this period have been debated for years. One is the series banking crises that occurred in waves, beginning in October 1930. Numerous bank failures in the South and the Midwest, associated with agricultural losses, occurred. The failures continued, until the December 11 collapse of the Bank of United States in New York City. Failure of the Bank of United States sent another shock wave throughout the financial community because this bank was not an ordinary bank: in terms of deposits at the time, it was the largest bank to fail in U.S. history.

The Federal Reserve, in the wake of this collapse, did not inject sufficient funds into the banking system. In other words, it did not act as **lender of last resort**. Rather, it operated under the mistaken belief that troubled banks were mismanaged and for the sake of efficiency should be closed. The Bank of United States and many others, lacking any support from the monetary authorities, simply closed their doors and denied depositors access to their funds. Of course, once word spread that a large bank failed and that the authorities did nothing to prevent it, a series of **bank runs** began. Depositors who feared that their bank could be next descended on banks to withdraw their deposits. Since the banking system operates on a **fractional reserve banking** basis—only a fraction of deposits are held in readily accessible form—many depositors were unable to complete withdrawals. Ultimately, many more banks closed their doors, some until funds could be gathered to meet depositor demands, others permanently.

Although there were other episodes of bank failures in intervening years, another significant round of bank failures took place in 1933. By March 1933, a total of 4,000 banks failed, representing more than $3 billion in lost deposits. (Between 1930 and 1932, 5,000 banks closed.) In the wake of this round of failures, newly inaugurated President **Franklin Roosevelt** called for the **Bank Holiday of 1933**, which began on March 6, and set aside a period of time when all banks would be closed for business. This allowed the government to inspect banks and to determine which were sound enough to reopen. Banks, enabled to get their financial affairs in order, reopened on firmer financial ground. This action, along with several pieces of legislation that increased depositor protection (*see* **Glass-Steagall Act of 1932**), reduced bank failures to 61 in 1934.

In conjunction with a failure of policy to respond adequately to the repeated waves of bank failures, some researchers have argued that monetary policy during this period was a major cause of the severity of the Great Depression. Associated primarily with the pioneering work of economists **Milton Friedman** and **Anna Jacobson Schwartz** (see Further Reading below), some argue that the Federal Reserve allowed itself to be swayed by the behavior of market interest rates in determining monetary policy. During the early 1930s, for example, market interest rates plummeted. Some in the Federal Reserve viewed this decline as an indication that there was an excess amount of money and credit in the economy. Because the interest rate is the "price" of credit, an excess amount of available credit relative to the amount demanded resulted in declining rates of interest. Because this is what was observed, the Federal Reserve did not see the need for a shift to an expansionary policy. This policy

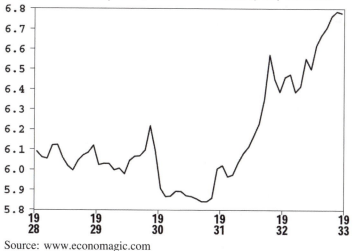

Adjusted Monetary Base; Billions of Dollars; SA; St. Louis

Source: www.economagic.com

decision is especially evident in the early stages of the depression. As shown in the previous chart, the adjusted **monetary base** (or base), a measure consisting of reserves and currency, declined sharply throughout 1930 and did not return to its pre-1930 level until mid-1932. This measure is often used to gauge monetary policy actions because it is believed that the Federal Reserve has a fair amount of direct control over its movements. Declines in the base thus represented conscious decisions by the Federal Reserve to either reduce the amount of money in the economy or not pursue sufficiently expansionary policies.

How did the behavior of the monetary base play out in terms of the money supply? Between 1929 and 1932, the money supply fell from about $47 billion to $36 billion, almost a 25 percent reduction. Even though the Federal Reserve undertook to expand the base in 1932, it was too little too late: the money supply fell further, from $36 billion in 1932 to $32 billion in 1933. Over the period 1929–1933, then, the money supply declined over 30 percent.

Whether this failure of monetary policy was *the* cause of the Great Depression's severity is a topic of continued debate. What most economists agree on is that the failure of monetary policymakers to act as lender of last resort during the wave of bank failures and their failure to reverse the dramatic decline in the money stock helps explain the severity of the recession that became the Great Depression.

FURTHER READING

Brunner, Karl, ed. *The Great Depression Revisited*. Boston: Martinus Nijhoff, 1981; Evans, Paul, Iftekhar Hasan, and Ellis W. Tallman. "Monetary Explanations of the Great Depression: A Selective Survey of the Evidence." Federal Reserve Bank of Atlanta *Economic Review* (Third Quarter, 2004): 1–24; Friedman, Milton, and Anna J. Schwartz, *A Monetary History of the United States, 1867–1960*. Princeton: Princeton University Press, 1963; Galbraith, John Kenneth. *The Great Crash of 1929*. Boston: Houghton-Mifflin, 1954); Kindleberger, Charles P. *Manias, Panics and Crashes*. New York: Basic Books, 1978; Lebergott, Stanley. *The American Economy: Income, Wealth and Want*. Princeton: Princeton University Press, 1976; Meltzer, Allan H. "Monetary and Other Explanations of the Start of the Great Depression." *Journal of Monetary Economics* (1976); Romer, Christina. "The Nation in Depression." *Journal of Economic Perspectives* (Spring 1993): 18–39.

GREAT INFLATION. When someone discusses the **Great Depression**, they mean the period 1929–1933, when the U.S. economy was in the throes of the worst economic downturn in its history. When someone refers to the "Great Inflation," they usually mean the period encompassing the 1960s and 1970s in the United States. Was the persistent increase in the price level—**inflation**—during this time on the same order of magnitude as the decline in output during the Great Depression? Hardly. But the period that begins in 1960 and ends in 1980 represents a unique period in U.S. history because the economy experienced a sustained increase in the rate of inflation. Indeed, it is this sustained increase in the rate of inflation that makes it of interest, because we wish to know why it occurred, whether monetary policy actions taken by the Federal Reserve contributed to its occurrence, and whether such an outcome can be prevented in the future.

To put the period in perspective, the figure below plots the rate of inflation, based on the Consumer Price Index (CPI), from 1951 through 1982. The chart begins with 1951 because it marks the Federal Reserve's independence from the U.S. Treasury in the conduct of monetary policy. (*See* **Treasury-Federal Reserve Accord of 1951**.) In response to the sharp

Inflation Rate
Quarterly Data, Consumer Price Index, 1951–82

Note: Shaded bars represent recessions.
Source: Hafer and Wheelock (2003).

increase in inflation that occurred in 1950 and early 1951, Federal Reserve officials wished to follow a policy of restraint but were committed to keep rates on Treasury securities low. The accord enabled monetary policymakers to pursue anti-inflation policies. As shown in the figure, these actions helped to reduce inflation in 1952 and to keep it low through 1956. Although inflation reached an annual rate of nearly 4 percent in 1957, it once again declined to under 2 percent and remained fairly close to that rate until 1965.

Beginning in 1965, the rate of inflation began to creep upward. From 1965 through the end of the decade, inflation rose from about 2 percent to nearly 6 percent. From there inflation continued to rise in successive waves. For example, after peaking at about 6 percent in 1970, it fell back to 3 percent only to rise again to over 12 percent by 1975. After that bout, it again retreated, but then jumped again in 1980 to its post-accord recent high of over 14 percent. Since 1980, inflation has decreased and, more recently, has behaved very similarly to the early 1960s.

What caused the Great Inflation? Some argue that a confluence of events brought about the rise in the rate of inflation. During this time policymakers' attention focused more on keeping the **unemployment rate** low than on keeping inflation at bay. A popular theory at the time was associated with the so-called **Phillips curve**. The Phillips curve plots the rate of inflation along with the unemployment rate. The notion was that one could view the two variables as a policy tradeoff: If an expansionary policy was followed that would increase the rate of inflation, then it also would reduce the unemployment rate. Or, if policy became restrictive and led to an increase in the unemployment rate, then the tradeoff would be a decrease in the rate of inflation. As shown in the figure below, this belief seemed to fit with the facts for the 1960s. Indeed, it appeared that policy actions could steer the economy along the Phillips curve, giving one a menu of choices for either lower unemployment with higher rates of inflation or lower inflation rates with higher rates of unemployment.

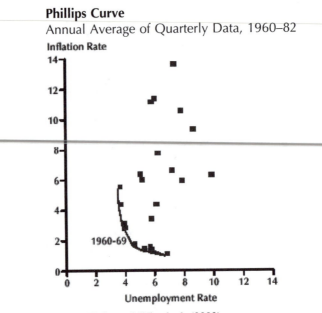

Phillips Curve
Annual Average of Quarterly Data, 1960–82

Source: Hafer and Wheelock (2003).

The other dots in the Phillips curve figure (above) are from the 1970s and early 1980s. One thing that is immediately apparent is that the 1970s and 1980s no longer lie along an established curve like it did in the 1960s. What the additional data suggest is that there is no one Phillips curve along which inflation and unemployment lie. In fact, the figure reveals that while the range of unemployment rates is somewhat limited—the unemployment rate appears to vary only between a low of about 4 percent to a high of about 10 percent—the associated rate of inflation is quite variable. In the data shown, for example, at an unemployment rate of 6 percent inflation varies from less than 2 percent to nearly 14 percent. The fact that there are multiple rates of inflation associated with a single unemployment rate reduces the value of the Phillips curve as a policy guide.

The existence of multiple inflation–unemployment combinations helps explain why the Great Inflation occurred. Suppose that a policymaker decides that the unemployment rate at which the economy operates at capacity is 4 percent. If every time economic growth slows enough to push the unemployment rate above that level the policymaker engages in an expansionary policy, the unemployment rate may fall back to 4 percent, but at the same time this policy puts upward pressure on the inflation rate. Now suppose that the policymaker's assumption that the full-capacity unemployment rate is 4 percent is incorrect. Let's assume it is actually 6 percent. This means that if the unemployment rate rises above 4 percent, then policy becomes expansionary. Because the economy strives to get to its "natural" unemployment rate of 6 percent, policy must be continuously expansionary as policymakers try to hit their 4 percent target unemployment rate. And because policy is continuously expansionary, it means that the Federal Reserve would put continuous upward pressure on prices as the **money** supply is expanded at a faster and faster rate.

Does this story fit the facts? To a large extent, the answer is yes. The figure below plots the rate of inflation along with the rate of growth of the money supply, here measured as the

Inflation Rate and M1 Growth

Quarterly Data, 1951–82

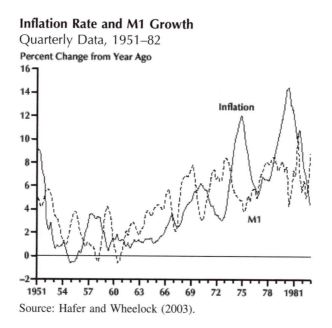

Source: Hafer and Wheelock (2003).

narrowest version called M1. (M1 includes **currency**, travelers' checks, and checking deposits.) As you can see, the two lines move upward in a roughly coincident manner. In other words, during this period the Federal Reserve was actively expanding the money supply in an effort to keep unemployment rates low or to decrease them. As you can see, the upward trend in the rate of inflation matches the upward trend in the growth of M1.

Is the increase in the rate of inflation over the period due solely to expansionary monetary policy? While increases in the growth rate of the money supply explain the upward trend in inflation during the Great Inflation, what explains the noticeable spike in the mid-1970s and again in 1979–1980? These spikes in the inflation rate are associated with the increase in oil prices engineered by the Organization of Petroleum Exporting Countries (OPEC). In each case, OPEC increased the price of crude oil very sharply, which led to increases in the prices of other goods. This effect, sometimes called an **aggregate supply shock**, stems from the fact that with higher oil prices come higher prices for gasoline and other inputs increasing the prices of production and transportation. In the end, however, the price shocks are temporary and inflation returns to its preshock rate of increase. As shown in the figure above, during the mid-1970s the level to which inflation returned was higher than before, and this was due to a higher underlying rate of money growth.

How could this prolonged period of increasing the rate of inflation occur without a policy change? There are a number of theories that attempt to explain how the Great Inflation occurred, but there is no one definitive explanation. For instance, Mayer (1999) interviewed Federal Reserve officials who were involved with the making of policy during this period. His research indicates that many believed that the cause of the rising inflation was outside the Fed's control. The removal of wage-price controls in 1974 and the oil price shocks later in the decade were often cited as reasons for the inflation. While these events may explain deviations of the inflation rate from its underlying monetary cause, they do not explain the upward trend in inflation. Nor do they explain why policymakers suddenly in the early 1980s altered their views of the causes of inflation. DeLong (1997) suggests that a primary cause of the Great Inflation was policymakers' mistaken belief in the inflation–unemployment tradeoff discussed earlier. With the vivid memory of the Great Depression and the 25 percent unemployment rates that occurred, DeLong argues that policymakers were willing to accept higher inflation as long as it would keep unemployment rates down. Blinder (1982) argues that bad luck is the culprit. Blinder suggests that the removal of wage and price controls in 1974 and the OPEC oil price shocks explain much of the inflation that occurred in the 1970s. His view does not, however, explain the upward trend that began in the mid-1960s or the upward trend that continued through the 1970s.

The debate over the causes of the Great Inflation will continue, because learning the nature of that experience will help future policymakers avoid the similar mistakes. Lansing (2000) argues that "focus on a single explanation for the historical episode [is common] because researchers wish to isolate the merits and drawbacks of a particular story. Nevertheless, researchers recognize that elements from many different theories could have been (and probably were) operating simultaneously within the U.S. economy."

FURTHER READING

Blinder, Alan S. "The Anatomy of Double-Digit Inflation in the 1970s." In *Inflation: Causes and Effects*. Robert Hall, ed. Chicago: University of Chicago Press, 1982; DeLong, J. Bradford. "America's Peacetime Inflation: The 1970s." In *Reducing Inflation: Motivation and Strategy*. Romer, Christina, and David Romer, eds. Chicago: University of Chicago Press, 1997; Hafer, R. W., and David C. Wheelock. "Darryl Francis and the Making of Monetary Policy, 1966–1975." Federal Reserve Bank of St. Louis *Review* (March/April 2003): 1–12; Lansing, Kevin J. "Exploring the Causes of the Great Inflation." Federal Reserve Bank of San Francisco *Economic Letter* (July 7, 2000); Mayer, Thomas. *Monetary Policy and the Great Inflation in the United States*. Cheltenham, UK: Edward Elgar, 1999.

GREEN BOOK. Prior to each meeting of the **Federal Open Market Committee (FOMC)**, the Fed's policymaking arm, the staff members of the **Board of Governors** prepare several documents that provide the FOMC with information on economic and financial developments since the last meeting. One of these documents is called the green book, so named because of its green cover. (The other two are the **blue book** and the **beige book**.) These "books" are provided to the FOMC members about five days prior to each meeting. This allows the FOMC to analyze the staff interpretations and forecasts and, especially in the case of the District Bank presidents, to compare the staff analysis with those produced by their own research staffs.

The opening sections of the green book present a description of developments in U.S. economic activity during the period since the last FOMC meeting, and perhaps over the previous several months. This discussion, meant to provide perspective for the current meeting's discussion, covers **inflation**, interest rate changes, changes in the growth rates of **money** and credit, and significant events in the international sector. Included in this section are staff forecasts of these variables for the next year or two. The remainder of the green book covers a wide variety of economic measures, such as, trends in unemployment, production, and prices in important sectors of the economy, such as oil production or autos. There also is a presentation on the current state of federal spending and revenues, in addition to any problems arising in the finances of state and local governments. Important developments in the banking industry and other **financial intermediaries** also may be discussed.

Because the green book is constructed by board staff members, it often represents their view of recent developments and how they may translate into some desired course for policy actions. One reason for providing the green book analysis to FOMC members prior to the meeting is to give them time to consider the staff's policy recommendations. For example, the staff prediction may be that the economy will grow at a too rapid a rate over the next one to two years and, given that prediction, monetary policy should become more restrictive. This policy action may entail raising interest rates or slowing the growth of the money supply, or some combination of the two. Research staffs at the District Banks may have a different outlook for the economy. If the research staff at the Federal Reserve Bank of Chicago believes that the economy is not likely to grow faster than its current rate, then they may advise their president not to advocate the green book's change in policy.

The green book's forecasts have been the subject of much analysis by economists who study the Federal Reserve and its policies. Because policy actions are predicated on the green book forecasts, a natural question to ask is how accurate are those predictions? If they are not very accurate at all, then policy actions could be attempting to correct a problem that does not even exist. This could lead to policy actions that are volatile and destabilizing. To address this, Gavin and Mandal (2002) compared forecasts of real output growth and inflation that were contained in the green book, the average of forecasts made by the FOMC, a collection of predictions by private sector forecasters and a naïve forecast. The latter essentially assumes that whatever happened in the past is going to continue into the future. How did the green book forecasts do? Looking at forecasts made over the past couple of decades, these authors find that the staff, FOMC and private forecasts were superior to the naïve predictions (that's reassuring) and that there was basically little difference between those of the board staff and the others. In other words, the forecasts underlying the green book discussion are no better and no worse than those produced by others.

FURTHER READING

Gavin, William T., and Rachel J. Mandal. "Evaluating FOMC Forecasts." Federal Reserve Bank of St. Louis (Working Paper 2001–005C); Joutz, F., and Herman O. Stekler. "An Evaluation of the Predictions of the Federal Reserve." *International Journal of Forecasting* (2000): 17–38.

GREENSPAN, ALAN (1926–). Alan Greenspan became the chairman of the Federal Reserve **Board of Governors** in August of 1987, filling an unexpired term as a member of the board. He was reappointed to a full 14-year term as governor in 1992 and was reappointed as chairman of the board by Presidents Reagan, George H. Bush, Clinton, and George W. Bush. Prior to his appointment, Greenspan was chairman and president of Townsend-Greenspan & Co., Inc., a New York–based economic consulting firm, from 1954 to 1974 and again from 1977 to 1987. He also has served in numerous government positions, including chairman of the President's **Council of Economic Advisers** under President Ford and as chairman of the National Commission on Social Security Reform. He holds a Ph.D. in economics (1977) from New York University.

As chairman of the **Board of Governors** and chairman of the **Federal Open Market Committee (FOMC)**, Greenspan is considered one of the most powerful individuals in the United States, second only to the president. During his tenure as chairman, there have been several events that demonstrated his skills in managing monetary policy. On October 19, 1987, the U.S. stock market experienced its largest one-day point decline in history. Dubbed "**Black Monday of 1987**," the Dow Jones Industrial Average declined over 500 points. The reaction of financial markets was swift: on the following day, they basically ceased to function. One reason was because with such a large decline in the value of the market, many financial firms needed additional funds to maintain their trading activity. Although similar to the stock market crash of 1929, the 1987 drop was not predicated on the bursting of a speculative stock market bubble. Even so, the financial system was in dire straits. Into this maelstrom stepped Alan Greenspan and E. Gerald Corrigan, the president of the Federal Reserve Bank of New York, working to prevent further collapse of the market. Before the market opened on Tuesday, October 20, Greenspan announced that the Federal Reserve System would stand ready to provide **liquidity** to the market. The Federal Reserve would, in other words, honor its commitment to act as **lender of last resort** in the face of this financial crisis. Not only would the Federal Reserve supply liquidity to the market through **open market operations**, but it also would provide discount **loans** to banks and other eligible institutions that agreed to support the financial market. Greenspan's quick response and decisive action, in many people's opinion, prevented a **financial panic**.

Under Greenspan's leadership, the Federal Reserve has dealt with other financial crises. Beginning in late 1999 and continuing for the next few years, the U.S. stock market again faced the turmoil of a deep correction. Coining the phrase "irrational exuberance," Greenspan warned of excessive stock market activity during the late 1990s. His belief was that the run up in stock prices was not supported by fundamentals, such as increasing earnings and profits by firms. Rather, he saw the rise of the stock market as one representing a financial bubble: stocks being purchased on the notion that their price, regardless of the firm or industry, would only rise since everyone would just continue to buy it. Of course, the bubble did burst and stock prices tumbled, falling more than 50 percent in some instances before the start of 2003. Greenspan and the Federal Reserve weathered this financial storm, again aggressively acting as lender of last resort to distressed financial firms.

In terms of how monetary policy is conducted, there have been several changes during Greenspan's tenure. When he became chairman in 1987, monetary policymakers were required by law (*see* **Humphrey-Hawkins Act of 1978**) to present to Congress their planned actions for the year. Although monetary policy used the monetary aggregates to some degree in the formation of policy, by the early 1990s the empirical relationship between the money supply measures and economic activity appeared to be breaking down. That is, changes in the growth of the money supply no longer seemed to predict the pace of economic activity as they had in the past. Never a champion of monetary aggregates as policy guides, Greenspan testified before Congress in July 1993 that the Federal Reserve would henceforth abandon the use of the monetary aggregates as a guide for monetary policy. Thereafter, the Federal Reserve has relied more heavily on manipulating the **federal funds rate** to attain their policy objectives.

This break with using the monetary aggregates and reinstating the federal funds rate as the key policy guide suggested to some that monetary policy might return to the high inflation days of the 1960s and 1970s. In contrast to those days, however, the Federal Reserve under Greenspan has been much more willing to aggressively adjust the funds rate up or down depending on the economic circumstances. For example, during the early 1990s the Federal Reserve lowered the funds rate in an attempt to promote economic growth following the recession of 1990–1991. While this was standard anticyclical policy, the Federal Reserve also reacted much more rapidly to raise the rate when it perceived that inflationary pressures were building in the economy only a few years later. Using the funds rate in this manner, some argue, was a break with past policy actions because the Federal Reserve was much more willing to change the rate in a proactive policy manner, raising it and lowering it on the basis of expected changes in the economy.

Not only was the Federal Reserve under Greenspan's leadership more willing and ready to engage in preventive policy actions, they also were more transparent about it. Instead of keeping secret their desired federal funds rate target, the FOMC began to announce its policy intentions following each meeting. This change reflects the growing belief that increased understanding of policy actions and the basis upon which they are made helps individuals adjust their behavior to expected outcomes. Unlike the Federal Reserve of his predecessors, monetary policy under Alan Greenspan has become much more open.

FURTHER READING

Tuccille, Jerome. *Alan Shrugged: Alan Greenspan, the World's Most Powerful Banker* (Wiley and Sons, 2002); Martin, Justin. *Greenspan: The Man Behind the Money*. Cambridge, MA: Perseus Publishing, 2000; Woodward, Bob. *Maestro: Greenspan's Fed and the American Boom*. New York: Simon and Schuster, 2000.

GROSS DOMESTIC PRODUCT (GDP). The objectives of monetary policy are a low, stable **inflation** rate, stable financial markets, and an economy that is operating as close to its full-employment capacity as it can. Policymakers use a variety of economic measures to see if they are achieving these goals: the inflation rate, often measured as the percentage change in the CPI; stable markets through observations of interest rate volatility; and sustained **economic growth** by observing measures that reflect economic activity, such as the **unemployment rate** or gross domestic product (GDP).

What is GDP? Economists define GDP as the total market value of all final goods and services produced in an economy in a given period of time. That standard definition may seem like a lot, but it is very specific for a reason. First, the notion of "total market value" means that GDP can be thought of as a broad measure of income being generated by an economy. Total market value translates into "price times quantity." That means that the income being generated by the sale of some good can be measured by how many are sold and the price. That gives a market value, a valuation determined in the market for shoes, chickens, hamburgers, and haircuts.

Note also that by requiring GDP to be a market value measure, there are numerous activities that are not included. Illegal activities, such as drug trafficking, prostitution, or illegal gambling, and some tax-evading activities are not included in the official GDP numbers because they are not legally recorded by any record of sale. This definition also means that nonmarket activities—the so-called underground economy—such as **barter** or individuals staying at home to raise the children instead of working elsewhere, are not measured. Even though the cost of hiring nannies and housekeepers is a good approximation for the market value of someone working in the house, the official numbers just do not include such a guess. In this sense, the official GDP numbers probably underestimate the true level of income being generated in an economy. This issue becomes important to policymakers because the size of the underground economy tends to grow during recessions.

The segment "produced in an economy" signifies that GDP is measuring income produced domestically, that is, within a country. Production abroad by domestically owned companies is not included, because GDP is trying to measure the value of goods produced domestically. In addition, the measure attempts to capture production and not simply sales. Finally, the notion of measuring GDP during a given time period means that we are trying to measure income generated today, not in the past. This means that the sale of a used 1966 Mustang will not be counted in today's GDP. The sale does not represent the creation of income, just the transfer of ownership. The sale of used goods is not included in GDP because they were already counted in a previous year. This brief overview of GDP gives a flavor of what is included.

To gauge the success of policy actions, most observers use a specific version of GDP. The measure discussed above is referred to as *nominal* GDP. It is nominal in the sense that it is calculated using current or nominal prices. A problem with this measure is that comparing GDP over time becomes difficult. For example, suppose in 2002 an economy produced one good: laptop computers. And suppose that the price of the laptop is $1,000. The GDP for 2002 would be $1 \times \$1,000$, or $1,000. Now suppose it is 2003 and GDP is given as $2,000. Even though it is twice as large as in 2002, does that mean that the economy grew? Are individuals in the 2003 economy better off? What if in 2003 the economy produced 2 laptops and the price did not change? That results in the $2,000 value for GDP. It also signifies that there are more goods for the same price, a better situation that in 2002. But what if the $2,000 GDP in 2003 is caused by a doubling of laptop prices and no increase in laptop production? If in 2003 laptops cost $2,000 and the economy still is producing 1, are individuals in the economy better off than before? Laptops cost twice as much but there are not more of them. Doesn't sound like an improvement, does it?

Because it is impossible to tell whether increases in nominal GDP over time are caused by increases in the price of goods and services or an increase in the output of goods and services or some combination of the two, economists use a measure called *real* GDP. Real GDP, unlike nominal GDP, accounts for changes in the price of goods over time. If prices double and output does not, then real GDP would not increase. If output doubles and prices remain fixed, however, then real GDP doubles as well. In other words, real GDP is GDP adjusted for price level changes. Real GDP, then, is a better measure to see how the output of an economy has changed over time, always using the prices in some base year as a reference point. For example, in 2004 the base year is designated as 1996.

It is useful to compare the behavior of nominal and real GDP over time to get a perspective on how price level changes affect the two measurements. The chart below shows nominal and real GDP for the United States over the past several decades. The crossover point is the base year. In the base year, nominal and real GDP are equal. Notice that as prices have risen since 1996, real GDP is less than nominal GDP. This indicates that even though the economy was growing, in the sense that there were more goods and services being produced, prices also were rising. This explains the gap between nominal and real GDP. Before the reference year, the gap indicates that prices were generally lower than in 1996.

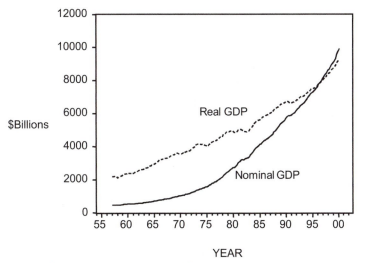

YEAR

Source: Federal Reserve Bank of St. Louis.

The chart also shows that the behavior of the two series has changed over time. For instance, note that the nominal GDP series begins to increase at a much faster rate beginning in about 1970 compared with real GDP. This faster growth reflects the fact that inflation was rising faster in this time, thus exaggerating the true increase in output being produced. While the increase in nominal GDP did reflect increased incomes, the fact that prices were rising rapidly meant that higher incomes were buying less than before.

Since about 1990, nominal and real GDP have tracked along at a fairly similar pace. This again shows the effect of price level changes (inflation). During this time, inflation rates were much less than during the 1970s. Consequently, nominal GDP and the price-adjusted real GDP tend to move together, indicating that the economy was producing goods and services and that inflation was not the kind of problem that it was during the 1970s. GDP data can be accessed through FRED at the Federal Reserve Bank of St. Louis Website (www.stlouisfed.org).

FURTHER READING

Taylor, John P. *Economics*. 4th edition. Boston: Houghton Mifflin Company, 2004.

GROUP OF 5, GROUP OF 7, GROUP OF 8, AND GROUP OF 10. These "groups" are made of countries, usually major industrial countries, that meet regularly to coordinate economic policies. This entry, based on the **International Monetary Fund**'s *Factsheet: A Guide to Committees, Groups and Clubs*, describes the membership of each group and its key activities.

The Group of Five (G-5) was established in the mid-1970s to coordinate the economic policies of the major industrial countries France, Germany, Japan, United Kingdom, and United States. The G-5 was the main policy coordination group among the major industrial countries through the **Plaza Agreement** of September 1985. It was subsequently superseded by the Group of Seven (G-7), which added Canada and Italy to the original G-5 members.

The Group of Seven (G-7) meets annually to hold economic summits. They have done so since 1975. The annual meetings are attended by the heads of each government. Sine the mid-1980s, finance ministers and central bank governors of the G-7 countries have tired to coordinate policies, especially domestic monetary policies and those that impact the foreign exchange markets. Beginning in 1987, the G-7 finance ministers and central bank governors, along with the managing director of the IMF, meet at least twice a year to discuss economic developments in their and in other countries and to assess economic policies.

In 1988 Russia joined the G-7 to form the G-8, which is sometimes referred to as the "Political 8" or "P8." Although Russia had participated in G-7 meetings previously, first at the 1994 Naples Summit and again in 1997 when Russia participated in political discussions at the Denver Summit, it was not until the 1998 Birmingham Summit that Russia joined the G-7 as a full participant. Even though Russia and the G-7 joined to form the G-8, the original G-7 continues to exist as a separate body. Each group issues statements and separate communiqués regarding economic and political issues.

The largest "group" is the Group of Ten (G-10). The G-10 consists of Belgium, Canada, France, Germany, Italy, Japan, the Netherlands, Sweden, United Kingdom, and United States. The G-10, comprising countries and central banks that agreed to abide by the General Arrangements to Borrow (GAB), was formed in 1962. Essentially, the G-10 countries agree to provide resources to the **International Monetary Fund** (IMF) for drawings by participants. In 1964 the group increased with the association of Switzerland, even though the name G-10 stuck. The activities of the G-10 are supervised by the Bank for International Settlements (BIS), the European Commission, the IMF, and the OECD.

FURTHER READING

G8 Information Centre. Website: www.g7.utoronto.ca/

HAMLIN, CHARLES (1861–1938). Charles Hamlin holds the distinction of being the first governor—the first chairman of the Board—of the Federal Reserve Board. Serving as assistant secretary of the U.S. Treasury at the time, Hamlin took the oath of office on August 10, 1914. He was appointed by President **Woodrow Wilson** to serve as governor for a one-year, renewable term. Hamlin served as governor until 1916 and he remained on the board until 1936.

Hamlin left a mixed record from his time at the board. Meltzer (2003) notes that Hamlin often was described as a weak leader, one who acquiesced to the requests of Treasury Secretary McAdoo, who served on the board as an ex officio member. The picture one gets from the record available is that Hamlin seldom participated in board meetings and often merely voted with the majority. Some questioned his capability to serve as governor. The record Hamlin left behind also indicates that he, like others of the time, did not place any blame for the **Great Depression** on the actions, or lack thereof, of the Federal Reserve. In November 1929, Hamlin reported to a group of New England bankers that the events of the stock crash were "inevitable and could not be avoided" (quoted in Meltzer [2003]). A year later, with the economy moving deeper into the recession, Hamlin observed in a speech that there was no need for any monetary stimulus on the part of the Federal Reserve.

FURTHER READING

Meltzer, Allan H. *A History of the Federal Reserve, Vol. 1: 1913–1951*. Chicago: University of Chicago Press, 2003; Yohe, William. "The Intellectual Milieu at the Federal Reserve Board in the 1920s." *History of Political Economy* (3:1990): 465–88.

HOOVER, HERBERT C. (1874–1964). Herbert Clark Hoover, born in the small town of West Branch, Iowa, served as the 31st President of the United States (1929–1933). Hoover was trained as a mining engineer at Stanford University in Palo Alto, California, graduating in one of its very first classes. Working for several private companies after graduation, some of the time being spent in China, Hoover was appointed by President **Woodrow Wilson** to head the Food Administration during World War I. Following the war, Hoover was a member of the Supreme Economic Council and headed the American Relief Administration, the organization responsible for administering relief shipments to war-torn Europe. During the 1920s, Hoover served as the Secretary of Commerce under Presidents Harding and **Calvin Coolidge**, became the presidential candidate in 1928 and beat Democratic candidate Alfred E. Smith for the presidency by an overwhelming majority of the popular vote.

Hoover was elected at a time when the nation enjoyed what many thought would be unending prosperity. Hoover set the tone for his administration's views in his inaugural address, given in March 1929, noting that "regulation of private enterprise and not Government ownership of operation is the course rightly to be pursued. . . ." Hoover believed that business worked best if left alone, with minimal government interference. He also believed that "business has by cooperation made great progress in advancement of service, in regularity of employment and in the correction of its own abuses." As a reading of history suggests, there were abuses in the business world at the time, abuses that became readily apparent in the financial markets with the stock market collapse in October 1929.

The policies of the Hoover administration are often blamed for the severity of the **Great Depression**. It is a mistake, however, to believe that Hoover stood idly by while the markets and the economy collapsed. The speculative activity of the stock market in the 1920s was recognized by Hoover as a serious problem. Hoover asked for an examination of the banking industry's involvement in the stock market's dizzying advance. He tried to convince leaders in the banking industry and policymakers at the Federal Reserve to step in and curtail the speculative loan making that some banks were engaged in, providing funds that only fueled the run-up in stock prices. In the end, Hoover was unsuccessful in stemming the speculative tide and the banks' involvement.

Blame for the stock market crash and the unraveling of the economic expansion was often laid at Hoover's feet. This is unfair. Hoover did try to fight the economic depression that was gripping the nation. In 1931, Hoover asked Congress to create the Reconstruction Finance Corporation to advance government loans to banks, businesses, and railroads in an attempt to prevent bankruptcies. He also called for relief for farmers who faced drought conditions in many parts of the country. On the financial side, Hoover called for banking reform. Still, by 1932 the recovery was not in sight. **Franklin Delano Roosevelt** stood as the Democratic Party candidate against Hoover, who had been renominated by the Republican Party, although without much passion. Roosevelt, who campaigned with great confidence that he would get the economy moving again, won in a landslide. Indeed, it was soon after his inauguration that Roosevelt declared the **Bank Holiday of 1933** that stemmed the tide of the downturn and bank closures. In fact, March 1933 often is considered to be the end of the Great Depression.

After his time in the White House, Hoover remained active in public service. In 1941 the Hoover Tower at Stanford University was dedicated. To this day Hoover's legacy to education remains as Stanford's Hoover Institution on War, Revolution and Peace, informally known as the Hoover Institute. Following World War II, President Harry Truman appointed Hoover to head the Famine Emergency Commission. In 1947 Hoover was asked by Congress to head a study of reorganizing the executive branch of the government. The Hoover Commission undertook this study and offered numerous suggestions to streamline the provision of government services. A second Hoover Commission study, this time of the federal government, was created in 1953 under the Eisenhower administration.

FURTHER READING

Barber, William J. *From New Era to New Deal: Herbert Hoover, the Economists and American Economic Policy, 1921–1933*. Cambridge, UK: Cambridge University Press, 1989; Burner, David. *Herbert Hoover: A Public Life*. New York: Athenaeum Publishers, 1984; Fausold, Martin L. *The*

Presidency of Herbert Hoover. Lawrence*:* University of Kansas Press, 1985; Herbert Hoover Presidential Library and Museum. Online at Website: http://hoover.archives.gov; Hoover, Herbert. *Memoirs*, 3 vols. New York: Macmillan, 1951–1952.

HUMPHREY-HAWKINS ACT OF 1978 (*See* **Full Employment and Balanced Growth [Humphrey-Hawkins] Act of 1978**)

INFLATION. Inflation is something that you hear about quite often. Every month a new inflation number is reported on the news and in the newspaper. People complain if the rate of inflation is too high, because they see the prices of things rising rapidly. People do not complain when inflation is low, because prices are relatively stable. So what is inflation? What causes inflation? Why is inflation bad? Let's answer those questions in order.

Inflation is defined as "a persistent increase in the general level of prices." That is a very specific definition. First, it requires that prices are rising *over time*—that is what is meant by persistent. And the price increase must occur for the general level of prices, measured by something like the Consumer Price Index (CPI). Inflation should not be thought of as an increase in the price of lettuce or the price of automobiles or the price of getting someone to repair your computer. While increases in these prices may contribute to the increase in the overall or general price level, an increase in each one is not thought of as inflation. So, to repeat, inflation is a sustained increase in the prices of all goods and services.

Inflation in the United States has taken a wild ride over the past 50 years. Using the CPI measure of the general level of prices, the figure below shows the path of inflation over time. Inflation started out after World War II at a relatively high level and dropped to nearly zero in 1955. By the early 1960s you can see that the inflation rate hovered between 0 and 2.5 percent. Beginning in the mid-1960s, however, it began to creep upward. (*See* **Great Inflation**.) During the 1970s, there are two noticeable spikes in the inflation rate. These spikes in 1974 and again in 1979 are associated with the oil price hikes engineered by the Organization of Petroleum Exporting Countries (OPEC). Still, while the actions of OPEC increased the rate of inflation for a short period of time, notice that inflation returned to a higher plateau in each instance. Peaking out in double digits in the early 1980s, inflation has declined over the past two decades. (The mini-spike in 1990 occurs with another oil price hike associated with the Gulf War.) Falling throughout the 1980s and 1990s, today inflation is about where it was in the early 1960s, around 2.5 percent.

Why be so concerned about the definition of inflation? The principal reason is that having a specific definition of inflation prevents us from making mistakes in deciding what causes inflation. For instance, did the OPEC oil price hikes cause inflation? From the figure you can see that the rate of inflation obviously increased in those times. But

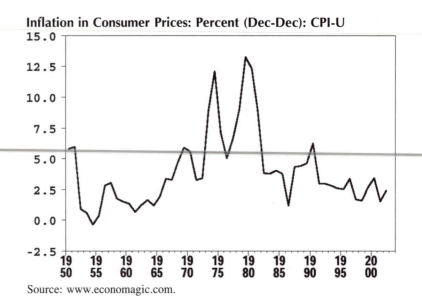

Inflation in Consumer Prices: Percent (Dec-Dec): CPI-U

Source: www.economagic.com.

notice also that the inflation rates did not go to a higher level and stay there. If they did, then oil price hikes would be a good explanation for inflation. The fact that inflation did not remain at the higher rates suggests that oil price hikes are not a good explanation for a *sustained* increase in the general level of prices.

This observation suggests the following way to think about the inflation process and how it relates to one-time kind of changes in the price level. The idea can be illustrated using the figure below. In this figure the price level is increasing at some rate, say 5 percent. This rate of increase actually can be measured as the slope of the line AB. Now, at some point in time, here designated as t_0, suppose OPEC raises oil prices, doubling the price for a barrel of oil from $28 to $56. If prices adjust quickly, then the *price level* would simply jump from B to C. But notice that if prices reacted instantaneously to the shock, the underlying rate of inflation would not be affected: the slopes (rate of increase) AB and CE are the same. In the real world, however, all prices simply do not change that rapidly. Contracts, slow recognition that there has been a change in oil prices, fixed wages, and a number of other factors help explain the more gradual adjustment of prices to such a shock. This adjustment is shown in the figure as the line BD. What is important to note is that while prices are adjusting to a higher *level*, the rate of their increase is faster than before. That is, *the rate of inflation from B to D is faster than from A to B*. This is shown in the bottom figure that plots the inflation rate. Going along at a rate of 5 percent, the shock in oil prices causes the price level to increase at a faster rate. This is shown as the higher rate of inflation in the bottom figure. Once the adjustment is completed, however, the rate of inflation returns to its preshock rate. As this suggests, a shock such as an oil price increase will not have a permanent effect on the rate of inflation. It will not cause a persistent increase in the general level of prices to occur.

So what causes inflation? If it is not shocks to the price level, then what is the cause? Most economists agree that the root cause of inflation—a persistent increase in the general level of prices—stems from excessive growth in the supply of **money**. The supply of money is, for all intents, determined by actions of the Federal Reserve or any other

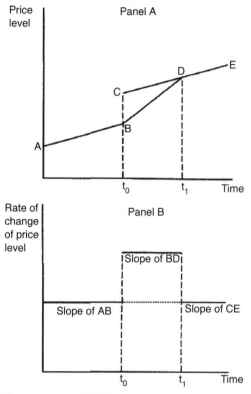

Effect of Transitory Nonmonetary Shock on the Trend Rate of Inflation

Source: Batten (1981).

central bank. Over time, the Federal Reserve has the ability to make the supply of money grow faster or slower. (For a discussion of how it brings about changes in the supply of money, see **Open Market Operations**.) How inflation and money supply growth are related can be shown in the **quantity theory** equation. This equation, the idea of which has been discussed for at least 200 years, simply says that if the output of goods and services in an economy is not related to money growth in the long run and the manner in which people chose to hold and manage their money is fairly predictable, then there is a direct relation between changes in the money supply and prices.

Is this true? First, does it make sense that money and output are not related? Consider this example. At the local Ford Motor Company plant, each line produces, say, 100 cars an hour. The people working on the line are making roughly $20 per hour. Now suppose we double their wages to $40 an hour. Will this make them doubly productive? Will the output of cars increase to 200 cars per hour simply because the workers now make more? The answer is no, because how many cars can be produced is essentially an engineering problem, not an economic one. Doubling the amount of money in the economy—giving everyone twice as much as they currently have—will not increase production of goods. What it will do, however, is increase individuals' demand for goods and services. And because there are not more goods out there to satisfy this increased demand, sellers will simply increase their prices to ration the amount of goods available.

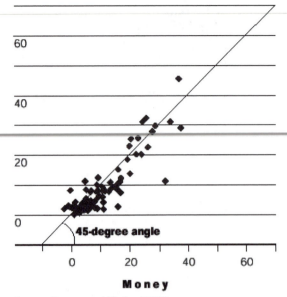

Source: Dwyer and Hafer (1999).

Does this example mean that doubling the growth rate of the money supply leads to an inflation rate that is two-times greater than the starting rate? Making links between variables in economics is not foolproof, but in this case the link between increased money growth and higher rates of inflation is pretty close. To test this, the chart above shows the relation between money growth rates and inflation rates across a large number of countries using data from the 1990s. If the relation between money growth and inflation is one-to-one, then all the points would lie on the 45-degree line. The fact that they do not suggests that there is some slippage in the money–inflation relationship. But the fact that they are on average very close to the 45-degree line indicates that the working explanation that inflation is caused by faster money growth is quite workable. Since the number of experiences covered in the sample of countries used is varied, it also suggests that the money–inflation link tends to hold across a diverse set of economic environments.

Finally, why is inflation bad? The most immediate effect of an increase in inflation is that it erodes **purchasing power of money**. Increases in the price level simply translate into a dollar being worth less in terms of what it can buy. This means that wages and salaries must keep pace with inflation if workers' purchasing power is to be constant. If inflation increases faster than the percentage increase in wages, the raise you get may not enable you to maintain your current living standards. A 3 percent raise when the inflation rate is running at 5 percent means that you are losing ground.

Increased rates of inflation also show up in higher **nominal interest rates**. (*See* **Fisher Effect**.) Lenders do not want to give up purchasing power, so when inflation rises, they want to make sure that those dollars you pay back on a loan are worth as much in the future as they are today. Lenders ensure this by raising the interest rate they charge on **loans**. A direct effect of inflation is that it increases costs of borrowing money, which in turn can slow economic activity. If businesses are not able to finance their activities at a profitable rate, then they may close their doors. If individuals cannot afford to purchase a house because the mortgage rates are too high, then the housing industry suffers and homes are not built.

In the extreme, inflation rates that are in the hundreds of percent—so-called *hyperinflations*—cause a breakdown in the pricing system. If you are unsure how much something will cost next month, you may simply wait to buy it. But if you know that it will be more expensive, then you will buy it now before the price increases. When prices are increasing at rates of 100 percent or 200 percent a *month*, then it is hardly worth the effort to post prices since they will soon change. Hyperinflations also make the money used for exchange—the dollar in the United States—worthless. Because everyone knows that money is rapidly losing its purchasing power, no one wants to hold it. Like the card game of Old Maid, no one wants to be holding money in the end when it becomes worthless.

FURTHER READING

Batten, Dallas S. "Inflation: The Cost-Push Myth." Federal Reserve Bank of St. Louis *Review* (June/July 1981): 20–26; Dewald, William G. "Money Still Matters." Federal Reserve Bank of St. Louis *Review* (November/December 1998): 13–24; Dwyer, Gerald P., Jr. and R. W. Hafer. "Are Money Growth and Inflation Still Related?" Federal Reserve Bank of Atlanta *Economic Review* (Second Quarter 1999): 32–43; Friedman, Milton. *Money Mischief: Episodes in Monetary History*. New York: Harcourt Brace Jovanovich, 1992; McCandless, George T., Jr., and Warren E. Weber. "Some Monetary Facts." Federal Reserve Bank of Minneapolis *Quarterly* Review (1995): 2–11.

INFLATION TARGETING. Monetary policymakers at the Federal Reserve and in other central banks have used a number of guideposts to determine the success, or failure, of their policy actions. For example, in the United States, at one time a key goal of policy was to maintain **unemployment rates** at relatively low levels. At another time financial market conditions drove policy decisions, meaning that policymakers often were more concerned about the reaction of the markets—interest rates becoming too high and volatile, for example—than they were about the long-term effects of their policies. Indeed, during the 1950s and 1960s, policy was driven as much by the "tone and feel" of the market as it was by any objective policy goal.

During the past decade or so, many central banks around the world have adopted some type of inflation target to guide their policy decisions. During the 1990s the number of countries that explicitly stated some inflation target increased from fewer than 10 to over 50. Those central banks currently using inflation targets include Australia, Canada, Finland, Israel, New Zealand, Spain, Sweden, and the United Kingdom. Although one might think that inflation targets would be attractive to countries that had experienced severe or prolonged bouts of inflation, this group of countries—characterized by low average rates of inflation—indicates that that is not the sole criterion.

One thing to notice from this list is that the United States is not one of the countries using an explicit inflation target to guide monetary policy. This absence is not for lack of trying. In 1995, Senator Connie Mack (R-Fla) introduced legislation that, in part, would require the Federal Reserve to set and make public a definition of price stability, one that would be paramount to all others. One point of debate centered on the notion of price stability. Did that mean that prices could not change, in which case the rate of inflation would be zero?

(The rate of inflation is calculated as the percentage change in a general price measure, such as the Consumer Price Index [CPI] or the broader GDP deflator.) Or did the Senator mean that the Federal Reserve should attempt to keep inflation in check, which meant that it would allow prices to increase but with some upper limit in mind? Also, would the price stability objective be ignored if a recession would occur, one that required the Federal Reserve to spur economic activity through expansionary policies, even though these may increase the rate of inflation? Needless to say, Senator Mack's proposal was not passed and the Federal Reserve today does not base its policies on an official inflation target.

Even though an inflation target is not used, does that mean that such a constraint on policy is not warranted? It is widely believed that, in the long run, the one economic variable that policymakers have the most influence over is the rate of inflation. Many studies have shown that the rate of growth of the money supply, relative to the rate of economic expansion, is directly related to the rate of inflation. That is, if the Federal Reserve were to double the growth rate of the money supply, it is highly likely that the rate of inflation would increase. Consequently, one positive aspect of an inflation target is that it is something that the Federal Reserve can attempt to achieve. If policy was to attempt to target the long-run growth of the economy, it probably would fail. Because the long-term growth of the economy is determined by the growth of the capital stock, by the growth of the labor force and by advances in technology, increasing or decreasing the growth rate of the money supply has little impact on real economic activity.

Rudebusch and Walsh (1998) suggest several reasons for adopting an inflation target. First, setting and announcing an explicit inflation target provides a clearer picture to the public about the intentions of policy and the framework in which such a goal will be achieved. As noted above, a reasonable inflation target is something that the Federal Reserve can achieve. An unreasonably low rate of unemployment is something that it cannot. Setting an inflation target and announcing it also helps in cementing inflation expectations among the public. This is important because it allows individuals and firms to make long-term commitments based on expectations of future price levels or inflation. For example, several studies have shown that when inflation is high and volatile, the informational content of prices is reduced—does a price increase really reflect the interaction of supply and demand or some change in inflation expectations?—and that long-term contracts get shortened. It makes perfect sense: Who is willing to lock in wages or prices for the future when inflation may be substantially higher or lower? Investments in financial assets and investment by firms in new plant and equipment both are affected when interest rates, which reflect in part the expected level of future inflation, become volatile and uncertain. More stable and predictable inflation produces an environment in which long-term interest rates are lower.

Another important argument in favor of inflation targets is that they make policy more transparent. Put another way, stating an inflation target commits policymakers to hit it. When the targets change or when the goals of policy vary, it becomes difficult to determine the success of policy actions. As Rudebusch and Walsh (1998) put it, inflation targets can "help insure that monetary policy is not dependent on always having the good luck to appoint the best people." Moreover, an inflation target provides the public and the Congress with a visible yardstick by which to measure policy success. It is in this sense that policy under an inflation target is more transparent than one in which the objectives are not well known or are stated in "soft" terms.

If these are the pluses to inflation targeting, what are the minuses? As with any rule, an inflation target makes policy more rigid than some would like. As mentioned earlier, if there is an external shock to the economy that results in a rapid run-up in the unemployment rate, a strict inflation target would not allow policymakers to undertake policy actions to cushion those effects. Even though in the long run the economy would return to full employment, the question is always how long that adjustment period would be without any policy intervention. Policy thus loses the flexibility that allows it to react to situations as they arise. Another aspect that detracts from the viability of an inflation target deals with informational lags. Policy effects take time to work through the economy. Changes in money growth rates today may not completely appear in prices for one to two years. Thus, by the time policymakers realize that the rate of inflation is running above or below the target, it may take quite a while to get it back on track. If this is true, then an obvious caveat to the setting of an inflation target is that there must be some flexibility in being able to react to misses. Such flexibility allows for rule breaking and an overall reduction in the credibility attached to any announced target.

As this discussion suggests, while adopting an inflation target may seem obvious if inflation is one of the Fed's policy objectives, it is not without complications. Because there has been little experience with such targets as a framework for monetary policy, it is likely that the debate will continue over the arguments for and against inflation targeting.

FURTHER READING

Bernanke, Ben S., Thomas Laubach, Frederic S. Mishkin, and Adam S. Posen. *Inflation Targeting: Lessons from the International Experience*. Princeton: Princeton University Press, 1999; Federal Reserve Bank of St. Louis. *Inflation Targeting: Prospects and Problems: Proceedings of the Twenty-Eighth Annual Economic Policy Conference of the Federal Reserve Bank of St. Louis*. Federal Reserve Bank of St. Louis *Review* (July/August 2004); Rudebusch, Glenn D., and Carl E. Walsh. "U.S. Inflation Targeting: Pro and Con." Federal Reserve Bank of San Francisco *Economic Letter* (May 29, 1998).

INTEREST RATE PEGGING. Interest rate pegging is a policy that focuses on keeping some **nominal interest rate** at a predetermined level. For example, in the period 1942–1953, the Federal Reserve's policy actions were aimed solely at keeping interest rates on government securities low. During World War II, this meant that the Federal Reserve stood ready to purchase or sell government securities in order to maintain interest rates at their prewar levels. This meant holding the rate on short-term Treasury bills at about 3/8 percent and 2.5 percent on long-term Treasury bonds. As discussed elsewhere (*see* **Intermediate Targets**), pegging interest rates means that the Federal Reserve gives up control over the money supply.

Although this was not a problem during the 1940s, the constraints of a pegging policy did raise concerns with the onset of the Korean War. At that time, inflation rates began to rise and with them interest rates. Because the Federal Reserve's policy was to peg rates, this meant that the Federal Reserve was forced to purchase larger and larger amounts of government securities in an attempt to keep the rates from rising further. The Federal Reserve increased purchases of securities increased the growth rate of the money supply and with it inflationary pressures: the inflation rate rose to about 8 percent in 1951.

Ultimately, the Federal Reserve and the Treasury agreed to abandon this policy. The **Treasury-Federal Reserve Accord of 1951** formally ended the Federal Reserve's official policy of pegging interest rates. Even though the Federal Reserve was no longer required to peg rates, it followed similar policies during the 1970s and again in the 1990s, policies that put much more emphasis on the control of nominal interest rates than the behavior of the money supply.

FURTHER READING

Humphrey, Thomas M. "Can the Central Bank Peg Real Interest Rates? A Survey of Classical and Neoclassical Opinion." Federal Reserve Bank of Richmond *Economic Review* (September/October 1983): 12–21; McCallum, Bennett T. "Some Issues Concerning Interest Rate Pegging, Price Level Determinacy, and the Real Bills Doctrine." *Journal of Monetary Economics*. January 1986): 135–60.

INTEREST RATE SPREAD (*See* **Term Structure of Interest Rates**)

INTERMEDIATE TARGETS. In setting monetary policy, the **Federal Open Market Committee (FOMC)** uses information available to it at the time it meets, such as recent changes in the **unemployment rate** or **gross domestic product (GDP)**. Because policy is forward looking, that is, it must try to guess the future effects of actions taken today, policymakers try to use economic measures that act as intermediate targets to get some feel for how they are meeting previous policy projections.

For example, consider the problems in setting a policy path whose goal is to meet some **inflation target**. Suppose the FOMC wishes to hit an **inflation** rate target of 3 percent. Because the lag between policy actions and eventual changes in the inflation rate are long and variable (*see* **Lags in Monetary Policy**), it may take almost two years before actions taken today are fully reflected in observed rates of inflation. Or, consider the problems associated with determining the effect of policy on real GDP. GDP statistics are available only on a quarterly (three-month) basis, and even then with a lag of at least two months. That is, when the FOMC meets in March, it may have a guess as to the value for GDP during the first three months of the year, but it is only a rough guess. Even so, the FOMC must make policy using that rough information.

Because the FOMC must make policy that looks forward and because it does not have final values for all of its economic goal variables (e.g., inflation, real GDP growth, etc.) at the time it makes its decisions, it often observes the behavior of *intermediate targets* to determine if they are on track toward their final policy goal. An analogy will help. Suppose scientists wish to send a scientific probe to Jupiter. Generally, this cannot be accomplished simply by firing the rocket in a straight line aimed at where Jupiter happens to be in the night sky. Policy—determining the trajectory of the spaceship to intersect with Jupiter's orbit—must be forward looking and must use certain intermediate observations to make sure the probe hits Jupiter and not some other planet. Scientists observe the flight of the probe, using various intermediate targets—this or that planet's moon—to see if the probe is on target. If the probe is supposed to travel by a moon of Venus and ends up close to Mercury, then something is terribly wrong and the likelihood of successfully getting the probe to Jupiter is dubious.

How does this apply to monetary policy? The notion of an intermediate target can be illustrated using a demand and supply model for the money supply. As shown in the

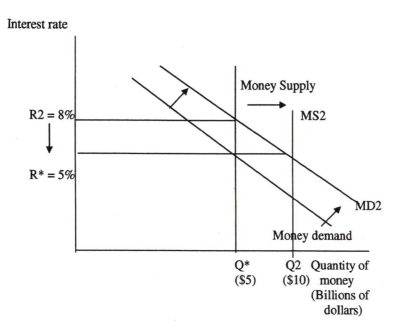

diagram above, there is some demand for **money**, which is related to the interest rate. In this case, the interest rate can be thought of as the "cost" of holding money. Hence, the demand curve is downward sloping, meaning that as the interest rate increases, individuals are less willing to hold money. The supply curve, shown as the vertical line, reflects the notion that the Federal Reserve determines the supply of money in the economy. While this is an assumption that actually may not hold over short periods of time, in the end it actually is the Federal Reserve, through its policies, that determines the money supply. For this discussion, there is little lost if we just illustrate the supply curve as a vertical line. With the demand for money and the supply of money, the intersection of the two determines the equilibrium rate of interest (shown here as R*) and the equilibrium amount of money in the economy (shown here as Q*).

The FOMC historically has used two intermediate targets: an interest rate or the supply of money. The diagram above illustrates potential problems with each. First, let's assume that the FOMC uses an interest rate, such as the **federal funds rate**, as its intermediate target. Also, let's assume that based on its analysis, the interest rate at 5 percent is optimal from the standpoint of achieving its goals of economic growth, low unemployment, and stable prices. This interest rate target is, as shown in the diagram, consistent with a money supply of $5 billion, as shown in parentheses below Q*. Note that if the demand for money increases, as shown in the shift to MD2, using the interest rate as an intermediate target means that the FOMC must increase the supply of money to MS2 in order to keep the interest rate from rising to R2, or 8 percent. Using the interest rate as the intermediate target in the face of money demand shifts means that the FOMC must relinquish control over the supply of money. This may have unwanted effects on the economy, such as increasing the rate of inflation in the long run.

What if the FOMC chooses the money supply (or its growth rate) as the intermediate target? Look at the diagram again. If the demand for money line shifts to MD2, this change would force the FOMC to let interest rates rise to 8 percent. As the diagram suggests, shifts in the demand for money, when the FOMC's intermediate target is the money supply, means that they must relinquish control over the interest rate. This may also have undesirable effects on the economy: rising interest rates may reduce business investment and reduce investment in financial assets.

So what are we to make of this? The most obvious answer is that rigid interest rate and money supply targets are not compatible. The FOMC can use one or the other, but not both if it expects to successfully hit either one. So how does it choose between the two? Economists who have studied this aspect of monetary policy believe that there are basically three criteria for selecting an intermediate target. One is measurability. Policymakers must be able to measure changes in the intermediate target if it is usable for policy. Included under this heading are considerations such as timeliness, how often the data are released, and whether the measure is subject to frequent and large revisions. Interest rates would seem preferable to the money supply measures under this criterion. Interest rates are determined in the financial markets and are available on a more timely basis than the money supply numbers. Also, interest rates are almost never subject to revisions. Still, the interest rate most appropriate for determining the impact of policy actions—the real rate of interest—is extremely difficult to measure accurately. Because policymakers have no foolproof way of measuring the real rate of interest, setting policy on the basis of movements in the nominal rate may lead to unexpected, and undesired, economic effects of certain policy actions. The money supply also is subject to measurement problems. The data on the money supply are available only with a lag of several weeks, and the data are subject to revisions, sometimes sizable. So, neither variable is free of measurement problems. What policymakers must decide is which is least harmful given the goal being considered. For example, if the goal is a low rate of inflation, then the measurement problems associated with the money supply may be less important given the known longer-term relation between changes in the money supply and inflation.

Another consideration in selecting between interest rates and the money supply as an intermediate target is the controllability of the measure. For a measure to be useful to policymakers, movements in that measure should reflect changes in policy actions. If interest rates or the money supply are changing for reasons unrelated to FOMC actions, then using the measure may give false signals to policymakers. For example, policymakers may be able to better control interest rates in the short run. But, as seen in the 1960s and 1970s, outside forces often push interest rates in directions that, if used as a target, lead to undesired consequences, such as rapid inflation. Money supply measures are not immune to such measurement problems either. Financial innovations alter the link between how individuals use money or bank deposits and the economy. If banks are able to offer deposits that provide higher rates of return and greater accessibility, then changes in the money supply may reflect these innovations and the public's reaction to them, not some policy action taken by the FOMC. For both interest rates and the money supply, therefore, each may give false signals that could confuse policymakers into thinking that their actions have been too restrictive or expansionary, even when they have not.

The third criterion is that the intermediate target variable should be related to the goal measure. For example, historical evidence suggests that increases in the growth rate of the money supply often precede higher rates of inflation. The evidence also suggests that interest rates move with, not before, those higher inflation rates. So, from the policymaker's viewpoint, which intermediate target measure is preferable? Clearly the money supply. But what if just the opposite is true when it comes to predicting future real GDP growth? That is, what if interest rates turn out to be a better intermediate target than the money supply if the goal is stable output growth? This presents a dilemma for policymakers and forces them to either pick one goal and therefore one intermediate target or switch between them over time. Although the Federal Reserve's stated goal is to keep inflation low, this goal is often at odds with the more immediate objective of increasing output growth rates.

Clearly this conflict between policy goals and the selection of the proper intermediate target is the subject of much ongoing debate among policymakers and those who observe policy actions. Financial innovations and the constant evolution of economic relations mean that this area of policy analysis is constantly under study by economists.

FURTHER READING

Brunner, Karl, ed. *Targets and Indicators of Monetary Policy*. San Francisco: Chandler Publishing, 1969; DeLong, J. Bradford. *Macroeconomics*. Boston: McGraw-Hill Irwin, 2002.

INTERNATIONAL BANKING FACILITY. International banking facilities, or IBFs, were created by the **Board of Governors** and established on June 18, 1981. It was announced that IBFs would commence operations beginning December 3 of that year to give state legislatures time to revise tax and banking laws. The official announcement marked the end of a three-year period of debate and discussion over the usefulness of IBFs: The New York Clearing House Association had originally proposed the concept to the Federal Reserve Board of Governors in July 1978 and in July 1981. By the end of the decade, over 500 IBFs had been established throughout the United States, with about half of them located in New York State alone. Of the total number of IBFs in operation at the time, 328 were opened by branches and agencies of foreign banks, 150 by banks and savings and loan associations, and 49 by **Edge Act corporations**.

What is an IBF? The primary function of an IBF is to allow depository institutions to offer deposit and loan services to foreign residents. For example, an IBF allows a U.S. bank to use its domestic offices to offer deposit and loan services to foreign customers who formerly would have used foreign offices. The depository institutions that are able to offer IBF include commercial banks, Edge Act corporations, savings and loan associations, mutual savings banks, and foreign commercial banks through their branches and agencies located in the United States. An enticing feature of an IBF is that it is not required to meet the Federal Reserve's **reserve requirements**, thus reducing its cost of operation relative to a domestic depository institution. In addition, some IBFs are not subject to certain state and local taxes on income. In essence, by lessening the cost of operation, an IBF allows depository institutions operating in the United States to compete with deposit and loan services provided by institutions in the Eurocurrency markets overseas. IBFs offer a number of services. For example, they may offer foreign residents large time deposits, and foreign banks and official institutions may place overnight funds with them. IBFs also can extend credit to foreign residents, other IBFs, or the U.S. offices of the IBF parent, and they may transact business in foreign currency.

The operations of an IBF fall under the auspices of several regulatory agencies, including the Federal Reserve and other federal and state regulators. An IBF's operations are subject to restrictions established by its chartering or licensing authority or by its primary supervisor. Regulators currently examine the foreign operations of U.S. banks through the U.S. head offices of the institutions and regularly conduct on-site examinations of selected branches and subsidiaries abroad.

FURTHER READING

Federal Reserve Bank of New York. "International Banking Facilities." *Fedpoints* (November 2002).

INTERNATIONAL MONETARY FUND. The International Monetary Fund (IMF) began operations in Washington, D.C., in 1946. The IMF was created almost two years earlier when delegates from 44 nations met at the New Hampshire resort of Bretton Woods. As World War II was drawing to a close, those delegates met to establish an international monetary system, one that would provide a framework within which **exchange rates** were determined. Eschewing the uncertainty of a freely floating exchange rate system, the **Bretton Woods System** established a managed exchange rate system with the U.S. dollar as the key international currency. With the signing of the Bretton Woods agreement in July 1944, that system was established. As part of the managed exchange rate system, an international organization was created to oversee and monitor the system. That organization was the IMF.

The rationale of the IMF was described in the *Articles of Agreement of the International Monetary Fund*. Originally adopted in July 1944 and amended in 1969, 1978, and 1992, the *Articles* describe a grand vision for the IMF. As described in Fieleke (1994, pp. 17–18) the purpose of the IMF is:

1. To promote international monetary cooperation through a permanent institution which provides the machinery for consultation and collaboration on international monetary problems;
2. To facilitate the expansion and balanced growth of international trade, and to contribute thereby to the promotion and maintenance of high levels of employment and real income and to the development of the productive resources of all members as primary objectives of economic policy;
3. To promote exchange stability, to maintain orderly exchange arrangements among members, and to avoid competitive exchange depreciation;
4. To assist in the establishment of a multilateral system of payments in respect of current transactions between members and in the elimination of foreign exchange restrictions which hamper the growth of world trade;
5. To give confidence to members by making the general resources of the Fund temporarily available to them under adequate safeguards, thus providing them with opportunity to correct maladjustments in their balance of payments without resorting to measures destructive of national or international prosperity; and
6. In accordance with the above, to shorten the duration and lessen the degree of disequilibrium in the international balances of payments of members.

Reading through this set of purposes, it is clear that the experiences of the past colored the vision of what the IMF should accomplish in the future. For example, the IMF sought to increase international policy coordination. During the **Great Depression**, for example, trade barriers were raised to levels that made the economic downturn even more severe than if the barriers had not been erected. The agreement also sought to reduce the uncertainty and economic effects of exchange rate fluctuations. Taking one characteristic from the **gold standard** period, the Bretton Woods System and the IMF tried to create an environment in which exchange rates were stable; that is, predictable. Like fixing the price of some good, exchange rate stability was viewed as reducing the pricing uncertainty that exists when exchange rates freely fluctuate. Of course, this approach also masked the need for exchange rate devaluations or appreciations when economic events warranted such changes.

The IMF was viewed as a permanent institution on the international monetary scene. Consistent with its status, the IMF's governing body, its **Board of Governors**, consists of finance ministers or central bank governors of the member countries. Each member country appoints one Governor to sit on the IMF's Board. The board normally meets once each year. The day-to-day operations of the IMF are conducted by the executive board. The executive board appoints a managing director, who serves as its chairperson and heads the IMF staff of some 2,000 international civil servants. Advisory to the board are two committees. One is the so-called "Interim Committee," which provides advice to the board on the functioning of the international monetary system. The other is the Development Committee. This committee, established jointly by the IMF and the World Bank, provides advice to poorer countries regarding special needs in the areas of financing or economic development issues.

Over time, an increasingly important role of the IMF has been to provide technical assistance to smaller economies. In recent years many of these economies have begun the process of transforming themselves from centrally planned economies to market-oriented ones. The nature of the assistance varies with the needs of the country, but the overall nature of such assistance can include instruction on fiscal, monetary, and foreign-exchange management and in related legal and statistical matters. It may also include training of officials from member countries, either at the headquarters in Washington, D.C., or abroad.

As stated in the *Articles*, a key role of the IMF, perhaps more important historically than today, is to oversee the international monetary exchange system. Although few governments are completely divorced from intervening in the foreign exchange market, there is much more flexibility in foreign exchange rates today than in the past. Since movements in foreign exchange rates are a key determinant of trade flows, the fourth purpose as stated above in the *Articles* recognizes that managing these exchange arrangements promotes trade. Thus, the IMF strives to remove restrictions to trade. This is done in part by requiring nations to remove payments restrictions on international transactions upon joining the IMF. Fieleke (1994) notes that "failure to honor this agreement could precipitate suspension of their borrowing privileges and, eventually, expulsion from the Fund. Members that have no such restriction are not to impose them without Fund approval. Similar bans apply to discriminatory currency practices."

A more controversial aspect of the IMF involves the fund's lending programs. Because one of the chief purposes of the fund is to maintain stability in the sphere of international trade, this can be done by providing assistance, in the form of loans, to nations that are struggling economically. In the past such assistance has been provided to nations that face payment difficulties, meaning that they are running substantial balance of payments deficits. Sometimes these difficulties arise as countries transition from planned to market economies. Other times they occur when governments simply mismanage economic policies. Countries have a variety of sources of fund support. As Fieleke (1994, p. 25) notes, "members may apply for loans from their credit tranches (percentages of their quotas), from the extended Fund facility, the compensatory and contingency financing facility, the buffer stock financing facility, the systemic transformation facility, the structural adjustment facility, or the enhanced structural adjustment facility." Where do the funds come from?

Upon joining the IMF, member nations pay a subscription. In addition, the IMF borrows from its members to finance loans to other nations.

What makes the IMF's lending programs controversial are the concessions that it often requires from borrowing nations. In the past such concessions have involved changing domestic policies to reduce inflation, the size of the government deficit, or a balance of payments problem. In some instances the requirements to gain funding have been so harsh that the domestic economy has suffered. As with most lending activities, the IMF faces the problem of **moral hazard**. That is, if the IMF makes the requirements of the loan too harsh, borrowing nations may simply agree to the IMF's stipulations, acquire the funds, and then renege. If the IMF is committed to maintaining international trade, such actions by borrowing nations may leave the IMF with no alternative but to bail them out again.

Although some of the IMF's activities draw criticism from various observers, it continues to promote international cooperation with a variety of programs. Through the IMF and other international agencies, countries are able to discuss policy coordination, provide technical assistance to needy nations, and monitor economic events around the world with an eye to fostering economic development worldwide.

FURTHER READING

Aufricht, Hans. *The International Monetary Fund: Legal Bases, Structure and Functions*. London: Praeger Publishers, 1964; Fieleke, Norman S. "The International Monetary Fund 50 Years After Bretton Woods." Federal Reserve Bank of Boston *New England Economic Review* (September/October 1994); International Monetary Fund. Website: www.imf.org/.

INVESTMENT BANKS. Investment banks are not like the bank where most of us deposit our paychecks and make cash withdrawals. Investment banks are, however, important **financial intermediaries**. The investment bank acts as the deal-maker in mergers and acquisitions, as brokers to corporations and individuals, and as underwriters for first-time sales of stocks and bonds. Unlike other brokers or dealers, though, investment banks earn their income by charging fees to the clients on whose behalf they are working. Because investment banks specialize in the collection of needed information and related tasks, they are more efficient at providing these services than are individual firms.

During the earlier part of the twentieth century, banking and investment activities often were housed in the same firm. Banks not only took in deposits and made **loans**; they also sold securities. This dual activity was especially evident in the larger New York money center banks. With the excesses of the 1920s laid bare with the crash of 1929 and the ensuing economic difficulties of the **Great Depression**, regulators sought to separate commercial banking and investment banking activities. The passage of the **Glass-Steagall Act of 1932** erected a regulatory wall that separated commercial banking from investment banking. This was done to protect depositors from imprudent investment activities on the other side of the bank.

With the passage of Glass-Steagall, banks that focused solely on securities-related activities were formed. As time has passed, the delineation between what constitutes a commercial bank and an investment bank has become blurred. Since the 1980s the regulatory wall between commercial and investment banking has been crumbling away. A major development has been the acquisition of investment banks by large commercial banking concerns. Not only has this trend effectively recombined commercial and investment banking, but it also has led to a further consolidation in the banking industry. In the late 1990s, for example, the investment bank of Alex Brown was acquired by Bankers Trust, and the combined firm subsequently was acquired by Deutsche Bank.

Investment banks are involved in many of the mergers and acquisitions that occur among firms. Activities in this area may include finding firms that are likely takeover prospects or firms that are looking for another to acquire them. Investment bankers serve both the interests of the acquired and the acquirers, although not at the same time. The funds used to finance such takeover attempts are often raised by the investment bank. One of the more infamous examples of this was the so-called junk bond craze of the 1980s. At that time, bonds of dubious value were used to raise funds to finance takeover activities. The individual credited with inventing this financial tool is Michael Miliken. In 1990, as these bonds began to default, Miliken's employer, Drexel Burnham Lambert, Inc., was forced to file for bankruptcy. This effectively killed the junk bond market and slowed the merger and acquisition activity, although both aspects of this intermediation again rose in popularity during the late 1990s.

Investment banks also serve as underwriters for stocks and bonds. The notion of *underwriting* refers to the practice of the investment bank purchasing the entire issuance of stocks or bonds at some predetermined price and then selling it on the market. For this service the underwriting investment bank charges a fee to the firm. While the investment bank takes on some risk by buying the issuance, there also is a large upside reward if the stocks or bonds are sold in the market for an amount greater than the predetermined price at which the investment bank purchased them. Firms are willing to hire investment banks to serve as underwriters due to the complexity of issuing new financial instruments and marketing them.

Investment banks also may assist companies that wish to sell divisions, or even the entire company. This often is done through sale of the company's stock, a process that requires a multitude of experts in areas such as firm valuation, legal expertise, financial analysts, and more. Investment banks specialize in such activities and, therefore, enable firms to more efficiently divest or be acquired than if they tried to accomplish this on their own.

FURTHER READING

Bruck, Connie. *The Predators' Ball: The Inside Story of Drexel Burnham and the Rise of the Junk Bond Raiders.* New York: Random House, 2001; Lewis, Michael. *Liar's Poker: Rising Through the Wreckage on Wall Street.* New York: Simon and Schuster, 1988; Lowenstein, Roger. *When Genius Failed: The Rise and Fall of Long-Term Capital Management.* New York: Random House, 2000.

JONES, HOMER (1906–1986). Homer Jones is best known for his role in the revival of monetary economic research within the Federal Reserve System. Jones accomplished this feat from his position as director of research at the Federal Reserve Bank of St. Louis. When Jones became research director, the prevalent view among macroeconomists and monetary economists was that (1) fiscal policy actions dominated monetary policy actions in affecting the economy and (2) that monetary policy was best guided by the judicious manipulation of market interest rates. In effect, monetary policy existed to provide the best environment within which fiscal policy could operate. For many, this meant a policy of keeping interest rates low, regardless of the longer-run implications. Concern about the behavior of monetary aggregates was lacking, as was the statistical research about the behavior of the aggregates.

When Jones arrived at the St. Louis Bank, the research department was much like those at other District Banks: monetary policy and its analysis were primarily the purview of the **Board of Governors** in Washington, D.C., except for the local use of the **discount rate** and banking supervision and regulation activities. During the late 1950s, there was a nascent emergence of the District Banks in the field of monetary research. The Atlanta Bank, under **Malcolm Bryan,** began to research the role of monetary aggregates. Even so, the research and statistical output of the research department at the St. Louis Bank set it apart from others. One aspect of this emerging reputation as a "maverick" in the Federal Reserve System came from the fact that Homer Jones was pushing the monetary research ideas associated with the so-called Chicago School, especially those of his former student, **Milton Friedman**. As Harry Johnson (1976, p. 437) puts it,

> Homer Jones and the Federal Reserve Bank of St. Louis in fact remained institutions of largely local Chicago repute and veneration during the first phase of the revival of professional and popular interest in monetary theory and conviction of the importance for good or ill of monetary policy.... It was Homer Jones and his staff in St. Louis ... who deserve the credit for shifting the focus of interest from a concept of a "test" of rival theories to the far more fruitful questions of the relative strengths, reliabilities, and speeds of monetary and fiscal impulses.

But Jones's contributions went beyond hiring the people who would produce the research for which the St. Louis Bank became famous. Jones pushed for reliable and timely statistics on the monetary aggregates. Because the Federal Reserve at the time was not providing much data on the movements in the monetary aggregates, Jones pushed for the compilation and publication of statistics that would show the growth of the monetary aggregates and their components over various time frames. This took the form of "growth triangles" that were made available in the bank's monthly and weekly publications. These growth triangles essentially allowed the reader to see the growth rate of a monetary aggregate over a period as short as the past month or as long as a year. This information thus allowed one to see patterns in the growth of the monetary aggregates that indicated changes in monetary policy. Although the focus of policy at the time was on financial market conditions, especially the behavior of interest rates, such policies also had an impact on the monetary aggregates. And because it was becoming more widely recognized that the behavior of the monetary aggregates in fact lead to predictable changes in the economy, this information was becoming more widely followed. This led some in the Federal Reserve System, especially individuals at the Board of Governors, to look upon the St. Louis Fed's actions as near heresy. As one governor was quoted as saying in a 1967 *Business Week* article, "It is a weakness for a regional bank to concentrate on national matters. We have a fine staff in Washington."

The importance of the St. Louis Bank's research orientation as led by Homer Jones (and his then-president **Darryl Francis**) is perhaps best stated by Milton Friedman (1976, pp. 435–36):

> Between them, Homer and Darryl Francis converted the St. Louis Bank into by far the most important unit in the System.... For the first time, a bank publication, *The Review of the Federal Reserve Bank of St. Louis*, began to be cited regularly in the academic journals. This academic revival was joined with similar penetration into practical affairs. Homer's insatiable curiosity about the facts, and his belief in the power of repeated exposure to the facts to erode illusion, led to the publication by the Bank of its now famed series of weekly and monthly collections of statistics ... the appearance week after week of those clearly drawn charts of the money supply did more than any other single thing, in my opinion, to bring about the change that has occurred from almost exclusive concentration in monetary policy on interest rates and on the esoteric 'tone and feel of the market' to stress on the quantity of money.

Although monetary policy actions today have retreated from placing the importance on the monetary aggregates that Friedman talks about, the now-accepted role of money and how its behavior affects economic activity and inflation are in no small part due to the research and analysis conducted at the St. Louis Bank under the direction of Homer Jones.

FURTHER READING

For more on Homer Jones and the role he and the St. Louis Fed played in the policy debates of the late 1950s and 1960s, see the contributions of Karl Brunner, Milton Friedman, Harry Johnson, and A. James Meigs in the special edition of the *Journal of Monetary Economics* (2:1976), from which the above quotations are taken. These are accessible at the Federal Reserve Bank of St. Louis's Website: www.research.stlouisfed.org/conferences/homer/jme.html.

JORDAN, JERRY. Jerry Jordan co-authored with **Leonall Andersen** the influential study "Monetary and Fiscal Actions: A Test of Their Relative Importance in Economic Stabilization." This article, which appeared in the Federal Reserve Bank of St. Louis's *Review* in November 1968, is widely recognized as shifting the focus in macroeconomics to testing the relative strengths and speeds of monetary and fiscal policy actions. Although the paper was subject to many criticisms on several different fronts—from the statistical approach to the underlying theory upon which the tests were based—the study remained a key analysis that helped propel the tenets of **Monetarism** into the forefront of policy discussion and academic debate. To this day it remains one of the most widely cited articles in economics.

Jordan came to the Federal Reserve Bank of St. Louis after receiving his Ph.D. in economics at UCLA. During his tenure at St. Louis, Jordan rose to the position of senior vice president and director of research. After leaving the St. Louis Bank, Jordan held several positions, including economist with Pittsburgh National Bank and First Interstate Bancorp in Los Angles and dean of the R. O. Anderson School of Management at the University of New Mexico. During 1981–1982, Jordan served as a member of President Ronald Reagan's **Council of Economic Advisors**, during which he also served as a member of the U.S. Gold Commission. In March 1992, Jordan became the president and chief operating officer of the Federal Reserve Bank of Cleveland, the position from which he retired in January 2003. A past president of the National Association of Business Economists, Jordan also is an adjunct scholar at the Cato Institute in Washington, D.C.

KEYNES, JOHN MAYNARD (1883–1946). John Maynard Keynes is undoubtedly the most influential economist of the twentieth century. Born in Cambridge, England, Keynes's father (John Neville Keynes) was a noted economist in his own right. After graduating from King's College, Cambridge, in 1905 with a degree in mathematics, Keynes worked in the British civil service. His first book in economics was written while he was a civil servant. The book, *Indian Currency and Finance*, described the Indian monetary system. In 1908 Keynes left government employment and returned to Cambridge as a lecturer. At the outbreak of World War I, he returned to government service, this time with the British Treasury. Keynes's intellect and persuasive personality allowed him to rise rapidly in the Treasury. By 1919 he was Britain's chief representative at the peace conference in Versailles, France, the conference that would establish the post-World War I reparations to be paid by the German government. Keynes resigned in a dispute over the drastic nature of the reparations, noting that the penalties imposed on Germany would undermine its ability to recover from the war and would instill destabilizing domestic nationalism. Indeed, one of Keynes's most famous books, *The Economic Consequences of the Peace*, separated him from the British government's position and made him a celebrity.

Keynes returned to his academic studies following the war. During the 1920s, Keynes pursued economic analysis along the lines of his mentor, Alfred Marshall and others (especially Arthur Pigou) associated with the so-called Cambridge School. This view of economics was primarily a long-run one, derived mostly from the **quantity theory**. This belief was that economies would tend toward their long-run equilibrium and that changes in the supply of money, over time, are related to changes in the price level. In the United States, a version of this theory was being worked on by **Irving Fisher**. Keynes's research in this area is summarized in two works: his *Tract on Monetary Reform* (1923) and the two-volume *Treatise on Money* (1930).

Keynes's work on monetary theory was mainline in many ways. He considered the role of the central bank to be one of stabilizing the price level over time, primarily by raising the "bank rate" (what we would call the **discount rate**) during times of rising prices and lowering it during times of falling prices. Even though Keynes's monetary work was published in 1930, he already had begun a change of heart in his views on the role of economic policy, both monetary and fiscal.

Following World War I, Britain was mired in economic stagnation. Due primarily to its attempt to return to prewar parity and the confines of the **gold standard**, Britain during the 1920s suffered persistently high rates of unemployment and negligible **economic growth**. Keynes, along with other economists of the time, began to reconsider the notion that economies would always return to their full-employment levels of output. Even though he believed that full employment would *eventually* return, he questioned the economic costs imposed by waiting for the adjustment to occur. Bringing together ideas from others and providing insights of his own led Keynes to write his most enduring work, *The General Theory of Employment, Interest and Money*. Although published in 1936, drafts of this work were being circulated much earlier than that. The policies promoted by Keynes and his tireless campaigning for his ideas led many governments, including the **Franklin Roosevelt** administration, to recognize the need for government action during the **Great Depression** to try to get the economy growing.

Keynes's insight, revolutionary then and commonplace today, was that the government, through expansionary spending programs, could maintain total demand for goods and services in times when demand in the private sector was falling off. That is, during recessions the government should, according to Keynes, engage in expansionary spending programs that would fill the void left by the private side of the economy. When the economy returns to full employment, such programs would be curtailed. Even though Keynes was a strong proponent of free markets, it was his view that there are times when economic forces come together in such a manner that free markets may not be able to combat the instabilities.

If Keynes's work focused on the fiscal side of policy, why include him here in a book about the Federal Reserve? One reason is that Keynes's theory and his approach to macroeconomics has dominated policy discussion from the appearance of the *General Theory* through today. A lasting feature of this movement, although not really part of Keynes's model, was the idea that through fiscal policy actions and a supporting monetary policy, governments could fine tune economic activity with such precision that recessions would become a thing of the past. By adjusting fiscal policy and with a monetary policy that would keep interest rates low, many Keynesian economists believed that full employment would be the norm.

Of course, such chutzpah was short lived. During the 1960s, the application of this policy approach created a lasting expansion but also led to increasing rates of inflation. (*See* **Great Inflation**.) The demand-side focus of such macroeconomic policies did not foresee the problems associated with supply-side disruptions, such as the Organization of Petroleum Exporting Countries (OPEC) oil price shocks of the 1970s. The inability of the Keynesian view to recognize and cope with these problems partly explains the rising popularity of the Monetarist arguments regarding the role of monetary policy. It also helped give rise to the **rational expectations** school, which is based on the idea that government policies to reduce the unemployment rate or increase real economic growth would only succeed if they were unexpected by the public. This requirement eventually would lead, according to the theory, to destabilizing policy actions.

Even though the macroeconomic movement associated with Keynes failed to foresee such problems, today's major macroeconomic models have morphed to incorporate these aspects. Indeed, the models that are used by governments, by central banks and by large private forecasting firms to predict economic behavior and forecast the effect of policy changes all are based on the model first laid out by Keynes in the *General Theory*.

FURTHER READING

Moggridge, Donald, ed. *The Collected Writings of John Maynard Keynes*. 30 volumes. New York: Macmillan Press, 1971 through 1989; Skidelsky, Robert. *John Maynard Keynes: Hopes Betrayed, 1883–1920*. New York: Viking Press, 1983; Skidelsky, Robert. *John Maynard Keynes: The Economist as Savior, 1920–1937*. New York: Penguin Press, 1992; Skidelsky, Robert. *John Maynard Keynes: Fighting for Freedom, 1937–1946*. New York: Viking Press, 2000.

LAGS IN MONETARY POLICY. To understand the issue of lags and how they affect the setting of monetary policy, an analogy is useful. Think of the last time you were sitting at a stoplight and you were, say, the tenth car back from the intersection. Everyone can see the stoplight. Given the speed of light and distances from it, when the light turns green, all drivers effectively see it at the same time. So why, then, as the tenth car back, do you have to wait before you move? The reason is because there are lags in individual responses to seeing the light change and these different reaction times lead to a lag in moving forward for cars farther back in the line.

How is this related to lags in monetary policy? The first lag is the time that it takes monetary policymakers to recognize that a change has occurred. Instead of a light going from red to green, the relevant change is an increase or a decrease in the rate of **inflation** or a jump in the **unemployment rate**. Because economic data are reported with a lag—inflation is reported monthly, meaning, for example, that the report released in June is for May inflation—changes may already be taking place before policymakers recognize them. This means that policymakers may already be behind the curve when it comes to reacting to observed changes in economic variables. For some variables, such as real **gross domestic product (GDP)**, which is reported only every three months, they are reported only as a preliminary number that gets revised at least twice before the "official" number is known. One reason for lags in policy setting comes from "recognition" lags.

Another reason lags arise is because once policymakers decide to institute a change, it takes time for them to implement this policy action. Although with their ability to change the level of the **federal funds rate** on very short notice through **open market operations**, it still takes time. And if the focus is on the growth rate of the money supply, a decision today to increase the growth rate of the **money** supply may take some time to realize. "Implementation" lags are another lag in policy that must be accounted for.

Once a policy action has been taken, there are lags in how quickly a policy action works its way through the economy. For example, suppose the **Federal Open Market Committee (FOMC)** increases interest rates in order to bring about a lower rate of inflation. How long does it take for everyone in the economy to recognize this change and alter their behavior in such a way that prices begin to increase at a slower pace? Existing research suggests that the lag between a policy action and the eventual change in inflation may be as long as two years. The same research suggests that, on average, a policy action to slow or increase growth in real GDP may be on the order to six to nine months. The very fact that the lagged responses of inflation and output to the same policy action differ suggests yet another complication in the formation of monetary policy.

And there are external effects that can influence the response of the economy to changes in monetary policy. In the post-9/11 world, policy actions were noticeably affected by uncertainties that had nothing to do with monetary policy. For example, the Federal Reserve aggressively began to push the federal funds rate down over the period from 2000 through 2003. Starting from a level of about 6.5 percent in June 2000, the Federal Reserve lowered the federal funds rate in a series of actions that left it at 1 percent, the lowest in more than 40 years, by mid-2003. As the Federal Reserve was pushing rates down, the economy did not show signs of increasing economic growth. In fact, the economy was sluggishly trying to rebound from the mild recession of 2001. But uncertainty, unwillingness to invest, the wars in Afghanistan and Iraq, and the continuing troubles in the Middle East all are looked upon as explanations for why the economy did not begin to expand at a faster pace that would be expected based upon the expansionary monetary policy implemented by the Federal Reserve.

Finally, the fact that such lags exist has led some economists, notably **Milton Friedman**, to call for monetary policies that focus more on long-term policy objectives. Because lags will make trying to stabilize economic activity in the short-term difficult, the Federal Reserve should focus on long-term relations, such as exists between money growth and inflation. Indeed, during the past two decades economists have come to believe that policies geared toward stabilizing short-run fluctuations in the economy are more likely to fail than those that focus on long-term relations.

FURTHER READING

Federal Reserve Bank of San Francisco. "U.S. Monetary Policy: An Introduction." *Economic Letter* (January 1, 1999); Friedman, Milton. "The Lag in Effects of Monetary Policy." *Journal of Political Economy*. (October 1961): 447–66.

LDC DEBT CRISIS. The LDC (less-developed-country) debt crisis became apparent to all in late-summer 1982 when the minister of finance of Mexico announced that the Mexican government would not meet a debt payment scheduled for August 16. At the time the amount of outstanding debt was about $80 billion. Within a year, the situation became even more dire as 27 other countries, owing a total of nearly $240 billion, were scrambling to reschedule debt payments: In effect, they could not pay off their **loans** on time and were negotiating for a different payment schedule and terms. Many of the countries were in Latin America, the four largest being Argentina, Brazil, Mexico, and Venezuela. As a group they accounted for about 75 percent of the total outstanding LDC debt.

Why the LDC debt crisis is of interest is because almost $40 billion of the debt was owed to U.S. banks, an amount that greatly exceeded the banks' capital and **reserves**. As stated by the **Federal Deposit Insurance Corporation (FDIC)** (1998, p. 191), "As a consequence, several of the world's largest banks faced the prospect of major loan defaults and failure." In other words, if these loans could not be paid off, not only could U.S. banks face bankruptcy but U.S. bank regulators, including the Federal Reserve, could face the difficult issue of dealing with a major banking and financial crisis.

Because the FDIC (1998) study provides a detailed discussion of the events leading to and around the LDC debt crisis, I summarize the points raised there. To do this, it is instructive to see how U.S. banks got into this mess, how regulators dealt with it, and how the aftershocks impacted not only how banks do business but also how regulators deal with such events.

The genesis of the LDC debt crisis occurred in the 1970s. During the mid-1970s, the price of oil, determined primarily by the actions of the Organization of Petroleum Exporting Countries (OPEC) producers, increased sharply. Between 1972 and 1980, for example, the price of crude oil, adjusted for inflation, increased fourfold to over $35 a barrel. This increase is often cited as a major **aggregate supply shock**, one that gave rise to a worldwide recession. Faced with falling output and declining incomes from their international trade, many of the less-developed countries were forced to borrow heavily in order to maintain current levels of economic activity. Many of the largest U.S. banks were willing to accommodate this demand, seeing this as an opportunity to expand their markets and new profit opportunities. Between 1977 and 1981, the amount of LDC debt due to the largest U.S. banks increased almost two thirds.

One aspect of these loans that made them onerous for the borrowing countries—and profitable for the banks—is that they often were priced using the London Interbank Offering Rate (LIBOR). The risk arose not in using the LIBOR rate but from the fact that the loans were often "repriced." In some instances, the rate on loans was changed every six months. This meant that borrowers could face substantially higher interest costs on their loans than originally contracted for. In times of economic uncertainty, such variable-rate loans can damage a borrower's ability to repay the loan. This raises the likelihood of default. On the banks' side of the equation, *if* the borrowing countries could continue to service their debt at the higher rates of interest, the profitability of the loan would just get greater. This led some banks to increase their activity in making more loans to countries that already appeared shaky.

The riskiness of such lending activity did not go without comment by high-ranking U.S. regulators. **Arthur Burns**, the chairman of the Federal Reserve, cautioned banks as early as 1977 against assuming too much risk through extended lending to LDCs. In 1979 the new chairman of the Federal Reserve **Paul Volcker** reiterated this concern. Along with other U.S. officials, Volcker warned that U.S. banks were assuming too much debt exposure in developing areas and were subjecting themselves to increased default risks as the countries were trying to reschedule debts. For some, the potential chain of events—default by the LDCs and either the collapse of the lenders or the bailout by the government—was sufficient to warrant increased oversight and regulatory intervention. Even so, many banks continued to lend to LDCs.

As noted at the beginning of this entry, by summer 1982 the problem reached a climax. Not only were LDCs continuing to borrow while they were actively rescheduling their outstanding debts, but U.S. banks continued to lend on the belief that things would get better. Of course, if the borrowers defaulted, as was becoming increasingly possible, the potential losses would be even greater. Banks were willing to take the gamble, especially as the regulators appeared ready to bail them out of trouble. (This is related to the problem caused by deposit insurance [*see* **Moral Hazard**] and the notion that some banks were simply too big to fail.)

The debt crisis was affected by outside events. In late-1979 and through 1982, the Federal Reserve embarked on a campaign to lower inflation by slowing the growth rate of the money supply and raising short-term interest rates. This policy had two major effects: First, it exacerbated a worldwide recession. Second, because the Federal Reserve pushed U.S. interest rates to such high levels, it in turn pushed up international interest rates. With the three-month **Treasury bill** rate hitting 16 percent in 1981, interest rates around the world increased, including the LIBOR rate. Recalling that most of the LDC debt was tied to the LIBOR rate, the Federal Reserve's actions thus made the funding difficulties faced by LDC debtors even worse. This confluence of events and their ill-advised decisions pushed the LDCs over the brink into bankruptcy. As mentioned above, in August 1982 Mexico's finance minister announced that his country would not longer be able to meet interest payments on its debt obligations. This announcement was followed by similar statements from the governments of 40 other nations, many of which were in Latin America.

What was the outcome of the LDC debt crisis? The years that followed are an illustration of **regulatory forbearance**. In the United States, banks were not required to set aside large amounts of reserves to cover the losses incurred in the debt crisis. Rather, they were given the opportunity to restructure the loans and attempt to resolve the issues. This meant that during the restructuring phase, many of the largest banks in the United States were technically insolvent (liabilities exceeded assets). If they used the market value of the loans to the LDCs, their capital positions were negative, bankrupt by definition. U.S. regulators chose not to take this route, however, largely because it could have led to a banking crisis on the widespread scale. In this instance, the regulators guessed correctly. While the profitability of the biggest lenders suffered for years as they restructured loans, built up loan-loss reserves, and simply wrote off the loans, there was no collapse of the banking system.

The LDC debt crisis is an example of how banks, in their attempt to maximize profits, sometimes put profitability ahead of caution, especially if they know that depositors' funds are insured by a government agency. It also shows how regulators sometimes are unwilling to stop potentially profitable activities by the banks they are regulating. In the end, the LDC debt crisis may not have led to an overall collapse of the banking system, but it was not costless. The combination of bad management and ineffective regulation during the LDC debt crisis cost stockholders in the major banks billions of dollars.

FURTHER READING

Cline, William R. *International Debt Reexamined*. Washington, D.C.: Institute for International Economics, 1984; Federal Deposit Insurance Corporation. "History of the Eighties—Lessons for the Future." Washington, D.C.: FDIC, 1997, Chapter 5 (This publication is available online from the FDIC.); Siedman, L. William. *Full Faith and Credit: The Great S&L Debacle and Other Washington Sagas*. New York: Times Books, 1993; Wellons, Phillip A. *Passing the Buck: Banks, Government and Third World Debt*. Boston: Harvard University Press, 1987.

LEAN AGAINST THE WIND. During the 1950s, Federal Reserve officials often noted that the goal of policy, in the short run, was to undertake actions that produced counter-cyclical movements in the market for credit and in the money supply. As discussed elsewhere, the **Federal Open Market Committee (FOMC)** and especially the chairman of the Federal Reserve at the time, **William McChesney Martin**, believed that maintaining orderly credit and financial market conditions and an evenly performing economy were the primary objectives of their actions. To do this, monetary policy would "lean against the wind," accomplished by being more expansionary in times of economic slowdowns and contractionary in times of expansion.

During the 1950s, this policy was thought to provide the best way to avoid sustained periods of **inflation** or **deflation**. Martin expressed the idea in testimony during his 1956 nomination to a full term as governor thusly: "Our purpose is to lean against the winds of deflation or inflation, whichever way they are blowing ..." (quoted in Friedman and Schwartz, 1963, p. 632). While such an approach to policy gave the FOMC maximum freedom of action, it also was a policy without content. Put another way, it was an approach that had no rudder, other than the desire to keep the economy on track. If inflation increased, how would the FOMC respond? Because there was no response written down and no policy rule, responses could and did vary over time. This meant that it became increasingly difficult for market participants to predict the stance of policy.

Another major problem with this policy, as noted by Friedman and Schwartz (1963) among others, is the fact that information upon which policy is decided arrives with a lag. If the FOMC bases its policy decisions on the best information available, the "wind" to which they are responding is outdated. Like light arriving from a distant star, information about inflation or economic growth available today actually reflects events that occurred several months earlier. Reacting to the "new" information puts policy behind the curve. And trying to foresee the effects of today's policy action on the economy in the future requires a degree of prescience that no policymaker, then or now, possesses. As Friedman and Schwartz (1963, p. 632) describe the situation, "the [Federal Reserve] System regarded the decision as one that had to be based on the balancing of numerous imponderables, which had best be left to the informed 'judgment' of the men in charge and could not be explicitly formalized."

Even though the notion of leaning against the wind may seem antiquated, it remains the underlying theme of monetary policy. Since its inception the Federal Reserve has sought to steer the economy and financial markets in its attempt, sometimes a failed one, to manage economic activity. Over time the FOMC has used various indicators and economic measures upon which to base their decisions. Unlike other central banks, the Federal Reserve has steadfastly rejected any formal policy rule that binds their decision making. Even though today's FOMC probably does not weight the day-to-day movements in financial markets as much as they did 50 years ago, they nonetheless are very concerned about prevailing against undesired changes in inflation or in economic growth. In this sense, leaning against the wind continues to be an important basis for monetary policy decision making.

FURTHER READING

Friedman, Milton, and Anna J. Schwartz, *A Monetary History of the United States, 1867–1960*. Princeton: Princeton University Press, 1963, especially Chapter 11.

LEGAL TENDER. In technical terms, legal tender is defined by Section 102 of the Coinage Act of 1965 (Title 31 United States Code, Section 392) to provide that *"All coins and currencies of the United States, regardless of when coined or issued, shall be legal tender for all debts, public and private, public charges, taxes, duties and dues."*

As stated by the Bureau of Engraving and Printing, "This statute means that you have made a valid and legal offer of payment of your debt when you tender United States currency to your creditor. However, there is no Federal statute which mandates that private businesses must accept cash as a form of payment. Private businesses are free to develop their own policies on whether or not to accept cash unless there is a State law which says otherwise." What does that mean? It means that legal tender, even though it is given a certain status by the government, is something that has long been subject to change. A short history of legal tender—**currency**—in the United States is illustrative of this dynamic nature.

Currency and legal tender have evolved throughout U.S. economic history. The Revolutionary War necessitated the issuance of paper currency by the Continental Congress. The same was true during the Civil War, when both the North and the South issued paper money to help finance their war efforts. In 1861, the U.S. Treasury (the North) issued what were called Demand notes. Printed in denominations of $5, $10, and $20, these bills were used by individuals to buy goods and were redeemable "on demand" for gold or silver coin. The printing of such notes was discontinued in 1862, replaced by Legal Tender notes. The South also issued paper currency, only they used cotton to back the value of their money.

Legal Tender notes were issued in the familiar $1 to $10 denominations as a move by the government to save money. How? By issuing paper currency that was backed only by the full faith of the government, gold and silver could be used to pay for the war, for example, buying materiel from foreign governments. It was not until 1879 that the government began once again to redeem Legal Tender notes for gold and silver coin.

In the late 1800s, both gold and silver certificates circulated as legal tender. First issued in 1863, gold certificates became a liability when, during the **Great Depression**, the public began to redeem their gold certificates for gold. Runs on banks and increased demands for gold led to passage of the Gold Reserve Act of 1933, which prohibited individuals from redeeming their paper currency for gold. Silver certificates, first issued in 1878, also circulated as money. In fact, until the 1960s, silver certificates were the primary currency. Originally available in denominations from $1 to $1,000, the rising price of silver in the 1960s led Congress to stop redeeming silver certificates for silver coin. As the price of silver rose, the value of the metal outpaced the value of the paper, leading to increased demands on U.S. holdings of the metal. To avoid the disappearance of silver coins, Congress stopped redeeming silver certificates in 1968. Instead, silver certificates were redeemed for Federal Reserve notes. Although the latter also are legal tender, they are backed only by the faith we have in the government. This type of money, one that is not backed by anything tangible, is referred to as *fiat* money.

FURTHER READING

Federal Reserve Bank of San Francisco. American Currency Exhibit. Website: www.frbsf.org.

LENDER OF LAST RESORT. The idea of a "lender of last resort" is an important concept in any discussion of central banking. Historically, some believed that central banks should stand ready to lend funds to banks during periods of **financial panics**. The constraint, however, was that such lending would be made only to solvent banks that were facing **liquidity** problems—with depositors wishing to withdraw funds not because the bank is failing but because depositors believe that it may—and that such lending would be made at a penalty rate. That is, funds could be borrowed from the central bank but at rates higher than those existing in the market. In this way the central bank could cushion the effects of financial panics, but it would do so in a way that clearly imposed significant costs on banks for not seeking alternative remedies. More modern treatments suggest that the lender of last resort functions of the central bank be broadened to mean that it should stand ready to lend funds to insolvent financial institutions. In this approach, the lender of last resort is acting to forestall financial panics and to stabilize the financial markets.

Why does the need for a lender of last resort exist? Modern banking systems generally operate in what is referred to as a **fractional reserve system**. In such systems, banks are required by law to hold some fraction of deposits on reserve, either as **vault cash** or on reserve with the central bank. Because banks have only a fraction of total deposits on hand at any point in time, an unexpected increase in demands to withdraw funds may leave the bank illiquid. Depositors wishing to withdraw funds may be turned away. Once the fact that a bank is not able to convert deposits to cash becomes known, depositors at other banks "run" their bank and demand to convert their deposits to cash. Because the other banks are in no better condition to supply these funds, a financial panic can ensue, where many banks, solvent or not, are unable to meet depositors' demands.

To satisfy the lender of last resort function, the **Federal Reserve Act of 1913** established the **discount window** mechanism by which banks could rediscount financial assets and receive **loans** from their Fed bank. As discussed elsewhere (*see* **Discount Window**), the willingness of the Federal Reserve to make loans to banks experiencing difficulties in meeting reserve requirements or in need of emergency funds illustrates the Federal Reserve acting as lender of last resort.

The history of the lender of last resort idea is a long one. The English economist Henry Thornton provides an early notion of how the central bank should behave in his *An Enquiry into the Effects of the Paper Credit of Great Britain,* published in 1802. In this book Thornton describes the role of the Bank of England during times of financial panic. Although the Bank of England was a private institution, it served as the government's bank and had a monopoly on issuance of currency within a 26-mile radius of London. For Thornton, the Bank of England should stand ready to provide liquidity to the market, loans to solvent but troubled banks, but not to provide aid to insolvent banks. Regardless of their size, Thornton did not believe that it was the duty of the Bank of England to save all banks from failure.

Perhaps the most famous work describing the early view of the lender of last resort is that of Walter Bagehot in his *Lombard Street,* which was published in 1873. Bagehot built on Thornton's ideas. As described in Bordo (1990), Bagehot laid out four basic tenets for the bank to use when acting as lender of last resort. These included lending but at a penalty rate; making clear to financial markets the bank's readiness to lend; lending to anyone with good collateral; and preventing illiquid but solvent banks from failing.

Against this backdrop, more recent writings on the role of central banks concern the scope of lending. Charles Goodhart, a leading contributor to this discussion, argues that central banks should provide assistance, albeit temporary, to insolvent banks. Goodhart (1985, 1987) breaks with the classic tradition by arguing that lending should be done without regard to whether a bank is solvent or insolvent. His point is that failure to support a bank facing difficulties will create more problems in the future. Unless the banking system is purged of depositor uncertainty with regard to their bank's liquidity, protecting one bank but not another will not dispel the effects of financial panic. By lending to any bank in trouble, Goodhart argues, the central bank is maintaining the stability of the financial market.

Goodhart's position is somewhat linked to the notion of the **"too-big-to-fail" doctrine**. In this view, the central bank will act to support a bank regardless of its solvency, as long as it is big. For example, in 1984 Continental Illinois, one of the 10 largest banks in the United States, became insolvent. The **Federal Deposit Insurance Corporation (FDIC)** stepped in to insure deposits up to $100,000, then stepped this up to deposits exceeding the $100,000 insurance limit and prevented losses for the bank's bondholders. The Federal Reserve in its role of lender of last resort acted promptly, increasing emergency lending through the discount window. Why this flurry of activity? Because Continental Illinois was on the list of banks that regulators considered too big to fail: if it did fail, they believed, the repercussions throughout the financial markets would be too severe. Within a year, the bank was taken over by another.

The actions of the Federal Reserve and the FDIC were hotly debated. Some argued that the lender of last resort function should not incorporate this idea of being too big to fail. Financial markets, it was argued, were sufficiently supple that shocks, even big ones, could be worked out through the market. There is some evidence that this view may be correct. In 1995, due to the speculative trading activities of Singapore-based Nick Leeson, one of England's oldest banks, Barings Bank, failed. Neeson's losses amounted to about $1.3 billion, more than the bank's capital. Did the Bank of England step in to save the Barings? Did the collapse of Barings cause the financial system to collapse with it? No on both counts. Indeed, this event suggested to some that the lender of last resort function as proscribed by Goodhart may not be needed in today's financial system where unforeseen shocks are hedged against and where shocks, when they do occur, are rapidly dispersed across many risk takers.

What's the broader evidence? In his survey of the historical record across many countries, Bordo (1990) finds that "monetary authorities following the classical precepts of Thornton and Bagehot can prevent banking panics [and that] contrary to Goodhart's view, successful [lender of last resort] actions in the past did not require assistance to insolvent banks." While it is clear that central banks should perform this function, it remains a subject for debate over the degree to which central banks should intervene to protect failing banks.

FURTHER READING

Bagehot, Walter. *Lombard Street: A Description of the Money Market.* London: H. S. King, 1873; Bordo, Michael D. "The Lender of Last Resort: Alternative Views and Historical Experience." Federal Reserve Bank of Richmond *Economic Review* (January/February 1990): 18–29; Goodhart, Charles. *The Evolution of Central Banks.* London: London School of Economics, 1985; Goodhart, Charles. "Why Do Banks Need a Central Bank?" *Oxford Economic Papers* (March 1987): 75–89; Humphrey, Thomas. "The Classical Concept of the Lender of Last Resort." Federal Reserve Bank of Richmond *Economic Review* (January/February 1975): 2–9; Thornton, Henry. *An Enquiry into the Effects of the Paper Credit of Great Britain.* (1802).

LIQUIDITY. Assets, both real and financial, possess some degree of *liquidity*. When economists use that term, what they are referring to is the ease with which an asset, such as a bond, can be converted into another good. For example, cash is generally considered the most liquid form of financial assets. That is because cash can be "sold" or exchanged for real goods (shoes, haircuts, DVDs, etc.) or other financial assets with ease. Now consider how easy it would be to convert the mortgage on a house to some other item, say a multicomponent home entertainment center. If you took a mortgage into the local electronics store and tried to buy the plasma screen TV, DVD player, speakers, etc., they would not allow it. Why? Because the owners of the electronic store know that it would be difficult for them to buy goods with the mortgage. In this sense, even though a mortgage is a type of financial asset, it is very different from cash in terms of the ease with which it can be converted from its current form into a real good or another asset. The less liquid an asset, the more steps are required to convert it into some other good.

There is a whole spectrum of financial assets with different degrees of liquidity. If cash is the most liquid, then demand deposits—checking accounts—probably are a close second. Checks and travelers' checks have the characteristics of being easily converted into goods or other assets: Buying a government bond or a bag of potato chips can be done with a personal check or a travelers' check if you're on vacation. Next on the list would be savings-type accounts. Here you need to first transfer funds in your account to your checking account before buying something. Or you need to visit the bank and get cash. Either way, buying that pizza becomes just a bit more complicated when using a savings account compared with using cash or writing a check. The degree of liquidity continues to decline—becoming less liquid—as we move farther out along the liquidity spectrum. **Treasury bills** are liquid in the sense that they can be sold, but they are less liquid than those assets already discussed. Still, they are more liquid than stocks or bonds issued by some major corporation.

Several aspects of this notion deserve mentioning. First, you may have wondered why there is no mention of **credit cards** or **debit cards**. After all, isn't using your Visa card easier than using a check? Visa is accepted almost everywhere and your check is not: just try cashing a check written on your hometown bank in Istanbul, Turkey. The reason that Visa is not included is because it is not a form of **money**: using your Visa card creates credit. In other words, when you buy that shirt with your credit card, you now owe Visa the $40. Visa pays the shop owner from Visa's checking account, and you pay Visa. In a strict sense, then, using a credit card does not create money, it just facilitates the use of it. Now you do not need to carry around money, just your credit card. Debit cards work in a similar fashion, except that they automatically transfer funds from your checking account to the store's account.

Second, determining the liquidity of a financial asset is important in creating measures of money. For example, in the United States, the Federal Reserve keeps track of four different measures of money: M1, M2, M3, and L. The Ms are determined by adding together the value of their components. M1, for instance, includes those measures that economists believe are "transactions" oriented: used primarily for buying goods and services. Consequently, the items included in M1 generally are the more liquid of financial assets, such as currency, checking accounts, and travelers' checks. M2 broadens that concept by adding to M1 small savings accounts and a few other measures that are believed to be held more for savings purposes than transactions. Thus, as we move from M1 through L, the degree of liquidity falls.

Third, and related to the preceding item, the liquidity of a financial asset is related to the interest rate associated with it. Have you ever wondered why cash pays no explicit interest rate while a bond does? Put another way, the rate of return from holding an asset usually is inversely related to its liquidity. The more liquid the asset, the lower is the rate of return to holding it. In some sense, the lower return reflects the idea that you are holding cash because of its usefulness in transactions. To get you to surrender some of that liquidity, you must be compensated: that is what interest rates do. They are payments for not buying goods today but withholding purchases until some time in the future. The lower interest rate on the more liquid assets thus reflects the "penalty" for not converting your liquid assets (cash) into less liquid but higher-return assets (**bonds**).

LIQUIDITY EFFECT. The underlying mechanics of the liquidity effect has been discussed in economics for many years, with its origins in the writings of economists from the 1800s. Still, it was not until 1968 that **Milton Friedman** first used the phrase *liquidity effect* in a speech sponsored by the United States Savings and Loan League. In his speech, Friedman suggested that the "liquidity effect in simplest form is the usual textbook relationship between the quantity of money and the interest rate which says that the larger the quantity of money, the lower the interest rate will have to be to induce people to hold it" (cited in Thornton, 2001, p. 60).

Friedman's notion of the liquidity effect is part of the story of how monetary policy actions are transmitted to the economy. To see how the liquidity effect works, consider the money demand and money supply diagram shown on p. 227. The money demand curve represents the public's desire to hold **money**—here defined as **currency** and deposits—based on several factors, such as income, expectations of future prices, etc. As you can see, changes in the interest rate lead to changes in the amount of money that an individual may wish to hold. This is because as the interest rate rises, the opportunity cost of holding money also increases. In this situation, the incentive is for an individual to reduce his or her money holdings and acquire financial assets that pay the higher interest rate. The money supply curve is drawn as a vertical line. This is done based on the assumption that the Federal Reserve controls the supply of money in the economy. While this may not be true in the short run, it is a useful working assumption of the longer term because in the end, the Federal Reserve does have the ability to offset decreases and increases in the money supply using various policy options.

To see how the liquidity effect works, suppose the Federal Reserve increases the supply of money in the economy. What happens? First, the increase in the money supply is depicted by the rightward shift in the money supply curve, from Ms to Ms1. With this new amount of money in the economy and the given money demand curve, the original equilibrium rate of interest (I1) will induce individuals to alter their money balances. That is, at I1, there is an **excess supply** of money, more money in the economy than people wish to hold, given their income. They react to this situation by getting rid of the money. No, they do not just throw it away or burn it; they spend it. One of the areas in which they spend their new found money is by buying financial assets, such as bonds. The increased demand for bonds drives bond prices up and the interest rate on bonds down. Because the interest rate on bonds is assumed to be the same as the one depicted in the diagram, the interest rate continues to fall until money demand and money supply are again in equilibrium. In the diagram, this is shown at the lower interest rate I2. If the demand for money does not change, the increase in the money supply and the subsequent decrease in the interest rate is what Friedman referred to as the liquidity effect.

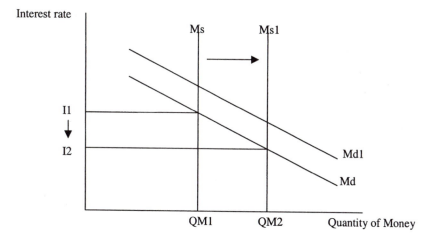

The liquidity effect is an important concept in discussions of monetary policy. When someone talks of expansionary policy, oftentime what they mean is a policy that is pushing down interest rates. As shown in the figure above, this would entail increasing the money supply relative to the demand for it. Why is this important? If the Federal Reserve is able to engineer a decrease in interest rates in the manner described by the liquidity effect, then it is able to lower borrowing costs throughout the economy. This enables businesses and individuals to borrow funds, expand their business operations, and purchase more goods at current incomes. Overall, the effect is to stimulate economic activity.

Friedman also realized that attempts to pursue lower and lower interest rates could have undesirable long-term consequences. For example, suppose that at the time the Federal Reserve increases the money supply in the above figure, the economy is operating at full employment. Increasing the supply of money may not lead to the economy producing more goods. This means that the increase in money holdings only increases nominal income and prices. The outcome is that the money demand curve in the figure will shift to the right (the demand for money increases). Note that if the demand for money increases—the curve Md is drawn to the right of its current position—then the interest rate where the money demand curve and the money supply curve intersect is now going to be higher than I2. This reflects the fact that expansionary monetary policy may eventually induce higher rates of **inflation** and these higher inflation rates will push up interest rates. Thus, while the Federal Reserve may be able to reduce interest rates in the short run (and some research suggests that the short run may be only a few weeks, if not shorter) via the liquidity effect, in the long run these policy actions may well lead to interest rates simply returning to their original levels, or even going higher.

FURTHER READING

Friedman, Milton. "Factors Affecting the Level of Interest Rates." *Proceedings of the 1968 Conference on Saving and Residential Financing.* Chicago: U.S. Saving and Loan League, 1969; Thornton, Daniel L. "Identifying the Liquidity Effect at the Daily Frequency." Federal Reserve Bank of St. Louis *Review* (July/August 2001): 59–82.

LIQUIDITY TRAP. The most popular version of a liquidity trap is a situation where **nominal interest rates** are at or near zero. Because most measure expansionary monetary policy by reductions in interest rates, monetary policy appears to be impotent in a liquidity trap because interest rates cannot be pushed any lower than zero. In such a situation, monetary policy is unable to stimulate total demand and raise spending because interest rates already are at zero. With interest rates at zero, or very close to it, most individuals would not be willing to hold bonds with negative returns instead of holding (zero interest-bearing) money.

The idea of the liquidity trap is credited to **John Maynard Keynes**, the famous British economist. Keynes offered the notion of a liquidity trap as a theoretical possibility in his famous book *The General Theory of Employment, Interest and Money* (1936). He saw it as having little practical application and only occurring in abnormal situations, such as currency crises, hyperinflations, or **financial crises**. Even so, the notion of a liquidity trap hampering the effective implementation of monetary policy has not been ignored, with some economists suggesting that Japan's decade-long lack of economic growth in the 1990s and early 2000s is caused by a liquidity trap in Japan. With interest rates hovering near zero for much of the time, some argue that Keynes's textbook example had been realized.

Does a liquidity trap really limit monetary policymaker's ability to increase spending? It does only if one believes that monetary policy actions work only through changes in the interest rate. For instance, in the case of Japan, some economists argued that expansionary policy actions could be taken by having the central bank buy real goods (cars, buildings, etc.) in the economy. Because the goal of an expansionary policy is to put more money into circulation, such purchases would accomplish that end in a very direct way.

FURTHER READING

Hutchinson, Michael. "Japan's Recession: Is the Liquidity Trap Back?" Federal Reserve Bank of San Francisco *Economic Letter* (June 16, 2000); Keynes, John Maynard. *The General Theory of Employment, Money, and Interest.* New York: Harcourt Brace, 1964; Krugman, Paul. "It's Baaack: Japan's Slump and the Return of the Liquidity Trap." *Brookings Papers on Economic Activity* 2 (1998): 137–205; Patinkin, Don. *Money, Interest and Prices.* New York: Harper & Row, 1965.

LOAN. A loan is an agreement between two parties. In one sense, a loan occurs when one party agrees to forego current spending so that the other party can spend more today than their current income permits. Bill lends $100 to Caitlin so she can purchase school books. That means that he does not have use of the $100, and so must reduce his spending from what it could have been. At the end of some agreed upon time, say a year, Bill expects Caitlin to repay him the $100. Unless the loan is made between good friends or relatives, it is customary that Bill expects not only to get the $100 back (the principal) but also something extra for the use of his money. This extra amount, the interest payment, is agreed to at the time the loan is made and is based on expected changes in the **purchasing power of money** over the year. If Bill expects money to be worth much less in a year, he will charge a higher interest rate than if prices are expected to remain constant.

This type of loan is referred to as a *simple* loan. It is simple because the borrower makes one payment at some future date. The payment of principal and interest terminates the loan. While simple, this type of loan is often used by banks to make commercial loans to businesses. If a loan is to be repaid over time, with multiple payments spaced out over the life of the loan, it is a *fixed-payment* loan. A home mortgage is a good example of a fixed-payment loan. When someone takes out a fixed-payment loan, they agree to pay the lender a fixed amount, say each month, to cover repayment of the principal and an interest payment. For example, when someone purchases a home, they may opt for a 30-year mortgage, which means that they will make monthly payments over the next 30 years. For example, a 30-year, $130,000 loan at 8.5 percent requires a monthly payment of approximately $999. If you do the math, you'll find that 30 years of monthly payments at $999 add up to $359,640. In other words, the lender is not going to lend someone $130,000 and extend the payments over 30 years for free. In fact, it is going to cost $229,640 in interest payments to borrow that money.

There are many types of bank loans. The list includes *self-liquidating* loans that are used by businesses to finance ongoing activities. *Term* loans, which are similar in spirit to the simple loans discussed above, often are used by business to purchase machinery or equipment. Banks also make credit available to firms or individuals through a type of loan referred to as a *line of credit*. This allows a firm or an individual to borrow up to some specified limit, the outstanding loan to be repaid according to some specified terms. What characterizes this type of loan is that they usually do not specify some future date at which the loan amount must be fully repaid. Often there is some minimum payment amount plus the interest payment that the bank expects. And, as illustrated in the home mortgage example, if an individual wishes to pay the minimum amount on the loan, the fact that the interest payment is nonzero means that extending the payment simply increases the total payments over and above the actual amount borrowed. Even though the borrower gets the use of the money today and is not obligated to pay it all off tomorrow, spreading the payments out over the indefinite future is not without a cost.

Loans are often constructed to meet borrowers' needs and to protect lenders from risk that the borrower will default on the loan. Protection against default risk is built into loans in several ways. Higher interest rates may be charged to those borrowers that the bank believes are more likely to default. Banks may write into loan agreements several *covenants,* which require the borrower to, for example, require bank approval for major changes in business operations. Covenants help protect the bank from loss by restricting the behavior of the borrower, whether it is a firm or a homeowner. Banks also may require collateral for loans. An example is when you take out a loan for a car, the car is the collateral: failure to pay the loan means the car is repossessed by the bank and sold off to recoup the loan amount.

FURTHER READING

Mishkin, Frederic S. *The Economics of Money, Banking, and Financial Markets.* 7th edition. Boston: Pearson Addison Wesley, 2004.

LONG-TERM CAPITAL MANAGEMENT. Long-Term Capital Management is a hedge fund that secured an interesting place in the history of the Federal Reserve. As a hedge fund, it was supposed to manage its funds in such a way that would minimize its exposure to risk. What the management of the fund did, however, was to "bet" that the unusually large spread between prices on long-term corporate and U.S. Treasury bonds would return to more normal levels. What the management team, which included two Nobel Prize winners in economics (Myron Scholes and Robert Merton), did not plan on was the collapse of the Russian financial system, which occurred in August 1998. This event caused investors to reevaluate their assessment of the riskiness of corporate and government bonds. Most favored government bonds, so instead of reducing the spread, as Long-Term had bet on, the spread widened even farther. The result was huge losses for Long-Term, which, by mid-September 1998, meant that the company was no longer able to meet its obligations to creditors.

The failure of every financial firm does not warrant an entry in this volume. But Long-Term Capital Management was not just any financial firm. To meet its obligations, Long-Term could have sold its portfolio of securities worth $80 billion and its $1 *trillion* in derivative securities. Fearing that such a fire sale would roil the financial markets, the Federal Reserve, already anxious because of the Russian collapse and the **Asian crisis**, moved in.

One action taken by the Federal Reserve was to lower the **federal funds rate** by 75 **basis points** (¾ of a percentage point). This moved signaled to the financial markets that the Federal Reserve recognized the seriousness of the situation and was injecting **liquidity** into the market. The other action, one more directly linked to Long-Term, was the bailout plan engineered by the Federal Reserve Bank of New York. On September 23, 1998 the bank brokered a rescue plan between Long-Term and its creditors. In the plan, creditors, banks and others were "asked" to invest an additional $3.6 billion in Long-Term in exchange for specific changes in the management of the fund. As it turns out, this infusion of funds and a turn around in the bond market eventually allowed Long-Term to recover its losses.

Was the Federal Reserve's bailout of Long-Term Capital Management a prudent policy action? Some argue that without the bank's intervention, the collapse of Long-Term could have led to a **financial panic**. Others suggest that by circumventing the discipline of the free market, the Federal Reserve's policy exacerbated the problem associated with **moral hazard**, the situation in which managers take greater risks knowing that the Federal Reserve will bail them of trouble.

FURTHER READING

Lowenstein, Roger. *When Geniuses Failed: The Rise and Fall of Long-Term Capital Management.* New York: Random House, 2000; Meyer, Laurence H. *A Term at the Fed: An Insider's View.* New York: HarperCollins, 2004 (Chapter 5).

LOUVRE ACCORD. The Louvre Accord, an agreement between industrial countries to maintain their foreign **exchange rates** at the then current levels, was announced on February 22, 1987. The accord is given the name Louvre because it was signed after a meeting of finance ministers and central bankers that took place in the Louvre Museum in Paris, France. Following the **Plaza Agreement**, signed at the Plaza Hotel in New York City in September 1985, the international exchange value of the U.S. dollar was lowered through the intervention of governments of the major industrial economies. By 1987, however, the falling value of the dollar began to raise concerns that if it were allowed to go even lower it would damage international trade, especially outside the United States. The Louvre Accord sought to stabilize exchange rates at their early-1987 levels.

The accord also represents an attempt to coordinate macroeconomic policies across countries. The signatories of the accord agreed "to intensify their economic policy coordination efforts in order to promote more balanced global growth and to reduce existing imbalances." A key component of this attempt was trying to get the counties involved—Canada, France, Germany, Japan, United Kingdom, and United States—to manage their domestic government budgets. For example, Canada, France, United Kingdom, and United States all agreed to reduce their budget deficits. Germany and Japan agreed to stimulate domestic growth.

In most instances, these agreements called on governments and central banks to follow policies that were not always in their own country's best interest. That is, international policy coordination, with a goal to fostering "more balanced global growth" may not foster domestic growth to the extent desired by domestic citizens and politicians. Consequently, these agreements are often not successful when looked at with hindsight. In this case, for example, the United States did not lower its deficit, and the German government was not particularly successful at expanding economic activity.

The accord did not result in much international policy coordination. There also is some question about whether intervention by central banks successfully brought about a reduction in the volatility of exchange rates. Catherine Bonser-Neal (1996) found in her study that during the period covered by the Plaza Agreement and the Louvre Accord, intervention by central banks did not lessen exchange rate volatility of the U.S. dollar, the Japanese yen, or the German Deutschmark. Her evidence indicates that, to the contrary, their actions actually increased exchange rate volatility.

FURTHER READING

Bonser-Neal, Catherine. "Does Central Bank Intervention Stabilize Foreign Exchange Rates?" *Federal Reserve Bank of Kansas City Economic Review* (First Quarter 1996): 43–71; Husted, Steven, and Michael Melvin. *International Economics*, 3rd edition. New York: HarperCollins, 1995; Louvre Accord: Official Statement. Accessed at www.g7.utoronto.ca/finance/fm870222.htm.

LUCAS, ROBERT, JR. (1937–). Robert Lucas is the John Dewey Distinguished Service Professor in Economics and the College at the University of Chicago. In 1995, he was awarded the Nobel Prize in economics. In its announcement of the prize, the Swedish Academy of Sciences noted that Lucas was awarded the prize "for having developed and applied the hypothesis of rational expectations, and thereby having transformed macroeconomic analysis and deepened our understanding of economic policy." Just what did he do, and why is he included in this volume?

Lucas's work followed the path of several predecessors, not the least of which was **Milton Friedman**. Friedman is best known for his development of the modern approach to the **quantity theory** of money, known more popularly as **Monetarism**. Beginning in the late 1950s, Friedman and his colleagues argued that the best approach to monetary policy was to reject the notion that a good policy is one being driven by the well-meaning though often mistaken beliefs of policymakers. It was suggested that because of lags and poor information, policymakers simply could not achieve the kind of fine tuning that they thought they could. Policy aimed at stabilizing the economy could instead increase economic fluctuations. Based on this research, Friedman argued for a simple rule, one that minimized the rate of inflation over time and reduced the policy-induced variability of output growth around its long-run trend.

Lucas suggested that because economics is based on the assumption that individuals make decisions rationally, how policy is carried out could have very different impacts on the economy from what policymakers think it will have. To illustrate this, Lucas suggested the thought experiment of an economy consisting of separate islands. Each island represents an individual or a firm. Now suppose that there is an event that affects all islands. Let's say that the event is an increase in the rate of money growth. Even though the effect of the event is general, the information that has occurred may not arrive at all islands simultaneously. Or, the information may not be processed as quickly or in the same manner by inhabitants of all islands. This time lag in information processing is similar in spirit to Friedman's notion of **lags in monetary policy**.

Lucas extended this idea and made it more formal through a rigorous mathematical presentation. Lucas argued that if the individuals made rational decisions, then it would be in their best interest to acquire as much information about the decision process as they could. Using standard economic principles, individuals would acquire information up to the point where the added cost of acquiring an additional piece of information was equal to the expected benefit of getting it. Lucas argued that it was in one's best interest to understand how and why monetary policy decisions were made. If everyone in the economy did this, then they understood observed policy actions and would react according to the expected outcomes.

By forming "**rational expectations**," Lucas argued, policies aimed at pushing economic growth above its long-run potential would fail, not only in the long run—Friedman's story—but also in the short run. This outcome flew in the face of the accepted wisdom derived from the Keynesian macroeconomic model (*see* **John Maynard Keynes**) and the reliance on the **Phillips curve** tradeoff between the unemployment rate and the rate of inflation. The logic of Lucas's analysis suggested that the only way in which a monetary policy could achieve even some short-run expansion of output would be if the policy action was unexpected. Until the public recognized to the change in policy, output would increase. But the output increase would only be temporary, because once the public realized the change in policy, the economy would retreat to its long-run trend. The lasting consequence, however, was a permanently higher rate of **inflation**. Thus, in order to achieve such short-run improvement in output, the monetary policymaker would necessarily have to behave in ever more unexpected ways in the future. The theory suggested that such policies would lead to larger gyrations in the economy and eventually a rejection of the policymaker's announcements. The upshot: Lucas's analysis suggested that the only stabilizing policy that a central bank could follow was **transparency** in its actions and to focus on the long-run consequences.

Lucas's rational expectations story greatly altered macroeconomic theory and policy analysis. Now economic models consider the policy environment in which decisions were made before historic relationships can be projected into the future. The so-call Lucas critique questioned the use of historical relationships between, for example, money growth rates and real output growth, to predict the outcome of some recent policy, because those historic relations are based on policies made at the time. If the factors that determine current policy decisions are different than in the past, increasing or decreasing money growth could lead to very different results than the policy's expected outcome.

Lucas's work, along with that of Thomas Sargent, Neil Wallace, and Robert Barro, has left a permanent mark on macroeconomic theory and on how monetary policy is conducted. Today, monetary policy is much more transparent than in the past: There is much less secrecy about the decision process, thus making it more accessible for the public to alter their expectations of policy and the future path of the economy. Monetary policy also is much more oriented to achieving long-term goals related to price level stability. In this way, the "rational expectations revolution" led by Robert Lucas transformed policy-making.

FURTHER READING

Barro, Robert J. "Rational Expectations and the Role of Monetary Policy." *Journal of Monetary Economics* (January 1976): 1–32; Fischer, Stanley, ed. *Rational Expectations and Economic Policy.* Chicago: University of Chicago Press, 1980; Holland, A. Steven. "Rational Expectations and the Effects of Monetary Policy: A Guide for the Uninitiated." Federal Reserve Bank of St. Louis *Review* (May 1985): 5–11; Lucas, Robert, Jr. "Expectations and the Neutrality of Money." *Journal of Economic Theory* (1972); Lucas, Robert, Jr. "Econometric Policy Evaluation: A Critique." *Carnegie-Rochester Conference Series on Public Policy* (1:1976): 19–46; Lucas, Robert, Jr., and Thomas Sargent. "After Keynesian Macroeconomics." Federal Reserve Bank of Minneapolis *Quarterly Review* (Spring 1979): 1–16.

MARGIN REQUIREMENT. A margin requirement limits how much an individual can borrow from brokers for the purchase of stock. For example, a margin requirement of, say, 10 percent allows someone to borrow 90 percent of the purchase price of the stock. Higher margin requirements mean that someone wishing to buy stock must put up more of their own money, thus reducing the potential profitability of a stock transaction. Authorized by Congress to set margin requirements, the Federal Reserve can use changes in the margin requirement as a policy tool. By raising margin requirements, the Federal Reserve attempts to reduce speculative stock purchases. By lowering margin requirements, the Federal Reserve makes it "cheaper" to buy stocks and thus encourages greater stock trading. Although many argued that the Federal Reserve's control over margin requirements was unnecessary, the stock market **Crash of 1987** reinforced the belief that it should continue to determine margin requirements.

The Federal Reserve's ability to set margin requirements comes under Regulations T, U, and X. Regulation T applies to broker-dealers, Regulation U to banks, and Regulation X to margin loans not covered under T and U. The history of these regulations stems largely from the stock market crash of 1929 (*see* **Great Crash**). At that time, investors often used large amounts of borrowed money to purchase stock. Fortune (2000) reports that it was not uncommon for brokers to advance 90 percent of the stock purchase price to prospective buyers. This meant that a buyer would provide only $10 for every $100 stock purchase. The margin was supposed to cover any shortfall in the stock's price. If stock prices fall, margin calls go out, requiring stockholders who bought on margin to provide more money for their margin account. Fortune notes that such lending increased speculative investment, elevated stock prices, and is likely to have contributed to the 1929 crash in stock prices.

The New York Stock Exchange responded to the 1929 stock market crash and subsequent economic hardships associated with the **Great Depression** by establishing that customers of member firms could borrow no more than 50 percent of a security's value. This change occurred in 1933. A year later, in 1934, passage of the Securities Exchange Act by Congress authorized a lending limit that applied to newly acquired securities. The power to regulate these standards was given to the Federal Reserve **Board of Governors**. Although there was some interest in changing margin requirements in the period between the end of World War II through the mid-1970s, the initial margin requirement as set under Regulation T has been 50 percent over the last quarter century.

Although the Federal Reserve has not changed the margin requirement, even in the face of the stock market crash of 2000, some argue that it should use margin requirements to actively manage stock market speculation. One of the key proponents of this position, Robert Shiller (2000) argues that if the Federal Reserve chooses to engage in such management of the margin requirement, it can help prevent the inefficient reallocation of wealth caused by market crashes.

FURTHER READING

Fortune, Peter. "Margin Requirements, Margin Loans and Margin Rates: Practice and Principles." Federal Reserve Bank of Boston *New England Economic Review* (September/October 2000): 19–44; Shiller, Robert. *Irrational Exuberance*. Princeton: Princeton University Press, 2000; Shiller, Robert. "Margin Calls: Should the Fed Step In?" *The Wall Street Journal* (April 10, 2000): A46.

MARKET EQUILIBRIUM. Understanding what is meant by the phrase "market equilibrium" is important for understanding how the Federal Reserve changes interest rates or how **open market operations** are employed in policy. Let's first establish what is meant by the term "equilibrium" and the conditions under which a market is in equilibrium.

When you think of equilibrium, you usually think of something that is stable. For example, when standing with both feet squarely under you, you are in an equilibrium: If there are no outside forces acting to move you one way or another, you will just stand there. When your equilibrium gets upset—someone pushes you from the side, for example—you may stumble before you regain your standing position. That stumble is an example of being out of equilibrium, regaining your standing position is an example of a new equilibrium. There are many other examples from the real world that help illustrate the idea that equilibrium occurs when there are no forces bringing about a change. For instance, the thermostat on the wall regulates the temperature of your house or apartment. When you set the temperature at 70 degrees, for example, the thermostat operates to turn on the furnace or the air conditioner whenever the temperature deviates too much from your desired setting. When the temperature rises, the air conditioning kicks in and pushes the temperature back down. When the temperature gets too cold, the furnace ignites and warms up the room. In this sense, the desired temperature—the setting on the thermostat—is the equilibrium temperature. Only when the temperature changes from its desired level, perhaps because someone left the front door open during winter, will the thermostat activate the furnace.

What does this have to do with the Federal Reserve? Think about a case where the Federal Reserve wishes to lower interest rates in an attempt to spur investment activity and raise the growth rate of economic output. To see this, the diagram below shows the supply of money and the demand for money. The supply of money is basically under the control of the Federal Reserve through open market operations, which include the buying and selling of government securities by the Federal Reserve. Briefly, when the Federal Reserve buys securities, it is attempting to increase the supply of money—that is, shift the supply curve to the right. When it sells securities, it is attempting to move the supply curve of money to the left.

Let's use this policy scenario and the figure on top of the next page to illustrate the concept of market equilibrium. The original money supply and money demand curves intersect at a unique rate of interest, here labeled as I*, and quantity of money, labeled as Q*. This interest rate-quantity of money pair represents the *equilibrium* interest rate and the

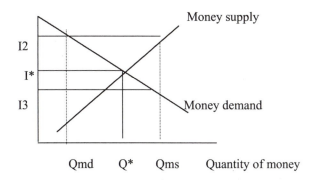

Interest rate

I2

I*

I3

Money supply

Money demand

Qmd   Q*   Qms   Quantity of money

equilibrium quantity of money for this market. Is this a stable outcome? Yes, because at I* the supply of money at this interest rate is equal to the quantity of money demanded. If an outside force bumped the market away from equilibrium, would it return to I*? To answer this, suppose the interest rate is above the equilibrium, say at I2. What's wrong in the money market? At I2 the figure shows that the quantity supplied of money (Qms) exceeds the quantity demanded (Qmd). (Read across from the interest rate I2 to where it intersects each curve and then look down to find the associated quantity of money.) At I2, the line intersects the supply curve at a quantity of money level that is to the right of the demand curve. When the quantity supplied of something exceeds the quantity demanded for it, it creates a situation known as a *surplus*. And when a surplus occurs, market forces act to push the price, in this case the interest rate, down to where the quantity supplied is exactly equal to the quantity demanded. In the diagram this only occurs where the supply and demand curves cross, at I*. If the interest rate was I3, below I*, then just the opposite condition would prevail in the market. At I3, the quantity of money demanded would be greater than the quantity supplied (a condition known as shortage) and the interest rate would get pushed back up to I*. Thus, I* is the market equilibrium interest rate given the money supply and demand curves.

To see how the equilibrium interest rate and the equilibrium quantity of money may change given open market operations, suppose the Federal Reserve buys government securities in the market (see figure below). This action increases the supply of money, depicted as a rightward shift in the money supply line. In effect, the Federal Reserve "pushed" the money market in one direction, upsetting its original equilibrium at I* and Q*. After the "push," what happens? At first, the original equilibrium interest rate of I* has

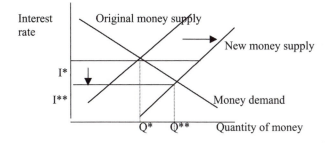

Interest rate

Original money supply

New money supply

I*

I**

Money demand

Q*   Q**   Quantity of money

not had a chance to adjust. With the new supply of money and the original equilibrium interest rate, there is a condition of *surplus* in the money market. That is, the quantity supplied of money at the original equilibrium rate of I* is greater than the quantity of money demanded at that rate. When there is a surplus in the market, the reaction is to push rates downward until the quantity supplied again equals the quantity demanded. This occurs at the interest rate I**, the new market equilibrium interest rate.

Is that what really happens? By and large, the answer is yes. When the Federal Reserve injects money into the banking system by buying their government securities, banks are paid with **reserves**. Because these reserves are not generating any income for the banks, they use them to make **loans**. If banks are trying to increase their lending activity, the only way they can accomplish this is by lowering the rates they charge on loans. In effect, the outcome of the process is exactly like that depicted in the figure on the bottom of page 237. And when the Federal Reserve is trying to raise interest rates, they engage in the opposite kind of behavior: They sell government securities to banks, thus reducing reserves in the system (pushing the supply curve to the left) and creating a condition of shortage in the market. With a shortage, interest rates get pushed upward as the market seeks the new equilibrium interest rate.

FURTHER READING

Miller, Roger LeRoy, and David D. VanHoose, *Modern Money and Banking*. 3rd edition. Boston: McGraw-Hill, 1993; Mishkin, Frederic S. *The Economics of Money, Banking, and Financial Markets*. 7th edition. Boston: Pearson Addison Wesley, 2004.

MARK-TO-MARKET. This phrase is often used in discussions of financial markets. When someone speaks of "mark-to-market," they usually mean establishing the value of a portfolio of financial assets based on existing market prices. So, for instance, if you purchased 100 shares of Wal-Mart stock several years ago at $50 and today the market price is $55, the value of your shares *today* is $550. In this way you are marking-to-market your portfolio or finding its current value. When estimating the market value of your portfolio, it really does not make much sense to rely on what you paid for it. The purchase value only becomes useful when you sell and are trying to determine your capital gain or loss.

The notion of mark-to-market also plays a role in measuring credit risk. When banks or other financial institutions make **loans**, they are concerned about the possibility that the borrower may not repay the entire loan amount. This is called default risk. Banks and bank regulators like the Federal Reserve would like to minimize it as much as possible. One of the issues that arises in discussions of bank regulation is how to measure the value of the bank's assets (loans, securities, etc.) and its liabilities (deposit accounts). The value of liabilities is fairly straightforward: Deposits usually are valued in current dollar terms. But what about loans?

Suppose a bank makes a loan to a developer to build a shopping center. To buy the land and build the buildings, the developer borrows $100 million. Construction crews are put to work, and in a year the shopping center opens for business. During construction, the developer pays installments required by the loan contract. Business at the new mall is initially good, but after a year business begins to fall off: maybe a newer, more upscale shopping center has sprung up in the vicinity. When a regulator looks at the bank's books, what value will she assign to the outstanding loan held by the developer? Should it be the original $100 million? If the value of the loan was measured using a mark-to-market approach, the current value of the loan would be based on what the shopping center is worth—in other words, its "market" value.

As you might imagine, the concept of mark-to-market is very appealing to regulators. After all, this gives them a much truer picture of the bank's net worth (the value of its assets minus its liabilities). For example, in our scenario, if the bank has liabilities of $95 million, valuing the shopping center loan (the bank's only asset) at its book value—the value of the original loan—indicates that the bank's net worth is $5 million (= $100 million – $95 million). But what if the bank had to liquidate the loan today? If the market value of the shopping center fell due to competition, selling it today would not fetch the original value of the loan. If the shopping center was sold today for $80 million, the bank's true net worth—one based on a mark-to-market approach—is a negative $15 million ($80 million – $95 million). A bank with a negative net worth—the technical definition of being bankrupt—is treated much differently by regulators than a bank with a positive net worth. (*See* **CAMELS**.)

While mark-to-market is fairly easy if one is only concerned about a few stocks, what about a portfolio that contains hundreds of stocks, government securities, and other financial assets? What about a bank's loan portfolio that contains loans for real estate, cars, and student loans? In the first instance, the cost is just managing the data collection: closing stock prices can be obtained fairly easily and on a daily basis. In the latter, however, the only way to obtain accurate information about the value of certain assets would be to actually sell them. This is very difficult, because banks do not want to sell their assets off just to discover their market value. In such instances, regulators may use estimates of the assessed valuations of assets in determining a bank's financial position.

FURTHER READING

Jones, David, and John Mingo. "Industry Practices in Credit Risk Modeling and Internal Capital Allocations: Implications for a Models-Based Regulatory Capital Standard." Federal Reserve Bank of New York *Economic Policy Review* (October 1998): 53–60.

MARTIN, WILLIAM McCHESNEY, Jr. (1906–1998). William McChesney Martin, Jr. seemed destined at birth to become a key figure in the financial history of the United States. Martin was born in 1906 to a prominent St. Louis banking family. For instance, Martin's father was called upon by President **Woodrow Wilson** to help draft the **Federal Reserve Act of 1913**. The younger Martin took to the financial business quite readily. After graduating from Yale University with a degree in Latin and English, Martin returned to St. Louis to begin his career with the brokerage house A. G. Edwards & Sons. After two years, at age 22, Martin became the company's youngest partner. A. G. Edwards sent Martin to the New York Stock Exchange as its representative in 1931. Martin arrived at the exchange during the tumultuous times of the **Great Depression** and soon realized that many changes were needed in the conduct of the exchange and its structure. Only four years after arriving at the exchange, Martin was elected to its board of governors. From his position on the board, Martin worked closely with the newly formed Securities and Exchange Commission (SEC) to bring about necessary stock market reforms. Testimony to Martin's influence, the SEC and the board of governors of the exchange elected him as the first president of the exchange in 1938. And all of this by the age of 31! This rapid ascent gave credence to the numerous labels that the popular press used about him, such as the "boy wonder" of Wall Street.

Martin served as president of the exchange until 1941, when he entered the U.S. Army for service during World War II. Martin's duties in the service utilized his ability for organization. He oversaw the disposal of raw materials from his position on the Munitions Allocation Board. Martin also served as the liaison between the Army and Congress and oversaw the Lend-Lease program for Russia. Although he entered the war as a private, he was discharged at its end as a colonel.

Martin did not return to New York and the financial world after the war. Instead, Martin accepted an appointed position as president of the U.S. Export-Import Bank. This appointment, made by President **Harry Truman**, was the first of several appointed positions that Martin would accept. After three years at the bank, Martin moved to the U.S. Treasury, where he served as assistant secretary for monetary affairs. It was in this role that Martin found his way to the Federal Reserve. As discussed elsewhere in this volume (*see* **Treasury-Federal Reserve Accord of 1951**), by the early 1950s the Treasury and the Federal Reserve were at odds over the policy role of the Federal Reserve. Since 1942, the Federal Reserve committed itself to peg interest rates on government securities to help finance the war effort. With the war over, however, many in the Federal Reserve argued that such a policy, if continued, would only lead to increasing rates of inflation if the Treasury persisted in pressuring the Federal Reserve to follow an expansionary low interest rate policy. With the economy heating up during the Korean War, continuation of such "easy money" policies was not viewed, in the Federal Reserve at least, as consistent with the policy objective of low inflation.

Martin was chosen by President Truman to broker a deal between the Treasury and the Federal Reserve. Although Truman openly sided with Treasury, Martin as the Treasury's representative devised a plan that would allow the Federal Reserve to free itself from the policy of pegging interest rates. At the same time, his solution allowed the Treasury to restructure its long-term debt and issue new securities at higher market rates. In the end, after much heated private and public debate, Martin's plan was accepted by both sides and by Truman.

Even though the accord was accepted, the then **Chairman of the Board of Governors Thomas McCabe** chose to resign his post after the accord had taken effect. The administration seized the opportunity to put "one of their own" into the chairman's position and nominated Martin for the job. On March 21, 1951, Martin became the chairman of the Board of Governors of the Federal Reserve System. What President Truman did not expect, however, was that Martin would steadfastly protect the Federal Reserve's new-found independence from the executive branch of the government. In fact, Martin's protection of the Federal Reserve's independence from the administration lasted through the next four presidents, including Eisenhower, Kennedy, Johnson, and Nixon. In all, Martin served as chairman of the board for 19 years.

Martin always was concerned about the independence of the Federal Reserve. In several instances, some of which were quite public, Martin pursued policies that he thought were correct even though the White House disagreed. In one of the most famous of such confrontations, Martin was summoned to the Texas White House by President Lyndon Johnson following an increase in the **discount rate** by the Board of Governors. Even after a heated and well-publicized confrontation, Martin held his ground and the rate increase stayed.

Aside from the longevity of his tenure as chairman, Martin left a legacy of policy actions that are not always viewed positively. Martin, by the nature of his training, was always a "market man." That is, his policy approach often focused on the reaction of the financial markets to the exclusion of other pertinent factors. Although he espoused the policy objectives of low inflation and stable economic growth, the policies actually followed by the Federal Reserve during the 1960s became quite inflationary. One explanation for this is Martin's (and others') disregard for policy indicators other than financial market conditions. For example, Martin eschewed the use of monetary aggregates as guides to policy decisions in meetings of the **Federal Open Market Committee (FOMC)** and disparaged, although always in a courteous and gentlemanly way, the use of monetary data and statistics as policy guides. Instead, Martin pressed for the use of the **tone and feel approach to policy** of the market as a better barometer to determine policy actions. Unfortunately, this guide often provided misleading clues about the pace of economic activity and the ongoing effects of monetary policy actions.

William McChesney Martin, Jr. stepped down as chairman on January 30, 1970, succeeded by Nixon appointee **Arthur Burns**. As Federal Reserve Governor **Andrew F. Brimmer** (2000) said of Martin, he "was the most outstanding central banker the United States has ever had. Blessed with exceptional ability and a strong head start in life, he turned aside numerous opportunities to become immensely wealthy in the financial world, to devote his talent to public service." After his retirement from the Federal Reserve, Martin remained actively engaged, holding various positions on numerous firms' boards of directors until his death in 1998 at the age of 91.

FURTHER READING

Bremmer, Robert P. *Chairman of the Fed: William McChesney Martin Jr. and the Creation of the Modern American Financial System.* New Haven: Yale University Press, 2004; Brimmer, Andrew F. "William McChesney Martin, Jr." *Proceedings of the American Philosophical Society* Vol. 144, No. 2 (June 2000); Federal Reserve Bank of Richmond. "Biography of William McChesney Martin, Jr." in *Fiftieth Anniversary of the Treasury-Federal Reserve Accord.* Available at the Richmond Bank's Website; Katz, Barnard S., ed. *Biographical Dictionary of the Board of Governors of the Federal Reserve.* Westport: Greenwood Press, 1992.

McCABE, THOMAS BAYARD (1893–1982). Thomas McCabe served as chairman of the Federal Reserve **Board of Governors** for only three years, from early 1948 through March 1951. Still, he holds a special place in the history of the Federal Reserve, because he played such an important role in the negotiations between the U.S. Treasury and the Federal Reserve which led to the **Treasury-Federal Reserve Accord of 1951**. As discussed elsewhere, the accord freed monetary policy from the shackles of requiring it to support interest rates on Treasury securities. After the accord, monetary policy under the Federal Reserve became much more independent from the government than at any time since the inception of the Federal Reserve.

Born in 1893 to a banking family, McCabe grew up in Selbyville, Delaware. He attended Swarthmore College, graduating in 1915 with a degree in economics. After a brief stint of working for his father in banking, McCabe began working for a paper company—the Scott Paper Company—in Chester, Pennsylvania, a job he would hold until he enlisted in the service at the outbreak of World War I. After the war, McCabe returned to Scott and advanced rapidly through the ranks of management, becoming CEO of the company by the time he reached his 34th birthday.

While at Scott, McCabe began his association with the Federal Reserve by serving on the board of the Federal Reserve Bank of Philadelphia. With the outbreak of World War II, McCabe served in various government positions. At the time of his appointment to the Board of Governors in 1947, McCabe was serving in the Truman administration as the liquidation commissioner, a position that put him in charge of the government's disposal of unneeded war materials. When McCabe was appointed to serve out the term of the recently deceased Federal Reserve Governor Ronald Ransom, President Harry Truman made it clear that McCabe was his chosen successor to become chairman. In April 1948, Truman named McCabe as his appointee for the chairman's position.

The events that led to the Treasury-Federal Reserve Accord and McCabe's subsequent resignation began in the late 1940s. In 1948, the economy suffered a recession that led the Federal Reserve to argue for a policy of lower interest rates. Because this meant that the Treasury could finance the government's activities at a lower rate, there was no conflict between the Treasury and the Federal Reserve. As the economy began to climb out of the recession in 1949, this changed. Federal Reserve policymakers began to call for a monetary policy that recognized the inflationary impact of previous expansionary policies. Amid this nascent debate, the war in Korea broke out in June 1950. The mix of policies became even more jumbled. The Treasury wanted the Federal Reserve to keep interest rates low as they had since World War II. The Federal Reserve, on the other hand, wanted to curtail credit expansion in order to dampen the inflationary pressures of previous low interest rate policies. Monetary policy, unlike the Treasury's desire, was geared to allow interest rates to rise. This was demonstrated forcefully, and publicly, by the Federal Reserve's increase in the **discount rate** in August 1950.

The Federal Reserve's move to raise rates set off an internal dispute between the Treasury Secretary, John Snyder, the White House, and McCabe. The not-so-secret debate between the different parties raged on for several months, some times spilling over to public criticisms of the Federal Reserve in the popular press. In an interesting flexing of its muscle, the Federal Reserve came out on top of the debate. In the end, the Treasury-Federal Reserve Accord freed monetary policy from the confines of an interest rate pegging policy. After the accord, interest rates on Treasury securities were allowed to float with the forces of demand and supply in the financial markets determining their levels. Although the Federal Reserve gained independence following the accord, McCabe's job as chairman of the Federal Reserve was a casualty of the fight. McCabe resigned as chairman on March 31, 1951. In an interesting twist, his successor was **William McChesney Martin, Jr.**, at the time the Treasury assistant secretary representative who had brokered the accord. If Martin's appointment was thought to represent a pulling in of the Federal Reserve by the Truman administration, it was not to be: Martin became a staunch defender of the Federal Reserve's independence.

After leaving the Federal Reserve, McCabe returned to Scott Paper and served as president of the company until 1962. On May 27, 1982, McCabe died at the age of 88.

FURTHER READING

Hetzel, Robert L., and Ralph F. Leach. "The Treasury-Federal Reserve Accord: A New Narrative Account." Federal Reserve Bank of Richmond *Economic Quarterly* (Winter 2001): 33–55; Katz,

Bernard S., ed., *Biographical Dictionary of the Board of Governors of the Federal Reserve.* Westport: Greenwood Press, 1992.

McFADDEN ACT OF 1927. On February 25, 1927, President **Calvin Coolidge** signed the McFadden Act into law. In essence the McFadden Act—named after its sponsor, Congressman Louis T. McFadden (R-Pa)—prohibited **commercial banks** from **branching** across state lines. Passage of the Interstate Banking and Branching Efficiency Act of 1994, otherwise known as the **Riegle-Neal Act of 1994**, dismantled the branching prohibition that the McFadden Act raised. Today, the United States has a nationwide banking system, with branches of major banks located throughout the country. If it is believed that a nationwide system is more efficient today, why was it that in 1927 exactly the opposite was thought to be true? This entry explores that question.

Branching by commercial banks was not always forbidden in the United States. For example, by the mid-1920s, 18 states permitted some form of branching. Sometimes this was limited to a single branch; other times, a bank could have multiple branches. Still, the idea that banks could branch outside of the state of their home office was not well received. Some feared the invasion of out-of-state banks that were larger and therefore posed an anticompetitive threat to the existing banks. The other aspect of the debate concerned the fact that the **National Banking Act of 1864** did not mention branching, meaning that national banks could not branch, even within state borders. This placed national banks at a competitive disadvantage. (If you drive through small towns, you might notice that many have their own "National Bank of ... ," a reflection of the fact that national banks could operate only as a unit bank; that is, as a single entity.) This omission of any discussion of branching often was taken as a prohibition against branching in general.

Although passed in 1927, the genesis of the McFadden Act occurred several years earlier. McFadden first introduced a bill that would enable national banks to branch. Since this meant that state banks, many of which were able to branch, would face increased competition, so the bill was opposed. But the move to allow national banks to branch was not dead. The **Comptroller of the Currency** lobbied for removing the restriction that denied national banks the right to branch within states. The Federal Reserve, however, came out in opposition to branching by national banks. Their reason for the opposition was based on the idea that protecting national banks from state bank competition would be better achieved not by allowing national banks to branch but by also denying state banks that opportunity. In 1923, the **Board of Governors** passed a resolution that sought to halt branching outside of the bank's home city and immediate area.

After several years of debate, with the addition and removal of many amendments, the bill was brought up again in 1927. This time it passed, although not without fierce opposition. One reason for its passage this time was the rising number of bank failures throughout the United States, failures that totaled nearly 1,000 in 1926. What the act did was to force national banks to comply with the branching regulations of the state in which they resided. While this put state banks and national banks on a similar footing, it also prevented large national banks from going across state lines. This effectively reduced the competition in the banking industry because it did not allow larger, possibly more efficient banks from entering markets across the country.

The success of the McFadden Act, when viewed from an economic perspective, is questionable. It was successful in keeping many banks open. But were these banks efficient? That is, because banks were limited in their ability to branch, it has been argued that poorly managed banks were kept open by the lack of competition. And when the **Great Depression** occurred, there was a vast wave of **bank failures**, a condition that was not experienced in Canada, where the banking system was characterized by a relatively small number of large banks with many branches. It is noteworthy that it took until the mid-1990s for this legislation to be completely repealed, an indication of the public's long-standing distrust of large, out-of-state banks. Still, with the advances in technology that have come about, interstate banking became inevitable.

FURTHER READING

Johnston, Verle B. "The McFadden Act: A Look Back." Federal Reserve Bank of San Francisco *Economic Letter* (August 19, 1983); Meltzer, Allan H. *A History of the Federal Reserve, Vol. 1: 1913–1951.* Chicago: University of Chicago Press, 2003.

MELTZER, ALLAN H. (1928–). Allan Meltzer is best known for his work with **Karl Brunner** which provided the early theoretical and empirical foundations for **Monetarism**. After receiving his Ph.D. from UCLA in 1958, Meltzer began to investigate the relationship between money, Federal Reserve policy, and the economy. In his early work, he examined the stability of money demand. This was an important area because a stable money demand relation—analogous to stable **velocity of money** within the context of the **quantity theory**—provided a key component to the Monetarist view that observed fluctuations in economic activity stemmed not from changes in the public's demand for money, an idea that many Keynesian economists and Federal Reserve policymakers believed to be true, but from changes in the supply of money. That is, by demonstrating that the velocity of money was relatively stable and predictable, Meltzer and other Monetarists showed that Federal Reserve policy actions might be responsible for causing or contributing significantly to **business cycles** and **inflation**.

One difference between the research path taken by Meltzer (along with Brunner) and other Monetarists was the formers' decision to question the current orthodoxy using its own accepted model, the so-called IS-LM model. While fellow Monetarist **Milton Friedman** never really used this model, Meltzer used it to demonstrate the importance of monetary policy actions in determining economic activity. Meltzer also investigated the nature of monetary policy by examining issues regarding policy **transparency** and **credibility**.

The bulk of Meltzer's academic career was spent at Carnegie Mellon University, in Pittsburgh, where he has been the University Professor of Political Economy since 1989. In addition to numerous visiting professorships at universities worldwide, Meltzer also served in numerous government capacities, including his time as a member of the President's Council of Economic Advisers (1988–1989) and as consultant to various government agencies, including the U.S. Treasury and the **Board of Governors**. On top of these activities, Meltzer co-founded with Brunner the Shadow Open Market Committee, a group of economists who meet regularly to analyze monetary policy. Policy statements by this group are often cited in the financial press.

Allan Meltzer has written hundreds of articles and numerous books on monetary policy and macroeconomics. His most recent book, *A History of the Federal Reserve: Volume I:*

1913–1951 (University of Chicago Press, 2003), is likely to become a classic reference. For more information on Meltzer, visit his Website at Carnegie-Mellon University (www.gsia.cmu.edu).

MEMBER BANKS. Member banks used to refer to those banks that were members of the Federal Reserve System. Today that means something different than it did a few decades ago. The changes that have taken place and the responses of policymakers and regulators to those changes offer an interesting insight into the structure of the Federal Reserve System and into how banks react to changes in incentives.

When the Federal Reserve System was formed after passage of the **Federal Reserve Act of 1913**, not all banks wanted to be members of the new system and not everyone wanted every bank to join. The decision was made to make every national bank a member of the system and to allow each **state bank** to join or not, as it wished. For the latter, membership in part required them to meet certain eligibility requirements. Of the 25,875 commercial banks in the United States in 1915, only 7,715 banks (about 30 percent) were members of the system. Of these, only 17 state banks (less than 1 percent) decided to join. Obviously, the vast majority of member banks were the national banks, but they had no choice in the matter. By 1925, however, the number of state banks belonging to the system had jumped to 1,472, representing 15 percent of the member banks.

These numbers changed following World War II. Between 1950 and 1975, for example, the number of member banks fell from 6,873 to 5,796, even though the total number of **commercial banks** in the United States remained fairly steady. Over this same time, the number of state banks that were members declined even more sharply, falling from 1,915 to 1,064, almost a 50 percent drop. Along with the decline in the number of member banks, the percentage of total deposits held by member banks relative to all commercial banks also declined.

There are several explanations for the decline. One is that state banks generally faced lower **reserve requirements** than did member banks. That is, banks are required by law to hold some percentage of their deposits on reserve, either with their Federal Reserve Bank or with a state regulator. For some states, these requirements could be met by holding interest earning financial assets. For member banks, however, reserves could be held in only two forms: reserves at a Federal Reserve Bank or as **vault cash**. In either case, member banks faced an opportunity cost in terms of lost interest income on the money held as reserves. This made member banks less profitable, all else the same, compared with their state bank competitors. What did membership provide? For member banks, they could avail themselves of discount loans through the Federal Reserve **discount window** in time of emergencies. Member banks also could use the Federal Reserve's check clearing system. But nonmembers could get such services, too. Smaller banks often used the clearing services of larger banks: with advancements in technology, and large banks effectively competed with the Federal Reserve to provide check-clearing services.

In the face of declining membership, Federal Reserve authorities warned that continued loss of banks weakened their ability to effectively conduct monetary policy. Think of it: If there are no member banks and one of the Federal Reserve's policy tools is to alter the reserve requirement, this tool is thereby totally ineffectual. The Federal Reserve thus lost some control over the supply of money with the decline in member banks.

Facing continued deterioration of membership, the Federal Reserve took action. As the **Depository Institutions Deregulation and Monetary Control Act (DIDMCA) of 1980** was being debated in Congress, the Federal Reserve actively lobbied for a change in membership rules. Federal Reserve officials testified before congressional committees and argued for universal reserve requirements applied to all commercial banks, savings and loan associations, mutual savings banks, and credit unions. The Federal Reserve would in one broad stroke solve the problem of monetary control stemming from declining membership and the increasingly important problems caused by the proliferation of money substitutes, such as **money market mutual funds**, **NOW accounts**, and the like. Against some stiff dissention, the DIDMCA was passed on March 31, 1980. As part of the act, all depository institutions—banks, savings and loans, credit unions—would be subject to the Federal Reserve's reserve requirements beginning in 1987, with reserves held either at the Federal Reserve or as vault cash. Banks that were forced to pay the tax of reserve requirements did get something for it: now all depository institutions were given access to the Federal Reserve's discount window, use of check-clearing services, shipment of currency and coin, use of wire facilities, etc. The provisions of the DIDMCA thus ended the debate over membership in the Federal Reserve System.

FURTHER READING

Gilbert, R. Alton. "Utilization of Federal Reserve Bank Services by Member Banks: Implications for the Costs and Benefits of Membership." Federal Reserve Bank of St. Louis *Review* (August 1977): 2–15; Meltzer, Allan H. *A History of the Federal Reserve, Vol. 1: 1913–1951.* Chicago: University of Chicago Press, 2003.

MILLER, G. WILLIAM (1925–). In the annals of Federal Reserve history, G. William Miller holds a rather dubious distinction: he served as chairman for the shortest interval in the postwar era. As President Jimmy Carter's selection to become the chairman of the Federal Reserve, Miller was sworn in on March 8, 1978. He left the chairman's position on August 6, 1979 to assume the position of Secretary of the U.S. Treasury. To some degree this changing of jobs was politically motivated: the president considered Miller's talents better utilized at the Treasury than at the Federal Reserve. Another view is that Miller was completely ineffectual during his time at the Federal Reserve, a time when **inflation** continued to rise into double-digit territory. Indeed, Miller's successor, **Paul Volcker**, generally is credited with changing the focus of monetary policy, placing more emphasis on reducing and controlling inflation than did Miller or his predecessors.

Before becoming chairman of the Board of Governors, Miller's career began as a member of the law firm of Cravath, Swaine & Moore in New York City. In the mid-1950s, he joined the firm Textron, Inc., rising to the position of chief executive officer by 1968. At the time of his nomination to the Board of Governors, Miller was serving as a director of the Federal Reserve Bank of Boston and several corporations and as chairman of the Conference Board and the National Alliance of Businessmen.

MONETARISM/MONETARIST. Monetarism is the term that describes a view or a body of work in which the behavior of the money supply is seen as playing a central role in explaining economic activity. Monetarists believe that observed changes in nominal income and prices are, over time, best explained by movements in the supply of **money**.

Changes in real output are not related to movements in the money supply in the long run but may be affected in the short run.

Like most "schools of thought," Monetarism should not be thought of as unified view of economics or how monetary policy should be conducted. While those economists included under the banner of Monetarism generally believe that changes in the supply of money and monetary policy actions are critical in explaining changes in the economy, the weight placed on money's role varies. For example, one version of Monetarism focuses on the long-run relation between money and the economy, a view that is directly linked to the **quantity theory** of money. The quantity theory posits that if the public's desired ratio of money holdings to nominal income is relatively stable over time, then changes in the supply of money and changes in nominal income (measured by **gross domestic product**) should move proportionally. More important, if real output over time is determined by "real side" factors, things like the growth of the labor force or improvements in technology, then changes in the money supply should be directly reflected in changes in the price level. (This money–price link occurs because real output is simply the product of nominal income and the price level.) Put another way, this long-run view of Monetarism suggests that changes in the growth rate of the money supply, relative to the growth of real output, are directly related to changes in the rate of **inflation**.

The foregoing is the basic foundation of Monetarism. Exactly what constitutes "Monetarism" varies as much as the number of individuals attempting to define it. Even though some would suggest additional entries to the following list, Monetarism can be thought of as a set of basic propositions. As described in Hafer (2001), these include the following:

- Monetarism refers to a set of testable propositions from which a set of policy prescriptions are determined. For example, **Milton Friedman's** famous X-percent rule and the more modern **Taylor Rule** for monetary policy are examples of policy prescription derived from a set of empirical findings.
- Movements in the money supply are a major factor explaining observed changes in nominal income and prices in the long run. While monetary impulses may affect real economic activity in the short run, money and real output are not likely to be related over time.
- The Federal Reserve is accountable for movements in the money stock over time.

These propositions are largely accepted by most economists today, even though at one time they were hotly contested. These propositions also form the basis of Monetarist policy prescriptions. To see this, it is useful to briefly examine the history of Monetarism's rise and fall as a policy guide.

Following the **Great Depression** and especially after World War II, the majority of economists believed that fiscal policy—government spending and taxation—was the most effective policy tool to manage economic activity. With a goal of maintaining full employment, monetary policy's role was to keep interest rates at levels necessary to maintain economic growth. In the 1950s there was an increased interest among academic scholars in the field of monetary theory and policy. Most notable in this regard is the work of Milton Friedman and his students at the University of Chicago. What Friedman's early work did was to shift the debate from money's role from its long-run effects, derived from the quantity theory, to its influence on the business cycle. That is, Friedman's work suggested that monetary policy, through its impact on the supply of money, could influence the behavior of real output over the short-term. Even though Friedman often emphasized the long-run nature of money's effect, the mounting evidence provided by the Monetarist research agenda contrasted sharply with the Keynesian orthodoxy in which money had no role.

Several publications in the 1960s established the Monetarist arguments against the accepted wisdom that changes in the supply of money were of secondary importance to movements in the interest rates. Friedman and David Meiselman (in "The Relative Stability of Monetary Velocity and the Investment Multiplier in the United States, 1897–1958") showed that changes in the money stock stemmed more directly from monetary policy actions than from other possible sources. Because movements in the money supply were related directly to policy actions, fluctuations in economic activity logically were tied to the Federal Reserve's policy actions. Their findings fueled a heated debate over the relative effectiveness of monetary and fiscal actions as countercyclical policies. Another publication by Friedman, this time with co-author Anna J. Schwartz, was *A Monetary History of the United States: 1867-1960*, published in 1963. A major contribution of the study was its description of monetary policy errors that led to and exacerbated the economic consequences of the Great Depression. Friedman and Schwartz laid much of the blame at the Federal Reserve's doorstep. While Friedman and Schwartz's *Monetary History* helped to establish a foundation for a link between monetary policy actions, especially with regard to movements in the monetary aggregates and the economy, their analysis was decidedly of a long-run nature.

One of the most important works linking movements in the money supply to *short-run* movements in the economy is the article "Monetary and Fiscal Actions: A Test of Their Relative Importance" written by **Leonall Andersen** and **Jerry Jordan** that appeared in the November 1968 issue of the Federal Reserve Bank of St. Louis *Review*. Andersen and Jordan's work demonstrated that movements in the supply of money not only were important in explaining changes in nominal income but also had a more direct and predictable impact on the economy than fiscal policy actions. The results of the Andersen–Jordan paper demonstrated that by manipulating monetary aggregates, monetary policymakers could achieve the kind of demand management outcomes once thought possible only through fiscal policy actions. The long-run Monetarist principles described earlier were given more credence than ever before because now they also appeared to hold over relatively short periods of time.

In his review of the debate, DeLong (2000) suggests that the Monetarist position received a further boost with the 1970 publication, again in the St. Louis Fed's *Review*, of Leonall Andersen and Keith Carlson's "A Monetarist Model for Economic Stabilization." The so-called St. Louis model, a streamlined version of modern economic models, was "Monetarist" in the sense that the affects from an increase in the growth rate of the money supply could be traced through to its effect on nominal spending, changes in the price level, real output, long-term interest rates, and unemployment. The St. Louis model moved the Monetarist debate into the realm of short-run policy dynamics, supported the notion that an exploitable long-run tradeoff between inflation and unemployment did not exist, and showed that monetary policy, not fiscal policy, was the more potent tool to achieve economic stabilization.

These studies and the many not listed provided empirical evidence that supported the Monetarist propositions. By the mid-1970s, the empirical work amassed at the time pushed Monetarism away from its roots in the long-term relations embodied in the quantity theory and into the arena of short-run stabilization issues.

During the 1970s, Federal Reserve policymakers grudgingly began to adopt parts of the Monetarist agenda. The **Federal Open Market Committee (FOMC)** started using monetary aggregate targets in policy analysis, even though later analysis suggests that their use of the monetary targets was more window-dressing than a serious change in policy. A dramatic shift toward a money-based policy occurred in October 1979 when the chairman of the Federal Reserve, **Paul Volcker**, announced that henceforth the Federal Reserve would follow a monetary policy aimed more at controlling **reserves** in the banking system rather than the level of the **federal funds rate**. This change, announced as a means to help reduce double-digit rates of inflation, suggested that the Federal Reserve would now attempt to control the behavior of the money supply in lieu of trying to control the level of interest rates. This experiment with Monetarism was unsuccessful and short-lived, however. (*See* **Monetary Targeting Experiment of 1979–1982.**)

Sweeping deregulations associated with the **Depository Institutions Deregulation and Monetary Control Act (DIDMCA) of 1980**, especially the spread of interest-bearing checking accounts, severely altered the historical relationship between movements in the supply of money and the economy. Further changes came about during the early 1980s with deregulation of the banking system and the quickened pace of financial innovations brought about due to changes in technology. With increased uncertainty over the link between movements in the money supply and changes in the economy, the FOMC in 1982 rejected the focus on the monetary aggregates. At that time, the FOMC announced that it was effectively returning to manipulating the federal funds rate as the tool to achieve their policy objectives. By the early 1990s, the historical relation between money and economic activity had, in the eyes of **Alan Greenspan**, chairman of the Federal Reserve Board, remained sufficiently uncertain to obviate the use of aggregates for policy purposes. He noted in July 1993 during congressional testimony that "The historical relationships between money and income, and between money and the price level have largely broken down, depriving the aggregates of much of their usefulness as guides to policy. At least for the time being, M2 has been downgraded as a reliable indicator of financial conditions in the economy, and no single variable has yet been identified to take its place."

Some have argued that the Federal Reserve's rejection of monetary targets indicates that Monetarism failed. While the notion that monetary policy should focus its attention on the behavior of the money supply in determining short-run policy objectives has not survived, it would be incorrect to conclude that Monetarism failed. DeLong (2000), for example, argues that many of the key tenets of Monetarism have become part of today's accepted wisdom. For example, the general acceptance of monetary policy rules is a legacy of the Monetarist agenda. In addition, the fact that monetary policy and not fiscal policy is considered the major weapon to combat economic fluctuations is a direct descendant of the early Monetarist arguments. Finally, recent empirical work (see Dwyer and Hafer [1988, 1999] and Hafer [2001]), while not addressing the version of Monetarism in which short-term manipulation of the monetary aggregates delivers direct and precise control over movements in income and inflation, supports the notion that changes in money growth have important affects on the long-run behavior of the economy.

FURTHER READING

Andersen, Leonall C., and Jerry L. Jordan. "Monetary and Fiscal Actions: A Test of Their Relative Importance in Economic Stabilization." Federal Reserve Bank of St. Louis *Review* (November

1968): 11–24; Andersen, Leonall C., and Keith M. Carlson. "A Monetarist Model for Economic Stabilization." Federal Reserve Bank of St. Louis *Review* (April 1970): 7–25; Brunner, Karl. "The Role of Money and Monetary Policy." Federal Reserve Bank of St. Louis *Review* (July 1968): 9–24; DeLong, J. Bradford. "The Triumph of Monetarism?" *Journal of Economic Perspectives* (Winter 2000): 83–94; Dwyer, Gerald P., Jr., and R. W. Hafer. "Is Money Irrelevant?" Federal Reserve Bank of St. Louis *Review* (May/June 1988): 3–17; Dwyer, Gerald P., Jr., and R. W. Hafer, "Are Money Growth and Inflation Still Related?" Federal Reserve Bank of Atlanta *Economic Review* (Second Quarter 1999): 32–43; Friedman, Milton, and Anna Schwartz, *A Monetary History of the United States, 1867–1960*. Princeton: Princeton University Press, 1963; Friedman, Milton, and David Meiselman, "The Relative Stability of Monetary Velocity and the Investment Multiplier in the United States, 1897–1958." In *Stabilization Policies*. New York: Prentice Hall, 1963; Hafer, R. W. "What Remains of Monetarism?" Federal Reserve Bank of Atlanta *Economic Review* (Fourth Quarter 2001): 13–33; Hafer, R. W., and David C. Wheelock. "The Rise and Fall of a Policy Rule: Monetarism at the St. Louis Fed, 1968–86." Federal Reserve Bank of St. Louis *Review* (January/February 2001): 1–24; Mayer, Thomas. *The Structure of Monetarism*. New York: W.W. Norton & Company, 1978; Meltzer, Alan H. "Monetarism: The Issues and the Outcome." *Atlantic Economic Journal* (March 1998): 8–31.

MONETARY BASE. In its simplest form, the monetary base consists of reserves of the banking system plus currency outstanding. The monetary base is a measure of money that links Federal Reserve actions to other more deposit-driven measures of the money supply. This means that the monetary base is largely determined by two forces: **reserves** held by banks at the Federal Reserve and the public's holdings of currency in circulation. (A smaller component, about 10 percent of the monetary base, consists of Treasury currency in circulation.) Indeed, even though the reserves component is the smaller fraction of the monetary base, it is the component that interests economists, because changes in bank reserves are affected by **open market operations,** which are directly under the control of the Federal Reserve.

Changes in the monetary base are brought about through changes in either the sources or the uses of the base. The Federal Reserve's consolidated balance sheet allows one to calculate the base using either. On the "sources" side, the base can be calculated by summing items such as holdings by the Federal Reserve of government securities, gold, and Treasury currency outstanding. If one turns to the "uses" side of the balance sheet, the base can be measured as the sum of banks' deposits at the Federal Reserve (reserves) and currency in circulation. The former measure provides an explanation for why the monetary base changes over time with the focus being on the supply side of the model. That is, the "sources" side tells us whether an increase or a decrease in the base came from a change in Federal Reserve holdings of securities (from open market operations), changes in Treasury currency holdings, etc. The latter measure tells us about changes in the base stemming from the demand side of the market. Because reserves are determined by multiplying the amount of bank deposits by the appropriate **reserve requirement**, changes in the "uses" measure usually stem from changes in deposits at banks. Thus, anyone can determine how a sustained increase in the base is related to Federal Reserve policy actions.

Because deposits held by banks at the Federal Reserve satisfy reserve requirements, the uses side of the balance sheet changes if the Federal Reserve changes reserve requirements. For example, the Federal Reserve may opt to lower reserve requirements. This in effect releases reserves to banks, allowing them to make loans or purchase securities.

Two economists, **Karl Brunner** and **Alan Meltzer**, developed a procedure that adjusts the monetary base for such reserve adjustments over time. When such a reserve adjustment is made, the resulting series is referred to as the *adjusted* monetary base. This series, currently calculated and published by the Federal Reserve Bank of St. Louis, is often thought to be the best measure of the monetary base. (For more detail and recent changes, see the series of articles by Anderson and Rasche listed below.)

Some economists believe that movements in the monetary base are a better indicator of changes in monetary policy than the broader monetary aggregates, such as M1 or M2. Indeed, there is some research, for example, Nelson (2002) and the relevant work cited therein, that indicates monetary policy actions that affect the growth of the monetary base are, over time, reflected in the behavior of the **inflation** rate and in movements of aggregate demand. Other research (see McCallum [2003]) suggests that in periods of low inflation, the nominal interest rate on low-risk financial assets, such as short-term Treasury securities, approaches zero, making movements in their observed yields less informative that changes in the monetary base. Data on the adjusted monetary base are available online from the Federal Reserve Bank of St. Louis Website.

FURTHER READING

Anderson, Richard G., and Robert H. Rasche. "A Reconstruction of the Federal Reserve Bank of St. Louis Adjusted Monetary Base and Reserves." Federal Reserve Bank of St. Louis *Review* (September/October 2003): 39–70; Anderson, Richard G., and Robert H. Rasche. "Measuring the Adjusted Monetary Base in an Era of Financial Change." Federal Reserve Bank of St. Louis *Review* (November/December 1996): 3–37; Anderson, Richard G., and Robert H. Rasche. "Eighty Years of Observations on the Adjusted Monetary Base: 1918-1997." Federal Reserve Bank of St. Louis *Review* (January/February 1999): 3–22; Brunner, Karl, and Allan H. Meltzer, "Liquidity Traps for Money, Bank Credit and Interest Rates." *Journal of Political Economy* (January/February 1968): 1–37; Burger, Albert E. *The Money Supply Process.* Belmont, CA: Wadsworth Publishing Company, 1971; McCallum, Bennett T. "Japanese Monetary Policy, 1991–2001." Federal Reserve Bank of Richmond *Economic Quarterly* (Winter 2003): 1–31; Nelson, Edward. "Direct Effects of Base Money on Aggregate Demand: Theory and Evidence." *Journal of Monetary Economics* (May 2002): 687–708.

MONETARY NEUTRALITY. Economists have, for at least the past 200 years or so, tried to determine what the effects of changes in the supply of **money** are on prices and output. David Hume's collection of essays, *Of Money and Interest*, published in 1752, was one of the first treatments to systematically consider the effects of changes in the money supply on the economy. An early statement of the **quantity theory**, Hume theorized that in the long run a permanent change in the money stock or its growth rate would have no effect on the level or growth rate of output. In effect, money was *neutral* in its impact on the real economy. The idea is that even if the money supply doubled, output of the machines and factories in the economy would not. But Hume theorized that an increase in the supply of money would have a proportional effect on prices in the economy. That is, a doubling of the money stock would lead to a doubling of prices in the long run.

The notion that money is neutral in the long run has been the focus of much modern debate. One reason is that this idea flies in the face of the view commonly held during the middle part of the twentieth century that by changing the growth rate of the money supply, the Federal Reserve could bring about permanent changes in the growth rate of real output and the **unemployment rate**. If the economy was growing at a rate of 3 percent, it was thought that by increasing the growth rate of the money supply, the Federal Reserve could boost economic growth, say to 4.5 percent. If this were not true, then the question becomes one of why it is not true. And does it hold in some "short-run" period?

To answer the first question, why should money be neutral in the long run? Suppose the money supply doubles overnight. In his now-famous example, **Milton Friedman** created the thought experiment of the Federal Reserve sending out a fleet of helicopters during the night, each laden with money. Their purpose was to drop bags of money onto each and every lawn in the country. In the morning when the inhabitants of the houses awoke, they would find that, upon opening the money bags on the front yards, each had exactly twice as much money compared with the previous night. Let's suppose that you went to bed with $10,000 and in the morning you awoke with $20,000. What would you do?

You'd likely spend some of it and maybe even save some of it. Let's suppose you and everyone else spend it all on new computers. What happens? Computer sellers and manufacturers initially see the surge in demand for computers: sales jump. But they do not know if the increased demand is permanent. So, in the short run, they try to produce more computers to meet market demand. They do not raise prices immediately, because they do not wish to alienate customers should the jump in sales be temporary. Even if they were already producing computers at their long-run capacity, producers will try to stretch production to meet the extra demand by, for example, using overtime. In this manner, producers are able, at least in the short run, to increase the production of computers.

So far in this example the increased production of computers is related to the increase in the money supply. Over time, however, this level of production is not sustainable. Computer factories, if they continued producing at this higher level, would face equipment problems as machines break down from overuse. Workers might even reject the offer of working more hours, unless they are compensated more. As demand continues to outstrip supply, sellers of computers begin to increase prices. As computer prices rise, reflecting the increase in demand relative to supply, fewer computers are purchased. This combination may lead to an eventual return of computer production to its original, pre–money-supply-increase level. What does not decline is the price of computers: After the increase in the money supply, computer prices stay at the new, higher level. What Hume hypothesized was that the money supply increase would, in the long run, be neutral with respect to output but would increase the price level proportionally.

Of course, helicopters do not fly around dropping money on people. But the Federal Reserve does affect the growth rate of the money supply. This means that if the real-world response of the economy is the same as in our example, the Federal Reserve or any other central bank is not able to bring about a permanent increase in the growth rate of real output. In the long run, however, the one economic variable that is affected by monetary policy is the price level. Faster money growth should be related to higher rates of inflation. Does this view of the world fit the facts? There are a number of studies that have examined the relationship between money growth, real output growth, and inflation for many different economies in many different eras. To encapsulate the relation over time and across countries, it is useful to simply plot the money growth and real output growth rates for different countries in one chart to see if there is a reliable relation. If money is neutral, then there should be no discernible relation between money growth and the growth rate of real output, on average. Such a plot is shown below.

Growth in Real GNP and Growth in Money: 1979 to 1984

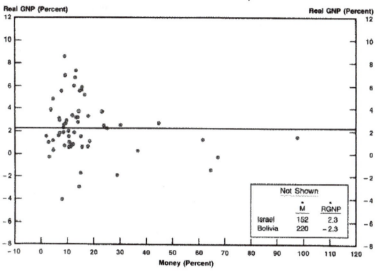

Source: Dwyer and Hafer (1989).

This chart shows the average rates of money growth and output growth across the five-year period 1979–1984 for about 70 countries. This averaging is done to smooth out the **business cycle** fluctuations in the data and to focus on the longer-run behavior of the variables. What is apparent from the chart is that, on average, there is no predictable relationship between money growth and real output growth across a large number of counties. In other words, over a period as short as five years, it appears that the effects of money growth rate changes are neutral with respect to changes in the growth rate of real output.

It thus appears that central bankers cannot flick the money growth switch and make the economy produce goods and services at a faster rate. While this is generally agreed upon today, there is still disagreement over the time frame that is needed to get to the "long-run" result. Is it possible that changes in monetary policy can change economic activity in the short run? This area of debate was sparked in the 1970s by the research of the Nobel Prize economist, **Robert Lucas, Jr.** Lucas suggested that what distinguishes the long run from the short run is that, in the long run, everyone knows that the money supply has been doubled, or that its growth rate has increased. Recall from above that the experiment was to double the money stock with a one-time dropping of money from the sky. This eventually showed up as a doubling of prices. Thought of in another way, it eventually became known to all that the money supply had doubled. Lucas asked if everyone, individuals and firms alike, knew from the very beginning that the money supply doubled over night, how would the economy respond?

Lucas's perfect knowledge assumption creates an interesting result. If *everyone* knows when they awake in the morning that the money supply doubled and that everyone now has twice as much money than they had last night, will there be a short-run increase in output? Using a mathematical model to describe his economy, Lucas showed that the answer is no.

His **rational expectations** model showed that if the monetary policy action was known by all, then all that would happen is that prices would immediately double—the long-run outcome—and output would not change. In other words, in a rational expectations world, the impact of changes in money growth rates is neutral in both the short run and the long run. Imagine what this result means to those policymakers who believed in managing economic activity: Unless you behave in an unpredictable manner, any action you take will be predicted by individuals in the economy. If policy is predictable, you can not increase the growth of output or reduce the unemployment rate.

Is money neutral even in the short run? Even though the models constructed by Lucas and others who helped focus attention on the role of expectations (most notably Thomas Sargent, Neil Wallace, and Robert Barro) suggested that expected monetary policy would have no impact on real output even in the short run, the data do not support this extreme view. Rather, as Milton Friedman and **John Taylor** demonstrated, because of "frictions" in the economy, such as wage contracts or the simple fact that prices and wages are not renegotiated minute by minute as new information arrives, the growth of output can be influenced in the short run by monetary policy actions. When prices and wages are "sticky," an increase in the growth rate of the money supply may result in an increase in output growth. (This notion is not, however, universally held. One group of economists believes that real business cycle models better explain real output behavior. In these models, there is no role for monetary policy actions in an explanation of observed fluctuations in real output.) Even with these frictions, the evidence suggests that monetary policy is not able to permanently raise or lower economic growth in the long run. In the long run, monetary policy actions affect only the price level and the rate of inflation.

FURTHER READING

Friedman, Milton, and Anna J. Schwartz. *A Monetary History of the United States, 1867–1960*. Princeton: Princeton University Press, 1963; Dwyer, Gerald P., Jr., and R. W. Hafer. "Is Money Irrelevant?" Federal Reserve Bank of St. Louis *Review* (May/June 1989): 3–17; McCandless, G. T., Jr., and Warren E. Weber. "Some Monetary Facts." Federal Reserve Bank of Minneapolis *Quarterly Review* (Summer 1995): 2–11; Lucas, Robert E., Jr. "Monetary Neutrality." *Journal of Political Economy* (August 1966); Bullard, James. "Testing Long-Run Monetary Neutrality Propositions: Lessons from the Recent Research." Federal Reserve Bank of St. Louis *Review* (November/December 1999): 57–77.

MONETARY TARGETING EXPERIMENT OF 1979–1982. For most of the period until 1979, monetary policy in the United States was conducted with an emphasis on manipulating short-term nominal interest rates in order to achieve some policy objective, such as maintaining a low rate of **inflation** or steady **economic growth**. As the 1960s progressed, monetary policy was largely responsible for the slow increase in the rate of inflation. At the start of the decade, inflation stood in the low single digits, around 2 percent. By the end of the 1960s, the rate of inflation had increased several-fold. Moreover, during the 1970s the United States experienced periods of high inflation together with deep **recessions**. On the heels of the Organization of Petroleum Exporting Countries (OPEC) oil price hikes in the mid-1970s, inflation soared to almost 15 percent while the economy tanked: the recession of 1973–1975 was the deepest of the postwar period. As these events were unfolding, there was a growing sentiment among economists that monetary policymakers should place greater emphasis on the behavior of the monetary aggregates in setting the direction of policy. The **Monetarist** revolution showed quite convincingly that monetary policy actions taken during the 1960s and 1970s were in large part responsible for the rise in the rate of inflation and the unstable economic activity.

The confluence of a change in economic views and poor economic conditions came to a head in the late 1970s. On October 6, 1979, the Federal Reserve announced that it would henceforth undertake actions to "assure better control over the expansion of money and bank credit, help curb speculative excesses in financial, foreign exchange, and commodity markets, and thereby serve to dampen inflationary forces." In making this statement, the Federal Reserve specified how it would accomplish this task: it would alter its day-to-day operations, shifting from a focus on the level of the **federal funds rate** to one that focused more on bank **reserves** and, therefore, the behavior of the supply of money. Although the Federal Reserve's official statement did not say that it was abandoning interest rates as policy indicators, it did suggest that it would place "greater emphasis in day-to-day operations on the supply of bank reserves and less emphasis on confining short-term fluctuations in the federal funds rate."

Thus began what many referred to as a "Monetarist" policy experiment. Even though the Federal Reserve had, under the constraints of the Federal Reserve Reform Act of 1977 and the **Humphrey-Hawkins Act of 1978**, been announcing growth ranges for the monetary aggregates, it was widely believed that in actuality the Federal Reserve paid little attention to the targets and did not follow policies that would force them to hit the targets. Even with targets for money growth, movements in the federal funds rate drove policy decisions and actions. With the official statement of October 6, apparently this was to change. Some took a somewhat jaundiced view of the Federal Reserve's new-found policy guide. For example, **Milton Friedman**, a founder of the Monetarism movement, wrote in his October 22, 1979, *Newsweek* column that, "those of us who have long favored such a change have repeatedly licked our wounds when we mistakenly interpreted earlier Fed statements as portending a change in operating procedures. I hope this time will be different—but remain skeptical until performance matches pronouncements." How successful the experiment would be was yet to be seen.

The experiment was short lived. In the summer of 1982, the Federal Reserve, citing unexpected swings in the **velocity of money**, abandoned the monetary targeting experiment. With velocity of money uncertain, it becomes more difficult to predict the outcome of policy actions on the economy. By October 1982, the Federal Reserve was once again using the federal funds rate as its main policy instrument, even though at the time it announced that it was targeting bank borrowing. The analysis by Gilbert (1985) and others illustrates that the Federal Reserve's use of a borrowing target was the same as using a federal funds target. In a few years, the Federal Reserve would officially announce that the federal funds rate was its main policy instrument and, by the mid-1990s, officially drop monetary aggregates from policy pronouncements.

A point of debate was whether the Federal Reserve actually undertook a policy change to follow the guidelines of a Monetarist strategy, or whether it simply used that public statement as cover for a policy aimed at raising interest rates to levels that an interest rate–oriented policy would not permit. There is much evidence to support the latter viewpoint. In a review of the episode, Milton Friedman (1984) argues that the Federal Reserve's policies were not what a Monetarist economist would argue for. For instance, Friedman notes that in the several years prior to the October change, the volatility of money growth was *lower* during the interest rate targeting period compared with the monetary aggregate targeting period. Not only did the Federal Reserve's policies increase the volatility of money growth, a condition that is not associated with the Monetarist view, but they also persistently missed preannounced money growth targets. In summary, Friedman considered the policies of 1979–1982 as ones that "deviated so widely from the policy recommended by Monetarists."

Benjamin Friedman (1984) (no relation to Milton) took a decidedly different view of the 1979–1982 experiment in monetary policy. Never a supporter of the Monetarist position, Benjamin Friedman argues that the volatility of money growth reflects not some devious plan of the Federal Reserve to discredit Monetarism but rather the basic inability of the Federal Reserve to control the money supply. Unforeseen changes in how and why individuals hold money balances—currency and checking accounts, for example—simply makes it impossible for the Federal Reserve to engage in policies that lead to stable money growth rates. And, given the fact that a number of **financial innovations** and changes in bank regulations were taking place at the time of the experiment, this further supported Benjamin Friedman's view was that the links between Federal Reserve policy actions and monetary aggregates were simply too loose to rely on. Not only could the Federal Reserve not control the aggregates, but the aggregates themselves were changing over time in response to the innovations in the financial markets. Benjamin Friedman also argued that relying on the monetary aggregates to achieve desired policy goals would not be successful. He pointed to the policy failures of the 1979–1982 experiment as supportive evidence. Not only did economic activity not stabilize, but the economy suffered through a deep recession on the heels of the policy change. True, inflation and **interest rates** began to fall in the early 1980s, but some argued that the price—economic recession and rising **unemployment rates**—was too high.

Who is correct? Actually, both are. The evidence amassed since the experiment, from analyses of the policy decisions to interviews with those individuals making the decisions, reveals that the underlying policy goal was not to adopt the Monetarist approach to policy. Following the announcement on October 6, 1979, the decision makers in the Federal Reserve were no more Monetarist than they were before, and the evidence makes clear that interest rates continued to be the key factor in policy decisions. Although interest rates were allowed to fluctuate more widely than before, oftentimes during the 1979–1982 period the growth targets for the monetary aggregates were abandoned in favor of unofficial interest rate targets.

FURTHER READING

Federal Reserve Bank of St. Louis. "Reflections on Monetary Policy 25 Years After October 1979." A Conference in Honor of the 25th Anniversary of October 1979 Change in Operating Procedures, October 7–8, 2004. Papers available at http://research.stlouisfed.org/conferences/; Friedman, Benjamin M. "Lessons from the 1979–82 Monetary Policy Experiment." *American Economic Review, Papers and Proceedings* (May 1984): 382–7; Friedman, Milton. "Lessons from the 1979–82 Monetary Policy Experiment." *American Economic Review, Papers and Proceedings* (May 1984): 397–400; Gilbert, R. Alton. "Operating Procedures for Conducting Monetary Policy." *Federal Reserve Bank of St. Louis Review* (February 1985): 13–21; McCallum, Bennett T. "Monetarist Rules in the Light of Recent Experience." *American Economic Review, Papers and Proceedings* (May 1984): 388–91; Pierce, James L. "Did Financial Innovation Hurt the Great Monetarist Experiment?" *American Economic Review, Papers and Proceedings* (May 1984): 392–6.

MONETARY VERSUS FISCAL POLICY DEBATE. This "debate" centered on the relative effectiveness of using monetary or fiscal policy to stabilize economic activity. The debate, which raged on for the 1960s and 1970s, is interesting on several fronts. One, many economists within the Federal Reserve System sided with those who believed that fiscal policy—changes in government spending and taxation—was the more powerful tool to use if one wished to increase or decrease the pace of economic activity. Monetary policy, on the other hand, was seen as fiscal policy's handmaiden: holding down interest rates so that fiscal policy could operate more effectively.

Two, pivotal publications in the 1960s moved the discussion toward recognizing the important role of money and monetary policy in explaining economic activity. The Friedman–Meiselman (1963) study showed that the public's demand for money was more stable than some economists believed. As such, changes in the supply of money led to predictable changes in both nominal income and prices. The Andersen–Jordan (1968) study showed that movements in the money supply were more important than measures of fiscal policy when it came to predicting movements in aggregate income. Although at the time the debate was fierce and raged on for some time, today it is widely believed that monetary policy is by far more important in explaining changes in economic activity and inflation over time. Although fiscal policy actions are seen as affecting short-term movements in income, they do not have the lasting impact as a permanent change in the growth rate of the money supply. (*See also* **Andersen, Leonall; Friedman, Milton; Jordan, Jerry;** and **Monetarism.**)

FURTHER READING

Hafer, R. W., ed. *The Monetary versus Fiscal Policy Debate: Lessons from Two Decades.* Totowa, NJ: Rowman & Allenheld, Publishers, 1986.

MONETIZATION. When someone mentions this term, they usually are referring to the idea that the Federal Reserve, by purchasing federal government debt, is "monetizing the debt." To understand this idea, it is necessary to first describe how the federal government finances its activities. With this foundation, we can then examine the idea of whether the Federal Reserve takes actions to monetize the debt.

Suppose the Federal government wishes to buy a new supersonic jet. How does it pay the airplane manufacturer for it? How does it finance this purchase? Answering this question is the same as answering the question, "How does the federal government get the funds to pay for new transportation systems, or more domestic security?" The answer is that the government can increase taxes on the public and use this money to pay for the additional expenses. Or, it can sell **bonds** in the financial markets and use the proceeds from the sale to purchase planes or mass transit. It could do both, but for this discussion let's assume that they choose the latter.

When the government sells bonds, it floats them in the market just like General Motors would. Suppose, however, that the Federal Reserve were to step in and purchase the government's bonds. That is, instead of trying to sell its bonds in the market, the government just sells them to the Federal Reserve. This means that the government gets the money—the Federal Reserve has to pay the government for the bonds as you or I would—and the Federal Reserve gets the bonds. Just like anyone else, the Federal Reserve is paid the interest on the bonds. But what the transaction has done is to increase the money supply. How did the Federal Reserve pay for the bonds? Essentially, it increases the U.S. Treasury's deposits, which are used to pay for the airplane. When all is accounted for, the money supply increases by the amount of the government bonds purchased.

If the Federal Reserve is buying the government's debt, isn't that better than having the government raise taxes or try to sell its bonds in the market and directly compete with private corporations? One worry that economists have about monetizing the debt is that it directly ties monetary policy to fiscal policy. In other words, if the Federal Reserve's policy objective is to keep money growth at some rate consistent with low **inflation** targets, the need to monetize the debt may push them off this path. If the government becomes profligate in its ways, then requiring the Federal Reserve to monetize the debt will lead to upward pressures on prices over time.

An interesting question for economists is whether increases in the federal debt lead to more rapid money growth as would occur if the Federal Reserve monetizes the debt. While there are a number of theoretical papers in which this positive relationship has been established, there is little evidence, at least for the United States, suggesting that the Federal Reserve has engaged in such practices. Since 1951, when the U.S. Treasury and the Federal Reserve agreed to let the monetary policymakers pursue policy objectives independent of the financing needs of the government (*see* **Treasury-Federal Reserve Accord of 1951**), the Federal Reserve has been free to follow its own policy course. This means that fiscal policy and monetary policy are not coordinated with an eye to keeping down the government's financing costs. Even so, for the period covering 1960 through the late 1970s, a period in which the Federal Reserve's policy was to try to fix the level of the **federal funds rate**, there is some evidence that the Federal Reserve may have engaged in some degree of monetization in an attempt to affect movements in short-term interest rates. The evidence is, however, mixed at best.

FURTHER READING

Blinder, Alan S. "On the Monetization of the Debt." In Laurence H. Meyer, ed., *The Economic Consequences of Government Deficits*. Boston: Kluwer-Nijhoff, 1983; Dewald, William G. "Deficits and Monetary Growth." Federal Reserve Bank of Atlanta *Economic Review* (January 1984): 11–20; Thornton, Daniel L. "Monetizing the Debt." Federal Reserve Bank of St. Louis *Review* (December 1984): 30–43.

MONEY. For this entry we split the discussion of money into two parts. The first deals with money as a theoretical concept, essentially how the functions of money help separate it from other goods in the economy. The second entry discusses empirical measures of money. This entry not only provides the reader with the modern measures of money but also provides a brief discussion of how money has changed over time, from shells, hides, and cotton bales to electronic impulses from a plastic card.

Money: Functions. An economist named Paul Spindt once suggested that "money is what money does." But what is *money*? Spindt's quip and this question may seem silly. After all, everyone knows that money is that stuff you carry around in your pocket or purse to pay for things like soda or hamburgers at the local fast food restaurant. Right? Wrong. If you were in London, those pieces of paper in your pocket (U.S. dollars) would not buy anything, just like someone from London trying to buy a hamburger here in the states with a five-pound note would be turned away. So the question of what constitutes money is not quite as odd as you may think.

Money, regardless of its shape or size or country of origin, has three primary functions: It serves as a medium of exchange; it serves as a unit of account; and it serves as a store of value. Of these three, the medium of exchange function is what separates money from other financial assets. In other words, even though a dollar bill and a government bond both can be considered a financial asset, only the dollar bill is considered money. (Try to buy groceries with a 10-year Treasury bond sometime and you'll see what we mean.)

So what is a medium of exchange? A medium sometimes is a go-between, like those individuals who purportedly can communicate with a lost relative. In a monetary economy, items that act as intermediaries in the transactions process serve as mediums. That is, money serves as the medium of exchange for buyers and sellers. For example, consider the situation when there is no money. Suppose I want some shoes and have only basketballs to offer in trade. First I have to find someone who wants to trade shoes, and then I must find out if any of them are willing to trade their shoes for basketballs. This very costly process trading process is called **barter**.

If the economy uses money, however, trading is made much easier. All I need to do is find someone selling shoes and offer my pieces of paper (money) to them for their shoes. But why on earth would they be willing to give up some tangible item like a pair of shoes for some pieces of paper? They are willing to do so because they know (or at least strongly suspect) that they in turn will be able to use those pieces of paper to buy things they want, like a vacation to Hawaii. The use of money, regardless of its physical form, significantly lowers the cost of buying and selling in an economy. In fact, the use of money is so important that nearly all but the most primitive societies use it.

If something is to be used as money, must it conform to certain characteristics? Yes. If everyone agrees to accept the item as money, then it must be standardized. In other words, everyone will be able to quickly determine its value before exchange takes place. This characteristic is why even the oldest of monies were standardized, whether it is by weight or by stamping the picture of the king or queen on it. To serve as an effective medium of exchange, the money item also must be accepted widely in exchange and be portable. It probably should be durable, too. These characteristics suggest the reason why most economies do not use fish as money. Fish may be widely accepted, but its easy portability and its rapid deterioration (we'll assume no refrigeration for this example) increase the likelihood that fish money would not be a widely occurring phenomenon. Other items, such as gold or silver, however, satisfy these conditions quite well. (In addition, precious metals are not in abundant supply thus limiting the supply of the money and maintaining its value.)

The money item also serves as the unit of account. That is just another way of saying that prices are denominated in the money item. This characteristic goes hand in hand with being a medium of exchange. For instance, think about our barter economy mentioned above. What is the "price" of my basketballs? In a barter economy the price would be whatever else they trade for. So, basketball prices may be stated as two pairs of shoes, or one turkey or a dozen cans of soda or 1/1,000th of a semester's tuition at college, etc. "Price" in a barter economy simply means the exchange ratio of a good relative to *each other good*. Calculating all of those prices quickly increases the cost of trading.

This can be easily demonstrated with a little math. If there are two goods, soda and basketballs, then there is only one price: so many basketballs for so many cans of soda.

(Because the soda price in terms of basketballs is just the inverse, we'll think of this as one price.) Suppose there are five goods in the economy: basketballs, soda, shoes, cars, and pizza. How many prices (exchange ratios) are there? The answer is 10: basketballs and soda (1); basketballs and shoes (2); basketballs and cars (3); basketballs and pizza (4); soda and shoes (5); soda and cars (6); soda and pizza (7); shoes and cars (8); shoes and pizza (9); and cars and pizza (10). As you can see, increasing the number of goods rapidly increases the number of prices one would have to know. In fact, the formula to determine the number of price-pairs is $[N(N - 1)]/2$, where N is the number of items in the economy. If N is 5, there are 10 prices. If N is 10, there are 45. In N is 100, the number of prices jumps to 4,950. Suppose the number of goods is equal to the number of separate items in a standard size grocery store, about 5,000. If there are 5,000 goods, the number of prices when money is not available as a unit of account is a whopping 12,497,500. And that is just for one store! As you can see, using money really reduces the cost of buying and selling.

Finally, money also serves as a store of value. Another way of putting this is that money serves as a "temporary abode" of purchasing power. Simply put, when you put money into a bank account in order to buy goods in the future, you are making use of money's store of value function. Of course, when money is put aside in this manner, it is hoped that when you take the money out it has at least the same or, preferably, greater purchasing power than we you deposited it. Of the three functions of money, this one is less certain than the others. In fact, depending on the circumstances, individuals may opt not to use money as a store of value but substitute other items, such as antique furniture, rare art, collectible cars, books, jewelry, baseball cards, land, or even stuffed animals. If storing your purchasing power in one of these nonmoney forms yields a higher return in the future, then they are a better store of value. The only drawback, other than they may lose value over time, is that most of these goods are not money. And because they are not money (i.e., a medium of exchange), they cannot very easily be converted into other goods. Try to pay for your tuition with Beanie Babies next time and you'll see what we mean.

These are the *functional* characteristics of money, generic features that most, if not all, monies have in common. The actual measures of money in use today vary widely across countries. In the following entry, we will deal with the modern empirical measures of money as defined by the Federal Reserve.

Money: Empirical Measures. Given the functional measures of money discussed above, economists try to figure out which existing money measures—things like currency, checking accounts, and savings accounts—perform these different roles. This is an important question because the Federal Reserve and other central banks sometimes monitor the behavior of the money measures to predict the effects of their policy actions on the economy.

The Federal Reserve collects and publishes data on three money supply measures. For lack of better titles, the measures are referred to as M1, M2, and M3. As you will see below, as one moves from M1 to M3, the money supply measures become broader and more inclusive. Put another way, M1 is often considered to be a "medium of exchange" measure—a money measure made up of components most likely to be used in the purchasing of goods and services—while M3 is more of a "store of value" measure—a money measure that is predominantly composed of savings-type accounts or other financial assets that are used as an abode of purchasing power.

As shown in the table below, the money measures move from the narrowest of money—determined by its liquidity, or the ease with which the monetary asset can be converted into some real good—to the broadest. The narrow M1 thus includes only the most liquid forms of money, currency in the hands of the public, travelers' checks, demand deposits, and other deposits against which checks can be written (e.g., **NOW accounts**). In December 2003, the total of these different components amounted to $1,286.9 billion. When we add on to M1 those monetary assets that are savings oriented, such as savings accounts, time deposits of under $100,000, and balances in retail money market mutual funds, the result is M2. As shown in the table, in December 2003 M2 amounted to $6,044.4 billion. Even though M1 is part of M2, it is clear from the table that it is a small part, approximately one sixth. If we take M2 and add to it other financial assets that are even less liquid, we get M3. M3 thus is composed of everything that is in M2 plus large-denomination ($100,000 or more) time deposits, balances in institutional money funds, repurchase liabilities issued by depository institutions, and **Eurodollars** held by U.S. residents at foreign branches of U.S. banks and at all banks in the United Kingdom and Canada. Adding up all of the components for M3 shows that by the end of 2003, M3 amounted to $8,806.6 billion. The table above shows not only the comparative sizes of M1, M2, and M3 but also the relative size of each measure's components. For instance, currency amounts to about half of M1, with the remainder split between check account balances. Looking at M2 you can see that its largest component is small savings deposits, which account for slightly over 50 percent of the total.

As stated in the Federal Reserve Bank of New York *Fedpoints* (2002),

the Federal Reserve began reporting monthly data on the level of currency in circulation, demand deposits, and time deposits in the 1940s, and it introduced the aggregates M1, M2, and M3 in 1971. The original money supply measures totaled bank accounts by type of

Components for M1, M2, and M3

M1 =	Currency	$664.0
	Travelers checks	7.3
	Demand deposits	306.5
	Other checkables	309.1
		$1,286.9
M2 =	M1	1,286.9
	Saving deposits	3,144.9
	Small time dep.	805.8
	Retail money funds	806.8
		$6,044.4
M3 =	M2	6,044.4
	Inst. money funds	1,102.6
	Large time	884.7
	RPs	493.8
	Eurodollars	281.1
		$8,806.6

Source: Federal Reserve Board. Data for December 2003.

institution. The original M1, for example, consisted of currency plus demand deposits in commercial banks. Over time, however, new bank laws and financial innovations blurred the distinctions between commercial banks and thrift institutions, and the classification scheme for the money supply measures shifted to one based on liquidity and on a distinction between the accounts of retail and wholesale depositors.

These changes in the financial markets and in the technology of transacting have given rise to alternative money measures. The existing money supply measures are often referred to as "simple-sum" measures. That is, they are determined by simply summing up the various components. How are those components determined? Trying to figure out what to include is not a matter of just picking this or that bank deposit. In theory, the choice is determined by what the final measure should capture. That is why the current M1 measure is thought of as a "transactions" measure of money: few people hold their savings in currency or checking accounts that pay no interest.

Due to the number of **financial innovations** in markets and transacting—for example, the advent of the **electronic money** card, the growth of **ATMs**, etc.—alternatives to M1 have been suggested. Some economists have suggested constructing money measures on the basis of each component's "money-ness," that is, the extent to which it is used in transactions. This money-ness characteristic of each component is used to create a weighted money supply measure, where currency gets the highest weight (it is used almost exclusively for transactions) and items like large time deposits gets a relatively small weight (it is hard to buy a new pair of shoes by showing the clerk the balance in your savings account). These alternative money measures can be constructed in a variety of ways. The bottom line, however, is that each is an attempt to more closely match the actual money measure with the theoretical notion of what is money.

For more on how money is measured, visit the Federal Reserve Board's Website and search under *monetary aggregates*. The Federal Reserve publishes weekly and monthly data on the three money supply measures and their components. These are available through a number of sources, a popular one being the Federal Reserve Bank of St. Louis's FRED database. It is available online at the St. Louis Bank's Website. Also, the Board of Governors reports the latest figures for the money supply at 4:30 P.M. every Thursday, and these updates appear in major newspapers, such as the *Wall Street Journal* or the *New York Times* on Friday.

FURTHER READING

Anderson, Richard G., Barry E. Jones, and Travis D. Nesmith. "Introduction to the St. Louis Monetary Services Index Project." Federal Reserve Bank of St. Louis *Review* (January/February 1997): 25–9; Federal Reserve Bank of New York. "Money Supply." *Fedpoint* (February 2003). Website: www.newyorkfed.org.

MONEY MARKET. When you read about the Federal Reserve and how it conducts monetary policy, oftentimes you will see the term "money market" used. For example, it may be stated that "Federal Reserve policy changes are impacting the money market and sending interest rates higher." Or, "Participants in the money market await the Fed's policy decision." What ever the context of the reference, money market is a term used to describe a broad swath of financial markets. For the most part, when someone refers to the money market, they mean that part of the financial system in which funds are transferred from lenders to borrowers for periods of less than one year. When borrowing takes place on terms of longer than a year, that is usually referred to as the *capital* market.

Why is the money market necessary? Businesses, governments, and banks often need funds to finance their activities. When their needs are for short periods of time, they turn to the money market. For example, a well-known financial instrument used in the money market is **commercial paper**. Commercial paper is a financial instrument that usually matures in six months or less and is used by firms to met day-to-day operating expenses. Firms sell commercial paper to buyers, effectively borrowing money directly from the lender and bypassing banks or other indirect channels of borrowing. Indeed, the increased use of the money market by firms to acquire operating funds has had a negative impact during the past few decades on banks' traditional role as the primary lenders to firms.

The financial instruments bought and sold in the money market are often used as ready sources of funds. For example, instead of holding financial assets that earn no interest income, such as demand deposits (checking accounts), some firms or individuals may chose to hold money market instruments that pay some explicit interest and are highly liquid. That is, they are easily convertible into spendable funds should some unexpected need arise. In addition to being highly liquid, money market instruments generally are safe investments. Finally, the market itself has no specific location. Because it is the financial center in the United States, New York is thought of as being the center of the money market. Even so, it is really an electronic market, so it is difficult to put geographic boundaries on it.

The Money Market

Instrument	Principal Borrowers
Federal Funds	Banks
Discount Window	Banks
Negotiable Certificates of Deposit (CDs)	Banks
Eurodollar Time Deposits and CDs	Banks
Repurchase Agreements	Securities dealers, banks, nonfinancial corporations, governments (principal participants)
Treasury Bills	U.S. government
Municipal Notes	State and local governments
Commercial Paper	Nonfinancial and financial businesses
Bankers Acceptances	Nonfinancial and financial businesses
Government-Sponsored Enterprise Securities	Farm Credit System, Federal Home Loan
Bank System	Federal National Mortgage Association
Shares in Money Market Instruments	Money market funds, local government investment pools, short-term investment funds
Futures Contracts	Dealers, banks (principal users)
Futures Options	Dealers, banks (principal users)
Swaps	Banks (principal dealers)

Source: Cook and LaRouche (1998).

What instruments are traded in this dispersed market? Who are the major participants? Cook and LaRouche (1998, p. 1) provide a summary answer to this question:

> The money market encompasses a group of short-term credit market instruments, futures market instruments, and the Federal Reserve's discount window. The major participants in the money market are commercial banks, governments, corporations, government-sponsored enterprises, money market mutual funds, futures market exchanges, brokers and dealers, and the Federal Reserve.

As the table above indicates, the money market is quite diverse, not only in terms of the instruments that are traded but also in terms of the participants. The table suggests that **commercial banks** are the largest single group actively trading in the money market.

How is the money market affected by Federal Reserve policies or actions? First, because the Federal Reserve, through its policy actions, directly impacts the amount of **reserves** in the banking system, changes in the supply of reserves often shows up as changes in the interest rates on the money market instruments. This is especially true for the **federal funds rate**, the interest rate that banks charge each other for overnight loans. Because the Federal Reserve brings about policy changes through buying and selling short-term Treasury securities in the open market, this, too, has a direct effect on the money market. Federal Reserve actions have a direct affect on the interest rates of these money market instruments, which, in turn, has a ripple effect on other longer-term rates. The Federal Reserve also may affect money market rates through its administration of the **discount window** and by changing the **discount rate**. Cook and LaRouche (1998) suggest that "under certain Federal Reserve operating procedures, changes in the discount rate have a strong direct effect on the funds rate and other money market rates. Because of their roles in the implementation of monetary policy, the discount window and the discount rate are of widespread interest in the financial markets." Although discount window activity historically had an important affect on other money market rates, the importance of the discount window and discount rate as a tool used by the Federal Reserve has declined appreciably in recent years.

FURTHER READING

Cook, Timothy Q., and Robert K. LaRoche. "The Money Market." *Instruments of the Money Market*. Richmond: Federal Reserve Bank of Richmond, 1998, Chapter 1; Stigum, Marcia. *The Money Market: Myth, Reality, and Practice*. Homewood, IL: Dow Jones-Irwin, 1990.

MONEY MARKET DEPOSIT ACCOUNTS. Money market deposit accounts (MMDAs) were created in the early 1980s. These accounts are similar to **money market mutual funds** in the sense that they pay an explicit interest rate on deposits that follows other market determined short-term rates. Unlike money market mutual funds, however, funds deposited in MMDAs are covered by federal deposit insurance because they are offered by commercial banks. MMDA funds are included under the checkable deposits category and are found in the M2 measure of money. They are not counted as part of the narrower, transaction-oriented M1 measure because it is thought that MMDA deposits, even though they are checkable, are more likely to serve as a savings-like deposit than as a transaction deposit. Indeed, the fact that most MMDAs pay interest and have limited check-writing capabilities suggests that they look more like a savings deposit than a checking account.

How did MMDAs come into existence? During the 1970s, banks were not allowed to pay interest on checking accounts and faced interest rate ceilings on other deposits. (*See* **Regulation Q**.) As the rate of **inflation** rose during the late 1960s, throughout the 1970s, and into the early 1980s, individuals seeking ways to offset the loss in **purchasing power of money** due to the rapid rise in prices shifted their deposits away from banks. Depositors withdrew funds from banks and put the money into, among others, money market mutual funds. These newly formed financial assets allowed individuals to earn market interest rates and have some limited check-writing ability. As funds flowed out of banks into these competing funds, the ability of banks to make loans was threatened. To deal with this, the banking industry lobbied Congress to pass legislation that removed the interest rate ceilings that banks faced and allowed banks to offer new deposits that let them compete with other, less-regulated financial institutions (such as the firms offering money market mutual funds). With the passage of the **Garn-St. Germain Act** of 1982, banks and other depository institutions were allowed to offer MMDAs to their customers for the first time. Not only were the interest rates on these new deposits unregulated—competition and market conditions would determine their level—but also the MMDAs were not subject to Federal Reserve **reserve requirements**. This meant that banks seeking such funds were not required to hold reserves with the Federal Reserve against such deposits, effectively making them less expensive to provide (in an opportunity cost sense) than standard checking accounts.

The fact that MMDAs offered competitive interest rates, had check-writing capabilities, and were covered by federal deposit insurance helped improve the competitive position of banks relative to other **financial intermediaries**.

FURTHER READING

Morris, Marc D., and John R. Walter. "Large Negotiable Certificates of Deposits." *Instruments of the Money Market*. Richmond: Federal Reserve Bank of Richmond, 1998, Chapter 4.

MONEY MARKET MUTUAL FUND. A money market mutual fund (MMMF) is a type of investment in which an individual purchases from a financial intermediary a share of a diverse pool of short-term, liquid financial assets, such as Treasury bills or commercial paper. The MMMF type of short-term investment is offered in two types: taxable and nontaxable.

The taxable MMMF first became available for public investment in 1972. The reason for the appearance of the MMMF was that existing regulations, which prohibited banks from paying market interest rates on deposits (*see* **Regulation Q**), made holding bank deposits, especially checking accounts, a losing proposition. In the early 1970s, the **inflation** rate began to rise rapidly. As the rate of inflation rose, money held in checking accounts and small savings and time deposits lost purchasing power. To combat this loss, individuals sought out alternative ways to hold their money while maintaining the ability to use the funds for check-writing purposes. The MMMF, offered almost solely by brokerage firms and mutual funds, served this purpose. Funds held in an MMMF account paid market rates of interest on short-term, liquid assets, and some accounts also offered limited check writing. For example, some funds allowed investors to write one or two checks from their accounts each month, usually with a $500 minimum imposed. What the MMMF did was to allow individuals to bypass commercial bank deposits, which paid below-market rates of interest, if any, without completely sacrificing some check-writing capability. MMMFs thus contributed to the problem of **disintermediation**; put another way, banks were finding it increasingly difficult to attract and keep deposits in the face of increasing rates of inflation and regulations that did not permit them to compete on deposit rates. While such regulation made some sense during the **Great Depression** when banks were protected from rate competition, in a world of inflation such constraints became barriers to profitability.

Needless to say, these options made MMMFs very attractive to customers who had heretofore been constrained to using only bank deposits as a means of saving and checking. Mutual funds allow an individual to invest for much less than the cost of purchasing the financial assets themselves. So, for a minimum investment of, say, $500, one could get market interest rates and still have ready access to one's investment. These characteristics made investment in MMMFs jump. Starting from zero in 1972, MMMF assets rose rapidly, reaching almost $4 billion by 1975. After this initial burst of interest, shares in MMMFs remained in the $3 to $4 billion range until the late 1970s. By the early 1980s, assets of taxable MMMFs stood at over $200 billion. Why the surge? Because the rate of inflation was pushing into double-digit ranges at the time, and the differential between what banks could pay on deposits and the rate of inflation was widening. Investors were looking for some means by which they could protect the purchasing power of their money and MMMFs offered such protection. As short-term interest rates began to climb with the rate of inflation, so, too, did the rates paid by MMMFs. Such competition for deposits did not go unchallenged by the banking industry. In 1982 Congress authorized banks to offer deposit accounts that were free of the earlier interest rate ceilings. These accounts, called **money market deposit accounts**, allowed banks to compete with MMMFs for depositors' money. Even with this competition, MMMF assets continued to grow through the 1980s. Today, the assets of taxable MMMFs are over $1.5 trillion. Even though investment in a MMMF is not covered by federal deposit insurance, many investors still prefer the chance of making higher interest rates from this investment compared with that offered by banks and other depository institutions.

What differentiates the taxable from the non-taxable MMMF? Taxable MMMFs consist of investments in short-term financial assets, the largest two components being U.S. securities, such as three-month **Treasury bills**, and **commercial paper**. Although there is some investment in different types of CDs (**certificates of deposit**), most of the assets of the MMMFs are in highly liquid, short-term assets. The interest income from these assets are taxable; hence the name "taxable MMMF." Nontaxable MMMFs invest in securities that are issued by state and local governments, from which the interest income is not subject to federal taxation. The first tax-exempt MMMF was offered in 1977, and the group experienced rapid growth beginning in the mid-1980s.

Why are MMMFs an important topic in a book about the Federal Reserve? As mentioned above, the problem of disintermediation was heightened by the growth of MMMFs, especially during the high inflation times of the 1960s and 1970s. With banks becoming less competitive due to constraining regulations, the Federal Reserve faced the possibility that the banking system was being weakened by competition from MMMFs. In its desire to maintain a stable banking industry and given the rapid rise of MMMFs that increased the instability of banking, the Federal Reserve backed legislation passed in the early 1980s that put banks back on a more competitive basis with the MMMFs. By deregulating deposit interest rates, it was believed that banks could compete more effectively. Unfortunately, this deregulation also gave rise to more instability and a massive shakeout of the banking and savings and loan industry during the 1980s. (*See* **Savings and Loan Crisis**.)

FURTHER READING

Cook, Timothy Q., and Jeremy G. Duffield. "Money Market Mutual Funds and Other Short-Term Investment Pools." *Instruments of the Money Market.* Richmond: Federal Reserve Bank of Richmond, 1998, Chapter 12; Johnson, Verle, and William Burke. "Funds and Their Critics." Federal Reserve Bank of San Francisco *Economic Letter* (March 20, 1981).

MONEY MULTIPLIER. The money multiplier is not an alchemist's scheme to turn one dollar into ten. But, in some sense, this is not far from what happens in the banking system. When someone takes a dollar in currency—a dollar bill—and deposits it into their checking account, the bank is required by law to hold some fraction of that dollar as **required reserves**. That is, the Federal Reserve requires the bank to keep back, say, a nickel out of each dollar and deposit that nickel with the Federal Reserve Bank. Or, the bank can hold the nickel as **vault cash**, simply thought of as money back in the vault. If the bank only holds a nickel in reserve for every dollar deposited, what happens to the other 95 cents?

The bank uses the 95 cents to make a **loan** to someone. For instance, let's say you want to open a Starbucks in your neighborhood. To do so you need exactly 95 cents, so you visit the bank, and lo and behold the loan officer is looking to lend someone 95 cents. The bank checks your credit history, you supply them with a business plan and the deal is done. You get a loan of 95 cents. And, to make things easy for you, since you'll be using the money to pay bills, wages, rent, etc., the bank simply opens a new checking account for you with a starting balance of 95 cents. While it may not seem like it, the money supply has just expanded. To see this, let's be clear how we define the money supply. Then we'll reconsider what took place.

In the simplest definition, the money supply is the sum of currency and bank deposits. To make the example even more tractable, let's assume that banks have only one type of deposit: checking accounts. Now let's reconsider the example. When my dollar was deposited, it had no immediate effect on the size of the money supply: since both the dollar in currency and the dollar in deposits are included in the money supply definition, moving money from one component to the other has no effect. At least not immediately. But what happens after my dollar is deposited? After the required reserve is deducted, the bank makes a loan to you. More important, when the bank makes the loan, it also created another checking account, this one worth 95 cents. So, moving money from currency to deposits had the effect of *increasing* the money supply—currency plus deposits—by 95 cents.

The process does not end there, however. When the bank creates the new checking account equal to 95 cents, it again holds a portion out to meet the reserve requirement. If we assume that the same percentage is used as above, then the bank would hold out 4.75 cents from the newly created 95-cent checking account. And, that's right, the bank keeps 4.75 cents in the vault to meet the reserve requirement and now has 90.25 cents to lend out again. The bank makes a 90.25-cent loan, creates yet another checking account and presto, the money supply now has increased by an additional 90.25 cents. By the end of this second round, my initial deposit of one dollar has generated an increase in the money supply of $1.85. In other words, the money supply has increased by a *multiplier* greater than 1.

The process continues until there is nothing to lend out after the last penny is deposited. What is the cumulative effect on the money supply of that initial dollar deposit? The answer to that depends on the size of the money multiplier. In our example, the cumulative increase in the money supply would equal $20. We know this because we can either sum all of the individual additions, or we can calculate the money multiplier. In this simple example, the multiplier is equal to the inverse of the reserve requirement, or $(1/0.05) = 20$. In words, a dollar increase in deposits eventually results in an increase in the supply of money amounting to $20.

The money multiplier plays an important role in the formation of monetary policy. First, by altering **reserve requirements**, the Federal Reserve can affect the size of the multiplier and, therefore, the impact of changes in deposits and reserves on the money supply. For example, if the reserve requirement is 5 percent, as in our example, the multiplier is 20. If it is 10 percent, however, the multiplier is only 10 $(= 1/0.10)$. And if it is 20 percent, the multiplier drops all the way to 5 $(= 1/0.20)$. By raising and lowering the reserve requirement, the Federal Reserve influences the growth of the money supply.

The second area in which the money multiplier plays a policy role can be illustrated by a situation where policymakers want to keep the money supply increasing by some constant amount. In the more realistic version of the multiplier than the one used above, we can relate the money supply to the **monetary base** using the relation $M = m(MB)$ where M is the money supply, m is the money multiplier and MB is the monetary base. (The monetary base equals reserves plus currency.) What this equation says is that if the multiplier is 5, then an increase in the monetary base of $1 will yield an increase in the money supply of $5. If the Federal Reserve wished the money supply to increase by $5 every period, it therefore would need to increase the monetary base by $1 each period.

During the **Monetary Targeting Experiment of 1979–1982**, one of the key proposals was that money supply growth rate should be controlled. If the Federal Reserve could control the behavior of the monetary base, then achieving a certain increase in the money supply required knowledge of what the money multiplier was. A number of studies found that the multiplier was relatively easy to forecast. This meant that if the Federal Reserve had a target level for the money supply, then all one needed to do was divide that desired amount by the forecast of the money multiplier to get the necessary level for the monetary base; that is $MB = (M/m)$. Even though this relationship was shown to hold, the Federal Reserve Board and the **Federal Open Market Committee (FOMC)** did not adopt such a policy strategy. Instead, the FOMC argued that following such a policy course would lead to wide swings in interest rates and would hamper policymakers' ability to react to unforeseen events in the economy and the financial markets. Even though there was evidence from other countries where monetary targets were being used, such as Switzerland, that interest rates did not become more volatile, or that such a policy approach did not limit policymakers from reacting to economic events, the Federal Reserve remained unconvinced. In the end, the Federal Reserve switched back to controlling the behavior of short-term interest rates as its primary mode of setting monetary policy.

FURTHER READING

Brunner, Karl, and Allan H. Meltzer. "Liquidity Traps for Money, Bank Credit and Interest Rates." *Journal of Political Economy* (January/February 1968): 1–37; Burger, Albert E. *The Money Supply Process*. Belmont, CA: Wadsworth Publishing Company, 1971; Hafer, R. W., and Scott E. Hein. "Predicting the Money Multiplier: Forecasts from Component and Aggregate Models." *Journal of*

Monetary Economics (November 1984): 375–84; Hafer, R. W., Scott E. Hein, and Clemens J. M. Kool. "Forecasting the Money Multiplier: Implications for Money Stock Control and Economic Activity." Federal Reserve Bank of St. Louis *Review* (October 1983): 23–33.

MONEY VERSUS CREDIT. Do you know the difference between money and credit? This question may seem silly, but it actually is a very important one. The answer is one that many get wrong. Is that dollar bill in your pocket money? Answer, yes. Is the $285 in you checking account money? Again, yes. What about your Visa card? When you buy shoes or tires with your Visa card, is it money? This time, a resounding no. (Did you say yes?)

Elsewhere in this volume we discuss the characteristics of money and what constitutes money in the real world. (*See* **Money**.) Nowhere in that discussion do we mention credit cards as money. The reason is because *credit* cards are a form of credit, and credit is not money. Even though a credit card and a ten-dollar bill can both be used to buy lunch, the transactions are really not the same. When you use your credit card, the credit card company is extending to you a loan to buy lunch. The loan is one measure of *credit*. So using a credit card is not the same as using money: you still get to eat, but in one case you incur a debt (the loan from the credit card company) and in the other you simply exchange money for goods (your $10 for a lunch).

Our example makes use of only one of the many forms of credit. Credit may be in the form of a student loan from the bank. It may take the shape of a bond that you buy from General Motors Corporation. In this case you are lending money to GM for some specified rate of return over some fixed time horizon. As these two examples suggest, credit has a mirror image in financial markets: debt. In some sense, credit is negative debt. My debt to a bank for a loan is the credit that they have extended to me. As McCallum (1989) notes, this zero-sum aspect of credit and debt makes the measurement of credit difficult. One approach is to simply confine attention to a specific sector, say bank credit, or a more inclusive measure such as domestic nonfinancial debt. Since this latter measure is the mirror image of credit, it could be used to track the amount of financial market debt (credit) that is owned by various groups in the economy.

A problem more difficult than simply measuring credit is whether changes in some credit measure are useful in setting monetary policy. To be sure, policymakers consider the information available from **financial markets** when they determine policy. But suppose "credit" is increasing. How would policymakers at the Federal Reserve interpret that piece of information? Does it indicate that households are taking on more debt by increasing their use of credit cards? Does that indicate goods times ahead? Or does it indicate that credit card holders are strapped for cash and are buying goods today with the idea that they'll pay off their debts when times get better? Movements in credit measures may thus have dual interpretations and complicate the setting of policy.

This problem is not totally avoided by using money measures in setting policy, but there is a long history of the relation between changes in the supply of money and the economy that just is not there when it comes to changes in outstanding credit and the economy. Although monetary policymakers once considered movements in credit to be a good indicator for policy, further analysis indicated that it is a flawed measure. Because movements in credit reflect both policy actions and the reaction of the economy to those actions—in effect, causation running from credit to the economy and back—it is not a sufficiently trustworthy measure upon which to base policy actions.

FURTHER READING

Friedman, Benjamin M. "The Roles of Money and Credit in Macroeconomic Analysis." in James Tobin, ed., *Macroeconomics, Prices and Quantities*. Washington, D.C.: Brookings Institution, 1983; McCallum, Bennett T. *Monetary Economics: Theory and Policy*. New York: Macmillan, 1989.

MORAL HAZARD. Moral hazard, like **adverse selection**, is a problem that is created by **asymmetric information**. In one area in which moral hazard arises, the insurance industry, the asymmetry of information concerns the actions of policyholders once they become insured. For example, suppose your neighbor decides to take out a health insurance policy. Prior to taking out the insurance policy, she may have behaved in a cautious manner: behaving otherwise—taking on riskier ventures, such as mountain climbing or skydiving—increases the probability of injury. With no insurance coverage, she would have been forced to cover the medical costs in the case of an injury. With insurance, however, she now bears the burden of only a portion of the cost. The *moral hazard* arises in this case if your neighbor, after getting insurance, behaves in a more risky manner than before she took out the policy. If she had behaved like this before the policy was written, the insurance company would have imposed a higher premium, or even decided against coverage.

In financial markets, moral hazard occurs when borrowers engage in activities after the **loan** is made that are riskier in the eyes of the lender. For instance, suppose the bank lends you $3,000 to set up shop as an economic consultant. The loan is made by a bank with repayment in mind: The bank expects you to actively seek business, advise customers, and with the proceeds, pay off the loan. Once you are out the door with their $3,000, what is to keep you from going straight to the local casino and letting it all ride on one spin of the roulette wheel? If you bet black and it comes up red, you lose the $3,000, and the bank will not get repaid. If the bank knew in advance what your post-loan action was going to be, it would add some stipulations in the loan agreement to prevent this behavior. Or, it might force you to put up something of value—collateral—to cover the loan in the event your business failed. Regardless, the presence of moral hazard increases the risk that banks face when making loans and, therefore, increases the costs of doing business.

The presence of moral hazard is also important when we consider government regulation of financial markets, especially banking. Although various forms of deposit insurance existed prior to the creation of the **Federal Deposit Insurance Corporation (FDIC)** in the 1930s, the federalization of such protection raises the question of how banks behave with and without deposit insurance protection. Think of the bank as the borrower of your funds: When you deposit money into an account at your local bank, you are in effect "lending" your money to the bank with the expectation that you can get it back whenever you wish. Once you have deposited the money in your bank, suppose that the banker decides to visit the aforementioned casino and use *your* money at the roulette wheel. Betting the deposits has two possible outcomes: a win means the bank is better off and you are no worse off. A loss, however, wipes out your deposits. But with insurance you do not really care because someone will pay you back, even if it is not the banker. This is the crux of the moral hazard problem when it comes to banking regulation: Deposit insurance may entice bankers to behave in a riskier manner than they would otherwise. This means that deposit insurance may actually increase the probability of **bank failure**, even though that is exactly what it was designed to prevent.

Are there ways to help prevent moral hazard while keeping deposit insurance? Economists and regulators have debated this question for some time. One example is the idea of using market signals to augment regulations. Gary Stern, president of the Federal Reserve Bank of Minneapolis, has suggested several approaches to using information available in financial markets to help mitigate the moral hazard problem. (See the two papers cited below for a sample of his arguments.) What information is out there? One of the issues about moral hazard and deposit insurance is that depositors have little incentive to monitor their bankers' behavior. Knowing that their deposits are covered by deposit insurance, most customers could care less what their bank does with their money, whether it is used at the casino or lent to a homebuilder. All they are concerned about is that when they write a check it gets cashed and that they get a statement every month for their records. But regulators, such as the Federal Reserve, the **Comptroller of the Currency**, and the FDIC all need to supervise bank activities to ensure, for the public's own good, that the banks are not engaged in undesirable activities. One way of using market signals is to reduce the coverage of insurance. If depositors bear a larger share of any potential bank failure, standard economic analysis suggests that depositors may find it advantageous to keep better track of where their bank is lending money and investing their deposits. In that manner, a market for bank information would arise, forcing banks to provide more detailed accounts of their activities, reducing the potential of moral hazard.

It also has been suggested that regulators may incorporate signals from the financial markets into their assessments of bank activity. For example, if movements in stock prices reflect the market's assessment of a bank's profitability, then perhaps such information could be used to augment the data already collected by regulators. If the stock market's collective wisdom is that Bank XYZ is making bad loans and the management is faltering, then its stock price is likely to fall relative to other, more-profitable banks. Using that information along with that collected to create a bank's **CAMELS** rating, for instance, could improve early detection of problem banks.

FURTHER READING

Stern, Gary. "Managing Moral Hazard with Market Signals: How Regulation Should Change with Banking." Federal Reserve Bank of Minneapolis *The Region* (June 1999); Stern, Gary. "Moral Hazard and Bank Protection." Remarks delivered at the Asia Pacific Finance Association Conference, July 23, 2001. Available from the Federal Reserve Bank of Minneapolis Website: www.minneapolisfed.org.

MORAL SUASION. Moral suasion occurs when the Federal Reserve uses its position to induce financial institutions to behave in certain ways. For example, through direct consultation with company officials or through public speeches, officials of the Federal Reserve may remind banks and other financial firms of their role in promoting various social goals, such as increased home ownership. (*See* **Community Reinvestment Act**.) Moral suasion also may take the form of delaying or denying bank mergers or acquisitions based on past behavior. In order for the Federal Reserve to achieve some desired policy goal, such as increasing economic growth, moral suasion may be as simple as encouraging banks to increase their lending activities in times of economic downturn. This occurred in the early 1990s when banks were reluctant to increase their outstanding loans following the recession of 1991.

FURTHER READING

Furfine, Craig. "The Costs and Benefits of Moral Suasion: Evidence from the Rescue of Long-Term Capital Management." Working Paper No. 2001–11, Federal Reserve Bank of Chicago.

MORGAN, J. P. (1837–1913). John Pierpont Morgan stands out as one of America's greatest financial figures. After his education in Boston and in Germany at the University of Göttingen, Morgan began his career as an accountant with the New York bank of Duncan, Sherman & Co. in 1857. Ten years later he moved to George Peabody & Company, a London-based company in which his father was a partner. Morgan moved again in 1871, this time to the firm of Drexel, Morgan & Co. as a partner. This firm was reorganized as J. P. Morgan and Company in 1895 and became one of the leading private banks in the United States.

Morgan is remembered for, among other attributes, his ability to gain control over large companies. In the mid-1880s, Morgan's firm controlled several railroad companies through stock ownership. By the late-1800s, Morgan arranged the consolidation of companies in several key industries, including electricity (the merger of Edison General Electric and Thompson-Houson Electric Company to form General Electric) and steel (Federal Steel was merged with Carnegie Steel to form the United States Steel Company). His activity led to his name being associated with others, such as Rockefeller and Carnegie, as a small group of individuals who controlled most of the basic industries in the United States.

In addition to his efforts at consolidating industrial production, Morgan was a great financial force. This is perhaps best illustrated by his actions during the **Panic of 1907**. Morgan and other financiers organized loan syndicates to rescue a number of failing financial institutions in New York City. While some argued that this action further consolidated Morgan's hold over the financial market, others believed that he helped the U.S. government weather this financial calamity. Although Morgan died in 1913 before the Federal Reserve was really operational, his shadow was cast across the new central bank: some argue that the role of the Federal Reserve—the overseer of the banking system—was simply a passing of Morgan's control to a new bureaucracy being run by his cronies.

FURTHER READING

Chernow, Ron. *The House of Morgan: An American Banking Dynasty and the Rise of Modern Finance.* New York: Atlantic Monthly Press, 1985; Strouse, Jean. *Morgan: American Financier.* New York: Random House, 1999.

MUTUAL SAVINGS BANK. A mutual savings bank is more like a savings and loan than a bank. Deposits at mutual savings generally are used to make mortgage **loans**. But, as the name implies, mutual savings banks are like mutual funds. That is, the depositors own the bank, each receiving a share of the profits in proportion to the amount of deposits they have at the bank. Mutual savings banks are concentrated mostly in the Northeast, where the first mutual savings banks opened in Boston and Philadelphia in 1816 (Savings Bank of Walpole). Throughout their long existence mutual savings banks have attempted to provide depositors with avenues to credit that may not have existed in the normal channels.

Like savings and loans, mutual savings banks suffered during the high **inflation** of the 1960s and 1970s. As inflation rose, mutual savings banks were forced to pay higher rates for funds. Since their main line of business is mortgages, many banks held low-interest, long-term loans on the books. This meant that the interest income from these loans was insufficient to make up for the high interest rates paid to acquire funds. This changed in 1980 with the passage of the **Depository Institutions Deregulation and Monetary Control Act (DIDMCA) of 1980** which effectively deregulated their business and allowed mutual savings banks to offer **checkable deposits** and make loans in areas other than mortgages. This freeing up of what the banks could do also had some cost: banks entering into more risky ventures suffered losses, forcing some to close their doors. After a period of consolidation, mutual savings banks changed with the times and today offer an array of financial services, such as investments, insurance and financial planning, in addition to traditional services.

FURTHER READING

Edwards, Franklin, and Frederic S. Mishkin. "The Decline of Traditional Banking: Implications for Financial Stability and Regulatory Policy." Federal Reserve Bank of New York *Economic Policy Review* (July 1995): 27–47.

NATIONAL BANKING ACT OF 1864. The National Banking Act of 1864, which predates the Federal Reserve System by 50 years, created a national banking system. On the heels of victory in the Civil War, the federal government set out to flex its legislative muscle in several areas, one of which was banking. For example, the National Banking Act effectively erased **free banking** from existence. This was accomplished by taxing **state bank** notes: by levying a tax on the issuance of state bank notes, banks no longer found it profitable to issue currency. As a result, national banks—a creation of the act—became the sole providers of bank notes. Granting national banks the monopoly over bank note issuance essentially gave the federal government control over the money supply. From this act, the federal government began to print and circulate uniform bank notes throughout the nation.

The National Banking Act also precluded banks from **branching**; that is, opening other offices in the state or in other states. After the act was passed, branching was permitted only for those state banks that converted to a national bank or banks that already had branches. Another feature of the act was that it imposed **reserve requirements** on banks. These **reserves** were to be held against deposits, either as **vault cash** (cash held in the vault of the bank) or deposited in a small group of large banks, known as reserve city or central reserve city banks. At the time, the only cities with central reserve city banks were New York, Chicago and St. Louis. Not only did the act require banks to hold reserves, it also stipulated what would constitute assets eligible to meet reserve requirements. Items that could be used included gold and gold certificates, greenbacks, and U.S. Treasury **currency**. What is missing from this list? National bank notes. Because they were held in distant banks and were not immediately available, reserves were not available to the banks to meet unexpected deposit demands. Consequently, this reserve system actually contributed to the occurrence of **financial panics** instead of preventing or cushioning them.

Yet another feature of the act was that it levied an additional tax on the national banks. After passage of the act all national banks were required to deposit with the **Comptroller of the Currency**—the national bank regulator—backing for their note issue. This backing amounted to $100 of 2 percent government bonds for every $90 of notes (currency) issued. This tax acted as an incentive not to issue currency, so banks reacted by creating deposits instead. The fact that banks issued few notes sometimes is considered a major drawback of the banking system during the late 1800s. As you see from reading the **Federal Reserve Act of 1913** entry, one of the key provisions of the act was to create an elastic currency.

This need stems directly from the problems arising from the lack of note issuance by banks following passage of the National Banking Act.

FURTHER READING

Hammond, Bray. *Banks and Politics in America*. Princeton: Princeton University Press, 1957; Miller, Roger LeRoy, and David D. VanHoose. *Modern Money and Banking*, 3rd edition. New York: McGraw-Hill, 1993, especially Chapter 15; Timberlake, Richard H. *The Origins of Central Banking in the United States*. Cambridge, MA: Harvard University Press, 1978.

NATIONAL MONETARY COMMISSION. The National Monetary Commission was created with the passage of the **Aldrich-Vreeland Act of 1908**. This act called on Congress to create a commission which would investigate the circumstances surrounding the **Panic of 1907** and recommend changes to the U.S. banking system that would help prevent similar catastrophes in the future. One of the charges of the commission was to determine what would be necessary to establish a central bank for the United States.

The commission, headed by Senator **Nelson Aldrich**, consisted of nine congressmen and nine senators. During the several years that the commission existed, numerous hearings were held and many studies made comparing the banking system of the United States to those in other countries. When it was over, the commission had generated more than 30 volumes of testimony and analysis, culminating in 1911 with the Aldrich Plan for a central bank.

As discussed in Miller and VanHoose (1993), the National Monetary Commission's three most important, or at least lasting, recommendations were (1) the creation of a central bank that had the ability to hold and create reserves; (2) establishment of a coordinated system of check clearing and collection; and (3) development of a fiscal agent that could assist the Treasury with its financing needs. Originally, the Aldrich Plan recommended a central bank with 15 branches. The commission, reflecting the popular view that too much centralization of power in the East was not good, proposed that the central bank should be governed by a "Reserve Association Board," made up of 45 members. This rather unwieldy board was to include several cabinet members, including the secretaries of treasury, commerce, labor, and agriculture; the comptroller of the currency; 14 individuals elected by the branch offices of the central bank; 24 members that would be comprised of those elected by owners of the stock in the central bank and representatives of both agriculture and business; and, finally, a governor (who today we would refer to as the chairman) and a deputy governor (today's vice chairman). Needless to say, the final plan, which became the Federal Reserve Act, did much to condense the breadth of representation and the size of the governing body.

FURTHER READING

Dewald, William G. "The National Monetary Commission: A Look Back." *Journal of Money, Credit, and Banking* (November 1972): 930–56; Miller, Roger LeRoy, and David D. VanHoose. *Modern Money and Banking*, 3rd edition. New York: McGraw-Hill, 1993; Meltzer, Allan H. *A History of the Federal Reserve, Vol. 1: 1913–1951*. Chicago: University of Chicago Press, 2003.

NATURAL RATE OF UNEMPLOYMENT. The so-called natural rate of unemployment does not really exist. It is not something that a government agency goes out and collects data on each month, like the published **unemployment rate**. Rather, the natural rate of unemployment is a conceptual measure of what the unemployment rate would be under certain conditions. Even though it is a theoretical concept, it is one of the most important in macroeconomics and in the analysis of monetary policy.

Milton Friedman, the Nobel Prize–winning economist, introduced the term natural rate of unemployment in his 1968 presidential address to the American Economic Association. Friedman suggested that there is a level of the unemployment rate at which there is no tradeoff between **inflation** and unemployment. The **Phillips curve** analysis was dominant at this time. That framework for analyzing policy suggested that there was a reliable, exploitable tradeoff between the rate of inflation and the unemployment rate. In other words, policymakers could predict what the cost of an expansionary monetary policy designed to lower the unemployment rate, measured in terms of higher rates of inflation. What the popular analysis did not consider was the long-term consequences of such policy actions. That is where Friedman's notion of the natural rate of unemployment comes in.

What Friedman (and, in a similar vein, Edmund Phelps) suggested was that there was some rate of unemployment around which the economy would naturally fluctuate. As expansionary policies push unemployment rates lower, the cost is higher inflation. But that is the transitory effect. Over time, as wages fail to keep pace with inflation, workers opt to leave the work force: they choose unemployment. As workers leave the labor force, the unemployment rate rises. Where it settles, Friedman argued, is the rate at which those in the labor force are willing to work for the going wage rate, given the higher level of prices. Stated formally, "the microeconomic structure of labor markets and household and firm decisions affecting labor supply and demand determine the natural rate of unemployment." (Walsh, 1998). If attempts by the Federal Reserve to push the observed unemployment rate lower are met with persistent increases in the rate of inflation, then perhaps they are trying to push the unemployment rate lower than its natural rate. In fact, if the Federal Reserve has no ability to affect the natural rate of unemployment over time, then its policy focus should be on something that it can affect, such as the rate of inflation.

If an economy fluctuates around this natural rate of unemployment, what is it and what determines it? Economists expend a lot of resources trying to measure the natural rate of unemployment. (Think of measuring the natural rate as trying to measure the presence of a photon: You cannot see it, but it leaves traces that you can see. Therefore, we know that photons exist.) The natural rate of unemployment has been estimated using various techniques, each differing in approach and sophistication. A crude measure is simply the average of the actual rate of unemployment over time. If one were to take the average unemployment rate since the early 1960s, the natural rate is about 6 percent. Indeed, a natural rate of 6 percent to 6.5 percent was often used in policy discussions during the last few decades. Other "guestimations" have put the natural rate at anything from about 4 percent to over 7 percent. Not knowing exactly what the natural rate is makes policy-making difficult, especially if one's goal is a specific unemployment rate. For example, how would you know if the policies taken to reduce the unemployment rate from 5.5 percent to 4.5 percent will be successful or just result in higher rates of inflation if you do not know the natural rate? During the 1990s, the Federal Reserve actively pursued an expansionary policy. As the unemployment rate fell, many economists and some Federal Reserve Governors argued that policy had gone far enough. Pushing the unemployment rate any lower—it reached 4.5 percent by 1998—would result in inflation. Well, the higher inflation never appeared, but a recession in 2000 solved the problem by pushing the unemployment rate back up above 6 percent.

Even though there is no official natural rate of unemployment statistic, economists know that this conceptual measure fluctuates over time. These changes are tied directly to the evolving demographics of the economy. During the past few decades, the make-up of the labor force in the United States began to include many more women than it used to. Because women in general exhibit different patterns of work than do men—they tend to move in and out of employment more than men—this altered the natural rate. The increased aging of the labor force, due to the coming retirement of "baby boomers," also impacts the natural rate. As this cohort ages, the natural rate is lowered since older workers tend to have lower unemployment rates than do younger ones. As the boomers retire, this also will affect the natural rate. Changes in worker productivity also explain changes in the underlying natural rate of unemployment.

If we're not sure what it is but we know that it changes over time, how can the natural rate of unemployment be a useful concept for monetary policymakers? As noted above, estimates of the natural rate act as benchmarks for policymakers. Because policy must be forward looking, policy actions that push the unemployment rate below what is generally perceived as the economy's natural rate should give pause to policymakers, sort of a "go slow" signal if further expansionary policy actions are contemplated. It also should remind policymakers that their actions probably have little impact on the long-term level of unemployment. In the long run, inflation and the unemployment rate are not related: that is Friedman's message.

FURTHER READING

Friedman, Milton. "The Role of Monetary Policy." *American Economic Review* (March 1968): 1–17; Staiger, Douglas, James H. Stock, and Mark W. Watson. "The NAIRU, Unemployment and Monetary Policy." *Journal of Economic Perspectives* (Winter 1997): 33–49; Walsh, Carl E. "The Natural Rate, NAIRU, and Monetary Policy." Federal Reserve Bank of San Francisco *Economic Letter* (September 18, 1998).

NEW CLASSICAL ECONOMICS. The so-called New Classical economics is diametrically opposed to the propositions that characterize the **New Keynesian economics**. New Classical economics is an extension of the work done in the early 1970s, starting with the **rational expectations** attack on the Keynesian orthodoxy in macroeconomics. The Keynesian models that proliferated after World War II were based on the notion that it is the demand side of the economy that drives economic activity. The idea that recessions are symptoms of too little demand leads naturally to the policy prescription that the government should step in and boost demand. This intervention can be done through policy actions that enable individuals to increase their purchases of goods and services; for example, lowering taxes or raising transfer payments from the government to individuals. It also can be accomplished by direct government spending. This latter avenue can be thought of as government-sponsored program to increase employment, or simply increases in government purchases from the private sector.

The difference between the Keynesian and the New Classical view is stark. In the Keynesian model, the consumption function—a relationship between one's income and how much one spends out of it, other effects held constant—is largely responsible for explaining observed changes in aggregate demand. But this relationship is based more on empirical observations of how consumption spending and income are related than on some underlying model of consumer behavior. In other words, if you plot out consumption spending and income, you'd find that the data suggest that out of every additional dollar of income, in the aggregate we spend from 70 to 80 cents of it. Knowing that, Keynesian economists would argue that if the government then gives you a dollar, you are going to spend, say, 75 cents of it. This suggests that one way to boost demand is to simply give people more money. Thus, the idea that increased government spending or make-work programs would increase aggregate demand and offer a method by which policymakers can offset **recessions**, or even manage the economy so that recessions never occur.

In the New Classical view, this ad hoc approach to explaining economic activity can lead to serious problems. For one, the New Classical view holds that people behave rationally. That is, they make choices based on the processing of all relevant and available information. For example, a Keynesian economist may observe behavior and note that for several weeks you left your house with no umbrella. Hence the prediction that you do not need to take an umbrella with you. The New Classical economist, on the other hand, will note that your decision not to take an umbrella in the past more likely reflects the fact that you looked at the weather report before leaving. If the weather report for the past several weeks indicated no rain, it is a rational decision not to carry an umbrella. Does that mean that you would never take one? No, because some day the weather report will forecast rain and, based on that information, you will take an umbrella with you.

The rule of thumb that people do not take umbrellas with them is easier to model than the New Classical approach which requires one to try and determine which information individuals do or do not use when deciding whether or not to carry an umbrella. How does this relate to monetary policy? Suppose monetary policymakers decide to use rules of thumb in setting policy. Suppose they believe that policies that lower the **unemployment rate** will lead to a predictable increase in the rate of **inflation**. This inverse relationship exists in the data and is called the **Phillips curve**. Even though the inverse relation can be shown in the data, is it a reliable foundation upon which to form policy? During the 1960s many economists believed that it was. Policy was oriented to lowering unemployment rates, or at least trying to keep the unemployment rate as low as possible. The idea was to manage economic activity in order to achieve some "full employment" unemployment rate. Such polices were unsuccessful because they merely pushed the rate of inflation higher and higher, while the unemployment rate rose and fell with each recession.

What is the New Classical take on this episode? The New Classical view is that any policy aimed at intervening in the market process is likely to meet with failure. In this example, government intervention was aimed at keeping the unemployment rate artificially below the level that was determined in the market through the interaction between businesses demand for labor and individuals decision on how much labor to supply. (*See* **Natural Rate of Unemployment**.) The New Classical view stresses that these demand and supply decisions are based on rational individuals using available information. Robert King (2002) suggests that "these decisions are presumed to be efficient for those who make them." In other words, an unemployment rate of 5 percent may be the efficient outcome of demand and supply interaction in the labor market even though monetary policymakers would like it to be 4 percent. Unless the labor market is not operating as it should, then policies to move the unemployment rate from its market-determined level to one that is desired by policymakers will lead to an inefficient outcome. In the 1960s, this inefficiency manifested itself in ever increasing-rates of inflation.

Another characteristic of the New Classical view is that, unlike the New Keynesian view, much more emphasis is placed on the supply side of the economy in explaining observed fluctuations in economic activity. Until fairly recently, most economists believed that most changes in economic activity came from changes on the demand side of the economy. That is, increases and decreases in **gross domestic product (GDP)** were explained by changes in consumption expenditures, business investment, or government taxes and spending. There was very little, if any, concern about the supply side of the economy. This, of course, changed dramatically in the 1970s, when, true to the predictions of **Milton Friedman** and Edmund Phelps, the dramatic rise in oil prices undermined predictions and policy responses based on the standard Keynesian model. This "**aggregate supply shock**" simply was not part of the orthodox model. The New Classical model, on the other hand, brought the supply side of the market into sharp focus. To understand movements in unemployment, it was necessary to model the behavior of the labor market, including the decision to supply or not to supply labor on the part of individuals. This knowledge also could lead one to predict the impact of tax cuts on labor income.

Some of the features of the New Classical model have been incorporated into the mainstream views of macroeconomics and monetary policy. Economists today are well aware of supply-side effects on the economy. Now the debate centers more on the extent to which supply-side or demand-side changes explain observed economic activity. If, as in the New Classical view, the preponderance of effect stems from the supply side, then monetary policies aimed at "fine tuning" the economy through demand-side policies will be unsuccessful. New Classical economists argue that economic fluctuations are likely to stem from supply-side disturbances and, therefore, monetary policy really has little impact on real output. King (2002) notes that "if a U.S. recession is due in part to real factors—such as a decline in U.S. competitiveness in world markets—monetary policy has limited ability to make things better." What monetary policymakers should focus on, in the New Classical view, is the longer-term behavior of prices. And in that sense, one can see the impact that the New Classical view has had on the debate over policy. More than in the past, discussions of monetary policy today are much more likely to concern the inflationary consequences of policy actions.

FURTHER READING

King, Robert. "New Classical Economics." in *The Concise Encyclopedia of Economics*. Website: http://www.econlib.org; Lucas, Robert E., Jr. "Econometric Policy Evaluation: A Critique." in Karl Brunner and Alan H. Meltzer, eds., *The Carnegie-Rochester Conference Series on Public Policy* (Vol. 1, 1976): 19–46; McCallum, Bennett T. *Monetary Economics: Theory and Policy*. New York: Macmillan Publishing, 1989.

NEW KEYNESIAN ECONOMICS. The branch of macroeconomics that goes under the label of "New Keynesian" arose in the 1980s, mostly in response to the theoretical attacks on Keynesian economics launched by followers of **New Classical economics**. The New Classical economists basically argued that market prices and wages adjusted very quickly to monetary policy changes. If true, then monetary policy—any economic stabilization policy, for that matter—would be more likely to fail than succeed in redirecting economic activity. In the strictest version of the New Classical view of the world, only when policy actions were unpredicted would the real economy react to a policy action. If policy actions are anticipated, then all that would happen is that prices would adjust and the real side of the economy—production, employment, etc.—would not be affected.

The New Keynesian economists took this view of the world to task. A key point of their argument against the New Classical proposition was that prices and wages simply do not adjust so rapidly, even in competitive markets, that resources do not shift in response to a change in policy. For example, suppose that the Federal Reserve announces that tomorrow it will begin to raise the growth rate of the money supply. Let's suppose that the money supply currently is increasing at a 5 percent rate of growth and that the Federal Reserve's announced new rate is 15 percent. In the New Classical view, inflation would simply jump once the announcement was made, and there would be no change in production or employment. New Keynesians argue that there are too many frictions in the economy for only price changes to occur. Consider how wages are determined. Many people sign annual contracts to set their wages. Unless everyone agrees to renegotiate those contracts, they fix wages over the year. In this case *nominal* wages simply cannot adjust, even though the policy was perfectly anticipated. (Real wages may adjust if nominal wages are fixed and the price level changes.) There are many areas in the economy other than wages where contracts limit price adjustment. Prices for many goods also do not adjust much over time. Newspapers, postage stamps, the price of a Big Mac—the prices of all of these items actually do not change much over time, because it is costly to change them. This is true even where there is no contract stating that the *Wall Street Journal* will cost $1.50 for the next 10 years.

New Keynesian economists recognize that because it is costly for firms to change prices and wage rates, prices and wages are sluggish, or "sticky." One explanation for this observed phenomenon used by New Keynesian economists is the notion of *menu costs*. This idea is based on the analogy to a restaurant changing prices on its menu. If customers see changes every time they visit the restaurant, then they may opt for another eatery that has more predictable prices. The notion that it is expensive for a restaurant to constantly change prices every time an ingredient to the soup de jour increases or decreases means that prices on the menu are not changing very often. If we expand this idea to most of the firms in the economy, you can see how even a small hesitation to change prices can lead to large macroeconomic effects.

Other areas in which the New Keynesian economists have focused their attention include wage and price staggering and the notion of efficiency wages. Many firms do not establish contracts or set prices with a specific calendar date in mind. For example, many university professors sign contracts in spring for the coming academic year, while workers in factories may renew contracts in the fall. Because there is no one date on which all contracts and prices change, this staggering of price and wage change can lead to observed stickiness in the movements of prices. In the area of efficiency wages, New Keynesian economists argue that some firms may set wages that, on average, are high enough to discourage workers from seeking other employment. While firms may be paying some workers more than their worth to the firm, it may actually be cheaper to pay a slightly higher wage than to go through the expense of constantly rehiring and training workers. Efficiency wages may thus reduce worker turnover and may make wages less susceptible to change.

Even though New Keynesian economics differs radically from the New Classical view, their propositions used to explain observed economic activity are very similar to the arguments put forth by early **Monetarist** economists, such as **Milton Friedman**. In the Monetarist story, the Federal Reserve increases the growth rate of the money supply with output at first increasing and then returning to its long-run trend. As output returns to trend, however, prices in the economy are rising. Thus, in the long run, money is neutral in its effects on output and employment, and changes in monetary policy, if maintained, alter only the price level. Even though the story is similar—and New Keynesian economists have greatly improved our understanding of how the economy works to generate this observed behavior—the implications for policy are quite different.

The Monetarist position, derived from the quantity theory, argues that even though there may be some short-term adjustment of output to an expansionary monetary policy, the long-run effect was nil. Hence, monetary policy should focus on the longer-term effects of its actions, essentially on the price level and **inflation**. The New Keynesian story is different. Because of these frictions in the market, there is a substantial role for the government to intervene. Policymakers in the New Keynesian model are thus encouraged to engage in activist, **countercyclical policy** as they attempt to overcome the imperfections in the market. Even though the track record of policy intervention is mixed, New Keynesian economists are more likely to encourage stabilization policy than would someone who adheres more to the Monetarist or New Classical views.

FURTHER READING

Mankiw, N. Gregory. "New Keynesian Economics." *The Concise Encyclopedia of Economics.* Website: www.econlib.org; Mankiw, N. Gregory, and David Romer, eds., *New Keynesian Economics.* Boston: MIT Press, 1991; Rotemberg, Julio. "The New Keynesian Microfoundations." In Stanley Fischer, ed., *NBER Macroeconomics Annual 1987.* New York: National Bureau of Economic Research, 1987.

NOMINAL INTEREST RATE. You put $100 into a savings account at your local bank. One year later you receive your bank statement, and your account now has $110 in it. The extra $10 that accrued in your account over the past year is the interest you earned on your initial deposit of $100. The *nominal interest rate* that you earned is equal to $10/$100, or 0.10. In other words, you earned an interest rate of 10 percent. In this sense, the nominal interest rate is the amount of interest earned ($10) relative to the initial deposit ($100).

Is that all there is to understanding what the nominal interest rate is? Hardly. **Irving Fisher**, a famous U.S. economist from the first part of the 1900s, actually wrote an entire book on the subject titled *The Theory of Interest* (1930). Sydney Homer looked at historical measures of and the behavior of interest rates in his *A History of Interest Rates* (1963), a study that spans the period from 2000 B.C.E. through the mid-1900s. And these are just two of the more prominent books on the single topic of the interest rate.

In this entry we will provide a bit more detail on what the nominal rate of interest is, how it is determined in financial markets, and how the Federal Reserve influences its behavior over time, both directly as a policy tool and indirectly as its policy actions lead to changes in economic activity and inflation, both of which impinge on movements in the nominal rate of interest.

The nominal rate of interest is a price. Many people think it is the price of **money**, but that is incorrect. The price of money, that stuff you carry around in your pocket or the balance in your checking account, is what it can buy. The price of a dollar, for example, is what it can purchase. If a can of soda is priced at 50 cents, then the "price" of a dollar is two cans of soda. The interest rate, on the other hand, is the price of *credit*. When you buy a pair of shoes and charge it, the interest rate you pay on the unpaid balance is a charge for the credit (i.e., **loan**) that Visa or American Express is extending to you. The interest rate also can be thought of as the price you charge the bank for using your money. In the example above, when you deposit money in the bank, you are letting the bank use your funds. But you are not letting the bank use your money for free: you charge them some rate of interest. While the bank sets the interest rate on deposits that it offers to you, you have the choice to deposit or not to deposit your money in a particular bank if the interest rate is not high enough. When we think of the interest rate in this sense, it really is the price you charge the bank for putting off your use of the money, say to buy a new car, until some later date. So, as you can see, the notion of the interest rate is a bit more complicated than simply what you get on a savings account or pay on a loan.

How is the nominal rate determined? Like most prices, it is determined in a market. In this case, the nominal interest rate is determined in the market for credit. Sometimes this is called the loanable funds market, because it reflects the interaction of suppliers of credit and demanders of credit. To see this, the figure below shows the loanable funds market, depicted by supply of and demand for credit curves.

The supply of credit is the amount of funds that is supplied to the market at various interest rates. For simplicity, let's assume that the only suppliers of credit are households. As the interest rate rises, households are willing to supply a greater quantity of credit to the market. For example, they may put more money into bank savings accounts as the interest rate offered rises. This positive relation is depicted by the upward sloping line. The demand for credit, on the other hand, is depicted by a downward sloping line. This means that as the interest rate rises, fewer demanders of credit—borrowers—will be willing to pay the higher price. Again for simplicity, let's assume that the only demanders for credit are businesses. As the interest rate rises, it is more costly for businesses to borrow funds. Because business must concern themselves with the profitability of borrowing funds, for

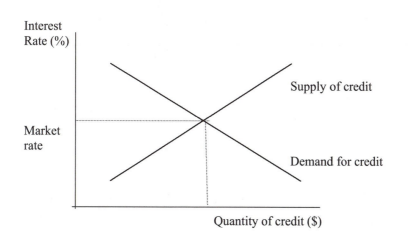

example, to invest in new equipment, the higher the price of credit, the fewer projects they will find profitable. Hence the negative relation between the interest rate and the amount of credit or funds demanded. The interest rate at which the quantity of credit demanded equals the quantity of credit supplied is the market (or **equilibrium**) nominal interest rate. As shown in the figure, given the supply and demand curves, there is only one market interest rate at which the quantity demanded equals the quantity supplied. Any rate above or below the equilibrium market interest rate will cause a shortage or surplus of credit in the market.

If the nominal rate of interest is determined by the interplay of the supply and demand for credit, what explains observed changes in the market determined, nominal rate of interest? The answer is changes in the supply and demand conditions in the market. For example, during economic expansions the demand for credit rises as firms are expanding operations, building new stores, etc. As the demand for credit curve in the above figure moves to the right, the intersection with the supply of credit curve occurs at a higher market rate of interest. This suggests that the nominal rate of interest is cyclical; that is, it tends to rise and fall with increases and decreases in business activity. This relation is indicted in the figure below, which plots the three-month **Treasury bill** rate over the past 50 years. The shaded areas represent **recessions**. As you can see, the nominal interest rate tends to rise during periods of economic expansion—the time between recessions—and fall during recessions.

Another factor that explains the behavior of nominal interest rates is **inflation**. Above we defined the nominal rate of interest as the ratio of the amount of money invested today relative to the amount you get in the future. In our example, you'd be willing to put down $100 today to get $110 in one year. Why? An underlying factor is what you think you'll be able to buy with your $110 in a year. If you think prices for things like shoes and CDs are going to change, then you expect to be able to buy at least as many shoes and CDs one year from now as you can today. So, the 10 percent nominal interest rate implicitly

3-Month Treasury Bill Rate, Secondary Market

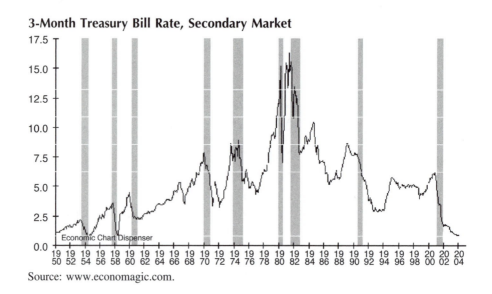

Source: www.economagic.com.

Inflation and the Three-Month Treasury Bill Rate: 1950–2004
(Shaded areas represent recessions)

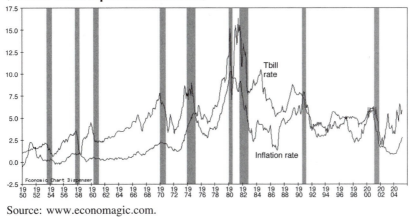

Source: www.economagic.com.

incorporates your expectation of what you think will happen to prices over the coming year. Since you're willing to let the bank use your money for a 10 percent fee, you must be assuming that prices are going to rise by less than 10 percent. Otherwise, putting your money into the savings account will prove to be a bad economic decision, one that you may make once, but hopefully not twice.

This suggests that expectations of inflation are another factor that affects the behavior of nominal interest rates over time. In terms of our demand and supply framework, an increase in expected inflation leads credit demanders to increase their demand for credit (a rightward shift in the demand curve) and credit suppliers to decrease their supply of credit (a leftward shift in the supply curve). The resulting market interest rate is higher than the one shown in the figure on the previous page. The notion that increases in the nominal rate of interest and expected inflation are positively related, known as the **Fisher effect**, shows up in the data. As you can see in the chart above, which plots the three-month Treasury bill rate and the rate of inflation over the past 50 years, there is a positive relation between the two series. Although both series fluctuate and do not move together at all times, the relationship is close enough to consider changes in inflation to be a fundamental cause of observed movements in the nominal rate of interest.

How does the Federal Reserve fit in with this discussion? In two ways: First, when the Federal Reserve engages in **open market operations**, it influences the demand for and supply of credit in the market. By choosing to either buy or sell government bonds, the Federal Reserve tries to bring about increases or decreases in nominal rates of interest, primarily the **federal funds rate**. Second, if the Federal Reserve lets it be known that it intends to pursue an expansionary monetary policy, this may have the secondary effect of increasing inflationary expectations. As we have already seen, increases in inflationary expectations are often accompanied by an increase in the nominal rate of interest. Such expansionary policies may also lead to more rapid **economic growth**. And as shown in the figure above, periods of economic expansion often are associated with increasing nominal rates of interest.

FURTHER READING

Fisher, Irving. *The Theory of Interest*. New York: McMillan Company, 1930; Homer, Sidney. *A History of Interest Rates: 2000 B.C. to the Present*. New Brunswick: Rutgers University Press, 1963; Mishkin, Frederic S. *The Economics of Money, Banking, and Financial Markets*. 7th edition. Boston: Pearson Addison Wesley, 2004.

NONACCELERATING INFLATION RATE OF UNEMPLOYMENT (NAIRU)
(*See* **Natural Rate of Unemployment**)

NONBANK BANKS. This seeming contradiction in terms refers to the creation of financial entities that were used to circumvent a banking restriction. In the **Bank Holding Company Act of 1956**, a "bank" was defined as a financial institution that made **loans** and took in deposits. The law was very clear that a "bank" did both of these activities. So, if a financial institution did just one but not the other, then technically it was not a bank, even though it operated for all intents like a bank. Once this loophole was discovered, banks realized that they could avoid **branching** restrictions by opening "nonbank" banks that would take in deposits but not make loans, or make loans but not take in deposits. Because nonbanks are not banks, they were not subject to antibranching laws. This meant that bank holding companies could effectively branch across state lines.

On the regulatory side, allowing nonbank banks to exist was viewed by some as non-competitive to those banks that were unable to take advantage of this loophole. This was evidenced by the fact that many companies, whose primary business was unrelated to banking, began opening nonbank banks. For example, firms such as Sears and J. C. Penney opened "limited-service" banks that focused on providing deposit services for customers. Some financial firms, such as credit card companies, also used nonbank banks to support their credit card business. Other financial firms, such as Merrill Lynch, opened nonbank banks in order to consolidate customer accounts. That is, a customer could process cash management accounts through their checking account in-house (England, 1987). Even though accounts at most nonbank banks were subject to **Federal Deposit Insurance Corporation (FDIC)** regulations, **reserve requirements**, audits, etc. many still believed that banks owned by non-traditional banking entities, would lead to instability in the financial markets. This lack of support for nonbank banks became law in 1987 when Congress passed the Competitive Equality Banking Act. This act closed the loophole in the Bank Holding Company Act by disallowing the opening of new nonbank banks.

Was the 1987 act passed to promote stability in the banking business or to protect the vested interests of existing bank owners? That question has been debated. On one side, it is arguable that limiting competition in the market is harmful to consumers. If nonbank banks offered a service that customers wished to use—evidenced by the fact that nonbank banks succeeded—then passing legislation that prohibits this activity damages customers. More choice is always preferable to less. On the other, if such competition leads to increased instability in larger, full-service banks, then perhaps specialty nonbank banks would actually harm the banking industry. For instance, some have cited the fact that during the **Great Depression** there was massive numbers of banks that failed in the United States but not in Canada. One explanation given is that the U.S. banking industry was characterized by numerous single banks that could not diversify. (Of course, one could argue that this arose because of antibranching laws in the United States.) The Canadian system, made up of many branches of a few large banks did not suffer such a calamity. If nonbank banks began to face difficulties, where was the parent bank to which they could turn?

This debate is but one of many continuous arguments swirling around the evolution of the financial system. As technology improves, attempting to circumvent existing regulations in search of more profits will continue to test regulators and lawmakers in the future.

FURTHER READING

England, Catherine. "Nonbank Banks Are Not the Problem." Cato Policy Analysis No. 85. The Cato Institute (April 28, 1987).

NOW ACCOUNTS. A NOW account is a *negotiable order of withdrawal* account. This is a relatively fancy name for a checking account that pays interest on the funds in the account. What makes NOW accounts so interesting, especially from an historical perspective, is that they represented a **financial innovation** that caused problems for monetary policymakers in the 1970s.

Prior to the passage of the **Depository Institutions Deregulation and Monetary Control Act (DIDMCA) of 1980**, banks were prohibited from offering explicit interest payments on checking accounts. The prohibition, due to **Regulation Q**, a relic of 1930s bank regulation, meant that banks could not openly compete for checking account funds using interest rates. Instead, banks offered *implicit* interest payments through promotions like "open an account and receive a free television!" Because a television has some monetary value, the notion was that because banks could not pay interest, they would pay you by giving customers televisions, trips, etc. As the rate of **inflation** increased throughout the 1960s, depositors looked for ways to protect their deposits from loss of purchasing power. That is, they looked for deposits that paid interest *and* provided check-writing privileges. NOW-type accounts had been made available to customers in the New England states since the 1960s and in 1978 the ability of banks in New York State to offer NOWs was granted. The impact of this decision was that the **Federal Open Market Committee (FOMC)** realized that NOW accounts, if more widespread, would impact the growth rate of the narrow monetary aggregate, M1, and could make its usefulness as a policy guide questionable. The reason for this is because customers would likely gravitate to NOW accounts, which were not in M1, because they allowed customers to earn interest and not lose their check-writing capabilities. The innovation of the NOW account was hampering monetary policy, because the innovation was muddying the distinction between transactions-type accounts—accounts used primarily to buy goods and services—and savings-type accounts, which are used to store wealth.

The popularity of NOW accounts grew tremendously after the passage of DIDMCA and the nationwide legalization of interest-bearing checking accounts. In the wake of this deregulation, the Federal Reserve redefined the monetary aggregates in February 1980. M1, which had consisted of currency and demand deposits, was redefined as M1A and M1B, the former measure very much like the "old" M1 and M1B essentially M1 plus interest bearing checking accounts at all depository institutions (banks, thrifts, and mutual savings banks). The effect of the nationwide legalization of NOW accounts was to make monetary policy very difficult. Which was the "correct" money measure to watch? M1A or M1B? Over a short transition period, it became clear that M1B dominated, and soon there was only one narrow measure, again called M1.

Today, NOW accounts are hardly noticed as anything revolutionary. Many individuals have interest-bearing checking accounts, often not even knowing that technically they may be NOW accounts.

FURTHER READING

Hafer, R. W. "The New Monetary Aggregates." Federal Reserve Bank of St. Louis *Review* (February 1980): 25–32.

OPEN MARKET OPERATIONS. When you read about the Federal Reserve conducting monetary policy, usually interpreted as raising or lowering the **federal funds rate**, you never hear about how they actually do this. Similarly, if you read elsewhere in this volume about how the Federal Reserve controls the growth rate of the money supply, the process by which they bring about this control is the same as the process by which they adjust interest rates. In both cases, they accomplish their policy objectives through open market operations.

Most textbooks refer to open market operations as one of three policy tool used by the Federal Reserve, the other two being changes in the **discount rate** and changes in **reserve requirements**. While these others are policy tools, they are, today, used so infrequently that open market operations has become the main policy tool used by the Federal Reserve. For this reason, it is very useful to understand what open market operations are and how they are related to the policy decisions made by the **Federal Open Market Committee (FOMC)**.

When the FOMC meets (approximately eight times a year), they decide on a direction for monetary policy. For example, the FOMC may decide that monetary policy should be more expansionary. To achieve this goal, the FOMC may wish to lower the prevailing interest rate in the **federal funds** market. At the conclusion of each FOMC meeting, the FOMC transmits the **directive** to the manager of the System Open Market Account at the Federal Reserve Bank of New York, who oversees the staff of the **Trading Desk** at the New York Federal Reserve Bank. In the directive, the FOMC provides the manager with a guide to policy actions. In this example, the FOMC directs the manager to lower the federal funds rate or increase the growth rate of the money supply. The manager uses this directive to decide on day-to-day purchases and sales of U.S. government securities in the open market—thus, the phrase "open market" operations.

Let's assume that the directive calls for a reduction in the federal funds rate. How is this achieved in open market operations? Because the federal funds rate is the rate determined in the market for excess bank reserves, one way to lower this rate is to increase the amount of reserves. Like the price of any item, when there is more of it relative to the demand, the price, in this case the interest rate, for it gets pushed down. And so it is in open market operations. By buying government securities from a group of government securities dealers, the Federal Reserve is able to increase reserves in the banking system and thus exert downward pressure on the federal funds rate. How does buying securities from dealers impact banks' reserves? Think of it this way. When the Federal Reserve buys securities, it gets claim to the securities and it pays for them by making an electronic deposit in the dealer's bank account. This shows up as an increase in the bank's reserves and thus reduces the federal funds rate.

What if the FOMC wishes to increase the federal funds rate? In this case exactly the opposite open market operation takes place: when the Trading Desk sells government securities to the dealers, this reduces the amount of reserves in the banking system and puts upward pressure on the federal funds rate. Dealers pay for the securities by reducing their accounts at banks thus reducing the banks' reserve positions.

The day-to-day operation of the Trading Desk is quite interesting. The following, reprinted from the Federal Reserve Bank of New York's *Fedpoint* (September 1998) provides an accurate description of the process:

> At the New York Fed's Trading Desk, the staff starts each workday by gathering information about the market's activities from a number of sources. The Fed's traders discuss with the primary dealers how the day might unfold in the securities market and how the dealer's task of financing their securities positions is progressing. The Trading Desk staff also talks with the large money center banks about their reserve needs and the banks' plans for meeting them.
>
> Reserve forecasters at the New York Fed and at the Board of Governors in Washington, D.C., compile data on bank reserves for the previous day and make projections of factors that could affect reserves for future days. The staff also receives information from the Treasury about its balance at the Federal Reserve and assists the Treasury in managing this balance and Treasury accounts at commercial banks. Following the discussion with the Treasury, forecasts of reserves are completed. Than, after reviewing all of the information gathered from the various sources, the Trading Desk staff develops a plan of action for the day.
>
> That plan is reviewed with a Reserve Bank president currently serving as a voting member of the FOMC during a conference call held each morning. Board staff sends a summary of this discussion to members of the FOMC later in the day, allowing the FOMC to monitor closely the Trading Desk's implementation of the committee's directive. Conditions in financial markets, including domestic securities and money markets and foreign exchange markets, also are reviewed each morning.
>
> When the conference call is complete, the Trading Desk is ready to enter the market to execute any temporary open market operation. The Desk initiates this process by sending an electronic message to all of the primary dealers, asking them to submit bids or offers within 10 to 15 minutes. The message states the term of the operation but does not specify its size. (The size of the operation is announced later, after the operation is completed.) The dealers' propositions are evaluated on a competitive best-price basis. Primary dealers whose offers have been accepted, and those whose offers have been turned down, are notified of the results, usually about five minutes after the bids or offers were due.

The Trading Desk and the **primary dealers** accomplish open market operations electronically. Although at one time such contacts were made by telephone, today the desk and the primary dealers are in contact through a computer system known as TRAPS, which stands for Trading Room Automated Processing System. It is through TRAPS that the dealers are notified and they make their bids or offers. Back at the Trading Desk, the different dealers' responses are displayed on a computer screen for evaluation by the staff of the desk. Once the desk has identified the best bids or offers, the dealers are notified through the TRAPS.

Even though the process by which open market operations are conducted may seem confusing, they are completed every day, usually in just a few hours. In addition to being implemented quickly, open market operations have several other advantages as a tool for policy. One is that any action taken can be quickly reversed. Since the TRAPS process makes contacting dealers very easy, and the system allows for rapid conclusion of the deals, in the advent that a trade needs to be reversed, it can be done in a matter of minutes. Another advantage of open market operations is that they allow the desk to achieve relatively small changes in either the federal funds rate or in **bank reserves**. Of course, this precision relies somewhat on the reserve forecasts made by the board staff. Even so, open market operations are precise enough to bring about small changes. Finally, open market operations allow the Federal Reserve to respond to unforeseen events quickly. Unexpected events, from major shocks like the terrorist attacks on September 11, 2001, to weather-related problems in the financial system, all can be addressed quickly using open market operations.

FURTHER READING

Akhtar, M. A. *Understanding Open Market Operations*. New York: Federal Reserve Bank of New York, 1997; Federal Reserve Bank of New York. "Open Market Operations." *Fedpoint* (September 1998).

OPERATION TWIST. The United States faced the problem of a growing balance of payments deficit and an outflow of gold in the early 1960s. The economy also was recovering from a **recession**. Monetary policymakers, with the encouragement of the new Kennedy administration, decided to conduct monetary policy in such a manner that would reduce this imbalance while maintaining their domestic policy goals, that is, low rates of **inflation**, a low **unemployment rate**, and sustained **economic growth**. The problem with this approach is that sometimes domestic and international policy goals may conflict. That is, the proper policy to handle one problem may lead to complications with the other.

In light of these dual policy objectives, in 1961 the Federal Reserve and the U.S. Treasury began a policy aimed at lowering long-term U.S. interest rates without lowering short-term rates. Known as "operation twist" or "operation nudge," the goal of policy was to twist the yield curve on U.S. government rates, pushing longer rates lower. If successful, this would flatten the yield curve: long-term interest rates would be lowered to a level closer to short-term interest rates.

This policy was clearly a departure from its earlier stated **bills only** approach, the Federal Reserve began to purchase Treasury notes and bonds (those securities with maturities of greater than one year) and sell short-term Treasury securities. Meulendyke (1998) reports that this action led to an increase in the Federal Reserve's holdings of notes and bonds by nearly $9 billion and a reduction in holdings of shorter-term Treasuries by about $7.5 billion. Even though operation twist continued through 1962, there is little evidence that it was very successful. Not only is there some question concerning whether it actually flattened the structure of interest rates as advertised, but there is also a debate whether the policy effectively reduced the balance of payments imbalance. By 1963, when short-term rates were rising, references to this policy disappeared from Federal Reserve documents.

FURTHER READING

Holland, Thomas E. "Operation Twist and the Movement of Interest Rates and Related Economic Time Series." *International Economic Review*. (October 1969): 260–5; Meulendyke, Ann-Marie. *U.S. Monetary Policy & Financial Markets*. New York: Federal Reserve Bank of New York, 1998; Ross, Myron. "'Operation Twist': A Mistaken Policy?" *Journal of Political Economy* (April 1966).

PANIC OF 1907. The Panic of 1907 is recognized as one of the most severe economic downturns in U.S. economic history. The downturn in business activity, which began in May 1907 and lasted through June 1908, was characterized by sharply lower output of goods and services in the economy, increases in the **unemployment rate**, and a decline in prices. What precipitated the onset of the business contraction? How did it evolve over the 14 months? What was the major outcome of this episode? This discussion addresses these questions.

In the period immediately preceding the panic, the economy experienced reasonably stable **economic growth**, expansion of industrial production, growth in real income, and increased immigration. At the same time, the general level of prices showed no signs of sharp increases, although by 1906 **inflation** had started to accelerate moderately. Overall the U.S. economy was enjoying a relatively stable and prosperous time. By late 1906, increasing gold imports from abroad were effectively expanding the money supply in the United States. Although these gold imports, mainly from the Great Britain and Germany, were having favorable effects on the U.S. economy, major foreign markets were suffering disruptions. To stem these exports, the Bank of England raised its bank rate several times between September 13 and October 19, 1906. (Raising the bank rate, or **discount rate**, was thought to make U.K. investments more attractive, thus stemming the outflow of gold from the United Kingdom.) In a little more than one month, the Bank of England's bank rate was increased from 3.5 percent to 6 percent. The German central bank—the Reichsbank—took similar measures. The most immediate effect of these actions was to stem the flow of gold to the United States.

Here in the United States, there was volatility in stock prices as the exchange was buffeted by increased speculative behavior in late 1906 and early 1907. March 1907 marked the beginning of a series of severe price reductions on stock market. One of the most documented and sensational involved trading for Union Pacific railroad stock. The early 1900s was a time of trust busting. The Roosevelt administration actively sought to break up the large conglomerates that had formed in the previous decade. Not only were these corporations known to undertake monopolistic behavior in their own markets, but they also were thought to be sources of much stock manipulation. In early 1907 the Interstate Commerce Commission opened hearings into the activities of Edward Harriman, a financier who held controlling amounts of stock in several railroad companies.

Through his control of the Union Pacific, Harriman sought control over terminal facilities in many towns and cities. If he could control the terminals, he would effectively control railway traffic. Although the hearings lasted only a few days, interest in the activities of the Union Pacific—and in its stock—was heightened.

By early 1907 the economy was entering into a **recession**. The National Bureau of Economic Research (NBER) dates the peak of the economic expansion as May 1907. Friedman and Schwartz (1963) suggest that the Panic of 1907 can be characterized as having two phases. The first phase lasted from May to September of 1907. The slowing of economic activity was not severe by previous standards. Due to the reversal of gold imports, the **monetary base** began to decline, thus causing the money stock to decline. Between May and September, the money supply declined by 2.5 percent.

The second phase began in October. This portion of the contraction is noted for several key events. One is a sharp decline in the stock of money. From September through early 1908, the money stock declined sharply, dropping by 5 percent. This drop, Friedman and Schwartz (1963) argue, reflects increased demand for currency by bank depositors. In other words, as depositors withdrew funds from their accounts and increased holdings of **currency**, the money stock shrank accordingly. This condition also made it increasingly difficult for businesses to obtain loans at profitable rates.

One reason that depositors withdrew funds from banks was the ongoing uncertainties about the stock market discussed above. Shocks to the market occurred as misdeeds of corporate giants were made public. At the annual meeting of the Union Pacific, held in Chicago in October 1907, Harriman announced that he would expose the well-known financier Stuyvesant Fish as a stock manipulator, an event that raised the market's level of anxiety. At the same time, stock prices in United Copper Company fluctuated dramatically on rumors of intervention by Standard Oil against one of the main directors of United Copper, F. Augustus Heinze. The fluctuation in United Copper's stock price rippled through to other companies, especially banks. For example, when United Copper's share prices fell, it caused a decline in the shares of the bank Mercantile National, because it was rumored that United sought to take over Mercantile National. Depositors started a run on Mercantile. Even though Mercantile was a member of the New York Clearing House—a reserve pool of funds deposited by financial institutions for emergency needs—and Mercantile's call for help was met by the Clearing House, depositors continued to withdraw funds in increasing amounts. As usually occurs with a **bank run**, this concern spread to other banks and contagion developed.

These events spawned a number of bank runs in October. During the week of October 14, five members of New York Clearing House and three other institutions required financial assistance to meet depositor demands. These requests were met by a consortium of banks formed by the Wall Street financier **J. P. Morgan**. Even with this rescue, problems in the New York banking community prevailed. In the very next week there began a substantial drain on deposits at the Knickerbocker Trust Company. Knickerbocker was one of the largest trust companies in New York, with approximately 18,000 depositors and deposits in the $62 to $64 million range. In addition, runs began on the second and third largest trust companies in New York. To help stem this panic, the New York Clearinghouse banks shipped currency to troubled trust companies that held reserve deposits with the clearinghouse. Currency also was being shipped to interior banks (outside of New York) that held deposits with New York banks and were seeking to preserve their funds by drawing down their deposits. All the while, banks were paying out funds to customers seeking **liquidity**.

The panic was short lived. J. P. Morgan's consortium of banks provided a pool of funds, distributing over $35 million to troubled banks and trust companies. By October 26, less than two weeks after the panic struck the New York financial industry, the clearinghouse was issuing loan certificates, in effect providing a currency substitute to those individuals still wishing to withdraw their deposits. In the end, this restriction of convertibility from deposits into currency helped to quell the panic. As New York banks began to restrict convertibility into currency, individuals began hoarding currency. This reaction lasted until February 1908. At that time, deposits began returning to banks.

A major outcome of the Panic of 1907 was the belief that changes needed to be made in the regulation and oversight of the banking industry, and with its relation to the stock market. Friedman and Schwartz (1963) argue that the bank failures and bank runs associated with the panic likely exacerbated the economic contraction. They also note, however, that early restriction of payments cut short the possible effects of continued bank runs and failures and the increased economic costs that such continued systematic failure of the banking system would have entailed. Indeed, the Panic of 1907 and how it was handled are sometimes considered as a viable policy reaction to bank runs. Unfortunately, a similar response was not followed in the **Great Depression** of 1929–1933.

Another major outcome of the Panic was setting into motion the currency and banking reform movement that eventually led to the **Federal Reserve Act of 1913**. While there were many cross-currents in the debate over the role of government in regulating business, there was general consensus that change was needed. In this vein, Senator **Nelson W. Aldrich** of Rhode Island, the recognized leader of the conservative side of the Republican Party and the head of the Senate Finance Committee, introduced a bill that called for the creation of the **National Monetary Commission** to investigate and recommend changes in the U.S. banking system.

FURTHER READING

Federal Reserve Bank of Boston. *The Panic of 1907*. Website: www.bos.frb.org; Friedman, Milton, and Anna Schwartz. *A Monetary History of the United States, 1867-1960*. Princeton: Princeton University Press, 1963, especially Chapter 4; Sprague, O. M. W. *History of Crises under the National Banking System*. National Monetary Commission. Washington, D.C.: Government Printing Office, 1910; Tallman, Ellis W., and Jon Moen. "Lessons from the Panic of 1907." Federal Reserve Bank of Atlanta *Economic Review* (May 1990): 2–13.

PATMAN, JOHN WILLIAM WRIGHT (1893–1976). Congressman John William Wright Patman deserves a mention in this treatment of the Federal Reserve not for his support of the Federal Reserve System but for his steadfast opposition to the Federal Reserve and its policies. Patman was elected to Congress for the first time in 1928 and served until his death in 1976. A died-in-the-wool Populist, Patman considered the Federal Reserve to be a creation of the federal government that would lead to no good. He feared the unfettered power of the Federal Reserve to create money with no backing. Patman understood that the Federal Reserve, through its policies, could inflate the money supply and, with it, the general level of prices. He therefore was staunchly opposed to the Federal Reserve's rather unique independence from the government. Because of this belief,

Patman was a constant source of criticism of the Federal Reserve and continually attempted to reign in its power.

PENN SQUARE. There are a few individual firms that have earned a place in this volume about the Federal Reserve: **Continental Illinois,** a bank whose failure sparked one of the largest emergency infusions of **reserves** by the Federal Reserve; **Long-Term Capital Management**, a hedge fund that, when its collapse was imminent in the late 1990s, caused the Federal Reserve to inject reserves into the banking system and the Federal Reserve Bank of New York to broker a deal that saved that firm from bankruptcy; and this entry, Penn Square.

Penn Square Bank, N.A., of Oklahoma City failed on July 5, 1982. Technically, it was closed by the **Federal Deposit Insurance Corporation (FDIC)**. Its closure and the events surrounding this failure are part of the story of banking in the early 1980s, a large part played by Continental Illinois. Penn Square thus provides a look into the **regulatory forbearance** of those overseeing banking at the time and the role of bad luck or poor management, depending on when and how one views it.

Penn Square, the seventh largest bank in Oklahoma when its doors were closed for business, was a one-office bank in Oklahoma City. In fact, the bank operated out of shopping mall. Penn Square's management aggressively made **loans** to the oil and gas industry. About 80 percent of Penn Square's loan portfolio was made to companies in the oil and gas industry, an amount that was much more heavily weighted toward this one sector than the bank's competitors. Even though Penn Square obviously did not heed the adage not to put all of their financial eggs in one basket, their lending strategy paid handsome dividends in the short run: between 1977 and 1982—before the collapse—Penn Square's assets as reported on their books (*see* **Mark-to-Market**) increased from $30 million to $436 million. Penn Square achieved this result by lending to speculative and profitable gas and oil producers and by having loan requirements that were quite easy by industry standards. In addition, Penn Square sold "participations" in many of its ventures: it sold other banks part of the loans and then collected fees for servicing the loans. Participation in Penn Square's lending activity is a major reason why Continental also failed.

Although risky, and even though regulators should have questioned Penn Square's lending practices both in terms of the loan requirements and in terms of the concentration of loans in one industry, their earnings growth muted much of the criticism. Until oil prices fell, that is. In 1982 oil prices fell sharply, and with this decline came the bankruptcy of the risky oil and gas producers to which Penn Square had made loans. These loan defaults meant that most of Penn Square's assets—those outstanding loans—were now worthless. Since Penn Square was lenient on requiring suitable collateral for the loans, when the loans defaulted there was nothing for Penn Square to sell off to recoup their funds. Penn Square was closed and, unlike Continental Illinois two years later, Penn Square did not get assistance from the Federal Reserve to remain in business.

FURTHER READING

Federal Deposit Insurance Corporation. *History of the Eighties—Lessons for the Future.* Washington, D.C.: FDIC, 1998, Chapter 9; Zweig, Phillip L. *Belly Up: The Collapse of the Penn Square Bank.* New York: Crown Publishing (1985).

PHILLIPS CURVE. The Phillips curve is the namesake of A. W. H. Phillips, a British economist who in 1958 published a study that related the movements of wages to the **unemployment rate** in the United Kingdom. Using data on wage rate **inflation** and the unemployment rate over the period 1861–1957, Phillips found that there was a negative or inverse relation between the two series. That is, when the unemployment rate was low, the data showed that wages began to rise at a faster rate, and when the unemployment rate was high, the rate of wage increase slowed. This suggested that in tight labor markets, markets in which employers had to compete more for workers, this competition pushed wages up. At the other end of the scale, during times of high unemployment, for example during **recessions**, there was surplus labor in the market and little pressure to push up wages.

During the late-1950s and especially into the 1960s, many economists believed that the government could accurately and methodically control the pace of economic activity. In the term of the day, policymakers could "fine tune" the economy, keeping it growing at or near the economy's full employment potential. Such a feat would enable governments to keep the unemployment rate low. Two U.S. economists named Paul Samuelson and Robert Solow (both future recipients of the Nobel Prize in economics) took Phillips's idea and made a simple change: instead of plotting wage inflation and unemployment, Samuelson and Solow (1960) substituted the rate of price inflation for wages—hence the modern Phillips curve of inflation plotted on the vertical axis and unemployment plotted along the horizontal axis. Such a Phillips curve appears in the figure below.

The data used in the figure covers the period 1960–1982. Note that we have highlighted the data from the 1960s, the period when the Phillips curve was thought to hold promise as a policy tool. As the 1960s experience suggests, the tradeoff between higher rates of **inflation** and lower unemployment rates appeared to be a reliable relationship. Note that the 1960s observations lie tightly along the curve superimposed on the data. Because

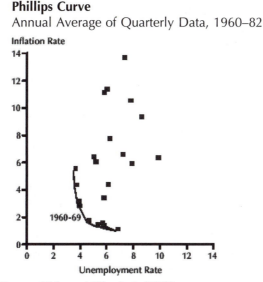

Phillips Curve
Annual Average of Quarterly Data, 1960–82

Source: Hafer and Wheelock (2003).

there occurred both economic booms and recession during this period, it was argued that the inverse relation between inflation and unemployment was robust to changes in the **business cycle**. This meant, at least to some, that the observed tradeoff could be used as a policy "menu." That is, the estimated relation could be used to predict the "cost" of lowering unemployment in terms of increased rates of inflation. For example, if the government preferred an unemployment rate of 4 percent instead of 6 percent, expansionary monetary and fiscal policies to lower unemployment would predictably increase inflation by so much. The curve also indicates that the lower the government tried to push the unemployment rate, the more rapidly the rate of inflation increased. The inflation–unemployment tradeoff depicted in the Phillips curve thus provided policymakers with the parameters that constrained their actions.

A major problem with the Phillips curve was that it relied on the public forming their expectations of inflation in a backward manner. Moreover, it presumed that when making decisions to supply labor, workers considered only their nominal wage and not the true purchasing power of their wages. If workers based their collective decision to supply labor on the behavior of their real wage rate—nominal wages adjusted for inflation—then policies that pushed the rate of inflation upward would in effect reduce real wages. As real wages fell with rising rates of inflation, workers opted not to work (chose unemployment). If true, then at some point the Phillips curve is not the downward sloping line seen in the figure above, but increases in inflation would lead to *increases* in unemployment as well.

This insight came from two economists, Edmund Phelps (1967) and **Milton Friedman** (1968). Friedman and Phelps argued that if workers determine their decisions to supply labor based on the real wage (in effect, the purchasing power of their wage) and if firms also based their hiring decisions on the real wage, then there would be one real wage that is associated with an unemployment rate that one could think of as the "full employment" unemployment rate. (This unemployment rate would exist when the economy is operating at its long-term potential.) This meant that a policy aimed at lowering the unemployment rate below that full employment or "**natural rate of unemployment**" would only push inflation higher. Their idea was that over time the labor market would adjust to bring the real wage back in to equilibrium at the natural rate of unemployment. The upshot of this theory is that while inflation rose and with it nominal wages, real wages would return to their original equilibrium values. Because the real wage was unchanged, so, too, was the unemployment rate. In other words, over time, an expansionary policy aimed at lowering the unemployment rate below the natural rate would only lead to permanently higher rates of inflation and no effect on the unemployment rate. The Friedman–Phelps view predicts just what is shown in the figure above: unemployment rates hovering around some natural rate (around 5 to 6 percent in the figure on the previous page) and inflation rates spiraling upward.

The Friedman–Phelps attack focused on the long-run effect of expansionary government policies. Their arguments meant that Federal Reserve policies aimed at lowering the unemployment rate would, over time, only lead to higher inflation. While Friedman and Phelps attacked the underlying logic of the Phillips curve, the reality of the 1970s indicated that they were correct. During the 1970s, the unemployment rate and the rate of inflation both increased dramatically, just the opposite of what the Phillips curve predicted would happen. Now it appeared that higher rates of inflation could be associated with higher unemployment rates as well. (*See* **Stagflation**.) As the Phillips curve became less reliable as a policy guide, Federal Reserve policymakers and some economists began to tout the usefulness of monetary aggregates to guide policy. Growing out of the **Monetarism** movement, Federal Reserve policymakers began to adjust the growth of the monetary aggregates in the short-run to try and manage economic activity. While money supply measures are useful indicators of inflation pressures over time, they, too, are not good tools to try and manipulate economic activity, a lesson that the Federal Reserve learned in the period 1979–1982.

Has the Phillips curve been tossed into the dustbin of economic ideas? Hardly. The insights of Friedman and Phelps suggested that the original unemployment–inflation relation could be augmented by accounting for changes in inflation expectations over time. The so-called expectations-augmented Phillips curve recognized that individuals base their labor decisions on expected future inflation, not past inflation. When expectations are accurate, there will be no tradeoff between inflation and unemployment: The Phillips curve is vertical at the natural or full employment rate of unemployment. If expectations are wrong, however, a short-run tradeoff might exist between the two measures. Why? Because until workers discovered that the real wage they were working for is not the one they expected, they will continue to supply labor. Once they discover that their actual real wage is less than what the expected, they quit work and the unemployment rate returns to the natural rate. This view suggests that monetary policymakers can, in the short run, exploit the lack of perfect adjustment in real wages—caused by, among other things, multiperiod wage contracts—in order to achieve some short-lived reduction in the unemployment rate. Once the market adjusts, however, the unemployment rate returns to the natural rate and inflation moves to a higher plateau.

Even though the Phillips curve has been subject to much criticism during its existence, it still remains a key component in many macroeconomic models. This is true even though the estimated relation has shown marked instability over time. Put another way, the predicted tradeoff between inflation and unemployment seems to change over time. Even though there was an inverse relationship between inflation and unemployment in the 1960s, in the 1970s it was positive. During the period since the mid-1980s, there appears to be little relation at all between the two series. In the 1990s, a study done by Federal Reserve economists found that the standard Phillips curve model grossly over-predicted the rate of inflation. Indeed, as Lansing (2002) notes in his review, "The need to update the short-run Phillips curve to account for changes in [the estimated relation and the natural rate of unemployment] poses a difficult challenge for anyone who wishes to use the model for the purpose of forecasting inflation."

FURTHER READING

Friedman, Milton. "The Role of Monetary Policy." *American Economic Review* (March 1968): 1–17; Hafer, R. W., and David C. Wheelock. "Darryl Francis and the Making of Monetary Policy, 1966–1975." Federal Reserve Bank of St. Louis *Review* (March/April 2003): 1–12; Hoover, Kevin D. "Phillips Curve." *The Concise Encyclopedia of Economics.* Website: www.econlib.org; Lansing, Kevin. "Can the Phillips Curve Help Forecast Inflation?" Federal Reserve Bank of San Francisco *Economic Letter* (October 4, 2002); Phelps, Edmund S. "Phillips Curves, Expectations of Inflation and Optimal Employment Over Time." *Economica* (August 1967): 254–81; Phillips, A. W. H. "The Relation Between Unemployment and the Rate of Change of Money Wages in the United Kingdom, 1861–1957." *Economica* (November 1958): 283–99; Samuelson, Paul A., and Robert M. Solow. "Analytical Aspects of Anti-Inflation Policy." *American Economic Review, Papers and Proceedings* (May 1960): 177–94.

PLAZA AGREEMENT. In September 1985, representatives of the so-called **Group of 5** countries—France, Germany, Japan, United Kingdom, and United States—met at the Plaza Hotel in New York City to discuss how they might coordinate policies to lower the international exchange value of the U.S. dollar. Following the demise of the **Bretton Woods System** of exchange rates, it was thought that the free movement of **exchange rates** had harmed the United States, because the value of the dollar was being pushed higher. A higher dollar meant that U.S. exports were often at a competitive disadvantage relative to other countries' goods. This is demonstrated by the fact that the United States was running large trade deficits while Germany and Japan were enjoying trade surpluses. This was not lost on the U.S. Congress: seeing U.S. trade deficits rising, talk of trade restrictions and threats of protectionism began to swirl.

The announcement of the Plaza Agreement took foreign exchange markets by surprise. Not only was the agreement hammered out in secrecy, but the nature of the agreement suggested that the United States, long an adherent of free markets in foreign exchange, now seemed willing to support intervention by central banks in order to bring about exchange rate stabilization. The agreement seemed to mark a change in the trend of the dollar's exchange value: following the announcement the dollar fell in value, declining about 35 percent relative to other currencies until the signing parties agreed to stabilize the dollar with the **Louvre Accord** in 1987.

FURTHER READING

Bonser-Neal, Catherine. "Does Central Bank Intervention Stabilize Foreign Exchange Rates?" Federal Reserve Bank of Kansas City *Economic Review* (First Quarter 1996): 43–61; Husted, Steven, and Michael Melvin, *International Economics*, 3rd edition. New York: HarperCollins, 1995.

POLICY CREDIBILITY. The idea of how credible a policy is can affect the outcome of policy decisions. This stems in large part from the **rational expectations** challenge to the orthodox Keynesian models of the post–World War II era. In the early Keynesian approach it was believed that the government could "manage" the economy by adjusting fiscal policy—taxes and government expenditures—and monetary policy. Monetary policy at the time was viewed as determining the level of **nominal interest rates** in the economy, with little interest paid to the behavior of the money supply, except as it might impact the behavior of interest rates.

This focus of monetary policy created inconsistencies in achieving policy objectives. While Federal Reserve officials often stated that maintaining low rates of **inflation** was a key policy objective, the policies actually followed had just the opposite result. We now know that the policy objective at the time was to keep the **unemployment rate** as low as possible. If policy needed to be more expansive in order to meet that objective, then its cost was higher rates of inflation. Such inconsistency between policy announcements and policy actions raised concerns about the credibility of monetary policy. If policy becomes less credible, it becomes more difficult for the public to predict how policymakers will react to certain economic events. This in turn raises the cost of trying to interpret policy, of trying to figure out just what the Federal Reserve is up to and how its actions are going to affect the economy.

Economists have a term for this situation: **time inconsistency**. This notion was first applied to monetary policy by Finn Kydland and Edward Prescott (1977). Consider the following scenario: The Federal Reserve announces that it is going to follow a policy that allows it to achieve its publicly stated inflation target, say a rate of inflation equal to 4 percent. The policymakers first act in such a way to make this pronouncement credible. If individuals start to believe that monetary policy is in fact aimed at hitting the inflation goal, this gets factored into their decisions. One such decision is a firm's decision to hire workers and a worker's decision to take the job. Kydland and Prescott showed that if expectations of inflation are embedded in economic decisions, it is in the Federal Reserve's short-term interest to follow a policy that actually is more expansive than expected. Even if the economy is operating at full employment, this policy creates a surge in economic activity and produces a decrease in the unemployment rate. Over time, however, the unemployment rate returns to its full-employment level and the rate of inflation rises to a permanently higher level. Unfortunately for policymakers, however, once the public catches on, future policy announcements become less credible and the ability of the Federal Reserve to affect economic activity, even in the short run, is jeopardized. Kydland and Prescott's insight was to show that even though such a policy may allow the Federal Reserve to achieve short-term gains in lowering the unemployment rate, it costs them in the long run. Not only will inflation be higher, but the credibility of future policy announcements is weakened.

How do monetary policymakers achieve a credible policy? One way is to behave in a consistent manner. With respect to policy's ultimate objectives, this may mean following some rule wherein the public knows how the Federal Reserve, or any central bank for that matter, will behave under certain conditions. For example, even with predetermined **inflation targeting** stated, a policy rule may allow the central bank to undertake policies that focus on curtailing short-term economic downturns. Even though a low and stable inflation rate may be the central bank's long-term goal, it may decide not to sit idly by while the economy suffers a recession. Quick policy responses to negative economic events, such as **recessions**, may be perceived by the public as a rational response to economic events, and one that does not push the central bank too far from its stated policy objectives. If this is the case, then the policy is not time-inconsistent.

Another approach is to increase the **transparency** of monetary policy. Over the years, policymakers have become more forthcoming about how policy decisions are made. They also now release their policy decisions on a timely basis. For example, today the **Federal Open Market Committee (FOMC)** meets about eight times a year and releases to the public its policy decisions immediately after each meeting. In the past, the release of such information did not occur until following the next meeting, if then.

Other central banks also have sought to increase the transparency of their policies as a means to improve the credibility of their decisions. In Canada, for example, the central bank issues the *Monetary Policy Report* several times a year to provide information about current policy and the economic conditions affecting policy decisions. The Bank of Canada also announced in the mid-1990s that it would focus on the overnight interest rate (like the **federal funds rate**) as its operating target. To clarify the use of this rate, the bank establishes and announces a range of acceptable levels for this rate.

Other banks have undertaken policies that strengthen their resolve to be more credible. New Zealand's Reserve Bank Act of 1989 specifies that it is the policy objective of its central bank to "achieving and maintaining stability in the general level of prices." Stated somewhat differently, the central bank of New Zealand has an inflation target that drives its policy actions. Such an inflation target also is at the core of policy decisions of the

European Central Bank. Interestingly, the Federal Reserve of the United States has refused to adopt an explicit inflation target.

Achieving a credible policy may depend on the structure of the central bank. In the United States, the Federal Reserve is considerably more "independent" of the government than in some other countries. When the FOMC makes decisions, they do not make them as part of a government body, as would a decision from the U.S. Treasury Department. In the United States, monetary policy is largely divorced from the political arena. In other countries, this usually is not the case. In some countries the central bank is part of the government, in the sense that bank decisions are made in concert with other government bodies. While this may make monetary policymakers more accountable for their actions— bad policy decisions could lead to being removed from one's position at the central bank— it also may hamstring policymakers from making tough decisions that are more long term in nature. Because a politician's planning horizon arguably is related to the election cycle, some have argued that giving elected officials a greater say in the conduct of monetary policy may induce **political business cycles**, where expansionary policies are followed prior to the election with contractionary policies followed soon thereafter.

FURTHER READING

Chang, Roberto. "Policy Credibility and the Design of Central Banks." Federal Reserve Bank of Atlanta *Economic Review* (First Quarter 1998): 4–15; Kydland, Finn, and Edward Prescott, "Rules Rather than Discretion: The Inconsistency of Optimal Plans." *Journal of Political Economy* (June 1977): 473–92; Perrier, Patrick, and Robert Amano. "Credibility and Monetary Policy." Bank of Canada *Review* (Spring 2000): 11–17.

POLICY INEFFECTIVENESS PROPOSITION (*See* **Rational Expectations**)

POLICY TRANSMISSION MECHANISM. This refers to the "channels" through which a change in monetary policy works its way through the economy. For example, the transmission of policy actions to the economy can occur when the Federal Reserve changes the amount of **reserves** in the banking system which in turn affects interest rates and the relative prices of real goods and their portfolio of financial assets. Due to these price changes, individuals in the economy alter their holdings of goods and financial assets, bringing about changes in production and income.

It is common to think of the transmission of policy as first influencing interest rates and in turn setting into motion a series of portfolio adjustments, both of real goods and financial assets. Ahktar (1997, p. 22) describes the impact of a policy of tightening—raising interest rates—as setting into motion a series of reactions:

> Sustained increases in short-term interest rates lead to lower growth of deposits and money as well as higher long-term interest rates. Higher interest rates raise the cost of funds, and, over time, have adverse consequences for business investment demand, home buying and consumer spending on durable goods, other things remaining the same. This is the conventional money or interest rate channel of monetary policy influence on the economy.

In general, economists agree that monetary policy actions affect the economy largely through interest rates and prices. What they do not agree on is the relative importance of these different channels. For those who believe that the main thrust of policy actions is through interest rates, the natural implication is for policy to manipulate interest rates in order to achieve a desired policy outcome. For those who believe that policy actions are transmitted through interest rates and other prices as well, controlling interest rates is a less clear-cut policy option.

FURTHER READING

Ahktar, M. A. *Understanding Open Market Operations.* New York: Federal Reserve Bank of New York, 1997; Bernanke, Ben, and Mark Gertler. "Inside the Black Box: The Credit Channel of Monetary Policy Transmission." *Journal of Economic Perspectives* (Fall 1995): 27–48; Taylor, John B. "The Monetary Transmission Mechanism: An Empirical Framework." *Journal of Economic Perspectives* (Fall 1995): 11–26.

POLITICAL BUSINESS CYCLE. Since the early 1970s, economists and political scientists have theorized about and tested for regularities in policy actions that may produce desired economic outcomes that coincide with election cycles. The idea of a political business cycle is that the government, perhaps with the assistance of the central bank, behaves in a manner that helps to increase economic prosperity in the period leading up to an election. Once in office or once returned to office, the government undertakes policies to cool economic activity down, hence raising the possibility of a **recession** or increases in the **unemployment rate**. On the monetary side, the argument would be that the Federal Reserve lowers interest rates (increase the growth rate of the money supply) prior to an election and then raises them (lowers the growth rate of the money supply) once the election is over.

There is a large literature on this topic, even though the weight of the evidence does not seem to support the generality of the claim. Aside from the case of Richard Nixon's 1972 run for reelection, there is little evidence of a political business cycle in the United States. Even so, it is instructive to briefly discuss the notion.

Although there had been a few studies done in the early 1970s looking at economic determinants of voting in congressional races, William Nordhaus (1975) is an example of formally modeling the political business cycle. Nordhaus's model recognizes that monetary policy could be a dominant force in manipulating economic activity to achieve some political goal. In this early model it was believed that the Federal Reserve could achieve these goals because voters were basically backwards looking creatures. That is, how one voted in his model was a function of past performance of the incumbent and past inflation. Since **inflation**, according to the model, would be lowered in the period running up to the election (and voters' memories are short), the Federal Reserve could assist incumbents in getting re-elected. As Drazen (2000, p. 7) puts it in his review, "The levels of monetary expansion and economic activity are those which maximize voter satisfaction in an election period alone. In the period immediately after the election, the government reverses course." After the election, the incumbent attempts to keep expected inflation low until the next election and then pursues another round of expansionary monetary policy. Hence the notion of a business cycle that is timed with the political cycle.

Does this view of how monetary policy is set conform to reality? The Federal Reserve is largely independent of the political process when it comes to setting monetary policy: A president does not exercise much power over monetary policy. While Federal Reserve policymakers are not totally devoid of being influenced by the administration or members of Congress, there is no direct mechanism that permits incumbents to pull the levers that can switch monetary policy from fast to slow to achieve political goals.

Another problem with this theory is that it presumes that voters are myopic or one-dimensional. In the early models, voters' decisions were modeled as affected only by the behavior of inflation relative to their expectations formed by looking backward: whatever inflation was in the past is what the model presumes voters think it will be in the future. More recent modeling of economic behavior suggests that rational individuals will take into account the behavior of past inflation when forming their expectations of the future, and that they also will consider other, more forward-looking information. In some economic models, for example, individuals form expectations based on the expected behavior of the monetary authority. (*See* **Rational Expectations**.) Because it is in everyone's best interest to figure out what causes inflation, if the Federal Reserve undertook expansionary policy actions in order to boost an incumbent's chances for reelection, the voters would see through the ploy and know that higher inflation—and a reversal of policy—would come after the election. This foresight might lead them not to reelect the incumbent.

While the foregoing may suggest that the political business cycle probably does not hold in the United States, in other countries, where the ties between different parts of the government are much closer, there is some evidence that government policies do change before and after elections. As surveyed in Drazen (2000), there is evidence that government policies, especially fiscal policies, have been more expansionary prior to than after national elections. There is evidence for such a relation in Israel, Turkey, various Latin American countries, India, and sub-Saharan Africa. In these countries, the evidence is more persuasive that it is fiscal policy changes being used to affect electoral decisions and not monetary policy. Indeed, it may be that the political business cycle cannot explain the behavior of monetary policymakers, but it does explain the decisions by politicians to raise or lower taxes or increase or decrease government spending.

FURTHER READING

Alesina, Alberto. " Macroeconomics and Politics," in *NBER Macroeconomics Annual*. Cambridge, MA: MIT Press, 1988; Drazen, Allan. "The Political Business Cycle after 25 Years." Unpublished paper, University of Maryland (May 2000); Nordhaus, William. "The Political Business Cycle." *Review of Economic Studies* (1975): 169–90.

PRICE INDEX. It is well established that monetary policy actions affect the behavior of prices over time. Even though the Federal Reserve may not be able to make economic output grow at a rate faster than its long-run potential, there is no upper limit on how fast prices can rise. In the final analysis, it is monetary policy actions that determine the rate of **inflation** in the long run.

In order to understand the link between monetary policy and inflation, it is important to consider the price index. Why? Because the way Federal Reserve economists and policymakers, or any other economist for that matter, measure inflation is by calculating the percentage change in some *price index* over time. By knowing what a price index is and what its weakness are, we have a better basis to see how the Federal Reserve uses price indexes and how it interprets movements in them to set policy.

To illustrate what a price index is, it is easiest to use the Consumer Price Index (CPI). The CPI measures the average change in prices paid by consumers for a given basket of goods and services. Because the CPI tells us about price *changes*, it measures prices over time. But simply knowing that prices change, some going up others going down, over time is not very informative. To make this information useful, the Bureau of Labor Statistics, the compiler of the CPI data, established a reference year to which all other prices are compared. This reference year, known as the *base year*, allows you to tell how much prices have changed over time. For example, in early 2004 the CPI was about 185. (Note that the CPI is expressed in hundreds, denoting the fact that an index number is really measured in percent terms.) Currently, the base year used by the BLS is an average of prices in 1982, 1983, and 1984, expressed as 1982–1984 = 100. A 2004 value of 185 means that, for the basket of goods included, it now costs 185 percent of the price paid in 1982–1984. That is, if a candy bar cost $1 in 1982–1984, in 2004 it cost $1.85. Stated in terms of percentage change—inflation—the price of the candy bar rose 85 percent over the past 20 years.

A useful aspect of a CPI-type of index is that it measures price changes by holding constant quantities purchased. For example, to simplify the calculation, think of the basket of goods and services as including pizza and hair cuts. Let's suppose that in 1983 you bought 10 pizzas and got 5 haircuts. What the CPI calculates is how much that same basket—those 10 pizzas and 5 haircuts—costs in other years as well. If you paid $75 for pizza and haircuts in 1983 and $93 for the same goods (and amounts) in 2004, the CPI in 2004 would be 124 (= 93/75). Notice that what this approach does is to give one a measure of pure price change without confusing the issue by mixing together price and quantity changes. By keeping quantities fixed we know that observed changes in the index measure price changes alone.

Because the Federal Reserve pays very close attention to the inflation rate, which again is measured as the percentage change in a price index, it also is important to realize that any price index is not perfect. Consider the effect of quality changes. Suppose that in 2004 you got better haircuts, so much better that you didn't get your hair cut as often. Suppose also that they were cheaper in 2004. But because the CPI uses base year quantities, it assumes that you'll still consume just as many haircuts as before. When measuring your total expenditures on pizza and haircuts in 2004, it may only add up to $85, or a CPI of 113. Because the price fell *and* the quality improved, you actually are much better off economically in 2004 than in the earlier year. So, does the inflation rate of 13 percent really reflect only price changes? No, because it cannot capture quality improvements.

The best good with which to illustrate this effect is the computer. Over time computers have done two things: they have become faster and they have become cheaper. In an economic sense, the real price of a computer has fallen sharply. There are a number of other areas where quality improvements and price changes are linked. New cars, for example, have many new features that did not even exist a few years back. Electronic equipment, from MP3 players to Palm Pilots, are items that were not around in the base year. How does the BLS account for them in the CPI? Such developments require the BLS to undertake periodic surveys to determine which items to include and exclude from their price indexes. While MP3s may get in, surely changes in the price of horseshoes have little effect on over all spending, at least much less than they once did.

These and other issues surrounding the use and interpretation of the CPI have led monetary policymakers to question the use of policy rules that focus solely on rates of inflation or price levels. A policy rule that mandates the Federal Reserve to keep the inflation rate within a narrow band is likely to fail, simply because there are many forces acting upon a price index that, aside from any monetary affect, may cause the index to rise or fall. (*See* **Inflation Targeting**.) For example, during the mid-1970s the price of crude oil doubled. This rippled through the economy and caused the CPI inflation rate to rocket into double-digit territory. In an inflation target environment, this increase in inflation, even though it was not caused by a change in monetary policy, would have necessitated a sharp reversal in the growth rate of the money supply. In fact, that is partly what the Federal Reserve did in response to the increased rate of inflation.

Unfortunately, it was the wrong thing to do. If an inflation rule is used to keep the *general level* of prices from rising too fast, then reacting to an increase in the price index that is caused by an increase in only one of its components, in this case, oil and petroleum prices, is detrimental. In the abstract, undertaking a contractionary monetary policy in such an environment is more likely to cause economic activity to slow than it is to cause inflation to drop. This is why the Federal Reserve, while maintaining that keeping inflation low on average, has never adopted the kind of inflation targets or objectives used by other central banks, such as the Bank of England or the Central Bank of New Zealand.

FURTHER READING

Federal Reserve Bank of St. Louis. *Inflation Targeting: Prospects and Problems*. 28th Annual Economic Policy Conference. Website: http://research.stlouisfed.org/conferences; U.S. Department of Labor, Bureau of Labor Statistics. Website: http://www.blas.gov/cpi.

PRICE STABILITY. In many entries in this volume we have made the point that the Federal Reserve's long-term policy objective should be the reduction of **inflation**. If monetary policy cannot, in the long run, affect the level of output in the economy— putting more money into the economy does not make machines produce more goods— then it must focus on the behavior of the price level. This notion has taken two paths in recent debates. One is that the Federal Reserve should act in such a way as to reduce the overall rate of inflation. Indeed, during the late 1970s and early 1980s, when inflation was in the double-digit range, this was the mantra of most policy critics. And it was the policy objective that led Chairman of the Federal Reserve **Paul Volcker** to institute policy changes that put much more emphasis on reducing inflation. Even though the short-term cost was a deep **recession**, the rate of inflation has trended downward and been relatively low ever since. In 2004, the rate of inflation was about 2.5 percent, well below the 12 percent rate of inflation that existed in 1980.

The other path in the discussion focuses on price stability. It may seem semantic, but price stability and low inflation are not the same. When the inflation rate is *low*, prices are still rising, albeit at a slower rate. Still, if the inflation rate is, say, 3 percent, the price level will double in 24 years. That is not price stability. Price stability can be interpreted as *no change* in prices: In other words, a zero rate of inflation on average. While no one believes that the Federal Reserve can achieve a zero rate of inflation at all times, some have argued that a zero average rate of inflation, sometimes a bit above zero, sometimes a bit below zero, could be the policy objective of the central bank.

One argument for price stability is that knowing what prices are likely to be in the future lowers uncertainty and makes planning easier and less costly. Knowing how much goods and services will cost in the future makes saving for the future easier. Another argument for price stability is that a stable price environment allows the price system to function more smoothly. When prices are unstable, the signals being sent by the price system get distorted. When prices are moving all over the place, it becomes difficult to distinguish between relative price changes—one good's price changing with respect to another's—and an overall price increase where all the prices of all goods are rising or falling. Because it is relative price changes that direct resources in the economy, upsetting this process can have consequences to the economy.

This breakdown of the price system's signaling function also can happen when all prices are rising at a very rapid pace. During periods of *hyperinflation*, when inflation rates are running in the hundreds of percent, prices become almost meaningless. The cost of trying to predict what prices will be in the future, something that wage earners try to figure out when negotiating new contracts, becomes a daunting task.

Price stability, usually thought of as maintaining a very low (though nonzero) rate of inflation over time, serves to reduce this noise-to-signal ratio in the price system. An analogy might help. When you tune your radio, there are markers to help find a station's frequency. With a strong signal, the music of your favorite group comes out loud and clear. But move the tuner around and what do you get? Static and the occasional bit of music. When the tuner is faulty, the noise (static) rises relative to the signal (music). Trying to achieve price stability is a lot like trying to keep your radio tuned. You can enjoy the music and do not have to divert your attention from more important activities, like driving down the highway.

Is there any downside to pursuing a policy of price stability? Perhaps. Suppose the Federal Reserve announces that it will undertake policies to keep the price level, measured by the Consumer Price Index (CPI), at its current value. In December 2003, that value was 185. In the strictest sense, if the price of lettuce increased in February 2004 because of a bad freeze in lettuce-producing states, the Federal Reserve would have to act. The reduction in the availability of lettuce would drive its market price upward and, because lettuce is one of the goods included in the CPI, the CPI would increase. Unless there was an offsetting price reduction somewhere else in the economy, the price level would increase and the directive of price stability would be violated. In this situation, the Federal Reserve would undertake restrictive policy actions, reducing the growth rate of the money supply or raising interest rates. But would this make sense? What would be the consequences?

The answer to the first question is no. Prices in an economy change all the time, some are rising and others are falling. Trying to fashion a coherent and predictable monetary policy around the vagaries of market price movements likely would plunge the Federal Reserve into destabilizing policy actions. A good monetary policy is not one that changes direction from month-to-month. The consequences of such a policy would be that individuals in the economy would not be able to decipher Federal Reserve actions or to predict what they would be in the future. This could lead to economic instability. In the end, most economists favor a monetary policy that aims at stabilizing the rate of inflation at a low level to one that tries to maintain a zero rate of inflation.

FURTHER READING

Svensson, Lars E. O. "How Should Monetary Policy Be Conducted in an Era of Price Stability?" In Federal Reserve Bank of Kansas City *New Challenges for Monetary Policy,* 1999; Walsh, Carl E.

"Should Central Banks Stabilize Prices?" Federal Reserve Bank of San Francisco *Economic Letter* (August 11, 2000).

PRIMARY DEALER. When the **Federal Open Market Committee (FOMC)**, the policymaking group of the Federal Reserve, wishes to undertake actions to raise or lower interest rates or change the growth rate of the money supply, their desires are transmitted to the Open Market **Trading Desk**, located at the Federal Reserve Bank of New York. Individuals at "the Desk," under the supervision of the Manager of Domestic Open Market Operations, bring about the FOMC's desired policies by buying and selling government securities (*see* **Open Market Operations**) through a group of government securities dealers, known as *primary dealers*. These primary dealers with whom the Desk deals are large securities firms or large commercial banks.

How does a firm become a primary dealer? Primary dealers are chosen by officials at the Federal Reserve Bank of New York after consultation with other regulatory agencies, the Securities and Exchange Commission when the applicant is a broker-dealer, or federal bank supervisors when the applicant is a commercial bank. In each case, an applicant must meet specific capital standards. When the applicant is a bank or a securities firm, it must meet minimum capital adequacy standards to ensure that the dealers can handle securities transactions of a size that is necessary for Federal Reserve policy actions. This means that the primary dealers are large enough to participate in the Federal Reserve's open market sales and purchases. In March 2002, for example, primary dealers accounted for an average trading volume of $375 billion *per day*. (The Federal Reserve Bank of New York publishes a weekly report, called the Primary Dealer Transactions, which reports the trading volume.) Primary dealers also are large enough to supply the Desk with information that is helpful in determining the appropriate policy action. Every day the staff at the Desk contacts some of the primary dealers to get their views on conditions in the financial markets and any changes that the dealers expect.

The list of primary dealers changes over time, but not too often. The Federal Reserve Bank of New York reviews the role of each primary dealer and assesses the viability of the dealer in this capacity. Dealers must meet capital adequacy requirements as mentioned above but also must demonstrate that they are active and significant trading partners with the Federal Reserve. Failure to satisfy the minimum performance standards results in a dealer being removed from the list of active traders.

There have been some changes made in the relationship between the Federal Reserve Bank of New York and the primary dealers. Beginning in the early 1990s, one of these changes eliminated a standard trading volume with customers. The Federal Reserve Bank of New York also disbanded its dealer surveillance unit, since it does not have regulatory authority over the dealers. In its place, the New York Bank instituted a market surveillance procedure that works with individuals from other regulatory agencies, including the Federal Reserve **Board of Governors**, the Securities and Exchange Commission, the U.S. Treasury, and the Commodity Futures Trading Commission.

As of February 2004 there were 23 primary dealers. Below is an alphabetical listing of the dealers who report to the Government Securities Dealers Statistics Unit of the Federal Reserve Bank of New York:

Primary Government Securities Dealers*

ABN AMRO Bank, N.V., New York Branch
BNP Paribas Securities Corp.
Banc of America Securities LLC
Banc One Capital Markets, Inc.
Barclays Capital Inc.
Bear, Stearns & Co., Inc.
CIBC World Markets Corp.
Citigroup Global Markets Inc.
Countrywide Securities Corporation
Credit Suisse First Boston LLC
Daiwa Securities America Inc.
Deutsche Bank Securities Inc.
Dresdner Kleinwort Wasserstein Securities LLC
Goldman, Sachs & Co.
Greenwich Capital Markets, Inc.
HSBC Securities (USA) Inc.
J. P. Morgan Securities, Inc.
Lehman Brothers Inc.
Merrill Lynch Government Securities Inc.
Mizuho Securities USA Inc.
Morgan Stanley & Co. Incorporated
Nomura Securities International, Inc.
UBS Securities LLC

Source: Federal Reserve Bank of New York,
February 2004.

Details of the change in administrative relations between the Federal Reserve Bank of New York and the dealers is provided in the Bank's memorandum of January 22, 1992, accessible at www.newyorkfed.org/markets/pridealers_policies.html.

FURTHER READING

Federal Reserve Bank of New York. "Primary Dealers Defined." *Fedpoint* (April 2002). Website: www.newyorkfed.org.

PRIME LOAN RATE. The prime loan rate, or simply the prime rate, is the interest rate that banks charge their favored corporate customers. Today the prime rate plays a much less important role than in the past, acting more as a signal or indicator of what the cost of business borrowing is than a firm rate charged to customers. The prime rate represents what a bank would charge a large, relatively low-risk customer. In reality, however, for many banks and businesses, the stated prime rate represents the beginning rate from which loan rates are negotiated. The prime rate also is used by banks to establish borrowing costs for other customers. For example, some loans may be stated as "prime plus," which is the prime rate plus some predetermined markup, such as 3 percentage points. So, if the prime rate is 7 percent and the markup is 3 percent, the loan rate would be 10 percent. Because of the prime's use in different lending situations, the prime rate is watched as a general barometer of borrowing costs.

Bank Prime Loan Rate

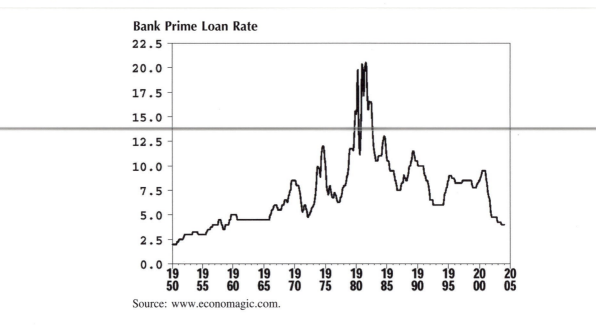

Source: www.economagic.com.

The prime rate, shown in the figure above from 1950 to early 2004, generally moves with other market rates, especially the three-month **Treasury bill** rate and the **federal funds rate**. This is because the prime rate reflects not only the cost to customers of borrowing from banks but also, in turn, the cost to banks of obtaining funds to lend out. If market rates of interest are rising, then the cost to banks of acquiring funds also is rising and banks pass this increase along to borrowers. How much of the bank's additional cost is passed on depends on the borrower's ability to negotiate a lower rate.

PRINCIPAL-AGENT PROBLEM. The principal-agent problem arises when owners (the principals) do not have the economic incentive or are unable to effectively monitor the managers (the agents). Although the problem can easily be generalized to many situations, it often times is discussed in the context of stockholders (the principals) who are unable to monitor the actions of the firm's managers (agents). For example, most stockholders probably do not even know who the management team is of the firms in which they own stock. Moreover, when the time arises for them to vote on the success or failure of management, usually through the annual stockholders' meeting, most stockholders simply defer that decision to others through proxy votes. While this often is an economically efficient route—most stockholders free-ride off the concerns and information-gathering activities of others who closely monitor the activities of company managers and resulting changes in the price of the stock—it can lead to significant losses. The collapse of Enron and the financial shenanigans of WorldCom during the early 2000s are two glaring examples of how the principal-agent problem can lead to serious problems.

In the context of the Federal Reserve, the principal-agent problem creates problems for bank and financial institution regulators. Mishkin's (2004) discussion makes clear that the principal-agent problem arises when the public (the principals) assumes that regulators (the agents) are acting in their—the public's—best interests. That is, we all assume that regulators act to quickly close problem banks or to make sure that managers of banks showing signs of trouble are warned or removed. But, as in the case of a manager who is not under the direct oversight of a stockholder, regulators operate with great freedom in making such decisions.

To illustrate the potential problem, consider the hypothetical situation of an auditor working for the Federal Reserve or the **Comptroller of the Currency**. Her job is to make sure that banks are operating in as safe a manor as possible. If the bank is not, then actions should be taken to replace existing management or at least change the bank's borrowing and lending activities.

Since the auditors are not under the scrutiny of the public, what is her incentive to behave in this manner? To be sure, most do their jobs quite diligently. But what if the auditor sees employment in banking as her future? Would this individual be more likely to look aside while a bank in trouble either attempts to correct the problems or just continues with their questionable practices? At what time does **regulatory forbearance** end and enforcing regulations "by the book" take over? In some cases, such forbearance can create widespread problems. Mishkin (2004) argues that the regulatory changes brought about in the early 1980s made it easier for savings and loans (S&Ls) to operate in a manner that increased the potential for failure. Because Congress reduced the funding for S&L regulatory staff at the same time, the large number of S&L failures across the nation imposed a huge cost on taxpayers from promoting regulatory forbearance in the name of some political goal. In the case of the **savings and loan crisis**, the failure of the taxpayers' agents to protect them from the risky behavior by some S&L managers is a costly example of the principal-agent problem.

FURTHER READING

Mishkin, Frederic S. *The Economics of Money, Banking, and Financial Markets*. 7th edition. Boston: Pearson Addison Wesley, 2004.

PURCHASING POWER OF MONEY. Sometimes you hear people say something like "a dollar just isn't worth what it used to be." Those who say this always seem to be your folks' friends, the ones who tell you stories of 25-cent Cokes, going to the movies for a couple of bucks, and paying 50 cents for a gallon of gasoline. Put another way, "Why has the purchasing power of a dollar fallen over time?" We can answer this question by first thinking about what **money** is and why its purchasing power changes over time. Then we can think about what the link is between money and prices and the Federal Reserve.

What is the price of money? Be careful: If you answered the question by saying it is the rate of interest, you'd be wrong. Credit—a **loan** for simplicity—is you borrowing from your future income to spend now. The price of credit is the interest rate that the bank, the loan shark, or your friend charges you for the use of their money. The interest rate reflects their decision about how trustworthy you are and about what they think goods will cost in the future. As discussed elsewhere, the **nominal rate of interest**—the loan rate—incorporates the lender's expectation of how fast they think prices may increase over the life of the loan. The higher the expected rate of **inflation**, the higher is the rate of interest they charge on a loan. Why? Because when you pay off the loan, the lender wants to be able to buy just as many goods as when they made the loan. In other words, they want to maintain purchasing power.

If the interest rate is not the price of money, what is? This may seem a bit circular, but the price of money is what money can buy. Suppose a can of Coke costs $1.00. You'd say that the price of a can of Coke is a dollar. What is the price of the dollar? The answer is a can of Coke. The dollar and the can of Coke exchange for each other; so the price of one is stated relative to the other. Because we live in an economy with millions of goods, measuring the price of money by calculating each and every relative price in this fashion would be a colossal exercise in futility. Instead, economists measure the price of money—its purchasing power—by using a **price index**.

One such price index is the Consumer Price Index (CPI). The CPI includes thousands of goods. Each month the Bureau of Labor Statistics (BLS) in Washington, D.C., conducts a survey of prices for a large number of goods and services and measures whether they have changed over the course of the month. When all of this information is collected, the BLS publishes its monthly CPI number. For instance, the CPI for December 2003 is 185.0. (Because it is an index, it is stated in hundreds.) This number means that compared with some base period (when the CPI = 100), in this case the span between 1982 and 1984, prices for all of the goods in the CPI are, on average, 185% higher than they were 20 years ago. Stated another way, if a candy bar cost $1 in 1983, in December 2003 the same candy bar cost $1.85. As you can see, the purchasing power of a dollar— what it can buy—has fallen over the past two decades. In this example, a dollar in December 2003 buys the same as 54 cents (= 100/185) did in the early 1980s.

The figure below plots the inverse of the CPI (100/CPI) for the period 1920 up to 2004. This is one measure of the purchasing power of a dollar, as just discussed. Because this series uses historic data, for this exercise the base year is 1967 when the CPI is set equal to 100. As you can see, the purchasing power of a dollar prior to 1967 was greater and less thereafter. This means that since 1967 inflation—the rate of increase in prices—has been positive. As the CPI increases over time, the ability of a dollar to buy the same amount of goods diminishes: its purchasing power falls. The figure also shows that the purchasing power of money did not always decline. This is most noticeable is in the period

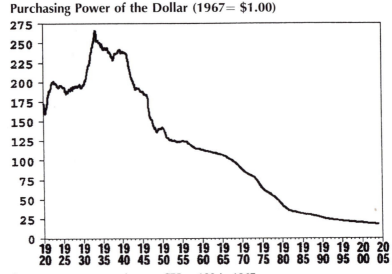

Purchasing Power of the Dollar (1967= $1.00)

Source: www.economagic.com. CPI = 100 in 1967.

from 1930 to about 1935—the **Great Depression**. During this time the purchasing power of money actually *increased*. This increase was caused by a fall in prices, sometimes referred to as **deflation**. While this may seem preferable to inflation, it actually is not. During this time of deflation, not only did prices fall, but so did income, a combination that led to massive unemployment and economic hardship.

If rising prices reduce money's purchasing power, what causes prices to increase? The answer is how rapidly the money supply is increasing. Think of it: If I give you more money, what do you do with it? The most likely answer is "spend it." You and everyone else get more money, go out and spend it and ... ? That's right, prices increase as people compete for a limited number of goods. As more and more money is put into circulation, its purchasing power is diminished. An increase in the supply of money lowers its value in exchange. Increasing the money supply, then, is likely to lower its purchasing power.

This is where the Federal Reserve comes in. In essence, the Federal Reserve controls the growth of the money supply in the United States. It's not like it can turn a spigot on and off and to get more or less money in the next few days. But Federal Reserve policy actions over time determine the growth rate of the money supply. Since it is the Federal Reserve (or any central bank in other countries) that ultimately determines how much money there is in the economy, they are the ultimate source of reductions in the purchasing power of money. So what explains the decline in the purchasing power of money during the past 50 years? The answer is Federal Reserve policy that increased the amount of money in the economy.

FURTHER READING

Fisher, Irving. *The Purchasing Power of Money: Its Determination and Relation to Credit, Interest and Crises*. New York: Macmillan, 1911; *How Much Is That Worth Today?* Website at www.eh.net/ehrresources/howmuch/dollarq.php.

QUANTITY THEORY. One of the most enduring monetary theories is the quantity theory of money. The quantity theory is described by the simple equation: $MV = PQ$. In this equation M represents the *money stock*, P is the price level (*see* **Price Index**), Q stands for total output of the economy, and V is velocity. This latter term is the linchpin to the economic relationship embodied in the quantity theory. Rearranging the equation reveals that velocity is measured as the ratio of the money stock (M) to the dollar value of output in the economy (PQ), or $V = PQ/M$. The **velocity of money** thus measures the "speed" with which a single dollar circulates through an economy. The higher is velocity, the faster a dollar circulates to support trade, which in turn creates income. An increase in velocity means money is being exchanged at a faster rate.

Early uses of the quantity theory focused on the link between movements in the money stock and the price level. Notable in this regard is the work of David Hume, an economist writing in the 1700s. Hume noticed that increases in the supply of money, then due to increased inflows of gold and silver from foreign explorations, were associated with subsequent increases in the prices of goods. If output (Q) and velocity (V) are stable over time, then the quantity theory predicts that changes in the money stock (M) will be directly reflected in changes in the price level (P).

The quantity theory took its modern form in the writings of **Irving Fisher** during the early 1900s. Fisher used the quantity theory to explain movements in the price level and observed swings from boom to bust in economic activity. (*See* **Business Cycles**.) Fisher believed that changes in the money supply are a major factor explaining whether the economy is growing rapidly or is in a **recession**. Even though he recognized that there were other sources of "shocks" that might explain changes in the pace of economic activity, he gave movements in the supply of money center stage.

The quantity theory continues to provide an important anchor to modern discussions of how monetary policy affects the economy. A number of studies show that sharp swings in the growth rate of the money supply often lead to similar swings in economic activity. This observation led many economists, notably **Milton Friedman**, to argue for monetary policies that produce a steady growth rate of the money supply. Many of these studies also show that, over time, changes in the rate of inflation are related directly to changes in the growth rate of the money supply. In countries where the money supply is increasing at a much faster rate than the economy is producing goods and services, it generally is the case that the inflation rate also is increasing. These findings suggest that the Federal Reserve or any other central bank must be concerned about the growth rate of the money supply in setting its policies.

For additional information, see the related entries **Equation of Exchange**, **Monetarism,** and the references cited.

FURTHER READING

Dwyer, Gerald P., Jr., and R. W. Hafer. "Are Money Growth and Inflation Still Related?" Federal Reserve Bank of Atlanta *Economic Review* (Second Quarter 1999): 32–43; Hafer, R. W. "What Remains of Monetarism?" Federal Reserve Bank of Atlanta *Economic Review* (Fourth Quarter 2001): 13–33.

RANDOM WALK. The notion of a random walk and its implications for financial markets is nowhere better described than in Burton G. Malkiel's classic book *A Random Walk Down Wall Street*. Malkiel describes a random walk in the following manner:

> A random walk is one in which future steps or directions cannot be predicted on the basis of past actions. When the term is applied to the stock market, it means that short-run changes in stock prices cannot be predicted. Investment advisory services, earnings predictions, and complicated chart patterns are useless. (p. 24)

Does Malkiel mean that investing in the stock market is as predictable as throwing darts at the stock page of a newspaper? Almost, but not quite. Notice that the definition of a random walk very clearly refers to *changes* in stock prices not their level. This distinction is critical to understand the notion of a random walk. In the chart below, the monthly open quote of the Dow Jones Industrial Average is plotted along with the percentage change of those opening quotes. The former is the level of the Dow Jones, the latter is its change. Note that the level is more predictable than the change: The level rises over most of the period shown, takes a turn south in late 1999, falls until 2003, and has since started to rise again. Could one come up with a model that explains this increase over time? This may be where investment advisors earn their money, recognizing changes in the economy or in technologies that may pay long-run dividends to someone who invests in that industry.

The percentage change in the Dow is the jagged line. You can see that it is much more volatile, shifting between positive and negative at almost every observation. Indeed, the percentage change varies between positive and negative 150 percent! This illustrates the idea that when someone asks what the closing value of the Dow will be tomorrow—what will be the change in the Dow—the best answer may just be whatever today's close is.

Let's put some meat on the idea of a random walk. Suppose I want to describe the behavior of stock prices mathematically. (Don't worry, it isn't very hard.) I can do so using the following equation:

$$SP_{\text{today}} = SP_{\text{yesterday}} + \text{noise}.$$

In words, the level of stock prices today (SP_{today}) is equal to the level of stock prices yesterday ($SP_{\text{yesterday}}$) plus some "noise." Noise is defined as the effect of random events that may increase or decrease stock prices on any given day. If you listen to the daily stock market wrap up, most of what passes for explanations of why the market rose or fell that

DJ Industrial Average Open

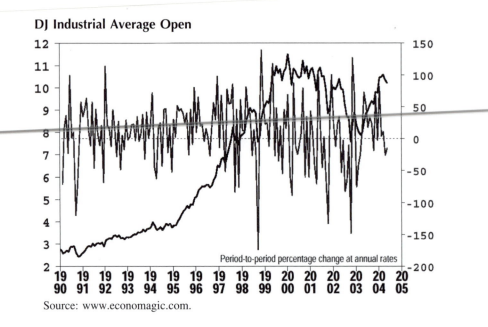

Source: www.economagic.com.

day is noise. For instance, commentators may suggest that changes in stock prices were due to investors getting spooked by the unemployment number or that the **Chairman of the Federal Reserve** today carried around a brief case more stuffed with papers than usual. So, day to day, this "model" isn't too bad of a predictor of stock prices. Not that it is always correct, just that it is, on average, better than any alternative.

To model a random walk, rewrite the preceding equation as:

$$SP_{today} - SP_{yesterday} = \text{noise}.$$

Now the equation says that the *change* in stock prices—measured as the differences between today's close and yesterday's—is just noise. That is, changes in stock prices are random events and therefore unpredictable over time. By the definition of random, this means that changes in stock prices are not predictable. This is what Malkiel means when he warns of financial advisors claiming that they can beat the market, especially over short time horizons: no one can consistently predict random events with much accuracy.

What does this have to do with the Federal Reserve and monetary policy? Stock prices reflect the underlying earnings of a firm. Some would suggest that those future earnings, stated in current dollar figures, determine the level and the direction of stock prices. For example, the fact that Amazon.com was not profitable during the first several years of its existence did not preclude its stock price from rising: investors were betting on the firm's future success, not its current growing pains. When the Federal Reserve enacts policies that affect expectations of **inflation** or future business activity, it impacts the stock market. Moreover, if monetary policy becomes less predictable or policymakers lose credibility, the uncertainty in the market—the "noise" in the equation above—becomes greater and the variability in stock prices increases. If stock prices become more volatile, investors switch to safer investments. If money is pulled from the stock market, this can have negative effects on the economy. If stock prices fall, people lose wealth and this may reduce their desire to spend on goods and services. If this effect is strong enough, a stock market decline may lead to a **recession**.

FURTHER READING

Fama, Eugene. "Efficient Capital Markets: A Review of Theory and Empirical Work." *Journal of Finance* (May 1970): 383–417; Malkiel, Burton G. *A Random Walk Down Wall Street*. New York: W.W. Norton & Company, 1990.

RATIONAL EXPECTATIONS. The idea of "rational expectations" is not a new one in economics, even though the modern version altered macroeconomic theory and the approach to policymaking. The role that expectations plays is an important one in most economic theories. **John Maynard Keynes**, who provided the foundation for modern macroeconomics in the 1930s, believed that individuals' expectations of the future helped explain **business cycles**. His notion of "animal spirits," by which he meant the changing expectations of businesses regarding future sales and profits, was part of his theory to model booms and busts in the economy. By the 1950s, economists adopted mathematical approaches to describing the process by which expectations are formed and tested the idea that expectations are based primarily on extrapolations of the past into the future. For example, if one wanted to generate a forecast of the rate of **inflation** for next year, one approach would be to simply take past rates of inflation, say over the past couple of years, add them together, and find the average. The average of the past rates of inflation could serve as a forecast of future rates.

One economist working in this field suggested that observed outcomes could depend on what was expected. That economist, John Muth of Indiana University, suggested in the early 1960s that, for example, agricultural output could be related to expectations by farmers of what future prices might be. If farmers expected prices for wheat to be higher by harvest time, they may plant more acres in wheat today. In this case, the higher *expected* price led to a greater future supply of wheat. This may seem like common sense, but the notion of rational expectations was to take a much more complicated and important turn following Muth's initial insights.

Robert Lucas, Jr., a Nobel Prize laureate in economics, took Muth's idea and extended it to monetary policy and the business cycle. Writing in the early 1970s, Lucas suggested that information flows through the economy with a lag. Using the analogy of separate islands, Lucas suggested that information reaches the islands—analogous to individuals or businesses in an economy—at different times. Some firms react immediately to the new information; others wait while they gather additional information. Using the basic economic principles that individuals act rationally—act in what they perceive to be their own best interests, given the information available at the time—Lucas suggested that rational expectations meant that information is gathered up to the point where the additional cost of gathering the information does not exceed the additional benefit from obtaining it. Think of this analogy: which weather forecast did you rely on when deciding whether to take an umbrella as you left your house in the morning? Is it the forecast heard on the radio as you walked out the door, or is it today's forecast that you remember from the newspaper five days ago? Given the questionable accuracy of five-day weather forecasts, you have learned over time not to put too much reliance in them. This is acting rationally. But the day's forecast provided in the morning has a much higher probability of being accurate, so that is the one you based your behavior on. What Lucas suggested was that information about weather forecasts reaches individuals with varying lags. Some people may only get the five-day forecast; others, the daily forecast. Even though one may be better than the other, the behavior of each individual is rational since they are acting on the basis of the set of information available to them. Even though the person using the five-day forecast may get wet, revealing that after the fact their forecast was wrong, at the time the forecast was made, it was the best available. Even though they get wet today, they have behaved rationally.

Can you have incorrect forecasts and still be rational? Yes. Rational expectations does not mean that forecasts are always correct. What rational expectations does mean, however, is that you will not knowingly repeat your mistake over and over. If you based your behavior on the five-day forecast and always get wet, it would not be rational to keep depending on that forecast. Rational expectations means that individuals change the information sets used to make decisions in order to minimize their losses (getting wet). If they see someone else who always seems to have an umbrella when it rains and leaves it at home when it is sunny, then it is rational to find out what information they use and adopt it.

What does this have to do with monetary policy? Quite a bit, actually. Suppose that you base your expectations of future inflation on past rates alone. You look back and see that inflation averaged 3 percent over the past several years. If you wish to make your friend a **loan**, then you might use this as the expected rate of inflation, to which you would add the costs of making the loan, etc., and come up with an interest rate on the loan of 5 percent. At the time when the loan is made, however, the Federal Reserve is engaging in behavior that is likely to raise the rate of inflation in the future. Since your expectations formation process does not use this information—what policymakers are up to—you ignore it. The cost of not using this information may be that in a year or two, the rate of inflation is no longer 3 percent but 6 percent. This means that that **money** you get back from the loan now is worth much less in terms of the **purchasing power of money**. The individual who used the information about the Federal Reserve's shift in monetary policy would have adjusted the interest rate on loans and not lost money. At the time the loan was made, both inflation forecasts were rational. After the fact, however, only one is based on the best approach. The next time, however, it is likely that the Federal Reserve's behavior is an additional piece of information that all lenders will incorporate into their expectations generation process.

How individuals incorporate changes in monetary policy into their expectations played a major role in the breakdown of **Phillips curve**–based policies of the 1960s and 1970s. This policy strategy was premised on the idea that policymakers could manipulate the rate of inflation and the **unemployment rate** to achieve some desired mix. That is, if policymakers wished to lower the unemployment rate, then they would take policy actions to spur economic activity, usually accompanied by an increase in the rate of inflation. Perhaps more importantly, they thought that this tradeoff was stable: whatever the relation was in 1965 is what it would be in the future.

In some sense, the idea was that policymakers could "trick" the public into acting in ways that were not in their own best interest. Suppose the Federal Reserve *announces* that its policies are aimed at keeping inflation at 3 percent, but the actions it takes are likely to push the rate of inflation higher. Would it be rational for individuals to think that the Federal Reserve is serious about its announced policy? Not if such expectations were wrong in the past. Rational expectations suggest that individuals should alter the information they use in forming expectations, basing them on outcomes, not on announced policies. This idea has been referred to as the "policy ineffectiveness proposition" and is associated with the work of Lucas, in addition to Robert Barro, Thomas Sargent, and Neil Wallace. Sargent (2002) says that, "If people have rational expectations, policies that try to manipulate the economy by inducing people into having false expectations may introduce more 'noise' into the economy but cannot, on average, improve the economy's performance."

This idea is perhaps one of the most lasting impacts of the rational expectations movement. Because it can be shown that attempting to manipulate the economy will fail—people simply figure out what the policies are and adapt their behavior accordingly—the best policy is one that does not deviate from its preannounced path. Policy **transparency** may deliver the best of economic outcomes: low inflation and economic growth that is not destabilized because of monetary policy actions. (*See also* **Efficient Markets Theory; Real Business Cycle Theory; Lucas, Robert, Jr.**)

FURTHER READING

Fischer, Stanley, ed. *Rational Expectations and Economic Policy*. Chicago: University of Chicago Press, 1980; Lucas, Robert E., Jr. "Econometric Policy Evaluation: A Critique." In Brunner and Meltzer, eds, *Carnegie-Rochester Conference Series in Public Policy* (Vol 1: 1976); Lucas, Robert E., Jr. *Studies in Business Cycle Theory*. Cambridge, MA: MIT Press, 1981; Muth, John. "Rational Expectations and the Theory of Price Movements." *Econometrica* (No. 6, 1961): 315–35.

REAL BILLS DOCTRINE. It often times is argued that the Federal Reserve's main policy objective should be to maintain full employment. This policy goal could be achieved by trying to keep interest rates low in order to encourage investment spending by businesses, which would in turn lead to increased economic activity. This notion of keeping borrowing rates low and encouraging investment to keep employment at its maximum that originates with the *real bills doctrine*. In its original form—the basic idea has been around for over 100 years—the real bills doctrine argued that monetary policy should not focus on the growth of the money supply or any specific level for interest rates. Rather, the real bills doctrine is premised on the belief that monetary policy actions should simply provide enough money and credit to meet the needs of commerce. Put another way, if banks experience and increase in the demand for loans, the central bank should increase available funds to meet this demand and encourage economic activity.

In the early days of the Federal Reserve, following the real bills doctrine meant that when banks appeared at the **discount window** and applied for **loans** from the Federal Reserve, these loans were granted as long as the bank provided evidence that the loans being made were for productive purposes. These loans were referred to as *eligible paper* and were used by banks to back their loans from the Federal Reserve. The real bills doctrine meant that increases in economic activity generated greater loan demand and increased the demand for **money** and credit. The supply of money, therefore, would passively adapt to the level of business activity. In a sense, the supply of money was demand determined. Supporters of the real bills doctrine argued that if monetary policy was guided by this doctrine, there would never be any inflationary effects of monetary policy: increases in the supply of money would never exceed the demand for it.

An inherent flaw in this doctrine is that it is based on the assumption that lending decisions are made in real terms. Consider the following scenario: economic activity begins to increase and with it the demand for loans. Suppose prices also begin to rise, reflecting the increased demand for goods and services pressing against a supply that is limited by labor productivity and the sheer physical limits of producing more. If a business wishes to maintain the same level of real activity, over time it will increase its demand for funds simply because of rising prices. According to the real bills doctrine, this increased loan demand—demand that increased simply to offset the effects of rising prices—should be met by the Federal Reserve increasing the supply of money. However, this drives prices still higher, which begets an increase in loan demand, etc., etc. What this exercise demonstrates is that if an economy is operating at full employment, an increase in demand is likely to show up in price increases, not further increases in the output growth. This means that following the real bills doctrine imparts an inflationary bias to policy. Ironically, reducing **inflation** is exactly what the supporters of the doctrine thought they could avoid.

The real bills doctrine dominated thinking about policymaking at the time of the Federal Reserve's founding. By 1920, however, the Federal Reserve's policymakers realized that such a passive policy was inconsistent with keeping the rate of inflation low. Following the real bills doctrine, combined with their attempt to keep interest rates low to help the U.S. Treasury finance World War I, there was a sharp increase in the rate of inflation. In 1919 and 1920 the rate of inflation averaged about 14 percent. In light of this inflationary experience, in 1920 the Federal Reserve began to more actively manage the money supply through the cumbersome use of the discount window. Even though a **recession** followed their policy of raising the **discount rate** and reducing the growth of the money supply, the Federal Reserve succeeded in their attempt to lower the rate of inflation.

What is most interesting about the real bills doctrine is that it reappears in various guises at different times. For example, the German central bank (the Reichsbank) used the real bills doctrine as the theoretical foundation for its policy of increasing the money supply in the early 1920s. Unfortunately, this policy led to rates of inflation that exceeded *1 million* percent in 1923. How could they continue to increase the money supply when the rate of inflation soared ever higher? The policymakers in charge at the Reichsbank simply did not believe that their actions were directly connected to the resulting inflation.

And in case you think that such a wrong-headed policy could no longer exist, policies calling for lowering interest rates to spur economic activity actually are based on the underlying premise of the real bills doctrine. If there is no excess production capacity in an economy, following a policy of lowering interest rates—and simultaneously increasing the rate of growth of the money supply—often leads to an increase in the rate of inflation. Although not to the extent which occurred in Germany in the early 1920s, Federal Reserve policy during the 1960s and 1970s are consistent with one based on the real bills doctrine. This is evidenced by policy actions that led to rapid **economic growth** and rising rates of inflation, followed by contractionary policies to fight inflation, followed by expansionary policies to get out the recession caused by the contractionary policies. Indeed, during 2004 the Federal Reserve's policy of pushing the **federal funds rate** to historic lows and keeping it there for a sustained period of time raised the question of whether it had gone too far and will, as past repudiations of the real bills doctrine have shown, create higher rates of inflation in the future.

FURTHER READING

Friedman, Milton, and Anna Schwartz, *A Monetary History of the United States, 1867–1960.* Princeton: Princeton University Press, 1963; Humphrey, Thomas M. "The Real Bills Doctrine." Federal Reserve Bank of Richmond *Economic Review* (September/October 1982): 3–14; Meltzer, Allan H. *A History of the Federal Reserve, Vol. 1: 1913–1951.* Chicago: University of Chicago Press, 2003; Thornton, Henry. *An Inquiry into the Nature and Effects of the Paper Credit of Great Britain* (1802), reprinted by Kelley Publishing, 1962.

REAL BUSINESS CYCLE THEORY. The development of macroeconomic theory over the period since World War II took several paths. The Keynesian view of how the economy works, based on the pioneering work of British economist **John Maynard Keynes**, focused on the demand side of the economy. In that model, changes in income-generating factors, such as household consumption expenditures, business investment spending, and government spending, determine the rate at which the output of goods and services increase. Monetary policy, in the earlier versions of the theory, was viewed as somewhat passive; that is, there to maintain interest rates at levels consistent with some desired rate of economic expansion. Another characteristic of this view is that it paid little attention was paid to the inflationary effects of monetary policy actions. The main thrust of policy in the Keynesian model came through fiscal policy, changes in government spending and taxation.

An early countertheory to this view was made by the so-called **Monetarism** movement. Monetarists believed that observed fluctuations in the economic activity—**recessions** and booms—could be explained by movements in the stock of money, and that inflation was directly to the growth rate of the money supply. In a nutshell, Monetarists considered monetary policy actions to be the driving force behind economic activity: changes in the areas emphasized by the Keynesians were simply responses to earlier monetary policy actions.

By the early 1970s another challenge to the Keynesian model emerged, that of **rational expectations**. What the rational expectations model did was to assume that markets tended to clear—quantities demanded were equal to the quantities supplied of some good—when wages and prices are flexible. The idea is that if markets are competitive, available information allows prices and wages to change, reflecting pertinent information that leads to an efficient allocation of resources. In the rational expectations model, real output of the economy is determined by real factors, such as changes in the size of the labor force, the amount of plant and equipment being used by business, and the productivity of workers. In this view, real output growth was not a function of changes in the growth rate of the money stock *as long as policy changes were anticipated*. In other words, any effect of monetary policy actions came only from unexpected changes in money growth. Monetary policy could affect real output growth in the short run, but only if policy actions were not anticipated, and in the long run monetary policy actions had no affect real output growth. Like the Monetarist view, however, monetary policy actions were considered the source of observed rates of **inflation** over time.

By the early 1980s, some economists were pushing the rational expectations model a bit further, arguing that fluctuations in real economic activity had nothing to do with monetary policy, regardless of whether policy actions were or were not anticipated. These economists argued that economic fluctuations could be explained solely by "shocks" to the supply side of the economy. More specifically, early proponents of this new "real business cycle" theory, or RBC as it came to be known, argued that observed fluctuations in real output growth could be explained as outcomes from changes in labor productivity. In other words, forces that acted to change the amount of output workers produced explained most of the ups and downs in economic activity.

Coined by Long and Plosser (1983) and based on earlier work by Kydland and Presscott (1982) (Kydland and Presscott won the 2004 Nobel Prize in economics), RBC theory followed the rational expectations model by assuming that markets equilibrate when there are changes in the economy. The basic idea is as follows: At a point in time, households establish their optimal distribution of labor and leisure—work and nonwork—over the future given current and expected conditions about production and the demand for their services. If prices for goods and services change, and therefore the purchasing power of labors' wage changes, laborers adjust their supply of labor—decisions to work or not—in a manner that leaves the growth of output unchanged.

Workers decision to supply labor also is based on firms' production decision, which is based on existing technology. What is meant by "technology"? Think of it in a broader context than computers. Technology here means the overall knowledge of producing goods and services. For example, the technology that existed during the 1970s was one that relied on relatively inexpensive energy. When the Organization of Petroleum Exporting Countries (OPEC) raised the price of oil in 1973, this meant that the existing "technology" of production was made obsolete: higher oil prices made the existing technology economically inefficient. Other examples of negative supply-side shocks include famines, natural disasters (floods, earthquakes, etc.) or wars. On the positive side, RBC theory also recognizes that there are "positive" shocks to the economy, which can take the form of improvements in management practices or production techniques. Positive or negative, RBC theory argues that it is unexpected shifts in production technologies, not monetary policy, that move economic output above or below its long-run trend.

If RBC theory relies on productivity shocks to explain economic fluctuations, what is the role for monetary policy? In the RBC version of the world, movements in the money supply simply reflect the changing needs of the economy. In fact, the RBC view assumes that the quantity of deposits held by individuals is determined by the interaction between depositors and banks: the monetary authority has little or no role in determining this distribution of funds. What the central bank does affect is the amount of reserves and currency outstanding in the economy. By altering so-called *outside money*, the Federal Reserve's actions determine the price level (and, therefore, inflation) in the long run. Since output is determined on the supply side of the economy, changes in money growth, according to RBC theory, only affects prices.

RBC theory relies on the underlying notion that markets clear and that prices and wages are highly flexible, able to change as conditions warrant. This assumption, shared with the rational expectations model, may not hold in the real world to the extent that RBC theorists suggest. Wages are often set by contract thus preventing their rapid adjustment. Prices also are sometimes slow to adjust to changes in the economy. Another aspect of RBC theory is that testing the models produced by RBC theorists often amounts to "calibrating" the models and not "estimating" them. In other words, RBC models often are used to generate a series of values for real output (such as real **gross domestic product [GDP]**), which are then compared with the historic actual values. If they two series move together closely, then it can be argued that RBC theory "fits" the data and is a reasonable explanation for what we see.

The RBC theory is the latest in a continuing series of attempts by economists to try and explain business cycles. By knowing how and why business fluctuations occur, we then have a better understanding of the role of monetary policy.

FURTHER READING

Chaterjee, Satyajit. "From Cycles to Shocks: Progress in Business-Cycle Theory." Federal Reserve Bank of Philadelphia *Business Review* (March/April 2000): 1–11; Kydland, Finn, and Edward C. Prescott. "Time-to-Build and Aggregate Fluctuations." *Econometrica* (1982): 1345–70; Long, John, and Charles I. Plosser. "Real Business Cycles." *Journal of Political Economy* (1983): 1345–70; Plosser, Charles L. "Understanding Real Business Cycles." *Journal of Economic Perspectives* (Summer 1989): 51–77.

REAL MONEY BALANCES. How much **money** do you have? This may seem like a silly question, but think about it for a second: How much money do you have in cash and in your checking account? The answer differs depending on your spending needs, on how much you earn, and what the alternatives are for not holding money. You decide how much to hold in some spendable form (cash, checking, etc.) and how much to put into a savings-type deposit, such as an IRA, a **certificate of deposit**, or a passbook savings account. Your decision on how much money to hold largely depends on the factors just described. Economists can predict the amount of money people hold—their money balances—by considering their income and the *opportunity cost* of holding money, measured by the rate of interest. The rate of interest is important because if it increases, then the lost interest income one could make if you did not hold cash and put your money into a savings deposit might make you decide to hold less cash and put more of your income into a savings account.

Economists and policymakers want to know what *real money balances* people hold. Note that we've changed it a bit and now are concerned with *real* money balances. Real balances a nominal balances—actual dollars and checking account balances—adjusted for the price level. We make this distinction because economic theory tells us that you hold money (the non–interest-earning kind) largely to buy things. If your ability to buy things diminishes due to increases in the prices of goods and services, then you will adjust your holdings of nominal balances in order to bring your purchasing power back to its original level. Real money balances are more meaningful in an economic sense, because they measure your command over goods and services.

Why should the topic of real money balances be discussed in a book about the Federal Reserve? How individuals change their real money balance holdings in response to a change in the supply of money is an important factor in how monetary policy actions affect the economy. Consider the following scenario. Given income, interest rates and the price level, suppose the Federal Reserve doubles the amount of money in the economy. Relative to the amount of money you were holding, now you have twice as much. Because your money holdings have doubled, you must decide about what do to with all that extra cash. You can spend it, which will increase income in the economy. This also impacts the price of goods, pushing them up and lowering the value of your new money holdings. (Even though you have more dollars, they buy less than before.) If the rate of **inflation** rises, banks and other lenders raise their rates on loans. Or, instead of spending it all, you may opt to invest in bonds or put the money in the bank. The decision also affects the level of interest rates. Unless you simply hoard the money or burn it, increasing the supply of money affects the level of income, interest rates, and prices in the economy.

Because of these links, the Federal Reserve monitors the behavior of real money balances. Real money balances are part of its statistical model of the economy, one that is used for policy analysis and to forecast the outcome from taking alternative policy actions. If the public suddenly changes its pattern of dealing with increases in the supply of money, this can have unexpected consequences on policy decisions. If policymakers predicted that the public wanted to hold $X billions and it turned out to be less, their policy actions to increase the money supply would overstimulate the economy and lead to inflation. If policymakers pump more money into the economy than individuals wish to hold, this sets into motion the inflationary reaction described above.

FURTHER READING

Federal Reserve Bank of San Francisco. *Monetary Targeting and Velocity*. San Francisco: Federal Reserve Bank of San Francisco, 1983; Laidler, David E. W. *The Demand for Money: Theories and Evidence*. 4th edition. New York: HarperCollins, 1993.

REAL RATE OF INTEREST. The real rate of interest often is measured as the difference between the **nominal rate of interest**—the rate stated in the newspaper or on your car **loan**—and the rate of **inflation**. For instance, if the interest rate on a three-month **Treasury bill** is 6 percent and the rate of inflation is 4 percent, then a quick measure of the real rate of interest is 2 percent ($6 - 4 = 2$). Although this is a quick way of calculating the real rate of interest, it actually can be misleading, especially when the real rate of interest plays a key role in determining the direction of monetary policy. In this entry we first explain what the real rate of interest is, how it can be measured, and what role it plays in monetary policy decisions.

Irving Fisher, a U.S. economist often associated with early analysis of the rate of interest, argued that the nominal and real rates of interest are distinguished on the basis of the standard of value used to measure them. In his book *The Theory of Interest*, originally published in 1930, Fisher noted that the nominal or money rate of interest fluctuates as individual's expectations about future prices changed. For example, if you lend someone $100, payable in one year, what you expect to get back in a year is the $100 plus any lost purchasing power. That is, if today an economics textbook cost $100 and in a year it cost $110, unless you get at least $110 back, your loan of $100 today means that you will be economically worse off in a year because you cannot afford to buy the book. In *real terms*, you have loss purchasing power: $100 in the future just doesn't buy the same amount of goods as $100 today.

Fisher recognized the importance of time in discussing the behavior of nominal and real rates of interest. He argued that nominal rates would fluctuate with expectations of price level changes (i.e., inflation) even though the real rate of interest might be relatively steady. If lenders had perfect foresight, if they knew the rate of inflation for the next year and could costlessly adjust nominal interest rates to reflect that expectation, the real rate of interest would not budge. In such a world, there would be no loss in purchasing power by lending money out today with future repayment having the same purchasing power. Fisher

Inflation and Inflation Expectations

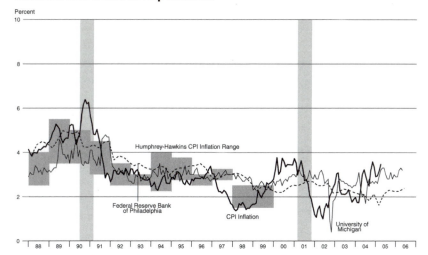

Source: Federal Reserve Bank of St. Louis, *Monetary Trends.*

(1954, p. 44) noted, however, that, "The business man supposes he makes his contracts in a certain rate of interest, only to wake up later and find that, in terms of real goods, the rate is quite different."

Fisher's relation between interest rates, both nominal and real, and price level changes is shown in the equation

$$\text{Nominal rate} = \text{Real rate} + \text{Expected inflation}$$

which today we call the Fisher equation. With a little algebra, the real rate of interest can be measured as

$$\text{Real rate} = \text{Nominal rate} - \text{Expected inflation}$$

Fisher suggested over 70 years ago that if the nominal rate of interest does not fully adjust to changes in the expected rate of inflation, and this expectation is correct, then lenders lose purchasing power when lending in an inflationary environment. For instance, if the actual rate of inflation turns out to be higher than the lender anticipated in setting the nominal rate, the real rate turns negative and purchasing power is lost.

Measuring an economically meaningful real rate of interest is tricky. It is complicated by the fact that what you might expect inflation to be over the next year is often quite different from what I expect it to be. If one compares inflation forecasts produced by economic forecasting firms, you would find that they usually do not match up perfectly, although they may be similar. And there are times when the professional opinion about what inflation might be in the future is far from the mark. During the mid-1970s, unexpected oil price hikes caused most economists to predict inflation rates that were far below the actual outcomes. At that time, bankers adjusted the nominal rates of interest higher, but not nearly enough to match the rapidly rising rate of inflation. During this time the measured real rate of interest was negative.

Different measures of the real rate of interest can be calculated since there are different forecasts of inflation. The figure above shows the actual rate of inflation, measured using the Consumer Price Index (CPI) and several well-known series of expected inflation. Two of the series are based on surveys—the University of Michigan and the Federal Reserve Bank of Philadelphia series—and the other is taken from testimony given by the chairman of the Federal Reserve before Congress. As you can see, even though the series move together over time, often times there is substantial differences in the inflation rate that is being forecast. And since the inflation forecast varies, this translates into different forecasts of the real rate of interest.

How is the real rate of interest important to a discussion of monetary policy? As you have seen, the real rate of interest is influenced by movements in the nominal rate of interest and the expected rate of inflation. The Federal Reserve exerts significant influence over both of these measures and, therefore, affects the level of the real rate of interest. For example, during the period following the 2001 recession, the Federal Reserve actively pushed the **federal funds rate** to lower and lower levels. For much of 2003 and 2004, the federal funds rate stood at 1 percent, a level not seen for over 40 years. At the same time the prevailing rate of inflation was less than 1 percent, although during 2004 the inflation rate began to rise. In this environment the real rate of interest on such short-term funds was effectively zero. In contrast, nominal interest rates on financial assets with longer maturities were about 4.75 in mid-2004. If Fisher is right, this divergence between short- and long-term interest rates in 2004 indicated that the financial markets anticipated higher inflation in the future: Given a real rate of interest, a higher nominal rate of interest reflects a higher expected rate of inflation. Levels of the real rate of interest can be used, therefore, to gauge the financial market's expectation about inflation that may affect (and reflect) the direction of monetary policy. Indeed, during mid-2004, most observers thought that the Federal Reserve's policy of maintaining low nominal rates of interest (and, given inflation, low real rates of interest as well) imparted a substantial inflationary bias into the economy. Hence, the higher level in long-term interest rates.

Another way in which the real rate of interest affects monetary policy is through several of the policy models used to guide decisions. One such model, the **Taylor Rule**, relates monetary policy actions to deviations in real output growth and inflation from their desired levels. A component of the rule, however, is the real rate of interest. If the Federal Reserve's notion of what this real rate of interest is does not match up with reality, then policy decisions will be biased. That is, policy may be more or less expansionary than if the policymakers had an accurate measure of just what the true underlying real rate of interest actually is. Indeed, the importance of accurately measuring the real rate of interest makes it a topic of continued interest (no pun intended) and research.

FURTHER READING

Antoncic, Madelyn. "High and Volatile Real Interest Rates." *Journal of Money, Credit and Banking*, (February 1986): 18–27; Darin, Robert, and Robert L. Hetzel. "An Empirical Measure of the Real Rate of Interest." Federal Reserve Bank of Richmond *Economic Quarterly* (Winter 1995): 17–47; Fama, Eugene F. "Short-Term Interest Rates as Predictors of Inflation." *American Economic Review* (June 1975): 269–82; Fisher, Irving. *The Theory of Interest*. New York: Kelley & Milllman, 1954. Originally published in 1930.

RECESSION. When you read in the newspaper or hear on the television that the economy is headed into another recession, what are they talking about? Or, if you prefer better news, maybe the newsperson is telling you that the economy is experiencing renewed **economic growth** and is heading out of a recession. In either case, when someone refers to a recession, what they are talking about is a downturn in economic activity. That is, during a recession, the amount of goods and services being produced (most often measured by real **gross domestic product [GDP]**) is declining.

A recession is part of a **business cycle**. A business cycle is composed of the expansion phase and the contraction phase. Suppose the economy is experiencing economic growth with real GDP increasing at a rate of 3 percent per year. If the growth rate of real GDP were to slow, say to 1.5 percent, that would not be a recession. Even though the pace of economic activity is slower, it is not a recession. The rule of the thumb used by most economists defines a recession as two consecutive quarters (six months) of *negative* real GDP growth.

In the United States, the National Bureau of Economic Research (NBER) organizes a panel of economists to meet and decide on the beginning and ending dates for recessions. The Cycle Dating Committee meets to review the relevant economic data (employment numbers, production statistics, etc.) and determines when they believe a recession began and when it ended. (The entry for **Business Cycle** lists the "official" recessions for the United States as designated by the NBER.) The chart below shows how recessions, designated by the shaded bars, are associated with growth rates of real GDP. Recessions occur when the growth rate of real GDP dips below zero. The record over the past 25 years indicates that some recessions are quite short, like the recession of 1980 which lasted six months, and some are prolonged, like the recession of 1981–1982. The chart also indicates that some recessions are more severe, in terms of negative real GDP growth, than others. For instance, the two most recent recessions, which occurred in 1990 and 2001, are relatively "mild" in terms of the decline in real GDP growth below zero compared with the 1981–1982 recession.

Another aspect about the historical record of recessions in the United States is that recessions in the post–World War II era are "different" than those occurring before the war. First, they seem to occur less often. Second, they appear to have a shorter duration. Although there is some research to suggest that this difference is due to statistical record keeping, it also may be that the recent record reflects policy actions taken by the government. In other words, the Federal Reserve engages in expansionary policies when the economic growth begins to slow. For example, when the economy fell into recession during 2001, the Federal Reserve aggressively pushed interest rates down in an attempt to reduce the severity and duration of the recession. Even though post-recession job growth did not match previous recoveries, this policy action was viewed by many as the appropriate response to a slowing economy. In this way, recessions have an important impact on monetary policy decisions.

There has been much research on recessions and economists continue to debate their cause. To be sure, almost every recession has some unique characteristic or event associated with it. In the mid-1970s the oil price increase engineered by the Organization of Petroleum Exporting Countries (OPEC) gets some of the blame for the 1974–1975 recession. In 2001 the terrorist attacks on New York City and Washington, D.C., are given

Real Gross Domestic Product

Percent change from year ago

Source: Federal Reserve Bank of St. Louis, *National Economic Trends.*

some of the blame for the slowdown in the economy. The question that remains is whether there is any single underlying event that occurs with every recession. In the past, some economists believed that fluctuations in money growth were largely to blame for observed economic fluctuations. Other economists argue that real factors, such as shocks to the productivity of workers, are the root cause of recessions. This view, associated with the **real business cycle theory**, contends that shocks such as the oil price increase in the 1970s are the type of events that send an economy into recession.

The weight of the evidence suggests that recessions probably result from some combination of the several effects. While the oil price shocks of the mid-1970s undoubtedly slowed economic activity, at the same time the Federal Reserve actively slowed money growth and raised interest rates. Though this policy was taken to fight the ensuing increase in **inflation** stemming from the oil price increase, monetary policy exacerbated slowing of the economy. In this case, which effect—oil price increase or contractionary monetary policy—is the cause of the recession? Recessions, business cycles, and what causes them are subjects of continued interest to economist and to monetary policymakers.

FURTHER READING

National Bureau of Economic Research. Website: www.NBER.org. Taylor, John B. *Economics*. 4th edition. Boston: Houghton Mifflin Company, 2004.

REDLINING. In 1977 Congress passed the **Community Reinvestment Act** (CRA) in large part to prevent the practice of "redlining." Redlining refers to a bank or other lending institution's refusal to lend money to anyone or any business that exists within a certain geographical area. Historically the practice of redlining was the method by which bankers allegedly discriminated against certain groups, refusing to make **loans**. Whether or not banks actually drew a red line around these areas is debatable. But the practice of not making the loans seems to have existed.

The CRA required banks to make loans in those areas from which they acquired deposits. For example, there is evidence that even though banks accepted deposits from individuals in low-income areas, the banks were not willing to make loans back to the people and businesses in those areas. Although there is some question about the force with which CRA was applied in its early days, beginning in July 1990 regulators began publicizing individual bank's CRA rating and evaluation. In other words, regulators let the public know just how compliant local banks were in following the CRA guidelines. Of course, this was a controversial move, because it was not always in a bank's best interest to have such information made public. Customers who had deposits at a bank could now see if their bank was making loans to their neighbors, or whether anyone in the deposit market was also getting loans. With the advent of public disclosure, however, the number of banks meeting CRA lending guidelines increased.

There is some debate about the merits of CRA. For example, one could argue that forcing banks to meet some lending guideline—in terms of percentage of loans made in a given geographical area, let's say—may not be economically sound. If the area is a high-risk area, regardless of who lives there, then banks are going to be reluctant to make loans. If banks make loans in such an area, the interest rate charged must be sufficiently high enough to compensate the bank for the increased risk that the loan will not be repaid (default). This conflict creates a problem within CRA-type regulation. Once banks are required to make loans in areas or to individuals and businesses that are higher risk, they also faced the issue of what rate to charge. If individuals in the risky area were being charged a higher interest rate than others, charges of discrimination would arise. Bank's arguments that individuals or businesses of similar risk would get similar rates often times was dismissed. Thus, compliance with CRA sometimes is viewed as an economically inefficient allocation of credit: it may be socially beneficial, but the economics is questionable.

Some also argue that forcing banks to make loans that they otherwise would be reluctant to make affects bank activity. That is, banks may restrict their lending activities over all simply to avoid CRA requirements. If true, this means that CRA reduces the pool of credit available to an entire community. Also, compliance with CRA raises the cost to a bank of making loans. If a bank now makes more loans in riskier areas, it is likely that it will expend more resources monitoring those loans. In addition, CRA regulations often required banks to create new departments that are dedicated to CRA compliance. These additional costs raise a bank's overall cost structure and could raise the level of interest rates charged for all loans, whether to risky customers or the safest.

Whether CRA succeeded in removing discrimination from the lending decision remains a topic of debate. A number of studies find that one cannot reject the belief that individuals in minority areas often are subject to higher loan rejection rates than individuals in non-minority areas. At the same time, when factors other than race are considered, such as income, job history, or borrower wealth or mortgage insurance, race may not be the single most important factor. Of course, the intertwining of all of these factors is what usually affects a lender's decision to make the loan or not.

FURTHER READING

Avery, R. B., and T. M. Buynak. "Mortgage Redlining: Some New Evidence." Federal Reserve Bank of Cleveland *Economic Review* (Summer 1981); Fettig, David. "In Light of Public Disclosure, CRA Gains Luster." Federal Reserve Bank of Minneapolis *fedgazette* (July 1993); Ross, S. L., and J. Yinger. *The Color of Credit: What Is Known about Mortgage Lending Discrimination.* Cambridge, MA: MIT Press, 2002.

REGULATION Q. When Congress passed the **Depository Institutions Deregulation and Monetary Control Act (DIDMCA) of 1980**, one aspect of the act was to phase-out the nearly 50-year-old interest rate ceilings imposed on bank deposits. By 1986, such

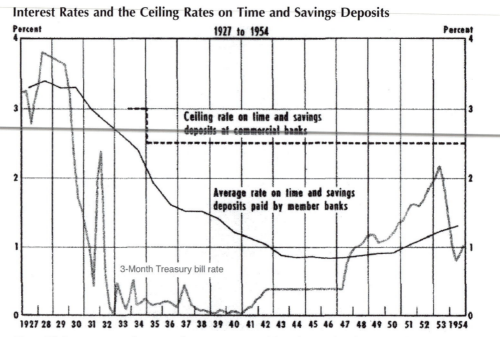

Interest Rates and the Ceiling Rates on Time and Savings Deposits
1927 to 1954

Percent

Ceiling rate on time and savings deposits at commercial banks

Average rate on time and savings deposits paid by member banks

3-Month Treasury bill rate

1927 28 29 30 31 32 33 34 35 36 37 38 39 40 41 42 43 44 45 46 47 48 49 50 51 52 53 1954

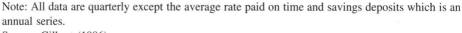

Note: All data are quarterly except the average rate paid on time and savings deposits which is an annual series.
Source: Gilbert (1986).

ceilings, enforced under the Federal Reserve's Regulation Q, were completely dismantled. What was Regulation Q? Why did it outlive its usefulness? We'll address those questions in this entry.

Regulation Q arose out of the **Great Depression** and represented an attempt by legislators to encourage changes in bankers' behavior. As part of the **Banking Act of 1933** and the **Banking Act of 1935**, Regulation Q imposed interest rate ceilings that banks could pay on checking accounts and savings deposits. This imposition was based on a couple of ideas. First, the notion was that with this ceiling country banks would be more likely to make **loans** to local borrowers than holding balances with large money center banks. Given the recent experiences of the Great Depression, some legislators, especially those from more rural areas, felt that the larger money center banks simply used the deposits from the smaller banks for their own speculative purposes. This not only deprived rural communities of funds needed for economic development, but also filled the coffers of the very banks that many associated with the speculative excesses of the 1929 stock market crash.

Another popular explanation of the need for interest rate ceilings was to reduce competition for deposits among banks. Because banks had to compete for deposits with each other, this reduced their profitability and arguably made them more vulnerable to failure. If banks could make more money off of their deposits—bank income is derived from the difference between what they pay to depositors and what they earn from making loans—then they would be less inclined to make it up somewhere else, such as in riskier loans or speculative investments. The bottom line is that many believed that banks should be protected from competition. While there is some evidence to support this notion, it also is true that even though banks stopped making explicit interest payments, they often substituted implicit interest payment means to compete for deposits. For example, banks offered incentives to open an account with their bank by "giving away" items such as televisions or toasters. If one calculated the cost of the "free" item and related that to the minimum balance often required, you could come up with a bank's implicit payment for deposits.

In the early days of Regulation Q it was relatively ineffective. Although the Federal Reserve sometimes used Regulation Q to harness in aggressive banks, the ceilings on interest rate payments generally were above existing market rates of interest. As shown in the chart above, from its inception until the mid-1950s, the Regulation Q ceiling rate was above rates being paid by banks on time and savings deposits, and above the three-month **Treasury bill** rate, a commonly used rate to gauge the level of short-term market rates.

From the mid-1950s until its demise, however, the rate ceilings imposed under Regulation Q were very restrictive. As the rate of inflation increased and with it **nominal interest rates**, the ceiling rate under Regulation Q began to lag behind market rates. Even though the Federal Reserve raised the ceiling rate several times, it never raised the rate high enough to match market rates. This meant that banks were operating at a competitive disadvantage: the rate paid on deposits was less than what the customer could get elsewhere. Deposits flowed from banks and thrift institutions into newly formed financial products, such as **money market mutual funds**. By the early 1980s, the regulation that was meant to provide some protection for banks (and to increase their profitability) was having exactly the opposite effect. Because Regulation Q prohibited banks from raising rates on deposits to match competition from nonbank sources, banks experienced what is called **disintermediation**.

The phase-out of Regulation Q lasted from 1980 through 1986 and did not occur without cost. Because the regulation had disproportionate effects on the allocation of deposits across different institutions over time—some institutions were harmed more by the regulation in terms of what they could and could not pay on deposits, which affected their profitability—the phase-out also altered the distribution of deposits across financial institutions. This is most notable in the allocation of deposits between commercial banks and thrift institutions, such as savings and loan institutions. As Regulation Q ceilings were lifted, banks were now able to more effectively compete with savings and loans for deposits. This competition put upward pressure on deposit rates at both financial institutions. But, because savings and loans had loan portfolios that were comprised much more heavily of long-term mortgages, the increase in the cost of funds squeezed their profits more so than it did for banks. Indeed, some suggest that this competition was a key factor explaining the failure of many savings and loans during the early 1980s. (*See* **Savings and Loan Crisis**.)

FURTHER READING

Gilbert, R. Alton. "Requiem for Regulation Q: What It Did and Why It Passed Away." Federal Reserve Bank of St. Louis *Review* (February 1986): 22–37.

REGULATORY FORBEARANCE. This term often is associated with the savings and loan debacle of the early 1980s, although its use is much more widespread. First, what do we mean by "regulatory forbearance"? Stern (2002, p. 4) provides two definitions. One is "withdrawing from the regulation of certain, previously regulated activities." In other words, if a regulation said you could not do some activity but then it is allowed anyway, this would be one example of regulatory forbearance. This is equivalent to "regulatory withdrawal." A definition that is used most often in discussions of financial institution is "refraining from applying regulatory conditions." This means that even though a regulation has not officially changed, regulators simply may opt not to apply it as stringently as before.

This latter version of regulatory forbearance was adopted by regulators dealing with the large number of failures of savings and loan associations (S&Ls) during the 1980s. Instead of closing bankrupt institutions, regulators often gave many failing S&Ls a pass, hoping that conditions would change and the S&Ls would be able to regain profitability. Part of this approach was to allow S&Ls to count as assets on their books items such as "goodwill" and other nonmarket items. Institutions were given credit for "good faith" tests, as noted by White (1991). Regulators essentially allowed S&L managers to claim false profits on their books when, according to the rules, they should have stepped in and closed them down. As economist Ed Kane aptly named them, these were Zombie S&Ls: still functioning but in reality bankrupt.

Why would a regulator allow an institution that is insolvent to continue operating? Mishkin (2004) suggests three reasons. One is that the insurance fund upon which failing institutions would draw to pay off depositors could not handle the volume of demand by depositors. Second, regulators turned a blind eye to the problems, not willing to admit their past mistakes. Finally, regulators often form close relationships with the individuals and institutions they are supposed to be regulating, relationships that may preclude them from taking harsh though necessary actions. All of these factors raise the **moral hazard** issue associated with regulatory forbearance. Managers of institutions that have been allowed to remain open even though they are insolvent may take a very different attitude to managing risks than before. The idea is that since they are bankrupt anyway, why not roll the dice and take big risks to see if they can dig themselves out of bankruptcy.

Obviously, regulatory forbearance can have negative side effects. Most recently, regulatory forbearance was viewed as a key factor explaining the problems associated with financial distress during the **Asian Crisis**. Indeed, some economists have shown that regulatory forbearance can lead to reductions in **economic growth**.

FURTHER READING

Degenarro, Ramon P., and James B. Thomson. "Capital Forbearance and Thrifts: Examining the Costs of Regulatory Gambling." *Journal of Financial Services Research* (1993); Mishkin, Frederic S. *The Economics of Money, Banking, and Financial Markets.* 7th edition. Boston: Addison Wesley, 2004; White, Lawrence J. *The S&L Debacle*. New York: Oxford University Press, 1991.

REPURCHASE AGREEMENT. The Federal Reserve uses repurchase agreements, or "repos" as they are often called, in the conduct of **open market operations**. For instance, a repo occurs when the Open Market **Trading Desk** at the New York Federal Reserve Bank buys a government security from one of its designated **primary dealers** and the dealer agrees to "repurchase" the security within some agree upon time period. Usually the repurchase takes place within one to seven days but may extend out to 15 days. When the dealer buys back the security, the dealer pays the original price plus some prespecified return to the Federal Reserve for the use of the money. Repos are granted on a competitive basis with primary dealers asked to submit rates that they (the dealers) are willing to pay for the repo. When the sum total of the bids equals the amount of reserves that the Federal Reserve wishes to inject into the banking system, the bidding ends. Because the Federal Reserve pays for the securities by crediting the reserve account of the bank in which the dealer has an account, repos are a method by which the Federal Reserve influences the level of reserves in the banking system, especially for short periods of time and especially when some technical adjustment is needed. For example, there may be a temporary reduction in reserve due to **float** that the Federal Reserve wishes to offset. Since the problem is a temporary one, using a repo is the most efficient approach to take, as it is reversed in a known period of time.

FURTHER READING

Bowser, Norman. "Repurchase Agreements," Federal Reserve Bank of St. Louis *Review* (September 1979); Federal Reserve Bank of New York. "Repurchase Agreements." *Fedpoints* (October 2002); Lumpkin, Stephen A. "Repurchase and Reverse Repurchase Agreements." *Instruments of the Money Market*. Richmond: Federal Reserve Bank of Richmond, 1998, Chapter 6.

RESEARCH DIVISION/DEPARTMENTS. Economic research at the **Board of Governors** is carried out in several areas: the Division of Research and Statistics; the Division of Monetary Affairs; and the Division of International Finance. Personnel in these three divisions consist of Ph.D. economists and support staff, totaling about 450. The Division of Reserve Bank Operations and Payments Systems conducts research focusing on the operational side of Federal Reserve activities, such as check clearing. In addition to the board's research divisions, each of the 12 District Banks have research departments that vary in size and composition. Most research is conducted by Ph.D. economists supported by a staff. The main goal of research conducted within the system is to provide policymakers with the most current evidence, both theoretical and empirical, on the relation between the economy and the impact of policy decisions. In some sense, the ultimate goal of research in the system is to advise members of the **Federal Open Market Committee (FOMC)** about policy options and to advise and inform other policymakers within the system about the effects of regulatory changes and changes in foreign economic activity and to provide economic forecasts. The research output from all of these various groups often is published in leading academic journals, Federal Reserve publications, and presentations at professional conferences.

The make-up of the Federal Reserve's research divisions and departments is an interesting anomaly compared with the structure of foreign central banks. Most other central banks do not have this kind of research diversity. The usual model for a central bank is to have a research department at the main bank without competing departments spread throughout the system. This aspect of research within the Federal Reserve System grew out of a long history of concerns in the United States over the centralization of decision making, both in politics and in the establishment of the Federal Reserve System. Even though the **Banking Act of 1935** largely concentrated monetary policy decisions in the Board of Governors and removed the regional policy focus of the District Banks— primarily through discount window decisions—a remaining feature of the system today is the independent nature of the research departments. Indeed, the "maverick" label applied to the Federal Reserve Bank of St. Louis during the 1960s and 1970s arose out of its views about the role of money and monetary policy. The St. Louis Fed was long recognized as a **Monetarist** bank within the system, publishing research results that often were diametrically opposed to the positions taken by the board. Similarly, during the 1980s the Federal Reserve Bank of Minneapolis became known as the "**rational expectations**" bank because of its publications extolling the virtues of the relatively new rational expectations view of macroeconomics. While these two banks may be the best examples, other banks also take policy positions that are not always in line with the board staff's views.

For information on the board's staff, visit the Website at www.federalreserve.gov/research, which provides links to directories, research resources, and career opportunities. For information about separate banks' research departments, visit the individual bank websites.

FURTHER READING

Wheelock, David C. "National Monetary Policy by Regional Design: The Evolving Role of the Federal Reserve Banks in Federal Reserve System Policy." In J. von Hagen and C. Waller, eds. *Regional Aspects of Monetary Policy in Europe*. Boston: Kluwer Academic Publishers, 2000.

RESERVE ACCOUNTING. The Federal Reserve requires depository institutions in the United States to hold a minimum amount of their deposits on reserve, either as **vault cash** (cash held on hand in the bank's vault) or as **reserves** with the Federal Reserve. The minimum amount that each bank must hold is determined by the **reserve requirement,** which is set by the **Board of Governors**. Within this framework, banks are not required to hold this minimum each and every day. Rather, required reserves are determined over a two-week period. Determining just how banks meet their reserve requirement and the period over which the requirement is calculated has changed over time, and has been the subject of significant analysis.

From 1968 through 1984, the Federal Reserve used a system known as *lagged reserve accounting*. Under this system, the period over which a bank calculated its average daily balances to determine its reserve requirement—called the reserve maintenance period— was a seven-day period ending each Wednesday. When a bank calculated how much it needed on reserve to meet its requirement, it took the daily average of reservable deposits over the same seven-day period, but one ended on Wednesday two weeks earlier. This earlier period was called the *computational period*. In effect, a bank held reserves today determined by the average of deposits two weeks earlier. Hence the name *lagged* reserve accounting.

Why would the Federal Reserve use such a system to determine reserve requirements? There have been a number of studies claiming that a system in which reserves are determined contemporaneously makes (more about that below) money growth and interest rates more volatile. The idea is that unless banks are able to smooth their reserve holdings over time, trying to meet reserve requirements on a weekly basis would send banks scrambling for funds every Wednesday. This would increase fluctuations in the **federal funds rate** around settlement days and lead to unnecessary volatility in financial markets. (See Thornton [1983] and the articles cited therein for a discussion of this research.)

Some economists (see articles cited in Thornton) argued that monetary policy, especially control over the growth rate of the money supply, could be improved if the Federal Reserve moved to a system of *contemporaneous reserve accounting*. The move to contemporaneous accounting in the 1980s meant that banks determined required reserves on the basis of their daily average deposits over a 14-day reserve maintenance period that began on a Thursday and ended on a Wednesday, two weeks hence. Under this scheme, the computational period started two days before the maintenance period. One of the changes with this move was to extend the reserve maintenance period from one to two weeks.

One reason why the Federal Reserve adopted contemporaneous accounting was that it believed it would enhance its ability to control money growth. The idea was that by moving to contemporaneous reserve accounting, a tighter relationship would develop between reserve growth and money growth. Even so, research by some economists (see Thornton) indicated that the type of reserve accounting system used actually has little impact on the long-run behavior of the money supply, but money growth may be more volatile in the short-run. After more than a decade, the Federal Reserve re-adopted the use of lagged reserve accounting in 1998.

FURTHER READING

Gilbert, R. Alton, and Michael E. Trebing. "The New System of Contemporaneous Reserve Requirements," Federal Reserve Bank of St. Louis *Review* (December 1982): 3–7; Thornton, Daniel L. "Lagged and Contemporaneous Reserve Accounting: An Alternative View." Federal Reserve Bank of St. Louis *Review* (November 1983): 26–33.

RESERVE REQUIREMENT. A reserve requirement is imposed by the Federal Reserve on deposits at banks. Since the passage of the **Depository Deregulation and Monetary Control Act (DIDMCA) of 1980**, the **Board of Governors** has set reserve requirements on transaction deposits (deposits like checking accounts) from 8 percent to 14 percent. Following passage of DIDMCA, the Federal Reserve was not able to set reserve requirements on personal time deposits except in unusual situations, and after consultation with Congress. Although the DIDMCA set out the general outline for reserve requirements, there have been changes since its passage. For example, the **Garn-St. Germain Act** of 1982 cushioned the reserve requirement against small banks, providing no reserve requirement for the first $2 million of a bank's deposits, a level that was intended to increase each year as the overall level of deposits in the banking system increases. By 2002, for example, that level is $5.7 million.

Reserve requirements are graduated, based on the amount of deposits in a bank. The current (2005) set of reserve requirements is as follows: 0 percent on transaction deposits up to $6 million, 3 percent on deposits from $6 million to 42.1 million, and 10 percent on deposits over $42.1 million. These requirements are applied to deposits over a two-week period. According to the Federal Reserve Bank of New York (2002), to calculate a bank's reserve liability "a bank's average reserves over the period ending every other Wednesday must equal the required percentage of its average deposits in the two-week period ending the Monday sixteen days earlier." Put slightly differently, a bank's reserve requirements are based on an averaging process so that fluctuations in deposits do not cause undue harm to banks. If reserve requirements were specified at some level for each day, banks facing a large influx of deposits would have to scramble to fulfill its reserve requirements. By using a two-week period, called the maintenance period, banks are able to manage their reserves in order to meet the Federal Reserve's requirements.

Reserve requirements are one tool used by the Federal Reserve to conduct monetary policy. Although the Federal Reserve seldom changes reserve requirements, a seemingly minor one can have dramatic affects on the reserve position of banks. Such reserve changes impact their lending decisions, the level of interest rates and eventually the growth of the money supply. For instance, increasing the amount that banks must keep on reserve for each dollar of deposits, the Federal Reserve can limit the banks' ability to make **loans** and expand deposits. (*See* **Money Multiplier**.)

Some argue that when the Federal Reserve changes the reserve requirement ratio it must offset the effects that the change has on banks' reserve positions. That is, if the Federal Reserve raises reserve requirements, then it offsets this action by injecting more reserves into the system through open market purchases of government securities. Since the last time that reserve requirements were officially changed was 1992, one could argue that its usefulness as a policy tool has diminished in recent times. Indeed, as noted in Hein and Stewart (2002), the notion that reserve requirement changes may not be a useful policy tool is demonstrated by the fact that the central banks of Canada, Great Britain, and New Zealand have eliminated cash reserve requirements. Since the Federal Reserve allows banks to offer **sweep accounts**, which effectively eliminate reserve liability by banks, one could argue that the Federal Reserve also has *de facto* lowered the reserve requirement to zero for many banks.

FURTHER READING

Federal Reserve Bank of New York. "Reserve Requirements." *Fedpoint* (February 2002). Website: www.newyorkfed.org; Goodfriend, Marvin, and Monica Hargraves. "A Historical Assessment of the Rationales and Functions of Reserve Requirements." Federal Reserve Bank of Richmond *Economic Review* (March/April 1983): 3–21; Hein, Scott E., and Jonathan D. Stewart. "Reserve Requirements: A Modern Perspective." Federal Reserve Bank of Atlanta *Economic Review* (Fourth Quarter 2002): 41–52; Meulendyke, Ann-Marie. *U.S. Monetary Policy and Financial Markets*. New York: Federal Reserve Bank of New York, 1990.

RESERVES. Banks acquire deposits and use these funds to make **loans** and other investments. To a bank your checking account deposit is a liability: it is money that the bank owes you. On the other side of the balance sheet, the car loan that you took out from the bank—a liability to you since you owe the money to the bank—is an asset to the bank. Assets—loans and investments—are how banks earn income. Before a bank is able to use your deposit money to make a loan, it must make sure that it has enough of the deposits on hand to meet depositors' demands. For example, when you go to the bank and ask to withdraw $100 from your checking account, the bank must have the $100 in **currency** on hand to satisfy your request. This "on-hand" money is held as **vault cash**, quite literally cash held by a bank in its vault.

In addition to vault cash, banks are required by law to hold *reserves* at the Federal Reserve. For each dollar in **checkable deposits**, a bank is required to hold a small fraction (say 10 percent) of it on reserve at their Federal Reserve Bank. These funds are call *required* reserves. Banks may chose to hold more than is required by law. Even though reserves do not earn banks any interest, they are the most liquid asset a bank can hold and thus are useful to meet unforeseen demands by customers. These reserves are called *excess* reserves because they are in excess of the amount required by law. If there is an unexpected outflow of deposits and the banks must borrow from other banks or sell of some of its investments to meet its reserve requirements, this is costly to the profitability of the bank. In order to guard against such loss, banks manage their excess reserves as a form of "**liquidity** management."

Banks manage their reserves to help maximize profits. For example, because reserves do not pay interest, banks try to avoid holding too many reserves. A clear indication of this is the growth of so-called **sweep accounts**, accounts where banks "sweep" funds from reservable deposit accounts into deposits that have no reserve requirements. The bank usually does this overnight, agreeing with the customer that the latter will get some fraction of a percent in interest. Since the customer sees no cost to sweeping the account—the money reappears the next morning as if it had always been there—they usually are willing to accept whatever return is offered.

Reserves play a key role in the conduct of monetary policy. Suppose a bank is holding just the correct amount of required reserves and wishes to hold zero excess reserves. When the Federal Reserve buys government securities in the open market (*see* **Open Market Operations**), it pays for those securities by electronically crediting the checking account of the seller. This means that the seller's bank now has more deposits and must increase its holding of required reserves commensurately. Because the initial deposit requires the bank to hold a small fraction as required reserves, this transaction also means that the bank now holds excess reserves. But the bank does not wish to hold excess reserves, so it tries to get rid of them. This can be done by making loans. When the bank makes a loan it creates more checkable deposits which in turn require the bank to hold additional required reserves. But for each new dollar of deposit and reserves, there is a large fraction left in excess reserves. Thee excess reserves again get loaned out and the process starts all over again. Even though each "round" uses fewer funds than the previous one—each required reserves take a bite out of each new dollar in deposits created—the process continues until there are no more funds to lend out. This purchase of securities by the Federal Reserve puts into motion a multi-step process where the initial increase in the bank's reserves leads to a multiple increase in deposits. (*See* **Money Multiplier**.) All of this occurs because banks are required to hold reserves.

Although monetary policy in the United States focuses on the level of the **federal funds rate**, achieving the desired rate is achieved through the manipulation of reserves in the banking system. The federal funds rate is the rate that banks charge each other for borrowing excess reserves in the overnight market. When the Federal Reserve bought securities in the above example, it created a condition in which the bank now held excess reserves. Between the time the bank could dispose of these excess reserves by making loans, the bank could lend excess reserves to another bank in the federal funds market. In this market, banks lend and borrow excess reserves on an overnight basis. As with any market, when there is an excess of funds available, the federal funds rate (the price) gets pushed down. In this way, how banks manage reserves and how the Federal Reserve alters the amount of reserves in the banking system have direct affects on the level of the federal funds rate, and how the Federal Reserve conducts monetary policy.

FURTHER READING

Meulendyke, Ann-Marie. *U.S. Monetary Policy & Financial Markets*. New York: Federal Reserve Bank of New York, 1998.

RIEFLER-BURGESS DOCTRINE. The Riefler-Burgess Doctrine refers to an attempt by Winfield Riefler, an economist at the **Board of Governors**, and New York Federal Reserve Bank economist W. Randolph Burgess to provide a framework for the conduct of monetary policy decisions. During the early years of the Federal Reserve System, there were competing ideas of how policy should be conducted. The favored policy approach was the **real bills doctrine**, a policy that expands and contracts the supply of money according to the pace of business activity. The Riefler-Burgess doctrine worked within the overarching framework of the real bills doctrine. It focused on the borrowing behavior of banks. A key proposition is that banks are unwilling to borrow from the Federal Reserve through the **discount window** mechanism. If this is true, the Federal Reserve could bring about changes in the availability of credit and money and affect market interest rates by actively managing the **discount rate**—the rate at which banks paid to borrow from the Federal Reserve. Discount rate policy was given an important role in the conduct of monetary policy. As interpreted by Meltzer (2003), when the Federal Reserve raised the discount rate, this would lower banks' borrowing from the Federal Reserve which in turn reduced the amount of credit and money, thus raising interest rates. According to this view, monetary policy could therefore alter market rates simply by adjusting the discount rate up and down.

The problem with the Riefler-Burgess doctrine is that banks often increased their discount window borrowing in times of business expansion. Applying the Riefler-Burgess view, such activity would be interpreted as banks' response to a restrictive policy when in fact it was just the opposite: bank borrowing would rise even though the money supply was increasing, too. As often occurred with monetary policy, the focus on interest rates caused Federal Reserve officials to misread the outcome of their intended actions.

FURTHER READING

Burgess, W. Randolph. *The Reserve Banks and the Money Market*, 2nd ed. New York: Harper, 1936; Meltzer, Allan H. *A History of the Federal Reserve, Vol. 1: 1913–1951*. Chicago: University of Chicago Press, 2003; Riefler, W.W. *Money Rates and Money Markets in the United States*. New York: Harper, 1930.

RIEGLE-NEAL ACT OF 1994. This is the shortened version for the Riegle-Neal Interstate Banking and Branching Efficiency Act of 1994. The Riegle-Neal Act repealed certain portions of the **McFadden Act of 1927,** which was passed to prevent large (mostly eastern) banks from crossing state boundaries to set up branches. The McFadden regulation was evaded when banks created **bank holding companies**. Even though a holding company owned banks in different states, it technically was not a bank operating across state lines: it was a corporation that just happened to won banks in different states. This activity came under regulation with passage of the **Bank Holding Company Act of 1956**. Especially through the Douglas Amendment to the 1956 Bank Holding Company Act, states regained some control over the ability of out-of-state bank holding companies to open banks. The Riegle-Neal Act repealed the Douglas Amendment and consequently ushered in interstate banking. On September 29, 1995, full nationwide banking was permitted.

An outcome of Riegle-Neal is evident in the growing consolidation of banking in the United States, consolidation that has led to an increase in the number of branches of large banks, such as Bank of America, operating in many towns and cities. In addition to a change in the regulatory environment, this change has been enabled by the rapid advances in communications technology. Today, unlike in the past, the ability of banks to rapidly disseminate and manage information means that the need for numerous banks is simply not economically efficient. Economies of scale are likely to lead to a continuation of consolidations in the banking industry.

FURTHER READING

Mishkin, Frederic S. *The Economics of Money, Banking, and Financial Markets,* 7th edition. Boston: Pearson Addison Wesley, 2004. See especially Chapter 10.

ROOSEVELT, FRANKLIN DELANO (1882–1945). Franklin D. Roosevelt is one of the most famous and influential U.S. presidents of the twentieth century, due to his vision and political tenacity. Roosevelt will be remembered for taking the United States out of the **Great Depression** and for his stewardship during World War II.

Born to an Eastern establishment family in Hyde Park, New York, Roosevelt attended Harvard University and Columbia Law School. Roosevelt, like his cousin, Theodore Roosevelt, entered politics at a relatively young age. Unlike his famous cousin, however, Franklin was a Democrat. After scoring his first political victory in the New York Senate race in 1910, Franklin rose to prominence in the Democratic Party. He was appointed by President **Woodrow Wilson** to be assistant secretary of the Navy, and in 1920 at the age of 38 he became the Democratic Party's nominee for vice president. In 1928, his political career took a major step forward when he became governor of New York. Four years later, while the nation was in the depths of the Great Depression, Franklin Roosevelt defeated **Herbert C. Hoover** to become the 32nd President of the United States.

This was a gloomy time to take office. Even though some relief programs had commenced under the Hoover administration, it was Roosevelt who ignited the public's spirit of overcoming the difficulties of the Great Depression. When he took office in early 1933, about 13 million workers were unemployed, hundreds of **commercial banks** had closed, and the economy was in shambles. In a bold political and economic move, Roosevelt ordered that there would be a bank holiday, beginning in March 1933. All commercial banks in the United States were closed for business during the **Bank Holiday of 1933**. The holiday would be used as a time for banks to get their books in order, a time when weak banks could be closed and others would reopen with renewed funds. The holiday helped restore public confidence in the banking system. Indeed, March 1933 is often considered as the end of the economic downturn and the beginning of recovery.

Roosevelt's administration initiated a number of public works projects designed to increase income by creating jobs. Many of these programs began in the first few months of his administration, the now-famous period referred to as the "first hundred days." Deficit spending ruled the day as the federal government stepped in to create jobs in agriculture and industry. The Tennessee Valley Authority was created to provide cheap electrical power to southeastern United States. Roosevelt's New Deal programs apparently worked: The economy started to recover from the depths of the Great Depression.

One of the lasting aspects of Roosevelt's policies was the concentration of power in Washington, D.C. This occurred also in the Federal Reserve System. Up to this time, most of the systemwide power resided in the Federal Reserve Bank of New York, primarily because it was the bank where system operations occurred and because New York was the money center of the United States. The onset of the Great Depression, and some would argue the death of **Benjamin Strong**, helped shift the center of power in the system to Washington. The **Board of Governors** in Washington took on more control within the system, usurping the power of **District Banks** that had previously guided policy through their control over **discount window** lending.

At this time Congress enacted many new pieces of legislation that regulated banking and financial markets. After the disaster of the depression, it was felt that markets, especially financial markets, were too unregulated. Free enterprise was good, but the Great Depression revealed the fact that, if unchecked, free enterprise occasionally would lead to severe economic contractions. With this in mind, Congress passed and Roosevelt signed sweeping legislation that constrained the behavior of banks and financial markets. The **Banking Act of 1933** and **Banking Act of 1935** reshaped banking with detractors arguing that too much power was put into the hands of large, Eastern banks. Others complained that the new regulations stifled competition, in some instances giving banks monopoly power over setting interest rates on deposit and loans. These concerns were largely ignored. Even though recent legislation has overturned almost every regulation passed in the 1930s, the banking system remained relatively stable during the period since the Great Depression.

Franklin Roosevelt served four terms as president (elected in 1932, 1936, 1940, and 1944). His last full term coincided with World War II. Although he tried to keep the United States neutral during the early years of the war in Europe, the United States supplied Great Britain with material and aid beginning in 1940. At the time France already had fallen to Germany and Great Britain was under attack. Reluctant to enter the war, Roosevelt saw no other choice when, on December 7, 1941, Japanese airplanes attacked Pearl Harbor, a day that Roosevelt said would "last in infamy." Suffering from polio since the summer of 1921, Roosevelt's health was always of concern. During his last term in office, his health deteriorated notably as he directed the U.S. war effort against the forces of Germany, Japan, and Italy. While visiting Warm Springs, Georgia, Roosevelt suffered a cerebral hemorrhage and died on April 12, 1945.

FURTHER READING

Barber, William J. *Designs within Disorder: Franklin D. Roosevelt, the Economists, and the Shaping of American Economic Policy*. Cambridge: Cambridge University Press, 1996; Leuchtenberg, William E. *Franklin D. Roosevelt and the New Deal, 1932–1940*. New York: Harper Colophon Books, 1963; Mitchell, Broadus. *Depression Decade: From New Era through New Deal, 1929–1941*. New York: Harper Torchbooks, 1969.

RULES VERSUS DISCRETION. Decisions made by the policymaking arm of the Federal Reserve, the **Federal Open Market Committee (FOMC)**, are guided by *some* process. This process may be as constraining as keeping the rate of interest at 5 percent, or as free-wheeling as changing policy based on whatever strikes the FOMC's collective fancy on a particular day. While the actual process lies somewhere in between, these extreme positions capture the nature of the argument over how policy decisions should be made: using rules or using discretion. In this discussion we cover suggested policy rules and provide examples from the most rigid to the most flexible.

A policy rule can take several forms. A policy rule could be "The Federal Reserve will keep the **federal funds rate** at 3 percent." Or, it might be "The Federal Reserve will keep the growth rate of the money supply at 5 percent." Gramlich (1998) refers to such rules as an "unconditional." An unconditional rule ties the FOMC's hands: policy actions must keep interest rates or **money** growth at the predetermined level or rate regardless of what is occurring in the economy. Even though this type of rule may seem extreme, it is, in fact, exactly the type of policy rule advocated by **Milton Friedman**, one of the most influential economists of the twentieth century. Why did he choose such a simple rule?

Friedman believed that policymakers are hampered not by lack of good intentions but by lack of timely information. Whether it is expanding or contracting is information that policymakers receive only with a time lag, and sometimes a substantial lag at that. In addition, how policy actions affect the economy is known only after time has passed, a period that may be several years. If policymakers are unsure of how the economy is behaving and at the same time unsure of how their actions are affecting the economy, Friedman argued that the safest approach was to remove one potential source of volatility to the economy: the economic effects of monetary policy actions. If individuals in the economy know that the Federal Reserve's policy is to keep the money supply growing at some x-percent rate, for example, then decisions could be made without having to worry about unpredictable policy actions as being an additional unknown. All's that would be necessary is to determine what the "X" should be in the X-percent rule. For Friedman, since real output growth averaged about 3 percent over time, a money growth of 3 to 5 percent would help ensure that **inflation** would be no more than 1 to 2 percent over time. (For a discussion of this relationship, *see* **Quantity Theory**.)

Would such a binding rule work? The answer to some extent depends on the time frame of the analysis. If one believes that monetary policy really only affects prices in the long run and has no impact on how fast real output increases over time, setting a fixed growth rate for the money supply "locks in" a long-run or average rate of inflation. Friedman also believed that substantial short-run fluctuations in the growth rate of the money supply leads to harmful swings in output growth. If monetary policy is constrained to keeping the growth rate of the money supply at some fixed rate—follow a rule—then this removes the source of this potentially destabilizing effect.

Critics argue that a fixed or X-percent money growth rate rule is premised on the notion that the demand for money or the **velocity of money** is predictable over time. If the demand for money is increasing at a predictable rate over time, then the link between changes in the growth of the supply of money and the economy also is predictable. If money demand changes unexpectedly, however, the link between the predetermined growth rate of the money supply and the rate of economic growth and inflation becomes uncertain and the usefulness of the X-percent rule is questionable. William Poole (1970) pointed out that if the demand for money shifts, a 5 percent increase in the supply of money may not deliver a long-run inflation rate of zero as was predicted. Depending on what the demand for money is, a policy that keeps the money supply increasing at a 5 percent rate may cause inflation to vary substantially from the desired rate. Once we relax the assumption of how stable the demand for money is, the efficacy of a fixed-rate policy rule becomes obvious. It should be noted that even though Friedman's X-percent rule is dismissed by economists as a workable monetary policy rule, it provides a foundation for discussing whether policymakers should behave if they wish to keep inflation low over time and reduce policy-induced volatility in the real economic activity.

A policy rule that loosens the constraints of an X-percent rule is called a feedback rule. A feedback rule is guided by the same objectives as Friedman's rule: prevent inflation in the long run, and prevent policy-induced fluctuations in real output in the short run. One example of such a rule allows the policymaker to adjust the growth rate of the money supply in response to long-term changes in the demand for money. This type of feedback rule recognizes that changes in technology influence how we hold money and that this alters historical relationships between money growth and the economy. For example, if money demand is trending upward, then in order to maintain a desired level of inflation (given output growth) the Federal Reserve would increase the rate of growth of the money supply. Since the increased availability of money is simply meeting demand, it is not creating an inflationary pressure. And, if this trend were to reverse, the feedback rule would tell the Federal Reserve to reduce the growth rate of the money supply.

Another type of feedback rule is suggested by **John Taylor** (1993). The so-called **Taylor Rule** is actually quite simple. Taylor suggests that the Federal Reserve could determine the federal funds rate by working backwards. That is, the policymaker knows what his desired rate of inflation is and what the actual rate of inflation is. He also knows how fast the economy is growing relative to its long-run trend. What Taylor suggested is that the Federal Reserve could use this information in the following formula to determine the federal funds rate, the Federal Reserve's policy tool:

$$FFR = r^* + p + 0.5(y - y^*) + 0.5(p - p^*)$$

where FFR is the federal funds rate, r^* is the equilibrium real federal funds rate, y is the growth rate of real output, y^* is the long-run trend in real output growth, p is the inflation rate, and p^* is the policymaker's desired or target rate of inflation. The value 0.5 in front of the output and inflation deviation values—the terms in parentheses—are adjustment coefficients, or amounts by which the Federal Reserve should move the federal funds rate for each percentage point deviation in output or inflation. Taylor's rule indicates is that if the economy is growing in at its long-run trend ($y = y^*$) and if inflation is at the policymaker's desired rate ($p = p^*$), the federal funds rate is equal to its real equilibrium rate. In this situation the Federal Reserve would not undertake any policy actions to raise or lower the federal funds rate.

The beauty of Taylor's rule is the simplicity of deriving its policy message: If the economy is growing faster than its long-run trend (a condition usually thought to create inflation), so that $y > y^*$, then the Federal Reserve should take actions to raise the federal funds rate. In other words, take a restrictive policy action. If inflation is exceeding the policymakers' desired rate, so that $p > p^*$, the Federal Reserve should raise the federal funds rate. Again, a restrictive action is implied to ward off higher rates of inflation. If the economy slows to a rate of growth less than its long run trend, or if inflation falls relative to the desired rate, Taylor's rule indicates that policymakers should undertake expansionary policy actions and lower the federal funds rate.

Even though the Taylor Rule is the most recent of the rules suggested for policymakers to follow, it, too, has problems. For example, what is the correct inflation target rate? Even more basic: What is the correct price measure to determine the target rate of inflation? Rates of inflation differ depending on which measure one uses: the Consumer Price Index

(CPI) and the GDP deflator sometimes give divergent messages of how high or low the rate of inflation is. Similarly, how should we measure the long-run trend in output? There are various measures and they each yield different policy outcomes when used in the Taylor rule.

If policy rules are problematic, should Federal Reserve policymakers rely on discretion to guide policy actions? Some argue that it is the only sensible approach in a world of uncertainty. Federal Reserve Governor Edward Gramlich (1998) argues that, "The uncertainties implicit in using any rule of thumb, however well it might have performed in the past, are probably sufficient that policy-makers should retain their discretion.... Myriad short term uncertainties and special factors mean that rules still cannot deal with many ad hoc situations."

This statement reflects a common viewpoint taken by most policymakers since the inception of the Federal Reserve. One of the best examples of using discretionary policy is the Federal Reserve's decision-making process in the 1950s and early 1960s. Policy during that time often was determined by the **"tone and feel" approach to policy** of the financial markets. In other words, policymakers were likely to use their "gut reactions" to events of the day in determining the direction of policy than some model. The chairman of the Federal Reserve during much of this period, **William McChesney Martin**, often described the policy process as one of **"leaning against the wind,"** a reference to the notion that if the economy seemed to growing to fast or financial markets seemed to "tight," then the Federal Reserve would react. Chairman Martin also disparaged and rejected the use of economic models or statistical analysis as the foundation for policy decisions. Unfortunately, the legacy of his approach to setting policy was a persistent increase in the rate of inflation that began in the early 1960s and continued until the early 1980s when inflation reached double-digits.

It is unlikely that human decision-making will be supplanted totally by fixed rules when it comes to monetary policy. But, to quote Federal Reserve Governor Gramlich, "in view of the deeper uncertainties about how hard monetary authorities should lean against what wind, rules of thumb might give good guidance to policy-makers. They might help authorities avoid large and persistent mistakes. Rather than replacing judgment, in the end rules may aid judgment."

FURTHER READING

Gramlich, Edward M. "Monetary Rules." The Samuelson Lecture, presented before the 24th Annual Conference of the Eastern Economic Association, New York, New York, February 27, 1998, accessed at the Board of Governors Website: www.federalreserve.gov; Hafer, R. W., Joseph H. Haslag, and Scott E. Hein. "Implementing Monetary Base Rules: The Currency Problem." *Journal of Economics and Business* (December 1996): 461–72; McCallum, Bennett T. "The Case for Rules in the Conduct of Monetary Policy: A Concrete Example." Federal Reserve Bank of Richmond *Economic Review* (September/October 1987): 10–18; Poole, William. "Optimal Choice of Monetary Policy Instruments in a Simple Stochastic Macro Model." *Quarterly Journal of Economics* (May 1970): 197–216; Simon, Henry. "Rules versus Authorities in Monetary Policy." *Journal of Political Economy* 44 (1936): 1–30; Taylor, John B. "Discretion versus Policy Rules in Practice." *Carnegie-Rochester Conference Series on Public Policy* (December 1993): 195–214.

SAVINGS AND LOAN CRISIS. The savings and loan (S&L) crisis is an example of how attempts to regulate financial institutions sometime backfire, especially if there is a confluence of deregulation and **regulatory forbearance**. All of these came together in the 1980s with the largest and most wide-reaching collapse of a segment of the financial market since the **Great Depression**. To illustrate the issues surrounding the regulation of financial institutions, whether they are savings and loans or **commercial banks**, this episode is a useful guide.

In the end, the savings and loan crisis was a cost to every taxpayer and created strains on the rest of the financial system, strains that were borne by other depository institutions and by the Federal Reserve as one of the regulators. It has been estimated that the cost of the bailout of the Federal Savings and Loan Insurance Corporation (FSLIC)—the savings and loan industry's counterpart to the banking industry's **Federal Deposit Insurance Corporation** (FDIC)—was over $175 billion. How did it happen? What lessons are to be learned from the experience? We'll try to answer those questions.

The savings and loan crisis (hereafter S&L crisis) was the culmination of numerous policy mistakes. One of these was the provision of **deposit insurance** to savings and loans that, similar to the deposit insurance provided to banks, created the problem of **moral hazard**. Since all savings and loans were charged the same rate for deposit insurance, the insurance fund was unsound from the start. Riskier savings and loans—riskier in the sense that their managers sought out riskier areas in which to lend funds—flourished because if they failed, depositors would be repaid by the government. This encouraged less profitable or even bankrupt S&Ls to gamble on making loans that had a high probability of not being repaid. But this problem with deposit insurance was exacerbated by other policy changes in the early 1980s. One was the desire by Congress, supported by the Federal Reserve, to deregulate banking. One aspect of this deregulation was the removal of **Regulation Q**. Reg Q prohibited banks from paying interest on checking accounts and put interest rate ceilings on certain types of deposits. Enacted during the Great Depression, Regulation Q was extended to savings and loans in 1966. This restriction allowed savings and loans to acquire funds at a low cost and profitably lend them in the home mortgage market. Since a large component of S&Ls income was generated by mortgages made 10 to 20 years earlier at very low rates, the removal of the Reg Q restriction meant that the cost of funds rose dramatically. Since S&Ls earnings were derived largely from low-interest mortgages, their profits were squeezed: it now cost them more to acquire funds than they made on outstanding loans.

The deregulation of banking created negative externalities for savings and loans. Federal Reserve monetary policies in the late 1970s and early 1980s caused even more problems for savings and loans. Beginning in 1979, Chairman **Paul Volcker** directed the Federal Reserve to undertake policies aimed at reducing **inflation**. This was accomplished by restraining the growth of the money supply and pushing market interest rates into double digit ranges, reaching 15 percent by mid-1980. This again squeezed savings and loans' profits. With low-interest long-term mortgages being the largest source of revenues, S&Ls now had to pay depositors interest rates that were twice of three times higher than the rate on mortgages. In other words, the spread between what savings and loans paid for funds and what they were earning on those funds turned negative.

The Federal Reserve's high interest rate polices came at the same time as the deregulations discussed above were enacted. In response, Congress in 1980 and 1982 lifted restrictions on savings and loans that determined the types of investments they could make. A key provision of this change was allowing savings and loans to invest directly in the commercial real estate market. The idea was that by allowing savings and loans access to markets that provided higher rates of return, struggling savings and loans could work their way back toward profitability. Unfortunately, this created a moral hazard problem. At the time, the combined net worth (assets minus liabilities) of all savings and loans was negative. In other words, they were technically bankrupt. Given the opportunity to take a chance on the "big score," many savings and loan managers took on much riskier investments than they had in the past. And why not: they already were bankrupt and being kept open only because of regulatory forbearance. If they took the risk and failed, they would be closed and depositors would be paid off by the government. If they did not take the risk, however, they would be closed down anyway. So, many took one riskier loans with the hope of hitting the big score that would return them to solvency. For many savings and loans, they turned to the commercial real estate market for financial redemption.

This market, which includes shopping malls, retail development and multi-family housing experienced a series of setbacks in the 1980s. With the decline in oil prices in the mid-1908s, there was a concurrent collapse of real estate in the oil-producing states. The boom in commercial real estate in Oklahoma, Texas and Louisiana that had followed oil prices up collapsed with the decline in oil prices. Savings and loans that loaned millions to mall developers now held mortgages on real estate that could only be sold for a fraction of the original loan. (*See* **Mark-to-Market**.) Regulatory forbearance, inept supervision and a desire to try anything to keep savings and loans operating culminated in the collapse of many savings and loans.

The cleanup of the S&L crisis continued throughout the 1980s. In 1987 Congress attempted to recapitalize the FSLIC with an infusion of about $11 billion, even though experts agreed that the necessary funding was actually many times that amount. More legislation followed in 1989 with the passage of the **Financial Institutions Reform, Recovery, and Enforcement Act of 1989**. Although it too provided insufficient funds to correct the mess, it was a step in the right direction.

Savings and loans still exist, though there are far fewer of them than before the S&L crisis. What does the future hold for this segment of the financial industry? One expert argues that savings and loans are not likely to survive into the future. As Bert Ely (2002) suggests "integrated, specialized housing lenders such as S&Ls are no longer need-ed ... Eventually, S&Ls probably will cease to exist as a separately regulated industry."

FURTHER READING

Ely, Bert. "Savings and Loan Crisis." *The Concise Encyclopedia of Economics.* Accessed at Website: www.econlib.org, 2002; Federal Deposit Insurance Corporation. "The S&L Crisis: A Chrono-Bibliography." Accessed at Website: www.fdic.gov; White, Lawrence. *The S&L Debacle: Public Policy Lessons for Bank and Thrift Regulation.* New York: Oxford University Press, 1991.

SCHWARTZ, ANNA JACOBSON (1915–). Anna J. Schwartz is recognized as one of the most prominent economic historians and monetary economists of the last 50 years. A scholar on British financial institutions and economic history, her first major work was *The Growth and Fluctuation of the British Economy 1790–1850*, published in 1953 and co-authored with A. D. Gayer and W. W. Rostow. It is her work with **Milton Friedman** that Schwartz gained the most recognition amongst monetary policymakers. Together they authored the controversial *A Monetary History of the United States* (1963) in which they demonstrated the importance of movements in the stock of money in explaining economic fluctuations. A key argument in the book was that if the Federal Reserve can control the behavior of the money supply over time, then its behavior during the onset of the **Great Depression** exacerbated the situation, turning a **recession** into the most severe economic downturn in U.S. economic history. Schwartz and Friedman showed the im-portance that a stable money monetary policy is to achieving stable **economic growth**.

Schwartz joined the staff of the National Bureau of Economic Research (NBER) in 1941 after receiving her Masters degree in economics from Columbia University in 1935 and working for the U.S. Department of Agriculture. Her connection to the NBER continues to this day: she was named emeritus research associate in 1985. During her time at the NBER, Schwartz has served as the staff director of the U.S. Gold Commission in 1981–1982. In that role she wrote Volume I of the Report of the Gold Commission and helped to organize a conference in 1982 which resulted in the book *A Retrospective on the Classical Gold Standard, 1921–1931*, published in 1984. Still active, Schwartz's research agenda spans monetary policy, international policy coordination and economic history.

FURTHER READING

Bordo, Michael D., and Milton Friedman. "Introduction." *Money in Historical Perspective.* Chi-cago: University of Chicago Press, 1987; Feldstein, Martin. "Anna Schwartz at the National Bureau of Economic Research," *Journal of Financial Services Research* (18:2/3, 2000): 115–7; Friedman, Milton, and Anna Schwartz. *A Monetary History of the United States, 1867–1960.* Princeton: Princeton University Press, 1963; Friedman, Milton, and Anna Schwartz. *Monetary Statistics of the United States.* New York: Columbia University Press, 1970; Friedman, Milton, and Anna Schwartz. *Monetary Trends in the United States and the United Kingdom: Their Relation to Income, Prices and Interest Rates, 1867–1975.* Chicago: University of Chicago Press, 1982.

SEASONAL CREDIT. "Seasonal" credit is extended to depository institutions—usually small and medium sized banks with deposits under $250 million—that demonstrate a recurring pattern of seasonal fluctuation in their **liquidity** needs. Seasonal credit is extended through the Federal Reserve's **discount window**. Seasonality affects banks that do a large share of their business with the agricultural or tourist related industries. For example, in the spring the demand for **loans** by farmers to pay for crop seed rises and their deposits decrease. In the fall when crops are harvested just the reverse is true: farmers repay loans and increase their deposits. During this fall period depository institutions repay their seasonal borrowings. The geography of seasonal borrowing reflects this relation: the Federal Reserve Bank of New York's district has very little seasonal borrowing, while the Midwestern District Banks, such as Kansas City or Minneapolis, have much more.

Seasonal credit extended to nonbank institutions is often viewed as a last resort to keep them operating. Most of these institutions, such as savings and loans or credit unions, have other resources available to them for seasonal credit. For example, the Federal Home Loan Banks help serve savings and loans and savings banks; credit unions can turn to the National Credit Union Administration's Central Liquidity Facility for seasonal borrowing needs; or the institutions may turn to the **federal funds market**. If these other sources are not adequate, a depository institution can apply to the Federal Reserve for seasonal credit. To qualify the institution must demonstrate that it has been subject to fluctuations in deposits during the previous three years that are related directly to seasonal factors. If officials at the Federal Reserve Bank believe that seasonal effects are existent and believe that the institution is being harmed by them, the bank can extend seasonal credit advances lasting for a period of up to nine months. To ensure that the institution is not abusing its seasonal borrowing, for example by lending the funds in the federal funds market, the Federal Reserve monitors their activity in the overnight lending market.

The borrowing rate set on seasonal credit historically was equal to the Federal Reserve's **discount rate**. In 1992 the Federal Reserve began to charge a seasonal credit rate that is calculated as an average of the current federal funds rate and the rate for negotiable 90-day certificates of deposit as determined in the secondary market.

For details about the use and administration of the discount window, visit the Website www.frbdiscountwindow.org.

FURTHER READING

Federal Reserve Bank of New York. "Seasonal Borrowing." *Fedpoint* (February 2003). Available online at Website: www.newyorkfed.org.; Wheelock, David C. "Replacement Windows: New Credit Programs at the Discount Window," Federal Reserve Bank of St. Louis *Monetary Trends* (May 2003).

SECONDARY MARKETS. Financial instruments, such as stocks, **bonds**, and government securities, are traded in primary and secondary markets. A primary market is one in which *newly issued* financial instruments are bought. A secondary market, by far the largest of the two, is one in which *existing* financial instruments are bought and sold. The most active secondary markets generally are for government securities, such as **Treasury bills** and bonds, and corporate stock. More recently there has been an expanding secondary market for other types of financial instruments, such as corporate bonds, state and local bonds, and **loans** made by consumer credit companies and banks.

Transactions in secondary markets take place through brokers. Brokers are individuals who intermediate transactions, whether it is an individual buying stock in Microsoft, or the Federal Reserve buying government securities. Brokers specialize in the information of trading financial assets in the secondary market. It is through brokers that Federal Reserve **open market operations** take place. The buying and selling of government securities in the secondary market is the most effective way in which monetary policy objectives can be carried out. Buying and selling government securities at prices determined in the open market is how the Federal Reserve changes the volume of **reserves** in the banking system, thus achieving its policy objectives for the level of the **federal funds rate** and the growth rate of the **money** supply. By manipulating these economic variables the Federal Reserve attempts to control inflation and keep the economy expanding at a steady rate.

FURTHER READING

Akhtar, M. A. *Understanding Open Market Operations*. New York: Federal Reserve Bank of New York, 1997; Federal Reserve Bank of New York. "Open Market Operations." *Fedpoints* (September 1998). Available online at Website: www.newyorkfed.org.

SECOND BANK OF THE UNITED STATES. The U.S. government granted a 20-year charter to the Second Bank of the United States in 1816. Need for such bank—the charter for the **First Bank of the United States** was allowed to expire just five years earlier— became apparent when the United States found it difficult to finance the War of 1812 and to deal with the **inflation** that followed. The Second Bank operated in a similar fashion to the First Bank: it acted as the government's fiscal agent; the majority of the bank's capital ($35 million) was owned by individuals, state and local governments; and the managers of the bank consisted of 25 directors, 20 of which were selected by private stockholders with the other 5 appointed by the president of the United States.

Soon after its charter was granted, however, the Second Bank was involved in controversy. The bank often presented for payment the notes of **state banks**; that is, the bank would return the notes to the state banks in exchange for gold. Because these notes were backed by gold, the expectation that the bank would redeem notes kept the issuance of state bank notes in check. Consequently, many felt that the bank was establishing a monopoly in the issuance of circulating notes. This helped create a uniform **currency** across the country, but it also deprived state banks from the gains that note issuance could deliver.

Second, the appointment of Nicholas Biddle as the bank's third president in 1823 ushered in a period of turmoil. Biddle tried to regulate the nation's banking system much more closely than his predecessors. This led to a number of positive developments. For example, the bank became the **lender of last resort** to state banks, largely because of its extensive holdings of gold and silver. The bank also aided private firms when others would not. When Biddle made the bank the largest dealer in foreign exchange, he enabled the bank to check drains of gold and silver, thus keeping check on the underlying base of the money supply.

Even though the bank seemed to satisfy the needs of a growing economy its fate did not rely on the positive things it had accomplished but on politics. In 1828 Andrew Jackson was elected President of the United States over Henry Clay, a firm supporter of centralized banking. Jackson opposed the bank and any other institution that further centralized power in Washington, D.C. During the 1828 campaign, Jackson spoke publicly about the dangers of banks in general, and the Second Bank in particular. (It seems that Jackson had earlier suffered substantial financial losses in a speculative land deal and blamed the banks involved.)

President Jackson had a powerful platform from which to rally his cause against the bank. His election in 1828 began the so-called Bank War as he campaigned to discredit the bank and Biddle. He argued that the bank was unconstitutional and a harmful government monopoly whose policies favored the economic interests of the urban over the rural areas of the country. To Jackson and his supporters the bank showed little or no knowledge of the business needs by "ordinary" citizens, especially those in the agrarian South and West. In the 1832 presidential campaign, Henry Clay made re-chartering the bank part of the political debate. Clay supported a bill for re-chartering the bank four years early, a bill that Congress passed in the summer of 1832. Jackson vetoed it and Congress could not muster the needed votes to override. Later that year Jackson overwhelmingly won re-election.

Once re-elected, Jackson directed the U.S. government to cease making deposits with the bank, the beginning of the end for the bank. Although there is some debate over whether the actions taken by the Biddle in 1834 accelerated the bank's downfall, the bank's charter was allowed to expire in 1836. The bank continued operations as a state bank until it failed in 1841. The country's second experiment with a central bank had, like the first, ended more because of politics than economics. It would not be until the **Federal Reserve Act of 1913** that the United States would have a central bank.

FURTHER READING

Govan, Thomas Payne. *Nicholas Biddle: Nationalist and Public Banker 1786–1844*. Chicago: University of Chicago Press, 1959; Walton, Gary M., and Hugh Rockoff. *History of the American Economy*, 8th edition. Orlando: Dryden Press, 1998; Temin, Peter. *The Jacksonian Economy*. New York: W.W. Norton, 1969; Hammond, Bray. *Banks and Politics in America*. Princeton: Princeton University Press, 1957; Timberlake, Richard H. *The Origins of Central Banking in the United States*. Cambridge, MA: Harvard University Press, 1978.

SEIGNIORAGE. Seigniorage is one of those words that you probably will not see anyplace but here or an economics text. Though obscure, it actually is an important concept. In its most basic form seigniorage is the profit that the government makes from its monopoly control over the production of **money**. This idea can be explained using an example suggested by Miller and VanHoose (1993). Suppose the economy uses gold coins for transactions purposes, and the government controls the production of gold coins. This means that the government incurs costs associated with acquisition of gold and the production of coin. If the market value of the gold coins is exactly equal to the cost of production, the government earns no monopoly profit from the production of coin. Seigniorage would, in this case, be zero. On the other hand, if the cost of producing a coin is less than its market value—that is, a coin that costs a dollar to produce is worth 5 dollars in terms of goods and services in the market—then the government benefits. Seigniorage in this case is 4 dollars.

Seigniorage amounts to rent paid to the government for its monopoly control over the production of money. Amongst other reasons, this form of taxation explains why counterfeiting money is illegal: the government does not wish to share its monopoly profits with anyone else. By maintaining its monopoly over the production of money, the government artificially keeps up the demand for its **currency**. And if you think that this is nonsense, the example of **free banking** in the United States during the mid-1800s and its demise following the Civil War is a perfect example of how the government sought to establish monopoly control over money production.

Seigniorage can have important implications for monetary policy. Countries that aim for high rates of **inflation** often are attempting to increase their seigniorage (tax revenue) from money production. The study by Gros (1993) shows that seigniorage can be a significant source of revenue for a country. Gros estimates that in Portugal during the 1980s seigniorage amounted to an average of about 3 percent of **gross domestic product (GDP)**. For Greece, the percentage was close to 2 percent of GDP. With one of the requirements of entering the European Community being a convergence of inflation rates to some low rate, these countries were forced to enact policies that lowered inflation and thus reduced their reliance on seigniorage as a source of tax revenue.

FURTHER READING

Gros, Daniel. "The Fiscal Implications of Price Stability and Financial Market Integration," *European Journal of Political Economy* (November 1993): 581–501; Haslag, Joseph H. "Seigniorage Revenue and Monetary Policy: Some Preliminary Evidence," Federal Reserve Bank of Dallas *Economic Review* (Third Quarter 1998): 10–20; Miller, Roger LeRoy, and David D. VanHoose. *Modern Money and Banking*. New York: McGraw-Hill, 1993.

SMITHSONIAN AGREEMENT OF 1971. The Bretton Woods **exchange rate** system, which began after World War II, was designed to replace the **gold standard** system in which the foreign exchange value of a nation's **currency** was determined by how many ounces of gold it exchanged for. Under the **Bretton Woods System**, instead of tying the value of a currency to gold, it effectively tied it to the U.S. dollar. Since the dollar's value was expressed in terms of gold, this was a roundabout way of using gold as the underlying determinant of exchange rates. In reality, it became clear over time that U.S. policies, especially monetary policy, was the driving force behind movements in international exchange rates. This created problems for the Bretton Woods System, problems that became apparent during the 1960s. At the time U.S. monetary policy was very expansionary. Since the Bretton Woods System was based on maintaining exchange rates in a very narrow range, this meant that when the U.S. money supply expanded, other countries were forced to follow suit in order to maintain agreed upon exchange rates.

The formal end of the Bretton Woods System came in December 1971 at a conference of international monetary policymakers held at the Smithsonian Institute in Washington, D.C. The purpose of the conference was to realign the exchange rates of the major currencies. Part of the Smithsonian Agreement was that the value of the U.S. dollar would fall relative to gold. Before the Agreement, the dollar was pegged at $35 per ounce of gold. After the Agreement, the dollar was $38 dollars per ounce of gold. This meant that the value of the dollar, relative to other currencies, was devalued by about 8 percent. For those countries with trade surpluses with the United States, (the value of exports to the United States exceeded the value of imports from the United States) their currencies were revalued upward. Similar to the Bretton Woods System, once this realignment took place countries agreed to maintain the new exchange rates within a band of 2.25 percent of the target rate.

The Smithsonian Agreement provided only temporary relief from the current exchange rate problems. U.S. monetary policy continued to increase the growth of the money supply, putting pressure on other central banks to expand their money supplies. In the summer of 1972, foreign exchange traders began to pressure the British pound and the Italian lira, eventually forcing the British government to let the foreign exchange value of the pound float. In other words, the foreign exchange value of the pound was now determined by the demand for and supply of pounds in the international currency market. This was a clear break with the Smithsonian Agreement. At the same time, those countries that saw increased demand for their currencies, notably Germany, imposed controls on the flow of funds into their country.

The Smithsonian Agreement led to a breakdown in the use of the dollar. During this period of speculative attacks on various currencies, the dollar was pegged to gold at $38 per ounce. The catch, however, was that the U.S. government was not converting dollars into gold. Even though the value of the dollar was devalued, the fact that it was inconvertible into gold really meant that the devaluation impacted the foreign exchange value of other currencies more than the dollar. Fearing that the dollar's value was declining, speculators began to sell dollars in massive amounts during 1972 and into 1973. In response the U.S. government raised the official gold price of the dollar to $42.22, but this had little effect on the dumping of dollars. By March 1973, all of the major trading countries had announced that they were allowing their currencies to float. March 1973 marks the end of the Bretton Woods System and the failure of the Smithsonian Agreement to patch up the exchange rate system.

FURTHER READING

Melamed, Leo. "Evolution of the International Money Market." *Cato Journal* (Fall 1988): 393–404.

SPECIAL DRAWING RIGHTS. A special drawing right, or SDR, is an international reserve asset that is issued by the **International Monetary Fund** (IMF). An SDR is used by central banks or government treasuries to supplement their official reserves of foreign currency. The original purpose of the SDR, which was created in 1969, was for IMF member countries to use it when purchasing international currencies. For example, if a country was experiencing a decline in the exchange value of its currency in international markets, it could use SDRs to purchase its currency as a means to increase its value (in effect, increase the demand for the currency). At the time when SDRs were created gold and the U.S. dollar served the purpose of international reserve assets. But the expansion of trade created a situation where the supplies of gold and dollars simply were not sufficient to meet the needs of the world economy. This led IMF member countries to think of SDRs as an additional international reserve asset. By the early 1970s the **Bretton Woods System** had collapsed and the SDR's role as an international reserve asset diminished. Today, the SDR serves as a unit of account for the IMF. That is, countries exchange SDRs for international currencies either through mutually agreeable exchange with the other member country, or through the IMF designating one country to purchase SDRs from another. This latter situation occurs when one country has a strong balance of payment position relative to the other. In both instances, the SDR has basically replaced gold as the international medium of exchange.

SDRs affect domestic monetary policy because they appear as an asset in the Federal Reserve's balance sheet. When the U.S. Treasury acquires SDRs in an international transaction, the Treasury issues an SDR certificate to the Federal Reserve. This is, in effect, a claim on the SDR. The Federal Reserve then credits the Treasury's account. On a wider scale by issuing SDRs to countries that then converted them into domestic currency, the IMF is essentially acting as a **lender of last resort**. But this is not the use for which SDRs were intended. Undertaking such a policy allows the IMF to act as a supernational lender of last resort, even though its decision may not depend of issues such as solvency of the rescued institutions. In one of the most recent manifestations of such actions, the bailout of the Asian and Russian economies during the 1990s, one prominent economist, **Anna Jacobson Schwartz** (1998), argued that "the bailouts have worsened their situations" and that the model upon which such actions were taken "is an abject failure."

FURTHER READING

International Monetary Fund. *Factsheet*. Accessed at www.imf.org/external/np/exr/facts/sdr.HTM.; Schwartz, Anna J. "Time to Terminate the IMF." Cato Institute Report (October 6, 1998) accessed at www.cato.org.

STABILIZATION POLICY. Stabilization policy most often is meant to describe policy actions that are intended to reduce fluctuations in the growth rate of real **gross domestic product (GDP)**. This focus characterizes policy though during much of the post World War II era, up until the late 1970s. As discussed in Hafer and Wheelock (2003), the macroeconomic policy framework that emerged after the **Great Depression** and World War II focused on keeping **unemployment rates** as low as possible. In the United States, unlike some European countries that experienced hyperinflation at times in their history, the experience of the Great Depression, when the unemployment rate reached about 25 percent, colored attitudes of what economic policy objectives should be. Indeed, the popularity of the **Phillips curve** policy analysis fit perfectly with this mindset: policy was viewed as balancing the tradeoff between higher rates of **inflation** and lower unemployment rates. Since unemployment was viewed as the worse of the two, monetary policy during the period from 1960 through 1980 was inflationary. Many economists and policymakers at the time considered moderate rates of inflation a small price to pay for full employment.

History tells us that attempts to keep the economy running at or above full employment created an inflationary environment. The policies followed in this period gave rise to what has been referred to as the **Great Inflation** in the United States. Did stabilization policy fail? What's the evidence? Are there any reasons to suspect that such policies are likely to be successful? We'll attempt to answer those questions in this entry.

Below is a table listing the timing of **business cycles** since 1854 as defined by the National Bureau of Economic Research (NBER). Notice that prior to World War II there are many more **recessions** and that they appear to last for much longer periods of time compared with the period since 1950. Looking at the period prior to 1929, chosen to exclude the Great Depression, the average economic downturn lasted almost 21 months and the average expansion lasted a bit more than 25 months. Since 1950 the frequency and severity of recessions are much less than before, and the length of economic expansions is much longer. Aside from the significant recession of the early 1980s, most post-war recessions have been relatively mild on an historical comparison. In fact, since the early 1980s there have been only two mild recessions, in 1990 and in 2001. In fact, the period since 1980 has been characterized more by economic growth than recessions, leading **John Taylor** (1998) to dub this period the "Great Expansion."

Business Cycles in the United States

Business Cycle Reference Dates		Duration in months	
Peak	**Trough**	**Contraction**	**Expansion**
November 1948	October 1949	11	
July 1953	May 1954	10	45
August 1957	April 1958	8	39
April 1960	February 1961	10	24
December 1969	November 1970	11	106
November 1973	March 1975	16	36
January 1980	July 1980	6	58
July 1981	November 1982	16	12
July 1990	March 1991	8	92
March 2001	November 2001	9	120

Source: National Bureau of Economic Research (www.NBER.org).

Even though the evidence in the table is appealing, there are some who question whether the data are comparable over time. Christina Romer of University of California at Berkeley has analyzed the data and argues that the pre-World War II data are of dubious quality and reliability. Making comparable changes in the data led Romer (1986, 1989, and 1991) to argue that business cycles in the post-war period have been no less severe than before. Her findings have been supported and rejected by others leaving the question open for debate.

Granting that post-war policy has dampened fluctuations in output growth, the cost has been higher rates of inflation. The chart below shows the rate of inflation over the period since 1950. Notice that the rate of inflation increases over time, spiking in the mid and

Inflation in Consumer Prices: Percent (Dec-Dec): CPI-U

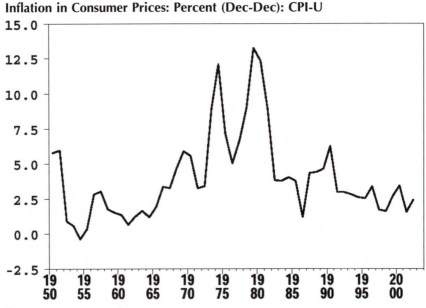

Source: www.economagic.com.

late 1970s. Even though these spikes are associated with sharp increases in oil prices at the time, the underlying rate of inflation also increased throughout this period. It was only after 1980, when the Federal Reserve decided to make lowering inflation its key policy objective that the rate of inflation began to fall and remain low.

Aside from arguments over data interpretation, changes in how economists model the economy raised questions about the efficacy of monetary policy actions aimed at stabilizing output growth. The economic theories developed after World War II are based on the premise that changes in policy had lasting effects. It was believed that monetary policy could permanently shift the economy from one level of output growth (or unemployment rate) to another by altering its policies. The problem is that if policymakers were trying to make the economy growth at a 5 percent rate when its long-run, full employment rate of expansion is 3 percent, policy was doomed to fail. Even though this policy might achieve a short-run growth rate of the economy that was faster than its long-run average, it was not sustainable. When the economy returned to its long-run rate of growth and associated unemployment rate, the only lasting effect was a higher rate of inflation. When the Federal Reserve attempted to again lower the unemployment rate and raise output growth, the outcome was the same: higher rates of inflation. The lesson learned from the 1960s and 1970s is that while the Federal Reserve may be able to cushion the short-run effects of a recession, it could not push the economy to a permanently higher level of output growth.

How successful is the Federal Reserve at minimizing the costs of a recession? Think about the requirements of doing this. First, policymakers must recognize that the growth of real output is slowing, or even beginning to slow. Although there are numerous pieces of economic information about this that are available to policymakers, the arrival of such information occurs with a time lag, one that is sometimes considerable. (*See* **Lags in Monetary Policy**.) Once policymakers realize and agree that the economy is in a recession, it is not uncommon that the worst of the decline is over and the economy is beginning to recover. Because policy affects the economy with a lag, the Federal Reserve may undertake an expansionary policy even if it really isn't called for. An overly aggressive policy speeds up the economic expansion, setting into motion a run-up in prices that must be dealt with at a later date. The sheer fact that policy is made in an informational vacuum, and the fact that policymakers cannot be sure how much of their policy is anticipated or not, makes it extremely difficult for a policymaker to design a stabilization policy that actually reduces the variability of the growth rate of real output.

FURTHER READING

Hafer, R. W., ed. *The Monetary versus Fiscal Policy Debate: Lessons from Two Decades.* Totowa, NJ: Rowman and Allenheld, 1986; Hafer, R. W., and David C. Wheelock. "Darryl Francis and the Making of Monetary Policy, 1966–1975." Federal Reserve Bank of St. Louis *Review* (March/April 2003): 1–12; Romer, Christina. "Is the Stabilization of the Postwar Economy a Figment of the Data?" *American Economic Review* (June 1986): 314–34; Romer, Christina. "The Prewar Business Cycle Reconsidered: New Estimates of Gross National Product, 1869–1908." *Journal of Political Economy* (February 1989): 1–37; Romer, Christina. "The Cyclical Behavior of Individual Production Series, 1889–1984." *Quarterly Journal of Economics* (February 1991): 1–31.

STAGFLATION. Stagflation is the term that economists use to describe a condition of rising rates of **inflation,** slowing **economic growth** and rising **unemployment rates**. This situation occurred in the United States during the 1970s during the aftermath of the oil price increases in 1973. Before that time, economists generally thought that higher inflation rates occurred only when unemployment rates declined. The Federal Reserve's policy dilemma in a period of stagflation is whether to fight the rising unemployment rates through expansionary policies, or attempt to reduce the rate of inflation through contractionary policies. The problem is that one set of monetary policies cannot do both. Although coinage of the tern is often attributed to Nobel Prize winning economist Paul Samuelson in the 1970s, apparently the term was used in a 1965 speech given by Iain MacLeod, a British Member of Parliament.

STATE BANK. A state bank is chartered by a state banking authority. This is not to be confused with a *national* bank, which is chartered to operate by the federal government. Because state and national banks operate in every state, this gives rise to the notion that the United States has a **dual banking system**, one comprised of state and federally chartered banks.

Historically, the choice to seek a federal or state charter often boiled down to whether one wished to be part of the Federal Reserve System or not. National banks were required to join the Federal Reserve System; state banks were not required to do so. Banks that were members of the System were accorded certain privileges, such as the ability to borrow from the Federal Reserve's **discount window** and the use of the Federal Reserve's check clearing facilities. Membership also imposed a cost: members were required to hold non–interest-bearing **reserves** against deposits, usually at their Federal Reserve District Bank. State banks also faced **reserve requirements**, but they often were less than those imposed on national banks. Banks that chose to be members of the Federal Reserve System also were required to have their deposits insured by the **Federal Deposit Insurance Corporation (FDIC)**. Although state banks did not face such a restriction, most opted to insure their deposits with the FDIC. Thus, the choice to seek a federal or state charter largely came down to weighing the costs and benefits of membership in the Federal Reserve System.

State banks today operate alongside nationally-chartered banks. Passage of the **Depository Institutions Deregulation and Monetary Control Act (DIDMCA) of 1980** lowered the barriers between state and national banks. After DIDMCA, all banks could avail themselves of the discount window, thus making the Federal Reserve the **lender of last resort** for all banks. In addition, state and national banks faced similar reserve requirements. This legislation expanded the Federal Reserve's ability to control reserves in the banking system and achieve its policy objectives. Thus, DIDMCA made the chartering decision less one of opting for the least costly version to which regulator to choose.

State banks have an interesting history. In one period, which lasted approximately from 1839 to 1865, the number of state banks expanded rapidly. This period, known as the **free banking** era in the United States, ceased with the onset of the Civil War. The number of state banks was sharply reduced once the war started, largely because of declines in the value of the banks' assets. The number of state banks also declined following passage of federal legislation, especially the **National Banking Act of 1864**, which created national banks. In this act the federal government levied a tax on state bank notes, effectively taxing them out of existence and creating a national currency. By the 1870s, however, the tide turned as individuals realized that obtaining a national bank charter was not necessary to run a successful banking operation and may have been prohibitively expensive. Consequently, the number of state banks grew, eventually outnumbering national banks by almost a two-to-one ratio by 1907.

State banks, like their federally chartered competitors, have experienced the trend of consolidation over the past 20 years. Based on FDIC data on insured institutions, the number of federally chartered institutions in 1984 stood at 1,707 compared with 1,711 state banks. By 2003, however, the number of federally chartered banks was 815 and the number of state chartered banks was 598. Thus, the recent data indicate that as a percentage of total banking institutions, state banks have declined proportionally more than federally chartered banks. This also is true if one compares the numbers of offices for each type of bank.

Data on the numbers of state banks and national banks is available online from the Federal Deposit Insurance Corporation (www.fdic.gov). For information specific to state banks, an informative site to visit is that of the Conference of State Bank Supervisors (www.csbs.org), an advocacy group for state banks in the United States.

FURTHER READING

Walton, Gary M., and Hugh Rockoff, *History of the American Economy.* 8th edition. New York: The Dryden Press, 1998.

STERILIZED AND UNSTERILIZED INTERVENTION. Economies throughout the world are much more closely linked than they were just a few decades ago. This means that policy actions taken by the Federal Reserve affect not only the U.S. economy, but also has affects that ripple across a number of other economies. And the reverse is true. Even though the U.S. economy remains relatively closed—the percentage of economic activity, measured by **gross domestic product (GDP),** due to international trade is lower for the United States than other countries like Japan or the United Kingdom—policymakers in the United States must be aware of actions taken by other governments.

One such area in which policy actions have a wider impact is in the **foreign exchange markets**. Until the 1980s, the Federal Reserve actively sought to influence the dollar's **exchange rate** by intervening in the foreign exchange market. During the late 1950s and early 1960s, members of the **Federal Open Market Committee (FOMC)** spent much of their time trying to determine how to influence the dollar exchange rate in order to affect the balance of trade. At times, the discussion suggested that more attention was paid to international affects of policy than to domestic ones. (See Hafer [1999] for a discussion of this episode.) Since the 1980s, in contrast, the Federal Reserve has been much less actively engaged in trying to move or protect the dollar exchange rate. To some extent this reflects a change in policy that began with the more free-market attitude of the Reagan Administration. The view espoused was that the value of the dollar in international markets should be determined by the forces of supply and demand, not by some pre-determined idea of what the "correct" value of the dollar should be.

Although there is less intervention today than in the past, the forces determining the value of the dollar in foreign exchange are not totally free of government intervention. Foreign central banks regularly buy and sell currencies to influence the exchange value of their currency. When such intervention occurs, it impacts the domestic stock of money unless specific actions are taken by the Federal Reserve to counteract or offset these effects.

The Federal Reserve System's balance sheet includes, among other items, international reserves—currencies of other countries—and domestic currency in circulation. The latter measure is part of the domestic **monetary base**, which includes domestic currency in circulation and **reserves** of the banking system. Suppose that the Federal Reserve decides to sell $1 billion worth of its holdings of international reserves (holdings of other countries' currencies) in exchange for $1 billion in U.S. dollars. The effect of this transaction is to reduce the Federal Reserve's holdings of international reserves by $1 billion, *and reduces* the amount of dollars in circulation by $1 billion. In other words, the Federal Reserve intervened in the foreign exchange market (the sale of $1 billion in foreign currency) and allowed this action to impact the domestic money supply, here measured by the monetary base (reserves plus currency). This type of intervention is referred to as *unsterilized* intervention. Unsterilized intervention occurs when the Federal Reserve allows its trading activity in the foreign exchange market to affect the domestic money supply. The transaction also could have been completed with the buyer of the foreign currency writing a check to the Federal Reserve, which would have reduced deposits with the Federal Reserve (reserves) and had the same effect on the monetary base.

Suppose that the Federal Reserve does not wish there to be any affect on the domestic money supply stemming from its international exchange activity. This is accomplished in the following manner. In the preceding example, the foreign exchange activity caused the monetary base to decline because the purchase of dollars (sale of foreign currencies) reduced the monetary base. To offset this, the Federal Reserve engages in **open market operations** where the Federal Reserve purchases $1 billion in government securities, thus increasing reserves in the banking system by $1 billion. Since the monetary base consists of currency and bank reserves, the reduction in currency by $1 billion is offset by the $1 billion injection of reserves into the banking system stemming from the open market purchase. In this way, the Federal Reserve has *sterilized* its foreign exchange transaction, completely offsetting any affects of the foreign exchange market intervention on the domestic money supply.

Each approach to trading of international currency has been used by the Federal Reserve. During the 1960s some believed that the FOMC's preoccupation with the foreign exchange value of the dollar and the trade balance led them to undertake interventions in the foreign exchange market that caused the domestic stock of money to increase more than desired. It has been shown that this policy provided a foundation to the inflationary bias that began in the 1960s and continued throughout the 1970s. It also can be shown that sterilized intervention may not affect the level of the dollar exchange rate. Because sterilized intervention does not, in the end, alter the size of the money stock, there is no change in domestic interest rates and therefore no change in the foreign exchange value of the dollar. This outcome, based on the assumption that domestic and foreign assets are substitutes, may lead one to wonder why the Federal Reserve would even engage in such activity. The reason is because through sterilized intervention policymakers are able to signal their intentions about the future level of the exchange rate. This notion, however, gets little support in research examining the role of Federal Reserve intervention in foreign exchange markets.

FURTHER READING

Mishkin, Frederic S. *The Economics of Money, Banking, and Financial Markets*. 7th edition. Boston: Pearson Addison Wesley, 2004, Chapter 20; Hafer, R. W. "Against the Tide: Malcolm

Bryan and the Introduction of Monetary Aggregate Targets." *Federal Reserve Bank of Atlanta Economic Review* (First Quarter 1999): 20–37; Branson, William H., Jacob A. Frenkel, and Morris Goldstein, eds. *International Policy Coordination and Exchange Rate Fluctuations*. Chicago: University of Chicago Press, 1990.

STRIPS. Strips are obtained by stripping—removing—the interest payment coupon from a government security with the intent of treating the coupon as a separate financial asset. Suppose one has a bond with 10 interest payment coupons, each guaranteeing a payment of $10. Stripping this bond of its coupons allows a dealer to sell off the coupons separately. If an investor, like a **commercial bank**, for example, wishes to fix a revenue source for some point in the future, buying that one coupon payment enables it to do so.

The use of strips has grown during the past several decades. During the 1970s some dealers traded government securities in the **secondary market** by removing one or more of their interest coupons. Referred to as "zeros" for the fact that the coupons or the original security now has no periodic interest payment—hence the idea of "zero coupons" or zeros, for short—U.S. Treasury officials worried that the existence of such financial assets could reduce tax revenues to the federal government. To thwart the use of strips to avoid taxes, the government passed the Tax Equity and Fiscal Responsibility Act (TEFRA) in 1983. This was short-lived, however, as the Treasury soon withdrew its objections to coupon stripping. In response to this change, a number of financial securities that are hybrids of the original asset began to appear. For example, in the early 1980s securities with names like "TIGRS" (Treasury Investment Growth Receipts) and "CATS" (Certificates of Accrual on Treasury Securities) began to be traded in financial markets. In 1985, the U.S. Treasury developed its own version of stripped securities when it began to offer STRIPS, which stands for Separate Trading of Registered Interest and Principal Securities. In its STRIPS program the Treasury uses the **Fedwire** system to offer securities with 10 years or longer to maturity. The Treasury wires notes and bonds to the New York Federal Reserve and receives separated components in return. The growth of the STRIPS program and similar innovations in the financial market has provided an increased amount of **liquidity** in the market and a wider array of financial instruments that enable investors to meet their specific funding needs.

FURTHER READING

Federal Reserve Bank of New York. "STRIPS." *Fednotes* (November 2002).

STRONG, BENJAMIN (1872–1928). Benjamin Strong served as the first governor (now referred to as president) of the Federal Reserve Bank of New York from 1914 until his death in 1928. Strong's time at the New York Bank represents one of tumultuous change and conflict within the Federal Reserve System. Strong was there at the birth of the System and helped shape monetary policy through World War I and its aftermath and guide it through the economic boom of the 1920s. Monetary policy was in its infancy and a state of flux. Strong, with a name that befits his stature in the System, carved out a position of power unrivaled by any other. As governor of the New York Bank, Strong wielded power that some have likened to that of today's **Chairman of the Board of Governors**.

Strong's position in the System makes him the subject of a large literature. For this entry we'll focus on just one area of debate: would the **Great Depression** have been avoided or at least mollified if Strong had lived beyond 1928? One set of researchers, for example **Milton Friedman** and **Anna Jacobson Schwartz** (1963), argue that had Strong's dominating policy position in the System and his track record through the 1920s suggest that he would have acted to mitigate the forces which led to the Great Depression. Their argument is that he would have recognized the need in the early 1930s for aggressive and expansionary monetary policies, and been willing to enact them. This view is countered by, among others, **Karl Brunner** and **Allan H. Meltzer** (1968) and Temin (1989), who believe that Strong had not developed an understanding of how to use monetary policy to achieve countercyclical results. In a more recent analysis, Wheelock (1992) argues that the redistribution of power within the System following Strong's death, power that shifted from the Federal Reserve Bank of New York to Washington, D.C., does not provide a credible explanation for the failed policies that were ultimately followed at the onset and during the Great Depression. Rather, Wheelock argues that Strong had always advocated the **gold standard** as the proper framework for policy and that he would not have jeopardized the convertibility of the dollar. Wheelock shows that policies taken during the Great Depression actually were similar to those taken during the 1920s, the time when Strong wielded the most power. Wheelock (1992, p. 27) states that "Benjamin Strong's death robbed the System of an intelligent leader at a crucial time and undoubtedly imparted a contractionary bias to monetary policy during the Great Depression. It seems clear, however, that Strong's death did not cause a fundamental change in regime." Policies taken during the Great Depression, like those advocated by Strong during his tenure at the New York Bank, focused on preserving the gold standard.

FURTHER READING

Chandler, Lester V. *Benjamin Strong: Central Banker*. Washington, D.C.: Brookings Institution, 1958; Friedman, Milton, and Anna Schwartz. *A Monetary History of the United States, 1867–1960*. Princeton: Princeton University Press, 1963; Roberts, Priscilla. "Benjamin Strong, the Federal Reserve and the Limits to Interwar American Nationalism: Part I: Intellectual Profile of a Central Banker." Federal Reserve Bank of Richmond *Economic Quarterly* (Spring 2000): 61–76; Roberts, Priscilla. "Part II: Strong and the Federal Reserve System in the 1920s." Federal Reserve Bank of Richmond *Economic Quarterly* (Spring 2000): 77–98; Wheelock, David C. "Monetary Policy in the Great Depression: What the Fed Did, and Why." Federal Reserve Bank of St. Louis *Review* (March/April 1992): 3-28; Wicker, Elmus. *Federal Reserve Monetary Policy, 1917-1933*. New York: Random house, 1966; Wueschner, Silvano A. *Charting Twentieth-Century Monetary Policy: Herbert Hoover and Benjamin Strong, 1917–1929*. Westport, CT: Greenwood Press, 1999.

SUPERREGIONAL BANKS. The history of banking in the United States is one of small banks versus large, rural versus urban. Into this mix one could put Eastern establishment versus Southern and Western banks. The bottom line is that the development of banking often has pitted the interests of the large money center banks, located in cities like New York and Chicago, against those located in small towns or cities of lesser size. This all changed, however, during the 1970s and 1980s.

With the advent of **bank holding companies**, firms could skirt **branching** regulations that limited their activities to one state. Increased geographical diversification allowed banks to increase the mix of **loans** held in their portfolio, thus decreasing the risk that a downturn in one industry or in one state would lead to an overall reduction in bank profitability. In addition, the technological advances that were being made allowed smaller banks to realize economies of scale in their operations that once were achieved only by large banks. New computer software and the ability to link banks together via high speed telecommunications networks meant that to become large did not mean a bank had to be located in New York or Chicago.

These developments and the eventual loosening of interstate branching restrictions (*see* **Riegle-Neal Act of 1994**) encouraged bank mergers, a movement that created what some call "superregional" banks. These bank companies grew rapidly as their management was often oriented toward acquisition of other banks in order to achieve a multi-regional presence. Another aspect of superregional banks is that their headquarters are not always located in the money center cities. A good example is NationsBank, which is head-quartered in Charlotte, North Carolina. Through numerous acquisitions across the country, NationsBank grew tremendously over the past 20 years. Its most recent move was to merge with Bank of America, a California-based bank, to create one of the nation's largest banks. This merger allowed both banks to achieve a national presence, with more than 1,000 branches and more than 10 million customers from coast to coast. Another super-regional bank is Wachovia Bank, also located in the Southeast. In July 2004, it acquired Southeast Bank to become one of the largest banks in the Southeastern United States.

FURTHER READING

Berger, Allen N., Anyil K. Kashyap, and Joseph Scalise. "The Transformation of U.S. Banking Industry: What a Long Strange Trip It's Been." *Brookings Papers on Economic Activity* (2:1995): 55–218; Hannan, Timothy, and Stephen Rhoades. "Future U.S. Banking Structure, 1990–2010." *Antitrust Bulletin* (37: 1992).

SUPERVISION AND REGULATION. The Federal Reserve is a key player in super-vising and regulating many aspects of the financial system in the United States. The Federal Reserve, along with other government agencies, is responsible for keeping the financial system, including depository institutions, operating in a safe and efficient man-ner. Even though the terms supervision and regulation are often combined into the short-hand "sup and reg," they actually are separate activities. Under its charge to supervise the banking system, the Federal Reserve monitors, inspects and examines banks to determine if they are operating in a safe and sound manner. The Federal Reserve issues many specific regulations that guide the behavior of banks and other financial institutions.

The Federal Reserve undertakes numerous supervisory activities. As an off-site su-pervisor of banks, the Federal Reserve periodically reviews the financial conditions of banks and **bank holding companies**. One of the most important of such reports submit-ted by banks to the Federal Reserve is the Call Report, officially known as the Consolidated Reports of Condition and Income, and for bank holding companies, the Consolidated Financial Statements for Bank Holding Companies. These reports are one source of in-formation that enables the Federal Reserve to review bank activities. Although the cov-erage of the Call Report varies across banks, differences that reflect bank size and scope of activity, they are one of the most important methods that the Federal Reserve uses to monitor bank activity.

The Federal Reserve uses automated screening systems in its offsite monitoring of bank activity. This system, known as the System to Estimate Examinations Ratings (or SEER for short), allows the Federal Reserve to determine which banks that have poor financial conditions. Use of SEER helps the Federal Reserve identify banks that are experiencing problems and to provide some means by which these problems can be addressed. One such solution also may to send examiners to the troubled institution. This is part of the Federal Reserve's on-site supervisory role. To insure safety and soundness, the Federal Reserve routinely sends a team of examiners to visit banks. Based on legislation passed in the 1990s, a team of Federal Reserve examiners visits every state bank, bank holding company and other depository institutions at least once a year. Large banks are examined jointly by the Federal Reserve and the relevant state bank agency; smaller banks usually are reviewed by these two on an alternating basis.

Enforcement of operating guidelines is part of the Federal Reserve's supervisory role. When it is determined that a bank or other depository institution is not operating in a manner that promotes sound and safe banking, the Federal Reserve takes corrective actions. Such actions may include communicating the areas of concern to the management of the institution and asking them to bring the bank into compliance. If the institution is unable or the management unwilling to correct the problems uncovered through examination, the Federal Reserve may call for the institution to cease all activities that the examination team deems questionable, assess a fine against the management, or even remove the officers of the bank. Such harsh actions are fairly rare, however.

In addition to supervising the activity of domestic banks, the Federal Reserve oversees the international operations of U.S. banks and the U.S. operations of foreign banks. The Federal Reserve works with regulatory agencies in other countries to ensure that foreign branches of U.S. banks operate in a sound and safe manner. Part of this activity is sanctioned under the International Lending Supervision Act of 1983, which directs the Federal Reserve to consult with authorities in other countries to adopt policies and practices that are consistent with United States and the foreign country's regulations. Passage of the International Banking Act of 1978 created a regulatory structure within which U.S. branches of foreign banks operate. Although the act gave state and federal licensing agencies a primary role in supervising foreign-owned branches, the Federal Reserve maintains some supervisory duties, especially in the area of approving applications by foreign banks to establish branches in the United States. Indeed, the stipulations that must be met in order for the Federal Reserve to grant applications are quite involved. With the passage of the Foreign Bank Supervision Enhancement Act of 1991, the Federal Reserve's role in the supervision of foreign–owned U.S. branches increased even further.

The Federal Reserve's activities as a bank regulator lies mostly in establishing standards of operation and conduct that promote safe and sound banking practices. The regulations established by the Federal Reserve cover a myriad of bank activities, from lending activities to consumer protection. (A complete list of current Federal Reserve regulations can be found in Appendix C.) Regulations of bank activity include setting **capital requirements** for banks that are in compliance with international standards (*see* **Basel Accord**) and making decisions on requests by banks to merge or to acquire other institutions. In making such decisions, the Federal Reserve weighs the costs and benefits to determine if there is any economic harm to the public at large. For example, will the merger lead to a monopoly condition in the local deposit market? They also determine whether there are negative effects in terms of the institution's financial viability. If the Federal Reserve believes that a merger of two banks will not promote safe and sound banking practices, then such a request could be denied.

In addition to its regulation of banking, the Federal Reserve also oversees various aspects of financial transactions. Passage of the Securities Exchange Act in 1934 gave the Federal Reserve the responsibility of regulating **margin requirements** in the securities trades, an area in which the Federal Reserve still operates though with much less vigor than during the years immediately following passage of the law. The stock market crash of 1987 and the more recent market troubles beginning in 2000 reminded many that the Federal Reserve still acts as the regulator of margin requirements.

Finally, the Federal Reserve aids the United States Treasury Department in the enforcement of the Bank Secrecy Act of 1970 which made it illegal to use foreign bank accounts to launder illicit funds. The act also requires financial institutions operating in the United States to report substantial currency transactions. The Federal Reserve works to ensure that banks are complying with this law, acquiring information on such activity during its periodic examinations of bank activity.

FURTHER READING

Board of Governors of the Federal Reserve. *The Federal Reserve System: Purposes & Functions*, 8th edition. Washington, D.C.: Board of Governors of the Federal Reserve System, available online at Website: www.bog.gov.

SWAPS. Swaps involve two parties entering into a contractual agreement to "swap" one's set of payments for another's. Swaps are a form of financial derivative used to manage risk that was developed in the 1980s. There are two general kinds of swaps: One involves an exchange of interest payments. The other is an agreement to swap a set of payments denominated in one **currency** for a set of payments denominated in another. Swaps provide institutions, both financial and nonfinancial, the means to manage risk. (A fuller discussion of how swaps work is beyond the scope of this work. For a good introduction, see Mishkin, 2004.)

Swaps may expose financial institutions to increased risk when they act as the intermediary to such transactions. Consequently, a series of regulations have been passed since the early 1980s requiring financial institutions engaged in this intermediary process to hold higher levels of capital than those banks not so engaged. Such regulation is not unwarranted. There have been several well-publicized events that justify concerns over the use and abuse of swap agreements. Two such examples are the collapse of Barrings Bank in 1995 and the bankruptcy of Orange County, California in 1994. In each case, due largely to a failure of the supervisory role of the relevant regulators, individuals took excessively risky positions in the financial markets using swaps and other derivative instruments. If they had been successful—if they had bet correctly—they would not have made the nightly news or made this discussion. But they were not. In the Barrings Bank case, Nick Lesson, the head clerk at Barrings's Singapore branch, speculated on the behavior of Japan's major stock index, the Nikkei, in July 1992. By the end of the year he had lost the bank $3 million. Trying to make it back by engaging in even riskier speculations, his losses mounted, reaching $1.3 billion by early 1995 at which time he fled Singapore. (He was soon apprehended and is now in jail.) These losses were greater than the bank's capital and thus brought down Barrings Bank, which had been in business over 100 years.

Even though such an event is not commonplace, the use of swaps and other financial derivatives remains an area of concern to regulators and policymakers at the Federal Reserve. If banks take on risky positions, this exposes them to failure when the value of the swap arrangements exceeds the capital value of the bank, as in the case of Barrings Bank. Unlike a **loan**, if there is a failure by one of the parties—recall that banks usually perform the service of intermediary—the bank's exposure can be contained. Although headline-grabbing events such as the collapse of Barrings Bank get attention, most banks and other financial institutions use swaps to effectively manage or help others manage risk. Still, they remain under the watchful eye of the regulators at the Federal Reserve.

FURTHER READING

Mishkin, Frederic S. *The Economics of Money, Banking, and Financial Markets*. 7th edition. Boston: Pearson Addison Wesley, 2004.

SWEEP ACCOUNTS. Sweep accounts, more correctly called retail sweep programs, are a relatively new development in how banks manage their **reserves**. Banks are required by law to keep a certain percentage of their transactions deposits on reserve with the Federal Reserve, or as **vault cash**. For example, suppose a bank is required to hold 3 percent of every dollar in transactions deposits (i.e., checking accounts and the like) in reserves. This **reserve requirement** means that the bank has 3 percent less in deposits to loan out. Even though a prudently managed bank would hold some reserves against deposits, most bankers would like to avoid doing so because reserves do not earn any interest income.

One way to avoid holding reserves is to reduce the amount of deposits against which reserves are required. Banks could simply refuse to take on new deposits, but that would not be wise in terms of profitability. Instead, banks discovered that one way to avoid holding reserves is to alter how the deposits of customers were being held at the time when reserve requirements are calculated. If a bank can "sweep" all of its reservable accounts into nonreservable accounts—accounts for which the Federal Reserve imposes no reserve requirement—at the end of the business day, then the bank's reserve liability goes to zero. But if the reserves are now just showing up in other bank accounts overnight, where's the profit in that? Usually a bank invests swept funds in overnight securities, such as **federal funds**, for which the bank pays the customer some portion of the interest income earned on the use of the funds.

The chart below plots estimates by the **Board of Governors** of the dollars swept from transactions accounts into nonreservable **money market deposit accounts** (MMDAs) beginning in 1994 through 2000. This start point reflects the fact that in January 1994 the Federal Reserve Board allowed a bank, First Union Bank, to use new computer software that enabled account sweeping—essentially reclassifying accounts on an overnight basis—to occur. Note that for the first couple of years, retail sweep programs were not that sizable. Beginning in mid-1995, however, the use of sweep programs increased dramatically. By 2000, about $400 billion was being swept out of transactions accounts and into MMDA accounts on a monthly basis.

How do sweep accounts affect monetary policy decisions? First, because sweep accounts lower the amount of reserves held by the banking system, sweep accounts impact

Sweeps of Transaction Deposits into MMDAs
Board of Governors Staff Estimates, Jan. 1994–Oct. 2000

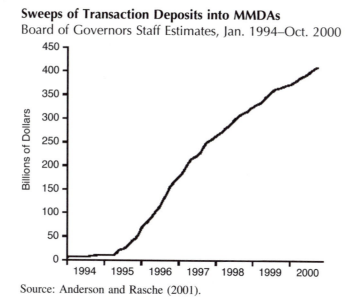

Source: Anderson and Rasche (2001).

several monetary measures. The most immediately affected measure is the **monetary base**. In it simplest form the monetary base consists of reserves held by the banking system plus currency. The monetary base is an important monetary measure, because changes in the monetary base reflect policy actions. For instance, when the Federal Reserve engages in **open market operations**, it changes the level of the monetary base by changing the amount of reserves in the banking system. If the Federal Reserve seeks to increase reserves by a certain amount, their ability to accomplish this may be impaired by the existence of sweep account activity.

Sweep accounts also affect other measures of money, most importantly those that consist mostly of transactions accounts (such as M1). The chart below dramatically illustrates how sweep accounts affect transactions balances (checkable accounts) in the banking system. When sweep programs began in earnest reported transaction deposits fell sharply. If one was watching this measure and using it to gauge the direction of policy, the immediate concern would be that policy was being very restrictive: deposits were falling. In response, policymakers might argue for expansionary actions. But what was really going on? When the sweep programs are added back into the data, a much different picture emerges. Now transaction account balances are no longer decreasing, but increasing. Obviously, if the solid line in the chart is reality but the policymaker was working on the assumption that the dotted line was the facts policy actions obviously would be far off the mark.

The upshot of sweep programs is that reserve requirements are, for many banks, now a "voluntary restraint," as Anderson and Rasche (2001) describe the situation. They note that if bank regulators are willing to allow banks to use sophisticated computer software to circumvent reserve requirements, then the regulators are sending a message that this avenue of monetary control is being minimized. In a policy environment where the main thrust of policy is control of short-term interest rates, such as the **federal funds rate**, the need to impose statutory reserve requirements may not be important to a successful policy.

Transaction Deposits

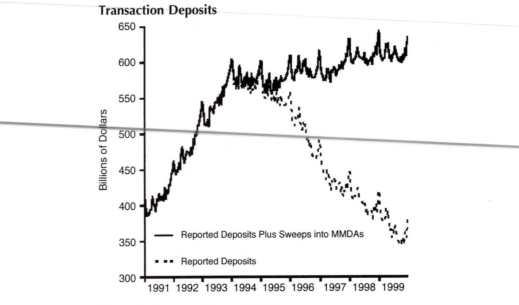

Source: Anderson and Rasche (2001).

Data on the amount of dollars in sweep accounts are available from the Federal Reserve Bank of St. Louis, accessible at www.stls.frb.org/research/swdata.html.

FURTHER READING

Anderson, Richard G., and Robert Rasche. "Measuring the Adjusted Monetary Base in an Era of Financial Change." Federal Reserve Bank of St. Louis *Review* (November/December 1996): 3–37; Anderson, Richard G., and Robert Rasche. "Retail Sweep Programs and Bank Reserves, 1994–1999." Federal Reserve Bank of St. Louis *Review* (January/February 2001): 51–72; O'Sullivan, Orla. "Counting Cash in the Dark." *ABA Banking Journal* (February 1998): 86–92.

TAYLOR, JOHN (1946–). John B. Taylor is perhaps best known as the creator of the **Taylor Rule**, a mathematical description of how the Federal Reserve sets policy. Taylor also is known for his early work in the development of **rational expectations** models of the economy that relaxed the stringent information requirements of earlier versions and his work on international policy coordination. Taylor most recently is the Mary and Robert Raymond Professor of Economics at Stanford University. He has held a number of government positions, recently as the undersecretary for international affairs at the U.S. Department of Treasury in the Bush administration.

FURTHER READING

Snowdon, Brian, and Howard R. Vane, eds. *Conversations with Leading Economists*. Cheltenham, UK: Edward Elgar Pubs, 1999.

TAYLOR RULE. The Taylor Rule is named after economist **John Taylor**. It is the most recent attempt in a long line of research to model the behavior of Federal Reserve policymakers. The Taylor Rule is an algebraic description of what drives policymakers' decisions to raise or lower the **federal funds rate**. The idea is that if we can pin down those variables that seem to be most important most of the time, then policy becomes more transparent or predictable.

Taylor's rule represents the latest attempt to model or describe policy actions. Its use represents a confluence of several more recent ideas in economics, including **rational expectations** and **time inconsistency**. Both of these concepts have been used to demonstrate that some type of policy rule is likely to deliver a better economic outcome than is a policy based purely on the discretion of the policymakers. In an earlier argument for policy rules, **Milton Friedman** argued that the Federal Reserve should simply set the growth rate of the money supply to some predetermined rate, say 3 percent, and work to meet that growth rate objective. Friedman was well aware that such a fixed-rate type of rule would not always be optimal, in the sense that such a rule would not always keep the economy growing at its long-run potential. Even so, within the context of his argument—that discretionary policy actions had led to more volatile economic growth and an upward bias in the rate of **inflation**—many believed that Friedman's fixed-rate rule was preferable to the Federal Reserve's actual record. It also had that characteristic that it would minimize inflation over time, a primary goal of monetary policy.

Taylor's rule inherited from this tradition the notion that some type of rule is preferable to discretion. But the basic idea in Taylor's rule is that the Federal Reserve would adjust its policy instruments as the economy changes in order to minimize deviations of real output from its full employment level (sometimes referred to as potential GDP) and to keep the rate of inflation low and close to some desired rate. In reality the Taylor rule is quite simple. The original version of the Taylor rule can be written as

$$r = p + 0.5y + 0.5(p - 2) + 2$$

where r is the **federal funds rate**, p is the rate of inflation over the previous year, and y is the percent deviation in real **gross domestic product (GDP)** from its potential. The number 2 in parentheses represents a target rate of inflation. This means that the value in parentheses (p − 2) represents the deviation in actual inflation (p) from the desired rate of inflation which Taylor assumed to be 2 percent. The other 2 that appears reflects Taylor's assumption that if real GDP is at its potential (so that y = 0) and the rate of inflation is equal to 2 percent, then the real federal funds rate (r − p) would be equal to 2 percent, a rate that he believed to be consistent with real GDP growing at its potential or long-term rate. Finally, the two 0.5 values represent the Federal Reserve's response to changes in either inflation or real GDP. If, for example, the rate of inflation increases to 4 percent, the Federal Reserve operating under Taylor's rule would increase the federal funds rate by 1 percentage point [= 0.5(4 − 2)].

What does the Taylor Rule mean in words? It translates into the following: When the Federal Reserve sees inflation rising above the 2 percent target rate, it should increase the federal funds rate. In theory, this would raise the general cost of borrowing and help slow the pace of economic activity, thus reducing inflationary pressures building in the economy. Similarly, when the economy begins to grow faster than its long-term or potential rate, the Federal Reserve should raise the federal funds rate in order to slow economic growth, again with the goal being to remove inflationary pressures in the economy. Of course, should just the opposite conditions occur, the Federal Reserve would take actions to lower the federal funds rate. The bottom line is that Taylor's rule shows what the Federal Reserve should do when the economy begins to deviate from (1) its long-term growth path and (2) the policymaker's desired rate of inflation. When Taylor applied his rule to the real world, he found that at least for 1987–1992, the equation explained actual movements in the federal funds rate quite well. In other words, plugging in the actual numbers for y and p and using his values of .5 and 2, etc. the generated value for the federal funds rate (r) closely matched the actual one.

Following publication of Taylor's rule (Taylor, 1993), numerous investigations examined the ability of the rule to replicate the actual behavior of the federal funds rate. One of many such studies, by Judd and Rudebusch (1998), showed that when applied to different time periods, Taylor's rule was less precise compared with the outcomes for his original 1987–1992 period. Of course, what this implies is that the underlying forces that drive monetary policy decisions likely shifted with those who set policy and with changes in the economic environment. For example, the 1990s, a period of relatively stable economic growth and low inflation, is much different that the 1970s, when inflation soared to double-digit levels and the economy suffered through a significant **recession**.

Federal Funds Rate and Inflation Targets

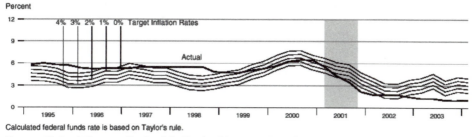

Calculated federal funds rate is based on Taylor's rule.

Source: Federal Reserve Bank of St. Louis, *Monetary Trends.*

Even though the precision of the Taylor Rule is debatable, it is useful as a tool that provides some indication of the inflationary impacts of current policy actions. For example, the Taylor Rule can be rewritten to yield the rate of inflation (p). Combined with the actual federal funds rate, one gets some notion of the underlying inflation target that the Federal Reserve had in mind as they adjusted the federal funds rate. Such an exercise is available in the Federal Reserve Bank of St. Louis's publication *Monetary Trends*, where the Taylor Rule is used to simulate the target rate of inflation. That is, the inflation rate target that, assuming the other factors of the rule hold, underlies the Federal Reserve's policy actions. Above is the outcome of such an exercise as it appeared in the June 2004 issue.

The chart above shows that the implied target rate of inflation shifted over time. Looking at the chart reveals the fact that the Taylor Rule assumes that the Federal Reserve responds to deviations in real output from its full employment potential. This is apparent prior to the 2001 recession. At that time the Federal Reserve aggressively lowered the federal funds rate in response to the mounting evidence of an economic slowing, and to offset the effects stemming from the September 11, 2001, terrorist attacks on New York and the Pentagon. According to the Taylor Rule, lowering the federal funds rate is consistent with raising the Federal Reserve's target rate of inflation. Because inflation did not materialize in this period or immediately thereafter, the evidence suggests that policy actions were weighted more toward promoting economic growth than fighting inflation. With this in mind, it may not be surprising that during the recession and slow growth years of 2001–2003, the Taylor Rule's simulation of inflation is not very accurate (it overpredicts inflation). Even so, this exercise allows one to see, all other factors held constant, how the Federal Reserve's policy actions relate to some underlying inflation target. As stated above, this is useful because it promotes increased policy **transparency**.

FURTHER READING

Hetzel, Robert H. "The Taylor Rule: Is It a Useful Guide to Understanding Monetary Policy?" Federal Reserve Bank of Richmond *Economic Quarterly* (Spring 2000): 1–33; Judd, John, and Glenn Rudebusch. "Taylor's Rule and the Fed: 1970–1997." Federal Reserve Bank of San Francisco's *Economic Review* (Number 3, 1998): 3–16; Taylor, John B. "Discretion vs. Policy rules in Practice." *Carnegie-Rochester Conference Series on Public Policy* (February 1993): 195–214.

TEETERS, NANCY HAYS (1930–). Nancy Teeters became the first woman to serve as governor of the Federal Reserve. Appointed by President Jimmy Carter, Teeters served from September 18, 1978, through June 27, 1984. Prior to her appointment as governor,

Teeters was the chief economist (1974–1978) of the U.S. House of Representatives Budget Committee. After leaving the board, Teeters became director of economics and vice president at the IBM Corporation, a position she held until her retirement in 1990.

FURTHER READING

For more on Nancy Teeters, the Oberlin College Archives (online at www.oberlin.edu/archive) houses the Nancy Hays Teeters Papers.

TERM STRUCTURE OF INTEREST RATES. Most central banks use **nominal interest rates** as a primary tool to achieve monetary policy objectives. In the United States, for example, the Federal Reserve closely monitors the **federal funds rate**—the interest rate banks charge each other for overnight funds—raising or lowering it as economic events dictate. During the period following the 2001 recession, for example, the Federal Reserve move aggressively to lower the federal funds rate, eventually pushing it to 1 percent, the lowest level in decades. At its June 25, 2003, meeting, the **Federal Open Market Committee (FOMC)**, the policymaking arm of the Federal Reserve, announced that, "the Committee continues to believe that an accommodative stance of monetary policy, coupled with still robust underlying growth in productivity, is providing important ongoing support to economic activity" and that it "decided today to lower its target for the federal funds rate by 25 basis points to 1 percent." As the economy rebounded, there was increasing belief that the Federal Reserve would increase the federal funds rate in order to offset any inflationary effects that their earlier expansionary policies may have created. Consequently, during 2004 the FOMC set about raising the federal funds rate.

As the FOMC moves the federal funds rate up and down, this in turn affects the level of other interest rates on financial instruments that have longer maturities than just overnight. This occurs because banks and other financial institutions use the federal funds rate as a base rate to determine their cost of acquiring funds. If the federal funds rate increases, then other rates are expected to follow suit. Even though rates of longer maturity may not increase or decrease by the same amount as the federal funds rate, changes along the "term structure" have implications for economic activity. Indeed, many believe that by adjusting the federal funds rate, the FOMC tries to alter the term structure of interest rates to influence the pace of economic activity.

The term structure of interest rates—the relation between short-term and long-term interest rates—can be a useful tool for monetary policymakers and for individuals attempting to predict the impact of policy actions on the economy. In other words, when the term structure changes, policymakers use that information to determine how the markets are reacting to their policy actions. Alternatively, changes in the term structure may help predict future changes in economic activity and provide useful information to forecasters.

How does the term structure work? Let's use a simple example to illustrate the relation. The accompanying chart plots the monthly values of the federal funds rate and the interest rate on 10-year U.S. government bonds. We use these two rates because they are often used in research to test the ability of the term structure to predict economic fluctuations.

The chart shows that even though the two rates display a common movement over time, at times they behave quite differently. For example, in 1974, note that the federal funds rate increased sharply relative to the 10-year rate. In 1984, exactly the opposite occurred. Also,

Economagic: Data and Charts

←Federal funds (effective)
←10-year Treasury Constant Maturity

Source: www.economagic.com.

note that the 10-year rate tends to be higher than the federal funds rate (although that, too, changes at times). This reflects the market's expectation that future short-term rates are likely to be higher than current short-term rates (an idea commonly referred to as the "expectations theory"). This may occur because the market expects higher inflation. In addition, because it is riskier to tie up one's money for longer periods, riskier in the sense that you may suffer loss of purchasing power, one might expect interest rates on long term financial instruments to be higher than short-term rates, simply because individuals must be compensated for this risk with higher rates of interest.

The chart also shows the occurrence of **recessions**. Does the differential movement of the federal funds rate and the 10-year rate provide predictive evidence of recessions? Suppose the FOMC decides that the economy is growing too fast and that **inflation** is a potential problem. In this case the FOMC would move to raise the federal funds rate. While this policy action also impacts longer-term rates, such as the 10-year rate, movements in the federal funds rate occur much more rapidly. Thus, a policy action to become more contractionary would be shown as an increase in the federal funds rate relative to the 10-year rate. Is the evidence in the chart consistent with this idea?

The answer is "sometimes." The most obvious case is the 1974 recession when the federal funds rate jumped to about 12.5 percent, a full 5 percentage points above the 10-year rate. This sharp increase in the federal funds rate relative to the 10-year rate suggests that monetary policy had become quite restrictive and the economy entered a deep recession soon thereafter. It should be noted that this increase in the federal funds rate occurred during a strange time in U.S. economic history. First, Franklin National Bank, at the time of the nation's largest banks, collapsed, thus requiring the Fed to step in and act as **lender of last resort**. This event put upward pressure on the federal funds rate and all short-term rates. Second, it also is associated with the Organization of Petroleum Exporting Countries (OPEC)-engineered oil price hike. This oil price increase set into motion a series of policy missteps: first the Federal Reserve attempted to fight the inflationary consequences of the oil price hike by constraining policy—hence the rise in the federal funds rate. Later they

373

reversed this course to fight the onset of a recession caused by some combination of their earlier policy and the effects of the oil price increase itself.

What about the other times? For the recessions of 1980–1982, the federal funds rate moved much higher than the 10-year rate. And more recently during the 1991 and 2001 recessions, the funds rate moved higher than the 10-year rate prior to the onset of the recession, although the magnitude of the gap and the timing are much different than the earlier instances. Still, one could argue that there were no "false" signals using this gap between the two rates as an indicator of future recession: at no time during the past 20 years has the federal funds rate moved higher than the 10-year rate without a recession occurring soon thereafter.

FURTHER READING

Campbell, John Y. "Some Lessons from the Yield Curve." *Journal of Economic Perspectives.* (Summer 1995): 129–38; Estrella, Arturo, and Frederic S. Mishkin. "The Yield Curve as a Predictor of U.S. Recessions." Federal Reserve Bank of New York *Current Issues in Economics and Finance* (June 1996); Friedman, Benjamin, and Kenneth N. Kuttner. "Money, Income, Prices and Interest Rates." *American Economic Review* (June 1992): 472–92; Rudebusch, Glen. "Interest Rates and Monetary Policy." Federal Reserve Bank of San Francisco *Economic Letter* (June 13, 1997).

TIME INCONSISTENCY. The Federal Reserve announces that it is going to follow a policy to prevent an increase in the rate of **inflation**. Let's say that it publicly announces an inflation target of 3 percent. At the time of the announcement, this inflation target seems appropriate, and following the announcement monetary policy shifts toward meeting that goal. Reacting to the announcement and the policy changes that give it some credibility, individuals come to believe that policymakers are in fact sincere in hitting the announced inflation goal. The low inflation target gets factored into economic decisions, such as what interest rate to charge for **loans** and what wage increases to expect. Over time, however, it becomes clear that the low-inflation policy that the Fed announced it would follow is no longer constraining their actions. The Fed opts not to implement the policy, even though expectations have been altered, in order to pursue an alternative objective, say lowering the **unemployment rate**. In this sense, the announced policy is time-inconsistent.

The work that is recognized as pioneering the idea of time-inconsistent policies is that by Kydland and Prescott (1977). (Kydland and Prescott were awarded the 2004 Nobel Prize in economics.) The Kydland–Prescott analysis was trying to explain the sharp increase in the rate of inflation that occurred in the United States during the 1970s. Even though the higher rates of inflation experienced during the 1970s is due to some extent to oil price increases in 1973 and again in 1979, there is a general upward trend in the rate of inflation. (*See* **Great Inflation.**) If one abstracts from the spikes in the inflation rate caused by the oil price increases, the underlying increase in inflation is explained by the increasing rate of money growth. In other words, many economists believe that the rising inflation rates were due to monetary policy decisions that led to excessively high rates of inflation. If maintaining low rates of inflation is a goal of policy, why did monetary policy fail to achieve that goal?

What Kydland and Prescott showed was that monetary policymakers focused more on lowering the unemployment rate than on inflation. This is where the inconsistency of their policy actions comes in. It is well known that expansive monetary policy—lowering interest rates or raising the growth rate of the money supply—can affect real output and unemployment, but only in the short run. Think of it this way. The plant that produces Fender guitars produces, say, 500 per year. There is an expansionary monetary policy enacted, incomes rise, and people start buying more guitars. In the short run, Fender tries to expand production by using overtime, adding an extra shift, etc. But in the end the production of guitars is limited by the sheer engineering of the plant. An artisan can only produce so many guitars, regardless of how much you pay her. As demand increases, output returns to its full production level, but Fender starts raising prices. How does this translate to the whole economy? If the Federal Reserve sees unemployment at a level higher than it would like, it tries to push it down with expansionary policy. Once it gets down to the desired level, they then turn their attention to reducing the rate of inflation. If the unemployment rate keeps bumping back up, however, this requires more expansionary policies. Over time, even though the policy of lowering the unemployment rate seemed optimal at the time, the consequence is an ever-higher rate of inflation, which is inconsistent with the policymaker's long-term goal. Thus, policy is time-inconsistent.

The inflation experience of the United States in the 1970s fits that scenario. Kydland and Prescott showed that by engaging in "inflation surprises" during the 1970s, the Federal Reserve was able, albeit temporarily, to influence the unemployment rate, but the cost was permanently higher inflation. The policy implication of time-inconsistency is derived from the same notion as the **rational expectations** ideas of **Robert Lucas, Jr.** If the Federal Reserve tries to impact unemployment in the manner described above, workers come to expect that the policy announcement is not credible. As workers come to expect higher rates of inflation, the only way for the Federal Reserve to engineer an inflation surprise is to make the surprise even bigger than the public expects. This policy soon degenerates and nobody believes future policy announcements. In this sense, the time-inconsistency analysis suggests that for policy to be credible, it should try to be consistent over time.

The idea of time-inconsistency has implications for other government policies. Because time-inconsistent monetary policies are thought to raise the average rate of inflation, they therefore affect the government's ability to fund its activities. Selling bonds to the public to pay for government programs requires the government to raise the interest rate paid on those bonds, thus reducing the net funds available to finance its programs. Put another way, a larger portion of the federal deficit goes to financing its own debt.

Time-inconsistent policies make it more difficult for a central bank to engage in stabilization policies. During the 1970s, for example, the oil price shocks that hit the economy created a situation where inflation rates rose along with the unemployment rate. This coincident behavior was not thought possible in models used up to this time. What's the proper policy response? If the Federal Reserve has announced that it is following a low-inflation/low-unemployment rate policy and the oil price shock raises both, what is the optimal response by the monetary policymaker? If it attacks the higher rate of inflation with contractionary polices, the unemployment rate will rise even farther. If it tries to lower the unemployment rate, the inflation rate will increase. (Indeed, this latter approach is what was done.) Under such conditions, the optimal policy may be to do nothing: the rate of inflation will return to the pre–oil price shock level and, over time, so will the unemployment rate. If the short-run demands on policy are to "solve" one or the other problem, the outcome is a time-inconsistent policy. (*See also* **Policy Credibility; Transparency**.)

FURTHER READING

Barro, Robert, David Gordon. "Rules, Discretion and Reputation in a Model of Monetary Policy." *Journal of Monetary Economics* (12:1983): 101–21; Dennis, Richard. "Time-Inconsistent Monetary Policies: Recent Research." Federal Reserve Bank of San Francisco *Economic Letter* (April 11, 2003); Kydland, Finn, and Edward Prescott. "Rules Rather than Discretion: The Inconsistency of Optimal Plans." *Journal of Political Economy* (June 1977): 473–92.

TONE AND FEEL APPROACH TO POLICY. During the 1950s and into the 1960s, there were numerous statements by Federal Reserve officials indicating that their decisions about monetary policy often were driven by their perceptions about financial markets. The notion of "tone and feel" was used to describe how financial markets were reacting to policy actions and how policymakers *thought* markets would react to their policies.

To understand how the tone and feel approach to policy worked, a few quotes from Federal Reserve officials may help. For example, in hearings before the Joint Economic Committee in 1961, Robert G. Rouse, the manager of the Federal Open Market Account (the **Trading Desk**) at the Federal Reserve Bank of New York, testified that

> . . . hour by hour developments, particularly in the Federal funds market, in the Government securities market, in the progress of Government securities dealers in finding the financing required to carry their portfolios of Government securities, provide the manager of the account with information which gives him an informed judgment of the degree of ease or tightness in the market—sometimes referred to as the 'feel' of the market." (quoted in Atkinson, 1969, p. 85)

In testimony before the same committee, the president of the Federal Reserve Bank of New York, Alfred Hayes, provided a similar view, noting that the manager of the desk uses "impressions" of trading and the "combination of a great many things," none of which are the actual amount of reserves in the banking system, money growth rates, the level of interest rates, etc., that describe the "tone" of the market and affect policy decisions.

During the 1950s, a debate among economists both inside and outside of the Federal Reserve System arose over the use of statistical information and forecasts to guide policy. The published minutes of the **Federal Open Market Committee (FOMC)** make it clear that the New York Federal Reserve and those working on the Trading Desk preferred a nonstatistical approach. That is, they preferred a policy that was not constrained by some rule that required them to act in this way or that. In one exchange at the October 22, 1957, meeting of the FOMC, Rouse stated that "operations depended on the judgment of the Manager of the account based not only on the figures [reserves, etc.] but also on the feel of the market." The problem with such an approach is that there often is no consistency in the reason for the decisions. For example, if **reserves** in the banking system were growing rapidly, this may indicate to policymakers that their actions have been very expansionary. The behavior of interest rates, however, may indicate that the market has not reacted to the reserve expansion in the manner expected. If interest rates have not declined in the face of rapidly growing reserves but in fact increased, which measure should the FOMC use in deciding their next action?

This debate heated up during the 1960s. Monetary policy became increasingly expansionary as the FOMC attempted to maintain full employment by artificially keeping interest rates low. Because of increased demands for funds in financial markets, interest rates naturally would have increased were it not for attempts by the FOMC to increase the flow of money into the economy as a means to offset these demands. The record indicates that this policy approach led to increased rates of **inflation** and put upward pressure on interest rates. This policy was attacked by many economists, most notably those associated with the **Monetarist** school of thought. The Monetarist view was that policy should focus on keeping the growth rate of the monetary aggregates at reasonably low levels. Making the growth rate of the monetary aggregates the principal policy indicator, it was argued, removed the uncertainty surrounding policy decisions that rely on someone's reaction to observed or potential developments in financial markets.

By the late 1960s, most economists continued to believe that monetary policy was not accurately described by the behavior of any single variable, thus providing a basis for the belief that an eclectic approach such as "tone and feel" was appropriate. For example, the 1968 **Economic Report of the President** stated that "In the formulation of monetary policy.... [S]ome consideration should be given to all of ... financial flows as well as to related interest rates in formulating any comprehensive program of analysis of financial conditions"(p. 89). Later in the *Report* it is stated that focusing on the growth of the money stock or the use of a simple rule for policy was not acceptable: "given the complex role of interest rates in affecting various demand categories and the likely variation in so many other factors, any such simple policy guide could prove to be quite unreliable" (p. 92). Indeed, in numerous FOMC meetings, the chairman of the Federal Reserve, **William McChesney Martin**, extolled the virtues of flexibility in policy, going so far as arguing that monetary policy should not be constrained by the "dead hand of statistics," something that he associated with reliance on the monetary aggregates. And if you think that this view was limited to the 1960s, consider the comments of Chairman **Paul Volcker** and the December 20–21, 1982, meeting of the FOMC:

> I think we're left with what could be termed an eclectic, pragmatic approach [to policy decisions]. It's going to involve some judgment as to which of these [aggregate] measures we emphasize, or we may shift from time to time ... [W]e're going to have to make judgments as to which one is more significant at any particular point in time against what nominal GNP is or what the goal is of what the real economy is doing and what prices are doing and all the rest ... [T]hat's the way the Federal Reserve used to operate, less elaborately, for years when policy by present standards looked pretty good." (quoted in Hafer, 1999, p. 23)

Although one is hard pressed to argue that current practices of monetary policy do not involve some "feel" by policymakers about the impact of their actions, it also is clear that over time there has been much more reliance on some statistical indicator of policy to guide decisions. During the 1960s Federal Reserve economists often employed the now discredited "tone and feel" approach, which gave way to explicit targets for the **federal funds rate**, then targets for bank reserves and more recently returning to a policy based on targeting the funds rate. Although each series of policy approaches varies in emphasis (today's federal funds targeting is more flexible than the approach used in the 1970s, for example), there is clearly a greater emphasis today on rules in policymaking rather than tone and feel. (*See* **Rules versus Discretion**.)

FURTHER READING

Atkinson, Thomas R. "Tone and Feel of the Market as a Guide for Federal Open Market Operations." In Karl Brunner, ed. *Targets and Indicators of Monetary Policy*. San Francisco: Chandler

Publishing Company, 1969; DeLong, J. Bradford. "The Triumph of Monetarism?" *Journal of Economic Perspectives* (Winter 2000): 83–94; Hafer, R. W. "Against the Tide: Malcolm Bryan and the Introduction of Monetary Aggregate Targets." Federal Reserve Bank of Atlanta *Economic Review* (First Quarter 1999): 20–37; Hafer, R. W., and David C. Wheelock. "The Rise and Fall of a Policy Rule: Monetarism at the St. Louis Fed, 1968–1986." Federal Reserve Bank of St. Louis *Review* (January/February 2001): 1–24; Mayer, Thomas. *Monetary Policy in the United States.* New York: Random House, Inc., 1968.

TOO-BIG-TO-FAIL DOCTRINE. The 1980s witnessed a series of **bank failures**, some on a very large scale. In 1982 **Penn Square**, a bank located in Oklahoma, failed. This by itself was not a unique event, except for the fact that Penn Square was one of the largest banks in the south-central United States. What was crucial about this failure was that another even larger bank located in Chicago—**Continental Illinois**—was closely tied to the activities of Penn Square. Penn Square had made millions of dollars in energy **loans** to regional oil producers and related businesses. When oil prices began to decline in this period, many oil businesses failed and with them went Penn Square. Continental Illinois, then the nation's seventh largest bank, had purchased from Penn Square over $1 billion in energy-related loans. When the value of Penn Square's loan portfolio declined dramatically this led to rumors that Continental Illinois also would become insolvent. In spring 1984 a run began on Continental Illinois deposits. Over the period of only a couple of months, customers began withdrawing deposits from the bank in alarming amounts and with great speed: between May and July, Continental's depositors withdrew over $10 billion in deposits. With the shadow of insolvency hanging over it, Continental could not raise additional funds and began to sell off assets.

Continental's troubles continued into 1985. The **Federal Deposit Insurance Corporation (FDIC)**, the federal insurer of bank deposits, purchased billions in notes from the bank. The Federal Reserve also stepped in, injecting **liquidity** into Continental by lending emergency funds through **discount window** loans. By summer 1985, Continental was getting assistance from government regulators to stay afloat. In August it was classified as a permanent recipient of $4.5 billion in assistance: in other words, the government was not necessarily looking for payback. By this time the FDIC owned nearly 80 percent of the outstanding shares of the bank. In effect, Continental was owned by the government.

Why did the government undertake such a massive and expensive rescue of this bank? As the **Comptroller of the Currency** announced in Congressional testimony in 1984, they had enacted a "too-big-to-fail" policy. This was outlined as a policy where the government would shore up failing banks in order to prevent **bank runs** and the kind of financial panic that characterized the **Great Depression**. The idea was that with government backing, such banks would continue to operate and, over time, return to profitability. Failure to act, on the other hand, was not an option: allowing large financial institutions to fail would cause other institutions like Continental to fail and severely strain the entire financial system. At least, that was the theory. This theory was used again in 1990 when the Bank of New England experienced difficulties. As before, federal regulators stepped in and propped up the bank.

This policy did not, however, extend to smaller banks. This, and the fact that the very action of propping up failed institutions exacerbated the **moral hazard** problem inherent with deposit insurance, brought about an end to this policy by the early 1990s.

FURTHER READING

Stern, Gary, and Ron J. Feldman. *Too Big to Fail: The Hazards of Bank Bailouts*. Washington, D.C.: Brookings Institution, 2004.

TRADING DESK. The trading desk, short for the open market trading desk, is comprised of a group of economists at the Federal Reserve Bank of New York. Headed by the Federal Reserve System's account manager, these individuals have the job of carrying out the policy objectives of the **Federal Open Market Committee (FOMC)**. This is done through the buying and selling of U.S. government securities. This activity takes place on a daily basis, generally commencing about 9:00 A.M. when the account manager begins discussions with individuals in the financial markets in order to obtain information about conditions in the government securities market and a feel for how prices on these securities may change during the day. By 11:00 A.M. the account manager and the staff of the trading desk have acquired information regarding changes in Treasury deposits, the timing of sales of Treasury securities, forecasted changes in the **monetary base**, and other factors that may influence **reserves** in the banking system and conditions in the financial markets. Around 11:30 A.M. the account manager and the staff reach agreement on the proper strategy to take and communicate this strategy in a conference call with at least two members of the FOMC. Traders on the desk then notify government securities dealers of the Federal Reserve's desire to buy or sell securities and take quotations for selling prices if the traders wish to purchases securities or bids if the purpose is for the Federal Reserve to buy securities. By 12:30 P.M., the traders at the desk have completed their task for the day, completing their purchase or sale of securities. With trading done, the rest of the day is then spent monitoring conditions in the financial markets, especially in the **federal funds market**, to see what the next day's activity may entail. (*See also* **Open Market Operations**.)

FURTHER READING

Akhtar, M. A. *Understanding Open Market Operations*. New York: Federal Reserve Bank of New York, 1997; Meulendyke, Ann-Marie. *U.S. Monetary Policy & Financial Markets*. New York: Federal Reserve Bank of New York, 1998.

TRANSPARENCY. The Federal Reserve historically has sought to maintain secrecy about its decisions and the processes by which those decisions are made. During most of the last 50 years the decisions made at meetings of the **Federal Open Market Committee (FOMC)** have not been made public until many months after the meeting. Indeed, the minutes of these meetings still are not made available on a timely basis. Although recently there has been a move to become more open about the process and the decisions—the FOMC now announces after each meeting what its policy decision is—how that decision is made still remains a mystery for several years.

The move to announcing policy decisions after each FOMC meeting is an example of increased transparency. The idea is that by announcing what policy it intends to follow, the FOMC reduces the need for individuals to expend resources in trying to guess what the Federal Reserve's policy intentions are. In the past, that is exactly what financial market participants would do. Many large banks and brokerage houses employed numerous economists whose job it was to watch Federal Reserve activity in the market and try to decipher which direction policy was moving. (*See* **Fed Watcher**.) While this provided income to those economists hired by the firms, it was, in a greater sense an inefficient allocation of resources: If the Federal Reserve would simply announce its intentions, those economists income could be used in other areas of the firm.

Walsh (2001) provides a useful summary of policy transparency. Transparency about the objectives of policy may reduce the public's uncertainty concerning the goals of policy. If the Federal Reserve announces that its objective is to keep inflation low, then that is a transparent policy, one to which the policymakers can be held accountable. This may then reduce the problem of **time inconsistency** in policy. That is, in the face of rising **unemployment rates**, if the Federal Reserve has announced that a low rate of **inflation** is its policy objective, it may make it more difficult for the FOMC to engage in expansionary policies that are aimed at lowering the unemployment rate in the short run. If the public perceives the FOMC from backing off on its promise, the public may then begin to expect higher rates of inflation.

Can transparency be a problem? Walsh suggests that if a central bank already has a good reputation for keeping policy aligned with its stated policy objectives, changing these objectives may negatively affect the public's expectations. For example, suppose a central bank has over time become known as an inflation fighter and has been able to hold inflation low, and announces a change in this policy (they may wish to focus on a current problem of increased unemployment rates, for instance). This may cause greater uncertainty among the public and financial markets than if the policymakers had not been so forthcoming.

An area where Walsh sees benefit in policy transparency concerns the breakdown of **asymmetric information** between policymakers and the public concerning which models the banks uses in making its policy decisions, and the information used in those models. With regard to the economic model, this may relate to which economic variables—money supply or interest rates—that the policymakers believe are the ones to focus on when making decisions. This is difficult since most economists have yet to agree on which is the better one to use for policy. Knowing which one the Federal Reserve is using at least reduces one source of uncertainty. Similarly, if the public is aware of what economic information the policymakers are using in their deliberations helps increase transparency. For example, if the FOMC makes it known that the increase in the unemployment rate is caused by something beyond their control, say a natural disaster that raises the number of unemployed in a section of the country, and that policy cannot change to meet this one-time event, then the public is better able to interpret the bank's nonaction. Indeed, increases in oil prices which impact inflation rates are sometimes cited as examples of economic events outside the Federal Reserve's control and should not lead to major shifts in policy.

FURTHER READING

Broaddus, J. Alfred. "Transparency in the Practice of Monetary Policy." Federal Reserve Bank of Richmond *Economic Quarterly* (Summer 2001): 1–9; Walsh, Carl. "Transparency in Monetary Policy." Federal Reserve Bank of San Francisco *Economic Letter* (September 7, 2001).

TREASURY BILLS. A Treasury bill is a short-term (a maturity of less than one year) obligation of the U.S. government. Treasury bills are a widely held financial instrument and represent a key tool used in the conduct of monetary policy. This is because they are quite *liquid*, in the sense that they can be easily converted into goods or into other financial assets. In this entry, we provide a brief introduction to how Treasury bills rates are computed, how they are sold, and what role they play in the implementation of monetary policy.

If you were to purchase a **bond**, you would expect a periodic payment over the life of the bond. For example, many retired individuals purchase bonds because bonds pay out a fixed amount—the coupon payment—in periodic increments, say, every six months or annually. The interest rate on the bond determines the size of the coupon payment. When the bond matures, it is sold. When someone purchases a Treasury bill, in contrast, there are no periodic interest payments. Rather, bills are sold by the U.S. Treasury at a discount from their face value, beginning at $10,000 and increasing in increments of $5,000. When the bill is sold, the interest rate that the investor gets is determined by the difference between the face value of the bill and the price at which it was sold. For instance, suppose you purchase a three-month bill for $9,500. If the face value of the bill is $10,000, then at the end of three months, when you sell the bill back to the government, you get $10,000. The interest rate you are being paid is 5.26 percent, or [($10,000 − $9,500)/$9,500]. If the price of bills rises, next week they are selling for $9,650, then the interest rate has fallen: a bill sold for $9,650 has a rate of 3.63 percent. If the price of bills falls to $9,200, then the interest rate has risen: a bill sold for $9,200 has a rate of 8.70 percent.

Treasury bills are sold at a weekly auction, every Monday at the Federal Reserve Bank of New York. The size of the offering usually is announced in the previous week. The auction is conducted through the Federal Reserve System, which acts as the fiscal agent for the Treasury. Bids must be entered by 1:30 p.m. New York time on the day of the auction. As in most auctions, investors bid on the bills being auctioned with winning bidders paying the following Thursday. Those actively engaged in the bidding process may include banks, state and local governments, and mutual funds, among others. The pecking order of bids is that any bid over $1 million, called a competitive bid, takes precedence over a bid less than $1 million, called a noncompetitive bid. If all of the bills available for auction are sold to competitive bids only, then those entering non-competitive bids will not be able to purchase any bills.

Treasury bills are an attractive investment vehicle for several reasons. One is that they are almost totally free of default risk. As an obligation of the U.S. government, only failure of the government would preclude one from being paid. This is unlike other investment vehicles, such as corporate bonds, where bankruptcy of the firm could mean that one will not be repaid their investment. Indeed, in financial models, when a measure of the "risk free" rate is used, the actual measure is the three-month Treasury bill rate. Another reason for the purchase of bills is that the market for them is very liquid. As mentioned elsewhere, **liquidity** is a characteristic whereby a financial asset can be quickly and at low cost converted into cash or real economic goods. Since the market for bills is so large and organized, it is very easy for someone to sell their holdings of bills in the **secondary market**. Although it may not seem like it, the minimum denomination of a Treasury bill ($10,000) actually is much less than some alternative financial assets. This third characteristic makes Treasury bills attractive to a much wider variety of investors, from large corporations to individuals. Last, Treasury bills also have tax advantages that some other financial assets do not possess. The most important is that the interest income from a Treasury bill is not taxable by state and local governments. Depending on the income taxes levied by one's state, Treasury bills may offer a better investment return even if the pre-tax interest rate is lower.

Treasury bills play an important role in the conduct of monetary policy. When the **Trading Desk** at the Federal Reserve Bank of New York undertakes **open market operations**, it does so by buying and selling Treasury bills in the secondary market. For instance, when the Federal Reserve buys bills from dealers it injects reserves into the banking system. When bills are sold, the Federal Reserve is trying to accomplish just the opposite: to remove reserves from the banking system. The buying and selling of Treasury bills allows the Federal Reserve to change the amount of **reserves** in the banking system and, concurrently, the level of the **federal funds rate**. Whether the Federal Reserve influences reserves and rates through outright purchases of bills in the market, or through **repurchase agreements**—the sale or purchase of bills today with an agreement to "reverse" the transaction in a few days—the Treasury bill market is an important element in the implementation of monetary policy.

FURTHER READING

Cook, Timothy Q., and Bruce J. Summers, eds. *Instruments of the Money Market*. Richmond: Federal Reserve Bank of Richmond, 1998, Chapter 2.

TREASURY DEPARTMENT. The U.S. Treasury Department is "the primary federal agency responsible for the economic and financial prosperity and security of the United States and as such is responsible for a wide range of activities...." So states the introductory paragraph on the Treasury Department's Website. These activities are diverse and include advising the President of the United States on economic matters, both domestic and international, managing federal finances and the federal debt, collecting taxes, to enforcing alcohol, drug and tobacco laws. The Treasury, mainly through the **Comptroller of the Currency** and the Office of Thrift Supervision, act to ensure the stability of the payments system by supervising and regulating banks and other depository institutions. In addition to the functions carried out by these two parts of Treasury, there are specific individuals within the Treasury's hierarchy that are responsible for advising and assisting the Secretary of the Treasury in certain areas. These include the Undersecretary of Domestic Finance, the Assistant Secretary of Economic Policy, the Assistant Secretary of Financial Markets, and the Assistant Secretary of Financial Institutions.

In addition to the complementarity of activities in the areas of financial institution supervision and regulation, the Federal Reserve and the Treasury have, in the past, been closely linked in terms of setting monetary policy. Prior to the **Treasury-Federal Reserve Accord of 1951**, Federal Reserve policy was dominated by the requirements of the Treasury. The role of monetary policy was viewed as having a single goal: keep interest rates a slow as low as possible to allow the Treasury to finance government activity at the lowest possible cost. To do this, the Federal Reserve was called upon to peg the interest rate on short-term government securities. Indeed, in 1942 the Federal Reserve announced that the interest rate on three-month **Treasury bills** would be maintained at a rate of 0.375 percent. Once the war was over, however, Federal Reserve officials argued that continuing to peg interest rates would simply lead to higher rates of **inflation**.

During the late 1940s and into 1950 there were numerous Congressional hearings on the link between Treasury financing and the Federal Reserve's monetary policies. In March 1951, in a joint announcement, monetary policy was made independent of Treasury needs. From that point on, Treasury debt management and Federal Reserve monetary policy were no longer officially linked. That said, Federal Reserve policy-makers in the 1950s and 1960s did not ignore the timing of Treasury financings and the impacts such sales of securities could have on financial markets. Reading the *Minutes* of the **Federal Open Market Committee (FOMC)** during this time, one often sees references to an "even keel policy," a euphemism for a policy that attempted to offset any impact on interest rates that may stem from Treasury activities. Today, monetary policy and the Treasury are linked by the fact that open market operations, the purchase and sale of government securities, deals solely with short-term Treasury securities.

FURTHER READING

Federal Reserve Bank of Richmond. "Fiftieth Anniversary of the Accord: Issues in Treasury-Federal Reserve Relations." *Economic Quarterly* (Winter 2001); U.S. Treasury Department. Website: www.ustreas.gov.

TREASURY-FEDERAL RESERVE ACCORD OF 1951. In the period immediately following World War II, Federal Reserve policies aimed primarily at fixing the interest rate on government securities. This policy was undertaken to keep interest rates low, based largely on the fears that the **unemployment rate** would increase sharply once the war-induced production of goods subsided once hostilities ended. A policy of pegging government interest rates at a low level meant that the Federal Reserve was expanding the money supply at rates that led eventually to increases in **inflation**. During the late-1940s and into 1950, officials at the Treasury and the Federal Reserve argued over the merits of such a policy. Treasury officials believed that the Federal Reserve's actions were necessary to sustain economic expansion. Federal Reserve officials, on the other hand, argued that being constrained to keep interest rates low—essentially keeping the government's cost of borrowing low—did not allow them enough flexibility to adequately fight the higher rates of inflation that occurred after war-time price controls were lifted. The requirement that the Federal Reserve buy government securities in the amounts needed to fix interest rates robbed the Federal Reserve of its ability to respond to other economic concerns.

In 1949 and 1950, economic growth and inflation both slowed and the controversy between the Federal Reserve and the Treasury subsided. The outbreak of war in Korea led to another round of surging prices as consumers and business increased their spending fearing the scarcity of goods like that experienced only a few years earlier during World War II. Increased inflation rekindled the Federal Reserve and Treasury's debate over the proper role of monetary policy. As long as the Federal Reserve was required to fix interest rates on government securities at low levels, the ability of the central bank to fight inflation would continue to be hampered.

In early 1951 the controversy came to a climax. In January the Secretary of the Treasury announced that government securities would be issued with an interest rate no higher than 2.50 percent. The announcement carried the implication that Federal Reserve officials had agreed to this, when in fact they had not. President **Harry Truman** announced his support for the policy of fixing rates, also suggesting that the Federal Reserve had agreed to this policy. The announcement and ensuing debate culminated in an official announcement by the **Board of Governors** to Treasury officials that monetary policy would no longer peg interest rates on government securities. Because the Federal Reserve is an independent agency in the government, it could enforce this decision. After additional negotiation, the Treasury and the Federal Reserve issued a joint statement— the so-called accord—in March 1951:

> The Treasury and the Federal Reserve System have reached full accord with respect to debt management and monetary policies to be pursued in furthering their common purpose to assure the successful financing of the Government's requirements and, at the same time, to minimize monetization of the public debt.

The Accord of 1951 was a key turning point in the conduct of U.S. monetary policy. Marking the end of policies aimed solely at supporting Treasury operations, the accord gave the Federal Reserve freedom to pursue other policy objectives, such as fighting inflation and improving economic stabilization.

An interesting side-bar to the negotiation leading to the accord is that the head negotiator for the Treasury, **William McChesney Martin**, became chairman of the Board of Governors of the Federal Reserve soon after the accord was reached. He served as chairman from April 2, 1951, until January 31, 1970.

FURTHER READING

Federal Reserve Bank of Richmond. *Fiftieth Anniversary of the Accord: Issues in Treasury-Federal Reserve Relations. Economic Quarterly* (Winter 2001).

TREASURY TAX AND LOAN DEPOSITS. The Federal Reserve acts as the federal government's bank, and in doing so perform several services. The Treasury holds its deposits at **commercial banks**. In the past, there were large weekly swings in these deposits, making it difficult for the Federal Reserve to manage weekly **reserves** in the banking system. In 1978 the Treasury altered its cash management approach, introducing the Treasury Tax and Loan (TT&L) Investment Program. This program was enacted with the objectives of payment of interest on the Treasury's cash balances at commercial banks and to reduce the fluctuations in Treasury deposits at commercial banks.

The history of such accounts is quite long. In 1917 Congress passed the Liberty Loan Act which created Liberty Loan accounts. (This discussion draws on Lang, 1979.) These accounts were used to facilitate the sale of war **bonds** used to help finance World War I. When a Liberty Bond was sold, the proceeds were deposited into the Liberty Loan accounts at commercial banks instead of in the Treasury's account at the Federal Reserve. This meant that the deposited funds remained in the banking system until spent by the government. In 1918 the Treasury extended the program to include income and excess profits taxes to be deposited in the Liberty Loan accounts, and renamed the accounts War Loan Deposits. Because banks were required to pay an interest rate of 2 percent and the accounts were checkable, passage of the **Banking Act of 1933** eliminated this feature of the accounts. The **Banking Act of 1935** also made the accounts subject to the same **reserve requirements** that were imposed on privately held checking accounts. These deposits increased sharply during the Treasury's financing of World War II. In addition, the Treasury continued to extend the scope of the program, including deposits with an increased number of tax receipts and withheld income taxes and Social Security payroll taxes. In 1950 the accounts were renamed Tax and Loan accounts.

The TT&L accounts work this way. Every day businesses and individuals pay taxes to the U.S. Treasury. These funds are deposited directly into TT&L accounts at more than 12,000 depository institutions and the amount is reported to a Federal Reserve Bank. Unlike regular **checkable deposits**, however, the TT&L deposits are not all covered by federal deposit insurance. Those deposits not covered by insurance are fully collateralized. At the end of business, the Federal Reserve Banks report to the Treasury's cash managers the total amount in the TT&L accounts and these managers determine how much of the tax receipts are needed to cover the daily operating expenses of the federal government. Once that amount is determined, the Treasury's cash manager notifies the Federal Reserve Bank of the needed amount and it is transferred from the TT&L account to the Treasury's account at the Federal Reserve.

FURTHER READING

Lang, Richard W. "TTL Note Accounts and the Money Supply Process." *Federal Reserve Bank of St. Louis Review* (October 1979): 3–14; Meulendyke, Ann-Marie. *U.S. Monetary Policy & Financial Markets.* New York: Federal Reserve Bank of New York, 1998.

TRUMAN, HARRY (1884–1972). Harry Truman was the 33rd President of the United States, serving from 1945 until 1953. As **Franklin Roosevelt**'s vice-president, Truman became president upon the death of Roosevelt on April 12, 1945. Truman was thrust into the position of making crucial decisions regarding the ending of World War II—Truman gave the order to drop the atomic bombs on Hiroshima and Nagasaki—and the aftermath. On the foreign affairs front, Truman faced several threats from the Soviet Union. In 1947, when the Soviet Union was threatening both Turkey and Greece, Truman sought aid for the two countries, giving rise to what is now referred to as the Truman Doctrine. When the Soviets blockaded western Berlin in 1948, Truman organized a massive airlift of goods to support West Berlin. He also helped negotiate the agreement that would create the North Atlantic Treaty Organization (NATO), a military alliance established in 1949 that was meant to protect western Europe from Soviet invasion. In June 1950, Truman also ordered the "police action" to protect South Korea. This decision, prompted by the June 1950 invasion of the South by North Korea, was the beginning of the Korean War.

In addition to his record in the field of foreign affairs, Truman also left a mark on domestic policy. In domestic policy Truman favored expanding the role of the federal government. Early in his tenure as president, Truman advocated programs to expand Social Security, employment programs and public programs to eradicate poverty. These programs fall under what has been called Truman's Fair Deal programs.

In the area of monetary policy, Truman and officials in his administration often were at odds with the Federal Reserve. During the 1940s, the Federal Reserve operated with the primary purpose of pegging interest rates on government securities. This was taken to reduce the cost to the government of funding the war effort. After the war, however, the policy came under much criticism by economists inside and outside of the Federal Reserve. Even so, Truman felt an obligation to peg the rates on government **bonds**, partly to protect their value to those who had purchased them, but also to assist the government in funding his desired pubic programs. When the Korean conflict broke out, there were renewed calls from the government to the Federal Reserve to follow a policy that kept interest rates on government securities low. The problem was that while the policy was being touted as a patriotic necessity in a time of war, economically it fueled a rapid rise in the rate of inflation. With the rate of **inflation** averaging about 8 percent in 1950, some monetary policymakers argued that unless policy was changed—even just raising the level of the peg—there would be dire inflationary consequences.

A series of meetings between the White House, the Federal Reserve and representatives of the U.S. Treasury were held in late 1950 and early 1951. As details of the meetings became public knowledge, it was clear that a growing chasm existed between the parties involved. The issue was forced in February 1951 when the Federal Reserve informed the White House that it no longer would peg interest rates on government securities. This announcement, which became public knowledge, set off a series of heated debates and acrimonious, public comments. For many in the Federal Reserve, actions by the White House were interpreted as simply trying to keep monetary policy under their control, albeit through the Treasury.

The dispute was resolved with the public announcement of the **Treasury-Federal Reserve Accord of 1951**. As part of the agreement, the chairman of the Federal Reserve **Thomas Bayard McCabe** agreed to resign. To replace him, Truman nominated **William McChesney Martin, Jr.**, Treasury's negotiator for the accord. Martin's appointment was approved by the Senate on March 21. In an interesting twist, Martin went on to become one of the most ardent advocates for Federal Reserve independence from the government. If Truman thought he was getting an ally and someone whom he could control, he was mistaken.

Truman did not seek reelection in the 1952 campaign. Following President-elect Eisenhower's inauguration in January 1953, Truman returned to his home in Independence, Missouri where he lived until his death on December 26, 1972, at age 88. For a brief biography of Truman, visit the Website www.whitehouse.gov/history/presidents and click on Truman.

FURTHER READING

Federal Reserve Bank of Richmond. *Fiftieth Anniversary of the Accord: Issues in Treasury-Federal Reserve Relations. Economic Quarterly* (Winter 2001); Hetzel, Robert L., and Ralph F. Leach. "The Treasury-Fed Accord: A New Narrative Account." Federal Reserve Bank of Richmond *Economic Quarterly* (Winter 2001): 33–55.

TRUTH IN LENDING. Regulations regarding "truth in lending" attempt to increase the transparency of credit transactions. These regulations require lenders to provide consumers with clear, understandable terms of lending arrangements and the cost of obtaining **loans**. Legislation which brought about the truth in lending laws originally was enacted by Congress in 1968 as part of the Consumer Protection Act, later refined in 1980 as part of the **Depository Institutions Deregulation and Monetary Control Act (DIDMCA) of 1980**. For the most part, this legislation was designed to help protect small businesses and individuals.

The truth in lending law is implemented through two key Federal Reserve regulations: Regulation M and regulation Z. (See Appendix C for a complete listing of all the Federal

Reserve regulations.) Regulation M covers rules for consumer leasing transactions. Essentially, this regulation covers transactions where the leased good or property is used for personal, family or household purposes. The time period of the lease is relatively short (but must exceed four installments) and the total amount of the contractual obligation must not exceed $25,000.

Regulation Z covers compliance with consumer credit parts of the Truth in Lending Act. Regulation Z applies to any individual or business that offers consumer credit, under the proviso that the lender meet several conditions. These are that the credit is offered periodically; that it is offered to consumers (as opposed to businesses); that the credit is subject to finance charges; and that the credit is for personal, family or household purposes. As you can see, the regulation is designed to cover the activity of financial institutions who lend to households and not businesses, whether commercial or agricultural.

Under Regulation Z lenders must disclose information about the credit terms of a loan. For example, the lender must inform the borrower about any finance charges incurred with the loan obligation, the annual percentage rate on the loan, the total amount of periodic principal and interest payments, and the total cost of the purchase, including the down payment and the periodic payments. What if a financial institution violates the truth in lending laws? Penalties can be substantial. For example, violating the disclosure rules may be fined by twice the amount of the finance charge, with costs of attorneys and fees added on.

Truth in lending laws recently have made the news in the area of subprime lending, more popularly known as predatory lending. The U.S. Department of Housing and Urban Development (2000) defines subprime lending as "providing credit to borrowers with past credit problems, often at a higher cost or less favorable terms than loans available in the conventional prime market." The belief is that such lenders engage in abusive practices by keeping borrowers uninformed of certain aspects of the obligation they are signing, or simply making loans to individuals at rates far above the standard rates. A popular view is that lenders would customize loans in such a way as to entrap unsophisticated borrowers who do not have alternative credit sources do draw upon. This type of activity is an example of the behavior that comes under the purview of the truth in lending activity covered by the Federal Reserve's implementation of Regulations M and Z.

FURTHER READING

Federal Deposit Insurance Corporation. Website: www.fdic.gov and search for "truth in lending."; Turner, M. A., and F. Skidmore, eds. *Mortgage Lending Discrimination: A Review of Existing Evidence*. Washington, D.C.: The Urban Institute, 1999; U.S. Department of Housing and Urban Development. *Unequal Burden: Income and Racial Disparities in Subprime Lending in America* (April 2000).

UNEMPLOYMENT RATE. The unemployment rate is announced every month by the Bureau of Labor Statistics (BLS), a government agency located in Washington, D.C. Of all the available economic statistics, the unemployment rate ranks high in importance to monetary policymakers. This is because the unemployment rate provides a first glimpse into the well-being of the economy. Available monthly—the March unemployment rate is announced in early April—the unemployment rate is a statistic that tells us whether the economy is producing new jobs, if workers are becoming discouraged and leaving the work force, or some combination of the two.

The unemployment rate in the United States is measured using one of two surveys. One is called the *household* survey. This survey is used to collect data on the size of the labor force and household employment. For example, the first question asked is "do you have a job?" If your answer is yes, then you are counted as part of the labor force. If the answer is no but you are currently looking for a job, then you are part of the labor force but considered unemployed. If you answer no and you are not seeking employment, then you are not part of the labor force. One caveat about the unemployment rate derived from the household survey is that if you become discouraged and simply quit looking for work, you are not officially considered to be unemployed even though you are out of work. The unemployment rate is calculated as the ratio of the number of people unemployed to the labor force. For example, if there are 7 million people counted as unemployed and 125 million in the labor force, the unemployment rate is 7/125, or 5.6 percent. This figure is usually referred to as the civilian unemployment rate because it excludes those in the military.

Some believe that the other survey, the *establishment* survey, is more accurate. This survey is conducted by collecting data from a large number of businesses. Because the establishment survey questions employers, it sometimes is thought that the answers given to the survey are more accurate than those collected through the household survey. Of course, even this survey is not without problems. For example, the establishment survey misses self-employed individuals. The guy who mows lawns for a living or the neighbor who babysits is not counted in the establishment survey but is captured by the household survey. The establishment survey also ignores those individuals who are out on strike. Even with these caveats, the establishment survey generally is regarded as the more accurate measure of unemployment.

Unemployment Rate; Percent SA

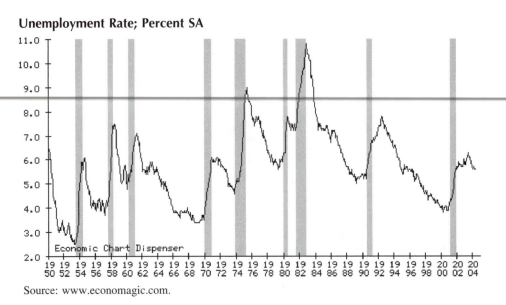

Source: www.economagic.com.

A key use of the unemployment rate is to gauge the pace of economic activity. In a booming economy firms are hiring workers and the unemployment rate should be relatively low. When a **recession** occurs, firms lay off or fire workers as the demand for their products declines. In this situation the unemployment rate is expected to increase. As shown in the chart above, the unemployment rate is very cyclical, meaning that it rises during economic downturns and falls during economic expansions. Looking at the timing of the movements in the unemployment rate, you will notice that it tends to lag the onset of a recession and the beginning of a recovery. This reflects the fact that the unemployment rate is considered to be a *lagging* indicator of economic activity. Why would this be? As you can see in the accompanying chart, the unemployment rate always seems to remain high even after a recession, shown by the shaded bars, has ended.

When the economy is coming out of a recession, firms often are unsure that any observed increased in the demand for their goods is permanent. Given this uncertainty, they use existing workers to produce more goods, sometimes resorting to overtime if demand continues to increase. Once firms believe that the recovery is for real, demand outstrips the productive ability of the reduced workforce and firms hire more workers. At this time the unemployment rate begins to recede.

The unemployment rate plays a major role in monetary policy actions. Following the 2001 recession, for example, the Federal Reserve pushed the **federal funds rate** to historic lows, down to 1 percent, and left it there for almost two years. The reason given for this action was that the recovery out of the 2001 recession was viewed as a "jobless" recovery, meaning that the creation of new jobs seemed to be lagging behind historic trends. The Federal Reserve reacted by engaging in an expansionary policy.

The most direct way in which the unemployment rate has entered policy discussions is through the **Phillips curve** analysis, most popular during the 1960s and 1970s. The Phillips curve basically relates the level of the unemployment rate to the rate of **inflation**. Some economists believed that there exists a stable trade-off between the two measures. That is, if the Federal Reserve engaged in expansionary policy to lower the unemployment rate this would "cost" the economy a higher rate of inflation. The idea was that the tradeoff could be measured with precision, so that an X percentage point reduction in the unemployment rate would be accompanied with an increase in the rate of inflation by Y percentage points. Because lowering the unemployment rate was given more policy weight than keeping the rate of inflation low, policies oriented to keeping the unemployment rate down gave rise to a 20-year period of rising rates of inflation, a period commonly referred to as the **Great Inflation**.

As a final note, a flaw with focusing on the unemployment rate is that there may be little monetary policy can do to affect it. Suppose the economy was operating at full tilt. In such a world, the unemployment rate may be at what some call the **natural rate of unemployment**. That is, at a level that simply reflects the dynamics of the labor market—people switching jobs to secure higher income or just to try something new—or the fact that some individuals are prone to being unemployed. Suppose the official unemployment rate associated with the natural rate of unemployment is 4.5 percent. If the Federal Reserve pursues a policy to lower the unemployment rate below 4.5 percent, the likely outcome is to cause an increase in the rate of inflation. Indeed, this is just what happened in the 1960s and 1970s. Once an economy reaches its "full employment" level of activity, trying to push the economy to grow faster may not lead to permanently lower unemployment rates, just to permanently higher rates of inflation. Even though the Federal Reserve may not have any impact over where the natural rate of unemployment is, its policies clearly affect the level of the unemployment rate in the short run. If the unemployment rate is cyclical and monetary policy is part of the explanation for business cycles (although there is some debate over this: *see* **Real Business Cycle Theory**), then the Federal Reserve is partly to blame for the fluctuations in the unemployment rate.

FURTHER READING

Bureau of Labor Statistics. Website: www.bls.gov; Friedman, Milton. "The Role of Monetary Policy." *American Economic Review* (March 1968): 1–17; Rissman, Ellen R. "What is the Natural Rate of Unemployment?" Federal Reserve Bank of Chicago *Economic Perspectives* (September/October 1986); Taylor, John B. *Economics*. 4th edition. Boston: Houghton Mifflin, 2004.

UNIT BANKING. During much of the United States' banking history, banks often were *unit* banks. That is, banks that could have only one office, with no branches in other parts of the city, state, or country. When people traveled they would either take cash or travelers' checks or hope that when visiting another city they could cash a check written on their bank. If they seemed so inconvenient, why did unit banks, and the laws that required them, persist?

One explanation is that unit banking limited competition. In many instances, especially in smaller towns, there was "the bank." The local bankers wielded power by being the only lending institution in town. If **branching** were allowed, it may be that a larger bank, located in a distant city, could open a branch office in town, thus reducing the original bank's monopoly position. Another reason for unit banking stems from the experience of the **Great Depression**. Some lawmakers believed that if unit banking was the norm, if a bank experienced difficulties those problems would be localized to that bank in that town. If branching was allowed, then the problems experienced in one locale could spread to others. As a bank with branches tried to keep its offices open, it could spread problems throughout a larger geographical region. As it turns out, this reasoning probably was mistaken. Because unit banks have no other resources to call upon, when difficulties did arise they often led to a failure of the bank. Other countries, such as Canada, had a banking system characterized by a small number of very large banks, each with many branches throughout the country. During the Great Depression, it appears that the banking system in Canada did not suffer the same collapse as in the United States. Some argue that Canadian banks were able to spread the impact of problems across a system of branches, allowing banks to diversify their portfolio of banking across different types of loans (agricultural, industrial, commercial, etc.) so that economic difficulties in any one area did not bring down the bank.

Another reason why unit banking may not make sense is that unit banks often cannot achieve economies of scale. Small unit banks simply do not have the level of activity that may pay for them to offer online checking, overdraft protection, or other consumer services. A bank that has grown large enough to make such services profitable thus offers the consumer more choices, and often at a lower cost.

The trend in the United States clearly is away from unit banking. Consider these numbers. In 1900 there were about 12,500 banks but only 87 had any branches. By 1935, following the **bank failures** of the Great Depression, there were about 14,000 banks, of which 796 had branches. As recently as 1960, banks with branches still were in the minority: of the 13,126 banking institutions, 10,740 were unit banks. Beginning in the 1970s, however, that ratio began to change. By 2003 there were 7,769 institutions, with 5,545 operating branches and only 2,224 operating as unit banks. Not only has branching spread across the United States, but the total number of banking institutions has decreased, thus reflecting the consolidation in the banking industry.

Why has branching become pervasive? One is the technology of banking. Improved computer technology allows a bank with a computer to handle many different customers at many different locations. Online banking, the explosion of **automated teller machines (ATMs)**, and similar "nonhuman" methods to deliver banking services allow a bank to operate in many places at the same time. It also is more cost-effective for one bank to run a large computer system to meet such customer needs than it is for every little bank to own and maintain its own computer system. These are the economies of scale mentioned earlier. Banks also have followed population shifts into suburban areas and into different parts of the country. Population growth in the southeast and the southwest meant that banks could follow their customers into new areas if they branched. Of course, recent legislation overturning of the **McFadden Act of 1927** and the **Glass-Steagall Act of 1932** (*see* **Riegle-Neal Act of 1994**), both of which were designed to prevent bank failures on the magnitude associated with the Great Depression, opened the doors to bank consolidation and increased branching activity. It is likely that in your town there are branches of one or more of the largest banks in the United States.

If branching and bank consolidation are the trend, why are there still a couple thousand unit banks? In many instances these banks are located in small towns where the banking market may be able to support only one bank. During the 1990s, there also occurred a movement in banking to what is sometimes referred to as "boutique" banks. These banks, usually small, often focus on customer relations and usually have a relatively small geographic market. Their key to success is personalized service and to provide a level of customer attention that some may feel is lacking from the branches of an out-of-state bank conglomerate.

FURTHER READING

Federal Deposit Insurance Corporation. Website: www.fdic.gov. (See "Historical Statistics of Banking."); Wells, Donald R., and L. S. Scruggs. "Historical Insights into the Deregulation of Money and Banking." *Cato Journal* (Winter 1986): 899–910.

VAULT CASH. Vault cash is, quite literally, the cash that banks have on hand in their vault. Vault cash serves several purposes. One is to meet currency demands of its customers. After all, if you go into your bank and ask for $100 out of your checking account, you hope that they have the cash on hand. Another is that vault cash is used by a bank to satisfy its **reserve requirements**. In both instances, vault cash is considered to be an asset to the bank.

The chart below shows the behavior of vault cash over the past decade. There are several points worth noting. First, vault cash has become a major component of **reserves** of the banking system. With the increased use of so-called **sweep accounts**, banks can satisfy reserve requirements on a smaller amount of transactions deposits. For some banks, such requirements can be met with vault cash. Total reserves in the banking system in mid-2004 was $46 billion. Because vault cash amounted to about $32 billion, this means that vault cash alone accounted for about 70 percent of reserves. (In terms of total currency outstanding, vault cash in 2004 amounted to less than 5 percent.)

Another observation from the chart is that vault cash is a fairly volatile series. At times banks may wish to hold additional funds on hand to meet customer demands. This increased demand for currency may occur during times of uncertainty. For example, look

Vault Cash Used to Satisfy Required Reserves, Not Adjusted for Changes in Reserve Requirements (Billions of Dollars)

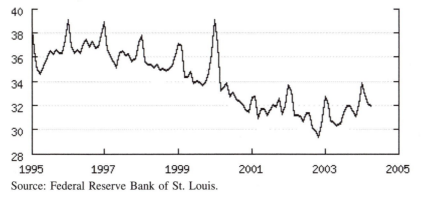

Source: Federal Reserve Bank of St. Louis.

at 2001 and you will see that there is a spike in vault cash holdings at the time of the September 2001 terrorist attacks. Also, because the series is not seasonally adjusted, vault cash holdings take fairly predictable upturns at certain times of the year, most notably during the Christmas holiday season.

FURTHER READING

Anderson, Richard G., and Robert H. Rasche. "Measuring the Adjusted Monetary Base in an Era of Financial Change." Federal Reserve Bank of St. Louis *Review* (November/December, 1996): 3–37; Mishkin, Frederic S. *The Economics of Money, Banking, and Financial Markets*. 7th edition. Boston: Pearson Addison Wesley, 2004.

VELOCITY OF MONEY. The so-called velocity of money, sometimes called the income velocity of money, is directly related to the idea of money demand. Velocity measures the number of times the stock of money in the economy "turns over" in each period. Put slightly differently, the velocity of money measures how many dollars of nominal income is supported by each dollar of the money supply. A higher value of velocity indicates that a dollar in circulation is traded more rapidly between individuals as they buy goods and services.

To see how velocity is measured, letting V stand for velocity,

$$V = \frac{\text{Nominal GDP}}{\text{Money supply}} = \frac{Py}{M}$$

where P is the price level and y is real **Gross Domestic Product (GDP)**. What this relation says is that if more and more income is generated by trades within the economy—nominal GDP is increasing—and there is no change in the supply of **money** (M), then the existing stock of money must be circulating at a faster rate than before. In other words, its velocity increased. In times when cash was the primary type of money used in transactions, the idea of a dollar bill being traded from hand to hand made much more sense than it does today. Still, the concept that money is being used more efficiently because of **financial innovations** also could be reflected in a rising velocity.

Velocity is fundamental to the workings of the **quantity theory**, a very simple model of the economy. As discussed in more depth elsewhere, the quantity theory is described by the equation

$$MV = Py.$$

What the quantity theory tells us is that if real output (y) is determined by factors such as labor productivity or the ratio of capital to labor, then there is a direct relation between the money supply (M), velocity (V), and the price level (P). *If* velocity is determined by factors such as payment practices or existing technologies of transacting—cash versus credit cards—then there may be a close relation between the money supply and the price level. That is, if one considered both velocity and real GDP as fixed values, then there is a direct, positive relation between changes in the money supply and the price level. Stated in dynamic terms, the rate of **inflation** is solely determined by the growth rate of the

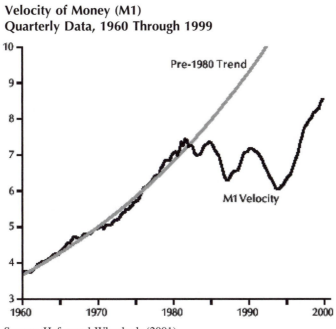

Velocity of Money (M1)
Quarterly Data, 1960 Through 1999

Source: Hafer and Wheelock (2001).

money supply. The quantity theory also tells us that if velocity is a constant, then nominal GDP (Py) also is related directly to movements in the money supply.

The idea that velocity is a constant is not born out by the data. As shown in the figure above, the velocity of money, here measured using the M1 definition of money, is not a fixed numerical value. For example, note that M1 velocity dropped from 1980 through 1985 and then began to increase. Note also that velocity rose at what appears to be a relatively constant rate during most of the 1960s and 1970s. If one believed that velocity was increasing at a relatively predictable rate, say, averaging about 2 to 3 percent per year, then this was a useful piece of information upon which to build a monetary policy.

To see why this might be true, write out the quantity equation in growth rate form, or

Money growth + velocity growth = inflation + real GDP growth.

If the average growth rate of velocity did not change much, then it was argued that monetary policymakers could effectively undertake policies that enables them to better control inflation and nominal GDP growth (= inflation + real GDP growth). This was the basis of the **Monetarist** attack on Federal Reserve policies in the 1960s and 1970s.

The problem with this approach was that velocity did not continue to increase in the 1980s as it had in the previous two decades. As seen in the figure above, the decline of velocity beginning in 1980, associated with the innovations associated with passage of the **Depository Institutions Deregulation and Monetary Control Act (DIDMCA) of 1980**, meant that predictions of inflation and nominal GDP growth based on pre-1980 velocity would be wrong. And this is what happened: forecasts of inflation given the money growth numbers available in the early 1980s were much higher than the actual outcomes. Since velocity had declined, a faster growth rate of the money supply would, according to the equation, not have the same effect compared with a decade earlier. Failure to recognize the consequences of the velocity shift led many to discount the Monetarist threats of higher inflation. It also led the Federal Reserve to discount the use of monetary aggregates in the setting of policy.

Although the debate continues, officials at the Federal Reserve pay little attention to the behavior of the monetary aggregates. They argue that shifts in velocity make them unreliable guides to policy. Today, as in the 1950s and 1960s, the Federal Reserve relies on movements in the market interest rates (the **federal funds rate**) to implement policy.

FURTHER READING

Fisher, Irving. *The Purchasing Power of Money*. New York: Macmillan, 1911; Hafer, R. W. "What Remains of Monetarism?" Federal Reserve Bank of Atlanta *Economic Review* (Fourth Quarter 2001): 13–33; Hafer, R. W., and David C. Wheelock. "The Rise and Fall of a Policy Rule: Monetarism at the St. Louis Fed, 1966-86." St. Louis Federal Reserve Bank *Review* (January/ February 2001): 1–24.

VOLCKER, PAUL (1927–). Paul Volcker was chairman of the Federal Reserve **Board of Governors** from 1979 until 1987, when he was succeeded by **Alan Greenspan**. Educated at Princeton, Harvard, and the London School of Economics, Volcker held a number of business, government, and academic positions before becoming chairman. During the summers of 1949 and 1950, he worked as a research assistant in the Federal Reserve Bank of New York. In 1952, following a year as the Rotary Foundation Fellow at the London School, Volcker returned to the New York Bank as an economist in the research department. In 1955, he moved to the securities department to serve as a special assistant. Between 1955 and 1975, Volcker served in several positions. He worked as a financial economist for Chase Manhattan bank, immediately following his time at the New York Bank; he moved to the U.S. Treasury Department, holding various positions between 1962 and 1965; returned to Chase in 1965; and in 1969 again returned to Treasury, where he served as Undersecretary for Monetary Affairs until 1974. Between 1974 and 1975, Volcker was a senior fellow at the Woodrow Wilson School of Public and International Affairs at Princeton University, a position he held until becoming president of the New York Bank in 1975.

Volcker will be remembered for the policy change that led to a significant reduction in the rate of inflation during the 1980s. On October 6, 1979, Volcker met with other members of the **Federal Open Market Committee (FOMC)** to change the approach to monetary policy. Prior to that date, monetary policy targeted the **federal funds rate** and tried to manipulate the rate within fairly narrow bands to achieve its policy goals. This policy and the fact that oil prices had spike upward in the late 1970s created a situation of high **inflation**. To fight inflation, then running at nearly a 15 percent rate, it was decided at that meeting that henceforth more weight would be given to the behavior of the monetary aggregates in formulating policy. Whether the FOMC faithfully followed policies that could be considered "**Monetarist**" or whether this was just lip service remains a topic of debate to this day. Regardless, Volcker led the FOMC at a time when policy became much more restrictive: interest rates were pushed above 20 percent and, not surprisingly, the economy responded. Not only did inflation begin to decline sharply, but the economy entered into a deep **recession**. The "Volcker recession" set off a widespread call for his resignation, from political pundits to academic scribblers. There were marches calling for his ouster, perhaps the most dramatic being the march on Washington by farmers who circled the Federal Reserve building on tractors. Volcker and the FOMC held their ground. As the recession waned, inflation fell and, by the time he left the Federal Reserve, the rate of inflation in the United States had dropped to a rate of less than 5 percent.

FURTHER READING

BookRags. *Biography of Paul Volcker*. Website: www.bookrags.com/biography/paul~volcker/; Neikirk, William R. *Volcker: Portrait of the Money Man*. Chicago: Congdon & Weed, 1987.

VREELAND, EDWARD (1856–1936). Edward Butterfield Vreeland is best known as the cosponsor of the **Aldrich-Vreeland Act of 1908**, the piece of legislation that pushed the United States closer to establishing a central bank. A representative from the state of New York, Vreeland was elected to Congress seven times, spanning the period 1899–1913. He served as chairman of the Committee on Banking and Currency in the 61st Congress and was appointed as member of the **National Monetary Commission**, serving as its vice chairman from 1909 to 1912. It was the work of the National Monetary Commission that laid the foundation for the Federal Reserve System. Upon leaving political life, Vreeland pursued business interests in Salamanca, New York, until his death in 1936.

WAGE AND PRICE CONTROLS. The idea behind wage and price controls is to establish some minimum, or some maximum, price for a good, service, labor, or credit. The idea is simple: By creating a price, the government is able to take the market mechanism out of play, and this is supposed to make the good available to a broader range of individuals than would occur if the market determined the price. A good example is rent control on New York City apartments. Rent control began as a gesture to service men and women returning home following World War II. The idea was commendable: by setting a maximum on rent, those who had served their country would be more able to find housing and get back into civilian life. Today, there still are apartments in New York City that are under rent control provisions with rent that is many times *below* the current market value. This bypasses the market mechanism that establishes rents in New York City and that fewer such apartments will be available.

For the purposes of a discussion about the Federal Reserve, the best example (or the worst) of wage and price controls occurred during 1971 to 1973. The Nixon Administration, seeing the rate of **inflation** rising to the then high of around 5 percent, sought to curtail the so-called wage–price spiral: by stopping the rapid increases in prices, rapid wage increases also would cease and this would put less pressure on firms to raise prices, etc. The argument by administration officials was that the controls would be temporary—only 90 days—and then they would be removed. By then, it was argued, policies could be put into place that would attack the causes of inflation. Of course, imposing wage and price controls had exactly the opposite reaction.

Inflation is caused by increases in the money supply at a rate that exceeds the productive output of an economy. To use the oft-quoted definition: inflation is "too much money chasing too few goods." During the 1960s and into the early 1970s, the rising rates of inflation experienced in the United States stemmed directly from an expansionary monetary policy. As policymakers tried to hold down the **unemployment rate**, they succeeded in pushing up the rate of inflation. Because there was debate at the time as to what causes inflation, this influence of monetary policy was not given much weight. So, on August 15, 1971, President Richard Nixon announced to the public that he was imposing a wage and price freeze.

Not only was the imposition of such controls bad economics, it also was bad timing. Monetary policy, which had up to this point been expansionary, did not change. Because prices were being held constant by controls, monetary policy continued with its expansionary ways. As the controls lasted into the mid 1970s—controls lasted until April 1974, going through "phases" I, II, and III—the economy was buffeted by some shocks. A bad harvest in 1973 should have pushed agricultural prices up (and hence inflation), but controls kept a lid on them. In late 1973 there was the Organization of Petroleum Exporting Countries (OPEC) oil price increase that also negatively affected prices. Once controls were dismantled the rate of inflation began to increase rapidly, from about a 3 percent rate in June 1972 to a rate of almost 13 percent by December 1974. Wage and price controls did not "cure" inflation; they merely contained it for a while.

One thing that the Nixon wage and price control episode did was to provide more ammunition to those economists who believed that the behavior of the money supply, and therefore the behavior of the Federal Reserve, is key to explaining inflation. (*See* **Monetarism**.) Since the controls prevented inflation from rising with the rapid growth in the supply of money, they provided the Federal Reserve with cover for their expansive policy actions. Even the chairman of the Federal Reserve at the time, **Arthur Burns**, favored the controls on the belief that inflation really had little to do with monetary policy and more with reactions to rising prices for labor (wages) and for raw materials. The utter failure of controls to limit inflation over time, and the dislocation they created by upsetting the market pricing mechanism, thoroughly discredited this approach to macroeconomic policy. In the end, most economists agree that inflation is a monetary problem, one that cannot be cured with setting limits on price movements.

FURTHER READING

Blinder, Alan S. *Economic Policy and the Great Stagflation*. New York: Academic Press, 1981; Rockoff, Hugh. "Price Controls." *The Concise Encyclopedia of Economics* (2002) accessed at Website: www.econlib.org.

WARBURG, PAUL (1868–1932). Paul Warburg was born to a prominent banking family in Hamburg, Germany. He was one of the architects of the **Federal Reserve Act of 1913** and a key figure in the early debates over monetary policy. After college, Warburg held numerous positions in banking, working in London and Paris. He also traveled extensively in India, China, and Japan. After this experience, Warburg returned to Germany to become a partner in the family banking firm of M. M. Warburg & Co. After marrying an American citizen, Warburg split his time between Hamburg and New York City. In 1901, Warburg moved to New York and accepted the position of partner at the financial firm of Kuhn, Loeb and Co. Not only was the firm one of the most influential on Wall Street, but it also was his father-in-law's (Warburg married Loeb's daughter, Nina). Soon after Warburg settled in New York, the American economy and financial markets experienced a series of **financial panics**, the most significant being the **Panic of 1907**.

Warburg believed that the Panic of 1907 reflected the underlying problems of the U.S. banking system. Warburg pushed for a banking system that was patterned after the European system of discounting. Warburg promoted a plan for implementing such a system in the United States. In essence, Warburg pushed for centralizing reserves in the banking system in a central bank. By concentrating reserves, banks could seek relief by borrowing from the central bank. By converting their assets into currency, banks could meet depositors' demands without undue effects to financial or business conditions. Warburg's ideas received a wide audience in financial circles in the United States. One individual who came to appreciate Warburg's views was Senator **Nelson Aldrich**. A senator from Rhode Island, Aldrich was the chairman of the Senate Finance Committee and head of the **National Monetary Commission**.

Warburg's ideas were crystallized in his paper "The Discount System in Europe," a study that became part of the commission's analysis of other banking systems. In numerous speeches, editorials, and papers, Warburg pushed for the establishment of a banking system where the central bank would meet the needs of business as the economy expanded and contracted. He combined the idea of a discount system patterned after the European model and with his belief that the United States needed a much broader **commercial paper** market.

In early November 1910, Warburg, Aldrich, and a small group of influential members of the New York bankers traveled to Jekyll Island, Georgia, ostensibly to hunt ducks. At this enclave, which lasted 10 days, they hammered out a plan for reforming the U.S. banking system, a scheme that later came to be known as the Aldrich Plan. The outcome of this meeting provided the basic structure of what would become the Federal Reserve System. There would be a "central reserve" organization (called the National Reserve Association), one that could meet emergency reserve needs of banks during financial distress. The plan also called for branches (15) located around the country. Through these branches, the association served as the **lender of last resort** to the banking system. Although there were some changes, the Aldrich Plan was the blueprint for the Federal Reserve Act.

After the Federal Reserve Act was passed in 1913, Warburg began his career as a central banker. Although there was much opposition, President **Woodrow Wilson** nominated Warburg to serve as a member of the first Federal Reserve Board. During his time on the board (1914–1918), Warburg provided leadership in the early days of learning how to make monetary policy. His knowledge of banking and finance and his international experience all elevated him in discussions of the day.

FURTHER READING

Dykes, Sayre Ellen, and Michael W. Whitehouse. "The Establishment and Evolution of the Federal Reserve Board: 1913–1923." *Federal Reserve Bulletin* (April 1989); Whitehouse, Michael W. "Paul Warburg's Crusade to Establish a Central Bank in the United States." Federal Reserve Bank of Minneapolis *The Region* (May 1989).

WILSON, WOODROW (1856–1924). Woodrow Wilson, born in Virginia to a Presbyterian minister, began his career not as a politician but as an academician. After graduating from the College of New Jersey (now Princeton University) and the University of Virginia Law School, Wilson continued his academic training at Johns Hopkins University in Baltimore, Maryland, where he earned his doctorate. After receiving his degree, Wilson returned to Princeton, where he taught political science. He was a rising star at Princeton, becoming president of the university in 1902.

Wilson's political career began with his election as governor of New Jersey in 1910. He moved away from the conservative side of the Democratic Party after the election, vowing to take a progressive stance in his political decisions. His actions and decisions gave rise to a national reputation, one that led to being the Democratic Party's presidential nominee in

1912. Stressing individualism and states' rights, Wilson became the twenty-eighth president of the United States with only 42 percent of the popular vote but a majority of the electoral votes.

Among the important pieces of legislation that Wilson pushed through Congress, one of the more lasting was his sponsorship of the legislation that became the **Federal Reserve Act of 1913**. (A complete version of the act is available in Appendix A.) Signed into law on Christmas Eve, 1913, Wilson's support for the act provided the backing that helped give the country its first true central bank.

Although Wilson tried to maintain the nation's neutrality, following his reelection in 1916 he asked Congress for a declaration of war on April 2, 1917. At that point, the United States was at war with Germany. Following the end of the war in 1918, Wilson pushed for the League of Nations, his version of what would one day become the United Nations. When presented with the treaty that contained the League of Nations, the Senate defeated it. Wilson then embarked on a nationwide tour to generate support for the league. During this tour, he suffered a stroke that nearly ended his life. From that point on, Wilson's health failed until he died in 1924.

FURTHER READING

Brands, H. W., and Arthur M. Schlesinger. *Woodrow Wilson 1913–1921: The American Presidents Series*. New York: Times Books, 2003; Heckscher, August. *Woodrow Wilson*. New York: Simon and Schuster, 1991; Link, Arthur Stanley. *Woodrow Wilson and the Progressive Era, 1910–1917*. New York: Harper Collins Publishing, 1972.

ZERO COUPON BONDS (*See* **STRIPS**)

APPENDIX A

THE FEDERAL RESERVE ACT

(Enacted December 23, 1913. The act as currently amended is available at the Federal Reserve Board of Governor's Website: www.federalreserve.gov.)

An Act To provide for the establishment of Federal reserve banks, to furnish an elastic currency, to afford means of rediscounting commercial paper, to establish a more effective supervision of banking in the United States, and for other purposes.

Be it enacted by the Senate and House of Representatives of the United States of America in Congress assembled, That the short title of this Act shall be the "Federal Reserve Act."

Wherever the word "bank" is used in this Act, the word shall be held to include State bank, banking association, and trust company, except where national banks or Federal reserve banks are specifically referred to.

The terms "national bank" and "national banking association" used in this Act shall be held to be synonymous and interchangeable. The term "member bank" shall be held to mean any national bank, State bank, or bank or trust company which has become a member of one of the reserve banks created by this Act. The term "board" shall be held to mean Federal Reserve Board; the term "district" shall be held to mean Federal reserve district; the term "reserve bank" shall be held to mean Federal reserve bank.

FEDERAL RESERVE DISTRICTS

SEC. 2. As soon as practicable, the Secretary of the Treasury, the Secretary of Agriculture and the Comptroller of the Currency, acting as "The Reserve Bank Organization Committee," shall designate not less than eight nor more than twelve cities to be known as Federal reserve cities, and shall divide the continental United States, excluding Alaska, into districts, each district to contain only one of such Federal Reserve cities. The determination of said organization committee shall not be subject to review except by the Federal Reserve Board when organized: Provided, That the districts shall be apportioned with due regard to the convenience and customary course of business and shall not necessarily be coterminous with any State or States. The districts thus created may be readjusted and new districts may from time to time be created by the Federal Reserve Board, not to exceed twelve in all. Such districts shall be known as Federal reserve districts and may be designated by number. A majority of the organization committee shall constitute a quorum with authority to act.

Said organization committee shall be authorized to employ counsel and expert aid, to take testimony, to send for persons, and papers, to administer oaths, and to make such investigation as may be deemed necessary by the said committee in determining the reserve districts and in designating the cities within such districts where such Federal reserve banks shall be severally located. The said committee shall supervise the organization in each of the cities designated of a Federal reserve bank, which shall include in its title the name of the city in which it is situated, as "Federal Reserve Bank of Chicago."

Under regulations to be prescribed by the organization committee, every national banking association in the United States is hereby required, and every eligible bank in the United States and every trust company within the District of Columbia, is hereby authorized to signify in writing, within sixty days after the passage of this Act, its acceptance of the terms and provisions hereof. When the organization committee shall have designated the cities in which Federal reserve banks are to be organized, and fixed the geographical limits of the Federal reserve districts, every national banking association within that district shall be required within thirty days after notice from the organization committee, to subscribe to the capital stock of such Federal reserve bank in a sum equal to six per centum of the paid-up capital stock and surplus of such bank, one-sixth of the subscription to be payable on call of the organization committee or of the Federal reserve Board, one-sixth within three months and one-sixth within six months thereafter, and the remainder of the subscription, or any part thereof, shall be subject to call when deemed necessary by the Federal Reserve Board, and payments to be in gold or gold certificates.

The shareholders of every Federal reserve bank shall be held individually responsible, equally and ratably, and not one for another, for all contracts, debts, and engagements of such bank to the extent of the amount of their subscriptions to such stock at the par value thereof in addition to the amount subscribed, whether such subscription have been paid up in whole or in part, under the provisions of this Act.

Any national bank failing to signify its acceptance of the terms of this Act within the sixty days aforesaid, shall cease to act as a reserve agent, upon thirty days notice, to be given within the discretion of the said organization committee or of the Federal Reserve Board.

Should any national banking association in the United States now organized fail within one year after the passage of this Act to become a member bank or fail to comply with any of the provisions of this Act applicable thereto, all of the rights, privileges, and franchises of such association granted to it under the national-bank Act, or under the provisions of this Act, shall be thereby forfeited. Any noncompliance with or violation of this Act shall, however, be determined and adjudged by any court of the United States of competent jurisdiction in a suit brought for that purpose in the district or territory in which such bank is located, under direction of the Federal Reserve Board, by the Comptroller of the Currency in his own name before the association shall be declared dissolved. In cases of such noncompliance or violation, other than the failure to become a member bank under the provisions of this Act, every director who participated in or assented to the same shall be held liable in his personal or individual capacity for all damages which said bank, its shareholders, or any other person shall have sustained in consequence of such violation.

Such dissolution shall not take away or impair any remedy against such corporation, its stockholders or officers, for any liability or penalty which shall have been previously incurred.

Should the subscriptions by banks to the stock of said Federal reserve banks or any one or more of them be, in the judgment of the organization committee, insufficient to provide the amount of capital required therefore, then and in that event the said organization committee may, under conditions and regulations to be prescribed by it, offer to public subscription at par such an amount of stock in said Federal reserve banks, or any one or more of them, as said committee shall determine, subject to the same conditions as to payment and stock liability as provided for member banks.

No individual, co-partnership, or corporation other than a member bank of its district shall be permitted to subscribe for or to hold at any time more than $25,000 par value of stock in any Federal reserve bank. Such stock shall be known as public stock and may be transferred on the books of the Federal reserve bank by the chairman of the board of directors of such bank.

Should the total subscriptions by banks and the public to the stock of said Federal reserve banks, or any one or more of them, be, in the judgment of the organization committee, insufficient to provide the amount of capital required therefore, then and in that event the said organization committee shall allot to the United States such an amount of said stock as said committee shall determine. Said United States stock shall be paid for at par out of any money in the Treasury not otherwise appropriated, and shall be held by the Secretary of the Treasury and disposed of for the benefit of the United States in such manner, at such times, and at such price, not less than par, as the Secretary of the Treasury shall determine.

The Federal Reserve Board is hereby empowered to adopt and promulgate rules and regulations governing the transfers of said stock.

No Federal reserve bank shall commence business with a subscribed capital less than $4,000,000. The organization of reserve districts and Federal reserve cities shall not be construed as changing the present status of reserve cities and central reserve cities except in so far as this Act changes the amount of reserves that may be carried with approved reserve agents located therein. The organization committee shall have power to appoint such assistants and incur such expenses in carrying out the provisions of this Act as it shall deem necessary, and such expenses shall be payable by the Treasurer of the United States upon voucher approved by the Secretary of the Treasury, and the sum of $100,000, or so much thereof as may be necessary, is hereby appropriated, out of any moneys in the Treasury not otherwise appropriated, for the payment of such expenses.

BRANCH OFFICES

SEC. 3. Each Federal reserve bank shall establish branch banks within the Federal reserve district in which it is located and may do so in the district of any Federal reserve bank which may have been suspended. Such branches shall be operated by a board of directors under rules and regulations approved by the Federal Reserve Board. Directors of branch banks shall possess the same qualifications as directors of the Federal reserve banks. Four of said directors shall be selected by the reserve bank and three by the Federal Reserve Board, and they shall hold office during the pleasure, respectively, of the parent bank and the Federal Reserve Board. The reserve bank shall designate one of the directors as manager.

FEDERAL RESERVE BANKS

SEC. 4. When the organization committee shall have established Federal reserve districts as provided in section two of this Act, a certificate shall be filed with the Comptroller of the Currency showing the geographical limits of such districts and the Federal reserve city designated in each of such districts. The Comptroller of the Currency shall thereupon cause to be forwarded to each national bank located in each district, and to such other banks declared to be eligible by the organization committee which may apply therefore, an application blank in form to be approved by the organization committee, which blank shall contain a resolution to be adopted by the board of directors of each bank executing such application, authorizing a subscription to the capital stock of the Federal reserve bank organizing in that district in accordance with the provisions of this Act.

When the minimum amount of capital stock prescribed by this Act for the organization of any Federal reserve bank shall have been subscribed and allotted, the organization committee shall designate any five banks of those whose applications have been received, to execute a certificate of organization, and thereupon the banks so designated shall, under their seals, make an organization certificate which shall specifically state the name of such Federal reserve bank, the territorial extent of the district over which the operations of such Federal reserve bank are to be carried on, the city and State in which said is to be located, the amount of capital stock and the number of shares into which the same is divided, the name and place of doing business of each bank executing such certificate, and of all banks which have subscribed to the capital stock of such Federal reserve bank and the number of shares subscribed by each, and the fact that the certificate is made to enable those banks executing same, and all banks which have subscribed or may thereafter subscribe to the capital stock of such Federal reserve bank, to avail themselves of the advantages of this Act.

The said organization certificate shall be acknowledged before a judge of some court of record or notary public; and shall be, together with the acknowledgment thereof, authenticated by the seal of such court, or notary, transmitted to the Comptroller of the Currency, who shall file, record and carefully preserve the same in his office.

Upon filing of such certificate with the Comptroller of the Currency as aforesaid, the said Federal reserve bank shall become a body corporate and as such, and in the name designated in such organization certificate, shall have power—

First. To adopt and use a corporate seal.

Second. To have succession for a period of twenty years from its organization unless it is sooner dissolved by an Act of Congress, or unless its franchise becomes forfeited by some violation of law.

Third. To make contracts.

Fourth. To sue and be sued, complain and defend, in any court of law or equity.

Fifth. To appoint by its board of directors, such officers and employees as are not otherwise provided for in this Act, to define their duties, require bonds of them and fix the penalty thereof, and to dismiss at pleasure such officers or employees.

Sixth. To prescribe by its board of directors, by-laws not inconsistent with law, regulating the manner in which its general business may be conducted, and the privileges granted to it by law may be exercised and enjoyed.

Seventh. To exercise by its board of directors, or duly authorized officers or agents, all powers specifically granted by the provisions of this Act and such incidental powers as shall be necessary to carry on the business of banking within the limitations prescribed by this Act.

Eighth. Upon deposit with the Treasurer of the United States of any bonds of the United States in the manner provided by existing law relating to national banks, to receive from the Comptroller of the Currency circulating notes in blank, registered and countersigned as provided by law, equal in amount to the par value of the bonds so deposited, such notes to be issued under the same conditions and provisions of law as relate to the issue of circulating notes of national banks secured by bonds of the United States bearing the circulating privilege, except that the issue of such notes shall not be limited to the capital stock of such Federal reserve bank.

But no Federal reserve bank shall transact any business except such as is incidental and necessarily preliminary to its organization until it has been authorized by the Comptroller of the Currency to commence business under the provisions of this Act.

Every Federal reserve bank shall be conducted under the supervision and control of a board of directors.

The board of directors shall perform the duties usually appertaining to the office of directors of banking associations and all such duties as are prescribed by law.

Said board shall administer the affairs of said bank fairly and impartially and without discrimination in favor of or against any member bank or banks and shall, subject to the provisions of law and the orders of the Federal Reserve Board, extend to each member bank such discounts, advancements and accommodations as may be safely and reasonably made with due regard of the claims and demands of other member banks.

Such board of directors shall be selected as hereinafter specified and shall consist of nine members, holding office for three years, and divided into three classes, designated as classes A, B, and C.

Class A shall consist of three members, who shall be chosen by and be representative of the stock-holding banks.

Class B shall consist of three members, who at the time of their election shall be actively engaged in their district in commerce, agriculture or some other industrial pursuit.

Class C shall consist of three members who shall be designated by the Federal Reserve Board. When the necessary subscriptions to the capital stock have been obtained for organization of any Federal reserve bank, the Federal Reserve Board shall appoint the class C directors and shall designate one of such directors as chairman of the board to be selected. Pending the designation of such chairman, the organization committee shall exercise the powers and duties appertaining to the office of chairman in the organization of such Federal reserve bank.

No Senator or Representative in Congress shall be a member of the Federal Reserve Board or an officer or a director of a Federal reserve bank.

No director of class B shall be an officer, director, or employee of any bank. No director of class C shall be an officer, director, employee or stockholder of any bank.

Directors of class A and class B shall be chosen in the following manner:

The chairman of the board of directors of the Federal reserve bank of the district in which the bank is situated or, pending the appointment of such chairman, the organization committee shall classify the member banks of the district into three general groups or divisions. Each group shall contain as nearly as may be one-third of the aggregate number of the member banks of the district and shall consist, as nearly as may be, of banks of similar capitalization. The groups shall be designated by number by the chairman.

At a regularly called meeting of the board of directors of each member bank in the district it shall elect by ballot a district reserve elector and shall certify his name to the chairman of the board of directors of the Federal reserve bank of the district. The chairman shall make lists of the district reserve electors thus named by banks in each of the aforesaid three groups and shall transmit one list to each elector in each group.

Each member bank shall be permitted to nominate to the chairman one candidate for director of class A and one candidate for director of class B. The candidates so nominated shall be listed by the chairman, indicating by whom nominated, and a copy of said list shall, within fifteen days after its completion, be furnished by the chairman to each elector.

Every elector shall, within fifteen days after the receipt of the said list, certify to the chairman his first, second, and other choices of a director of class A and class B, respectively, upon a preferential ballot, on a form furnished by the chairman of the board of directors of the Federal reserve bank of the district. Each elector shall make a cross opposite the name of the first, second, and other choices for a director of class A and for a director of class B, but shall not vote more than one choice for any one candidate.

Any candidate having a majority of all votes cast in the column of first choice shall be declared elected. If no candidate have a majority of all the votes in the first column, then there shall be added together the votes cast by the electors for such candidates in the second column and the votes cast for the several candidates in the first column.

If any candidate then have a majority of the electors voting, by adding together the first and second choices, he shall be declared elected. If no candidate have a majority of electors voting when the first and second choices shall have been added, then the votes cast in the third column for other choices shall be added together in like manner, and the candidate then having the highest number of votes shall be declared elected. An immediate report of election shall be declared.

Class C directors shall be appointed by the Federal Reserve Board. They shall have been for at least two years residents of the district for which they are appointed, one of whom shall be designated by said board as chairman of the board of directors of the Federal reserve bank and as "Federal reserve agent." He shall be a person of tested banking experience; and in addition to his duties as chairman of the board of directors of the Federal reserve bank he shall be required to maintain under regulations to be established by the Federal Reserve Board a local office of said board on the premises of the Federal reserve bank. He shall make regular reports to the Federal Reserve Board, and shall act as its official representative for the performance of the functions conferred upon it by this Act. He shall receive an annual compensation to be fixed by the Federal Reserve Board and paid monthly by the Federal reserve bank to which he is designated. One of the directors of class C, who shall be a person of tested banking experience, shall be appointed by the Federal Reserve Board as deputy chairman and deputy Federal reserve agent to exercise the powers of the chairman of the board and Federal reserve agent in case of absence or disability of his principal.

Directors of Federal reserve banks shall receive, in addition to any compensation otherwise provided, a reasonable allowance for necessary expenses in attending meetings of their respective boards, which amount shall be paid by the respective Federal reserve banks. Any compensation that may be provided by boards of directors of Federal reserve banks for directors, officers or employees shall be subject to the approval of the Federal Reserve Board.

The Reserve Bank Organization Committee may, in organizing Federal reserve banks, call such meetings of bank directors in the several districts as may be necessary to carry out the purposes of this Act, and may exercise the functions herein conferred upon the chairman of the board of directors of each Federal reserve bank pending the complete organization of such bank.

At the first meeting of the full board of directors of each Federal reserve bank, it shall be the duty of the directors of classes A, B and C, respectively, to designate one of the members of each class whose term of office shall expire in one year from the first of January nearest to date of such meeting, one whose term of office shall expire at the end of two years from said date, and one whose term of office shall expire at the end of three years from said date.

Thereafter every director of a Federal reserve bank chosen as hereinbefore provided shall hold office for a term of three years. Vacancies that may occur in the several classes of directors of Federal reserve banks may be filled in the manner provided for the original selection of such directors, such appointees to hold office for the unexpired terms of their predecessors.

STOCK ISSUES; INCREASE AND DECREASE OF CAPITAL

SEC. 5. The capital stock of each Federal reserve bank shall be divided into shares of $100 each. The outstanding capital stock shall be increased from time to time as member banks increase their capital stock and surplus or as additional banks become members, and may be decreased as member banks reduce their capital stock or surplus or cease to be members. Shares of the capital stock of Federal reserve banks owned by member banks shall not be transferred or hypothecated. When a member bank increases its capital stock or surplus, it shall thereupon subscribe for an additional amount of capital stock of the Federal reserve bank of its district equal to six per centum of the said increase, one-half of said subscription to be paid in the manner hereinbefore provided for original subscription, and one-half subject to call of the Federal Reserve Board. A bank applying for stock in a Federal reserve bank at any time after the organization thereof must subscribe for an amount of the capital stock of the Federal reserve bank equal to six per centum of the paid-up capital stock and surplus of said applicant bank, paying therefore its par value plus one-half of one per centum a month from the period of the last dividend. When the capital stock of any Federal reserve bank shall have been increased either on account of the increase of capital stock of member banks or on account of the increase in the number of member banks, the board of directors shall cause to be executed a certificate to the Comptroller of the Currency showing the increase in capital stock, the amount paid in, and by whom paid. When a member bank reduces its capital stock it shall surrender a proportionate amount of its holdings in the capital of said Federal reserve bank, and when a member bank voluntarily liquidates it shall surrender all of its holdings of the capital stock of said Federal reserve bank and be released from its stock subscription not previously called. In either case the shares surrendered shall be canceled and the member bank shall receive in payment therefore, under regulations to be prescribed by the Federal Reserve Board, a sum equal to its cash-paid subscriptions on the shares surrendered and one-half of one per centum a month from the period of the last dividend, not to exceed the book value thereof, less any liability of such member bank to the Federal reserve bank.

SEC. 6. If any member bank shall be declared insolvent and a receiver appointed therefore, the stock held by it in said Federal reserve bank shall be canceled, without impairment of its liability, and all cash-paid subscriptions on said stock, with one-half of one per centum per month from the period of last dividend, not to exceed the book value thereof, shall be first applied to all debts of the insolvent member bank to the Federal reserve bank, and the balance, if any, shall be paid to the receiver of the insolvent bank. Whenever the capital stock of a Federal reserve bank is reduced, either on account of a reduction in capital stock of any member bank or of the liquidation or insolvency of such bank, the board of directors shall cause to be executed a certificate to the Comptroller of the Currency showing such reductions of capital stock and the amount repaid to such bank.

DIVISION OF EARNINGS

SEC. 7. After all necessary expenses of a Federal reserve bank have been paid or provided for, the stockholders shall be entitled to receive an annual dividend of six per centum on the paid-in capital stock, which dividend shall be cumulative. After the aforesaid dividend claims have been fully met, all the net earnings shall be paid to the United States as a franchise tax, except that one-half of such net earnings shall be paid into a surplus fund until it shall amount to forty per centum of the paid-in capital stock of such bank.

The net earnings derived by the United States from Federal reserve banks shall, in the discretion of the Secretary, be used to supplement the gold reserve held against outstanding United States notes, or shall be applied to the reduction of the outstanding bonded indebtedness of the United States under regulations to be prescribed by the Secretary of the Treasury. Should a Federal reserve bank be dissolved or go into liquidation, any surplus remaining, after the payment of all debts, dividend requirements as hereinbefore provided, and the par value of the stock, shall be paid to and become the property of the United States and shall be similarly applied.

Federal reserve banks, including the capital stock and surplus therein, and the income derived therefrom shall be exempt from Federal, State, and local taxation, except taxes upon real estate.

SEC. 8. Section fifty-one hundred and fifty-four, United States Revised Statutes, is hereby amended to read as follows:

Any bank incorporated by special law of any State or of the United States or organized under the general laws of any State or of the United States and having an unimpaired capital sufficient to entitle it to become a national banking association under the provisions of the existing laws may, by the vote of the shareholders owning not less than fifty-one per centum of the capital stock of such bank or banking association, with the approval of the

Comptroller of the Currency be converted into a national banking association, with any name approved by the Comptroller of the Currency:

Provided, however, That said conversion shall not be in contravention of the State law. In such case the articles of association and organization certificate may be executed by a majority of the directors of the bank or banking institution, and the certificate shall declare that the owners of fifty-one per centum of the capital stock have authorized the directors to make such certificate and to change or convert the bank or banking institution into a national association. A majority of the directors, after executing the articles of association and the organization certificate, shall have power to execute all other papers and to do whatever may be required to make its organization perfect and complete as a national association. The shares of any such bank may continue to be for the same amount each as they were before the conversion, and the directors may continue to be directors of the association until others are elected or appointed in accordance with the provisions of the statutes of the United States. When the Comptroller as given to such bank or banking association a certificate that the provisions of this Act have been complied with, such bank or banking association, and all its stockholders, officers, and employees, shall have the same powers and privileges, and shall be subject to the same duties, liabilities, and regulations, in all respects, as shall have been prescribed by the Federal Reserve Act and by the national banking Act for associations originally organized as national banking associations.

STATE BANKS AS MEMBERS

SEC. 9. Any bank incorporated by special law of any State, or organized under the general laws of any State or of the United States, may make application to the reserve bank organization committee, pending organization, and thereafter to the Federal Reserve Board for the right to subscribe to the stock of the Federal reserve bank organized or to be organized within the Federal reserve district where the applicant is located. The organization committee or the Federal Reserve Board, under such rules and regulations as it may prescribe, subject to the provisions of this section, may permit the applying bank to become a stockholder in the Federal reserve bank of the district in which the applying bank is located. Whenever the organization committee or the Federal Reserve Board shall permit the applying bank to become a stockholder in the Federal reserve bank of the district, stock shall be issued and paid for under the rules and regulations in this Act provided for national banks which become stockholders in Federal reserve banks.

The organization committee of the Federal Reserve Board shall establish by-laws for the general government of its conduct in acting upon applications made by the State banks and banking associations and trust companies for stock ownership in Federal reserve banks. Such by-laws shall require applying banks not organized under Federal law to comply with the reserve and capital requirements and to submit to the examination and regulations prescribed by the organization committee or by the Federal Reserve Board. No applying bank shall be admitted to membership in a Federal reserve bank unless it possesses a paid-up unimpaired capital sufficient to entitle it to become a national banking association in the place where it is situated, under the provisions of the national banking Act.

Any bank becoming a member of a Federal reserve bank under the provisions of this section shall, in addition to the regulations and restrictions hereinbefore provided, be required to conform to the provisions of law imposed on the national banks respecting the limitation of liability which may be incurred by any person, firm, or corporation to such banks, the prohibition against making purchase of or loans on stock of such banks, and the withdrawal or impairment of capital, or the payment of unearned dividends, and to such rules and regulations as the Federal Reserve Board may, in pursuance thereof, prescribe.

Such banks, and the officers, agents, and employees thereof, shall also be subject to the provisions of and to the penalties prescribed by sections fifty-one hundred and ninety-eight, fifty-two hundred, fifty-two hundred and one, and fifty-two hundred and eight, and fifty-two hundred and nine of the Revised Statutes. The member banks shall also be required to make reports of the conditions and of the payments of dividends to the comptroller, as provided in sections fifty-two hundred and eleven and fifty-two hundred and twelve of the Revised Statutes, and shall be subject to the penalties prescribed by section fifty-two hundred and thirteen for the failure to make such report.

If at any time it shall appear to the Federal Reserve Board that a member bank has failed to comply with the provisions of this section or the regulations of the Federal Reserve Board, it shall be within the power of the said board, after hearing, to require such bank to surrender its stock in the Federal reserve bank; upon such surrender the Federal reserve bank shall pay the cash-paid subscriptions to the said stock with interest at the rate of one-half of one per centum per month, computed from the last dividend, if earned, not to exceed the book value thereof, less any liability to said Federal reserve bank, except the subscription liability not previously called, which shall be canceled, and said Federal reserve bank shall, upon notice from the Federal Reserve Board, be required to suspend said bank from further privileges of membership, and shall within thirty days of such notice cancel and retire its stock and make payment therefore in the manner herein provided. The Federal Reserve Board may restore membership upon due proof of compliance with the conditions imposed by this section.

FEDERAL RESERVE BOARD

SEC. 10. A Federal Reserve Board is hereby created which shall consist of seven members, including the Secretary of the Treasury and the Comptroller of the Currency, who shall be members ex officio, and five members appointed by the President of the United States, by and with the advice and consent of the Senate. In selecting the five appointive members of the Federal Reserve Board, not more than one of whom shall be selected from any one Federal reserve district, the President shall have due regard to a fair representation of the different commercial, industrial and geographical divisions of the country. The five members of the Federal reserve Board appointed by the President and confirmed as aforesaid shall devote their entire time to the business of the Federal Reserve Board and shall each receive an annual salary of $12,000, payable monthly together with actual necessary traveling expenses, and the Comptroller of the Currency, as ex officio member of the Federal Reserve Board, shall, in addition to the salary now paid him as Comptroller of the Currency, receive the sum of $7,000 annually for his services as a member of said board.

The members of said board, the Secretary of the Treasury, the Assistant Secretaries of the Treasury, and the Comptroller of the Currency shall be ineligible during the time they are in office and for two years thereafter to hold any office, position, or employment in any member bank. Of the five members thus appointed by the President at least two shall be persons experienced in banking or finance. One shall be designated by the President to serve for two, one for four, one for six, one for eight, and one for ten years, and thereafter each member so appointed shall serve for a term of ten years unless sooner removed for cause by the President. Of the five persons thus appointed, one shall be designated by the President as governor and one as vice governor of the Federal Reserve Board. The governor of the Federal Reserve Board, subject to its supervision, shall be the active executive officer. The secretary of the Treasury may assign offices in the Department of the Treasury for the use of the Federal Reserve Board. Each member of the Federal Reserve Board shall within fifteen days after notice of appointment make and subscribe to the oath of office.

The Federal Reserve Board shall have power to levy semiannually upon the Federal reserve banks, in proportion to their capital stock and surplus, an assessment sufficient to pay its estimated expenses and the salaries of its members and employees for the half year succeeding the levying of such assessment, together with any deficit carried forward from the preceding half year.

The first meeting of the Federal Reserve Board shall be held in Washington, District of Columbia, as soon as may be after the passage of this Act, at a date to be fixed by the Reserve Bank Organization Committee. The Secretary of the Treasury shall be ex officio chairman of the Federal Reserve board. No member of the Federal Reserve Board shall be an officer or director of any bank, banking institution, trust company, or Federal reserve bank nor hold stock in any bank, banking institution, or trust company; and before entering upon his duties as a member of the Federal Reserve Board he shall certify under oath to the Secretary of the Treasury that he has complied with this requirement. Whenever a vacancy shall occur, other than by expiration of term, among the five members of the Federal Reserve Board appointed by the President, as above provided, a successor shall be appointed by the President, with the advice and consent of the Senate, to fill such vacancy, and when appointed he shall hold office for the un-expired term of the member whose place he is selected to fill.

The President shall have power to fill all vacancies that may happen on the Federal Reserve Board during the recess of the Senate, by granting commissions which shall expire thirty days after the next session of the Senate convenes.

Nothing in this Act contained shall be construed as taking away any powers heretofore vested by law in the Secretary of the Treasury which relate to the supervision, management, and control of the Treasury Department and bureaus under such department, and wherever any power vested by this Act in the Federal Reserve Board or the Federal reserve agent appears to conflict with the powers of the Secretary of the Treasury, such powers shall be exercised subject to the supervision and control of the Secretary.

The Federal Reserve Board shall annually make a full report of its operations to the Speaker of the House of Representatives, who shall cause the same to be printed for the information of the Congress.

Section three hundred and twenty-four of the Revised Statutes of the United States shall be amended so as to read as follows: There shall be in the Department of the Treasury a bureau charged with the execution of all laws passed by Congress relating to the issue and regulation of national currency secured by United States bonds and, under the general supervision of the Federal Reserve Board, of all Federal reserve notes, the chief officer of which bureau shall be called the Comptroller of the currency and shall perform his duties under the general directions of the Secretary of the Treasury.

SEC 11. The Federal Reserve Board shall be authorized and empowered:

(a) To examine at its discretion the accounts, books and affairs of each Federal reserve bank and of each member bank and to require such statements and reports as it may deem necessary. The said board shall publish once each week a statement showing the condition of each Federal reserve bank and a consolidated statement for all Federal reserve banks. Such statements shall show in detail the assets and liabilities of the Federal reserve banks, single and combined, and shall furnish full information regarding the character of the money held as reserve and the amount, nature and maturities of the paper and other investments owned or held by Federal reserve banks.

(b) To permit, or, on the affirmative vote of at least five members of the Reserve Board to require Federal reserve banks to rediscount the discounted paper of other Federal reserve banks at rates of interest to be fixed by the Federal Reserve Board.

(c) To suspend for a period not exceeding thirty days, and from time to time to renew such suspension for periods not exceeding fifteen days, any reserve requirement specified in this Act: *Provided*, That it shall establish a graduated tax upon the amounts by which the reserve requirements of this Act may be permitted to fall below the level hereinafter specified: *And provided further*, That when the gold reserve held against Federal reserve notes falls below forty per centum, the Federal Reserve Board shall establish a graduated tax of not more than one per centum per annum upon such deficiency until the reserves fall to thirty-two and one-half per centum, and when said reserve falls below thirty-two and one-half per centum, a tax at the rate increasingly of not less than one and one-half per centum per annum upon each two and one-half per centum or fraction thereof that such reserve falls below thirty-two and one-half per centum. The tax shall be paid by the reserve bank, but the reserve bank shall add an amount equal to said tax to the rates of interest and discount fixed by the Federal Reserve Board.

(d) To supervise and regulate through the bureau under the charge of the Comptroller of the Currency the issue and retirement of Federal reserve notes, and to prescribe rules and regulations under which such notes may be delivered by the Comptroller to the Federal reserve agents applying therefore.

(e) To add to the number of cities classified as reserve and central reserve cities under existing law in which national banking associations are subject to the reserve requirements set forth in section twenty of this Act; or to reclassify existing reserve and central reserve cities or to terminate their designation as such.

(f) To suspend or remove any officer or director of any Federal reserve bank, the cause of such removal to be forthwith communicated in writing by the Federal Reserve Board to the removed officer or director and to said bank.

(g) To require the writing off of doubtful or worthless assets upon the books and balance sheets of Federal reserve banks.

(h) To suspend, for the violation of any of the provisions of this Act, the operations of any Federal reserve bank, to take possession thereof, administer the same during the period of suspension, and, when deemed advisable, to liquidate or reorganize such bank.

(i) To require bonds of Federal reserve agents, to make regulations for the safeguarding of all collateral, bonds, Federal reserve notes, money or property of any kind deposited in the hands of such agents, and said board shall perform the duties, functions, or services specified in this Act, and make all rules and regulations necessary to enable said board effectively to perform the same.

(j) To exercise general supervision over said Federal reserve banks.

(k) To grant by special permit to national banks applying therefore, when not in contravention of State or local law, the right to act as trustee, executor, administrator, or registrar of stocks and bonds under such rules and regulations as the said board may prescribe.

(l) To employ such attorneys, experts, assistants, clerks, or other employees as may be deemed necessary to conduct the business of the board. All salaries and fees shall be fixed in advance by said board and shall be paid in the same manner as the salaries of the members of said board. All such attorneys, experts, assistants, clerks, and other employees shall be appointed without regard to the provisions of the Act of January sixteenth, eighteen hundred and eighty-three (volume twenty-two, United States Statutes at Large, page four hundred and three), and amendments thereto, or any rule or regulation made in pursuance thereof: *Provided*, That nothing herein shall prevent the President from placing said employees in the classified service.

FEDERAL ADVISORY COUNCIL

SEC. 12. There is hereby created a Federal Advisory Council, which shall consist of as many members as there are Federal reserve districts each Federal reserve bank by its board of directors shall annually select from its own Federal reserve district one member of said council, who shall receive such compensation and allowances as may be fixed by his board of directors subject to the approval of the Federal Reserve Board. The meetings of said advisory council shall be held at Washington, District of Columbia, at least four times each year, and oftener if called by the Federal Reserve Board. The council may in addition to the meetings above provided for hold such other meetings in Washington, District of Columbia, or elsewhere, as it may deem necessary, may select its own officers and adopt its own methods of procedure, and a majority of its members shall constitute a quorum for the transaction of business. Vacancies in the council shall be filled by the respective banks, and members selected to fill vacancies, shall serve for the un-expired term.

Federal Advisory Council shall have power, by itself or through its officers, (1) to confer directly with the Federal Reserve Board on general business conditions; (2) to make oral or written representations concerning matters within the jurisdiction of said board; (3) to call for information and to make recommendations in regard to discount rates, rediscount business, note issues, reserve conditions in the various districts, the purchase and sale of gold or securities by reserve banks, open market operations by said banks, and the general affairs of the reserve banking system.

POWERS OF FEDERAL RESERVE BANKS

SEC. 13. Any Federal reserve bank may receive from any of its member banks, and from the United States, deposits of current funds in lawful money, national-bank notes, Federal reserve notes, or checks and drafts upon solvent member banks, payable upon presentation; or, solely for exchange purposes, may receive from other Federal reserve banks deposits of current funds in lawful money, national-bank notes, or checks and drafts upon solvent member or other Federal reserve banks, payable upon presentation.

Upon the endorsement of any of its member banks, with a waiver of demand, notice and protest by such bank, any Federal reserve bank may discount notes, drafts, and bills of exchange arising out of actual commercial transactions; that is, notes, drafts, and bills of exchange issued or drawn for agricultural, industrial, or commercial purposes, or the proceeds of which have been used, or are to be used, for such purposes, the Federal Reserve Board to have the right to determine or define the character of the paper thus eligible for discount, within the meaning of this Act. Nothing in this Act contained shall be construed to prohibit such notes, drafts, and bills of exchange, secured by staple agricultural products, or other goods, wares, or merchandise from being eligible for such discount; but such definition shall not include notes, drafts, or bills covering merely investments or issued or drawn for the purpose of carrying or trading in stocks, bonds, or other investment securities, except bonds and notes of the Government of the United States. Notes, drafts, and bills admitted to discount under the terms of this paragraph must have a maturity at the time of discount of not more than ninety days: *Provided*, That notes, drafts, and bills drawn or issued for agricultural purposes or based on live stock and having a maturity not exceeding six months may be discounted in an amount to be limited to a percentage of the capital of the Federal reserve bank, to be ascertained and fixed by the Federal Reserve Board.

Any Federal reserve bank may discount acceptances which are based on the importation or exportation of goods and which have a maturity at time of discount of not more than three months, and indorsed by at least one member bank. The amount of acceptances so discounted shall at no time exceed one-half the paid-up capital stock and surplus of the bank for which the rediscounts are made.

The aggregate of such notes and bills bearing the signature or endorsement of any one person, company, firm, or corporation rediscounted for any one bank shall at no time exceed ten per centum of the unimpaired capital and surplus of said bank; but this restriction shall not apply to the discount of bills of exchange drawn in good faith against actually existing values. Dealing in foreign trade paper by member banks allowed.

Any member bank may accept drafts or bills of exchange drawn upon it and growing out of transactions involving the importation or exportation of goods having not more than six months sight to run; but no bank shall accept such bills to an amount equal at any time in the aggregate to more than one-half its paid-up capital stock and surplus.

Section fifty-two hundred and two of the Revised Statutes of the United States is hereby amended so as to read as follows: No national banking association shall at any time be indebted, or in any way liable, to an amount exceeding the amount of its capital stock at such time actually paid in and remaining undiminished by losses or otherwise, except on account of demands of the nature following:

First. Notes of circulation.

Second. Moneys deposited with or collected by the association.

Third. Bills of exchange or drafts drawn against money actually on deposit to the credit of the association, or due thereto.

Fourth. Liabilities to the stockholders of the association for dividends and reserve profits.

Fifth. Liabilities incurred under the provisions of the Federal Reserve Act.

Regulation of rediscounts, etc. The rediscount by any Federal reserve bank of any bills receivable and of domestic and foreign bills of exchange, and of acceptances authorized by this Act, shall be subject to such restrictions, limitations, and regulations as may be imposed by the Federal Reserve Board.

OPEN-MARKET OPERATIONS

SEC. 14. Any Federal reserve bank may, under rules and regulations prescribed by the Federal Reserve Board, purchase and sell in the open market, at home or abroad, either from or to domestic or foreign banks, firms, corporations, or individuals, cable transfers and bankers' acceptances and bills of exchange of the kinds and maturities by this Act made eligible for rediscount, with or without the endorsement of a member bank.

Every Federal reserve bank shall have power:

(a) To deal in gold coin and bullion at home or abroad, to make loans thereon, exchange Federal reserve notes for gold, gold coin, or gold certificates, and to contract for loans of gold coin or bullion, giving therefore, when necessary, acceptable security, including the hypothecation of United States bonds or other securities which Federal reserve banks are authorized to hold;

(b) To buy and sell, at home or abroad, bonds and notes of the United States, and bills, notes, revenue bonds, and warrants with a maturity date of purchase of not exceeding six months, issued in anticipation of the collection of taxes or in anticipation of the receipt of assured revenues by any State, county, district, political subdivision, or municipality in the continental United States, including irrigation, drainage, and reclamation districts, such purchases to be made in accordance with rules and regulations prescribed by the Federal Reserve Board;

(c) To purchase from member banks and to sell, with or without its endorsement, bills of exchange arising out of commercial transactions, as hereinbefore defined;

(d) To establish from time to time, subject to review and determination of the Federal Reserve Board, rates of discount to be charged by the Federal reserve bank for each class of paper, which shall be fixed with a view of accommodating commerce and business;

(e) To establish accounts with other Federal reserve banks for exchange purposes and, with the consent of the Federal Reserve Board, to open and maintain banking accounts in foreign countries, appoint correspondents, and establish agencies in such countries wheresoever it may deem best for the purpose of purchasing, selling, and collecting bills of exchange, and to buy and sell with or without its endorsement, through such correspondents or agencies, bills of exchange arising out of actual commercial transactions which have not more than ninety days to run and which bear the signature of two or more responsible parties.

GOVERNMENT DEPOSITS

SEC. 15. The moneys held in the general fund of the Treasury, except the five per centum fund for the redemption of outstanding national-bank notes and the funds provided in this Act for the redemption of Federal reserve notes may, upon the direction of the Secretary of the Treasury, be deposited in Federal reserve banks, which banks, when required by the Secretary of the Treasury, shall act as fiscal agents of the United States; and the revenues of the Government or any part thereof may be deposited in such banks, and disbursements may be made by checks drawn against such deposits.

No public funds of the Philippine Islands, or of the postal savings, or any Government funds, shall be deposited in the continental United States in any bank not belonging to the system established by this Act: *Provided*, however, That nothing in this Act shall be construed to deny the right of the Secretary of the Treasury to use member banks as depositories.

NOTE ISSUES

SEC. 16. Federal reserve notes, to be issued at the discretion of the Federal Reserve Board for the purpose of making advances to Federal reserve banks through the Federal reserve agents as hereinafter set forth and for no other purpose, are hereby authorized. The said notes shall be obligations of the United States and shall be receivable by all national and member banks and Federal reserve banks and for all taxes, customs, and other public dues. They shall be redeemed in gold on demand at the Treasury Department of the United States, in the city of Washington, District of Columbia, or in gold or lawful money at any Federal reserve bank.

Any Federal reserve bank may make application to the local Federal reserve agent for such amount of the Federal reserve notes hereinbefore provided for as it may require. Such application shall be accompanied with a tender to the local Federal reserve agent of collateral in amount equal to the sum of the Federal reserve notes thus applied for and issued pursuant to such application. The collateral security thus offered shall be notes and bills, accepted for rediscount under the provisions of section thirteen of this Act, and the Federal reserve agent shall each day notify the Federal Reserve Board of all issues and withdrawals of Federal reserve notes to and by the Federal reserve bank to which he is accredited. The said Federal Reserve Board may at any time call upon a Federal reserve bank for additional security to protect the Federal notes issued to it.

Every Federal reserve bank shall maintain reserves in gold or lawful money of not less than thirty-five per centum against its deposits and reserves in gold of not less than forty per centum against its Federal reserve notes in actual circulation, and not offset by gold or lawful money deposited with the Federal reserve agent. Notes so paid out shall bear upon their faces a distinctive letter and serial number, which shall be assigned by the Federal Reserve Board to each Federal reserve bank. Whenever Federal reserve notes issued through one Federal reserve bank shall be received by another Federal reserve bank they shall be promptly returned for credit or redemption to the Federal reserve bank through which they were originally issued. No Federal reserve bank shall pay out notes issued through another under penalty of a tax of ten per centum upon the face value of notes so paid out. Notes presented for redemption at the Treasury of the United States shall be paid out of the redemption fund and returned to the Federal reserve banks through which they were originally issued, and thereupon such Federal reserve bank shall, upon demand of the Secretary of the Treasury, reimburse such redemption fund in lawful money or, if such Federal reserve notes have been redeemed by the Treasurer in gold or gold certificates, then such funds shall be reimbursed to the extent deemed necessary by the Secretary of the Treasury in gold or gold certificates, and such Federal reserve bank shall, so long as any of its Federal reserve notes remain outstanding, maintain with the Treasurer in gold an amount sufficient in the judgment of the Secretary to provide for all re-demptions to be made by the Treasurer. Federal reserve notes received by the Treasury, otherwise than for redemption, may be exchanged for gold out of the redemption fund hereinafter provided and returned to the reserve bank through which they were originally issued, or they may be returned to such bank for credit of the United States. Federal reserve notes unfit for circulation shall be returned by the Federal reserve agents to the Comptroller of the Currency for cancellation and destruction.

The Federal Reserve Board shall require each Federal reserve bank to maintain on deposit in the Treasury of the United States a sum in gold sufficient in the judgment of the Secretary of the Treasury for the redemption of the Federal reserve notes issued to such bank, but in no event less than five per centum; but such deposit of gold shall be counted and included as part of the forty per centum reserve hereinbefore required. The board shall have the right, acting through the Federal reserve agent, to grant in whole or in part or to reject entirely the application of any Federal reserve bank for Federal reserve notes; but to the extent that such application may be granted the Federal Reserve Board shall, through its local Federal reserve agent, supply Federal reserve notes to the bank so applying, and such bank shall be charged with the amount of such notes and shall pay such rate of interest on said amount as may be established by the Federal Reserve Board, and the amount of such Federal reserve notes so issued to any such bank shall, upon delivery, together with such notes of such Federal reserve bank as may be issued under section eighteen of this Act upon security of United States two per centum Government bonds, become a first and paramount lien on all assets of such bank.

Any Federal reserve bank may at any time reduce its liability for outstanding Federal reserve notes by depositing, with the Federal reserve agent, its Federal reserve notes, gold, gold certificates, or lawful money of the United States. Federal reserve notes so deposited shall not be reissued, except upon compliance with the conditions of an original issue.

The Federal reserve agent shall hold such gold, gold certificates, or lawful money available exclusively for exchange for the outstanding Federal reserve notes when offered by the reserve bank of which he is a director. Upon the request of the Secretary of the Treasury the Federal Reserve Board shall require the Federal reserve agent to transmit so much of said gold to the Treasury of the United States as may be required for the exclusive purpose of the redemption of such notes.

Any Federal reserve bank may at its discretion withdraw collateral deposited with the local Federal reserve agent for the protection of its Federal reserve notes deposited with it and shall at the same time substitute therefore other like collateral of equal amount with the approval of the Federal reserve agent under regulations to be prescribed by the Federal Reserve Board.

In order to furnish suitable notes for circulation as Federal reserve notes, the Comp-troller of the Currency shall, under the direction of the Secretary of the Treasury, cause plates and dies to be engraved in the best manner to guard against counterfeits and fraudulent alterations, and shall have printed therefrom and numbered such quantities of such notes of the denominations of $5, $10, $20, $50, $100, as may be required to supply the Federal reserve banks. Such notes shall be in form and tenor as directed by the Secretary of the Treasury under the provisions of this Act and shall bear the distinctive numbers of the several Federal reserve banks through which they are issued.

When such notes have been prepared, they shall be deposited in the Treasury, or in the subtreasury or mint of the United States nearest the place of business of each Federal reserve bank and shall be held for the use of such bank subject to the order of the Comptroller of the Currency for their delivery, as provided by this Act.

The plates and dies to be procured by the Comptroller of the Currency for the printing of such circulating notes shall remain under his control and direction, and the expenses necessarily incurred in executing the laws relating to the procuring of such notes, and all other expenses incidental to their issue and retirement, shall be paid by the Federal reserve banks, and the Federal Reserve Board shall include in its estimate of expenses levied against the Federal reserve banks a sufficient amount to cover the expenses herein provided for.

The examination of plates, dies, bed pieces, and so forth, and regulations relating to such examination of plates, dies, and so forth of national-bank notes provided for in section fifty-one hundred and seventy-four Revised Statutes, is hereby extended to include notes herein provided for.

Any appropriation heretofore made out of the general funds of the Treasury for engraving plates and dies, the purchase of distinctive paper, or to cover any other expense in connection with the printing of national-bank notes or notes provided for by the Act of May thirtieth, nineteen hundred and eight, and any distinctive paper that may be on hand at the time of he passage of this Act may be used in the discretion of the Secretary for the purposes of this Act, and should the appropriations heretofore made be insufficient to meet the requirements of this Act in addition to circulating notes provided for by existing law, the Secretary is hereby authorized to use so much of any funds in the Treasury not otherwise appropriated for the purpose of furnishing the notes aforesaid: *Provided*, however, That nothing in this section contained shall be construed as exempting national banks or Federal reserve banks from their liability to reimburse the United States for any expenses incurred in printing and issuing circulating notes.

Every Federal reserve bank shall receive on deposit at par from member banks or from Federal reserve banks checks and drafts drawn upon any of its depositors, and when remitted by a Federal reserve bank, checks and drafts drawn by any depositor in any other Federal reserve bank or member bank upon funds to the credit of said depositor in said reserve bank or member bank. Nothing herein contained shall be construed as prohibiting a member bank from charging its actual expense incurred in collecting and remitting funds, or for exchange sold to its patrons. The Federal Reserve Board shall, by rule, fix the charges to be collected by the member banks from its patrons whose checks are cleared through the Federal reserve bank and the charge which may be imposed for the service of clearing or collection rendered by the Federal reserve bank.

The Federal Reserve Board shall make and promulgate from time to time regulations governing the transfer of funds and charges therefore among Federal reserve banks and their branches, and may at its discretion exercise the functions of a clearing house for such Federal reserve banks, or may designate a Federal reserve bank to exercise such functions, and may also require each such bank to exercise the functions of a clearing house for its member banks.

SEC. 17. So much of the provisions of section fifty-one hundred and fifty-nine of the Revised Statutes of the United States, and section four of the Act of June twentieth, eighteen hundred and seventy-four, and section eight of the Act of July twelfth, eighteen hundred and eighty-two, and of any other provisions of existing statutes as require that before any national banking associations shall be authorized to commence banking business it shall transfer and deliver to the Treasurer of the United States a stated amount of United States registered bonds is hereby repealed.

REFUNDING BONDS

SEC. 18. After two years from the passage of this Act, and at any time during a period of twenty years thereafter, any member bank desiring to retire the whole or any part of its circulating notes, may file with the Treasurer of the United States an application to sell for its account, at par and accrued interest, United States bonds securing circulation to be retired.

The Treasurer shall, at the end of each quarterly period, furnish the Federal Reserve Board with a list of such applications, and the Federal Reserve Board may, in its discretion, require the Federal reserve banks to purchase such bonds from the banks whose applications have been filed with the Treasurer at least ten days before the end of any quarterly period at which the Federal Reserve Board may direct the purchase to be made: *Provided*, That Federal reserve banks shall not be permitted to purchase an amount to exceed $25,000,000 of such bonds in any one year, and which amount shall include bonds acquired under section four of this Act by the Federal reserve bank.

Provided further, That the Federal Reserve Board shall allot to each Federal reserve bank such proportion of such bonds as the capital and surplus of such bank shall bear to the aggregate capital and surplus of all the Federal reserve banks.

Upon notice from the Treasurer of the amount of bonds so sold for its account, each member bank shall duly assign and transfer, in writing, such bonds to the Federal reserve bank purchasing the same, and such Federal reserve bank shall, thereupon, deposit lawful money with the Treasurer of the United States for the purchase price of such bonds, and the Treasurer shall pay to the member bank selling such bonds any balance due after deducting a sufficient sum to redeem its outstanding notes secured by such bonds, which notes shall be canceled and permanently retired when redeemed.

The Federal reserve banks purchasing such bonds shall be permitted to take out an amount of circulation notes equal to the par value of such bonds.

Upon the deposit with the Treasurer of the United States of bonds so purchased, or any bonds with the circulating privilege acquired under section four of this Act, any Federal reserve bank making such deposit in the manner provided by existing law, shall be entitled to receive from the Comptroller of the Currency circulating notes in blank, registered and countersigned as provided by law, equal in amount to the par value of the bonds so deposited. Such notes shall be the obligations of the Federal reserve bank procuring the same, and shall be in form prescribed by the Secretary of the Treasury, and to the same tenor and effect as national-bank notes now provided by law. They shall be issued and redeemed under the same terms and conditions as national-bank notes except that they shall not be limited to the amount of the capital stock of the Federal reserve bank issuing them.

Exchange of two per cent bonds, for gold notes and bonds. Upon application of any Federal reserve bank, approved by the Federal Reserve Board, the Secretary of the Treasury may issue, in exchange for United States two per centum gold bonds bearing the circulation privilege, but against which no circulation is outstanding, one-year gold notes of the United States without the circulation privilege, to an amount not to exceed one-half of the two per centum bonds so tendered for exchange, and thirty-year three per centum gold bonds without the circulation privilege for the remainder of the two per centum bonds so tendered: *Provided*, That at the time of such exchange the Federal reserve bank obtaining such one-year gold notes shall enter into an obligation with the Secretary of the Treasury binding itself to purchase from the United States for gold at the maturity of such one-year notes, an amount equal to those delivered in exchange for such bonds, if so requested by the Secretary, and at each maturity of one-year notes so purchased by such Federal reserve bank, to purchase from the United States such an amount of one-year notes as the Secretary may tender to such bank, not to exceed the amount issued to such bank in the first instance, in exchange for the two per centum United States gold bonds; said obligation to purchase at maturity such notes shall continue in force for a period not to exceed thirty years.

For the purpose of making the exchange herein provided for, the Secretary of the Treasury is authorized to issue at par Treasury notes in coupon or registered form as he may prescribe in denominations of one hundred dollars, or any multiple thereof, bearing interest at the rate of three per centum per annum, payable quarterly, such Treasury notes to be payable not more than one year from the date of their issue in gold coin of the present standard value, and to be exempt as to principal and interest from the payment of all taxes and duties of the United States except as provided by this Act, as well as from taxes in any form by or under State, municipal, or local authorities. And for the same purpose, the Secretary is authorized and empowered to issue United States gold bonds at par, bearing three per centum interest payable thirty years from date of issue, such bonds to be of the same general tenor and effect and to be issued under the same general terms and conditions as the United States three per centum bonds without the circulation privilege now issued and outstanding.

Upon application of any Federal reserve bank, approved by the Federal Reserve Board, the Secretary may issue at par such three per centum bonds in exchange for the one-year gold notes herein provided for.

BANK RESERVES

SEC. 19. Demand deposits within the meaning of this Act shall comprise all deposits payable within thirty days, and time deposits shall comprise all deposits payable after thirty days, and all savings accounts and certificates of deposit which are subject to not less than thirty days' notice before payment.

When the Secretary of the Treasury shall have officially announced, in such manner as he may elect, the establishment of a Federal reserve bank in any district, every subscribing member bank shall establish and maintain reserves as follows:

(a) A bank not in a reserve or central reserve city as now or hereafter defined shall hold and maintain reserves equal to twelve per centum of the aggregate amount of its demand deposits and five per centum of its time deposits, as follows:

In its vaults for a period of thirty-six months after said date five-twelfths thereof and permanently thereafter four-twelfths.

In the Federal reserve bank of its district, for a period of twelve months after said date, two-twelfths, and for each succeeding six months an additional one-twelfth, until five-twelfths have been so deposited, which shall be the amount permanently required.

For a period of thirty-six months after said date the balance of the reserves may be held in its own vaults, or in the Federal reserve bank, or in national banks in reserve or central reserve cities as now defined by law.

After said thirty-six months' period said reserves, other than those hereinbefore required to be held in the vaults of the member bank and in the Federal reserve bank, shall be held in the vaults of the member bank or in the Federal reserve bank, or in both, at the option of the member bank.

(b) A bank in a reserve city, as now or hereafter defined, shall hold and maintain reserves equal to fifteen per centum of the aggregate amount of its demand deposits and five per centum of its time deposits, as follows:

In its vaults for a period of thirty-six months after said date six-fifteenths thereof, and permanently thereafter five-fifteenths.

In the Federal reserve bank of its district for a period of twelve months after the date aforesaid at least three-fifteenths, and for each succeeding six months an additional one-fifteenth, until six-fifteenths have been so deposited, which shall be the amount permanently required.

For a period of thirty-six months after said date the balance of the reserves may be held in its own vaults, or in the Federal reserve bank, or in national banks in reserve or central reserve cities as now defined by law.

After said thirty-six months' period all of said reserves, except those hereinbefore required to be held permanently in the vaults of the member bank and in the Federal reserve bank, shall be held in its vaults or in the Federal reserve bank, or in both, at the option of the member bank.

(c) A bank in a central reserve city, as now or hereafter defined, shall hold and maintain a reserve equal to eighteen per centum of the aggregate amount of its demand deposits and five per centum of its time deposits, as follows:

In its vaults six-eighteenths thereof.

In the Federal reserve bank seven-eighteenths.

The balance of said reserves shall be held in its own vaults or in the Federal reserve bank, at its option.

Any Federal reserve bank may receive from the member banks as reserves, not exceeding one-half of each installment, eligible paper as described in section fourteen properly indorsed and acceptable to the said reserve bank.

If a State bank or trust company is required by the law of its State to keep its reserves either in its own vaults or with another State bank or trust company, such reserve deposits so kept in such State bank or trust company shall be construed, within the meaning of this section, as if they were reserve deposits in a national bank in a reserve or central reserve city for a period of three years after the Secretary of the Treasury shall have officially announced the establishment of a Federal reserve bank in the district in which such State bank or trust company is situate. Except as thus provided, no member bank shall keep on deposit with any nonmember bank a sum in excess of ten per centum of its own paid-up capital and surplus. No member bank shall act as the medium or agent of a nonmember bank in applying for or receiving discounts from a Federal reserve bank under the provisions of this Act except by permission of the Federal Reserve Board.

The reserve carried by a member bank with a Federal reserve bank may, under the regulations and subject to such penalties as may be prescribed by the Federal Reserve

Board, be checked against and withdrawn by such member bank for the purpose of meeting existing liabilities: *Provided*, however, That no bank shall at any time make new loans or shall pay any dividends unless and until the total reserve required by law is fully restored.

In estimating the reserves required by this Act, the net balance of amounts due to and from other banks shall be taken as the basis for ascertaining the deposits against which reserves shall be determined. Balances in reserve banks due to member banks shall, to the extent herein provided, be counted as reserves.

National banks located in Alaska or outside the continental United States may remain nonmember banks, and shall in that even maintain reserves and comply with all the conditions now provided by law regulating them; or said banks, except in the Philippine Islands, may, with the consent of the Reserve Board, become member banks of any one of the reserve districts, and shall, in that event, take stock, maintain reserves, and be subject to all the other provisions of this Act.

SEC. 20. So much of sections two and three of the Act of June twentieth, eighteen hundred and seventy-four, entitled "An Act fixing the amount of United States notes, providing for a redistribution of the national-bank currency, and for other purposes," as provides that the fund deposited by any national banking association with the Treasurer of the United States for the redemption of its notes shall be counted as a part of its lawful reserve as provided in the Act aforesaid, is hereby repealed. And from and after the passage of this Act such fund of five per centum shall in no case be counted by any national banking association as a part of its lawful reserve.

BANK EXAMINATIONS

SEC. 21. Section fifty-two hundred and forty, United States Revised Statutes, is amended to read as follows:

The Comptroller of the Currency, with the approval of the Secretary of the Treasury, shall appoint examiners who shall examine every member bank at least twice in each calendar year and oftener if considered necessary: *Provided*, however, that the Federal Reserve Board may authorize examination by the State authorities to be accepted in the case of State banks and trust companies and may at any time direct the holding of a special examination of State banks or trust companies that are stockholders in any Federal reserve bank. The examiner making the examination of any national bank, or of any other member bank, shall have power to make a thorough examination of all the affairs of the bank and in doing so he shall have power to administer oaths and to examine any of the officers and agents thereof under oath and shall make a full and detailed report of the condition of said bank to the Comptroller of the Currency.

The Federal Reserve Board, upon the recommendation of the Comptroller of the Currency, shall fix the salaries of all bank examiners and make report thereof to Congress. The expense of the examinations herein provided for shall be assessed by the Comptroller of the Currency upon the banks examined in proportion to assets or resources held by the banks upon the dates of examination of the various banks.

In addition to the examinations made and conducted by the Comptroller of the Currency, every Federal reserve bank may, with the approval of the Federal reserve agent or the Federal Reserve Board, provide for special examination of member banks within its district. The expense of such examinations shall be borne by the bank examined. Such examinations shall be so conducted as to inform the Federal reserve bank of the condition of its member banks and of the lines of credit which are being extended by them. Every Federal reserve bank shall at all times furnish to the Federal Reserve Board such information as may be demanded concerning the condition of any member bank within the district of the said Federal reserve bank.

No bank shall be subject to any visitatorial powers other than such as are authorized by law, or vested in the courts of justice or such as shall be or shall have been exercised or directed by Congress, or by either House thereof or by any committee of Congress or of either House duly authorized.

The Federal Reserve Board shall, at least once each year, order an examination of each Federal reserve bank, and upon joint application of ten member banks the Federal Reserve Board shall order a special examination and report of the condition of any Federal reserve bank.

SEC. 22. No member bank or any officer, director, or employee thereof shall hereafter make any loan or grant any gratuity to any bank examiner. Any bank officer, director, or employee violating this provision shall be deemed guilty of a misdemeanor and shall be imprisoned not exceeding one year or fined not more than $5,000, or both; and may be fined a further sum equal to the money so loaned or gratuity given. Any examiner accepting a loan or gratuity from any bank examined by him or from an officer, director, or employee thereof shall be deemed guilty of a misdemeanor and shall be imprisoned not exceeding one year or fined not more than $5,000, or both; and may be fined a further sum equal to the money so loaned or gratuity given; and shall forever thereafter be disqualified from holding office as a national bank examiner. No national-bank examiner shall perform any other service for compensation while holding such office for any bank or officer, director, or employee thereof.

Other than the usual salary or director's fee paid to any officer, director, or employee of a member bank and other than a reasonable fee paid by said bank to such officer, director, or employee for services rendered to such bank, no officer, director, employee, or attorney of a member bank shall be a beneficiary of or receive, directly or indirectly, any fee, commission, gift, or other consideration for or in connection with any transaction or business of the bank. No examiner, public or private, shall disclose the names of borrowers or the collateral for loans of a member bank to other than the proper officers of such bank without first having obtained the express permission in writing from the Comptroller of the Currency, or from the board of directors of such bank, except when ordered to do so by a court of competent jurisdiction, or by direction of the Congress of the United States, or of either House thereof, or any committee of Congress or of either House duly authorized. Any person violating any provision of this section shall be punished by a fine of not exceeding $5,000 or by imprisonment not exceeding one year, or both.

Except as herein provided in existing laws, this provision shall not take effect until sixty days after the passage of this act.

SEC. 23. The stockholders of every national banking association shall be held individually responsible for all contracts, debts, and engagements of such association, each to the amount of his stock therein, at the par value thereof in addition to the amount invested in such stock. The stockholders in any national banking association who shall have transferred their shares or registered the transfer thereof within sixty days next before the date of the failure of such association to meet its obligations, or with knowledge of such impending failure, shall be liable to the same extent as if they had made no such transfer, to the extent that the subsequent transferee fails to meet such liability; but this provision shall not be construed to affect in any way any recourse which such shareholders might otherwise have against those in whose names such shares are registered at the time of such failure.

LOANS ON FARM LAND

SEC. 24. Any national banking association not situated in a central reserve city may make loans secured by improved and unencumbered farm land, situated within its Federal reserve district, but no such loan shall be made for a longer time than five years, nor for an amount exceeding fifty per centum of the actual value of the property offered as security. Any such bank may make such loans in an aggregate sum equal to twenty-five per centum of its capital and surplus or to one-third of its time deposits and such banks may continue hereafter as heretofore to receive time deposits and to pay interest on the same.

The Federal Reserve Board shall have power from time to time to add to the list of cities in which national banks shall not be permitted to make loans secured upon real estate in the manner described in this section.

FOREIGN BRANCHES

SEC. 25. Any national banking association possessing a capital and surplus of $1,000,000 or more may file application with the Federal Reserve Board, upon such conditions and under such regulations as may be prescribed by the said board, for the purpose of securing authority to establish branches in foreign countries or dependencies of the United States for the furtherance of the foreign commerce of the United States, and to act, if required to do so, as fiscal agents of the United States. Such application shall specify, in addition to the name and capital of the banking association filing it, the place or places where the banking operations proposed are to be carried on, and the amount of capital set aside for the conduct of its foreign business. The Federal Reserve Board shall have power to approve or to reject such application if, in its judgment, the amount of capital proposed to be set aside for the conduct of foreign business is inadequate, or if for other reasons the granting of such application is deemed inexpedient.

Every national banking association which shall receive authority to establish foreign branches shall be required at all times to furnish information concerning the condition of such branches to the Comptroller of the Currency upon demand, and the Federal Reserve Board may order special examinations of the said foreign branches at such time or times as it may deem best. Every such national banking association shall conduct the accounts of each foreign branch independently of the accounts of other foreign branches established by it and of its home office, and shall at the end of each fiscal period transfer to its general ledger the profit or loss accruing at each branch as a separate item.

SEC. 26. All provisions of law inconsistent with or superseded by any of the provisions of this Act are to that extent and to that extent only hereby repealed: *Provided*, Nothing in this Act contained shall be construed to repeal the parity provision or provisions contained in an Act approved March, fourteenth, nineteen hundred, entitled "An Act to define and fix the standard of value, to maintain the parity of all forms of money issued or coined by the United States, to refund the public debt, and for other purposes," and the Secretary of the Treasury may for the purpose of maintaining such parity and to strengthen the gold reserve, borrow gold on the security of United States bonds authorized by section two of the Act last referred to or for one-year gold notes bearing interest at a rate of not to exceed three per centum per annum, or sell the same if necessary to obtain gold. When the funds of the Treasury on hand justify, he may purchase and retire such outstanding bonds and notes.

SEC. 27. The provisions of the Act of May thirtieth, nineteen hundred and eight, authorizing national currency associations, the issue of additional national-bank circulation, and creating a National Monetary Commission, which expires by limitation under the terms of such Act on the thirtieth day of June, nineteen hundred and fourteen, are hereby extended to June thirtieth, nineteen hundred and fifteen, and sections fifty-one hundred and fifty-three, fifty-one hundred and seventy-two, fifty-one hundred and ninety-one, and fifty-two hundred and fourteen, of the Revised Statutes of the United States, which were amended by the Act of May thirtieth, nineteen hundred and eight, are hereby reenacted to read as such sections read prior to May thirtieth, nineteen hundred and eight, subject to such amendments or modifications as are prescribed in this Act: Provided, however, That section nine of the Act first referred to in this section is hereby amended so as to change the tax rates fixed in said Act by making the portion applicable thereto read as follows:

National banking associations having circulating notes secured otherwise than by bonds of the United States, shall pay for the first three months a tax at the rate of three per centum per annum upon the average amount of such of their notes in circulation as are based upon the deposit of such securities, and afterwards an additional tax rate of one-half of one per centum per annum for each month until a tax of six per centum per annum is reached, and thereafter such tax of six per centum per annum upon the average amount of such notes.

SEC. 28. Section fifty-one hundred and forty-three of the Revised Statutes is hereby amended and reenacted to read as follows: Any association formed under this title may, by vote of shareholders owning two-thirds of its capital stock, reduce its capital to any sum not below the amount required by this title to authorize the formation of associations; but no such reduction shall be allowable which will reduce the capital of the association below the amount required for its outstanding circulation, nor shall any reduction be made until the amount of the proposed reduction has been reported to the Comptroller the Currency and such reduction has been approved by the said Comptroller of the Currency and by the Federal Reserve Board, or by the organization committee pending the organization of the Federal Reserve Board.

SEC. 29. If any clause, sentence, paragraph, or part of this Act shall for any reason be adjudged by any court of competent jurisdiction to be invalid, such judgment shall not affect, impair, or invalidate the remainder of this Act, but shall be confined in its operation to the clause, sentence, paragraph, or part thereof directly involved in the controversy in which such judgment shall have been rendered.

SEC. 30. The right to amend, alter, or repeal this Act is hereby expressly reserved.

Approved, December 23, 1913.

APPENDIX B

MEMBERSHIP OF THE BOARD OF GOVERNORS: 1913–2004

Appointive Members

Name	Federal Reserve District	Initial appointment	Other information
Charles S. Hamlin	Boston	August 10, 1914	Reappointed in 1916 and 1926. Served until February 3, 1936.
Paul M. Warburg	New York	August 10, 1914	Term expired August 9, 1918.
Frederic A. Delano	Chicago	August 10, 1914	Resigned July 21, 1918.
W.P.G. Harding	Atlanta	August 10, 1914	Term expired August 9, 1922.
Adolph C. Miller	San Francisco	August 10, 1914	Reappointed in 1924. Reappointed in 1934 from the Richmond District. Served until February 3, 1936.
Albert Strauss	New York	October 26, 1918	Resigned March 15, 1920.
Henry A. Moehlenpah	Chicago	November 10, 1919	Term expired August 9, 1920.
Edmund Platt	New York	June 8, 1920	Reappointed in 1928. Resigned September 14, 1930.
David C. Wills	Cleveland	September 29, 1920	Term expired March 4, 1921.
John R. Mitchell	Minneapolis	May 12, 1921	Resigned May 12, 1923.
Milo D. Campbell	Chicago	March 14, 1923	Died March 22, 1923.
Daniel R. Crissinger	Cleveland	May 1, 1923	Resigned September 15, 1927.
George R. James	St. Louis	May 14, 1923	Reappointed in 1931. Served until February 3, 1936.
Edward H. Cunningham	Chicago	May 14, 1923	Died November 28, 1930.

(continued)

Appointive Members *(Continued)*

Name	Federal Reserve District	Initial appointment	Other information
Roy A. Young	Minneapolis	October 4, 1927	Resigned August 31, 1930.
Eugene Meyer	New York	September 16, 1930	Resigned May 10, 1933.
Wayland W. Magee	Kansas City	May 18, 1931	Term expired January 24, 1933.
Eugene R. Black	Atlanta	May 19, 1933	Resigned August 15, 1934.
M.S. Szymczak	Chicago	June 14, 1933	Reappointed in 1936 and 1948. Resigned May 31, 1961.
J.J. Thomas	Kansas City	June 14, 1933	Served until February 10, 1936.
Marriner S. Eccles	San Francisco	November 15, 1934	Reappointed in 1936, 1940, and 1944. Resigned July 14, 1951.
Joseph A. Broderick	New York	February 3, 1936	Resigned September 30, 1937.
John K. McKee	Cleveland	February 3, 1936	Served until April 4, 1946.
Ronald Ransom	Atlanta	February 3, 1936	Reappointed in 1942. Died December 2, 1947.
Ralph W. Morrison	Dallas	February 10, 1936	Resigned July 9, 1936.
Chester C. Davis	Richmond	June 25, 1936	Reappointed in 1940. Resigned April 15, 1941.
Ernest G. Draper	New York	March 30, 1938	Served until September 1, 1950.
Rudolph M. Evans	Richmond	March 14, 1942	Served until August 13, 1954.
James K. Vardaman, Jr.	St. Louis	April 4, 1946	Resigned November 30, 1958.
Lawrence Clayton	Boston	February 14, 1947	Died December 4, 1949.
Thomas B. McCabe	Philadelphia	April 15, 1948	Resigned March 31, 1951.
Edward L. Norton	Atlanta	September 1, 1950	Resigned January 31, 1952.
Oliver S. Powell	Minneapolis	September 1, 1950	Resigned June 30, 1952.
Wm. McC. Martin, Jr.	New York	April 2, 1951	Reappointed in 1956. Term expired January 31, 1970.
A.L. Mills, Jr.	San Francisco	February 18, 1952	Reappointed in 1958. Resigned February 28, 1965.
J.L. Robertson	Kansas City	February 18, 1952	Reappointed in 1964. Resigned April 30, 1973.
C. Canby Balderston	Philadelphia	August 12, 1954	Served through February 28, 1966.
Paul E. Miller	Minneapolis	August 13, 1954	Died October 21, 1954.
Chas. N. Shepardson	Dallas	March 17, 1955	Retired April 30, 1967.
G.H. King, Jr.	Atlanta	March 25, 1959	Reappointed in 1960. Resigned September 18, 1963.

Name	Federal Reserve District	Initial appointment	Other information
George W. Mitchell	Chicago	August 31, 1961	Reappointed in 1962. Served until February 13, 1976.
J. Dewey Daane	Richmond	November 29, 1963	Served until March 8, 1974.
Sherman J. Maisel	San Francisco	April 30, 1965	Served through May 31, 1972.
Andrew F. Brimmer	Philadelphia	March 9, 1966	Resigned August 31, 1974.
William W. Sherrill	Dallas	May 1, 1967	Reappointed in 1968. Resigned November 15, 1971.
Arthur F. Burns	New York	January 31, 1970	Term began February 1, 1970. Resigned March 31, 1978.
John E. Sheehan	St. Louis	January 4, 1972	Resigned June 1, 1975.
Jeffrey M. Bucher	San Francisco	June 5, 1972	Resigned January 2, 1976.
Robert C. Holland	Kansas City	June 11, 1973	Resigned May 15, 1976.
Henry C. Wallich	Boston	March 8, 1974	Resigned December 15, 1986.
Philip E. Coldwell	Dallas	October 29, 1974	Served through February 29, 1980.
Philip C. Jackson, Jr.	Atlanta	July 14, 1975	Resigned November 17, 1978.
J. Charles Partee	Richmond	January 5, 1976	Served until February 7, 1986.
Stephen S. Gardner	Philadelphia	February 13, 1976	Died November 19, 1978.
David M. Lilly	Minneapolis	June 1, 1976	Resigned February 24, 1978.
G. William Miller	San Francisco	March 8, 1978	Resigned August 6, 1979.
Nancy H. Teeters	Chicago	September 18, 1978	Served through June 27, 1984.
Emmett J. Rice	New York	June 20, 1979	Resigned December 31, 1986.
Frederick H. Schultz	Atlanta	July 27, 1979	Served through February 11, 1982.
Paul A. Volcker	Philadelphia	August 6, 1979	Resigned August 11, 1987.
Lyle E. Gramley	Kansas City	May 28, 1980	Resigned September 1, 1985.
Preston Martin	San Francisco	March 31, 1982	Resigned April 30, 1986.
Martha R. Seger	Chicago	July 2, 1984	Resigned March 11, 1991.
Wayne D. Angell	Kansas City	February 7, 1986	Served through February 9, 1994.
Manuel H. Johnson	Richmond	February 7, 1986	Resigned August 3, 1990.
H. Robert Heller	San Francisco	August 19, 1986	Resigned July 31, 1989.
Edward W. Kelley, Jr.	Dallas	May 26, 1987	Reappointed in 1990; resigned December 31, 2001.
Alan Greenspan	New York	August 11, 1987	Reappointed in 1992.
John P. LaWare	Boston	August 15, 1988	Resigned April 30, 1995.
David W. Mullins, Jr.	St. Louis	May 21, 1990	Resigned February 14, 1994.

(continued)

Appointive Members *(Continued)*

Name	Federal Reserve District	Initial appointment	Other information
Lawrence B. Lindsey	Richmond	November 26, 1991	Resigned February 5, 1997.
Susan M. Phillips	Chicago	December 2, 1991	Served through June 30, 1998.
Alan S. Blinder	Philadelphia	June 27, 1994	Term expired January 31, 1996.
Janet L. Yellen	San Francisco	August 12, 1994	Resigned February 17, 1997.
Laurence H. Meyer	St. Louis	June 24, 1996	Term expired January 31, 2002.
Alice M. Rivlin	Philadelphia	June 25, 1996	Resigned July 16, 1999.
Roger W. Ferguson, Jr.	Boston	November 5, 1997	Reappointed in 2001.
Edward M. Gramlich	Richmond	November 5, 1997	
Susan S. Bies	Chicago	December 7, 2001	
Mark W. Olson	Minneapolis	December 7, 2001	
Ben S. Bernanke	Atlanta	August 5, 2002	
Donald L. Kohn	Kansas City	August 5, 2002	

Chairmen	Term	Vice Chairmen	Term
Charles S. Hamlin	August 10, 1914– August 9, 1916	Frederic A. Delano	August 10, 1914– August 9, 1916
W.P.G. Harding	August 10, 1916– August 9, 1922	Paul M. Warburg	August 10, 1916– August 9, 1918
Daniel R. Crissinger	May 1, 1923– September 15, 1927	Albert Strauss	October 26, 1918– March 15, 1920
Roy A. Young	October 4, 1927– August 31, 1930	Edmund Platt	July 23, 1920– September 14, 1930
Eugene Meyer	September 16, 1930– May 10, 1933	J.J. Thomas	August 21, 1934– February 10, 1936
Eugene R. Black	May 19, 1933– August 15, 1934	Ronald Ransom	August 6, 1936– December 2, 1947
Marriner S. Eccles	November 15, 1934– January 31, 1948	C. Canby Balderston	March 11, 1955– February 28, 1966
Thomas B. McCabe	April 15, 1948– March 31, 1951	J.L. Robertson	March 1, 1966– April 30, 1973
Wm. McC. Martin, Jr.	April 2, 1951– January 31, 1970	George W. Mitchell	May 1, 1973– February 13, 1976
Arthur F. Burns	February 1, 1970– January 31, 1978	Stephen S. Gardner	February 13, 1976– November 19, 1978
G. William Miller	March 8, 1978– August 6, 1979	Frederick H. Schultz	July 27, 1979– February 11, 1982
Paul A. Volcker	August 6, 1979– August 11, 1987	Preston Martin	March 31, 1982– April 30, 1986
Alan Greenspan	August 11, 1987–	Manuel H. Johnson	August 4, 1986– August 3, 1990
		David W. Mullins, Jr.	July 24, 1991– February 14, 1994
		Alan S. Blinder	June 27, 1994– January 31, 1996
		Alice M. Rivlin	June 25, 1996– July 16, 1999
		Roger W. Ferguson, Jr.	October 5, 1999–

Source: Federal Reserve Board of Governors.

APPENDIX C

FEDERAL RESERVE REGULATIONS

Regulation	Subject	Purpose
A	Extensions of Credit by Federal Reserve Banks	Governs borrowing by depository institutions at the Federal Reserve discount window
B	Equal Credit Opportunity	Prohibits lenders from discriminating against credit applicants, establishes guidelines for gathering and evaluating credit information, and requires written notification when credit is denied
C	Home Mortgage Disclosure	Requires certain mortgage lenders to disclose data regarding their lending patterns
D	Reserve Requirements of Depository Institutions	Sets uniform requirements for all depository institutions to maintain reserve balances either with their Federal Reserve Bank or as cash in their vaults
E	Electronic Funds Transfers	Establishes the rights, liabilities, and responsibilities of parties in electronic funds transfers and protects consumers when they use such systems
F	Limitations on Interbank Liabilities	Prescribes standards to limit the risks posed by obligations of insured depository institutions to other depository institutions
G	Securities Credit by Persons other than Banks, Brokers, or Dealers	Governs extension of credit by parties other than banks, brokers, or dealers to finance the purchase or the carrying of margin securities; see also regulations T, U, and X
H	Membership of State Banking Institutions in The Federal Reserve System	Defines the requirements for membership by state-chartered banks in the Federal Reserve System and establishes minimum levels for the ratio of capital to assets to be maintained by state member banks
I	Issue and Cancellation of Capital Stock of Federal Reserve Banks	Sets forth stock-subscription requirements for all banks joining the Federal Reserve System

(continued)

Federal Reserve Regulations *(Continued)*

Regulation	Subject	Purpose
J	Collection of Checks and Other Items by Federal Reserve Banks and Funds Transfers through Fedwire	Establishes procedures, duties, and ties among (1) Federal Reserve Banks and (2) the senders and payors of checks and other items, and (3) the senders and recipients of wire transfers of funds
K	International Banking Operations	Governs the international banking operations of U.S. banking organizations and the operations of foreign banks in the United States
L	Management Official Interlocks	Restricts the management relationships that an official in one depository institution may have with other depository institutions
M	Consumer Leasing	Implements the consumer leasing provisions of the Truth in Lending Act by requiring meaningful disclosure of leasing terms
N	Relations with Foreign Banks and Bankers	Governs relationships and transactions between Federal Reserve banks and foreign banks, bankers, or governments
O	Loans to Executive Officers, Directors, and Principal Shareholders of Member Banks	Restricts credit that a member bank may extend to its executive officers, directors, and principal shareholders and their related interests
P	Minimum Security Devices and Procedures for Federal Reserve Banks and State Member Banks	Sets requirements for a security program that state-chartered member banks must establish to discourage robberies, burglaries, and larcenies
Q	Prohibition against Payment of Interest on Demand Deposits	Prohibits member banks from paying interest on demand deposits (for example, checking accounts)
R	Relationships with Dealers in Securities Under Section 32 of the Banking Act of 1933	Restricts employment relations between securities dealers and member banks to avoid conflict of interest, collusion, or undue influence on member bank investment policies or advice to customers
S	Reimbursement to Financial Institutions for Assembling or Providing Financial Records	Establishes rates and conditions for reimbursement to financial institutions for providing customer records to a government authority
T	Credit by Brokers and Dealers	Governs extension of credit by securities brokers and dealers, including all members of national securities exchanges; see also regulations G, U, and X
U	Credit by Banks for Purchasing or Carrying Margin Stocks	Governs extension of credit by banks to finance the purchase or the carrying of margin securities; see also regulations G, T, and X
V	Loan Guarantees for Defense Production (Dormant)	Facilitates the financing of contracts deemed necessary to national defense production
W	Vacant	

Regulation	Subject	Purpose
X	Borrowers of Securities Credit	Extends to borrowers who are subject to U.S. laws the provisions of regulations G, T, and U for obtaining credit within or outside the United States for the purpose of purchasing securities
Y	Bank Holding Companies and Change in Bank Control	Governs the bank and nonbank expansion of bank holding companies, the divestiture of impermissible nonbank interests, and the acquisition of a bank by individuals
Z	Truth in Lending	Prescribes uniform methods for computing the cost of credit, for disclosing credit terms, and for resolving errors on certain types of credit accounts
AA	Unfair or Deceptive Acts or Practices	Establishes consumer complaint procedures and defines unfair or deceptive practices in extending credit to consumers
BB	Community Reinvestment	Implements the Community Reinvestment Act and encourages banks to help meet the credit needs of their communities
CC	Availability of Funds and Collection of Checks	Governs the availability of funds deposited in checking accounts and the collection and return of checks
DD	Truth in Savings	Requires depository institutions to provide disclosures to enable consumers to make meaningful comparisons of deposit accounts
EE	Netting Eligibility for Financial Institutions	Defines financial institutions to be covered by statutory provisions regarding netting contracts—that is, contracts in which the parties agree to pay or receive the net, rather than the gross, payment due

Source: Federal Reserve Board of Governors.

INDEX

ABOUT THE AUTHOR

R. W. Hafer is a Professor of Economics in the Department of Economics and Finance at Southern Illinois University Edwardsville. He also is Director, Office of Economic Education and Business Research at SIUE. Before joining the SIUE faculty he was a Research Officer at the Federal Reserve Bank of St. Louis.

Professor Hafer has taught economics and finance at several institutions, including St. Louis University, Washington University—St. Louis, the Stonier Graduate School of Banking, and Erasmus University in Rotterdam, The Netherlands. He served as a Consultant to the Central Bank of the Philippines (1998), was a Research Fellow with the Institute of Urban Research (2001) and has been a Visiting Scholar with the Federal Reserve Banks of Atlanta and St. Louis.

The author and co-author of nearly 100 scholarly articles and the editor/co-editor of three books on monetary policy and financial markets, his commentary pieces have appeared in several newspapers, including the *Wall Street Journal*. He also has appeared on local and national radio and television programs.